CONTINUUM ENCYCLOPEDIA OF
POPULAR MUSIC
OF THE WORLD

VOLUME V
ASIA AND OCEANIA

CONTINUUM ENCYCLOPEDIA OF
POPULAR MUSIC
OF THE WORLD

VOLUME V
ASIA AND OCEANIA

EDITED BY
JOHN SHEPHERD, DAVID HORN
AND DAVE LAING

continuum

First published 2005 by
Continuum
The Tower Building, 11 York Road, London SE1 7NX
15 East 26th Street, New York, NY 10010

Reprinted 2005

**British Library Cataloguing-in-Publication
Data**
A catalogue record for this book is available from the
British Library
ISBN 0-8264-7436-5 (set)

**Library of Congress Cataloging-in-Publication
Data**
Continuum encyclopedia of popular music of the
world/edited by John Shepherd ... [et al.].
        p. cm.
Includes bibliographical references and index.
    ISBN 0-8264-6321-5–ISBN 0-8264-6322-3 (v.2)–
    ISBN 0-8264-7436-5 (v.3-7)
    1. Popular music–Encyclopedias. I. Shepherd, John,
1947–
    ML102.P66C66 2003
    781.63'09-dc21
                                        2002074146

Typeset by BookEns Ltd, Royston, Herts.
Printed and bound in Great Britain by
Antony Rowe Ltd., Chippenham, Wiltshire

Contents

Contents

Contents

Introduction

The *Continuum Encyclopedia of Popular Music of the World* had its genesis in the International Association for the Study of Popular Music (IASPM) in the mid-1980s.

IASPM was established in the early 1980s as a response to the increasing number of scholars publishing in the field of popular music. These scholars needed an organization through which to share and comment on their work, through which to advocate the legitimacy and desirability of work on popular music, and through which to advocate the inclusion of popular music studies in the academy.

Early in the life of IASPM, there was a recognition of the need for a comprehensive and reliable reference work on popular music that would serve the needs of scholars, researchers, students, and information and media professionals, as well as the general public.

The *Continuum Encyclopedia of Popular Music of the World* was planned as a response to that need. The first volume to be produced from the *Encyclopedia* project was *Popular Music Studies: A Select International Bibliography*, published in 1997.

Part 1 of the *Encyclopedia* proper was published in 2003, and comprises two volumes: Volume I, *Media, Industry and Society*; and Volume II, *Performance and Production*. The title of this, Part 2 of the *Encyclopedia*, is *Locations*. It is divided into five volumes: Volume III, *Caribbean and Latin America*; Volume IV, *North America*; Volume V, *Asia and Oceania*; Volume VI, *Africa and the Middle East*; and Volume VII, *Europe*. Part 2 will be followed by Part 3, *Genres* and Part 4, *Biographies*.

Because no model existed for this kind of comprehensive, scholarly reference work on popular music, extensive research was undertaken to develop a systematic, subject-based taxonomy for such a new field of study. These *Locations* volumes form part of that taxonomy. It is for this reason that, rather than alphabetically, the entries in this Part of the *Encyclopedia* are organized geo-culturally by volume, and then in terms of sections and subsections within volumes. Subject areas that, in an alphabetical sequence, would have been scattered arbitrarily throughout the *Encyclopedia*'s volumes are in this way brought together and organized coherently to constitute an unprecedented body of knowledge. Because the volumes are organized in this way, it is important for the reader to consult the Table of Contents (and the pages setting out the Arrangement of the Material in Volumes I and II) at the beginning of each volume. Each volume also has its own index, making it easy to locate discussions of specific terms within a range of entries.

It is in part the subject-based character of the *Encyclopedia*'s volumes that makes them distinctive among popular music reference works. The scholarly character of the volumes is apparent also in the comprehensive end matter that is provided for most entries: bibliographies, discographies, sheet music listings, filmographies, and listings of visual recordings. The volumes draw on the expertise of the world's leading popular music scholars. They are additionally distinctive in covering the popular music of the whole world rather than only specific regions of it, a motivation responsible for the genesis and character of the *Locations* volumes.

The five *Locations* volumes contain entries on virtually all the countries in the continental areas covered by each volume. In addition, there are entries on many of the major regions and cities within each country as well as, in some instances, important districts within cities. In the case of Russia, the only country in the world whose contiguous land mass straddles two continents (Europe and Asia), it was decided to include the main entry on Russia in Volume VII (*Europe*), and the entry on Siberia, a region of Russia, in Volume V (*Asia and Oceania*). The same principle has been applied to countries whose land mass is not contiguous. Thus, for example, the coverage of the United States in Volume IV (*North America*) is restricted to the continental United States. As a consequence, the entry on Hawai'i is to be found Volume V (*Asia and Oceania*), while the entry on Puerto Rico – a self-governing Commonwealth of the United States whose citizens are American – is to be found in Volume III (*Caribbean and Latin America*). In addition to entries on countries and regions and cities within countries, there are entries on distinct cultural groups that straddle countries (such as Native North Americans and the people of the Basque Country), as well as on distinct cultural groups within countries and regions of countries (for example, the entry on Acadia in Volume IV, which discusses the popular music of the francophone population of Canada's three maritime provinces). Distinct cultural groups that straddle countries also include diasporas. The *Locations* volumes include entries on diasporas, to be found following entries on the countries or regions from which the diaspora in question originates. Thus, the entry on the Italian diaspora is to be found following the entries on Italy the country, its regions and major cities. The entry on the Jewish diaspora is to be found in a separate section on this subject in Volume VII (*Europe*) since most – but by no means all – Jews can trace their ancestry to Central and Eastern Europe or the Iberian peninsula. Each volume contains maps showing the geographical location of each entry.

The *Locations* volumes can be regarded as a microcosm of the *Encyclopedia*. Entries begin with a summary of the location's outstanding characteristics, including information on its environment, its history, geography, and principal social, political, economic, cultural and linguistic features, its industries and transportation networks (the development of popular music is often significantly affected by the growth and decline of industries and transportation networks), its ethnic and age profiles, and other pertinent demographic information. Entries then proceed to discuss the history, development and contemporary situation of popular music in the location, as well as the importance of the location to the history and development of popular music generally. For this, the structure of the *Encyclopedia* as a whole serves as a model.

Entries include accounts of social and cultural contexts (for example, the ways in which issues of class, ethnicity and gender might have affected the development of popular music in the location in question – entries on all three of these topics are to be found in Volume I), the music industry (to which a complete section is devoted in Volume I) and musical practices (covered in Volume II), including notable genres (genres will be covered in Part 3 of the *Encyclopedia*), musicians and other individuals, such as producers, engineers or industry personnel (all to be covered in Part 4 – *Biographies*). If the location is more local in character, there is a discussion of significant venues, such as neighborhoods, streets, theaters, dance halls, clubs and bars (Volume I contains a section on venues as a general topic). Entries also contain discussions of the role of significant institutions, such as music publishers, recording companies, studios, radio and television stations and government regulatory agencies (also covered as general topics in Volume I), as well as educational establishments with courses in popular music (Volume I contains a section on popular music studies).

Because the structure of the *Encyclopedia* as a whole serves as a model for *Locations* entries, more extensive and detailed information on genres and individuals of importance in locations will be found in Parts 3 and 4 of the *Encyclopedia*. Equally, because the first two volumes (Part 1) of the *Encyclopedia* contain entries on significant aspects of the music industry (e.g., recording, publishing, marketing, promotion, copyright and performing rights), as well as on music technologies, technical musical characteristics, performance techniques, and social and cultural contexts (e.g., ethnicity, gender, class, politics, education), *Locations* entries do not contain detailed discussions of these topics.

A word of explanation is in order concerning the spelling of genre names. In many parts of the world, genres names were originally an aural-oral phenomenon. The manner in which such names were then rendered in written form frequently varied both within and between locations. The policy has therefore been not to strive for consistency, which could be misleading, but to accept the spelling supplied by the contributor, an expert on the location in question.

A word of explanation is also in order concerning the end matter of entries. If a particular piece of music is referred to in an entry, every effort has been made to include a reference to it in the entry's end matter, either in the sheet music listing or in the discographical references (and sometimes both). In areas of the world where 'cassette culture' has predominated this has, however, not always been possible. Discographies, which are distinct from discographical references, provide a list of representative recordings of relevance to the entry in general. It must be stressed that these discographies are solely representative, and are not intended to be comprehensive. A distinction is drawn in discographical references and discographies between dates of recording and dates of issue where these differ. Dates of recording are in roman type; dates of issue are italicized. The aim of the sections on discographical references and discography is twofold: to provide information on original recordings, and to lead readers to recordings that they can hear. For this reason, reissues of early recordings are on occasion listed. The reissues listed are those that were available at the time the entry was signed off for publication. The period during which entries for this volume were signed off stretched from September 2003 to August 2004. Reissues listed in the discographical references and discographies of these entries may as a consequence no longer be available. However, the likelihood is that these particular recordings have been reissued elsewhere since that time.

Bibliographies contain information on virtually all publications referred to in the body of entries. They also list items of relevance to entries' subject matter that readers may wish to consult as further reading. Details of all films and visual recordings (videos) referred to in an entry are provided in a filmography or visual recordings listing at the end of the entry. Items in filmographies contain references to those responsible for the films' music. On occasion, items of relevance to an entry are listed in the filmographic and visual recordings section that are not referred to in the body of the entry.

Editing a comprehensive reference work on the world's popular music raises the question of 'what counts as popular music?' In other words, what are the criteria according to which information and topics are included in the *Encyclopedia*. The definition of popular music is an issue that continues to be debated. The Editorial Board has resisted the temptation to offer a precise definition of the term 'popular music' in its instructions to contributors, recognizing that the terms 'popular,' 'classical' and 'folk' are discursive in character, and changing products of historical, social, political and cultural forces rather than terms that designate easily distinguishable musics. The question of where 'the popular' ends and 'the folk' begins has proved particularly difficult. The advice given to contributors has been that music created and disseminated in rural situations in an exclusively oral-aural fashion with little currency outside its location of origin does *not* constitute a prime focus for these volumes. However, it does not follow from this that such music should not be discussed if it is commonly accepted as 'popular,' or if it forms an important source for later styles or genres commonly accepted as 'popular.' While the principal emphasis of the *Encyclopedia* is on the urban, the commodified and the mass disseminated rather than on the rural, the oral-aural and the restrictedly local, therefore, this emphasis is far from exclusive. The principal test for including music as 'popular' has been whether it has been so regarded by communities of practitioners or users. The tendency has therefore been to be inclusive rather than exclusive. As a consequence, 'classical' music is included if its use has been popular in character.

Ottawa, Canada
September 2004

Acknowledgments

The Editorial Board's first debt of gratitude is to Philip Tagg, Professor of Music at Université de Montréal, who, over a two-year period at the Institute of Popular Music at the University of Liverpool in the early 1990s, developed a detailed taxonomy of popular music, its practice and its study. This taxonomy served as a basic model for developing the structure of the *Encyclopedia*, as well as its major sections and headword lists.

A special word of thanks is due to Alyn Shipton, whose vision and dedication in the formative period of the *Encyclopedia* were vital to the development and long-term viability of an ambitious publishing project. Thanks are also due to Janet Joyce and Veronica Higgs, both formerly of the Continuum International Publishing Group, whose unwavering support and guidance were crucial to the realization of Part 1 of the *Encyclopedia*, and to laying the foundations for Part 2.

Thanks are also due to the University of Liverpool, the University of Exeter, the University of Göteborg (Sweden), and especially Carleton University (Ottawa), all of which have made significant financial contributions, as well as contributions in kind, in support of this project. In the context of the *Locations* volumes, special thanks go to Professor Michael Smith, Dean of the Faculty of Arts and Social Sciences at Carleton University.

The Editorial Board wishes to place on record its sincere appreciation for the work undertaken at Carleton University by Jennie Strickland, who was central to the commissioning of the entries for Part 2 of the *Encyclopedia* and was, until 2002, responsible for communicating with contributors and tracking entries. Thanks are also due to Jennifer Wilson, who at Carleton University made a major contribution to the editing of Volume III and Part II (Oceania) of Volume V.

Finally, the Board wishes to express its gratitude to Jo Allcock of the Continuum International Publishing Group, who took over as the *Encyclopedia*'s Managing Editor in September 2002, and who has played a major and critical role in bringing Part 2 of the *Encyclopedia* to publication.

List of Contributors

Alison Arnold is Adjunct Assistant Professor, Department of Music, North Carolina State University.

Carol M. Babiracki is Associate Professor of Ethnomusicology, Department of Fine Arts, Syracuse University.

Jonas Baes is Assistant Professor of the Department of Composition and Theory, College of Music, University of the Philippines.

Nimrod Baranovitch is Assistant Professor, Department of East Asian Studies, University of Haifa, Israel.

Guy L. Beck teaches courses in World Music and Religious Studies at Tulane University, New Orleans, Louisiana.

Dagmar Bernstorff is a writer and editorial consultant living in New Delhi, India.

Jayeeta Bhowmick is a teacher, a research assistant with the Indian Music Project at the City University, London, and a co-editor of *A Collection of Bengali Songs for Many Occasions*.

Gregory Booth is a Senior Lecturer in Ethnomusicology at the University of Auckland, New Zealand.

Charles Capwell is Associate Professor of Music, University of Illinois.

Jim Chopyak is a Professor of Music, Department of Music, California State University, Sacramento.

John Clewley is a freelance journalist and photographer living in Bangkok and the Southeast Asia correspondent/photographer for *Songlines* magazine.

Jeroen de Kloet is Assistant Professor of Media Entertainment at the Department of Communication Science, University of Amsterdam.

Keila Diehl is a Lecturer in Cultural Anthropology, Music and Religious Studies at Stanford University.

Gavin D. Douglas is Assistant Professor, School of Music, University of North Carolina at Greensboro.

Za Tawn Eng (Salai Tawna), Ph.D. candidate, Department of Ethnomusicology, University of Zürich, Switzerland and a musician (composer, songwriter, arranger and performer) in Myanmar. He holds an M.A. in Music (liturgical), Colchester Institute, UK.

Gerry Farrell was Senior Lecturer in Music, the City University, London.

Joseph Getter is a doctoral candidate in Ethnomusicology at Wesleyan University, Middletown, Connecticut.

Jason Gibbs is a librarian at the San Francisco Public Library.

David Goldsworthy is a Senior Lecturer in Ethnomusicology, University of New England, Armidale, Australia.

Virginia Gorlinski is Assistant Professor, School of Interdisciplinary Arts, Ohio University.

List of Contributors

Paul D. Greene is Associate Professor of Ethnomusicology, Pennsylvania State University.

Phil Grinham is a music and audio teacher at Hobart College, Hobart, Tasmania, and a musician and music historian.

Hideko Haguchi is a doctoral candidate at Kyoto University, Japan.

Seilen Haokip is a research worker on Kuki indigenous people and a freelance writer living in Aizawl, Mizoram.

Rachel Harris is Lecturer in Ethnomusicology at SOAS, London.

D.J. Hatfield is visiting assistant professor of Anthropology and East Asian studies at the College of William and Mary.

Shane Homan is a Lecturer in Media and Cultural Studies at the University of Newcastle, Australia.

Keith Howard is Reader in Music, SOAS, University of London, and Director of the AHRB Research Centre for Cross-Cultural Music and Dance Performance.

Joyce Hughes is a Ph.D. candidate in Ethnomusicology at New York University.

Okon Hwang is Associate Professor, Performing Arts Department, Eastern Connecticut State University.

Bruce Johnson is Professor in the School of English, University of New South Wales, Sydney, and an active jazz musician.

Subhash Kak is Delaune Distinguished Professor of Electrical Engineering and Professor of Asian Studies and Cognitive Science at Louisiana State University, Baton Rouge.

James Kippen is Associate Professor, Faculty of Music, University of Toronto.

Dznamilya Kurbanova lives and works in Ashkhabad, Turkmenistan.

Dave Laing is an author and lecturer, London.

Joanna C. Lee is an Honorary Research Fellow, Centre of Asian Studies, University of Hong Kong.

Craig Macrae is an Associate Professor at Berklee College of Music in Boston.

Peter Manuel is a Professor in the Music Department of the CUNY Graduate Center and John Jay College, New York.

Deirdre Marshall is a freelance writer living in Stratford, Victoria, Australia.

Tony Mitchell is a Senior Lecturer in Cultural Studies, University of Technology, Sydney.

Tôru Mitsui is Professor of Music and English, Kanazawa University, Japan.

Sarah Morelli is a doctoral candidate in Ethnomusicology at Harvard University, Cambridge, MA.

Karl Neuenfeldt is a Senior Lecturer in Music, Central Queensland University, Australia.

Yasushi Ogasawara lives and works in Tokyo.

Joseph J. Palackal is an accomplished singer of north Indian classical music and a doctoral candidate in Ethnomusicology at New York University.

Carole Pegg is a freelance researcher and lecturer based in the Faculty of Music, University of Cambridge, UK.

Ashok Ranade is a musicologist and composer who was previously the Director of the Music Centre at the University of Mumbai, India.

Sam-Ang Sam is a Cambodian ethnomusicologist living in Arlington, Virginia.

Anna Schultz is a doctoral candidate at the University of Illinois, Urbana-Champaign, and is an Adjunct Faculty Member at the State University of New York, Morrisville.

Manira Shahidi is at the Shahidi Museum of Musical Culture, Dushanbe, Tajikistan.

Roy Shuker, Media Studies Programme, Victoria University of Wellington, New Zealand.

Andreas Steen is research assistant at the Seminar of East Asian Studies, Free University Berlin.

Amy Ku'uleialoha Stillman is Associate Professor of Music and American Culture, and Director of Asian/Pacific Islander American Studies, at the University of Michigan.

Tan Sooi Beng is Professor, Department of Music, School of Arts, Universiti Sains Malaysia, Malaysia.

Tom Vater is a freelance writer and photographer based in London and Bangkok. www.tomvater.com

Michael Webb is an Ethnomusicologist and teaches music at St Paul's Grammar School, Sydney, Australia.

Philip Yampolsky is Program Officer for Media, Arts and Culture, the Ford Foundation, Jakarta, Indonesia.

Jin Zhaojun is a member of China's Musicians' Association, Senior Editor for *People's Music*, and music critic.

List of Maps

Abbreviations

A&R	artist and repertoire
A.D.	Anno Domini
ABC	Australian Broadcasting Commission (later, Corporation)
AFKN	American Forces Korean Network
AFN	American Forces Network
AIR	All India Radio
aka	also known as
AM	amplitude modulation
AMCOS	Australasian Mechanical Copyright Owners Society
AMI	Anugerah Musik Indonesia
APRA	Australasian Performing Right Association
ARIA	Australian Record Industry Association
ASIRI	Indonesian Recording Industry Association
ATV	Asia Television
B.C.	before Christ
BBC	British Broadcasting Corporation
BCC	China Broadcasting Service
BMG	Bertelsmann Music Group/Bertelsmann Musik Gesellschaft
CAAMA	Central Australian Aboriginal Media Association
CAC	Christian Arts and Communications
CASM	Centre for Aboriginal Studies in Music
CBS	Columbia Broadcasting System
CCTV	China's Central Television
CD	compact disc
CR	Commercial Radio (China)
CRC	China Record Company
DPRK	Democratic People's Republic of Korea
DVD	digital versatile disc/digital video disc
EDSA	Epiphania de los Santos Avenue (The Philippines)
EMI	Electrical and Musical Industries Ltd.
FEN	Far East Network
FM	frequency modulation
ft	feet
GCL	Gramophone Company Limited
GHQ	General Headquarters
GI	government issue (any member of the US armed forces)
HMV	His Master's Voice
ICRT	International Community Radio T'aipei
ISBS	Indian State Broadcasting Service

Abbreviations

JASPM	Japanese Association for the Study of Popular Music
JASRAC	Japanese Society for Rights of Authors, Composers and Publishers
KBS	Korean Broadcasting System
km	kilometer
KMC	Kwangmyong Umaksa (North Korea)
KMT	Kuomintang (nationalist Chinese administration, Taiwan)
KTV	Karaoke Television
LP	long-playing record
MBC	Munhwa Broadcasting Corporation
MCA	Music Corporation of America
MIB	Melayu Islam Berjaya
MIDI	musical instrument digital interface
MMC	Music Ministry for Christ (Myanmar)
MOR	middle-of-the-road [music]
MP3	MPEG Layer III
MTV	Music Television
NHK	Japanese Broadcasting Corporation
NIROM	Netherlands-Indische Radio Omroep Maatschappij
OECD	Organization for Economic Co-operation and Development
PAPPRI	Association of Indonesian Song Writers and Recorded Music Arrangers
PBC	Pusan Broadcasting Corporation
PRC	People's Republic of China
R&B	rhythm and blues
RCA	Radio Corporation of America
RLV	Rama Laxmi Vilasam
ROC	Republic of China
Rpm	revolutions per minute
RTB	Radio Television Brunei
RTHK	Radio Television Hong Kong
RTM	Radio Television Malaysia
SCS	Suara Cipta Sempurna
SLORC	State Law and Order Restoration Council (Myanmar)
sq	square
TAR	Tibetan Autonomous Region
TIPA	Tibetan Institute of Performing Arts
UNESCO	United Nations Educational, Scientific and Cultural Organization
URC	Underground Record Club
USSR	Union of Soviet Socialist Republics
VCD	video compact disc
WEA	Warner-Elektra-Atlantic
WOMAD	World of Music, Arts and Dance
YKCI	Indonesian Creative Work Foundation
ZAS	Zomi Artist Society (Myanmar)

Australian States

ACT	Australian Capital Territory
NSW	New South Wales
NT	Northern Territory
Qld	Queensland
SA	South Australia
Tas	Tasmania
Vic	Victoria
WA	Western Australia

Part I
Asia

1. Central Asia

China

Population: 1,286,975,500 (2003)

China is the most populous country in the world and the third-largest country (after Russia and Canada) with a total area of 3.7 million sq miles (9.6 million sq km). The country's land boundaries total 13,840 miles (22,143 km) and it borders 14 countries: North Korea, Russia and Mongolia in the north; Kazakhstan, Kyrgyzstan, Tajikistan, Afghanistan, Pakistan, India and Nepal in the west; and Bhutan, Myanmar, Laos and Vietnam in the south. China's territory spans a distance of 3,250 miles (5,200 km) from west to east and 3,440 miles (5,500 km) from north to south. In the east it has a coastline of 9,060 miles (14,500 km) that extends from the Yellow Sea in the north to the South China Sea in the south. The country's climate ranges from tropical in the south to subarctic in the north. In the west there are mainly deserts, high plateaus and mountains, while in the east mainly plains and deltas.

The great majority of China's population is concentrated in the eastern part of the country, where the climate and the terrain are the most hospitable. The east, especially the coastal region, is also the most developed and modern part of the country, where its major cities are located. Most of the interaction with the West in modern history took place along the coastline, and major cities in this region have developed in the context of semi-colonization by Western powers and Japan. In sharp contrast to this region, the western part of the country and its northernmost part have inhospitable climates and terrain, are sparsely populated and relatively underdeveloped.

In the early 1980s, approximately 80 percent of China's population were peasants, whereas urbanites constituted only 20 percent of the population. These proportions, however, started to change during the 1980s and 1990s as tens of millions of peasants started to migrate to cities as a result of Deng Xiaoping's economic reforms and the lifting of former restrictions on geographical mobility. In addition to the urbanite–peasant divide, ethnicity constitutes another major social division in China. The country is a multiethnic state and its population is made up of 92 percent Han Chinese and 55 national minorities that together constitute 8 percent of the total population. Minority groups usually inhabit the less hospitable and less developed parts of the country, and although significantly smaller in terms of population size, they still dominate demographically much of western China (most notably Tibet and Xinjiang) despite massive Han settlement in recent decades.

While the cultural differences between China's minorities and the Han majority are most obvious, the culture of the latter is by no means homogenous, exhibiting significant regional differences. Side by side with multiple regional dialects and cuisines there also exist in Han China multiple and very different regional forms of folk music. Within this regional diversity, the major cultural division is between the south and the north, the border being the Yangtze River, which starts in the Tibet-Qinghai Plateau in the west and flows out to sea near Shanghai in the east. In the domain of music this major cultural division revealed itself traditionally in that the southern China preference has been toward more moderate tempos, softer rhythms, stepwise melodies and more restrained singing, whereas in the north music has tended traditionally to be more bold (*haofang*), more percussive, and with more disjunct melodies. These different musical preferences are also evident in contemporary popular music.

Modern Chinese History and Modern Popular Music before the Reform Era: 1920s to Late 1970s)

The beginning of China's modernization is usually traced back to the Opium Wars of 1840–42. Following the attack by British warships on Chinese ports as a retaliation to the empire's attempt to put an end to the smuggling of opium from India to China by British merchants, the empire was forced to open itself to trade with the West on the basis of unequal treaties and started to cede territories to Western powers and later also to Japan. As part of this process, increasing numbers of Westerners started to move into China and began to establish extraterritorial settlements, mainly along the coastline. The presence of Westerners and the introduction of Western culture and technologies that followed shook the foundations of traditional society and culture and led in 1911 to the downfall of the Chinese Empire.

The focus of Western influence in China was Shanghai. An average Chinese, walled city until the Opium Wars, Shanghai emerged at the beginning of the twentieth century as a modern cosmopolitan metropolis, often referred to as 'The Paris of the East.' In the 1920s and 1930s one could watch films from Hollywood, dance to jazzy rhythms in night-clubs and dance halls, and at the same time listen to Soviet-style revolutionary songs in the city. Shanghai not only imported culture but also boasted a thriving record and film industry of its own. It was in this context that modern Chinese popular music came into being, combining indigenous elements with foreign ones and relying on modern technology for its dissemination in Shanghai and other major Chinese cities.

The modern popular music that emerged in Shanghai was influenced by Euro-American popular music and Soviet revolutionary music. Music that emulated the former dominated urban culture and was named *liuxing* ('popular') music. The lyrics of songs belonging to this genre were mainly about romantic love and were often set to rhythms of contemporary Western popular dances. Songs inspired by the Soviet model on the other hand were named *qunzhong gequ* or later *geming gequ* ('songs of the masses' and 'revolutionary songs,' respectively),

were normally produced by leftist musicians, and were disseminated mainly among students and workers. These songs were typically sung in choruses in a militant and heroic march style, and their lyrics were usually about national salvation.

The course of modernization in China and the development of popular Chinese music saw a dramatic turn in 1949 when the Communists, inspired by the Soviet Union and headed by Mao Zedong, defeated the Nationalists and established the People's Republic of China (PRC). The Communists established a powerful central government in Beijing, collectivized the country's agriculture and industry, and brought cultural production and distribution under the tight control of the Communist Party. Following Mao's prescriptions in his famous Yan'an Talks of 1942, literature and art were heavily politicized and were used intensively from that point on as tools for education and propaganda. As a result, from the 1950s, China was gradually taken over by an omnipresent, highly politicized and highly standardized revolutionary mass culture that was disseminated all over the country.

The affective quality of music, the fact that it could be sounded in public spaces and performed collectively, and no less importantly, its ability to communicate to millions of illiterate and semi-illiterate peasants, made music one of the most important political tools used by the Communists to legitimize their regime, indoctrinate the masses and mobilize them for revolutionary action. The Maoist era saw the emergence of a whole new kind of popular music culture, which in many ways was the antithesis of the dominant popular music culture that had emerged in Shanghai a few decades earlier. No longer a commercial and pleasure-oriented product, the main driving force behind the popularization of songs and the dominant content were now political. In addition, popular music ceased to be an exclusively urban phenomenon, as the new government made every effort to popularize revolutionary songs also among the rural majority. The strong link of the new regime to the countryside revealed itself also in the massive collection, arrangement and composition of folk songs. These were popularized locally and nation-wide along with the totally Westernized militant and heroic *geming gequ*, which after 1949 gradually started to dominate the music scene. The development of the new musical culture in the 1950s came hand in hand with the disappearance of *liuxing* music. The Euro-American-style, leisure-oriented, urban popular music was now seen as an anathema and came to symbolize the decadence of the urban bourgeoisie and Western imperialism.

Another dramatic turning point in the modern history of China and its popular music came after Mao's death in 1976 and the rise to power of Deng Xiaoping, who from 1978 led China to a new era of reform. Deng opened China to the world in a reform that was named the 'open door' policy, and established full diplomatic relations with the United States. Emphasis was now put on modernization and economic growth and the country gradually moved from an extremely centralized economy toward a free market economy. Although reforms skipped the authoritarian political system, they nevertheless brought with them significant liberalization in many social and cultural domains and people's lives became much less politicized.

Deng's reforms changed the nature of the popular music scene in China. Music production and distribution were no longer monopolized by the Party, and as a result the homogeneity that had characterized the previous era was replaced by vibrant diversity. The introduction of new technologies like cassette recording, television, and later video, karaoke, CD/VCD/DVD and Internet, all contributed in the 1980s and 1990s both to a wider dissemination of popular music and to its diversification. In many respects popular music culture in the reform era was a return to its pre-

1949 form. It was once again linked to leisure, to nightclubs, to romance, to the city and to the market. This change came hand in hand with the return of Euro-American-style pop, which started once again to dominate the popular music scene and replaced the Soviet-style revolutionary song. But the revival was nonetheless heavily mixed with practices that were inherited from the Maoist era. Folk songs in their various forms, for example, were still very important. So were officially sponsored propaganda and other politicized songs, which still constituted an integral part of popular music culture. The importance of such songs indicated that the state was still a major agent in popular music culture despite the fact that it no longer monopolized the production and distribution of popular songs.

The History and Characteristics of Major Genres and Styles in the Reform Era: From 1978

Although no clear-cut line can be drawn between genres because of considerable crisscrossing of musical style and content, four major genres were distinguishable in China during the 1980s and 1990s.

(a) Liuxing/tongsu *and* Gangtai

The first major change that took place in the popular music scene in Deng's era was the return of *liuxing* music in its more contemporary form. As

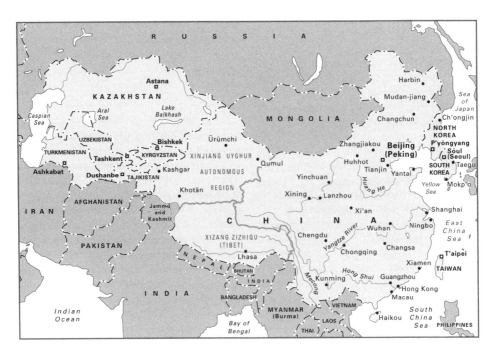

soon as China opened itself to the outside world, cassettes carrying soft love songs in moderate tempo and accompanied by crooning strings and electric guitars started to be smuggled into the country from Taiwan and Hong Kong. These songs, the most famous singer of which was the female Taiwanese singer Deng Lijun, were accepted with enormous enthusiasm because they reintroduced a whole array of artistic possibilities, topics and sentiments that had been suppressed for many years. Because it came from outside China, *liuxing* music also satisfied the desire of many to reconnect to the rest of the world after decades of isolation. Moreover, with their electric guitars, bass and keyboards, and Western drumsets, instruments that were completely unknown to musicians in China before the introduction of the 'open door' policy, *liuxing* songs also represented a longed-for modernity, which further increased their appeal.

The reintroduction of *liuxing* music was accompanied by a heated public debate and strong official resistance because the genre was stigmatized for decades as pornographic and decadent, and was blamed for lulling people's will for struggle. So negative were the associations that when 'light music' (*qing yinyue*) started to be legitimized in China in the early 1980s, another term, *tongsu* (which like *liuxing* means 'popular' or 'common'), was used for several years to denote 'healthy' light music as opposed to *liuxing*. The distinction between the two labels, however, became increasingly blurred as the 1980s progressed. For over half a decade, *liuxing* songs were officially considered as 'spiritual pollution' and were excluded from most of the official media, officially organized live events and music competitions. It was only in late 1985 and early 1986 that this genre became accepted by officialdom and began to be incorporated into official culture. Since the mid-1980s, *liuxing* music has dominated the popular music scene and the term has been used either to denote popular music in general, as opposed for example to Western classical music or traditional Chinese opera, or sometimes to denote pop as opposed to rock.

Like *liuxing* music of the 1920s, 1930s and 1940s, *liuxing* music of the reform era strongly resembled contemporary Euro-American pop. And yet, despite its obvious Westernized character it was unmistakably Chinese. It was sung in Chinese, the singing often retaining some degree of the nasality that characterizes traditional Chinese singing, and the tunes often showing traces of traditional tunes. Moreover, taken as a whole, *liuxing* music demon-strated considerable continuity with the traditional Chinese aesthetic preference for refinement, moderation and restraint, resulting in softer sounds, slower tempos and less accentuated beats and rhythms than those common in Euro-American pop.

The flow of songs from Taiwan and Hong Kong into China was the beginning of the formation of a transnational popular Chinese culture in which the former two were to play a dominant role. Music coming from these two places was named in China as *gangtai*, a name that combined the Mandarin Chinese names of the two places (Xianggang and Taiwan). Beginning from the late 1970s and early 1980s, *gangtai* music exerted an important influence on mainland musicians and helped to introduce into China many of the concepts and practices that became common in pop culture all over the world.

Although the popular music scene in Taiwan and Hong Kong has never been homogenous, the label *gangtai* has usually been understood in China to denote music that basically overlaps in terms of style with *liuxing/tongsu* music. For the majority of people in China, however, the label simultaneously stood for a better pop, more professional, modern, sophisticated and glittering, and was a signifier of a better life and real urban culture. At the same time, for some people, particularly in northern China and especially among rock fans, *gangtai* music represented a highly commercialized music that was nothing but light entertainment as opposed to real art, and inferior southern aesthetics of softness and sweetness, which were often also referred to as 'traditional' and 'feminine.'

(b) Min'ge

Songs labeled *min'ge* constituted the most characteristically Chinese genre in the popular music scene. Often identified in their titles by a reference to a particular locale or ethnic group (e.g., *Shaanxi* folk song, *Tibetant* folk song, *Hakka* folk song), these songs were sometimes arrangements of pre-existing folk songs associated with those areas or peoples, or alternatively were new compositions that drew on a certain folk style. In both cases, however, famous songs that were popularized nationwide were usually arranged or composed by urban professional musicians who in most cases received formal training in Western art music and consciously worked to 'improve' the original material by combining it with Western musical elements. This typical combination was the result of the widespread conviction among professional musicians in China beginning from the early decades of the twentieth century that Western art music was synonymous with modern music. One of the most important characteristics of *min'ge*, the national/folk singing style (*minzu/min'ge changfa*), was a good example of such a combination, being a hybrid that combined the high, nasal and highly ornamented traditional Chinese singing with Western bel canto singing. Similarly, although *min'ge* often employed traditional Chinese instruments, such as the *erhu* (two-string fiddle), *dizi* (bamboo flute), *zheng* (zither) and *pipa* (four-string lute) for slower and softer songs, and *suona* (double-reed oboe), gongs, cymbals and barrel drums for faster and more rhythm-oriented songs, they were normally also accompanied by Western instruments (classical and pop), and usually employed tempered tuning and harmony. Another important Western musical element that was sometimes combined with folk songs, particularly during the Maoist era, was choral singing.

Min'ge were also characterized by their lyrics, which often depicted rural life and natural scenery. Many songs were, for instance, about traditional festivities and often constructed the typical sonic image of such festivities by employing the screaming *suona*. Some songs also used folksy vocabulary, and typical nonsense vocables and accents, which immediately invoked rural setting. In addition, when performing folk songs, singers (especially female ones), often wore traditional-style costumes, and when videoclips accompanied the songs, they typically included shots of the countryside.

The large amount of *min'ge* and their persistent popularity in modern China owe much to the fact that peasants constitute the great majority of the country's population. Other important factors that contributed to their popularity, especially during the Maoist era (the 1950s through the 1970s), however, are political and ideological. The Party always drew its power and legitimacy from the countryside and China's peasants and, at least on the rhetorical level, always considered the village a more healthy and politically correct place than the city. Thus on the symbolic level, folk songs (as opposed to urban popular music) represented official ideals and values such as collectivism and production, as well as the masses of the toiling people. No less importantly, the songs helped to construct and assert distinctive national identity after a century of Western and Japanese imperialism. On the more practical level, *min'ge* also helped

the Party to promulgate official messages among the peasants, who could hardly relate to the Soviet-style marches that mobilized the urbanites.

The label *min'ge* was widely used in the Maoist era and was still attached to many songs from that period that were rearranged in the reform era. In the latter period, the production of *min'ge* also continued and in the early 1990s several songs in folksy style that were labeled *xin min'ge* (new folk songs) became big hits (e.g., 'The Love of the Boat Tower' ['Qianfu de ai'], 1994). After the mid-1990s, however, fewer songs in folksy style were produced, presumably because the style did not fit the general trend and official agenda of increasing modernization. The label *min'ge* nonetheless was still occasionally used to refer to new songs that carried collective messages, especially patriotism, even if the conformity of such songs to the above characterization was very partial.

(c) Official Pop

This genre was not identified by any Chinese term and that which is used here – 'official pop' – might appear to be an oxymoron in the context of China studies where 'official' and 'popular' have often been perceived as two mutually exclusive categories. However, there is no doubt that in reform China there exists a significant body of songs that are strongly associated with the state and officialdom and nevertheless enjoy wide popularity among significant portions of society and constitute an integral part of the popular music scene.

The link between the state and official songs was manifested in the 1980s and 1990s in the fact that many of the artists involved in the production and performance of these songs were employed by government and army working units. Dong Wenhua, for example, who was one of the most popular singers in the 1990s and who specialized in the performance of official songs, was employed by the Song and Dance Troupe of the General Political Department of the Chinese People's Liberation Army. Her affiliation with the army was rather obvious as she often performed her songs in army uniforms, which immediately identified her as representative of the state.

During the 1980s many official songs gradually departed from the heroic and militant style of the revolutionary era and moved closer to the softer style of *liuxing* music. This transformation seemed to be the result of a realization among state officials that in order to communicate with China's post-revolutionary disaffected youth they had to adapt themselves to their new taste and new sensibilities. Moreover, officials apparently also realized that the traditional aesthetics of restraint and moderation that characterized much of *liuxing* music were actually much more suitable to the neo-traditional ethos of stability, order and harmony that they propagated rather than the stirring aesthetics of revolutionary mass songs. But despite this general transformation, official songs maintained a distinctive style. They were typically sung either in Western bel canto singing style (*meisheng changfa*), or in the national/folk singing style, both of which are orthodox, professional singing styles that require formal training. Official pop songs were also usually more moderate in tempo than most other popular songs, they were often accompanied by Western classical musical instruments such as strings and in some cases brass and timpani, and often incorporated Western-style choirs, which helped to communicate the collectivist spirit that the regime still propagated. The performance of official songs tended to be solemn and ceremonious, presentational and highly choreographed, characteristics that helped to communicate power, discipline, authority and control.

As for their lyrics, official popular songs were usually highly didactic and they normally propagated messages such as patriotism, praise of Chinese culture, good citizenship and sacrifice for society, hard work and unity. Many songs also praised the regime by pointing to its achievements in leading China to modernity. The common denominator in most of these songs was the positioning of the state and the nation at the center. The videoclips, like the lyrics, made extensive use of national symbols, like the flag, Tiananmen Square, the Great Wall, soldiers, images of development like skyscrapers and highways, and universal images of hope and happiness such as children, white doves and flowers blooming. Conforming to the old revolutionary principle of socialist realism, all official songs depicted reality in idealized colors and optimistic tone.

Official pop songs demonstrated how the state in the 1980s and 1990s still used popular music for propaganda, for education purposes and, in general, to maintain a central position for itself in popular culture, despite the significant liberalization of the reform era. The songs were performed on a daily basis in official media – most notably on CCTV (China's Central Television), which broadcasts nationwide and in the 1990s turned out to be the most powerful official media in China – as well as in

officially organized live events. While this genre was not very popular among urban young people, who sought more fashionable and less politicized pop and had a considerable choice, it did enjoy considerable popularity among urban adults and certainly among peasants, who consumed popular music primarily through television.

(d) Yaogun

Rock was introduced into China around the mid-1980s and emerged as a significant genre in the early 1990s. Since its emergence it has been a purely urban phenomenon associated mainly with urban youth and with the capital, Beijing. The close association between rock and Beijing can be attributed to the massive presence of Westerners in the capital. Western students, business people, journalists, diplomats and others brought with them cassettes of rock music, patronized local venues that became greenhouses for the development of Chinese rock bands, and in some cases also performed rock themselves. Performances of Western bands in the capital (e.g., Wham! in 1985) also played an important role in introducing the style to local youth. Another possible cause for the link between rock and Beijing may be the compatibility of the style with musical aesthetics of the north.

Since its emergence in China, rock has been an exclusive subculture that has challenged consciously the government, official culture, traditional culture and the mainstream. Most Chinese rockers were independent musicians who did not work for the state and therefore had more artistic liberty. Rockers adopted not only the musical style, which with the exception of the language and some use of Chinese musical instruments did not differ in any significant way from Western rock, but also much of the ideology that traditionally accompanied rock in the West. Thus the style came to symbolize for Chinese rockers and rock fans values such as truthfulness, authenticity and originality, freedom, direct expression, rebellion and protest, as well as individuality and nonconformism. In addition to all these, it represented the ultimate modernity in popular music. For all Chinese, rock also represented the West, its best and its worst.

Since the emergence of rock in China, officials have recognized the political threat that was embodied in its Western liberal ideology and practices, and the style was consequently banned from official media and restrictions were often imposed on rock performances. Despite or perhaps because of the ban, rock thrived from the early to the mid-1990s. Many bands were established, numerous cassettes were released, and the rock 'underground' (*dixia*) subculture that emerged in the late 1980s and was confined hitherto to a few nightclubs rose to the surface and attracted the attention of increasing numbers of youngsters all over the country. The focus of this subculture was on rock 'parties' (the word 'party' was used in English), events that like rituals of reversal were designed as the opposite of officially organized live concerts: small in scale, casual and without anchors reading official propaganda texts between songs. At these parties, rockers and rock fans intermingled with one another without any distance between them. They danced, smoked, drank alcohol and got wild, and established an alternative exclusive community that challenged official order and the rest of society. The exclusivist nature of the rock subculture and the challenge that it posed to mainstream culture were enhanced by hippy-style behavior, jeans, long hair for males, drug use and more liberal sexual behavior.

After the mid-1990s, however, only a few years after it rose to the surface and emerged into the general public sphere, rock started to decline. Despite the appearance of a new generation of young radical rockers in the late 1990s and the fact that around the same time a few rock bands started to be shown on television, it was clear that rock had moved back to the margins of Chinese culture and society. The performances of the new radical rockers were normally relegated to small pubs, while the music of those bands that were permitted to perform on television was drained of the subversive, independent and alternative spirit that characterized earlier Chinese rock and even then, despite its tame nature, it still occupied a very marginal position in the mainstream. Several interrelated factors seemed to be responsible for the decline of rock in China. First was the systematic suppression of this genre by the state, combined with the radical consumerism of the 1990s, which the state appropriated successfully to serve its political interests. Another important factor was the tide in popular nationalism which swept China during the 1990s and which emerged hand in hand with disillusionment with the West, particularly with the United States, which now appeared as an aggressive competitor. The latter trend was accompanied by a resurgence of traditional Confucian values like order, authority, harmony, stability and unity, all of which the government enthusiastically propagated after the 4 June incident at Tiananmen Square in 1989. Against this background, rock was increasingly perceived as something alien, wild, vulgar and harmful.

The failure of rock to become a significant part of mainstream culture in China reflects the persistence of significant cultural and political differences between this country and the West despite the country's rapid modernization and increasing globalization. Similarly, whereas in the West rap, hip-hop and trance appeared in the 1990s as major genres, none of them really made significant inroads into Chinese popular music. Reflecting a complex combination of traditional and revolutionary values and aesthetic preferences, and a powerful authoritative regime that played an important role in shaping and controlling those values and aesthetics, Chinese popular music in the 1980s and 1990s showed an obvious preference for the singing of words (best illustrated in the enormous popularity of karaoke) as opposed to dance and instrumental music, for moderate tempos and rhythms as opposed to stimulating ones, and for more restrained, refined and highly choreographed and stylized musical expressions as opposed to more direct, bold and 'natural' expressions, and improvisation.

Politics, Economy and Technology

Political Uses of Popular Songs before the Reform Era

Massive and systematic political uses of popular music in China were already evident in the 1930s. After the Japanese army invaded Manchuria in 1931, leftist songwriters in Shanghai started to produce large numbers of patriotic mass songs in order to awaken the Chinese people and mobilize them to resist Japanese (and Western) imperialism. The production of patriotic songs reached unprecedented scale during the war of resistance against Japan (1937–45), in the course of which their dissemination also extended to the countryside.

Parallel to this activity the Communists were engaged in the countryside in the transformation of folk songs to advance a broader political agenda. As part of this effort, folk songs were collected in mass quantities and new politicized lyrics were set to their tunes. The new lyrics propagated resistance to the Japanese but also propagated the Party, Mao Zedong and socialist ideology. The use of preexisting tunes was intended to facilitate acceptance among peasants, but also helped to overcome the shortage in composers. The new songs were usually labeled 'folk songs' (*min'ge*), a label that provided legitimacy to the Party and naturalized its power because it suggested that the songs were spontaneous, authentic *vox populi*. Also propagating resistance to the Nationalists and delegitimizing their regime, the new folk songs that the Communists composed and disseminated among the rural population made a significant contribution to their seizure of power in 1949.

The link between music and politics was institutionalized in 1942 in Mao's famous Talks at the Yan'an Conference on Literature and Art. In his talks Mao stated that there is no art for art's sake and that all art is political. He also prescribed that art should serve the masses and the revolution and should be used as a weapon in uniting and educating the people and destroying the enemies. The Talks became the authoritative guidelines for writers and artists, who were expected from 1942 on in the Communist-controlled areas and from 1949 on all over China to conform to Party ideology and obey its instructions.

After 1949 the control that the Party practiced over music revealed itself in the organization of musicians in tightly controlled, state-sponsored associations, conservatories and song-and-dance troupes (*gewutuan*). The party not only controlled the production of music but also its dissemination, as all printed and electronic media and every large-scale public event started to be controlled by the party-state and its branches, which were omnipresent in every city and every village. As part of this process the entire record and film industry in China was nationalized.

The politicization of music reached its peak during the Cultural Revolution (1966–76), the most politicized period in the history of the PRC, during which music, like all other art forms, turned into a pure propaganda tool. Much of the musical repertory that existed prior to the revolution was banned, perceived to be inadequately or counter-revolutionary. This repertory was replaced by a new one, which included a handful of modernized Beijing operas and two ballets, which were labeled together 'model plays' (*yangbanxi*), and numerous new revolutionary songs. Never before was the range of style and content of music in China so narrow and standardized as during this period. The songs and operas praised Mao, cited from his famous quotations and slogans, and eulogized the revolution, class struggle, work, production and other socialist values. Many of them were created collectively and were intended for collective performance either by professional choirs or by the common people in mass rallies or other gatherings.

In addition, all music was militant and heroic, while soft, lyrical songs (*shuqing gequ*) were considered bourgeois. The revolutionary songs and modern operas were heard everywhere and at all times, as many people testify, and played an important role in triggering and inspiring the revolution and in providing the fuel that kept it going for a whole decade.

Seen from a wholly different perspective, with its homogenized, revolutionary mass culture and suppression of many regional and traditional cultures and individualistic artistic expressions, the Maoist era also played an important role in fulfilling one of the top targets set forth by Chinese nationalists at least since the end of the nineteenth century, namely, the establishing of a politically and culturally unified modern nation-state.

It is important to note, however, that even during the extremely politicized decade of the Cultural Revolution, the Party did not have absolute control over the production of music and its dissemination. Although much more research on this topic is still needed, it is known that during that period there also existed other forms of popular music that did not conform to official prescriptions. The best-known alternative body of music was disseminated among the rusticated educated youth (*zhiqing*), who were sent from the cities to remote rural areas for re-education through hard labor. It is estimated that close to 20 million young urbanites were sent to the countryside during the Cultural Revolution. Several scholars have pointed out that, in addition to popular revolutionary song, many of these young-sters also sang and composed other songs like love songs and other forbidden songs from China and abroad, as well as many that depicted their experience in a much less idealized light than the official representation of that experience. These songs were labeled *zhiqing gequ* (songs of educated youth) and some of them were recorded and released on cassettes in the late 1980s and early 1990s.

Popular Music, Politics, Economy and Technology in the Reform Era

In the late 1970s and early 1980s China saw the introduction of cassette and tape-recording technology, which had an enormous impact on its popular music culture. Cheap and technologically simple, the new technology combined with nascent market and non-official distribution networks of private entrepreneurs (*getihu*) had a decentralizing and democratizing effect in challenging the tight control of the state over music production and dissemination and its homogenizing impact. People could now import easily from outside the country (initially through smuggling); they could also produce alternative musics that were not available through state-controlled radio, television, films or performances, and distribute them independently. The introduction of cassette technology into China was crucial to the introduction and dissemination of *liuxing* music in the late 1970s and early 1980s, to the introduction of rock music half a decade later, to the revival and development of regional and ethnic varieties of popular music, and also to the making of a popular music market.

Parallel to the cassette revolution, the new liberalization and relative retreat of the state from much of people's daily lives also resulted in the reemergence of non-state spaces such as nightclubs and dance halls in which non-official popular music could be performed publicly. Emerging initially in the 'special economic zones' in southern China, which enjoyed a higher degree of autonomy, such venues soon spread to other parts of the country. In the context of emergent non-official venues and new market economy, many musicians started during the 1980s to engage in moonlighting (*zouxue*), that is, to perform outside their state-controlled song-and-dance troupes and other working units. Moonlighting enabled musicians not only to earn more money but also to perform songs that were not included in the narrow, conservative and highly politicized repertory of their troupes. The law of supply and demand and the need to compete for popularity in a free market economy soon affected governmental units, which experienced severe cuts in governmental subsidies during the 1980s. In order to survive, many such units also started to cater to popular taste and were clearly willing to compromise official ideology. It is reasonable to assume that the government tolerated much of this new activity because popular music benefited the new economy, the development of which the government considered one of its main goals.

Popular music not only reflected a changing political reality but also contributed to the change, as many of the new songs that started to circulate in China during the 1980s carried with them messages that were in obvious dissonance with official ideology. Deng Lijun's and other *gangtai* and locally produced *liuxing/tongsu* songs had an important impact on popular thought and behavior, particularly in urban centers. These songs celebrated romantic love and individuality and thus trivialized the collectivist ideology of the party-state. In celebrating sexuality (albeit in a very restrained and implicit manner) and leisure, they also violated communist puritanism and the ethos of hard work and discipline. In addition, *liuxing* songs also legitimized melancholy and despair, sentiments that conflicted with socialist realism and as a result disappeared from the public sphere in the Maoist era.

While *liuxing* songs challenged the state by marginalizing it and by offering escape and autonomy from official discourse and ideology, rock challenged the state by confronting it and its ideology in the most straightforward manner. Like *liuxing* songs, rock celebrated individuality but it also introduced a whole set of alternative values like freedom, criticism, protest, rebellion, non-conformism and the celebration of an out-of-control style, all of which posed a much more serious challenge to the dominant ideology with its emphasis on order, authority and discipline. The link between rock and politics was revealed as early as the mid-1980s. The famous eruption of student unrest in Shanghai in December 1986 came right after a rock concert during which students violated the accepted norms of public order and one of them was beaten by security men. More significantly, three years later rock played a central role in inspiring the Tiananmen student movement of 1989 as Wu'er Kaixi, one of the student leaders, testified a few weeks after he escaped to the United States following the 4 June crackdown. During the movement a song named 'Yiwusuoyou' (Having Nothing) by China's most prominent rocker Cui Jian became the anthem of protesting students all over China, and on 19 May the famous rocker himself arrived at the square and dedicated a new song he had written to the student hunger strikers. The song, 'Toujifenzi' (Opportunists) or 'Youjifenzi' (Guerilla Fighters) as it was originally named, encouraged students to seize the opportunity, express their feelings, show their power and carry on their struggle. Thus after four decades in which the power of music to mobilize the masses was utilized in China exclusively by the Communist Party, which used it to establish its hegemony and control, rock introduced the opposite possibility of using popular music to resist the government.

Despite the considerable liberalization of the reform era, however, the state continued to practice a high degree of control over the popular music scene. The most conspicuous manifestation of state control was the banning of certain types of music, the best example being the long-term exclusion of Chinese rockers from official media and the restrictions that the state regularly imposed on rock performances. An official ban was also practiced in relation to individual musicians who were not necessarily rockers but had a problematic political record. Taiwan superstar A-Mei (Zhang Huimei), for example, was officially banned in China after she sang the Taiwanese anthem at the ROC presidential inauguration in 2000. Likewise, Hong Kong superstar Anita Mui (Mei Yanfang) was prevented from giving live concerts in China after she performed her famous song 'Huan nühai' (Bad Girl) during one of her concerts in the country in 1995, despite official requests not to do so.

Another form of official control was censorship. In the reform era, state-owned publishers still controlled the release and distribution of new albums, and although many record companies were not owned by the state, official license was still required in order to release a new album. Receiving permission for releasing a new album meant that the content, especially song lyrics, had to be inspected and sometimes censored. The long history of tight censorship in China led to a situation in which musicians normally practiced self-censorship prior to submitting their albums for inspection in order to avoid trouble. Censorship was also practiced in live concerts. Prior to receiving a license for holding a large-scale concert (normally of over several hundred people), the organizers had to submit for inspection to officials at the Culture Bureau a list of all the songs that were going to be performed in the event and their lyrics. In addition, when allowed to participate in large-scale concerts, rockers were often warned not to try to stir up the audience and were instructed not to speak to the audience in between songs. Television officials would also inspect and censor song lyrics prior to televised events.

The Chinese state, however, did not only engage in restricting and banning, but also used positive means of control and influence. A good example of this form of control was the use of large-scale pop concerts to propagate official ideology among audiences of thousands and sometimes tens of thousands. Official values and messages were disseminated at such events through slogans on huge placards, through propaganda speeches that were read between songs by well-trained anchors, through the dates on which the concerts were held, which normally had political significance, and

through the songs themselves. While some of the songs in these concerts typically carried political messages, such events nevertheless usually included songs in all genres and thus simultaneously communicated a sense of diversity, pluralism and artistic freedom, which helped to present the state as liberal and democratic. At the same time, by having a diverse program that included minority folk songs on one hand, and rock songs on the other, state officials also hoped to propagate unity and no less importantly to tame the exclusivist rebelliousness associated with rock. Famous singers from Hong Kong and Taiwan were often invited to participate in such concerts, certainly to increase profits, but also to help propagate the idea of one China.

Another important aspect of the politicization of large-scale concerts was embodied in their structure and style. The delivery of pre-written politicized speeches, the fact that performers rarely interacted with the audience, that concerts ran according to strict, pre-written plan, and that the audience were normally expected to remain seated throughout the event, all turned pop concerts into disciplining rituals that helped to dramatize and re-establish state authority and control, and perpetuate the norms and sense of social order.

State-sponsored song competitions were another manifestation of the important role that the state played in controlling and shaping the popular music scene. Such competitions normally had clear political-artistic standards. They encouraged musicians to produce 'healthy' and 'positive' songs that expressed 'love for the homeland' and which the state could use for propaganda and education purposes. The state rewarded conformity to its prescribed standards in various ways, the most important of which was the promotion of award-winning songs in official media and particularly on television.

In the 1990s, television was the most important means that the state used to shape and control popular music culture. Aware of the enormous popularity and powerful impact of modern popular music and its political and economic potential, officials at the state-run CCTV established in 1993 China's own MTV. Named Zhongguo yinyue dianshi (Chinese Music Television), this body became part of the CCTV responsible for producing video-clips for selected popular songs, and from the mid-1990s China's national television started to broadcast popular music programs on a daily basis to hundreds of millions of television sets throughout the country. These programs presented a mixture of songs and clips, some of which had no political message at all, while others were always used as vehicles for propaganda. China's MTV thus satisfied in a controlled manner the growing demand for modern pop, for fashion, beautiful stars, entertainment and romance, at the same time enabling the state to use popular music in a most effective way to propagate official ideology and values.

Political Economy in the 1990s

In the early 1990s economic activity in China intensified to an unprecedented extent and the country was taken over by radical commercialization and consumerism. In this context many foreign record companies started to invest in the local market, new local companies were born and popular music turned into an important industry. Musicians now signed contracts with companies and were packaged and marketed as commodities.

Hand in hand with the commercialization of popular music there was a dramatic increase in piracy and in the early 2000s it was estimated that approximately 95 percent of music recordings that circulated in China were pirated versions. Many of these versions were not simple replication of existing originals but rather independent new productions with new design, title and content. In many cases such versions included songs that were recorded in live performances or from television shows and had never appeared on any original album. The widespread piracy in China led to a situation in which pop musicians relied for their livelihood mainly on live performances. The increase in commercialization made pop concerts in China an extremely profitable business so that in the early 2000s famous musicians could earn more than 100,000 yuan (US$12,500) in a single performance of just two or three songs. At that time the average monthly salary in China was around 600 yuan. This widespread piracy, combined with the economic potential that was embodied in live concerts, consequently led record companies to start functioning also as agents and to charge musicians with whom they signed contracts a certain percentage of the profits they earned from live performances (usually 20–50 percent).

A more significant implication of piracy, however, was the dependency of musicians on the state. If, during the 1980s and early 1990s, the emergent free market economy and the introduction of new technologies posed a serious challenge to state hegemony, by the mid-1990s it was clear that the state had adapted to the new conditions and learned how to appropriate both the market and some of the new technologies to consolidate its hegemony and control. The maintenance of tight control over television and the massive incorporation of popular music into this medium meant that the government controlled the most effective promotional tool in the country in the context of capitalist market. The same also applied to state control over large-scale pop concerts. Combined with piracy, this control meant that if pop musicians wanted to survive artistically, not to mention make a decent living, they had to maintain good relationship with officialdom and play the game according to official rules, at least to a certain extent. This situation led to a symbiotic system in which self-employed musicians often participated in highly politicized events and sometimes even wrote several 'healthy' songs that served the interests of the state in return for exposure. Thus, despite the fact that, in sharp contrast to the Maoist era, artists in the reform era were not pressured or persecuted politically as in the past, most of them nonetheless still submitted to the state (albeit to a significantly lesser degree), because the state now occupied a privileged position in the newly born market economy on which all of them depended. The link between the state on the one hand and important media and the market on the other helps to explain how the state was able to maintain a central position in popular music culture in the reform era, and why rock declined in the mid-1990s.

Ethnicity and Nationalism

One of the most impressive cultural projects in China after 1949 was the organized production and popularization of a massive body of artistic representations of ethnic minorities. As part of this project, songs about minorities (hereafter 'minority songs') started to be produced on a large scale, and with the support of the government became an important part of the new revolutionary mass culture. Minority songs normally incorporated elements from minority music and languages, and described local scenery and customs. They were often performed by minority singers dressed in colorful traditional-style ethnic costumes to the accompaniment of ethnic dance. Many of these songs were love songs and songs about local festivities and nature. The majority of the songs, however, including those just mentioned, carried political messages either in explicit or implicit form.

Minority songs have usually been referred to as 'folk songs' (*min'ge*) and the creation of many of them, like the creation of many Han Chinese folk songs, followed the pattern of setting new politicized lyrics to preexisting tunes or newly composed tunes that drew upon old ones.

The production and popularization of minority songs was part of the effort of the new regime to advance national integration and unity, and solidarity among China's different nationalities. They also constituted part of the effort to assert control over minority territories and peoples, and at the same time to foster a sense of belonging and loyalty to the new state among the latter by offering them representation in the new culture. In addition, the songs legitimated the new regime and propagated official ideologies among minority people. As part of the effort to incorporate ethnic minorities, minority musicians began to be trained in state institutions and were integrated into state-run song-and-dance troupes. Party officials often spoke about the commitment of the Party to preserving and developing minority cultures, and nothing demonstrated this commitment in the domain of music better than the establishing of song-and-dance troupes that specialized in minority music and dance. Labeled *minzu gewutuan* ('nationalities song-and-dance troupes'), these organizations and others provided much support to minority musicians and contributed to their professionalization and to the development and modernization of minority music. They also encouraged minority musicians to produce minority songs, and promoted them all over the country. Minority songs and dances added much diversity to the musical landscape on the mainland, which otherwise became increasingly standardized and homogenized.

At the same time, however, because they were state run and Han dominated, the activities of song-and-dance troupes and other institutions that incorporated minority musicians and music also resulted in the Sinification of minority music. Sinification was manifested most conspicuously in the language that was usually used in the songs. Although many songs incorporated a few words in a minority language and some had a complete minority-language version, the large majority of minority songs were sung in Mandarin Chinese. Similarly, although aiming to demonstrate diversity and pluralism in their explicit references to minority cultures, minority songs simultaneously neutralized significant otherness. This neutralization

revealed itself in standard messages such as calls for the unity of all ethnic groups and expressions of loyalty to Mao, the Communist Party and socialism, all of which left little room for real difference. Furthermore, many of the songs were composed or arranged so they would fit 'modern' (Western) musical standards and the obligatory aesthetics of socialist realism, both of which further decreased difference. Socialist realism was seen in the idealization of minority life in song lyrics and in the standard disciplined and highly choreographed and presentational cheerful performance.

In addition, although carrying explicit messages about solidarity, unity and equality, minority songs simultaneously reflected and promulgated the clear asymmetrical power relationship between the minorities on one hand and the Han majority and the Chinese state on the other. Much of the new repertoire was produced by Han musicians working directly for the government or the People's Liberation Army, in the hands of whom local material was transformed to fit Han ears. The central role that Han musicians and songwriters played in the production of minority songs and the impact of the dominant culture were also manifested in the content of the lyrics. These often revealed Han subjectivity in exoticizing the minorities and their customs, and in using trivial if not denigrating stereotypic images that turned minorities into inferior others. Most minority songs, therefore, were more *about* minorities than by or even for them.

Minority songs from the revolutionary period were still very popular in the post-Mao era and many of them were now performed in new, more contemporary renditions in unorthodox singing styles, to the accompaniment of amplified instruments, and sometimes to rock and disco beats. Furthermore, many old minority songs that were not overtly politicized, and as a result were banned during the Cultural Revolution, were now revived and new ones composed along the same lines. Normally these songs did not mention Mao, Deng or the Party, and did not praise socialism and the unity of all nationalities or assert loyalty to the Chinese state, at least not explicitly. Nevertheless they still communicated strong Han subjectivity and usually trivialized and neutralized minority otherness by presenting minority people and culture as colorful exotic objects, or alternatively by focusing on the beautiful landscapes of minority areas while completely ignoring the people who lived there. These seemingly non-politicized songs also conformed to the old principle of socialist realism in the fact that, when not ignored and actually referred to or involved in performance, minority people usually smiled and danced cheerfully in colorful costumes and avoided any meaningful statements or expressions that did not conform to official discourse.

This continuity notwithstanding, with the general liberalization of the reform era, a powerful resurgence of ethnicity and ethnic nationalism, and the commodification of ethnicity, there also emerged some new minority songs. The most conspicuous addition to the orthodox repertoire was offered, beginning from the mid-1990s, by several young musicians of ethnic minority origin who started to offer a conscious challenge to the orthodox songs and to the way minorities were being represented in general in China. These musicians were typically born in minority areas, moved during the late 1980s and early 1990s to Beijing, and were not affiliated with state-sponsored song-and-dance troupes. While in some of their songs they perpetuated the stereotypical exotic images associated with their ethnic group, they simultaneously struggled to expand the range of topics and style of representation that characterized orthodox minority songs and to assert modernity, subjectivity and authenticity. This struggle revealed itself in the fact that most of them adopted rock at least to a certain degree, and avoided performing their songs in the traditional-style exotic costumes of their ethnic groups. More significantly, in some of their songs several of these young minority musicians went even further, voicing dissatisfaction with the position of minority people in China and the orthodox narratives relating to their identity. An example of this new independent and challenging minority voice is 'Cang lang dadi' (The Land of the Blue Wolf), a song in rock style sung in Mandarin by the Mongolian Chinese musician Teng Ge'er, in which he expresses discontent over the loss of Mongolian identity and land, and longing for the times when the Mongols dominated China.

The powerful assertions of a different ethnicity in the works of young minority musicians in the 1990s clearly reflected and inspired the growing sense of ethnic identity and in some cases also of ethnic nationalism among China's minorities. However, these assertions were simultaneously targeted as satisfying the growing market demand in the 1990s for ethnic things, and ironically also indicated increasing integration of minorities and minority cultures in the general Chinese cultural sphere. Two factors that contributed to the popularity of minority songs were their ability to offer an exotic alternative to the highly 'homogenized' and 'oppressive' mainstream and, paradoxically perhaps, their capacity to assert Chineseness in the context of increasing Westernization and globalization.

In addition to minority musicians who gained fame at the national level and who, despite their assertions of otherness, catered also (if not mainly) to a Han audience, Deng's reforms led to the re-emergence of local pop stars in minority areas who maintained closer ties with their communities and their traditional music. These musicians, whose music was disseminated through locally produced cassettes and at best through local television and radio stations, sang in minority languages and used local instruments and musical idioms that were significantly different from the Han Chinese mainstream. Their music was the best example of the resilience and vitality of regional and ethnic cultures amid the homogenization of the Maoist era and the globalization that came about in the following era. For minority people this music was obviously instrumental in maintaining and asserting different identity vis-à-vis the Han majority and its dominant culture.

Gender and Sexuality

Traditional Chinese concepts and practices relating to romance and sexuality are characterized by strong emphasis on concealment, restraint and implicit expression. In literature and the performing arts, romantic love thus has normally been expressed through metaphors and indirect exchange of tender words, rather than through straightforward expression of carnal desire or physical contact. Moreover, in accordance with the Confucian ideology that generated these preferences, although popular literature and art in traditional China boasted strongly built and tough warriors who mastered martial (*wu*) arts, the ideal man, at least in the last millennium, was often a refined, delicate and sometimes extremely sentimental figure who mastered calligraphy, the writing of poetry and other civil (*wen*) arts. The physical and mental attributes of this ideal model of manhood suggest that gender in traditional China was grounded less in physical difference and more in social role. Despite the obvious preference for qualities that in China, as in the West, have often been referred to as 'feminine,' women in traditional society and culture were far from privileged. They were not allowed to participate in any public activity and were confined for centuries to the domestic sphere (footbinding helped to keep them there). Women were even excluded from traditional Chinese opera, one of the most popular art forms in traditional China, in which all female roles were impersonated by male actors.

Traditional practices and ideology that relate to gender and sexuality started to change in the early decades of the twentieth century under Western influence, and as with Chinese opera in traditional China, *liuxing* music and *qunzhong gequ* reflected and shaped many of these changes. In the former women sang in public in their own voice, and no less important, they often sang about romantic love and even about kisses. These songs reflected and contributed to the spread of new liberal ideas regarding romantic love and sexuality that started to gain popularity in major Chinese cities, and also projected and promulgated the controversial nascent image of 'the new/modern woman.' While many of these songs maintained the traditional aesthetics of restraint, moderation and concealment, others were totally Westernized and used lively Western dance rhythms, like tango and swing, and a full and powerful voice, all of which represented a much more radical break from tradition. *Qunzhong gequ*, on the other hand, in which men and women sang together heroically about the rescuing of the nation and avoided any reference to romantic love or sexuality, introduced a new, Western-style masculine, militant ethos, revolutionary puritanism and the communist interpretation of equality between the sexes.

The emergence of *qunzhong gequ* as a dominant musical genre during the Maoist era and the simultaneous disappearance of *liuxing* music both reflected and contributed to the radical shift during that era from the traditional aesthetics of refinement, delicacy and restraint to the militant and masculine revolutionary proletariat ethos that emphasized strong bodies, physical power, hard physical work and bold expression. The new musical landscape also reflected and shaped the radical transformation in the domain of gender and sexuality that took place during that era. The Mao years saw the development of a unisex culture in the context of which ideal women were supposed to look and behave like men and conform like the latter to the new masculine ethos that the revolution introduced. This trend reached its peak in the Cultural Revolution, during which gender differences were erased. If hitherto women were expected to wear the same working uniforms that men wore, not to adorn themselves and not to use

makeup, they were now also expected and often forced to wear their hair short, and in some cases also to tie their breasts so that it would look as if they did not have any. This new concept of womanhood revealed itself most forcefully in the much-celebrated officially sponsored image of the 'iron girls' (*tie guniang*), which emerged in literature and art right before the Cultural Revolution and depicted women doing traditionally male jobs like drilling for oil and repairing electricity lines. The heroic and militant mixed-group singing that was so popular during the Maoist period was both informed by and played an important role in the dissemination of the new unisex ethos. Such singing blurred the male/female dualism that was always a major ingredient in popular and folk songs. Even when singing alone women could no longer sing in the soft and sweet voice that was always considered an inseparable part of femininity, because the songs that required such singing simply disappeared from the public sphere. Instead, they too normally had to conform to the new masculine musical style and sing in a militant, loud and powerful voice, in fast tempo, and to a strong, march-like beat, all of which reinforced their newly masculine image.

Gender erasure during the Cultural Revolution came hand in hand with the elimination of any public expression of sexuality and romance, and, as gender distinctions and everything that was considered feminine disappeared in music, so the theme of romantic love disappeared also. Love songs were considered *huangse* (yellow), meaning pornographic, and were blamed for relaxing people's morale and for being decadent and part of Western capitalist bourgeois individualism and liberalism. Militant, mass singing helped to eliminate the intimacy and softness that has always been associated with love songs and, after 1949, such songs were gradually replaced in public culture by songs that articulated instead love for the Party, the homeland and chairman Mao.

Gender ideology and practice, and attitudes toward romance and sexuality changed drastically once again as a result of Deng's reforms. The extreme popularity that Deng Lijun's soft, slow, sweet, and breathy (*qisheng*) love songs gained as soon as they were introduced into China in the late 1970s suggested a powerful reaction to the gender erasure and the elimination of romance during the Cultural Revolution. By patronizing Deng Lijun's songs, people expressed their desire to revive gender distinctions, romance and traditional-style, soft femininity. Deng Lijun's songs were admired by both men and women. For the latter in particular they served as a powerful model for emulation, which was instrumental in regaining a sense of distinctive gender identity after years in which women were 'liberated' but at the same time were denied the right to be different.

Another expression of the post-Mao revival of gender was a crisis in masculinity among Chinese male writers and artists that emerged in the mid-1980s. By now it became clear that the masculine ethos of the Maoist era did not mean that men were necessarily empowered during those three decades. On the contrary, many men felt emasculated by the oppressive political order of that period and the fact that women started to participate in domains that were traditionally considered an exclusive male territory. Against this background, rock and a hybrid style named *xibeifeng* (northwest wind) proved extremely useful for regaining and asserting masculinity. The close association between masculinity and rock was demonstrated first and foremost in the fact that the style was performed and patronized predominantly by men. It was also revealed in the lyrics of many rock songs, which usually expressed male subjectivity and asserted male superiority. Many songs objectified women, often as sex objects and sometimes as competitors, and some even articulated overt misogyny. Rock not only served as a vehicle to express masculinity but actually introduced a new, Western model of masculinity, one that emphasized the male body, overt sexuality, independence, individualism, coarse and tough behavior, direct and bold expression, and defiance. In addition, rock also provided Chinese rockers and rock fans with a way to regain a sense of power because it signified Westernization and modernity.

The *xibeifeng* fad, which emerged simultaneously with rock and swept China in the late 1980s, was perceived as masculine too, but was used to assert masculinity in somewhat different way. Songs belonging to this style constituted one of numerous hybrid musical forms that emerged in China in the 1980s and 1990s. They combined melodic folk music from northwest China, which aimed to articulate Chinese identity, with synthesized disco and rock beats, which aimed to assert modernity. They were sung in a powerful, yelling, coarse and casual voice that was meant to imitate crude authentic peasant singing (but was actually heavily influenced by rock), and their lyrics focused on images of the countryside. The fad was part of the

Root Seeking (*xungen*) cultural movement that swept China in the mid-1980s, in which Chinese writers and artists tried among other things to establish their distinctive and superior Chinese identity as a reaction to the influx of pop from Hong Kong, Taiwan and the West. In sharp contrast to the soft and 'feminine' aesthetics of *gangtai* songs and their urban refinement, *xibeifeng* songs celebrated a kind of primitive, rustic virility that was meant to assert authentic and powerful Chineseness. The fad was said to be the revival of the *yang* (masculine) forces after several years in which the *yin* (feminine), embodied in *gangtai* songs, dominated the popular music scene on the mainland.

One of the most popular *xibeifeng* songs was 'Meimei qu' (Young Sister's Song) (also named 'Meimei ni dadan de wangqian zou' [Young Sister Go Boldly Forward]), which was first sung in Zhang Yimou's 1987 film *Red Sorghum*. The song was performed in the film after the male protagonist, a strongly built porter who is often shown half naked, makes love to a woman whom he was hired to carry to her wedding. After the love scene, which starts more like a rape and takes place in the middle of a sorghum field, the man shouts the song, the lyrics of which express male desire, with a powerful masculine husky voice. Indicating that the style was also related to politics within China, one Chinese critic suggested that 'Young Sister's Song' was 'the rise of a real man who is under profound oppression' (Yang and Zhang 1990, 410).

Despite the masculine aesthetics of *xibeifeng*, many songs in this style were sung by female singers. These singers projected an image that was much closer to that of the 'iron girls' of the revolutionary era than the soft image associated with Deng Lijun and the many female singers who started to imitate her on the mainland. Taken together, the two groups of singers indicated that in reform China, in contrast to the Maoist era (and traditional China), the public sphere accepted the simultaneous existence of multiple models of womanhood, multiplicity that implied among other things unprecedented choice for women with regard to their gender identity.

Yet the pop scene in the reform era also revealed the limits of women's choice. This was most obvious in the exclusion (with few exceptions) of women from rock, which since its emergence in China was men's territory. Since rock was intimately tied to modernity, independence, rebelliousness and direct and subjective expression, the exclusion of women from rock meant that women had limited access to important practices and a narrower range of artistic possibilities. Significantly enough, the few female voices that emerged in the popular music scene in China in the mid-1990s – and problematized the position of women and challenged male dominance and male hegemonic discourse of love – all drew upon rock and related styles. Thus the exclusion of women from rock could be seen as a male strategy to silence women, put them back in their traditional place, and keep them under control. Western rock, in other words, helped Chinese youth to subvert the authoritarian state, but simultaneously was appropriated to articulate and reconstruct old hierarchies in the domain of gender.

Men not only dominated rock but also all other musical styles. They controlled (as, for example, composers, songwriters, producers and record company managers) most of the music industry and produced most of the songs, including those of the most famous female singers. This resulted in a situation in which women in the pop scene of the reform era, as in the past, were often objectified, and it was often a male subjectivity that one heard even in songs that women performed. The dominance of men in the music industry also implied that men played a privileged role in the construction of popular female images in the Chinese pop scene.

The revival or persistence of traditional values and practices relating to gender and sexuality was also demonstrated in the decline of rock in the mid-1990s. It could be argued that, among other reasons, rock declined because of its celebration of overt sexuality, which contrasted sharply with traditional (and official) codes that stressed concealment and modesty. Similarly, since the celebration of the rough and rebellious macho-type masculinity was one of the most important elements in rock, it could also be argued that the genre declined because this Western-inspired masculinity did not fit the resurgent traditional ideals regarding manhood, which stressed restraint, moderation and gentleness. This resurgence was revealed in the mid-1990s in the increased popularity of male singers who sang slow and sweet songs about lost love in soft voices accompanied by slushy violins. For sure, the rebellious cowboy-type masculinity that was celebrated in rock posed a serious threat to the state, and it may have constituted another cause for the systematic suppression of the genre by officialdom. The state obviously preferred more docile and obedient subjects who would fit the post-1989 neo-Confucian order that stressed stability, harmony, order and authority.

Bibliography

Baranovitch, Nimrod. 2001. 'Between Alterity and Identity: New Voices of Minority People in China.' *Modern China* 27(3): 359–401.

Baranovitch, Nimrod. 2003. *China's New Voices: Popular Music, Ethnicity, Gender, and Politics, 1978–1997*. Berkeley, CA: University of California Press.

Baranovitch, Nimrod. 2003. 'From the Margins to the Centre: The Uyghur Challenge in Beijing.' *The China Quarterly* 175: 726–50.

Barmé, Geremie. 1992. 'Official Bad Boys or True Rebels.' *Human Rights Tribune* 3(4): 17–20.

Bernoviz (Baranovitch), Nimrod. 1997. *China's New Voices: Politics, Ethnicity, and Gender in Popular Music Culture on the Mainland, 1978-1997*. Unpublished Ph.D. dissertation, University of Pittsburgh, PA.

Blake, Fred. 1979. 'Love Songs and the Great Leap: The Role of a Youth Culture in the Revolutionary Phase of China's Economic Development.' *American Ethnologist* 6(1): 41–54.

Brace, Timothy. 1991. 'Popular Music in Contemporary Beijing: Modernism and Cultural Identity.' *Asian Music* 22(2): 43–66.

Brace, Timothy. 1992. *Modernization and Music in Contemporary China: Crisis, Identity, and the Politics of Style*. Unpublished Ph.D. dissertation, University of Texas at Austin.

Brace, Timothy, and Friedlander, Paul. 1992. 'Rock and Roll on the New Long March: Popular Music, Cultural Identity, and Political Opposition in the People's Republic of China.' In *Rockin' the Boat: Mass Music and Mass Movements*, ed. Reebee Garofalo. Boston, MA: South End Press, 115–28.

de Kloet, Jeroen. 2000. '"Let Him Fucking See the Green Smoke Beneath My Groin": The Mythology of Chinese Rock.' In *Postmodernism and China*, ed. Arif Dirlik and Xudong Zhang. Durham, NC: Duke University Press, 239–74.

Dujunco, Mercedes M. 2002. 'Hybridity and Disjuncture in Mainland Chinese Popular Music.' In *Global Goes Local: Popular Culture in Asia*, ed. Timothy J. Craig and Richard King. Honolulu: Association for Asian Studies and University of Hawai'i Press, 25–39.

Efird, Robert. 2001. 'Rock in a Hard Place: Music and the Market in Nineties Beijing.' In *China Urban: Ethnographies of Contemporary Culture*, ed. Nancy Chen et al. Durham, NC: Duke University Press, 67–86.

Friedlander, Paul. 1991. 'China's "Newer Value"

Pop: Rock-and-Roll and Technology on the New Long March.' *Asian Music* 22(2): 67–81.

Gold, Thomas B. 1993. 'Go With Your Feelings: Hong Kong and Taiwan Popular Culture in Greater China.' *The China Quarterly* 136: 907–25.

Guy, Nancy. 2002. '"Republic of China National Anthem" on Taiwan: One Anthem, One Performance, Multiple Realities.' *Ethnomusicology* 46(1): 96–119.

Hamm, Charles. 1991. 'Music and Radio in the People's Republic of China.' *Asian Music* 22(2): 1–42.

Han, Kuo-huang. 1980. Sleeve Notes to *Vocal Music of Contemporary China: Vol. 2 – The National Minorities* (LP Record). Folkways Records.

Harris, Rachel. 2002. 'Cassettes, Bazaars, and Saving the Nation: The Uyghur Music Industry in Xinjiang, China.' In *Global Goes Local: Popular Culture in Asia*, ed. Timothy J. Craig and Richard King. Honolulu: Association for Asian Studies and University of Hawai'i Press, 265–83.

Harris, Rachel. n.d. 'Wang Luobin: "Folksong King of the Northwest" or Song Thief?: Copyright, Representation and Chinese "Folksongs".' Unpublished paper.

Holm, David. 1984. 'Folk Art as Propaganda: The *Yangge* Movement in Yan'an.' In *Popular Chinese Literature and Performing Arts in the People's Republic of China 1949-1979*, ed. Bonnie S. McDougall. Berkeley, CA: University of California Press, 1–35.

Huang Liaoyuan, et al., eds. 1997. *Shi nian: 1986–1996 Zhongguo liuxing yinyue jishi* [Ten Years: Account of Popular Chinese Music, 1986-1996]. Beijing: Zhongguo dianying chubanshe.

Huot, Claire. 2000. 'Rock Music from Mao to Nirvana.' In *China's New Cultural Scene: A Handbook of Changes*, ed. Claire Huot. Durham, NC: Duke University Press, 154–81.

Jin Zhaojun. 2002. *Guangtianhuari xia de liuxing: Qinli Zhongguo liuxing yinyue* [Under the Naked Sun: My Personal Experience of Chinese Popular Music]. Beijing: Renmin yinyue chubanshe.

Jones, Andrew F. 1992a. *Like a Knife: Ideology and Genre in Contemporary Chinese Popular Music*. Ithaca, NY: East Asian Program, Cornell University.

Jones, Andrew F. 1992b. 'Beijing Bastards.' *Spin* (October): 80–90, 122–23.

Jones, Andrew F. 1994. 'The Politics of Popular Music in Post-Tiananmen China.' In *Popular Protest and Political Culture in Modern China*, ed. Jeffrey N. Wasserstrom and Elizabeth J. Perry. 2nd ed. Boulder, CO: Westview Press, 148–65. (First published Boulder, CO: Westview Press, 1992.)

Jones, Andrew F. 2001. *Yellow Music: Media Culture and Colonial Modernity in the Chinese Jazz Age*. Durham, NC: Duke University Press.

Kraus, Richard Curt. 1989. *Pianos and Politics in China: Middle-Class Ambitions and the Struggle Over Western Music*. New York: Oxford University Press.

Lee, Coral. 2000. 'From Little Teng to A-Mei: Marking Time in Music.' *Sinorama* 25(3): 33–44.

Lee, Gregory. 1995. 'The "East is Red" Goes Pop: Commodification, Hybridity and Nationalism in Chinese Popular Song and Its Televisual Performance.' *Popular Music* 14(1): 95–110.

Lee, Joanna Ching-Yun. 1992a. 'All for the Music: The Rise of Patriotic/Pro-Democratic Popular Music in Hong Kong in Response to the Chinese Student Movement.' In *Rockin' the Boat: Mass Music and Mass Movements*, ed. Reebee Garofalo. Boston, MA: South End Press, 129–47.

Lee, Joanna Ching-Yun. 1992b. 'Cantopop on Emigration from Hong Kong.' *Yearbook for Traditional Music* 24: 14–23.

Liang Maochun. 1988. 'Dui wo guo liuxing yinyue lishi de sikao' [Reflections on the History of Our Country's Popular Music]. *Renmin yinyue* 7: 32–34.

Ling Ruilan, ed. 1994. *Zhongguo xiandai youxiu gequ jingcui jicheng: Tongsu gequ 1978-1990* [A Pithy Collection of Excellent Modern Chinese Songs: Tongsu Songs 1978-1990]. Shenyang: Chunfeng wenyi chubanshe.

Ling Xuan. 1989. '"Xibeifeng" yu "qiu ge"' ('Northwest Wind' and 'Prison Songs'). *Renmin yinyue* 5: 37–38.

Mackerras, Colin. 1984. 'Folksongs and Dances of China's Minority Nationalities: Policy, Tradition, and Professionalization.' *Modern China* 10(2): 187–226.

Micic, Peter. 1995. '"A Bit of This and a Bit of That": Notes on Pop/Rock Genres in the Eighties in China.' *CHIME* 8: 76–95.

Micic, Peter. 1999/2000. 'A Selective List of Pop 'n' Rock Loan Words and Neologisms in the PRC.' *CHIME* 14–15: 103–23.

Samson, Valerie. 1991. 'Music as Protest Strategy: The Example of Tiananmen Square, 1989.' *Pacific Review of Ethnomusicology* 6: 35–64.

Schell, Orville. 1994. 'Nothing to My Name.' In *Mandate of Heaven: A New Generation of Entrepreneurs, Dissidents, Bohemians, and Technocrats Lays Claim to China's Future*, ed. Orville Schell. New York: Simon & Schuster, 311–20.

Steen, Andreas. 1996. *Der Lange Marsch des Rock 'n' Roll: Pop-und Rockmusik in der Volksrepublik China* [The Long March of Rock and Roll: Pop and Rock Music in the People's Republic of China]. Hamburg: Lit Verlag.

Steen, Andreas. 1999/2000. 'Tradition, Politics and Meaning in 20th Century China's Popular Music; Zhou Xuan: "When will the Gentleman Come Back Again?".' *CHIME* 14–15: 124–53.

Stock, Jonathan. 1995. 'Reconsidering the Past: Zhou Xuan and the Rehabilitation of Early Twentieth-Century Popular Music.' *Asian Music* 26(2): 119–135.

Sun Ji'nan. 1993. *Li Jinhui pingzhuan* [Annotated Biography of Li Jinhui]. Beijing: Renmin yinyue chubanshe.

Upton, Janet L. 2002. 'The Politics and Poetics of *Sister Drum*: "Tibetan" Music in the Global Marketplace.' In *Global Goes Local: Popular Culture in Asia*, ed. Timothy J. Craig and Richard King. Honolulu: Association for Asian Studies and University of Hawai'i Press, 99–119.

Wang Ruijiang, and Li Yuzhen, eds. 1994. *Zhongguo xiandai youxiu gequ jingcui jicheng: Yingshi gequ 1978-1990* [A Pithy Collection of Excellent Modern Chinese Songs: Film and Television Songs 1978–1990]. Shenyang: Chunfeng wenyi chubanshe.

Wang Xiaofeng. 1995. 'He Yong nao Xianggang' [He Yong Stirs Hong Kong]. *Yinxiang shijie* 3: 2–3.

Wheeler-Snow, Lois. 1972. *China on Stage: An American Actress in the People's Republic*. New York: Random House.

Witzleben, Lawrence. 1999. 'Cantopop and Mandopop in Pre-Postcolonial Hong Kong: Identity Negotiation in the Performances of Anita Mui Yim-Fong.' *Popular Music* 18(2): 241–58.

Wong, Cynthia P. 1996. 'Cui Jian, Rock Musician and Reluctant Hero.' *ACMR Reports* 9(1): 21–32.

Wong, Isabel K.F. 1984. '*Geming Gequ*: Songs for the Education of the Masses.' In *Popular Chinese Literature and Performing Arts in the People's Republic of China 1949-1979*, ed. Bonnie S. McDougall. Berkeley, CA: University of California Press, 112–43.

Wu Peng. 1990. 'Zhongguo 1949–1979 nian shuqing gequ, qunzhong gequ gaishu' [A General Description of Chinese Lyrical and Mass Songs Between 1949 and 1979]. In *Zhongwai tongsu gequ jianshang cidian*, ed. Yang Xiaolu and Zhang Zhentao. Beijing: Shijie zhishi chubanshe, 85–88.

Xue Ji. 1993. *Yaogun meng xun: Zhongguo yaogunyue shilu* [The Search for the Rock and Roll Dream: The True Story of Chinese Rock]. Beijing: Zhongguo dianying chubanshe.

Yang Xiaolu. 1990. 'Zhongguo dangdai tongsu gequ gaishu' [A General Description of Contemporary Chinese *Tongsu* Songs]. In *Zhongwai tongsu gequ jianshang cidian*, ed. Yang Xiaolu and Zhang Zhentao. Beijing: Shijie zhishi chubanshe, 225–27.

Yang Xiaolu, and Zhang Zhentao, eds. 1990. *Zhongwai tongsu gequ jianshang cidian* [An Appreciative Dictionary of Chinese and Foreign *Tongsu* Songs]. Beijing: Shijie zhishi chubanshe.

Yung, Bell. 1984. 'Model Opera as Model: From *Shajiabang* to *Sagabong*.' In *Popular Chinese Literature and Performing Arts in the People's Republic of China 1949-1979*, ed. Bonnie S. McDougall. Berkeley, CA: University of California Press, 144–64.

Zeng Yi. 1988. 'Qiu ge de fengxing shuoming le shenme?' [What Does the Popularity of Prison Songs Mean?]. *Guangming ribao* (19 October).

Zha, Jianying. 1995. 'Islanders.' In *China Pop: How Soap Operas, Tabloids, and Bestsellers Are Transforming a Culture*, ed. Jianying Zha. New York: New Press, 165–99.

Zhang Guangtian. 1996. 'Miao wu qing ge, chun lai hu? Guanyu "liuxing yinyue" de ji dian sikao' [Good Songs and Wonderful Dances, Has Spring Arrived?: Some Thoughts About 'Popular Music']. *Bailaohui* 1: 50–51.

Zhang Zhentao. 1990. 'Zhongguo san si shi niandai liuxing gequ, qunzhong gequ gaishu' [A General Description of Mass and *Liuxing* Songs in China During the 1930s and 1940s]. In *Zhongwai tongsu gequ jianshang cidian*, ed. Yang Xiaolu and Zhang Zhentao. Beijing: Shijie zhishi chubanshe, 1–5.

Zhao Jianwei. 1992. *Cui Jian zai yiwusuoyou zhong nahan: Zhongguo yaogun beiwanglu* [Cui Jian Cries Out in Having Nothing: A Memorandum on Chinese Rock]. Beijing: Beijing shifan daxue chubanshe.

Zhou You, ed. 1994. *Beijing yaogun buluo* [Beijing's Rock Tribe]. Tianjin: Shehuikexueyuan chubanshe.

Discographical References

Cui Jian. 'Toujifenzi.' *Cui Jian: Jiejue* [Cui Jian: Solution]. Zhongguo beiguang shengxiang yishu gongsi BSL 029. *1991*: China.

Cui Jian. 'Yiwusuoyou.' *Cui Jian: Xin changzheng lu shang de yaogun* [Cui Jian: Rock and Roll of the New Long March]. Zhongguo lüyou shengxiang chubanshe BZJ01. *1989*: China.

Mui Anita Yim-Fong (Mei Yanfang). 'Huai nühai.' *Huai nühai* [Bad Girl]. Capital Artists CD-04-1029. *1985*: Hong Kong.

Teng Ge'er. 'Cang lang dadi.' *Teng Ge'er: Meng sui feng piao* [Teng Ge'er: Dreams Float with the Wind]. Baidai (EMI)/Zhonghua wenyi yinxiang lianhe chubanshe ISRC CN-A49-94-348-00/A. J6. (94C009). *1994*: China.

Yu Wenhua, and Yin Xiangjie. 'Qianfu de ai.' *Qianfu siji diao* [Four Season Songs of the Boat Tower]. Zhongguo zhigong yinxiang chubanshe ISRC CN-A47-94-313-00/A. J6. *1994*: China.

Discography

Ai Jing. *Ai Jing: Wo de 1997* [Ai Jing: My 1997]. Dadi changpian/Magic Stone/Shanghai yinxiang chubanshe CD021. *1993*: China.

Chen Ming. *Chen Ming: Jimo rang wo ruci meili* [Chen Ming: Loneliness Makes Me So Beautiful]. Zhongguo changpian Guangzhou gongsi ISRC CN-F13-94-384-00/A.J6. *1994*: China.

Cheng Lin. *Cheng Lin: Hui jia* [Cheng Lin: Returning Home]. Dianyin chuanbo qiye youxian gongsi ISRC CN-F12-94-432-00/A. J6. (P-2529). *1995*: China.

Cui Jian. *Cui Jian: Beijing yanchanghui* [Cui Jian: The Beijing Concert]. Zhongguo lüyou chubanshe ISRC CN-M29-93-0009/A. J6. *1993*: China.

Cui Jian. *Cui Jian: Hongqi xia de dan* [Cui Jian: The Egg Under the Red Flag]. Shenzhenshi jiguang jiemu chuban faxing gongsi ISRC CN-F27–94-361-00/A. J6. *1994*: China.

Cui Jian. *Cui Jian: Wuneng de liliang* [Cui Jian: The Power of the Powerless]. Zhongguo changpian zonggongsi EL-1043 ISRC CN-A01-98-0086-0/A. J6. *1998*: China.

Dadawa (Zhu Zheqin), He Xuntian, He Xunyou, and Lu Yimin. *A jie gu* [Sister Drum]. Feidie changpian. *1995*: Taiwan.

Dedema. *Tianshang de feng* [The Wind in the Sky]. Shanghai shengxiang chubanshe ISRC CN-E04-97-388-00/A. J6. (Y-1329). *1997*: China.

Dong Wenhua. *Chuntian de fengcai* [The Charm of Spring] (VCD). Guizhou dongfang yinxiang chubanshe ISRC CN-G08-99-187-00/V. J6. *1999*: China.

Dou Wei. *Dou Wei: Hei meng* [Dou Wei: Black Dream]. Shanghai shengxiang chubanshe/Gunshi yousheng chubanshe youxian gongsi ISRC CN-E04-94-325-00/A. J6. *1994*: China.

Gao Feng. *Gao Feng: Tian na bian de ai* [Gao Feng: Love Over There in the Sky]. Baidai changpian (EMI)/Zhonghua wenyi yinxiang lianhe chubanshe ISRC CN-A49-94-349-00/A.J6. *1994*: China.

He Yong. *He Yong: Lajichang* [He Yong: Garbage Dump]. Shanghai shengxiang chubanshe/Gunshi yousheng chubanshe youxian gongsi ISRC CN-E04-94-326-00/A. J6. (Y-1132). *1994*: China.

Hong taiyang: Mao Zedong songge xin jiezou lianchang [Red Sun: Praise Songs for Mao Zedong Sung in Succession to a New Beat]. Zhongguo changpian zonggongsi Shanghai gongsi L-133. *1991*: China.

Lin Yilun. *Lin Yilun: Huo huo de geyao* [Lin Yilun: Fire Hot Songs]. Guangzhou xin shidai yingyin gongsi ISRC CN-F21-95-303-00/A. J6. (MTS-9503). *1995*: China.

Lolo. *Lolo yao* [Lolo's Swing]. Guoji wenhua jiaoliu yinxiang chubanshe/Guangzhou xin shidai yinxiang faxing gongsi ISRC CN-A26-95-315-00/A. J6. (IAM94011). *1995*. China.

Mao Amin. *Mao Amin* [Mao Amin]. Beijing dongfang yingyin gongsi/Huaxing changpian ISRC CN-A13-94-382-00/A.J6. (CAL-33-1158M). *1994*: China.

Mao Ning. *Mao Ning: '95 zui xin jinqu da fengxian* [Mao Ning: The Newest Golden Hits of 1995]. Guangdong wenhua yinxiang chubanshe/Gunshi yousheng chubanshe ISRC CN-H03-94-328-00/A. J. (MG-415). *1995*: China.

Na Ying. *Na Ying: Wei ni zhaosi muxiang* [Na Ying: I Yearn for You Day and Night]. Fumao changpian (DECCA)/Zhongguo kangyi yinxiang chubanshe ISRC CN-A53-94-301-00/A. J6. *1994*: China.

Peng Liyuan. *Peng Liyuan: Tiandi xiyangyang* [The World is Full of Joy] (VCD). Wuhan yinxiang chubanshe ISRC CN-F05-0007-00/V. J6. *2000*: China.

Shan ying (Mountain Eagle). *Shan ying: Zouchu Daliangshan* [Mountain Eagle: Getting Out of Daliangshan]. Guangzhou taipingyang yingyin gongsi ISRC CN-F12–94-415-00/A. J6. (P-2522). *1994*. China.

Tang chao (Tang Dynasty). *Tang chao yuedui* [Tang Dynasty]. Gunshi yousheng chubanshe youxian gongsi/Zhongguo yinyuejia yinxiang chubanshe Z421 H062. *1992*: China.

Tian Zhen. *Tian Zhen* [Tian Zhen]. Hunan wenhua yinxiang chubanshe ISRC CN-F37-96-301-00/A. J6. *1996*: China.

Wayhwa. *Wayhwa: Xiandaihua* [Wayhwa: Modernization]. Zhongguo guoji wenhua jiaoliu yinxiang chubanshe ISRC CN-A26-95-334-00/A. J6. *1995*: China.

Yaogun Beijing [Beijing Rock]. Beijing wenhua yishu yinxiang chubanshe/Yongsheng yinyue changpian youxian gongsi ISRC CN-C02-93-308-00/A. J6. *1993*: China.

Yaogun Beijing II [Beijing Rock II]. BMG Music Taiwan Inc. 9022-4/74321225664 (ISRC CN-A13-94-316-00/A. J6). *1994*: China.

Zang Tianshuo. *Zang Tianshuo: Wo zhe shi nian* [Zang Tianshuo: My Last Ten Years]. Shanghai yinxiang gongsi ISRC CN-E02-95-305-00/A. J6. *1995*: China.

Zhang Guangtian. *Zhang Guangtian: Xiandai gequ zhuanji* [Zhang Guangtian: Album of Modern Songs]. Zhongguo yinyuejia yinxiang chubanshe ISRC CN-A50-93-0008/A. J6. *1993*: China.

Zhongguo huo [Chinese Fire]. Gunshi yousheng chubanshe youxian gongsi/Zhongguo yinyuejia yinxiang chubanshe Z427 H064. *1992*: China.

Zhongguo ju xing shouchang yuanban [Original Edition of Original Renditions of Songs by China's Giant Stars]. Zhongguo changpian zonggongsi ISRC CN-A01-96-0120-0/A. J6. (EL-721). *1996*: China.

Zhongguo min'ge jingdian (2), MTV 42 shou [Chinese Folksongs Classics 2, 42 Songs with MTV] (video cassette). Heilongjiang yinxiang chubanshe ISRC CN-D10-95-355-00/V.J6. *1995*: China.

Zhongguo yaogunyue shili [The Power of Chinese Rock Music]. Gunshi yousheng chubanshe youxian gongsi/Shanghai shengxiang chubanshe ISRC CN-E04-95-358-00/A. J6. (Y-1175) (MSC-002). *1995*: China.

Zhou Xuan. *Zhou Xuan* [Zhou Xuan]. Zhongguo changpian Shanghai gongsi (4 cassettes: CL-51-54) ISRC CN-E01-93-326-00/A. J6. *1993*: China.

Filmography

Red Sorghum, dir. Zhang Yimou. 1987. China. 91 mins. Drama. Original music by Zhao Jiping.

NIMROD BARANOVITCH

REGIONS

Tibet
Population: 2,700,000 (2003)

Tibet, situated on the high plateaus of the Himalayan mountains at altitudes between 6,500 ft and 16,000 ft (2,000m–5,000m), has been a state since the seventh century. It had its greatest expansion in 790, when it reached the Oxus River in the West. Its relations with neighboring countries such as Mongolia, China, India and Nepal have been of intense cultural exchange, but of conflict as well. A priest-patron relationship was founded between the Mongol Chief Godan Khan and the Lama of the Sakya Monastery in 1244, the Lama having been the spiritual mentor, the Khan offering military protec-

tion. This was revived by Altan Khan, who conferred the title of Dalai Lama (Ocean of Wisdom) on Sonam Gyatso, the abbot of the Drepung Monastery in 1578. The theocratic political system, where the Dalai Lama was the spiritual as well as the temporal head of the Tibetan state, was institutionalized after 1660. The centralized state was ruled from the capital, Lhasa. Tibet's seclusion from the rest of the world set in only at the beginning nineteenth century for fear of threats to its culture.

When a Mongol tribe ascended to the throne of China and founded the Yuan Dynasty, this priest-patron relationship became the basis of Chinese efforts to control Tibet, which never fully succeeded. Since 1911, after the Chinese Revolution, Tibet has been de facto independent. But due to its policy of isolation, the Tibetan government did not perceive the need to press for self-determination and worldwide diplomatic recognition. When the army of the Chinese People's Republic invaded Tibet in 1950, the Tibetans were neither militarily nor diplomatically strong enough to resist.

The Chinese Government integrated the former Tibetan provinces of Kham and Amdo and termed the core province Ü Tsang the 'Tibetan Autonomous Region' (TAR), with a population of 2.4 million. A census of 1990 lists another 2.5 million Tibetans scattered in neighboring provinces. The Tibetan Exile Government maintains that there are 6 million Tibetans under Chinese rule. 130,000 Tibetan refugees live in exile, approximately 104,000 in India and Nepal, and 26,000 in other Asian countries, Europe and North America.

Tibet's rich musical heritage is a lesser-known aspect of its culture. Tibetans sing at work, at weddings, while walking on mountain trails and while drinking beer. Tibetan monks have developed the most elaborate ritual music of any Buddhist society, and there is a centuries old tradition of *lhamo*, the opera. The boundaries between ritual chanting, opera performed by professionals, court music and folk songs are fluid; these forms are interwoven and all carry the message of *dharma*, the Buddhist ethics. In a highly hierarchical society, music was a great leveler, not elitist, but open to all.

Traditionally, there were mainly three types of Tibetan music: folk songs, *lhamo* (the Tibetan opera), and Monastic ritual music and dance.

Tibet abounds in folk songs, which vary from one region to another. The melodies are well known, but the texts may change. There are the songs sung at work, particularly where teamwork is necessary, for example, when building a house. The women employed to flatten the floor by stamping sing to the rhythm of their feet. Peasants sing while sowing, plowing and threshing, and their yaks understand the rhythm. The nomads and the traders sing to the steps of their mules or donkeys on their months-long journeys across mountains and deserts. Some songs reflect the monotony of work, others the burden of the *corvée* for the monasteries; many express the loneliness of the nomad, separated from his family. The authors of the texts are usually unknown, some texts fade away and new texts are sung to the old melody. There are some exceptions though; the sage Milarepa (eleventh century) is said to be the author of folk songs, and the poetry of the unorthodox sixth Dalai Lama is still alive and popular.

Folk songs usually consist of one or two stanzas of four lines, with six syllables per line (for monastic songs an uneven number of syllables are de rigueur). Sometimes, they are accompanied by the *dhamyen*, the Tibetan six-stringed lute.

Wedding songs, which survive in Sikkim, are very important. The songs are sung partly by the bridegroom's party and partly by the bride's party, some by both, and they contain blessings and praises. A custom from Central Tibet has been revived in the Tibetan diaspora community since the 1980s: the wedding hostesses' *trung-shuma*. A group of women, well versed in wedding songs, welcome the guests, initiate the songs and dances, and encourage the guests to drink *chang* (Tibetan beer). Reluctant drinkers are mercilessly teased until they join the merry-making.

Another genre confined to Lhasa and other towns were the 'street songs.' These were witty, highly sarcastic songs commenting on political events, sung to the melodies of folk songs. In a highly hierarchical society, without political participation, and in which, traditionally, no media such as radio or newspapers existed, these street songs provided an outlet for political and social criticism, for lampooning the follies and misdeeds of the mighty, including ministers, abbots and even the Dalai Lama. The street songs even survived the Chinese occupation.

Some of these songs may not have been spontaneous verses by the 'man in the street,' but were composed by members of the aristocracy, the civil service or even high-anking monks to highlight discontent or embarrass their enemies. However, they were enthusiastically accepted by the people, sung and disseminated in the streets.

Another very popular form of music, as mentioned, is the Tibetan opera, *lhamo*. It originated in the fourteenth century, but may have had forerunners in the ritual dances at the royal courts. The performances are in the open air, with the audience sitting in a semicircle. There are no props, but splendid costumes. The actors sing, dance and recite, accompanied only by the Tibetan cymbals and drums. The themes of the dramas are taken from Tibetan history, from the Jataka stories (of Gautama Buddha's previous incarnations), or are adaptations of Indian classical plays, like Kalidasa's 'Shakuntala.' The texts swing between the hilarious and the poignant and, in the end, good always triumphs over evil. The actors spice their texts with satire and jokes on current events, sparing no one.

The impact of the Chinese occupation of Tibet – particularly the Cultural Revolution of the 1970s – on Tibetan music cannot be ignored. *Lhamo*, the opera, has been sinicized: the stories have been changed to suit the Maoist message; even the artists are often not Tibetans, but Chinese. The music echoes the sound of the Chinese opera. Similarly, folk songs have been rewritten to convey ideology but, given the multitude of folk songs, many have survived and often cryptically spread the Buddhist message or praise the Dalai Lama. The number of monks and monasteries has been drastically reduced. The novices, though, who still take the vows, learn the art of blowing the long horns and beating the drums.

Folksongs, *lhamo*, and ritual music do survive among the indigenous Buddhist minority living near the Indo-Tibetan border in the Indian states of Himachal Pradesh, Sikkim and Arunachal Pradesh, in Bhutan and in Nepal. The arts thrive in the Tibetan exile community. A well-planned mosaic of institutions maintains different aspects of Tibetan culture, from philosophy to medicine, and from Thangka painting to literature. The opera and Tibetan folk music are taught, researched and practiced in the Tibetan Institute of Performing Arts (TIPA) at Dharamsala. There are music and opera groups in the larger refugee settlements, as well as in some of the Tibetan schools and Tibetan Children's Villages in India. Once a year in the spring the opera groups assemble at Dharamsala for the *lhamo* festival, as was the custom in traditional Lhasa. As in Lhasa, the shows are open for everybody, rich or poor, young and old, men, women and children, and the Dalai Lama himself presides.

There is communication between the Tibetans in exile and in their home country. Travelers carry music cassettes, there are three broadcasting stations operating from India (Voice of America, Radio Free Asia, Voice of Tibet) and beaming into Tibet, and the Internet links exiles with the Tibetans under Chinese control.

Meanwhile, the Chinese government recognizes that the Tibetans have a rich folk culture and have even started a research project to document the heritage.

Bibliography

Bernstorff, Dagmar. 2004. 'Vibrant Culture.' In *Exile as Challenge: The Tibetan Diaspora*, ed. Dagmar Bernstorff and Hubertus von Welck. New Delhi: Orient Longman, 295–311.

Crossland-Holland, Peter. 2000. 'The Ritual Music of Tibet.' In *Song of the Spirit: The World of Sacred Music*, ed. Ragunath Sudhamaki. New Delhi: Tibet House, 137–44.

Diehl, Keila. 1996. 'The Wedding Hostesses (khrung zhu ma) of Central Tibet.' In *Chö Yang*, ed. Pedron Yeshi and Jeremy Russell. Sidhpur: Norbulingka Institute, 102–105.

Goldstein, Melvyn C. 1982 'Lhasa Street Songs: Political and Social Satire in Traditional Tibet.' *Tibet Journal* 7(1–2): 56–66.

Hauptfleisch, Wolfgang. 1998. *Bibliography: Tibetan Music and its Cultural Background*. Muenster/Westfalen: www.Uni-muenster.de/musikwissenschaft/hauptbiblio.htm

Nebesky-Wojkowitz, René de. 1976. *Tibetan Religious Dances: Text and Translation of the chams-yig*. Paris/The Hague: Mouton.

Ross, Joanna, l995. *Lhamo: Opera from the Roof of the World*. New Delhi: Paljor Publications.

Tucci, Guiseppe. 1966. *Tibetan Folk Songs from Gyantse and Western Tibet*. Ascona: Artibus Asiae Publications (second revised edition, first edition 1941).

Discography

Ache Lhamo. *Théatre Tibétain 'Prince Norsang.'* Sonodisk ESP 8433. *1985*: France.

Songs of Tibet. Loten Namling. n.d.: Switzerland.

Songs of Tibet. Ritual Records. *1994*: U.K.

Namgyal Monastère de sa Sainteté le Dalai Lama. *Chants et musique de la sagesse*. CDing International. n.d.: Nepal.

Nawang Khechog. *The Best of Ten Years*. CDing International. *1999*: Nepal.

Tibetan Folk Music. Saydisc 427. *1999*: USA.

Tibetan Monastic chants (World Festival of Sacred Music). Tibet House. *2000*: India.

TIPA. *Heritage of Tibet (Opera)*. Nextmusic SAS. *l986*: India.

DAGMAR BERNSTORFF

Tibetan Diaspora

Population: Approximately 130,000 Tibetans live in exile, with the largest concentrations living in India and Nepal (104,000), with 26,000 in other Asia countries, Europe and North America.

The Tibetan diaspora began in 1959, when an estimated 80,000 Tibetans escaped from Tibet over the Himalayas. Traveling mostly on foot, they were following their leader, the fourteenth Dalai Lama, into exile after a failed uprising against Chinese rule. For over 40 years, Tibetans have continued to escape from their homeland in an erratic flow that can be divided into three waves of migration. The first escapees (between 1959 and the mid-1960s) mostly came from Lhasa and southern border areas of Tibet. Few Tibetans escaped during the Cultural Revolution (1966–76), but in the 1980s a second wave of refugees, many of whom had been imprisoned during the first decades of Tibet's occupation, fled Tibet. Since the early 1990s, a third wave of refugees from northeastern Tibet has arrived in exile. Many 'new arrivals' are children or young adults who have been sent out of Tibet by their parents to be educated in one of the schools run by the Tibetan government-in-exile in India.

The capital-in-exile of the Tibetan diaspora is Dharamsala, a former British hill station located in the middle of a narrow finger of the Indian state of Himachal Pradesh, squeezed between Pakistan and the mountains that create India's border with Tibet. It was in this setting, amid Pahari-speaking shepherds and other Hindu townspeople, that the Dalai Lama settled and established his government-in-exile in 1960. Other important settlement centers for Tibetan refugees, including Darjiling, Delhi and Kathmandu, are scattered throughout India and Nepal. Tibetan refugees in South Asia have largely depended on petty business, the tourism and craft industries, and direct aid to support themselves. Since the early 1990s, a wave of resettlement has resulted in the establishment of significant Tibetan communities in cities throughout the United States, Canada and Europe.

Throughout the diaspora, Tibetan refugees have attempted to preserve their traditional cultural heritage, at the same time that they remain concerned with obtaining the education and skills necessary to participate successfully in their host societies. The dual goals of cultural preservation and modernization – drawing on traditional resources and learning from contemporary, non-Tibetan cultures – have inevitably influenced the form and content of the musical genres that have emerged out of the international Tibetan diaspora.

Modern Tibetan Songs

One of the Dalai Lama's first priorities in exile was to set up an institution dedicated to the preservation of traditional Tibetan music and dance. The Tibetan Institute for Performing Arts (TIPA) in Dharamsàla, with its opera company, instrument and costume-making sections, and teacher training program, has contributed to the appreciation of traditional genres by Tibetan refugee youth. However, due to the multi-local nature of refugee life and the global circulation of music videos and cassettes, many non-traditional or foreign musics, such as Hindi film music, Western rock 'n' roll and Nepali pop music, have also found a receptive audience among Tibetans living in exile. Other musical genres, such as Chinese-influenced Tibetan pop music, have been explicitly rejected on political grounds by all but the newest arrivals in exile. One result of this musical mélange has been the production of a new genre of 'modern Tibetan songs' by young refugees living throughout the diaspora. These songs bring together the foreign and the familiar, the modern and the traditional, and effectively challenge the usefulness of those categories.

The first modern Tibetan songs composed in India were, perhaps ironically, written by young artists at TIPA. These songs, accompanied by simple chord progressions on a Western guitar or paralleled by a melody line plucked on the *sGra sNyan* (a six-stringed Tibetan lute, pronounced 'dranyen'), circulated quickly throughout the Tibetan diaspora and have remained favorites. Beginning in the late 1960s, Western cassettes were widely available in the Himalayas, and Dharamsala's residents were occasionally exposed to live rock music by visiting Westerners. It was not until 1988, however, that the first cassette of original Tibetan songs influenced by the Western folk-rock sound was recorded and produced in exile by Tibetans themselves. This cassette, entitled *Modern Tibetan Folk Songs*, was released by three young refugees living in Dharamsala who called themselves Rang bTsan gShon Nu ('Rangzen Shonu' or 'Freedom Youth'). Their

songs, originally composed to accompany historical dramas in the refugee schools, were set to acoustic guitar supporting simple vocal harmonies. The group's accomplished guitarist and songwriter, Tsering Paljor Phupatsang, had grown up listening to Western hit songs in the context of Christian missionary schools in Darjeeling. Phupatsang went on to produce a popular solo cassette called *Rang bTsan Son rTsa* ('Rangzen Söntsa' or 'Seed and Root of Freedom') in 1990, the same year that TIPA's newly formed modern music group, later named the Ah-Ka-Ma Band, recorded a cassette titled *Tibetan Songs* in celebration of the Dalai Lama's 1989 Nobel Peace Prize. This experimental cassette featured an uneasy mix of traditional songs and new songs set to the beat of a synthesized drum machine. The group's most important contribution to the development of modern Tibetan music was, and still is, its dedication to incorporating traditional instruments, vocal techniques and folk tunes into pop-rock compositions.

At the beginning of 1995, two new cassettes were released in Dharamsala which in some ways broke through the formulas that had been quickly established for modern Tibetan songs: *Rang bTsan* ('Rangzen' or 'Self-Rule') by Phupatsang's Yak Band and *Modern Tibetan Songs* by the Ah-Ka-Ma Band. Unlike earlier sounds, these two cassettes fit squarely into the category of rock 'n' roll, with their electric lead and rhythm guitars, bass guitars and drum sets. The Yaks included a keyboard and male vocalists, while Ah-Ka-Ma, drawing from its members' traditional training in Tibetan performing arts, incorporated both the *sGra sNyan* and the *RGyud Mangs* (hammer dulcimer, pronounced 'gyumang') and added female vocalists to its sound. While the Yak Band has disbanded, the Ah-Ka-Ma Band, supported by the Tibetan government-in-exile, has since released several other albums, including *Ah-Ka-Ma 2000* (produced in honor of the sixtieth anniversary of the Dalai Lama's enthronement) and *Ah-Ka-Ma 2002* (promoting peace through the arts).

In the 1990s, approximately a dozen other Tibetan individuals and groups from other parts of the diaspora released cassettes featuring original Tibetan songs. Many were imitative of either the mellow 'folk-rock' acoustic guitar sound of Rang bTsan gShon Nu or of smooth Asian karaoke lounge music featuring keyboard synthesizers and solo vocalists heavily dependent on echo effects. More recent releases, such as the numerous popular cassettes produced since 1997 by Tsering Gyurmey in Nepal, have reflected the increasing influence of Hindi film music and Nepali pop songs on modern Tibetan music, while others have reflected the growing popularity of North American rap music among Tibetan youth living in Europe and North America.

Of note during 1990s, a decade of musical experimentation and recording by Tibetan refugees, were the 1991 cassette entitled *Ja* (Rainbow) and subsequent CDs *Renewal* (2000) and *Phayul* (2002), which largely featured contemporary Tibetan music played on traditional instruments. These songs were composed and recorded by a group of ex-TIPA artists who founded Chaksampa, a Tibetan dance and opera company based in San Francisco. In addition to his dedication to preserving traditional genres, the group's director, Tashi Dhondup (also known as 'Techung'), recorded his own CDs of original songs, *Yarlung* (1996), *Sky Treasure* (2000) and *Nyingtop* (2002). Due to his diverse talents, entrepreneurial spirit and continuing commitment to presenting traditional Tibetan performances, Techung has remained at the forefront of the Tibetan music scene and is deeply admired by the international Tibetan community. His group has been invited to participate in Tibet House's annual fundraising concert at Carnegie Hall and was featured at Smithsonian Folk Life Festival in Washington DC in the summer of 2000.

Other contemporary Tibetan artists living in 'double exile' in the West have found market niches for themselves in the international music scene, reaching out primarily to Western audiences. Flautist Nawang Khechog, has, for example, created a place for himself in the New Age market, tapping into the spiritual expectations many Westerners have with regard to Tibetan culture. Khechog, who typically incorporates instruments from all over the world in his recordings, has recently invented what he calls the 'universal horn,' a combination of the Tibetan ritual long horn and the Australian didgeridoo. Yungchen Lhamo has recorded haunting a cappella songs, seeking to encourage her listeners to awaken their spiritual awareness, and a Tibetan nun named Chöying Drolma has teamed up with North American guitarist Steve Tibbetts to provide Western audiences with appealing adaptations of sacred Tibetan chants.

A few Tibetan musicians trained in Chinese-ruled Tibet have found some popularity among Tibetans living in the diaspora, although for political and aesthetic reasons their fans are generally limited to those refugees who have recently escaped from the homeland. These include Dadon, a singer who escaped from Tibet in 1992 and whose life story is told in the 1998 film *Windhorse*, the late Jampa Tsering, who recorded several cassettes of original Tibetan pop music in Lhasa, and Yadhong, an extremely popular Tibetan musician living in China (outside of the Tibetan Autonomous Region or TAR) who is walking a fine line by recording and performing both Chinese and Tibetan songs.

Despite the seeming diversity and energy behind this story of the development of modern Tibetan music, the number of musicians involved in the movement has been very small, and the amount of new music being produced has been limited, due to a number of social, cultural and financial constraints that face aspiring musicians both in Tibet and in the Tibetan refugee community. For example, the limited range of acceptable topics for modern Tibetan song lyrics and the limited ability of the young generations in exile to compose formal, poetic lyrics in the Tibetan language greatly complicate the contemporary songwriter's task. Whereas folk songs in pre-1950 Tibet addressed a wide variety of topics and served many purposes (accompanying work, negotiating marriage arrangements, expressing political satire and so on), the themes of the freedom struggle, rigorous Red China-bashing, and nostalgic recalling of the solemn past have become canonized as the most appropriate sources for lyrics today. Therefore, song lyrics composed in exile are generally highly predictable, patriotic calls for Tibetans to put aside their differences, unite and fight for independence. Other acceptable topics include historical stories, expressions of sadness over the loss of a beautiful homeland and loved ones who have passed away or been left behind, and devotional poems for political martyrs, the Dalai Lama and other religious figures. As Hindi and English are not considered appropriate languages for addressing these solemn topics, young songwriters commonly depend on older, erudite aristocrats or monks to compose Tibetan lyrics for them.

Other constraints on the modern song genre include: (a) the overarching challenge of innovating within a community that is deeply concerned about cultural preservation; (b) the historically informed perception of music making and any form of entertainment work as an inferior position of service; (c) the stigma in Tibetan society of immodestly setting oneself apart from the group; (d) the difficulty of justifying to families and employers the time needed for rehearsals and the money needed for equipment or financing recordings; and (e) in the case of musicians working in the TAR or China, the surveillance by Chinese authorities of the lyrics and activities of musicians feared to be encouraging Tibetan nationalism.

The challenge facing Tibetan musicians at the beginning of the twenty-first century involves overcoming all of the challenges mentioned and finding the perfect balance between old and new, and unique and shared sounds. The efforts of artists toward achieving these goals were honored at a first-ever Tibetan Music Festival held in Bylakuppe, India in 2004. The event, attended by an estimated 18,000 Tibetans, provided musicians and singers with an opportunity to interact and support their shared goals of making music that has not been influenced by Chinese aesthetics (for detailed information about the event, see http://www.gon-poentertainment.com/festival2004.htm).

Conclusion

The popular music being made by Tibetans living outside of their homeland provides an interesting case study of what happens to culture 'on the road,' of musical creativity unhooked from a particular geographical place. In fact, the boundaries of cultural practices rarely coincide with the lines drawn on maps; refugee culture is, then, just an extreme example of the very common twenty-first-century experience of living multi-local or multi-cultural, hybrid lives. Paradoxically, due to the pressure to preserve Tibetan culture in exile, Tibetan refugee musicians may be less free to borrow from foreign cultures and genres than others whose communities are not threatened by the dual forces of colonization in the homeland and assimilation in the diaspora. Underlying these dynamics is a call to revisit the meaning and usefulness of the concept of 'cultural preservation,' including the risks of canonizing particular traditions as 'authentic' and dismissing contemporary or popular innovations as 'inauthentic' or even threatening to the community's cultural and ethnic integrity.

Bibliography

Diehl, Keila. 2002. *Echoes From Dharamsala: Music in the Life of a Tibetan Refugee Community*. Berkeley, CA: University of California Press.

Discographical References

Ah-Ka-Ma Band. *Ah-Ka-Ma 2000*. Tibetan Institute of Performing Arts. *2000*: India.

Ah-Ka-Ma Band. *Ah-Ka-Ma 2002*. Tibetan Institute of Performing Arts. *2002*: India.

Ah-Ka-Ma Band. *Modern Tibetan Songs*. Tibetan Institute of Performing Arts. *1995*: India.

Chaksampa. *Phayul*. Chaksampa Sound. *2002*: USA.

Chaksampa. *Rainbow Tibetan hJah*. *1991*: USA.

Chaksampa. *Renewal: Contemporary Tibetan Folk Songs*. Chaksampa Sound . *1999*: USA.

Dhondup, Tashi. *Nyingtop*. Kunga Records. *2002*: USA.

Dhondup, Tashi. *Sky Treasure*. *2000*: USA.

Dhondup, Tashi. *Yarlung: Tibetan Songs of Love and Freedom*. Music Tibet. *1996*: USA.

Phupatsang, Tsering Paljor. *Rang bTsan Son rTsa*. *1990*: India.

Rang bTsan gShon Nu. *Modern Tibetan Folk Songs*. *1988*: India.

TIPA Modern Music Group. *Tibetan Songs*. Tibetan Institute of Performing Arts. *1989*: India.

Yak Band. *Rang bTsan*. *1995*: India.

Discography

Ah-Ka-Ma Band. *Ah-Ka-Ma 2003*. Tibetan Institute of Performing Arts. *2003*: India.

Drolma, Chöying, and Tibbetts, Steve. *Chö*. Hannibal HNCD 1404. *1997*: USA.

Gyurmey, Tsering. *Pha Ma (Tsawai Lama Vol. 5)*. *2000*: Nepal.

Khechog, Nawong. *Rhythms of Peace*. Sounds True 294. *1996*: USA.

Khechog, Nawong. *Sounds of Peace*. Sounds True 296. *1996*: USA.

Khechog, Nawong. *Quiet Mind: The Musical Journey of a Tibetan Nomad*. Gemini Sun 1. *1997*: USA.

Lhamo, Yungchen. *Tibet, Tibet*. Real World CDRW59. *1996*: UK.

Lhamo, Yungchen. *Coming Home*. Real World CDR72. *1998*: UK.

Filmography

Windhorse, dir. Paul Wagner. 1998. USA. 97 mins. Drama.

KEILA DIEHL

Xinjiang Uyghur Autonomous Region

Population: 18,462,600 (2000); Uyghur: 8,139,458 (2000)

Xinjiang Uyghur Autonomous Region, sometimes known in the West as Chinese or Eastern Turkestan, is a region of oasis towns separated by great distances and, until the development of infrastructure under the People's Republic of China (PRC), accessible only by arduous overland journeys by

27

camel train through deserts and over mountains. The inhabitants of its oasis towns have for centuries traded in the goods that have passed along the Silk Road from China to the Near East and to Europe. The Uyghurs trace their ancestry back to the Uyghur Turks whose steppe kingdom flourished on China's northwestern borders during the eighth and ninth centuries. They first adopted Islam in the tenth century, of a type strongly influenced by Sufism. The Uyghurs are closely related culturally and musically to the peoples of the neighbouring Central Asian states, such as Kazakhstan, Kyrgyzstan and especially Uzbekistan. Politically, the history of this strategically important region is chequered with warfare and waves of conquests. It was a part of Genghis Khan's huge Mongol empire, and was later reconquered by the Manchu Qing dynasty, who gave it the name Xinjiang (in Chinese literally 'New Territories') in 1884. In spite of Russian and British jockeying for influence during the late nineteenth century (the 'Great Game'), China retained control of the region and, in the twenty-first century, the Uyghurs are recognized as the largest minority group in the Xinjiang Uyghur Autonomous Region of the PRC.

Uyghur traditional music-making revolves around the *mäshräp* (gathering or party) which draws villagers together for food, music and dancing. Weddings, circumcision parties, the major Islamic festivals and pilgrimages to saints' shrines are also important occasions for music. Singers are accompanied by the long-necked plucked and bowed lutes (*tämbur*, *dutar* and *satar*) and the *dap* frame drum, which are all found across Central Asia, often with the addition of the *skirupka* (violin, from the Russian) or accordion. Kettle drum and shawm bands (*naghra-sunay*) provide raucous, celebratory outdoors music. The singing style is highly ornamented, and the songs often employ the *aqsaq* or 'limping' assymetrical rhythms, which are also found in the rhythms of the Sufi *zikr* chants. Each oasis has its own distinctive musical style and repertoire, ranging from the more purely pentatonic sounds of the eastern town of Qumul (Hami), to the modally more complex style of the old Silk Road town of Kashgar in the southwest. Historically, the local kings in the various oasis kingdoms patronized musicians who sang the prestigious Muqam suites. The term is derived from the Arabic maqam, but the style is local, and each of the major oases boasts its own Muqam tradition.

Since the 1940s, Uyghur traditions have been professionalized and modernized through the So-viet model of state-run performance troupes. Beginning in the 1950s, local traditions formed the basis for new composition from revolutionary folk songs praising Chairman Mao, to large-scale operas, choral and orchestral works. In the early years of the twenty-first century, the troupes have performed song-and-dance spectaculars celebrating the region's inclusion in the People's Republic of China. State radio stations were established in the 1950s, and several local television channels arrived in the 1980s. These include not only Chinese-language channels, but also channels in the major languages of the region, Uyghur and Kazakh, which devote considerable air space to troupe performances.

Commercially recorded music in Xinjiang has a rather short history, beginning in the 1980s when recording technologies, especially the cheap medium of cassettes and cassette recorders, became widely available. Whilst numerous singers have released cassettes, the scene is dominated by a few influential male singers, most notably Abdulla Abdurehim, Ömärjan Alim and Abdurehim Heyit, who maintained their position throughout the 1990s and into the new century, expanding their medium from audiocassettes to VCD music videos. Many singers and musicians active in the pop music scene are also employed and trained within the state-run folklore troupes.

Mainstream Uyghur pop has a wide audience, crossing the generational and the urban-rural divide, although the more Western-influenced end of the market appeals mainly to urban youngsters. Pop music is widely disseminated on television. Pop singers perform live sets for dancing in high-class restaurants in the regional capital Ürümchi. Cassettes of pop music fill the bazaars in smaller towns around the region. This broad appeal increases the opportunities for pop performers to disseminate new sounds and ideas. Uyghur pop music can also be downloaded from several web sites maintained by the exiled community in the United States, most of whom have a strong political agenda. Clearly, the songs of artists working within the PRC appear on such websites without the knowledge or permission of the artist.

It is hard to draw a clear line between traditional and pop music in Xinjiang. Most popular composers strive to maintain some local flavor in their songs. Continuity with tradition lies in the maintenance of traditional rhythms (though the drum machine renders these somewhat inflexible), the use of traditional instruments alongside the synthesizer, the adaptation of specific folk melodies, but especially in singing style and its communication of emotion. Traditional folk songs are frequently set to synthesized beats, regional traditions may be combined with electric guitar and drumset, and new songs are composed with traditional instrumental accompaniment, notably the *dutar* (a long-necked two-stringed lute).

The scene also looks outwards. Black market copies of foreign films and audio CDs are everywhere. In the music shops of Ürümchi's main bazaar you may find the Sex Pistols *Never Mind the Bollocks* alongside Turkish pop and the latest Hindi film songs. It is reputed that the most recent Hollywood films appear in Xinjiang even before they reach US cinemas. New musical styles have an impact on the Uyghur pop scene in a rather unpredictable way. A reggae version of a folksong from the southern town of Khotän, called 'Katlama' and released by Shiräli in 1995, made one amusing addition to the global mix. Rock and heavy metal began to make inroads into the urban youth market in the mid-1990s with the bands Täklimakan and Riwäyat; this kind of sound arrived in Xinjiang via the rock scene of Beijing. Popular flamenco guitar, introduced into Xinjiang largely through the music of the Gipsy Kings, has been greatly in vogue since the mid-1990s, and is being incorporated into the Uyghur popular music repertoire, most famously by the Beijing-based cross-over star singer Äskär and his band Grey Wolf, who sings both in his native Uyghur and, aiming at the wider market, in Chinese.

Uyghur pop also draws on the Uyghur communities in Turkey and across the border in the Central Asian states. The Uyghur Theater of Musical Comedy was established in Kazakhstan in the 1930s. Originally briefed to perform Soviet-style agitprop opera, since the 1960s the theater has served as a training ground for pop stars on both sides of the border, providing a model for the later development of pop within Xinjiang. One band to emerge from its doors has been the Dervishes, musically one of the most exciting Uyghur bands at the turn of the twenty-first century. Formed in July 1999 by four mainly Russian-speaking Uyghur singers with Western classical musical backgrounds, the Dervishes' first appearance was at the Voice of Asia pop festival (a sort of sub-Eurovision song contest held annually in a ski resort in Kazakhstan). Their music is based in a heavy rock sound, mixed with Uyghur folk influences, and they are enthusiastic samplers of sounds from Mongolia to Brazil,

Turkish electronica to London clubland breakbeats. In 2003, their music was mainly available in Xinjiang via bootleg recordings, and the Dervishes were keen to profit from this fan base. They negotiated their first official release and tour with the Chinese Ministry of Culture in the same year. It remains to be seen if the political climate in Xinjiang will make space for rock stars from Kazakhstan and if the Dervishes will be able to maintain their resolutely apolitical stance.

Love and desire are, of course, the most common themes of pop songs, typically expressed in terms of burning fire, suffering and pain. Also striking is the dominance of the figure of the idealized mother, careworn, weeping, nurturing and self-sacrificing. In Uyghur culture the language of maternal tears is very much part of traditional sung expression. In contemporary Uyghur pop however, there is an added layer to the discourse on mother love: the notion of Mother as the central icon in the nationalist agenda. Uyghur nationalism often takes the form of social engagement and rather didactic songs, like those sung most famously by Abdulla Abdurehim about the serious problem of heroin addiction among Uyghur youth, such as 'Sirliq Tuman' (Strange Smoke; see http://www.uyghura-merican.org/uyghurche/muzika/). Abdulla, Ürümchi's leading pop singer since the early 1980s, exemplifies the respected position that many pop composers and singers occupy in the Uyghur community: one of moral leadership, and quite the obverse of the Western notion of the rebel rock star. However, it is the group of singers who perform traditional-style songs, setting contemporary lyrics, accompanying themselves on the *dutar* lute, who have done most to catch and express the zeitgeist. These singers include the superb female singer Sänubär Tursun, the more established star singer Abdurehim Heyit of Kashgar, and Ömärjan Alim from the northern town of Ghulja (Yining).

In a region often compared to Tibet, where political expression is limited and ethnic tensions simmer, pop song lyrics have often been a site of political contest, usually expressed in veiled allegories and metaphors. Ömärjan Alim's song 'Ana-mni Äsläp' (Remembering Mother) (1994) represents the clearest and perhaps most powerful expression of this use of allegory. In this song we find a lament for mother; her death symbolizes the death of the nation, and alongside the forceful expression of grief, a call for vengeance echoes. This song was released at the height of Ömärjan's popularity. At that time his cassettes formed a constant soundtrack to the bustle of Ürümchi's main bazaar, blaring from every cassette stall and restaurant. His songs, with their traditional *dutar* accompaniment and popular style of language, 'earthy' as one Uyghur recording engineer put it, also enjoyed unprecedented sales in rural areas where some 70 percent of the Uyghur population still make their living from the land. 'Remembering Mother' was one of Ömärjan's most emotive and radical calls to arms. Already, by the following year (1995), the government was beginning its 'crackdown on the cultural market' as part of a range of measures to combat Uyghur separatism, and it was becoming increasingly difficult to reference Uyghur discontent in the public forum, even through such veiled allegories. In the early 1990s, Uyghur musicians had taken advantage of the burgeoning free market in China to strike recording deals with newly established independent Chinese recording companies from Shanghai to Guangzhou. After 1995, such out-of-town deals were restricted, and the state-owned Xinjiang Recording Company kept a much tighter rein on lyrical content of Uyghur cassettes.

In February 1997, Uyghur discontent culminated in large-scale demonstrations in Ghulja and their brutal suppression by the authorities. In the years following this crackdown it seemed that the Uyghurs had more to grieve, both politically and literally, and over the next few years a spate of personal laments were released in the public sphere of pop. Without referencing the sphere of public action, these were nonetheless expressing a popular grief for which there were few other outlets. In 2000, Ömärjan Alim released a new lament for mother, 'Kättingiz Ana' (Mother, You Have Gone). Musically, this new lament was a close echo of the earlier 'Remembering Mother' but, in terms of performance style and lyrics, a very different mood was expressed. This time grief was accompanied not by anger but rather by fatalistic resignation and acceptance. In the accompanying music video the singer makes a journey from modernity – working at his computer in a city office, traveling along the newly-built highway to the impoverished Uyghur village to attend the funeral of his mother – mourning, it seems, not only the fading national dream but also the passing of a way of life.

Bibliography

Harris, Rachel. 2002. 'Cassettes, Bazaars and Saving the Nation: The Uyghur Music Industry in Xinjiang, China.' In *Global Goes Local: Popular Culture in Asia*, ed. Tim Craig and Richard King. Vancouver, BC: University of British Columbia Press.

Smith, Joanne. Forthcoming. 'Barren Chickens, Stray Dogs, Fake Immortals and Thieves: Coloniser and Collaborator in Popular Uyghur Song and the Quest for National Unity.' In *Music, National Identity and the Politics of Location: Between the Global and the Local*, ed. Ian Biddle and Vanessa Knights. Aldershot: Ashgate.

Uyghur Music. http://www.uyghuramerican.org/uyghurche/muzika/

Discographical References

Ömärjan, Alim. 'Anamni Äsläp' [Remembering Mother]. *Pärwayim Peläk* [Destiny Is My Concern]. Confiscated: no publishing details. *1994*.

Ömärjan, Alim. 'Kättingiz Ana' [Mother, You Have Gone]. *Tarim*. Xinjiang Recording Co. *2000*: China.

Shiräli. 'Katlama.' *Tarim*. Xinjiang Recording Co. *2000*: China.

Discography

Heyit, Abdurehim. *Ömüt* [Hope]. Nationalities Recording Co. *2002*: China.

Äskär. 'Tiläg' [Blessing]. DMVE Co. *2001*: China.

Dervishi. 'Dunya' [World]. Ala Music Enterprises. *2002*: Kazakhstan.

Tursun, Sänubär. 'Yollughum' [My Gift]. Xinjiang Recording Co. *2000*: China.

RACHEL HARRIS

CITIES

Beijing
Population: 14,560,000 (2003)

Beijing is the capital of the People's Republic of China. It is the country's political, cultural and economic center, and the center of external communications. Located in northern China, 75 miles (120 km) from the harbor city of Tianjin and the Bohai Sea, the city was the capital of China for over 650 years between 1258 and 1911, and became the capital once again on 1 October 1949, the date of the establishment of the People's Republic. Early in the twenty-first century, Beijing had a population of approximately 14.5 million, 11 million of whom were permanent residents, while most of the rest were internal immigrants from rural areas (often referred to as the 'floating population'). The city also had the largest foreign population of all the cities in the country; over 50,000 of the foreigners, according to official statistics, were long-term residents. In addition, there are 120 universities and other institutions of higher education in the city, in which approximately 550,000 students are enrolled. The last two groups in particular have exerted important influence on the development of popular music in the city and in the country as a whole.

Popular Music in Beijing Before the Reform Era

From the 1920s to the late 1940s, modern popular music existed in Beijing mainly in the form of radio broadcasts from Shanghai, where this music emerged and flourished. During that period no production of such music took place in the city and little activity related to this music existed. One notable exception was the dance parties that were held in the Six Countries Hotel (Liuguo Fandian, now Beijing Hotel), where people danced to the rhythms of Western popular music.

This situation changed in 1949 after the establishment of a new centralized government in Beijing, as a result of which most of the media infrastructure in China was relocated to the new capital. As part of this reorganization, the record industry was transferred from Shanghai to Beijing, where it was gradually organized under the monopoly of China Record Company (Zhongguo changpian gongsi). The main task of CRC was to produce and popularize a new kind of music, which consisted mainly of Chinese opera (xiqu), folk songs and revolutionary art songs, as opposed to the popular music in Euro-American style that flourished in Shanghai. The privileged position of Beijing in China's new popular music scene revealed itself most forcefully during the Cultural Revolution (1966–76), when Beijing opera (Jingju) was transformed into the famous revolutionary 'model operas' (yangbanxi), which became the core of the unitary revolutionary mass culture that was popularized all over the country and replaced numerous varieties of local opera.

Popular Music in the Reform Era

In 1980, the Beijing Baihua Sound Equipment Factory began to produce cassette tapes, marking a new phase in the development of popular music in the city and nationwide. A few years later, influenced by popular music from Hong Kong, Taiwan and the West, several Beijing-based organizations and schools started to train musicians in the new art of popular music. These included the Eastern Song and Dance Troupe, the Gu Jianfen Training Center for Singing Stars of the Central Song and Dance Troupe, the China Light Music Troupe and the Fulin Singers Class. These schools and troupes produced some of China's leading pop singers and composers of the late 1980s, including Mao Amin, Wei Wei, Su Hong and Li Jie.

Beijing's large-scale concerts played an important role in the domain of popular music. In May 1986, the China Audio and Video Publishing House and the Film and Audio Company of the Eastern Song and Dance Troupe jointly organized China's first large-scale pop concert, which was held in Beijing. The event, named Let the World be Filled with Love, was held in Beijing's Workers' Stadium and featured over 100 singers. It signaled that Euro-American-style popular music had started once again to dominate China's popular music scene and that it was now officially accepted.

After 1986, large-scale pop concerts were held regularly in Beijing and brought together many of China's most famous pop musicians. Some of the most significant concerts that served as landmarks in the history of China's pop include: The First Annual Awards-Granting Concert of the Billboard of Chinese Popular Songs, organized by Beijing Music Radio and held in August 1994 in the Capital Gymnasium; a marathon of performances entitled the Brilliant 1994 Popular Song Concert, which was organized by the Han and Tang Culture Company and the *Shopping Guide for Top-Quality Products* (a local newspaper) and was held in December 1994 in the Beijing Exhibition Hall Theater; and a concert named Ten-Year Retrospect on China's Pop Scene, which was held two nights in a row in the Capital Gymnasium in November 1996. The latter drew together over 1,000 musicians and other people from the music business, from all over the country, 800 of whom got a 'Medal for Achievements in Chinese Popular Music.'

These and other large-scale concerts exerted an important influence on the popular music scene in China, in part because of the capacity of the venues in which they took place; Beijing Workers' Stadium, Beijing Capital Gymnasium and Beijing Workers' Gymnasium have 45,000, 18,000 and 15,000 seats, respectively. (The Beijing Exhibition Hall Theater is relatively smaller with 1,800 seats.) The impact of large-scale concerts also derived from the fact that they were sometimes recorded and later broadcast on national and local television. The main producers of large-scale concerts include China Performing Arts Agency, China National Culture and Art Co., Beijing Great Dragon Culture Co., Beijing

Gehua Culture and Art Co. and others, all of which are governmental companies.

In addition to the large-scale concerts held regularly in Beijing, there also emerged during the late 1990s a tradition of annual musical events organized by nongovernmental companies and usually held in Chaoyang Park. These included the Beijing Jazz Festival and the Heineken Jammin' Festival, both held in the summer.

Rock in Beijing

One popular music genre that became strongly associated with China's capital was rock 'n' roll. This music was introduced into the city in the early 1980s by North American students who attended local universities. One such student, David Hoffman, established China's first rock band, Dadi (Mother Earth), made up of both Chinese and foreign students. Soon after the establishment of Dadi, local musicians started to organize their own bands. Among the earliest Chinese rock bands were Qiheban (Seven-Tier Boards) and Baitouweng (Bald Eagle), both of which were established in 1984, the former by Cui Jian and Liu Yuan and the latter by Zang Tianshuo and Sun Guoqing.

The popularity of rock in Beijing increased dramatically between 1989 and 1993. Many bands were established and they regularly played small-scale rock performances, referred to as 'parties' (in English). Many of these performances were held in restaurants located near the area of the foreign embassies or in downtown Beijing, and they were popular among foreign diplomats and business-people. Maxim's Restaurant in Beijing played a particularly important role in the development of Chines rock: Cui Jian and his friends often held rock parties there between 1989 and 1993.

A landmark in the history of rock in Beijing was a large-scale all-rock concert that was held in the Capital Gymnasium in February 1990, organized by Cheng Jin and Zang Tianshuo. The concert was named the 1990 Modern Music Concert and featured six of the most famous bands at that time: ADO, 1989, Baobei xiongdi (Baby Brother), Cobra, Huxi (Breathing) and Ziwo jiaoyu (Self-education).

Beginning in 1989, Beijing rock started to gain popularity in other parts of the country and to gain some recognition abroad. As Cui Jian released China's first rock album, *Rock and Roll of the New Long March* (1989), he was invited to participate in the Asia Music Festival in Europe. One year later he also launched a nationwide concert tour in China, which was cut halfway by government officials.

Another important contribution to the spread of rock from Beijing to other parts of China and beyond came from a Taiwanese label named Magic Rock. In 1992–3 a branch of the Taiwanese Rolling Stones record company, Magic Rock produced the first albums of two Beijing-based rock bands, Hei bao (Black Panther) and Tang chao (Tang Dynasty), which soon became two of China's most famous rock bands. These early rock albums, *Hei bao* and *Tang chao* respectively, achieved great success and were followed by numerous others, many of which were also produced by Magic Rock. After Cui Jian's 1989 performance at the Asia Music Festival in Europe, several other Beijing-based rockers were invited to perform abroad and gained some inter-national recognition. In the late 1990s, after several years of depression, rock music saw a limited revival in Beijing with the birth of several young rock bands such as Qingxing (Sober), Hua'er (Flowers), Tongku de xinyang (Miserable Faith), Zi yue (Confucius Says), Cangying (Flies), Xin kuzi (New Trousers) and Ershou meigui (Secondhand Rose).

At the beginning of the twenty-first century, live performances of Chinese rock were being held regularly in Beijing in small bars and nightclubs, the most famous of which include Poachers Inn, Hard Rock Café, CD Café, and many of the bars in the Sanlitun Bar Street, which emerged in the early 1990s. The CD Café was already known for hosting regular jazz jam sessions, led by the famous local sax player Liu Yuan. All of these venues are located in the northeastern part of Beijing, in or near the foreign embassies, and are attended by many foreign customers.

An Original Contribution

Another musical style that was closely associated with Beijing was *xibeifeng* (northwest wind), which enjoyed enormous popularity in 1987 and 1988. This music combined the style of Chinese folk songs from northwest China with rock 'n' roll and was China's first original popular music.

Record Companies

Between 1997 and 2002, most of the foreign record companies operating in China – Sony Music, Warner Music, BMG, EMI and others – moved their offices to Beijing. This relocation was another indication that the city had become the center of popular music in China. Beijing also has numerous local record companies which play an important role in producing and marketing local pop. These include: Jing wen, Chin tai, DMVE, Star Maker,

Kirin Kid, Rye, Tian zhong, Pulay, Zhu shu, Modern Sky and CZ.

Other Venues and Electronic and Printed Media

Karaoke bars are a major arena for the daily performance of popular music, both in Beijing and throughout China. The first karaoke bar opened in Beijing in early 1989, and by the end of that year the city already had over 70 such bars. In the 1990s, karaoke bars were found all over the city. Discothèques, too, are important; from the mid-1990s on, several opened in Beijing, among the most famous of which were NASA, Gunshi/Rolling Stones, JJ and Night-man. Most of the famous discothèques had a capacity of several hundred people and were located in the northern and eastern parts of the city, in between the universities and the foreign embassies.

Television

During the late 1980s and early 1990s popular music became an important ingredient in television broadcasts in China. This fact, combined with the fact that the headquarters of China's Central Television (CCTV – the country's most influential station, which broadcasts nationwide) are located in Beijing, was undoubtedly a major reason for the emergence of Beijing in the early 1990s as the unchallenged center of China's popular music scene in the reform era. Beijing, also has its own television station, BTV, which was established in 1979, has 10 different channels, and which broadcasts popular music daily. At the turn of the century, *Happy Weekend* and *The Public Welfare Song Competition* were among the favorite BTV music programs, watched throughout Beijing and further afield.

Radio

Beijing Music Radio station was established in 1993 and broadcast 24 hours a day. One of the most popular programs on this station was the *Chinese Popular Music Billboard*, which the station co-produced with China's Central Radio and 20 more provincial radio stations from all over the country.

Newspapers and Magazines

Several newspapers and magazines dedicated to music and other performing arts are published in Beijing and distributed nationwide. These include the *Music Weekly* and *Musical Life*, both of which are weeklies, and *Chinese Broadway* and the *Entertainment Circle*, both of which are monthlies.

Discographical References

Cui Jian. *Xin changzheng lu shang de yaogun* [Rock and Roll of the New Long March]. BJ201 *1989*: China.

Hei bao (Black Panther). *Hei bao* [Black Panther]. Z426 HO63. *1992*: China.

Tangchao (Tang Dynasty). *Tang chao* [Tang Dynasty]. Z421 HO62. *1992*: China.

Discography

He Yong. *Lajichang* [Garbage Dump]. CN-E04-94-326-00/AJ6. *1994*: China.

Qingxing. *Qingxing* [Sober]. CN-A26-97-355-00/A.J6. *1997*: China.

Zhang Chu. *Gudu de ren shi kechi de* [A Lonely Person is Shameful]. CN-E04-94-324-00.A.J6. *1994*: China.

Zheng Jun. *Chiluoluo* [Naked]. CN-A50-94-306-00/AJ6. *1994*: China.

Zhu Zheqin (Dadawa). *A jie gu* [Sister Drum]. CN-E02-94-338-00/A.J6. *1995*: China.

JIN ZHAOJUN (trans. NIMROD BARANOVITCH)

Hong Kong
Population: 6,787,000 (2002)

Hong Kong, a territory made up of three main areas (Hong Kong Island, Kowloon Peninsula and the New Territories), was ceded to Britain after two Opium Wars in the middle of the nineteenth century. Since 1997, when its sovereignty reverted to China, it has been run by a local government as a Special Administrative Region of the People's Republic of China.

A former fishing village with one of the world's best natural harbors, Hong Kong became a financial capital of Asia during the 1980s. Situated at the southern tip of China, Hong Kong has been the recipient of immigrants throughout its history. From Shanghai tycoons escaping from the Communist revolution to Vietnamese boat people, the influx of new inhabitants transformed Hong Kong into a vibrant and multicultural metropolis. Although Hong Kong still has more than 95 percent native Cantonese people (speaking the southern dialect, distinctly different from Mandarin, the official Chinese dialect), imported Anglo-American popular music has always found a market.

Popular music in Hong Kong during its colonial days included dance bands imported from Britain, and European traveling jazz musicians en route to 1930s Shanghai, then known as the 'Paris of the East,' situated further north along the Chinese coast. However, such 'Western' popular music would be exclusively performed in colonial establishments, to which few Cantonese would have had access. Popular musical entertainment for the Cantonese was Cantonese opera, a musical production that combined singing, instrumental music, acrobatic stage fights and elaborate costumes and makeup. Although there was a nascent recording industry for Cantonese music (mainly operatic numbers), Hong Kong did not have the market to support any sizable commercial venture.

The one-time sleepy fishing village and trading town first became a bustling city after 1949, when the founding of the People's Republic brought many refugees. Popular music in the 1950s and 1960s was divided into two drastically different worlds, with Shanghai émigrés still producing Mandarin songs, heavy on nightclub Latin and fox trot dance rhythms (and connecting Hong Kong to Taiwan), and a more local music appealing to urban young people who came into contact with Western popular music, including the Beatles, who performed live in 1964 on tour. Not only was this music fully derivative of Western pop and rock, but the songs were composed with English lyrics, and the bands all had English names.

Hong Kong did not gain international prominence until the 1970s, when rapid economic growth led to a rise in local consciousness. Hong Kong people took increasing pride in their Cantonese origins. By the early 1970s, Hong Kong's industrialization had also resulted in greater disposable income for urban young people – a stark contrast to the dwindling support for Mandarin popular songs, whose target audience was older and more conservative. Another contributing factor to the growth of popular entertainment was the founding of multiple commercial television stations (at one point in the early 1970s, there were rival stations with three Chinese and two English channels). Only two Chinese and two English channels have survived following fierce competition (the two English channels are the Hong Kong Television Broadcasting Corporation [TVB] and Asia Television [ATV], formerly Redifusion Hong Kong). All these stations staged their own television variety shows, in which popular singers would appear, singing either in Mandarin (imported Taiwanese popular songs) or English (from Beatles to Carpenters hits). The dissemination of such music contributed to the general awareness of such stars and songs as more people could afford to buy television sets for their homes.

As early as 1973, Sam Hui (Xu Guanjie) and his elder brother Michael (Xu Guanwen) starred in their own television show, which broadcast the first 'televised' Cantonese popular song. Entitled 'The Soul of Eiffel Tower' (Tieta Lingyun), this guitar-accompanied ballad became an overnight sensation, its title and lyrical content assuring people that no matter how much they traveled around the world, Hong Kong was still the best place to be because it was home.

From the mid-1970s onward, television stations such as TVB and ATV, and radio stations such as the popular Commercial Radio (CR, separated into channels 1 and 2, 2 being the youth culture pop music channel) and Radio Television Hong Kong (RTHK, the multi-channeled government radio station modeled after the BBC), not only disseminated music but also offered annual awards for outstanding composition, singing and production. It is through these televised awards, weekly radio pop charts and the high number of radio airplay hours that *cantopop* gradually took shape as a style and a genre. The first hit songs that took the entire population by storm (from young children to adults) were television soap opera theme songs, since they were broadcast daily. Written in the ballad style borrowed from Cantonese folk tunes, these hits were normally three to four minutes in duration, most of them with repetitive, memorable tunes. *Cantopop* as a style was characterized by heavily synthesized accompaniment, lilting melodies befitting the Cantonese dialect and lovelorn, amorous themes. By the late 1970s, regional community organizations also hosted annual popular song contests to nurture and discover new talents, both in singing and in composition. Through such channels, Leslie Cheung, Anita Mui, Jacky Cheung, Andy Hui and Sammi Cheng found international stardom. Other singers such as Andy Lau and Leon Lai rose through local television's actor-training program, and others came by way of modeling and acting.

Cantopop of that era also owed heavy debts to Japanese popular music, with frequent Cantonese covers of Japanese hits. Many *cantopop* stars received some training in Japan (just as Taiwanese stars did earlier), resulting in a similar style of delivery and packaging in Hong Kong, Taiwan and Japan. Of particular note is the rise of Teresa Teng (Deng Lijun), a Taiwanese singer who, during her heyday, enjoyed popularity in China, Taiwan, Hong Kong and Japan. Taiwanese authorities would drop illegal shipments of her cassette tapes along the coast of southern China as propaganda. People living in mainland China circulated illegal cassettes of Teng in the late 1970s, and many dubbed her 'little Deng' (of a China that was ruled by 'old Deng' Xiaoping). *Cantopop* reached new heights with the growth of

Hong Kong's film industry in the late 1980s, when Leslie Cheung starred and sang in such classics as *A Better Tomorrow* and *A Chinese Ghost Story*. Anita Mui's rendition of 'Rouge,' from a 1987 film *Yin Ji Kau* (whose international title was *Rouge*) directed by Stanley Kwan, also garnered international attention. At this time, during the zenith of Hong Kong popular culture, entertainment empires extended their reach into other products, appealing to audiences around the world.

The 12,000-seat Hong Kong Coliseum, which opened in the late 1980s, gave live performances a serious boost. Higher ticket prices and more extravagant productions soon followed. Even the Hong Kong Philharmonic Orchestra hosted its own annual series of popular music concerts, playing *cantopop* to packed houses. When a concert series was advertised, sometimes up to 10 to 15 consecutive sold-out shows took place.

The 1990s saw a general migration of marketing resources into the Chinese mainland, with the loosening of media control by the Chinese government. Such liberalization came hand in hand with the privatization of Chinese industries and businesses, and Hong Kong stars became the first generation of 'advertisement spokespersons,' a development which in turn allowed their presence as singers and actors to be promoted on the mainland.

Stylistically, *cantopop* has been in a musical stalemate since the early 1990s. Songs came to be written and produced on short notice, and record companies eager to make a better profit margin would cut down creative budgets but continue to spend on image and marketing. Few singers could withstand the pressure of live shows – too many of them lip-synched to recordings, even on television.

There have been isolated musical breakthroughs since the early 1990s: in 1993, a rap duo by the name of Softhard took the city by storm with a new release of fun rap, including political satires on pre-1997 Sino-British relations; another rap group, LMF (acronym for certain English-language obscenities), used foul language but managed to sell copies of their CDs in record shops despite a broadcast ban. In 2001, Eason Chan's 'Shall We Dance' used orchestral accompaniment, creating a hit that paid tribute to Fred Astaire and Ginger Rogers. In 2003, Ding Fei Fei (a star originally from Shanghai who was discovered and signed in Hong Kong) released a world music influenced album entitled *Origins*, containing new instrumental and vocal compositions including her own rendition on the electric *erhu* (traditional Chinese two-stringed fiddle).

Bibliography

Ho, Wai-Chung. 2000. 'The Political Meaning of Hong Kong Popular Music: A Review of Sociopolitical Relations Between Hong Kong and the People's Republic of China Since the 1980s.' *Popular Music* 19(3): 341–54.

Ho, Wai-Chung. 2003. 'Between Globilisation and Localisation: A Study of Hong Kong Popular Music.' *Popular Music* 22(2): 143–58.

Lee, Joanna C. 1992. 'Cantopop Songs on Emigration from Hong Kong.' *Yearbook for Traditional Music* 24: 14–23.

Witzleben, John Lawrence. 1998. 'Localism, Nationalism, and Transnationalism in Pre-postcolonial Hong Kong Popular Song.' In *Popular Music: Intercultural Interpretations,* ed. Toru Mitsui. Tokyo: Graduate Program in Music, Kanazawa University.

Witzleben, John Lawrence. 1999. 'Cantopop and Mandapop in Pre-Postcolonial Hong Kong: Identity Negotiation in the Performances of Anita Mui Yim-Fong.' *Popular Music* 18(2): 24–58.

Discographical References

Chan, Eason. 'Shall We Dance? Shall We Talk?' Emperor Entertainment Group EG 78692. *2001*: China (Hong Kong).

Ding, Fei Fei. *Origins*. Universal Music 981058-0. *2003*: China (Hong Kong).

Mui, Anita. 'Jinghuashuiyue.' Capital Artists CD-04-1220. *1997*: China (Hong Kong).

Discography

Cheung, Leslie. *Leslie*. Capital Artists CD-03-1263. *1998*: China (Hong Kong).

Cheng, Sammi. *Living Language*. WEA 3984-21495-2 *1997*: China (Hong Kong).

Hui, Sam. *Complete Collection of Sam Hui*. Universal Music 960259-0. *2002*: China (Hong Kong).

Polygram Hits. Polygram 557 069-2. *1998*: China (Hong Kong).

Softhard. *Softhard Special*. Cinepoly 157306-2. *1993*: Hong Kong.

Tam, Alan. *Continue Romance*. Philips 838 282-2. *1989*: Hong Kong.

Filmography

A Better Tomorrow, dir. John Woo. 1986. Hong Kong. 95 mins. Action Thriller. Original music by Joseph Koo.

A Chinese Ghost Story, dir. Ching Siu Tung. 1987. Hong Kong. 93 mins. Romantic Fantasy. Original music by Romeo Diaz, James Wong.

Yin Ji Kau (Rouge), dir. Stanley Kwan. 1987. Hong Kong. 96 mins. Drama. Original music by Siu-Tin Lei.

JOANNA C. LEE

Shanghai
Population: 17,000,000 (2002)

Shanghai is China's most prominent harbor and a city with a booming economy in the early twenty-first century. It is located along the Huangpu River on China's east coast, midway between the northern capital Beijing and the southern cities Guangzhou (Canton) and Hong Kong. The city has 17 million inhabitants, many of whom originate from provinces such as Zhejiang, Anhui, Jiangsu and Jiangxi. One should add an extra 20 percent to this figure, to account for migrant workers (*waidi ren*). Whereas Beijing is the political center of China, Shanghai can be considered its commercial center. Since the end of the 1990s, the city has competed with Hong Kong for being the primary commercial gateway to China for foreign entrepreneurs. Given its semi-colonial history, Shanghai is said to be very receptive to foreign influences, hence functioning as one of the fashionable trendsetters of the country.

Shanghai has developed its own musical culture and can be considered the birthplace of a modern and 'westernized' popular music in China. The revival of and nostalgia for Shanghai's glamorous popular culture of the Republican Era (1911–49) in the early 1990s connects this period with more recent contemporary culture, and is not to be separated from the city's political history. Following China's defeat in the Opium War and the 'Unequal Treaties' (1843), Shanghai was among the five cities that were forcefully opened to Western trade. Throughout the following 100 years the city was divided into three geographically defined and politically independent entities, which provided the basis for a new and hybrid popular culture: the 'old' Chinese City and two 'extraterritorial' regions, namely the French Concession (1849) and the International Settlement (1863), governed by the Great Britain and the United States. Following the Taiping Rebellion (1850–64) – China's biggest upheaval of the nineteenth century – the number of Chinese refugees in Shanghai rose tremendously and turned the city into the cultural center of the 'Jiangnan region' (south of the Yangzi-River, between the provinces of Jiangsu, Anhui and Zhejiang). Up to the 1940s, the city's extraterritorial status, its strengthening economy, industrialization,

commercial opportunities, relative freedom from the Chinese government and safety in times of war prepared the ground for a new and urban 'modern' synthesis of both Chinese and Western music genres. These developments were largely influenced and organized by the Western entertainment industry, which was concentrated in Shanghai.

Recording Industry – Beginnings
In 1896, the people of Shanghai saw their first film performance, and in 1903 foreign companies recorded their first Chinese shellac records there. In the 1920s, the film and the music industry – Chinese and foreign – began to flourish in Shanghai. During World War I, French Pathé-Orient established China's first record pressing plant, followed in 1924 by the Chinese-owned pressing plant of the Great China Record Company (Dazhonghua), British EMI-China and US RCA-Victor in the early 1930s. These factories, together with numerous production companies, imports of foreign music, US sound films and more than 30 broadcasting stations in Shanghai formed the unique commercial and musical platform on which the city's popular music began to take shape. Shanghai attracted various artists from different provinces and maintained its status as China's leading center of popular entertainment, despite many difficulties during the years of the Chinese-Japanese War (1937–45) and Japanese occupation (December 1941–August 1945). After four years of civil war, and at the time of the founding of the People's Republic of China in 1949, Victor Records disappeared and EMI-China moved to Hong Kong (a British dependency until 1997), followed by many of its songwriters and artists (e.g. Yao Min, Chen Dieyi, Yao Li, Zhang Lu). By the end of the year, the Great China Record Company had been transformed into the state-owned People's Records Factory (Renmin changpian chang). In 1955, it was renamed the China Record Factory (Zhongguo changpian chang), and remained the only pressing plant until 1964. Afterwards, subsidies were established in Guangzhou and, in 1968, in Beijing and Chengdu, supported by Premier Zhou Enlai himself.

Popular Chinese Genres in the Republican Era (1911–1949)
During the Republican Era a large variety of musical forms enjoyed popularity in Shanghai. Due to the heterogeneous population of Shanghai (which in the 1930s consisted of nearly four million inhabitants) and growing nationalist and anti-foreign sentiment, different genres gradually found

their way into the city's commercial entertainment industry. Among the traditional and most popular forms were genres such as Beijing Opera; story-telling genres that originated from Suzhou (*pingtan, tanci*); local opera styles from Ningbo, Shaoxing and Canton (Guangzhou); and the Shanghai Opera (*shenqu*, later, *huju*), which, as a hybrid synthesis of different genres, emerged in the 1930s.

While these urbanized but rather traditional forms of entertainment were performed on numer-ous stages in Shanghai, a new form of commercially organized modern popular entertainment songs also began to appear around this time. The new popular music (*liuxing yinyue*), or 'Songs of the Times' (*shidaiqu*), as the songs were usually called in the late 1930s, were sung in Mandarin Chinese. They derived from so-called 'little tunes' (*xiao diao*) or 'folk ditties' (*minjian xiaodiao*), based on old folk and love songs that were sung in brothels by prostitutes and courtesans. Despite their immoral and negative image, both the actresses and their songs enjoyed much popularity, the performers being among the first artists to be approached by record companies.

Western Influences

During the 'warlord period' (1917–27), Shang-hai's film and entertainment industry had pros-pered, and the first post-war US ragtime and jazz recordings had entered the harbor. A new middle class began to enjoy Hollywood films and 'social dancing' (mainly the fox trot), which were slowly becoming popular among Western-oriented Chi-nese audiences. Also in this decade, female opera actors and sing-song girls took to the stage; the Beijing opera star Mei Lanfang (1894–1961) rose to fame in Shanghai; and Li Jinhui (1881–1967), a progressive language teacher, patriot and composer of children songs, established the Bright Moon Song and Dance Troupe (Mingyue gewutuan). Its mem-bers were a group of young girls and boys who combined sentimental Chinese songs with Western instrumentation and thereby created a modern and attractive repertoire. By the end of the 1920s, Li Jinhui's daughter Li Minghui had several songs recorded, among them 'Maomaoyu' (Drizzling, 1929), which became one of the most well known songs of the Republican Period. 'Li-style music,' the new romantic sound combination of Chinese folk melodies (*minjian xiaoqu*) and Western instruments, as a new modern style, became the dominant popular music in the following years. Simulta-neously, dance halls (*yinyue ting*) were set up, the recording industry boomed and ensemble members

rose to stardom, both in the fields of music and film (e.g., Wang Renmei, Li Lili, Yan Hua, Zhou Xuan). While composers like Yan Gongshang and Yan Gefan adopted this commercially successful style, a large number of songs taken from Hollywood revue films and popular US jazz tunes were translated into Chinese, e.g. those sung by Maurice Chevallier and Jeanette MacDonald. Simultaneously, and partly in opposition to US jazz and entertainment culture, another popular genre developed within the circle of Western-trained, nationalist and cosmopolitan composers who were affiliated with the newly established Shanghai Music Conservatory (1927). Influenced by the German 'Kunstlied,' composers such as He Luting (1903–99) and Huang Zi (1904–38) wrote art songs (*yishu gequ*) with both senti-mental and patriotic lyrics.

Nationalism of the 1930s

During the 1930s, resistance to Japanese aggres-sion in Manchuria grew among cultural circles, and their struggle over ideological issues became visible. In principle, many musicians and composers were nationalistic. They either supported the ruling Nationalist Party (*Guomindang*) under Chiang Kai-shek (e.g., Xiao Youmei, Director of the Shanghai Music Conservatory), or left-wing class struggle (e.g., composers as He Luting, Ren Guang, Xian Xinghai). In contrast to 'Western-style' popular songs, they composed a new national music (*guoyue*) and so-called 'progressive songs' (*jinbu gequ*), 'mass songs' (*qunzhong gequ*) or 'revolutionary songs' (*geming gequ*), which were also inspired by Russian worker songs, and often sung by those stars mentioned above. The political usage of music was an important aspect of the 1930s, reflecting the ideological struggle between the nationalists and the communists. Among the most popular songs of the time was the leftist film song 'Yiyongjun' (March of Volunteers, 1935), composed by Nie Er (1912–35), which in 1949 became the national anthem of the People's Republic of China. Most of these songs were recorded by EMI-China and also served as film songs.

Shortly before Japan began to attack Shanghai in the summer of 1937, the actress Zhou Xuan (1920–57) recorded her two famous sentimental film songs 'Siji ge' (Song of the Seasons, 1937) and 'Tianya genü' (Sing-Song Girl at the Ends of the World, 1937), which became instant hits. By then, the popular 'Songs of the Times' were being identified with a particular Shanghai sound. In the 1940s, composers such as Yao Min, Li Jinguang, Chen

Gexin and Chen Dieyi supplied the lyrics and arrangement for new jazz and swing songs, while actresses such as Zhou Xuan, Yao Li, Gong Qiuxia, Bai Hong, Li Xianglan (Yoshiko Yamaguchi) and others became the stars of the war period. By the time of her early death, Zhou Xuan alone recorded 114 film songs and 97 others. Since the whole entertainment industry was occupied by Japanese forces and operated under strict censorship, non-political and occasional cynical love songs constituted the main genre of those years.

The Music Industry Post-World War II

When the war ended in 1945, Shanghai was for the first time solely governed by China. It was during this time that Zhou Xuan recorded her still famous film-song 'Night in Shanghai' (Ye Shanghai, 1946) for EMI-China, which reflected the hope for a happy and peaceful restoration of the city. Simultaneously, US culture began to flourish again in the form of Hollywood movies and jazz. However, increasing inflation and the civil war between nationalist and communist forces allowed only a short revival of Shanghai's pre-war entertainment culture. When the People's Liberation Army entered Shanghai in May 1949, recording companies and film studios were immediately liquidated and reorganized for propaganda purposes. One month later, the Shanghai newspaper *Jiefang ribao* (*Liberation Daily*) announced that the first songs had been recorded and were soon to be broadcast. In the early 1950s, the People's Record Factory began to release songs such as 'Zanmen gangren you liliang' (Our Workers have Strength), 'Xin Zhongguo de qingnia' (The Youth of New China), 'Gongren jinxingqu' (Workers' March) and folk-style songs like 'Funü ziyou ge' (Women's Freedom Song).

In the 1950s, as a former metropolitan center of capitalist, bourgeois and decadent Western culture, Shanghai became the target of several political campaigns that were attempting to eradicate its past. Meanwhile, the Shanghai song style survived in Taiwan and Hong Kong, where it underwent certain local changes. The revival of this genre came nearly half a century later, after Deng Xiaoping decided to rebuild Shanghai as the new economic center of South China. By then, Taiwanese singer Deng Lijun (also known as Teresa Teng, 1953–95) had already gained fame with modern adaptations of old Shanghai songs. In the early 1990s, EMI-Hong Kong began to distribute a series of more than 60 CDs, entitled 'Zhongguo shidaiqu mingdian' (The Legendary Chinese Hits). The revival of the

past has also been portrayed by the popularity of jazz since the 1990s; rather than experimenting with new styles, the jazz performed in Shanghai is mostly filled with nostalgia and decadence.

The period between the Great Leap Forward (*Dayuejin*) and the Cultural Revolution (*Wenhua dageming*) (1959–76) was a highly politicized one, during which music mainly served as a way to instruct and control the masses. In June 1958, the China Record Company (Zhongguo changpian she) was founded and became the only organization for editing and publishing records in the 20 years that followed. Only after Deng Xiaoping launched his open door policy in 1978 did the situation change, rapidly. Since 1978, but particularly after 1992 – when Deng Xiaoping traveled to the southern economic zones in order to help accelerate the development of an open market economy – China has indeed witnessed unprecedented economic growth. Shanghai can be considered emblematic for these changes. In the 1980s, while the city was slowly opening up to the outside world, the China Record Company merged with all its branches (factories and distribution company) in 1982 and became the China Record Corporation (1985), which began publishing its own journal *Audio & Video World* (*Yinxiang shijie*) in 1987. During the 1990s, the cityscape was dramatically transformed. Skyscrapers competed with one another for height, and neon lights turned the center of town into a permanent brightly lit shopping and entertainment zone. Shanghai's soundscape was transformed equally as fast yet, unlike in the Republican Era, Shanghai did not develop a sound of its own. Instead, the melodic songs of aforementioned Deng Lijun, the Taiwanese pop diva of the 1980s, resonated well with the changes of a Shanghai that was opening up. It was said in popular discourse that Deng Xiaoping ruled by day, but that Deng Lijun ruled by night. Perhaps because of this conflation of political and musical power, Deng's songs were deemed dangerously sensual by the authorities and, during the 1990s, her soft and melodic songs were replaced by the more upbeat and fashionable sounds of Hong Kong and the Taiwan pop stars of the day (*Gangtai liuxing yinyue*).

The Shanghai Conservatory of Music played a pivotal role in the promotion of Western and Chinese classical music, genres deemed less dangerous by the authorities when compared with either rock or pop. The conservatory also trained, albeit unintentionally, popular musicians. Zhang Ya-guang studied trumpet during the 1980s, to become later what was coined Shanghai's Cui Jian (the Beijing rock star who incidentally also studied the trumpet), when he formed the rock band Blue Forest (Lan senlin) in the early 1990s. This band was part of what was considered the first stage of rock in Shanghai, during which covers of Western rock were very popular. Other bands belonging to this era were Vexing Practice (Naohuo lianxi), Fuse (Baoxiansi) and Iron Orchid (Tie yulan). Iron Orchid was the only band from this early generation to release an album, in 1998, for the Beijing label Jingwen. The album received little critical or popular acclaim. Parallel to its release, at the end of the 1990s, a new generation of rock proliferated in Shanghai, with bands such as Crystal Butterfly (Shuijingdie), the Honeys (Tianmi de haizi), Bus for the Night (Yeban bashi) and Godot (Gedou). New styles were incorporated, such as the post-punk of One Stone Shot Birds (Jingong zhiniao), a hybrid form of rock with traditional Chinese music from Cool Fairyland (Lengku xianjing), the noise from Junkyard, and the experimental sound of Circus on Roof (Dinglou maxituan). These more established bands performed regularly in the Shanghai's bar street Xintiandi, at the Japanese-owned venue Ark, where Shanghai's most prominent rock critic Fei Qiang was in charge of the program. The more underground bands performed at bar and art gallery Room with a View (Dingcenghualang), or at the SUS2 Music Factory (Gua'er). The latter is also a modern music school, where one could learn to play popular music instruments, such as the guitar and drums. In 2001, Shanghai's first independent record label was founded, Fanyin, which released the first album of the Honeys. The company – which, like all record companies in China, has to deal with censorship practices as well as a high piracy rate – aims to give a voice to an alternative Shanghai sound. However promising this may seem, the rock scene from Beijing still dwarfs the one in Shanghai.

Despite its limited impact, rock as a signifier of rebellion and modernity exercised a strong influence on the literary realm in Shanghai in the late 1990s. Both *Shanghai Baby* (1999) written by Wei Hui, as well as *La La La* (1999) and *Candy* (2000) from Mian Mian, depict a lifestyle saturated with the clichéd triple, sex, drugs and rock 'n' roll, all pointing to a strong sense of anxiety on the part of young people. Translations into different languages ensured that these provocative female authors, whose work depicts the lifestyle of a new generation born after the Cultural Revolution,

gained a global audience, unlike their sonic counter-parts in both Shanghai and Beijing. Both writers are controversial in China. Wei Hui's book, for example, was banned at a book fair in Beijing in May 2000. Such a ban only applies to big cities like Beijing and Shanghai, and is bound to be ineffective, given the flourishing piracy market. As of 2004, the ban had not officially been lifted, yet bookshops had reached a silent agreement with the censorship department and were allowed to sell the book. Despite the availability of their works, both writers achieved less popularity locally when compared to their global reception.

The Music Scene at the Turn of the Twenty-First Century

Shanghai has remained, as it was in the 1930s, highly receptive to foreign cultural trends. At the turn of the twenty-first century, lounge bars such as the China-In and the Buddha Bar were joining in the global lounge and ambient trend, and DJing had become increasingly popular. Although the scene was by and large dominated by foreign DJs, local stars such as DJ V-Nutz were gaining recognition. In addition, hip-hop was gradually taking root in Shanghai. The first annual rap battle in the Pegasus club took place in 2002, initiated by US born Dana Burton. The 2004 final featured rapper Webber (Wang Bo) from Beijing battling against Black Bubble (Wang Fan) from Shanghai. The final once again underlined the importance of 'place' in popular music. Similar to rock culture, in the domain of hip-hop it is the capital that reigns: Webber, who was considered the top rapper of China, won the battle for the third year in a row. Hip-hop, lounge, DJing, as well as digital music may have established niche markets in Shanghai, but they remain too small to be called vibrant scenes.

This all reflects a fairly gloomy musical picture: neither during the 1980s, nor during the 1990s, did Shanghai play a pivotal role in terms of musical production in China. However, the city did, and has continued to function as an important cultural interface. Shanghai is a significant gateway for trends and fashions, including popular music, from Hong Kong, Taiwan, Japan, South Korea (rapidly increasing in importance as a regional cultural trendsetter) and the West.

Shanghai consequently seems to be caught up in a nostalgia for a decadent, flamboyant past, a nostalgia exemplified by the eagerness in the early twenty-first century to portray itself as the city of jazz, as well as by the revival in the 1990s of the old songs of the 1930s and 1940s. This decadent past is subsequently projected upon an imaginary cosmopolitan future. New musical cultures, ranging from hip-hop to ambient, are attempting to carve out a space in a city that acts upon its stereotype as being governed by the spirit of money. Shanghai is struggling against triple hegemonic forces in popular music: Beijing is the center of Chinese rock, Taiwan and Hong Kong are the centers of Chinese pop and the West is perceived as 'the origin' and hence the producer of 'the real, authentic' popular music. This leaves little room for contemporary Shanghai.

Bibliography

Benson, Carlton. 1995. 'The Manipulation of Tanci in Radio Shanghai during the 1930s.' *Republican China* 20(2) (April): 116–46.

Benson, Carlton. 1999. 'Consumers are also Soldiers: Subversive Songs from Nanjing Road During the New Life Movement.' In *Inventing Nanjing Road. Commercial Culture in Shanghai, 1900–1945*, ed. Sherman Cochran. New York/Ithaca: Cornell University, 91–132.

Chang, Michael G. 1999. 'The Good, the Bad, and the Beautiful: Movie Actresses and Public Discourse in Shanghai, 1920s–1930s.' In *Cinema and Urban Culture in Shanghai, 1922–1934*, ed. Zhang, Yingjin. Stanford, CA: Stanford University Press, 128–59.

Chen, Gang. 2002. 'Meigui meigui wo ai ni.' Gexian Chen Gexin zhi ge ['Rose, Rose I love You': Songs of the Immortal Chen Gexin]. Shanghai: Cishu Publishing House.

Chen, Yiping. 2000. *Zhongguo zaoqi dianying gequ jingxuan* [Collection of Songs from old Chinese Movies]. Beijing: Zhongguo Dianying Publishing House.

de Kloet, Jeroen. 2002. 'Commercial Fantasies: China's Music Industry.' In *Media Futures in China, Consumption, Content and Crisis*, ed. Stephanie H. Donald, Michael Keane and Yin Hong. London & Surrey: Routledge/Curzon Press, 93–104.

de Kloet, Jeroen. 2003. 'Confusing Confucius: Rock in Contemporary China.' In *Policing Popular Music*, ed. Martin Cloonan and Reebee Garofalo. Philadelphia: Temple University Press, 166–86.

Fei, Qiang. 2003. 'San Huang Ji.' *Quote* 3 (5): 16–17.

Gao, Chunming. 2002. *Shanghai yishu shi* [History of Shanghai Arts], 2 Vols. Shanghai: Renmin Meishu Publishing House.

Huang, Hao. 2001. 'Yaogun Yinyue: Rethinking Mainland Chinese Rock 'n' Roll.' *Popular Music* 20: 1–11.

Huang, Hao. 2003. 'Voices from Chinese Rock, Past and Present Tense: Social Commentary and Construction of Identity – *Yaogun Yinyue* from Tiananmen to the Present.' *Popular Music and Society* 26: 183–202.

Huang, Qizhi. 2000/2001. *Shidaiqu de liuguang suiyue 1930–1970* [The Age of Shanghainese Pops, 1930–1970]. Hong Kong: Joint Publishing Co. (Includes CD.)

Hung, Chang-tai. 1994. *War and Popular Culture: Resistance in Modern China, 1937–1945*. Berkeley, CA: University of California Press.

Jones, Andrew. 2001. *Yellow Music: Media Culture and Colonial Modernity in the Chinese Jazz Age*. Durham/London: Duke University Press.

Ko, Dorothy. 1999. 'Jazzing into Modernity: High Heels, Platforms, and Lotus Shoes.' In *China Chic: East Meets West*, ed. Valerie Steele and John S. Major. New Haven/Conn.: Yale University Press, 141–53.

McDaniel, Laura. 2001. '"Jumping the Dragon Gate." Storytellers and the Creation of the Shanghai Identity.' *Modern China* 27(4) (October): 484–507.

McDougall, Bonnie S. 1984 (ed.). *Popular Chinese Literature and Performing Arts in the People's Republic of China 1949–1979*. Berkeley CA: University of California Press.

Mian Mian. 1999. *Lalala*. Kunming: Yunnan Renmin Chubanshe.

Mian Mian. 2000. *Tang* [Candy]. Beijing: China Opera Publication House.

Mittler, Barbara. 1997. *Dangerous Tunes: The Politics of Chinese Music in Hong Kong, Taiwan, and the People's Republic of China since 1949*. Wiesbaden: Harrassowitz Publishing House.

Movius, Lisa. 2001a. 'Selling Their Souls for Rock 'n' Roll: Another Revolution Takes Hold in Shanghai.' *Asian Wall Street Journal*, 28 September. Retrieved at www.movius.us on June 3, 2004.

Movius, Lisa. 2001b. 'The Cat King's Blues: Shanghai Singer Zhang Yaoguang Proves That Old Stars Don't Die, They Just Keep Fish.' *City Weekend*, 23 April. Retrieved at www.movius.us on June 3, 2004.

Movius, Lisa. 2002. 'Shanghai's Heavy Thread: Lashing the Cities Underground Band Scene Together.' *City Weekend*, 11 April. Retrieved at www.movius.us on June 3, 2004.

Movius, Lisa. 2003. 'Rock in a Hard Place.' *Far Eastern Economic Review* 22 May. Retrieved at www.movius.us on June 3, 2004.

Schimmelpenninck, A. and Kouwenhoven, F. 1993.

'The Shanghai Conservatory of Music: History & Foreign Student's Experiences.' *CHIME* 6 (Spring): 56–91.

Steen, Andreas. 1999/2000. 'Tradition, Politics and Meaning in 20th Century China's Popular Music: Zhou Xuan, "When will the Gentleman come back again?"' *CHIME* 14/15, 124–53.

Steen, Andreas. 2003. '"Liebeslieder waren keine Revolutionslieder!" Die Schallplattenzensur im Shanghai der Republikzeit (1934–1949)' ['Love Songs Were Not Revolutionary Songs': Record Censorship in Shanghai during the Republican Period, 1934–1949]. In *Zensur: Text und Autorität in China in Geschichte und Gegenwart*, ed. Bernhard Führer. Wiesbaden: Harrassowitz Publishing House, 169–93.

Steen, Andreas. Forthcoming. *Zwischen Unterhaltung und Revolution: Grammophone, Schallplatten und die Anfänge der Musikindustrie in Shanghai 1877–1937* [Between Revolution and Entertainment: Gramophones, Records and the Beginning of Shanghai's Music Industry, 1877–1937], Wiesbaden: Harrassowitz.

Stock, Jonathan P.J. 2003. *Huju: Traditional Opera in Modern Shanghai*. Oxford: Oxford University Press.

Sun Jinan. 1993. *Li Jinhui pingzhuan* [Critical Biography of Li Jinhui]. Beijing: Renmin Yinyue Publishing House.

Sun, Mengjin. 1999. 'Jujue, Chengshou yu Pangguangde Yidai' [Refusal, Forebearing and a Generation of Onlookers]. *Modeng Tiankong* 5: 118–19.

Tuohy, Sue. 1999. 'Metropolitan Sounds: Music in Chinese Film Songs of the 1930s.' In *Cinema and Urban Culture in Shanghai, 1922–1943*, ed. Zhang Yingjin. Stanford, CA: Stanford University Press, 200–21.

Wang, Renmei. 1985. *Huiyilu: Wo de chengming yu buxing* [Memories: My Life and My Misfortunes]. Shanghai: Wenyi Publishing House.

Wang, Wenhe. 1995. *Zhongguo dianying yinyue xunzong* [Traces of Chinese Film Music]. Beijing: Zhongguo Guangbo Dianshe Publishing House.

Wang, Yuhe. 2002. *Zhongguo jinxiandai yinyueshi* [History of Modern Music in China]. Beijing: Renmin Yinyue Publishing House.

Wei, Hui. 1999. *Shanghai Baobei* [Shanghai Baby]. Shenyang: Literature and Art Publication House.

Witzleben, John Lawrence. 1995. *'Silk and Bamboo' Music in Shanghai: The Jiangnan Sizhu Instrumental Ensemble Tradition*. Kent/Ohio: Kent State University Press.

Xiang, Yansheng. 1994 (ed.). *Zhongguo jinxiandai yinyuejia zhuan* [Biographies of Chinese Composers in the Modern Period], 4 Vols. Shenyang: Chunfeng Wenyi Publishing House.

Yan, Jun. 1999. *Beijing Xinsheng* [New Sound of Beijing]. Hunan: Wenyi Publishing.

Zhang, Yingjin, ed. 1999. *Cinema and Urban Culture in Shanghai, 1922–1934*. Stanford, CA: Stanford University Press.

Zhao, Shihui. 1995 (ed.). *Zhou Xuan zishu* [Zhou Xuan in Her Own Words]. Shanghai: Sanlian Shudian Publishing House.

Zhang, Xiaozhou. 2000. 'New Music Guangzhou, Zai Guangzhou Zhao Le' [New Music Guangzhou, Looking For Fun in Guangzhou]. *Modeng Tiankong* 7: 16–17.

Zhou, Wei. 2002. *Wo de mama Zhou Xuan* [My Mother Zhou Xuan], 2nd ed. Taiyuan: Shanxi Jiaoyu Publishing House.

Discographical References

Beijing jinghua yinshuju geyongdui [Beijing Jinghua Publishing Chorus]. 'Zanmen gongren you liliang' [Our Workers have Strength]. People's Record Factory. 38127. *1949*: China.

Guo, Lanying. 'Fünü ziyou ge' [Women's Freedom Song]. People's Record Factory 38257. *1949*: China.

Li, Minghui. 'Maomaoyu' [Drizzling]. Pathé Baidai, 33777. *1930*: China.

Tie Yulan [Iron Orchid]. 'Tie Yulan' [Iron Orchid]. Jingwen. *1998*:China.

Yuan, Muzhi, Gu Menghe. 'Yiyongjun jinxingqu' [March of the Volunteers]. EMI-China A2395. *1935*: China.

Yun Mindu. 'Gongren jinxingqu' [Workers March]. People's Record Company 7018. *1951–52*: China.

Zhou, Xuan. 'Siji ge' [Song of the Seasons]. EMI-China 35335b. *1937*: China

Zhou, Xuan. 'Tianya genü' [Singsong Girl at the Ends of the World]. EMI-China 35335a. *1937*: China.

Zhou, Xuan. 'Ye Shanghai' [Night in Shanghai]. EMI-China B966. *1946*: China.

Zhou Xuan et al. 'Zhongguo shidaiqu mingdian' [The Legendary Chinese Hits]. EMI. *1992*: China.

Zhongyang yinyue xueyuan Shanghai fenyuan yingongtuan [Central Music Conservatory, Shanghai Branch, Workers Music Troupe]. 'Xin Zhongguo de qingnian' [The Youth of New China]. People's Record Company 6996. *1951–52*: China.

Discography

Junkyard. *Junk and Retain Junk*. Isolation Music. *2004*: China.

ANDREAS STEEN and JEROEN DE KLOET

Korea: Historical Background

Korea is situated on the Korean Peninsula. The Amnokgang and the Dumangang rivers separate the Peninsula from its northern neighbors, China and Russia. Japan is to its east beyond the Sea of Japan. About two-thirds of the country is mountainous, and Mount Baekdusan, bordering China, is the highest point at 8,900 ft (2,744 m) above sea level. The Koreans are one ethnic family, believed to be descendants of several Mongol tribes that migrated onto the Peninsula from Central Asia. All Koreans speak and write the same language, the reason for the country's homogeneity and strong national identity.

The history of Korea dates back to 2333 B.C., with Dangun as its first ruler. The town-states of ancient Korea gradually evolved into complex political structures, and the Korean Peninsula was eventually divided into three different kingdoms: Goguryeo in the north (37 B.C.–A.D. 668), Baekje (18 B.C.–A.D. 660) in the southwest and Silla (57 B.C.–A.D. 935) in the far south. By the mid-sixth century, Silla consolidated all the neighboring regions, and eventually occupied the area previously governed by Baekje, thus creating Unified Silla (668–935). In turn, the people of Goguryeo, along with a large Malgal population, established the Kingdom of Balhae (698–926) to the north of Unified Silla.

Although frequently invaded by neighboring countries, most of the Korean Peninsula has nevertheless been ruled by a single government since the Silla unification of 668. Silla rule lasted until the beginning of the tenth century, when the leaders began to fight among each other. In 918 Wang Kon founded the Koryo Dynasty. It was from this dynasty that the name 'Korea' was derived. In the twelfth century, the Koryo dynasty experienced conflicts between its civilian and military structures and later, in the thirteenth century, Korea was invaded several times by the Mongolians from the north. In 1392, the Koryo Dynasty was succeeded by the Chosun Dynasty, which was ruled by the Yi family from 1392 until 1910. Korea eventually lost its political independence in 1910, when Japan annexed the Peninsula and instituted colonial rule. The lives of Koreans deteriorated under Japanese colonialism until Japan was defeated in World War II. The Korean Peninsula then became divided into two different political entities based on ideological differences.

OKON HWANG

North Korea
Population: 22,466,481 (2003)

Music in the Democratic People's Republic of Korea (DPRK) (North Korea) is by definition popular music. Kim Il Sung, who ruled the northern state from its founding in 1948 until his death in 1994, filtered Andrei Zhdanov's socialist realism through Mao Zedong's 1942 Yan'an forum speeches in his 1951 'Talks with Writers and Artists.' In this, artists were told to 'learn from the lofty spirit of ordinary people,' since they 'should know that the genuine creator of great art is always the people.'

North Korea inherited a style of song known in Korean as *yuhaengga* (literally, 'popular songs'), based on Japanese *enka*, and produced locally from the 1920s onward. Many texts were patriotic, while melodies were typically set to a fox-trot rhythm (hence, the onomatopoeic term *ppongtchak* by which they are known in the Republic of Korea). Early Korean *yuhaengga* included 'Hoemangga' (Song of Hope); 'Saui ch'anmi' (Beautiful Death; set to a tune by Ivanovitch), first published in 1923; and 'Hwangsŏng yet'ŏ' (Footprints of the Ruined Castle), first recorded by the actress Yi Pojŏ (known under her Japanese name, Ierisu) in 1932. From the early 1940s, these songs were increasingly referred to as 'popular songs' (*taejung kayo*), and this term, with nationalist overtones, has continued to be used in the DPRK. Instrumental arrangements are similarly called 'popular music' (*taejung ŭmak*) or 'light music' (*kyŏng ŭmak*).

As the DPRK developed a political dogma, so artistic production was made to reflect socialism. Korean revolutionary songs, similar to the *geming guqu* of China, actually predate the founding of the northern state, beginning in the final days of the Pacific War with the composers Kim Sunnam, An Kiyŏng and Ri Kŏnu. Ri's 'Haebang chŏnsae ŭi norae' (Song of the Independence Fighters), 'Kanŭn kil' (The Way to Go) and 'Yŏmyŏng ui norae' (New Era Song), and Kim's 'Kŏn'guk haengjin'gok' (Foundation March for the Nation) are representative. Although these three artists, along with many others, had crossed the border from Sŏul (Seoul) into the DPRK, by 1948 they represented an elite, and some were trained in Japan. Kim was sent to study in Moskva (Moscow) with Khachaturian in 1952, but was ordered to return barely a year later.

He, like many others, was purged. In his place, the state promoted more proletarian artists such as Kim Wŏn'gyun (b. 1917). Kim had been a farmer, but in 1946 he produced 'Kim Ilsŏng changgŭn ŭi norae' (Song of General Kim Il Sung). A year later he completed the 'Aegukka' (National Anthem). These two are the most frequently heard of all DPRK songs and they are given a prominent position in popular collections. Kim was promoted to the rank of 'people's artist' (*inmin yesulga*), and from the 1970s onward was central to the Sea of Blood Opera Company (P'i pada kagŭk tan) in P'yŏngyang. He too was sent to study in Moskva (Moscow), where his graduation piece was the symphonic poem *Hyangt'o* (Birthplace). Songs have remained the dominant music genre in the DPRK, as witnessed by the prodigious output of composers such as Ri Myŏnsang and Kim Oksŏng (both now dead), and the massive collection of 2,000 Korean songs published in 1994 as *Chosŏn Kayo 2000 Kokchip*.

In the late 1950s, reflecting Sino-Soviet tensions following the death of Stalin, the DPRK launched its 'Galloping Horse Movement' (Ch'ŏllima undong). Partly imitative of Mao's '100 Flowers' policy, this initiative sought to increase production through a unitary ideology that gave the state absolute control. Control meant that a correct political content replaced notions of style or structure in musical production. However, patriotism reasserted itself above socialist revolution; hence, on the grounds that the vernacular alone exhibited a proper spirit, folk arts were researched, recovered and enriched. For a period, folk songs were collected, and what was termed 'resurrectionism' was avoided by the changing of lyrics to match socialist ideals and by the adjustment of melodies to fit diatonic scales. Folk songs about labor, farming, woodcutting, milling and weaving were part of a peasant past and had no place in classless socialism. Similarly, regional styles of folk song were not considered suitably popular, notably those from the eastern seaboard (tainted also because they were based on a Japanese mode), the southwest (because of their complexity and typical vocal sadness) and the northwest (because of the characteristic nasal vibration in many songs). A genre of so-called 'new folk songs' (*shin minyo*), developed in the late nineteenth or early twentieth century, often associated with specific writers and distinguished by the adoption of a lyricism characteristic of urban Sŏul (Seoul), met the requirements. 'Toraji' (The Bellflower), for example, was revised as 'Hwanggumsan ui paek toraji' (The White Bellflower on Yellow Gold Mountain), with a new text describing a socialist land of abundance; 'Ch'angbu t'aryŏng,' which originally described a girl waiting for her lover in veiled moonlight, as 'Moran Hill' tells of the magnificent rebuilding of the capital city by Kim Il Sung.

In the 1960s, themes were rationed, and hence instrumental pieces were written around revolutionary song or folk-song melodies. Central control was further enhanced as a new ideology took hold. *Juche*, often glossed as 'self-reliance,' enhanced group responsibility through 'seed theory' (*chŏngjaron*) and 'collective art' (*chipch'e yesul*). Seed theory was meant to guarantee profundity by placing ideology above but alongside mature talent, but it effectively denied individual creativity. Collectives of artists were jointly charged with developing popular music. In 1971, the first revolutionary opera, *P'i pada* (Sea of Blood), was completed by such a collective. All subsequent operas from the same company have been labeled 'immortal' for their patriotic and heroic stories, including *Kkŏt panun ch'ŏnyŏ* (The Flower Girl), *Ch'unhaengjŏn* (The Story of Spring Fragrance), *Tang ŭi ch'amdwin ttal* (A True Daughter of the Party), *Kŭmgangsan ŭi sori* (Song of the Diamond Mountains), *Yŏnp'ungho* (Gentle Breeze) and *Millima iyagi hara* (Tell the Story, Forest). Operas incorporate folk song, and arias are replaced by company choruses known as *pangch'ang* – a subgenre for which Kim Jong Il, the son of Kim Il Sung, is credited as inventor. Many *pangch'ang* have become standard concert items and popular songs in their own right, and are also frequently heard in orchestral arrangements. The best-known within the DPRK and northern China is 'Haemada pomi omyŏn' (Spring Comes Every Year) from *Kkŏt panŭn ch'ŏnyŏ*.

It is clear that popular music in the DPRK has always reflected state policy. This does not preclude development: 'popular music' in the DPRK contains many features of *yuhaengga*, but also folk-song elements and tunes arranged from revolutionary opera. Commercial recordings similarly mix these elements. Controlled through the Ministry of Culture and Art (*Munhwa yesulbu*), popular music groups have access to modern technology and electronic instruments, but have little control over what they perform. The two key groups working during the 1990s were Poch'ŏnbo (also known as the Poch'ŏnbo Electronic Ensemble) and Wangjaesan (also known as the Wangjaesan Light Music Band). Both took their names from revolutionary battles fought during the 1930s by Kim Il Sung and his guerrilla forces against the Japanese. Both were in effect troupes fronted by sets of singers who performed solo or in any variety of combinations. Both were popular in the sense that people flocked to see them; a 1991 tour of Japan by Poch'ŏnbo played to packed houses of mainly Korean-Japanese, while a 1992 three-week concert season by Wangjaesan in P'yŏngyang sold out before it opened. The two bands functioned as state-controlled vehicles for commercial production and, by 2002, the P'yŏngyang Foreign Languages Publishing House had listed for purchase 129 CDs of Poch'ŏnbo and 52 of Wangjaesan. However, songs continued to reflect state dogma, as witnessed by the 1992 Wangjaesan hit 'Sahoe chu ŭl' (Socialism Is Ours), which discussed the collapse of socialism in the former Soviet Union but concluded that socialism remained the path that the people of the DPRK wanted to follow forever.

Bibliography

(Excluding speeches by Kim Il Sung and Kim Jong Il on music and art, in Korean and English versions, contained in pamphlets and collected works.)

Academy of Sciences, ed. 1988. *Chosŏn ŭi minsok nori* [Folk Games of Korea]. Sŏul: P'urŭnsup. (Originally published 1980 P'yŏngyang: Institute of Archaeology, Academy of Sciences.)

Bunge, Frederica M., ed. 1981. *North Korea: A Country Study*. Washington, DC: American University, Foreign Area Studies.

Freeland, Nina, et al. 1976. *Area Handbook for North Korea*. 2nd ed. Washington, DC: American University, Foreign Area Studies.

Han Chungmo and Chŏng Sŏngmu. 1983. *Chuch'e ŭi munye riron yŏn'gu* [Studies on the Theory of *Juche* in Culture and Art]. P'yŏngyang: Sahoe kwahak ch'ulp'ansa.

Howard, Keith. 1996. '*Juche* and Culture: What's New?' In *North Korea in a New World Order*, ed. Hazel Smith et al. Basingstoke: Macmillan, 169–95.

Kim Ch'oewŏn. 1991a. *Chuch'e ŭmak ch'ongsŏ* [Collection of *Juche* Music], Vols. 4 and 5. P'yŏngyang: Munye ch'ulp'ansa.

Kim Ch'oewn. 1991b. *P'i pada-shik hyŏngmyŏng kagŭk* [Sea of Blood Style Opera], Vols. 1 and 2. P'yŏngyang: Munye ch'ulp'ansa.

Kim, Yol Kyu. 1992. 'A Study on the Present Status of Folklore and Folk Arts in North Korea.' *Korea Journal* 32(2): 75–91.

Lee, Byongwon. 1993. 'Contemporary Korean Musical Cultures.' In *Korea Briefing, 1993: Festival of Korea*, ed. Donald N. Clark. Boulder, CO: Westview Press, 121–38.

No Tongŭn. 1989. *Han'guk minjok ŭmak hyŏndan'gye* [Attaining a Korean People's Music]. Sŏul: Segwang ŭmak ch'ulp'ansa.

Sheet Music

No authors/composers are given unless otherwise noted below.

Chosŏn ŭmak chônjip [Collection of Korean Music] 1–15, 1985–1999. P'yŏngyang: Munhak yesul chonghap ch'ulp'ansa.

Chosŏn minjok ŭmak chônjip [Collection of Korean People's Music], *Minyo p'yŏn* [Folksong Volumes] 1–2, 1998. P'yŏngyang: Yesul kyoyuk ch'ulp'ansa.

Kim Yŏngsuk, ed. 1987. *Chosŭn ŭmak chŏnjip* [Collection of Korean Music]. P'yŏngyang: Munye ch'ulp'ansa.

P'i pada kyohyanggok [Sea of Blood Symphony]. 1975. P'yŏngyang: Munye ch'ulp'ansa.

Ro Ikhwa, ed. 1989. *Ri Myŏnsang chakkok chip* [Composition Collection of Ri Myongsong]. P'yŏngyang: Munye ch'ulp'ansa.

Ŭmak tosŏ p'yŏnjippu, eds. 1994. *Chosŏn Kayo 2000 Kokchip* [Collection of 2000 Korean Songs]. P'yŏngyang: Munhak yesul chonghap ch'ulp'ansa.

Yŏnghwa norae 100 kokchip [Collection of 100 Film Songs], 1993. P'yongyang: Munhak yesul chonghap ch'ulp'ansa.

KEITH HOWARD

CITIES

P'yŏngyang
Population: 2,741,260 (1993)

P'yŏngyang is the administrative capital of the Democratic People's Republic of Korea (DPRK) (North Korea) and, because of a centralized bureaucracy, it is the center of musical production. Socialist dogma has it that all music must come from the people and is for the people, and is therefore popular.

Seven large troupes are sponsored by the Ministry of Culture and Art in the capital: an opera troupe (the Sea of Blood Opera Company), two people's choruses, three art troupes (Moran Hill, Mansudae and P'yŏngyang) and an orchestra. Two 'light music' bands, Poch'ŏnbo Electronic Ensemble and Wanjaesan Light Music, are also centered in P'yŏngyang, as is film production at the P'yŏngyang Film Studios. There are two 'art palaces' at which children receive specialist music training. There is also a dedicated college, the P'yŏngyang Music and Dance College, and an institute named after Korea's foremost composer, the Isang Yun Music Research Institute.

Popular music is disseminated from the capital. Recordings are issued by one state organization, the Kwangmyong Umaksa (KMC), which issues recordings through a set of companies that include Meart, Naenara, P'yŏngyang and Mansudae. Most recordings contain assorted songs: revolutionary songs typically dating from the first period of North Korea's existence; folk-song arrangements collected and revised in the 1960s; songs from 'immortal' and 'people's' operas created by the Sea of Blood Opera Company from the 1970s and 1980s; and 'popular songs' (*taejung kayo*) or 'light music' (*kyŏng ŭmak*) from the 1980s onward. Composers and lyricists are distinct from singers and are often not credited because of the collective nature of North Korean socialist production, although celebrated song composers include Kim Wŏn'gyun, Ri Myŏnsang and Kim Oksŏng. Composers typically train in P'yŏngyang, but some have also studied in China and the former Soviet Union. A few film scores by Ri Chongo, Sŏng Tongch'un, Chŏn Ch'angil, Ko Suyŏng and Kim Yŏngsŏn have also been released. Cassettes remained dominant until the late 1990s; CDs began to appear after 1992. Following the trend elsewhere in East Asia, the 1990s also saw the appearance of karaoke bars, located in P'yŏngyang's hotels. Mokran Video released 70 songs under the title *Korean Songs and Karaoke* between 1993 and 1995.

KEITH HOWARD

South Korea
Population: 45,985,289 (2000)

In 1948 the first elections in Korea were carried out in the areas south of the 38th parallel, with Syngman Rhee becoming the first President of South Korea (aka Republic of Korea). In June 1950 North Korea invaded South Korea, this beginning the Korean War which was to last for three years and leave almost 3 million Koreans dead or wounded, and millions of others homeless and separated from their families. The country experienced political and economic difficulties, and a military coup d'état led by Major General Park Chung-hee in 1961 opened a new chapter in Korean history. While restricting people's political rights and civil liberties, Park Chung-hee, who became President in the 1963 election, led the country to rapid industrialization and high economic growth during the 1960s and 1970s. These developments effectively transformed the country. Once known as one of the world's poorest agrarian societies, South Korea became a technologically advanced industrialized nation, and aspired to become one of the top seven such nations during the first quarter of the twenty-first century. Park Chung-hee's assassination in 1979 and the ensuing political situation intensified the pro-democracy movement throughout the 1980s, and Kim Young-sam, a long-time pro-democracy activist, was elected the first civilian President in 1992. 1997 was also a landmark year for the maturing Korean democracy. The first ever transfer of power from the ruling to an opposition party was successfully accomplished through a peaceful presidential election with Kim Dae-jung, a leader of the major opposition party and the 2000 Nobel Peace Laureate, the successful candidate.

Although the musical landscape of South Korea features a variety of musical tastes from Western-style operas to Korean traditional lyric songs, Korean popular music is the most dominant type of music in the country.

Popular music, known in Korean as *yuhaengga* or *daejung gayo*, first developed in Korea at the beginning of the twentieth century. Korean popular music originated from a style of music called *changga*. Compared to most traditional folk songs, with melodies built upon various Korean scales and a guttural timbre, *changga* utilized Korean words with existing or newly composed Western-style melodies and a less throaty vocal projection. An early example of *changga* is a version of the Korean national anthem sung during King Gojong's birthday party in 1896. This was a recycled Protestant hymn with a newly composed Korean verse for that specific occasion.

Changga, favored by intellectuals who were open to new ideas and cultural trends, was taught at newly established Western-style schools. While the lyrics of many *changga* songs emphasized wholesome messages (for example, the importance of diligence, reverence for parents and the value of education), other *changga* songs, known as *yuhaeng* (popular) *changga* – which were recorded and distributed to a wider public – relied on the metaphor of a doomed love affair or a harsh life to reflect the gloomy reality of a colonized nation. The oldest recording of *yuhaeng changga* is 'I pungjin sesang' (This World of Woe and Tumult, recorded by the singer Kim San-wol), a Korean cover version of a Japanese popular song recorded by a Japanese record company, Nipbo nohong, in 1925.

In 1931, Chae Gyu-yeop made his debut as the first full-time professional popular singer in Korea by singing cover versions of foreign – mostly Japanese – songs. But the most significant event in relation to the birth of Korean popular music was the 1926 release of a *yuhaeng changga* called 'Sa-ui chanmi' (Adoration of Death) sung by Yun Sim-deok, a Western classical singer trained in Japan. Set to Ivanovitch's 'Blue Danube' (see Park 1987, 173), its Korean lyrics depict a bleak life. The singer was said to be in love with a married man, and her eventual suicide with her lover as she was returning to Korea after the recording of the song in Japan became one of the biggest scandals to hit Korea at that time. Koreans interpreted the gloomy and nihilistic view of her song as an expression of her doomed love. The song also resonated with many Koreans as a metaphor for the fate of a colonized nation. Because of the sensational circumstance surrounding the release of the song it became an instant hit, generating unprecedented record sales. Recognizing the potential for profit, record companies started to record other *yuhaeng changgas* for mass consumption, and a modern popular music industry began to take shape in Korea.

The two major genres during the early days of Korean popular music were *sinminyo* and *teuroteu*. *Sinminyo* (new folk song) is a genre that uses the rhythms, melodic shapes and singing styles of Korean traditional folk song. For example, a *sinminyo* entitled 'Sin bang-a taryeong' (New Wooden Press *Taryeong*), sung by Wang Su-bok in a 1933 recording, utilizes *taryeong* (a genre in Korea traditional folk song) as a basis for its composition. Many *sinminyo* singers came from a group of female entertainers called *gisaengs*, who were trained in singing and dancing mostly for the pleasure of men. Their training in traditional musical genres was tapped by the burgeoning popular music industry and some *gisaengs*, such as Wang Su-bok, became stars in this new medium. *Sinminyo* songs tend to describe themes commonly found in Korean traditional folk songs, such as love and breakups between lovers, or they depict indigenous scenery or seasons. By anchoring their content in a comfortable past, *sinminyo* songs were able to provide a safe haven from the rapidly changing world. Although *sinminyo* was successful at utilizing the nation's indigenous musical heritage, this also meant that the genre could not effectively capture the intensity of the time or capture the colonial reality of the nation.

Whereas the main theme of *sinminyo* was indulgence in the simple enjoyment of life, songs that belonged to a genre called *teuroteu* depicted a different world. *Teuroteu*, influenced by Japanese *enka*, owes its name to the fox trot, as its duple-meter structure was a striking departure from the triple-meter structure of most indigenous musics in Korea. (In fact, Koreans also identify this genre by a two-syllable onomatopoeic term, 'ppongjjak,' to emphasize its duple-meter structure.) Although many popular songs from Korean and other cultures and eras have routinely taken the parting of lovers as one of their main themes, the pathos of *teuroteu* songs was not just based on tearful sorrow. It was based also on the bitter lamentation of the defeated. In other words, the subject in *teuroteu* songs was always defeated by the cold and hard reality of a world full of impossibilities, and was always denied fulfillment of basic human desires such as the desire to be with loved ones or to return to one's beloved home. For example, the first verse of 'Tahyang sari' (Living in a Strange Land), released by Go Bok-su in 1934, depicts a homesickness that could never be cured. As in the case of the song 'Sa-ui chanmi,' the success of *teuroteu* as a genre was also based on the fact that the unquenchable desire of an individual again became a metaphor for the nation's desperation under colonial reality.

During the tumultuous period that followed the end of World War II and characterized the division of Korea, *teuroteu* maintained its dominance without any noticeable stylistic changes from the Japanese colonial period. It continued to be relevant because the pathos of the genre was easily transferable from the reality of a colonized nation to that of a war-torn country. Some *teuroteu* songs vividly depicted the hardship Korean people had to endure during the bloody war. Even at the beginning of the twenty-first century, songs such as 'Danjang-ui miari gogae' (Heartbreak *Miari* Hill), released by Yi Hae-yeon in 1956, were bringing tears to older Koreans who had lived through the war.

The Korean War (1950–53) brought soldiers from many different nations onto Korean soil, the most prominent being soldiers from the United States. Indeed, the presence of the United States as South Korea's chief ally became the dominant cultural force and has remained so since. Although the initial contact between Korea and the United States was made prior to the twentieth century, it was during the middle of the twentieth century that the impact of US culture was felt for the first time on a massive scale. US movies were imported to Korea and a large quantity of US goods was sold on the black market. American Forces Korean Network (a radio station) became the primary disseminator of US pop music, and envy for US economic and military strength was clearly evidenced in domestically produced popular songs in various ways. Sometimes, names of Western popular musical genres appeared in song titles: for example, 'Doraji mambo' (Balloon Flower Mambo, released in 1953 and sung by Sim Yeon-ok), 'Daejeon bureuseu' (Daejeon Blues, released in 1956 and sung by An Jeong-ae) and 'Bi-eu taengo' (Rain Tango, released in 1956 and sung by Do Mi). English words sometimes appeared in both the title and the lyrics of a song without Korean translation: for example, 'Leoki seoul' (Lucky Seoul) or 'Leoki moning' (Lucky Morning). Some songs blatantly displayed US envy, as in the case of 'Saen pransisko' (San Francisco), released by Jang Se-jeong in 1952.

Compared to the 1940s and the 1950s, the 1960s can be characterized as a rather stable period. The most notable event during this decade was the country's efforts to establish economic infrastructure. A series of five-year economic plans was launched, and modernization brought rural exodus and urbanization. *Teuroteu* continued to survive during this era by addressing the homesickness of the lower classes with 'countrified' themes. As in 'Gaseum apeuge' (Aching Heart), released in 1967 by Nam Jin, the genre also symbolized the social and psychological distance between the urban and the rural through the metaphor of geographical separation. If *teuroteu* songs were considered the domain of the rural population at that time, 'easy listening songs' were viewed as their stylish urban counterpart. As in Hyeon Mi's 'Bogo sipeun eolgul' (Face [That I] Miss), released in 1964, easy listening songs were full of urban imagery. Easy listening songs, as a genre, emerged when Korean singers who had previously sung for the US soldiers stationed in Korea started to migrate to the Korean domestic market. In contrast to *teuroteu* singers, whose singing was characterized by a wide and dramatic vocal vibrato, easy listening singers exhibited relatively stable pitch. By imitating the vocal characteristics of various US singers, South Korean easy listening singers also introduced new types of vocal timbre, which was a significant departure from the nasal guttural timbre that had dominated up until that point. In fact, some singers deliberately used English for their stage names (for example, Patti Kim, Lee Sisters and Blue Bells).

Korean popular music of the 1970s was primarily influenced by the shift from the prewar to the postwar generation. By then, Korean youngsters in their teens and twenties had no direct experience with Japanese colonialism or the Korean War. Until the early 1970s, the biggest genre in the Korean

popular music industry had been *teuroteu*. But by this time *teuroteu* was enjoyed by mostly older Koreans who had grown up during the Japanese colonial period and were already steeped in its aesthetics, or less educated Koreans who identified themselves with the lyrics of *teuroteu* songs, which typically depicted various hardships in life. Most young and educated people who were looking for fresh alternatives listened to neither *teuroteu* songs nor 'easy listening songs.' This was because of their overtly professional – and therefore 'stale' – presentation. In this cultural vacuum, they turned to the US popular music featured on various late night radio music programs. Meanwhile, leisure activities that moved beyond the necessities of basic existence came to be recognized by these young Koreans as important elements by which to judge the quality of one's life. The advent of the mass consumption of consumer electrical goods, especially of those of compact-size radio and cassette technology, bolstered the spread of US popular music. From this background, *tong-guitar* music emerged in the early 1970s.

Tong-guitar music developed as a Korean reproduction of the US folk song movement led by Bob Dylan and Joan Baez. It was a part of Korean youngsters' overall fascination with US culture, along with blue jeans, long hair and draft beer. The term '*tong-guitar*' derives from the Korean word '*tong*,' meaning 'a box,' plus the English word 'guitar.' Koreans called an acoustic guitar a '*tong-guitar*' because the resonating body of the instrument resembles a box. *Tong-guitar* music began when a few like-minded singers gathered in a music hall called Cheong Gaeguri Hall (Green Frog Hall) in downtown Sŏul (Seoul). Influenced by the US folk song movement of the 1960s, these Korean singers utilized the acoustic guitar as an integral part of their presentation, and they were eventually labeled '*tong-guitar* singers.' *Tong-guitar* singers were like a breath of fresh air to many young and educated people in Korea because of their amateurish and non-choreographed stage presence, the variety in their vocal timbre, the lyricism of their lyrics and the simplicity of their melody (with folk guitar accompaniment). The lyrics of almost all *tong-guitar* songs describe either the sentimental or joyful aspects of love. Even in the Korean-language *tong-guitar* cover versions of US protest songs (such as Bob Dylan's 'A Hard Rain's A-Gonna Fall'), most *tong-guitar* singers stripped the original words of their defiant spirit. Lacking any inflammatory political messages in their songs, most *tong-guitar* singers were able to avoid major government censorship. Wide distribution of their songs on radio and television music programs stimulated successful sales of their records, and *tong-guitar* music quickly became the most dominant force in the popular music scene during the early 1970s. One of the most popular *tong-guitar* songs from this period is 'Toyoil toyoil bame' (Saturday Saturday Night), released by Kim Se-hwan in the mid-1970s, which depicts a young boy's puppy love for a stylish girl.

Teuroteu as a genre continued to demonstrate resilience throughout the 1970s and into the 1980s. But, by the end of the 1980s, it was clear that its life cycle had almost expired. The only bright spot for this genre was Jo Yong-pil, who produced a string of hits by absorbing elements from other genres such as rock and *tong-guitar* music. Although Jo expanded the artistic boundaries of *teuroteu* with daring musical experiments, the core of his music continued to be *teuroteu* in its lyrical content and vocal timbre. One of the greatest hits by Jo Yong-pil was 'Dorawayo Busanhang-e' (Return to Pusan Harbor) (1975). Like other *teuroteu* songs from previous periods, this song also represented the plight of the underclass through a separation of loved ones.

The 1980s marked the appearance of a new genre, the ballad. Owing its musical genealogy to the 'easy listening' of the 1960s and the *tong-guitar* songs of the 1970s, the ballad provided a counterpoint to *teuroteu*. But unlike the *tong-guitar* songs, the ballad employed an extended orchestral accompaniment and clearly defined musical climaxes. Typical ballads made no reference to the plight of the country's underclass or had any other political connotations. Instead, they focused on the self-indulgence of love, as illustrated in Lee Yong's 'Ichyeojin gyejeol' (Forgotten Season), released in 1982.

By the mid-1990s, Korea was able to benefit from the results of various economic measures that had been taken over previous decades. From a war-torn country of the 1950s, Korea rose to be the ninth-largest economy in the world, with a gross national product equal to that of Spain. Since the 1990s, the pop music industry has been catering to youngsters in their early teens who have reaped the benefits of economic prosperity. Slow ballads and highly choreographed rap songs have become the corner-stone genres of any musical programming that targets this young audience. As South Korea entered the new millennium, major television networks continued to routinely air a variety of music programs featuring the Top 10 or the Top 100 songs of the week, alternating the two genres. Although these two genres can evidence totally different musical styles and stage presentations (exaggerated and mechanical dance movements for rap), the lyrical content of the songs from both genres features for the most part the same kind of love-song themes as before. This is illustrated in Seotaijiwa aideul's (Seotaiji'n Boys) 'Nan arayo' (I Know), an enormous hit in 1992.

Bibliography

Heulleogan norae [Song from Olden Days], Vol. 1. 1990. Sŏul: Samho.

Hwang, Moon-pyong. 1989. *Hanguk daejung yeonye-sa* [History of Korean Popular Entertainment]. Sŏul: Burukanmoro.

Hwang, Moon-pyong. 1991. 'Daejung eumak' [Popular Music] and 'Daejung gayo' [Popular Song]. In *Encyclopedia of Korean Culture*. Gyeonggi-do, Korea: Academy of Korean Studies.

Hwang, Okon. 1995. 'But Music Still Goes On: Popular Songs During the Korean War.' Paper presented at Society for Ethnomusicology Annual Conference, Los Angeles, CA.

Hwang, Okon. 2000. 'Korean Pop.' In *World Music: The Rough Guide. Vol. 2: Latin & North America, Caribbean, India, Asia and Pacific*, ed. Simon Broughton and Mark Ellingham. 2nd ed. London: Rough Guides, 164–69.

Hwang, Okon. 2001. 'Korea – Modern Developments – Popular Music.' In *The New Grove Dictionary of Music and Musician*, ed. Stanley Sadie. London: Macmillan, 814–15, 818.

Kim, Chang-nam. 1986. *Kim Min-ki*. Sŏul: Hanwul.

Kim, Chang-nam. 1991. *Salmui munhwa, huimang-ui Norae* [Living Culture, Hopeful Song]. Sŏul: Hanwul.

Kim, Chang-nam. 1995. *Daejung munhwa-wa munhwa silcheon* [Popular Culture and Cultural Practice]. Sŏul: Hanwul.

Kim, Chang-nam, et al. 1984. *Norae [Song] I: Truthful Song and Untruthful Song*. Sŏul: Silcheon Munhak-sa.

Kim, Chang-nam, et al. 1986a. *Norae [Song] II: Music for Human Being*. Sŏul: Silcheon Munhaksa.

Kim, Chang-nam, et al. 1986b. *Norae undong-ron* [The Theory of Song Movement]. Sŏul: Gong-dongche.

Kim, Chang-nam, et al. 1988. *Norae [Song] III: Ethnic Music and Song Movement*. Sŏul: Iron-gwa shil-cheon.

Kim, Chang-nam, et al. 1993. *Norae [Song] IV: Ethnic Music Movement in the Era of Popular Culture*. Sŏul: Silcheon Munhaksa.

Kim Young-jun. 1994. *Hanguk gayosa iyagi* [Korean Song History]. Sŏul: Areum.

Park, Chan-ho. 1987. *Hanguk gayosa* [History of Korean Popular Music], trans. from Japanese by An Dong-rim. Sŏul: Hyonam.

Seon, Seong-won. 1993. *8 kun shyo eseo raep kkaji* [From 8th Army Show to Rap]. Sŏul: Areum.

Yee, Sang-man. 1975. 'Hyondae eumak-daejung eumak' [Modern Music, Popular Music]. In *Hanguk hyondae munhwasa daegye*, Vol. I. Sŏul: Koryeo University Research Center for National Culture.

Yee, Young-me. 1991. *Minjok yesul undong-ui yeoksa-wa iron* [History and Theory of National Art Movement]. Sŏul: Han-gil sa.

Yee, Young-me. 1993. *Norae iyagi jumeoni* [Song Story Sack]. Sŏul: Nokdu.

Yee, Young-me. 1998. *Hanguk daejung gayosa* [History of Korean Pop Music]. Sŏul: Sigongsa.

Sheet Music

Jeon, O-seung, comp., and Yu, Gwang-ju, lyr. 1956. 'Leoki moning.' (Score appears in *Heulleogan norae* [Song from Olden Days], Vol. 1. Sŏul: Samho, 1990, 92.)

Kim, Bu-hae, comp. and lyr. 1956. 'Daejeon bureuseu.' (Score appears in *Heulleogan norae* [Song from Olden Days], Vol. 1. Sŏul: Samho, 1990, 74.)

La, Hwa-rang, comp. and lyr. 1953. 'Doraji mambo.' (Score appears in *Heulleogan norae* [Song from Olden Days], Vol. 1. Sŏul: Samho, 1990, 82.)

La, Hwa-rang, comp., and Im, Dong-cheon, lyr. 1956. 'Bi-eu taengo.' (Score appears in *Heulleogan norae* [Song from Olden Days], Vol. 1. Sŏul: Samho, 1990, 143.)

Park, Si-chun, comp., and Son, Lo-won, lyr. 1952. 'Saen pransisko.' (Score appears in *Heulleogan norae* [Song from Olden Days], Vol. 1. Sŏul: Samho, 1990, 161.)

Park, Si-chun, comp., and Yu, Ho, comp. & lyr. 1940s. 'Leoki seoul.' (Score appears in *Heulleogan norae* [Song from Olden Days], Vol. 1. Sŏul: Samho, 1990, 93.)

Yi, Bong-jo, comp., and Hyeon, Am, lyr. 1964. 'Bogo sipeun eolgul.' (Score appears in *Heulleogan norae* [Song from Olden Days], Vol. 1. Sŏul: Samho, 1990, 132.)

Yi, Jae-ho, comp., and Ban, Ya-wol, lyr. 1956. 'Danjang-ui miari gogae.' (Score appears in *Heulleogan norae* [Song from Olden Days], Vol. 1. Sŏul: Samho, 1990, 70.)

Discographical References

Dylan, Bob. 'A Hard Rain's A-Gonna Fall.' *The Freewheelin' Bob Dylan*. Columbia 8786. *1963*: USA.

Go, Bok-su. 'Tahyang sari.' 1934: Korea. (Discussed in Chan-ho Park. *Hanguk gayosa* [History of Korean Popular Music]. Soul: Hyonam, 1987, 316–19.)

Jo, Yong-pil. 'Dorawayo Busanhang-e.' *1975*: Korea. (Discussed in Kim Young-jun. *Hanguk gayosa iyagi* [Korean Song History]. Sŏul: Areum, 1994, 600.)

Kim, San-wol. 'I pungjin sesang.' *Nipbo nohong jyoseon soripan*. 1925: Korea. (Discussed in Chan-ho Park. *Hanguk gayosa* [History of Korean Popular Music]. Sŏul: Hyonam, 1987, 167–68.)

Kim, Se-hwan. 'Toyoil toyoil bame.' *ca. 1975*: Korea. (Discussed in Yee Young-me. *Hanguk daejung gayosa* [History of Korean Pop Music]. Sŏul: Sigongsa, 1998, 205.)

Lee, Yong. 'Ichyeojin gyejeol.' *Lee Yong Best*. Jigu JCS-2722. *1996*: Korea.

Nam, Jin. 'Gaseum apeuge.' *Nam Jin Jeongok 1 jib*. Super Star Records Stereo/SSCD-020. *1990*: Korea.

Seotaiji'n Boys. 'Nan arayo.' *Yo! Taiji!*. Bando Records BDCD-014. *1992*: Korea.

Wang, Su-bok. 'Sin bang-a taryeong.' *Yuseonggiro deutdeon gayosa*. Sinnara SYNCD-015. *1992*: Korea.

Yun, Sim-deok. 'Sa-ui chanmi.' *Yuseonggiro deutdeon gayosa*. Sinnara SYNCD-015. *1992*: Korea.

OKON HWANG

CITIES

Pusan

Population: 3,474,300 (2004)

Pusan (or Busan), South Korea's second-largest city with a land area of 168 sq miles (436 sq km), is also its largest port. The city is located at the southeastern tip of the Korean peninsula, just a ferry ride away from Japan. With the conclusion of World War II, ending with it the Japanese occupation of Korea, the city expanded with foreign nationals returning from overseas. The population again swelled with refugees from further north when the city became the temporary capital of the Republic of Korea during the Korean War (1950–53).

In the years following World War II and the Korean War, popular song reflected the tragedy and loss of loved ones that affected most Koreans. During these difficult years, many songs were written nostalgically remembering lost ones through verse rich in imagery. Pusan was memorialized in one such *trot* (popular ballad), 'Come Back to Pusan Harbor.' Re-recorded in 1980 by popular singer Jo Yong-Pil, the song has continued to resonate with Korean audiences.

The name Pusan, meaning 'Cauldron Mountain,' aptly describes the valley in which the early city was built. From its original natural borders, the city has spread along the coastline and into the surrounding hills. These two factors make for an unusually long city in which mountains seem to simply rise up out of its carpet of apartment high-rises.

Because of this city's length, there are two main centers. As is the case in Sŏul (Seoul), many of the clubs for people to dance or listen to bands are located around the universities and the heavily foreign-populated sections. Pusan's best-known foreign area is known as Texas Street or Texas Town. Originally named as such because of the presence of the US army, the area has more recently become heavily populated by Russian nationals. However, the influence of the US armed forces continues to be felt in the remaining military bars and jazz clubs situated alongside other venues for popular music.

In the summers, Pusan's many beaches – including Haeundae Beach – in the northeastern section of the city, are crowded with sunbathers and swimmers. These beaches provide an attractive backdrop for several professional and nonprofessional musical performances and competitions. These events are often broadcast on the national television networks, including the Pusan Broadcasting Corporation (PSB).

Discographical Reference

Yong-Pil, Jo. 'Come Back to Pusan Harbor.' *Come Back to Pusan Harbor. 1981*: South Korea.

SARAH MORELLI

Sŏul (Seoul)

Population: 10,280,523 (2002)

Sŏul (Seoul) is the capital of South Korea. According to the official Sŏul Metropolitan Government website, 'Hi Seoul,' (www.seoul.go.kr), people were believed to be living in the Sŏul area along the lower reaches of the Han River in the Paleolithic Age, and archeological evidences of settled lives were found from the Neolithic Age. But Sŏul came to its prominence in 1394 when the founder of the Joseon Kingdom chose Sŏul as its new capital. Sŏul is the most populous city in South Korea, accounting for approximately a quarter of the total national

population. Located only 37 miles (60 km) south of the Demilitarized Zone that separates South Korea from North Korea, the city's geography is dominated by four inner and four outer mountains, as well as the Han River which divides the city into almost two equal parts. The rapid population growth during the second half of the twentieth century led to the formation of many satellite cities around the capital, and now the cultural life of the capital includes not only Sŏul proper but also its surrounding vicinities.

Sŏul is not only the center of political and military activities for South Korea but also the hub of culture, including popular music. All major Korean recording companies are located in Sŏul, as are the headquarters of all major broadcasting companies. For example, the government-operated Korea Broadcasting System (KBS) airs three television channels, three AM radio channels and two FM channels. Munhwa Broadcasting Corporation (MBC) runs a television channel, one AM radio channel and two FM channels. More than 50 cable television channels are available, among them two foreign-run music television stations (MTV Korea and Channel [V] Korea). Two domestic music television stations (M-Net and KMTV) offer music videos and live shows 24 hours a day, 7 days a week.

Although people of more than 90 nationalities reside in the city, the percentage of foreign residents is less than 1 percent of its total population, and their presence as such does not have any measurable impact on the popular music scene in Sŏul. Instead, the primary source of contact with foreign – especially US – culture is through Korean and foreign media, as well as the American Forces Korean Network (AFKN, renamed AFN in 1997), which provides 24-hour English-language programming through AM and FM radio channels, as well as television channels. Both young and old people in Sŏul rely on the programming of these various broadcasting companies as the major source of entertainment, and pop musicians use these avenues as the premiere outlet for their creative activities.

During the 1960s and 1970s the sale of foreign popular music dominated 80 percent of the country's music market. The situation had completely changed by the beginning of the twenty-first century. Domestically produced pop music accounted for 84 percent of sales in 2003. This drastic change was due to the fact that youngsters in their early teens emerged as the major consumer group. These teenagers enthusiastically attend live concerts staged by major broadcasting companies. They are also the target consumers for new releases. A common sight in Sŏul is young people listening to music through headphones while riding a subway or walking. In fact, headphones have become ubiquitous in the city landscape.

Streets of Sŏul are dotted with many outlets for popular music CDs and cassettes. In addition, illegal copies of old and new popular songs are readily available for purchase at steeply discounted prices from street vendors, who usually set their movable carts in busy streets with loud speakers blaring the newest hits to attract customers.

One of the most prominent developments since the 1980s has been the explosive popularity of *noraebang* ('karaoke room'). During the last few years of the twentieth century, about 20,000 *noraebangs* sprang up nationwide, taking in more than two billion dollars annually in revenues. *Noraebangs* have become a permanent fixture in almost every commercial district and neighborhood in Sŏul. A *noraebang* facility usually holds several individualized chambers. Customers are provided with several song menus. In this way, they can choose from about 10,000 songs that are programmed into the karaoke machine, ranging from Korean oldies to the newest hit tunes.

Bibliography

1998. *Facts about Korea*. Sŏul: Korean Overseas Culture and Information Service.

Hwang, Okon. 2001. 'Asian American Musics: Korean Music.' *The Garland Encyclopedia of World Music Vol 3: The United States and Canada*, ed. Ellen Koskoff. New York: Garland Publishing Inc., 975-79.

Sutton, R. Anderson. 2003. 'Bounded Variation? Music Television and its Aesthetics in South Korea.' Paper presented at the Society for Ethnomusicology Annual Conference, Miami FL.

Taylor, Chris. 1993. *Seoul: City Guide*. Hawthorn, Australia: Lonely Planet Publications.

Hi Seoul – Official Seoul Metropolitan Government Website. www.seoul.go.kr

OKON HWANG

Taiwan

Population: 23,000,000 (2004)

Taiwan, also known as the Republic of China on Taiwan, is an island country straddling the Tropic of Cancer. Shaped by the movement of the Pacific Plate and the Asiatic Continental Shelf, Taiwan is divided by the rugged central mountain range,

Chungyang Shanmo. Consequently, most of the island's population live on the alluvial plains of the west coast. By the beginning of the twenty-first century, Taiwan had undergone nearly two decades of democratic reform. Tensions concerning national identity, political direction and economic development informed cultural life on the island, including popular music.

While Taiwan had been an outpost of fishers, pirates and merchants as early as the eleventh century, Chinese settlement did not occur until the period of Dutch colonial administration (1624–62). Early Chinese settlers hailed from Fukien's southeast coast. Hakka people from Kuangtung soon followed. Both groups displaced and assimilated much of the island's indigenous Malayo-Polynesian population. Immigrants brought regional styles of Chinese music to Taiwan, where these styles began to grow into popular forms. Formation of local institutions among Chinese immigrants entailed music that was native to Taiwan, often incorporating indigenous motifs, as evident in the genre for voice and three-string lute (*yüeh-ch'in*) known as *su siang ki*.

Popular Music of the Japanese Colonial Period (1895–1945)

The advent of Japanese rule in 1895 launched a period of rapid transformation. Besides extensive development of the island's agriculture and forestry, the colonists brought a fascination with technology, which was evident in city planning for the capital, T'aipei (Taihoku), and in the embrace of novel forms of mass culture. Colonial institutions produced both educational systems that would modify musical styles (Tsurumi 1977) and regional audiences for popular music.

Popular music developed in association with the theater, which introduced Peking Opera, the popular music of Shanghai, Western-style brass bands and Japanese music. These influences began to mature with the invention, in Ilan, of *koa-ah hi* (Taiwanese opera) (Ch'iu 1992; Silvio 1998). Cinema was introduced in T'aipei during the 1920s, and silent films provided opportunities for Taiwanese writers to produce music for the new medium. A Shanghai silent film was the inspiration for the first piece of Taiwanese popular music to have regional impact, 'Peach Blossoms, Blood, and Flowers,' written by Wang Yun-feng and Tan T'ien-ma in 1933.

Writers and performers of the Japanese colonial period were an itinerant group. Many traveled throughout the cities of Japan and China, seeking instruction and opportunities for performance. Some of the vitality of Taiwanese popular music in this period can be attributed to these peregrinations: in their travels, performers and writers encountered a wide variety of genres and explored their possibilities. Wandering performers within Taiwan and the presence of music in cinema, popular theater and teahouses made music available to a wide public without the expense of record players and recordings.

Popular music of the 1930s set the tone for subsequent Taiwanese-language music. Written in minor modes, with a preference for pentatonic scales, and often demanding a wide range and exacting control of vibrato from the singer, the tunes resembled a genre that became known in Japan as *enka*. Songwriters came from various occupations, ranging from Taiwanese opera performers to elementary school teachers, and often received additional training in Japan or lived there to compose for the Japanese subsidiaries of Victor-Victrola or Columbia. Like their Japanese counterparts, Taiwanese songs of the 1930s lamented lost love or expressed hope for reunion with loved ones. This correspondence in expressive form discounts any simple interpretation of these lyrics as resistance to colonialism, even if the romantic image remains a metaphor for political concerns.

Taiwanese popular music stalled in the 1940s with the intensification of hostilities in China. Wartime cultural policy strongly opposed borrowing from Chinese sources, the use of any language but Japanese in the mass media, and the development of autonomous cultural institutions, forcing most popular music and theater underground.

Popular Music of the 1950s and 1960s

The Nationalist Chinese (*Kuomintang*, hereafter KMT) administration of the island commenced with retrocession on 25 October 1945. KMT policy restricted the use of Taiwanese in mass media and exacted fines for even speaking the language in public. With the retreat of the KMT government to T'aipei in 1949 and the cold-war settlement of the 1950s, the task of representing China to the world fell to Taiwan. Nonetheless, Taiwanese-language popular music flourished in the 1950s and 1960s amidst newly introduced popular music in Mandarin.

Tensions between the Taiwanese people and their new rulers came to a head in 1947 with the 'February 28 incident' ('2-28'), in which KMT abuses

sparked violent popular protest. Following the incident, the KMT persecuted local intellectuals and activists in a wave of white terror that continued through the 1950s. At least 20,000 people perished during 2-28, setting the tone for enmities between people of pre-1949 and post-1949 origins. The incident and subsequent white terror have infused Taiwanese music with an undertone of violence that, as in the films of Hou Hsiao-hsien, manages to remain just subliminal. In this light, tunes from the late 1940s and early 1950s such as 'Hoping You Return Soon' or 'Fixing Broken Nets,' which in later decades became anthems of the opposition to KMT rule, stand out as real achievements of popular commentary within a musical medium.

Although frowned upon in official media, Taiwanese-language music continued to develop. In 1962, the appearance of televised Taiwanese opera gave added impetus to the creation of songs for this theater form. Music in the Taiwanese language remained vital in the teahouses and night-market medicine shows, which continued to foster the music as it deepened its dialog with Japanese Showa period *enka*. While many fine writers and singers left music altogether, others such as Hung Yi-feng toured the south of the island, where Taiwanese-language music remained popular (Huang 1988).

Popular music in Mandarin derived inspiration from Hong Kong, which was in touch with musical currents from the United States and Britain. Popular music in Mandarin thus developed along two lines: one that followed the sounds of Shanghai film music of the 1930s, and one that translated the rhythms and chord structures of rock 'n' roll for a Chinese audience. Dance halls, such as those in Tamsui and in the Westgate district of T'aipei, were major sites for performance of both types of music. The second trend became dominant after the arrival of US Armed Forces Radio T'aipei (now International Community Radio T'aipei [ICRT]) in 1954; soon, Taiwanese popular music charts began to resemble those in the United States (Wang 1997, 211). Launched in 1965, the China Broadcasting Service (BCC) music network radio program, *Songs of Youth*, introduced popular music in a wide variety of styles. Due to the restrictions that the KMT government placed on the media until the end of martial law, both radio and television were largely Mandarin language media.

Film and television also brought popular music to a wide audience during the 1950s and 1960s. In 1955, the film *Rainy Night Flowers* took a Taiwanese-language tune of the 1930s as its title, sparking the song's renewed popularity. In 1969, Theresa Teng, who became popular through the television variety shows of the 1960s, provided the theme song ('Hai Yün') for the first Taiwanese soap opera. Ironically, the height of Teng's popularity in the late 1970s coincided with the beginning of a movement that would shift the locus of popular music to the university campus.

The New Folk Music Movement (1975–82)

The new folk music involved both the adoption and rejection of Western models. The music bore little resemblance to the folk music of Taiwan or China, but was more like that of Bob Dylan or John Denver. However, the movement portrayed its struggle as a challenge to the dominance of North American popular music. 'Folkies' supplemented their music with lyrics that were 'deliberately "orientalizing"' in terms of attachment to 'motherland China' (Yang 1994, 58). The new folk movement thus expressed an anti-Western sentiment within a Western form.

The movement emerged among university students whose families had immigrated to Taiwan after 1949 with the KMT military. Their music expressed nostalgia for the loss of Chinese culture, which they knew only at second hand, and was an attempt to reconceptualize this culture within Taiwan's new landscape of factories and export-processing zones (Yang 1994, 55). The 'folkies' derided KMT economic policy and the party's international failures, particularly following the loss of the Republic of China's United Nations seat to the People's Republic of China in 1971. However, they did not hesitate to make use of KMT programs in their attempt to create a Chinese cultural renaissance. They also found allies in university faculty and in poets writing in the nostalgic mode, such as Yu Kuang-chung, whose poems were set to music by Yang Hsuan and recorded on *A Collection of Contemporary Chinese Folk Songs* (Jaivin 1996).

'Folkies' rejected prevailing conventions of popular music – the orchestras, flamboyance and perceived inauthenticity – in favor of singers who wrote songs and, in simple garb, performed them on acoustic guitar. This music was suited to venues that university students preferred, such as the teahouses near National Taiwan, Cheng-chih and Tamkang universities; the Astor Café off Chunking South Road; and gathering places with pastoral names such as Scarecrow (Jaivin 1996, 119). Some of the 'folkies' founded their own labels. Many

others flourished in existing institutions through the many music festivals and campus songwriting contests launched during the late 1970s. Recording companies recognized that the movement represented a vital, previously untapped market. The music, soon repackaged as 'campus songs,' was the catalyst for a shift in audience from an older one focused on the dance hall to a youth market focused on the college campus and coffeehouse (Wang 1997). Both Rock Records and UFO Records were instrumental in the expansion of the new folk music beyond the university campus to a broad youth audience.

Popular Music of the 1980s

Lee Shuang-tse, one of the proponents of new folk music, asked the crowd at a performance of Western folk music, 'Where are *our* songs?' Some on the periphery of the folk movement wondered whether music in the style of John Denver constituted 'our songs' after all. These critics, notably Lin Er and Chien Shang-jen, began investigations of Taiwanese folk music, attempting to write a new Taiwanese music that would be faithful to native melodies, even though set for conventions of the folk movement such as guitar accompaniment (Chien and Lin 1979). In 1977, influences from Taiwanese folk music became more pronounced with the appearance in T'aipei of a traditional *yüeh-ch'in* performer from the extreme south of the island, Ch'en Ta.

A new form of popular music was karaoke, introduced in 1976. Often performed in karaoke bars and distributed on cheaply produced cassette tapes were songs in the Taiwanese language that were, in the opinion of the 'folkies,' an embarrassment (cf. Hsiang Yang 1991). Speaking through a working-class awareness of struggle, despair and lack of trust, the songs both represented the underworld connections of Taiwanese-language music and expressed a popular sense of marginality common among Taiwanese in the 1980s. The disabled singer Ah-kiak-ah is most representative of this genre. In addition to addressing the endemic violence of Taiwanese society before the repeal of martial law, these gangster songs made oblique references to the systematic exclusion of Taiwanese from official media.

In the 1980s, a great influx of Mandarin-language music from Hong Kong, as well as the availability of music from the West, led to the increasing heterogeneity of the music produced on Taiwan. Local recording companies, aware of the popularity of various musical styles from the United States, Hong Kong and Japan, packaged these styles in Mandarin-language pop. Mandarin-language rock, hip-hop and boy-band performers, along with performers who specialized in covering songs in English, soon became prominent (Yang 1993). Companies that had formed initially to distribute new wave, punk or world music also began to cultivate Taiwan's alternative music scene. These companies, such as Wind, Crystal and Magic Stone became central in the promotion of new Taiwanese music in the 1990s.

New Taiwanese Music of the 1990s

The repeal of martial law in 1988 allowed new forms of musical expression to emerge. Ch'en Ming-chang was a major figure in this burgeoning movement. In his film scores from the mid- and late 1980s, such as that for Hou Hsiao-hsien's *Dust in the Wind*, his string music shows the influence of his encounter with Ch'en Ta and other folk performers. In 1989, Ch'en (with Wang Ming-hui) joined the band Blacklist Studios, creating the album *Songs of Rage*.

Blacklist sang in very colloquial Taiwanese set to music inspired by rap, elements of Taiwanese opera, and highly lyrical tunes based on Taiwanese folk music, sometimes incorporating the *yüeh-ch'in*. The music expressed the sentiment of a society that was undergoing rapid political-economic change yet looked to unrecoverable spaces and language with nostalgia.

New Taiwanese music matured through the 1990s with the music of Baboo, Chu Iok-sin ('Pork Rind'), Lim Giong, and the New Formosa Band. These performers shared a desire to create a music that sounded like Taiwan. Consequently, the differences between Mandarin-language and Taiwanese-language popular music seemed to be dissolving in favor of music that shifted among languages, engaged in cross-linguistic puns or used a dialogic strategy. Chu Iok-sin, who began as a singer in a folk-influenced genre, for example, sampled Taiwanese folk music, aboriginal songs, popular music of the 1930s and 1940s, and elements of mass culture arriving in Taiwan from the West. The result was a texture of sound that expressed Taiwan's ambivalent modernity and cultural quandaries. The New Formosa Band made musical reference to divisions among Taiwanese ethnic groups, hoping to defuse them with the knowledge of shared voices and stories. Lim Giong enveloped the gangster style of 1970s and 1980s

Taiwanese music in dark, electronic sounds, particularly on his soundtrack for Hou Hsiao-hsien's *Goodbye, South, Goodbye* (1996).

The attention paid by these and other musicians to Taiwan's musical heritage also led to rediscoveries of previously obscure performers, such as Kin Men-wang and Lee Bin-hue, blind teahouse performers from northern Taiwan. A proclivity toward borrowing and experimentation also marked these works, whether Chu's parodic rap or Wu Pai and China Blue's Taiwanese blues music.

Conclusion

Popular music production on Taiwan owes much to the cinema, which has embraced new musical ideas and recycled old ones (Yeh 1996). It has benefited from the development of independent production studios relying on MIDI technology (Tan Shih 1991) such as Taiwan Colors, Index, Mandala Works and True Voice. MIDI technology has also aided music production among Taiwan's indigenous population. Aboriginal popular music is centered in the cities of Taitung and Hualien on the Pacific coast, and involves writers and performers of many indigenous groups.

In 1996, an intellectual property dispute between an indigenous singer, Difang, and the German electronic band Enigma brought Taiwanese indigenous music to public attention, launching a popular fascination with aboriginal culture (Munsterhjelm 1999). This fascination has been part of the popular reappraisal of national identity in the wake of martial law reforms, as when one indigenous singer, Chang Hui-mei (A Mei), sang the national anthem at the 2000 inauguration of Taiwan's first non-KMT President (Guy 2002). Indigenous Taiwanese performers have also been the mainstay of the self-consciously 'alternative' music production of the Taiwan Colors and Wind labels. Other studios, such as Flying Fish/Cloud Leopard Synectics, have combined music production with aboriginal activism.

The influence of Taiwanese popular music seems limited. However, the new folk movement has certainly influenced popular music in the People's Republic of China, while the presence of new Taiwanese-language music in the films of Hou Hsiao-hsien and other directors has brought the music to an international audience. Although some Taiwanese music producers fear that digital media may promote a Karaoke parlor (KTV) culture (Jen et al. 2003), Taiwan seems posed to play a central role in the dissemination of popular music styles throughout greater China. Taiwanese popular music should be of interest to those who wish to examine popular music and the formation of linguistic ideology, the relationship between popular music and cinema, and popular music among multiethnic communities. Previous scholarship on Taiwanese popular music focused on the problems of creating music with an authentic voice within the constraints of musical production systems emanating from the West (Jaivin 1996; Tan Shih 1991; Wang 1997; Yang 1993, 1994). However, the problem seems to have become an internal one: how is Taiwan with its rival ethnic groups and colonial history to create a popular music that does not reproduce the exclusions of colonialism or the KMT period? The popular music on Taiwan at the beginning of the twenty-first century, a music that is experimenting with a variety of sounds and languages, would seem to be an indication that Taiwan's popular music may play a role in re-creating a vibrant public sphere in a country whose sovereignty has continued to be challenged.

Bibliography

Chang Li-wei, ed. 1991. 'Liu-hsing Ko-yao Tzu-ch'ü Tsuo-chia Ta-shih Chi' [An Historical Record of Composers and Lyricists of Popular Songs]. *Lien-ho Wen-hsüeh (Unitas Monthly)* 82: 130–51.

Chang Nan-sheng. 1991. 'Min-ko Mo-lo-liao! Ts'ung Chung-kuo Hsien-tai Min-ko K'an 70-nien-tai Taiwan Chih-shih-fen-tzu yü Liu-hsing Wen-hua ti Kuan-hsi' [Folk Songs Have Declined – An Examination of the Relationship Between Taiwanese Intellectuals and Popular Culture of the 1970s Through the Contemporary Folk Movement]. *Lien-ho Wen-hsüeh (Unitas Monthly)* 82: 112–13.

Chien Shang-jen. 1990. *Taiwan Min-yao* [Taiwan's Folk Songs]. T'aipei: Chung-wen Ch'u-pan-she.

Chien Shang-jen and Lin Er. 1979. *Taiwan Min-su Ko-yao* [Taiwan's Folk Songs]. T'aipei: Chung-wen Ch'u-pan-she.

Ch'iu K'un-liang. 1992. *Jih-chih Shih-ch'i Taiwan Hsi-chü chih Yen-chiu: Chiu-chü yü Hsin-chü 1895–1945* [Taiwanese Theater During the Japanese Colonial Period: Old Theater and New Theater, 1895–1945]. T'aipei: Tzu-li-wan-pao-she Wen-hua Ch'u-pan-she.

Guy, Nancy. 2002. '"Republic of China National Anthem" on Taiwan: One Anthem, One Performance, Multiple Realities.' *Ethnomusicology* 46(1): 96–120.

Hsiang Yang. 1991. 'Ch'ing-ch'un ho Yu-ch'ou ti Pi-chi: Ts'ung Taiwan Ko-yao ti "Pi-cheng ChhiaN-chhi" Tsou-ch'u' [A Diary of Youth and Longing: Walking Out from the 'City of Sadness' of Taiwanese Popular Songs]. *Lien-ho Wen-hsüeh (Unitas Monthly)* 82: 90–94.

Huang Mei-ying. 1988. 'Pao-tao Liang-tai Ko Wang – Hung Yi-feng yü Hung Jung-hung' [Two Generations of Taiwanese Kings of Song – Hung Yi-feng and Hung Jung-hung]. In *Taiwan Wen-hua Ts'ang-seng* [Vicissitudes of Taiwanese Culture]. T'aipei: Tzu-li-wan-pao-she Wen-hua Ch'u-pan-she, 177–84.

Jaivin, Linda. 1996. 'Hou Dejian and the Rise of Popular Music in Taiwan in the 1970s.' *CHIME* 9: 118–23.

Jen Chiang-ta, Lan Yung-cheng, and Cheng Keng-chang. 2003. 'Culture Industries: Their Viability and Economic Potential.' www.etaiwannews.com/forum/2003/04/23/1051426160.htm (accessed 16 May 2004).

Liao Pin-hui. 1991. '90-nien-tai Liu-hsing Ko-ch'ü chung ti Ch'eng-hsiang Yi-shih – yi Ch'en Ming-chang ho Chu Yüeh-hsin wei Lieh' [Ideologies of City and Country in Popular Songs of the 90s – Ch'en Ming-chang and Chu Iok-sin as Examples]. *Lien-ho Wen-hsüeh (Unitas Monthly)* 82: 115–19.

Ma Yeh-fang. 1997. *Yung-yuan ti Wei-yang Ko: Hsien-tai Min-ko, Hsiao-yuan Ko-ch'ü 20 nien chi-nien ts'e* [Eternal Vesper Songs: A 20-Year Commemorative Book of Contemporary Folk Songs and Campus Songs]. T'aipei: Kun-shih Wen-hua Ch'u-pan-she.

Munsterhjelm, Mark. 1999. 'Aboriginal Today, Taiwanese Tomorrow: The Packaging of A-Mei.' *M/C Reviews* 18 August 1999. www.uq.edu.qu/mc/reviews/sounds/amei.html (accessed 17 May 2004).

Silvio, Teri Jayne. 1998. *Drag Melodrama/Feminine Public Sphere/Folk Television: 'Local Opera' and Identity in Taiwan.* Unpublished Ph.D. thesis, Department of Anthropology, University of Chicago.

Tan Shih. 1991. 'Taiwan Liu-hsing Yin-yüeh ti Li-shih Fang-an' [An Investigation of the History of Taiwanese Popular Music]. *Lien-ho Wen-hsüeh (Unitas Monthly)* 82: 72–80.

Tsurumi, E. Patricia. 1977. *Japanese Colonial Education in Taiwan, 1895–1945.* Cambridge, MA: Harvard University Press.

Wang, Georgette. 1997. 'Seeking the Best Integration: Popular Music on Taiwan.' In *Whose Master's Voice*, ed. Alison J. Eubank and Fouli T. Papageorgiou. Westport, CT: Greenwood Press, 209–19.

Yang Feng-chih Irene. 1993. 'Genre Analysis of Pop Music in Taiwan.' *Popular Music and Society* 17(2): 83–112.

Yang Feng-chih Irene. 1994. 'History of Popular Music in Taiwan.' *Popular Music and Society* 18(3): 53–66.

Yeh, Y.Y. 1996. *A National Score: Popular Music and Taiwanese Cinema.* Unpublished Ph.D. thesis, University of Southern California.

Discographical References

Ch'en Ta. 'Su Siang Ki.' *Shan Ch'eng Tsou-Ch'ang* [Fulo Folk Songs in Taiwan Island]. Wind Records TCD 1519. *2000:* Taiwan.

Ch'iu Lan-fong. 'Bang Li Cha Kui' [Hoping You Return Soon]. *Tai-yü Huai-nien Lao-ko* [Nostalgic Taiwanese Songs], v. 10. Ming Yüeh Video Record Company MR 9483. *2000:* Taiwan.

Ch'iu Lan-fong. 'Iu Ia Hue' [Rainy Night Flowers]. Tai-yü Huai-nien Lao-ko [Nostalgic Taiwanese Songs], v. 5. Ming Yüeh Video Record Company MR 9478. 2000: Taiwan.

Hei-ming-dan Kung-tsuo-shih [Blacklist Studios]. *Liah-kong Koa* [Songs of Rage]. Rock Records RD1052. *1989:* Taiwan.

Huang Hsiu-chen. 'Tho-hoe Li Soeh Ki' [Peach Blossoms, Blood, and Flowers]. *Tho-hoe Li Soeh Ki*. Sunrise Records CD 8528. *ca. 2000:* Taiwan.

Lim Giong, Murky Creek Commune, and Lei Kuang-hsia. *Nan-kuo, Tsai-chien, Nan-kuo* [Goodbye, South, Goodbye] (Soundtrack). Magic Stone Music Company MSD022. *1996:* Taiwan.

Teng Li-chün Theresa. 'Hai Yün' [Rhythm of the Sea]. *Kuo-yü Chin-ch'ü* [Golden Mandarin Songs] v. 6. Rock Records IMAR 003-06. *1997:* Taiwan.

Yang Hsuan. *Chung-kuo hsien-tai min-ko hsüan* [A Collection of Contemporary Chinese Folk Songs]. *1975:* Taiwan.

Yu Hsueh-fong. 'Po Pho Bang' [Fixing Broken Nets]. *Tai-yü Huai-nien Lao Ko* [Nostalgic Taiwanese Songs], v. 10. Ming Yüeh Video Record Company MR 9483. *2000:* Taiwan.

Discography

Ah-kiak-ah. *Kang-oo Hue-gueh* [Gangster Years]. Chin-yuan Records CKYD041. ca. 1978–88; *ca. 1995:* Taiwan.

Ah-kiak-ah. *Tai-yü Jin-ch'ü* [Golden Taiwanese Hits] (3 vols.). Kuang-mei Records KMCD 6651-6653. ca. 1978–88; *ca. 1995:* Taiwan.

Baboo. *Sin Tai-peu* [New Taiwan Dollars]. Pony Canyon PCTA 00003. *1992:* Taiwan.

Biung (Wang Hong-en). *BIUNG.* Wind Records TCD 5603. *2001:* Taiwan.

Chang Chen-yüeh and Free Night. *Mi-mi chi-ti* [Secret Base]. Magic Stone Music Company MSD048. *1998:* Taiwan.

Ch'en Ming-chang. *Ch'en Ming-chang ti Yin-yüeh, Hsien-ch'ang Tsuo-p'in I* [Ch'en Ming-chang's Music, Live Recording I]. Crystal Records CIRD0001-4. 1989; *1990:* Taiwan.

Ch'en Ming-chang. *Ch'en Ming-chang ti Yin-yüeh, Hsien-ch'ang Tsuo-p'in II* [Ch'en Ming-chang's Music, Live Recording II]. Crystal Records CIRD1014-4. *1991:* Taiwan.

Ch'en Ming-chang. *E-po e Chit-cu Hi* [An Afternoon's Play]. Index Music/Rock Records RC259. *1989:* Taiwan.

Ch'en Ming-chang. *Hsi-meng Jen-sheng* [In the Hands of a Puppetmaster] (Original soundtrack). Index Records/Pony Canyon PCTA 00020. *1993:* Taiwan.

Chi Yü. *Kuo-yü Ching-hsüan* [Mandarin Greatest Hits Selection]. Rock Records RD1250. ca. 1979-92; *1992:* Taiwan.

Chu Iok-sin (alias Ti Thao-phoe, 'Pork Rind'). *Chhio-khoe liam-koa II: Goa-ho Li Kam Chai* [Funny Rap II: Happy New Year]. Mandala Works MW017. *1995:* Taiwan.

Chu Iok-sin (alias Ti Thao-phoe, 'Pork Rind'). *Ti Thao-phoe Chhio-khoe Liam-koa* [Pork Rind's Funny Rap]. Mandala Works MW012. *1994:* Taiwan.

Fei-yü Yun-pao Kung-t'uan [Flying Fish/Cloud Leopard Synectics]. *Hei-an chih Hsin* [Heart of Darkness Series] (11 vols.). WATA 001-011. *ca. 2002:* Taiwan.

Hou Te-chien. 'Lung ti Ch'uan-jen' [Heirs of the Dragon]. *1979:* Taiwan. Performed by Li Chien-fu on *Kun-shih min-ko hsi-lieh 6: ch'i-yüeh liang shan* [Rock Records Folk Songs Collection 6: The Cool Mountains of July]. Rock Records SND1006. *1992:* Taiwan.

Hsiao Hu Tui [Little Tigers]. *Tsai-chien* [Goodbye]. Warner Taiwan 912032. *1990:* Taiwan.

Hsiao-yuan Min-ko [Campus Folk Songs]. Rock Records IMAR002. 1975-85; *1995:* Taiwan.

Hsin Pao-tao K'ang-le Tui [New Formosa Band]. *H.P.K.T.* Rock Records RC328. *1992:* Taiwan.

Hung Yi-feng. *Chüeh-pan Tai-yü huai-nien lao-ko 20: Hung Yi-feng chuan-chi* [Out of Print Nostalgic Taiwanese Songs 20: Hong Yi-feng Compilation]. Ying-lun Records IL9648. ca. 1946–70; *ca. 1993:* Taiwan.

Kang-oo Sueh-lo [Gangster Road of Blood]. Wu-fei Music EBD002. *2000:* Taiwan.

Kin Menwang and Lee Binhue. *Formosa 2000.* Magic Stone Music Company MSD 079. *2000:* Taiwan.

Kin Menwang and Lee Binhue. *Liu-long kao Tamsui* [Wandering to Tanshui]. Magic Stone Music Company MSD024. *1997*: Taiwan.

Kun-shih Min-ko Hsi-lieh [Rock Records Folk Songs Collection] (9 vols.). Rock Records SND1000-SND1008. 1975–85; *1997*: Taiwan.

Lai-tzu Taiwan Ti-ts'eng ti Sheng-yin [Voices from Taiwan's Lower Strata]. Crystal Records CIRD1037-4. *1995*: Taiwan.

Lee Tsung-sheng. *Sheng-ming-chung ti Ching-ling* [The Spirit in My Life]. Rock Records RD1012. *1986*: Taiwan.

Lim Giong. *Iu-lok e Se-kai* [Entertainment World]. Mandala Works MW-011. *1994*: Taiwan.

Lim Giong, Baboo, Wu Pai, and Hou Hsiao-hsien. *Siao-lien-e An-na!* [Dust of Angels] (Original Soundtrack). Pony Canyon PCTA 00004. *1992*: Taiwan.

Pan-to [Banquet Table]. Crystal Records CIRD1030-4 and CIRD1031-4. *1994*: Taiwan.

Purdur (Ch'en Chien-nien) and Panai. *Purdur and Panai Unplugged Live*. Taiwan Colors Music TCM 012. *2001*: Taiwan.

Samingad (Ji Hsiao-chun). *Ye Huo. Ch'un Fong* [Wild Fire. Spring Wind]. Magic Stone Records MSD 100. *Taiwan*: 1999.

Taiwan Liu-hsing Yin-yüeh 1980–1990 Shih-nien Ching-tien Ta-ch'üan-chi [A Complete Collection of Ten Years of Classics of Taiwanese Popular Music, 1980–1990] (8 vols.). Rock Records DDD9001. *1993*: Taiwan.

Tai-yü Huai-nien Lao-ko [Nostalgic Old Taiwanese Songs] (20 vols.). Yinglun Records IL7701-IL7720. ca. 1935–75; *1990*: Taiwan.

Tai-yü Huai-nien Lao-ko [Nostalgic Old Taiwanese Songs] (10 vols.). Ming Yüeh Video Record Company MR 9476 – MR 9485. *2000*: Taiwan.

Teng Li-chün Theresa. *The History of Theresa Teng* (10 vols.). Taurus Records TACL9019-28. ca. 1970–85; *1995*: Japan.

Ts'ai Chen-nan. *Lan-ko e Taiwan Lio-li* [Big Brother Nan's Taiwanese Cuisine]. Warner Music Taiwan WEA398429157-2. 1979–99; *1999*: Taiwan.

Ts'ai Chen-nan. *Tho San* [A Borrowed Life] (Original soundtrack). UFO Records 97284-4. *1994*: Taiwan.

Ts'ai Lan-ch'in. *Che-ko Shih-chieh* [This World]. UFO Records UC 8744. *1987*: Taiwan.

Wang Fu-mei. *Wang Fu-mei chu ch'ang: Paiwan tsu 1* [Paiwan Collection 1: Wang Fu-mei Sings]. Hsin Hsin Records SN1025. *ca. 1993*: Taiwan.

Wu Pai and China Blue. *Lang-jen Ch'ing Ko* [A Wanderer's Love Songs]. Mandala Works MS016. *1994*: Taiwan.

Yuan Lang-ch'ao. [Het Eyland Formosa]. Magic Stone MSD 084. *2000:* Taiwan.

Filmography

Dong [The Hole], dir. Tsai Ming-liang, 1999. Taiwan. 95 mins. Songs performed by Ke Lan (Grace Chang).

Lien-lien Hung-ch'en [Dust in the Wind], dir. Hou Hsiao-hsien. 1987. Taiwan. 109 mins. Original music by Ch'en Ming-chang.

Nan-kuo, Tsai-chien, Nan-kuo [Goodbye, South, Goodbye], dir. Hou Hsiao-hsien. 1996. Taiwan. 112 mins. Original music by Lim Giong.

D.J. HATFIELD

CITIES

T'aipei
Population: 2,880,000 (2000)

T'aipei is the capital of the Republic of China on Taiwan. As the country's administrative and commercial center, the city has long been a site for the introduction of new musical currents. It has played this leading role because of the location of universities there, the greater availability of imported equipment and recordings, and the presence of International Community Radio T'aipei (ICRT), which has been influential in the introduction of popular musical styles from the United States and Europe. In addition, Taiwan's three national television companies are based in T'aipei. While these companies have been undercut by the prevalence of cable and satellite broadcasting, televised variety shows and dramatic series have remained instrumental in the dissemination of popular music on Taiwan.

T'aipei is divided into the West district, focused on Westgate Town, and the newer East district. From the 1930s through the 1960s, Westgate Town was the site of many theaters, as well as of a dance hall, all of which served as performance venues for a wide variety of popular music. In the 1970s and 1980s, the East district became more predominant, first as a result of the introduction of karaoke bars, and later with the establishment of discothèques, video-viewing parlors and karaoke parlors (KTV). Many of the pubs where live music is performed are also located in the East district.

Another factor that has influenced popular music in T'aipei is labor migration to the metropolis, particularly during the 1960s and 1970s. This experience was a catalyst for songs of homesickness and longing, such as 'T'aipei Is Cold Tonight,' and songs about the relationship between T'aipei and

Taiwan's disappearing small-town life, such as Luo Ta-yu's 'Small Town Lukang.' Lim Giong's 'Forward!' also belongs to this genre.

Bibliography

Hatfield, D.J. 2001. '"T'aipei Is Cold Tonight," or Finding Fate in Taiwanese Karaokes.' *Anthropology and Humanism* 26(1): 71–79

Selya, Roger Mark. 1995. *Taipei*. New York: John Wiley & Sons.

Discographical References

Lim Giong. 'Hiong Tsien KiaN' [Forward!]. Rock Records RD1103. *1990*: Taiwan.

Luo Ta-yu. 'Lukang hsiao chen' [Small Town Lukang]. *Chih Hu Che Yeh*. Rock Records RD1008. *1982*: Taiwan.

'Taipak Kim-ia Leng-chheng-chheng' [Taipei Is Cold Tonight]. *PhaiN Lo M-thang KiaN* [You Should Not Walk This Evil Road]. K & M Music KMCO968. *ca .1995*: Taiwan.

Discography

Ch'en Ming-chang. 'Sin-chng koe' [A Street in Hsinchuang]. *E-po e Chit-cu Hi* [An Afternoon's Play]. Index Music/Rock Records RC259. *1989*: Taiwan.

Hei-ming-tan kung-tsuo-shih [Blacklist Studios]. 'Tai-pei Ti-kuo' [Taipei Empire] and 'Bin-chu a-chhao' [Democracy Bumpkin]. *Liah-kong Koa* [Songs of Rage]. Rock Records RD1052. *1989*: Taiwan.

Hsin Pao-tao K'ang-le Tui [New Formosa Band]. 'Taipak e Hu-kim' [Somewhere Near Taipei]. *Hsin Pao-tao K'ang-le Tui II*. Rock Records RC448. *1994*: Taiwan.

Yuan Yin She [Aboriginal Voice Society]. *Am tao T'ien-liang* [Am Until Dawn]. Taiwan Colors Music TCM990101. *1999*: Taiwan.

Filmography

Ch'ing-shao-nien Nuo-cha [Rebels of a Neon God], dir. Tsai Ming-liang. 1992. Taiwan. 106 mins. Original music by Huang Shu-jun.

Dong [The Hole], dir. Tsai Ming-liang. 1999. Taiwan. 95 mins. Songs performed by Ke Lan (Grace Chang).

Lien-lien Hung-ch'en [Dust in the Wind], dir. Hou Hsiao-hsien. 1987. Taiwan. 109 mins. Original music by Ch'en Ming-chang.

D.J. HATFIELD

Tajikistan

Population: 6,177,000 (2002)

The Republic of Tajikistan is the only Persian-speaking state of Central Asia. It shares borders with Kyrgyzstan to the north, Uzbekistan to the west, China to the east and Afghanistan to the south. Mountains cover 90 percent of the land area of 54,922 sq miles (140,600 sq km). Dushanbe is the capital with a population of 523,000 (1999). Tajikistan has extensive mineral reserves including uranium, lead, iron and zinc. The only cash crop is cotton. The population is 64 percent Tajik, 24 percent Uzbek and 6 percent Russian. The state religion is Islam.

In the nineteenth century, the north of present-day Tajikistan was part of the Russian Empire, while the south was the eastern region of the independent Khanate of Bukhara. After the 1917 revolution, the north immediately joined the new Soviet state, and Bukhara was conquered by the Red Army in 1922. In 1924 the newly created Tajikistan was made an Autonomous Republic within the Soviet Federal Republic of Uzbekistan and, in 1929, it was granted the status of the Soviet Federal Republic of Tajikistan. This left two major Tajik cities, Bukhara and Samarkand, inside Uzbekistan, a fact that underlines the similarity between the classical and traditional music of the two republics.

Between 1924 and 1929, Tashkent (capital of Uzbekistan) and Moskva (Moscow) together controlled the policy, economy and culture. While part of the new Soviet leadership directed their energies to industrialization and collectivization, another part worked on building the cultural infrastructure. Tajikistan included what had been a provincial part of the Bukharan emirate, and it was now able to create modern theater and media, literature and music.

However, the Sovietization of Tajikistan led to its de facto withdrawal from the multilingual and multiethnic cultural arena of Central Asia. The country became estranged from cultures to which it had been relatively close, such as those of India and Pakistan, Iran, Afghanistan and China. This imposed isolation during the Soviet period involved the gradual reform of pre-revolutionary styles of thinking that had been mostly rooted in the Persian-Tajik literary heritage of Central Asia.

The only artistic space where that style of thinking was protected and preserved was, and has remained, music. Soviet musical institutions were established, and music provided a linkage between different parts of the cultural infrastructure, and resounded from the universities and academies of science, opera and ballet houses, theaters and cinemas, libraries and clubs, publishing houses and media.

The first music college was organized between 1925 and 1929 in Bukhara, while the first institute of music and dance was opened in 1928 in Samarkand. One year later, the musical college and a music school were opened in Khojand in northern Tajikistan. The Tajik state drama theater was founded in 1929 and was divided in 1934 into two parts: drama and music. Tajik musicians gained greater cultural power as they upgraded their skills at modern music courses, and at the Tashkent or Moscow conservatoires. At the beginning of the twenty-first century, the Mirso Tursun-zoda Institute of Art, Ziodullo Shahidi Musical College and Malika Sobirova Musical School were the basic institutions for a wide variety of careers in music and the music industry.

Tajikistan inherited the rich Persian culture of the region with its world-renowned literature, music, architecture and horticulture, which has its basis in the Islamic concept of the world as unity. In practice, this concept was steadily eroded by the nationalistic movements of the twentieth century, expressed in Central Asia in a national-Bolshevik interpretation. Although the roots of Tajik music were closely connected with Arab, Chinese, Indian, Iranian, Afghani, Turkish and Russian music, these features have been poorly recognized and developed as such.

During the almost 70 years of the Soviet period, the population of eastern Bukhara, now known as Tajikistan, increased due to a flow of immigrants sanctioned by the Soviet system. The first new arrivals were Russians, Caucasians, Iranians and Afghans and, during World War II, Europeans such as Germans and people of the Baltic States.

Flowing into this 'virgin' environment, the new inhabitants used Russian as their lingua franca. The Tajik language, as a *khorasanian* version of Persian, became a language of the indigenous elite, while music served to smooth over contradictions, transforming the fundamental values of the regional culture, such as respect, hospitality and interactivity into the public consciousness. In addition, music provided an effective instrument to bridge the gap between the cultures of the 'indigenous' people and those newly arriving.

The 1930s brought the first musical ensembles, and musical-theatrical societies and courses for both amateur and professional artists blossomed. The leading musicians, such as Ota Jalol, Khoja Abdulaziz (Rasulov), Sodirckon, Usto Shodi, Domullo Khalim, Levicha and N.N. Mironov, created a basis for the first generation of professional modern musicians and composers such as Bobokul Fayzullaev, Fasliddin Shahobov, Shohnazar Sohibov, Muravin and Cvetaev. The strategy of these artists was to conserve and prolong the vitality of musical heritage in modern forms. But Tajikistan remained a place of great upheaval, and conflicts between political and cultural forces prevented the actualization of that policy until the 1950s. A young musician, Ziodullo Shahidi, who became the leading composer of the Soviet period described one of the instances of conflict in the story 'Rafiki naynavozi man' (My Friend, the Flute-Player).

During the late 1920s and 1930s, Tajikistan drew in many musicians, actors and amateur actresses from Central Asia and Russia. Theater and music formed the principal arenas for different cultures in the region to converge. The first amateur theaters of Samarkand, formed by Tajiks, Uzbeks, Jews and Russians, told stories of love and struggles for freedom, and presented the whirling dances of a Sufi style known as *charh*. New interpretations of well-known melodies for piano and violin were another phenomenon of those times.

At the end of 1930s and early in the 1940s, Dushanbe (then called Stalinabad) established itself as an important location for three forms of popular music. The first was a new brand of 'indigenous' music from Darvoz and Hisor, whose best-known performer was Aka Sharif Juraev (and his family). His vivid and original interpretation of *mavrigi* and other old Bukharan styles was seen as a liberation of the music from the 'backwardness' of the famous traditional cultural cities such as Samarkand and Bukhara.

Secondly, another 'northern' style of interpretation, associated with young Samarkand musicians such as Sharifjon Bobokalonov, A'zam Kamolov, Fozil Soliev and Ziodullo Shahidi, attracted audiences through the use of a variety of instruments and the novelty of its sound. These artists synthesized traditional genres with international musical techniques, notably forms of Russian and European music such as opera and ballet.

Thirdly, the second half of the 1930s was marked by the creation of the first musical dramas and operas. The first musical plays, such as *Rozia* by C. Balacyanyan of Armenian origin and Z. Shahidi from Samarkand, and *Lola* by C. Balacyanyan and the Jewish writer C. Urbach, were based on political ideas, such as the emancipation of woman and the re-evaluation of traditional and folk music. In 1937, the musical drama *Shurishi Voce* (Revival of Voce) by

Sergey Balacyanyan, based on the libretto of the poets Abdusalom Dehoti and Mirso Tursun-Zade, was performed (it was later transformed into an opera). Based on well-known folk songs and the songs of Abulkasim Lohuti, a poet of Iranian origin, it restated the native revolutionary story in newly borrowed musical forms such as arioso, recitative, chorus and other styles of vocal.

At this time also, musical comedies such as *Arshim-Mal-alan* by the Azerbaijani composer Uzeir Gajibekov brought the sounds of the Caucasus region to Tajikistan. Affairs of the family served as the core subject matter for these comedies, which were accompanied by lyrical songs, with the singing and dancing by performers young and old. These received a rapturous reception in the new city of Dushanbe. The 'borrowed' ideas provoked a renewal of the old folk songs in the poetic genre of *du-bayty'* or *ruboi*.

The newly developed genres of music of the 1920s–40s attracted the attention of Russian musicologists, who initiated projects to preserve them. The most important of those activities was a project of recording the fundamental source of Central Asian musical heritage, known as *shashmaqom*. Performances by the Bukharan musicians Bobokul Faysulloev, Shohnazar Sohibov (one of the last surviving musicians of the Bukharan court, who died in Dushanbe in 1962) and Fasliddin Shahobov were recorded. Their performances, accompanied by traditional singing, were transcribed in the modern system of musical notation by a group of Tajik and Russian musicians. The final edition of *shashmaqom* in five volumes was finished in the 1960s under the direction of Russian professors V. M. Belyaev and E. E. Bertels.

During the late 1930s and early 1940s, dancing and singing groups from the cultural centers of different Tajikistan localities, together with their bands, traveled from city to city. They played *tanbur* and *dutor* (lutes), *gijjak* (spike fiddle), *nay* (flute) and *doyra* (frame drum), instruments common throughout Central Asia. The most popular dances with vocals were '*chor zarb*' (four rhythms) from Darvaza and 'the dance of horsemen' from Kuhistoni Badakhshon.

Eventually, these groups were invited to perform in Dushanbe. In the capital, performances took place in theaters, clubs, gardens/parks, stadiums and concert halls, bringing together thousands of people. The opening of the Opera House in 1937 became a great political and cultural event. This was not strictly an opera house in the European sense,

but more of a place to bring together the music of many different genres.

The construction of the railroad to Dushanbe (at that time 'Stalinabad'), the first in the most mountainous part of southern Central Asia, gave easy access to the capital for amateur musicians from the small, scattered *kishlaks* (settlements) among the Pamir mountains and along the Hisor and Fergana Valleys. The Stalinabad railroad linked Dushanbe directly to Moscow, a phenomenon praised by the young poets of those times.

In 1941, a festival of *Tajik Decade of Literature and Art* was held in Moscow. This accelerated the influx of Bukharan-Samarkandi-Darvasa-Pamir musicians into the Soviet capital. Their performances included traditional national instruments together with the new European ones: violin, cello, double bass, flute, oboe and tuba.

With the start of World War II, the fusion styles and instrumentation of Tajik musicians were often oriented toward the anti-fascist movement, in the form of patriotic songs. Traditional melodies were given solemn and victorious intonations. 'Aziz Moskva' (Dear Moscow), a march by the leading Tajik composer Ziodullo Shahidi, became a favorite for communal singing all over the USSR, and was heard at the all-union parade of sportsmen in 1944 in Moscow. Another popular composition was 'Idi Zafar' (The Day of the Victory), a celebration of the end of the war. Deeply lyrical, peaceful songs, based on *shashmaqom*, were also popular.

The foremost bands of the 1940 and 1950s were those of Aka Sharif Juraev, Gulomhaydar Gulomaliev and Gaffor Vallamad-zoda. While northern-style bands played sad and gracious music such as *munojot* (an appeal to God), with a dance by Ashura Nosirova, the southern style – in the dance of Musharafa Karimove – circled in a quick rhythm, *zarb*. The music performed by the string orchestras of women *rubab* (lute) players was a mixture of the two. The variety of musicians, singers and dances formed a basis for the development of new musical ideas, such as interpretations of national melodies on piano and violin.

Revolutionary French and Russian songs inspired compositions by Tajik musicians with improvisation on *doyra*, *tanbur*, *dutor* and *nay*. The first recordings of these and of an original Tajik genre, *rez*, were made in the Baltic States. At this time, recordings were also made of solos and collective improvisations of ritual songs for occasions such as weddings and funerals.

New Tajik songs grew from many external influences. Students based in Moscow and elsewhere brought back songs. The collaboration between musicians of different nationalities in previous decades led to the creation of new Tajik music in the 1950s and 1960s. Apart from Aka Sharif Juraev and Laylo Sharipova, of Iranian origin, the most well-known singers were from the Bukhara Jewish community: Rena Galibova, Barno Ischakova and Shoista Mulodjanova. The most popular songs included 'Chor Zarb,' 'It's Nice in Tajikistan,' 'Our House is not so Far,' 'The Toast,' 'Khush on zamon' (Those Good Times), 'Oshig shudam' (I am in Love) and 'Meparvaram' (Praising Love).

Films were another source of popular songs. In 1957, songs from the films *Man bo duhtare vohurdam* (I Met a Girl) and *Pisar boyad zan girad* (The Son Has to Marry) caught on from Dushanbe to Tashkent and from Tashkent to Moscow, Kiev and the Baltic states. This popularity gave birth to many other films, such as *Charoge dar Kuhsor* (The Light in the Mountains), whose songs were played throughout the country.

Between 1960 and 1980, a new light and easy genre, *estrada*, was popularized by the band Gulshan, and singers Mugaddas Nabieva, Tojiddin Muhiddinov and Karamatullo Kurbanov. The years since the 1970s have been dominated by figure of Daler Nazarov. In the 1980s, the genre *falak* was very popular, with Odina Khoshim and Davlammand Kholov as leading figures.

Parvina Shukrulloeva, a young singer (b 1984), became very popular among Tajik young people after her first appearance in the 1990s. With albums like *Lalaika Pamir* (1994), Oleg Fezov drew large audiences. In the early twenty-first century, new ensembles such as Baht (Happiness) and Trans, with the singers Malika Kurbonova and Parviz Nazarov, were established.

The sudden collapse of the Soviet Union, followed by five years of civil war (1992–97), almost completely destroyed the musical infrastructure of Tajikistan. It also created another danger for musical life in Tajikistan – a very strong emphasis on purely local music and a forced folklorization. Nevertheless, a gradual recovery could be realized by raising international interest in a re-evaluation of the musical heritage of the Silk Road to a new level. The Silk Road Ensemble project led by cellist Yo Yo Ma was one step towards this. Its multi-national personnel included two Tajikistan composers, Alisher Latif-Zadeh and Tolib-hon Shadidi.

Bibliography
Slobin, Mark and Slobin, Greta. 1975. *Central Asian Music: A Partial Translation of Vol. 1 of Sketches of the Music History of the Peoples of the USSR by V. Beliaev*. Middletown, CT.: Wesleyan University Press.

Discographical Reference
Fesov, Oleg. *Lalaika Pamir*. Miramar 203071. *1994*: USA.

Discography
Ma, Yo Yo and the Silk Road Ensemble. *Silk Road Journey: When Strangers Meet*. Sony Classical 89782. *2002*: USA.
Nabiev, Jurabeg and Ensemble Dorrdâne. *Maqam d'Asia Centrale 2. Tadjikistan: Tradition de Bukhara*. Ocora C 560102. *1997*: France.

MUNIRA SHAHIDI

Turkmenistan
Population: 4,930,000 (2002)

The Republic of Turkmenistan is situated in the southwest of Central Asia, and borders on Iran and Afghanistan to the south, Uzbekistan to the east, the Caspian Sea to the west and Kazakhstan to the northwest. Eighty percent of Turkmenistan's territory is covered by the Karakum Desert (Peski Karakumy), whose oil and gas deposits constitute the primary source of economic wealth. The population is 77 percent Turkmeni, seven percent Russian and nine percent Uzbek. Modern Turkmenistan is divided into five *velayats* (regions), each having its own administrative center. Each *velayat* has its own distinctive culture and dialect of the national language, Turkmen. The capital of the republic is Ashgabat (Ashkhabad) with a population of 525,000 (1999).

Russia conquered present day Turkmenistan in the 1880s. After the civil war in Central Asia of 1917–1922 and the establishment of the Bolshevik regime, the Soviet Socialist Republic of Turkmenistan was founded. The country proclaimed its independence in 1991. After that date, it was ruled by Sapormurad Niyazev Turkmenbashi, the former leader of the Turkmenistan communist party. He was later voted the President-for-life by the legislature.

The desert environment and arid continental climate significantly influenced the cultures of the Turkmen tribes, of which the great majority led a nomadic existence until the beginning of the twentieth century. For the nomad, life represented constant movement and renewal. This way of life affected the nature of Turkmen music and instruments, which had to be compact and easily transportable. The most ancient and widely used instrument was the *dutar*, an indispensable accessory of every *yurta* (nomad tent). The construction of this two-stringed plucked instrument was very simple, but the preparation of its component materials was a lengthy process, which meant that every instrument had to be treated with care and respect. It was carried on the back in a special felt cover that protected it from scorching heat and winds. According to legend, the first *dutar* was mute until its creator – Baba Gammar – struck a deal with the *sheitan* (devil), who in exchange for endowing the *dutar* with sound, demanded that he be commemorated in the names of certain parts of the instrument: *sheitan-perde, sheitan-deshik*.

In the pre-Islamic era, the *dutar* was used primarily by *baksy* (shaman healers), as it was believed that the dulcet sounds of the instrument attracted heavenly spirits. Gradually, *dutar* performance lost its magic significance and acquired the status of an independent instrumental tradition. Nevertheless, it continued to be thought that musicians possessed supernatural powers endowed by their 'patron saints,' Baba Gammar and Ashyk Aydyn Pirom. For this reason, when singers and instrumentalists first begin to learn their art, they consider it their duty to visit the graves of the great saints.

Soon afterwards, Turkmen musical culture diverged into two branches, the folk culture of everyday life and the oral-professional one. The many genres of folk music served various applied functions: they might be used to summon rain, banish evil spirits, calm cattle, or put a child to sleep; or else to accompany weddings, funerals and everyday activities. They also formed a part of divining rituals. The performance of folk melodies did not require great skill or training, but it was strictly confined to certain times of day or season, to specific places or circumstances.

Unlike its folk counterpart, professional music was intended to give purely aesthetic pleasure to an audience. Only professional musicians called *bagshy* (singer-instrumentalists) performed it. In order to become a true *bagshy*, a musically gifted male youth would accompany an established master for several years and learn the subtleties of the national tradition. Having achieved the necessary skill and obtained *pata* (the tutor's blessing), the youth obtained the right to stage independent public performances.

The *bagshy* spent most of their lives on the road. Moving from place to place, they brought not only their art, but norms of interaction, traditional etiquette and news of important events in the region and in neighboring states. Ever since the shamanic times, the Turkmen had held the *dutar* performer and his instrument in high esteem and, for every Turkmen tribe, the arrival of the *bagshy* musician was an important occasion and his performance was incorporated into a traditional ritual of hospitality. The *bagshy* musician was first and foremost a guest; he was met with great rejoicing, and sent on his way with gifts reflecting the tribe's admiration for his talent and skill.

Depending on the repertoire of the performer, the Turkmen *bagshy* were classified into *tirmechy* (singers), *destanchy* (performers of epic poetry) and *sazanda* (instrumentalists). During the Middle Ages, these groups were amalgamated into distinct schools of performance based on tribal origins: Akhal-Teke *yoly*, Damana *yoly*, Yemut-Goklen *yoly*, Salyr-Saryk *yoly* and Chovdur *yoly*. In the first half of the twentieth century, these names were replaced by new ones based on territory: Akhal *yoly*, Mary *yoly*, Balkan *yoly*, Lebap *yoly* and Dashoguz *yoly*. Each school was characterized by the types of instruments employed, the genres performed and the particular ways of playing folk music.

Thus, the main distinguishing feature of performers belonging to the Akhal *yoly*, from the central region of Turkmenistan, was a high level of proficiency on the *dutar*. Outstanding representatives of this school included Amangeldy Gonibekov, Shukur bagshy, Tachmammet Sukhangulyyev, Mylly Tachmyradov, Purli Saryyev, Chary Tachmamedov and Yagmyr Nurgeldyev. Their repertoire was remarkable for its highly developed forms, rich imagery and technical difficulty. The authorship of most *dutar* compositions is unknown, although the history of their creation is postulated in a number of folk legends. The Akhal region has been the source not only of short *dutar* pieces, but also of multipartite compositions and the *dutar* cycles *Mukambar, Gyrklar* and *Saltyklar*.

At the end of the nineteenth century, a northern regional instrument, the *gijak*, became widely used by the Akhal *yoly*. The *gijak* is a three-stringed bowed instrument with a loud, full-bodied sound and broad technical scope, used both as a solo and accompanying instrument. In 1953, the *gijak* was redesigned so that it might be included in orchestral ensembles of traditional instruments; the traditional quintal tuning was replaced by a quartal one.

In the northern region, the Dashoguz *yoly* was renowned for the performance of epic poetry. The vast repertoire of Turkmen *bagshy-destanchy* included the numerous chapters of the monumental *Gorogly* epic, as well as many individual and anonymous *destans* (epics) such as *Shassenem and Garyb*, *Zokhre and Takhir* and *Leyly and Mejnun*. These epic works were composed of alternating segments of poetry and prose; the storyteller would animatedly recite the prose and transform the poetry into song. During his recitation, the orator would now and then accompany himself on the *dutar*, producing a chord by gently touching the open strings of the instrument. It was almost obligatory for sung poetry to be accompanied by the *gijak*. It not only accompanied and enhanced the melodic base of the performance but, at times, even 'competed' with the singer. The founder of the northern epic tradition was Garadaly Goklen; his followers Chovdur Kor, Nazar Baga and Magtumguly Garlyyev created a variety of new styles that were still well-received at the beginning of the twenty-first century.

The songs of the traditional music schools of the eastern and western regions were remarkable for the originality of their thematic contents, which focused on the special features of the natural landscape. Many singers and musicians of the Lebap *yoly* in the eastern region found a source of inspiration in the self-willed character of the fast-moving, ever-shifting Amudar'ya River.

Boundless seascapes and majestic mountain ranges constituted the primary themes of the musical poetic works of the western performing school, the Balkan *yoly*, whose folkloric genres have been the best preserved in Turkmenistan. The tribes of this region, located by the Caspian Sea, occupied themselves mainly with fishing and navigation. The Balkan *bagshy* tradition was solely a sung form which was characterized by an 'open voice' method and an abundance of vocal ornamentation, accompanied by a *dutar* and *gijak* ensemble. Representatives of the Balkan singing school included Nurbedy Gulov, Ashirmamed Daudov, Mollo Chekliyev and Sarykhan Sapayev.

The traditional performing style in the southwestern part of Turkmenistan – the Mary *yoly* – was also remarkable for a particular vocal technique. In this school, the singer's unique vocal quality and guttural ornamentation were very similar to the sound produced by an ancient wind instrument, the *tuiduk*. The *tuiduk* had several variations: the *gargy-tuiduk* (with a body 80–82 cm in length), *dilli-tuiduk* (3–5 inches [8–12 cm]) and the now obsolete *gosha-dilli-tuiduk* (twinned *dilli-tuiduks*). Although all were made from reed, they varied in sound and appearance. The *gargy-tuiduk* had a husky timbre characterized by a distinctive whistling, while the *dilli-tuiduk* sounded piercingly and brightly in the high range. Vocal performance to the accompaniment of the *tuiduk*, as well as the playing of *tuiduk* melodies, demanded great technical skill, although for many centuries use of the instruments was limited to cowherds. The rise of industry in the twentieth century caused the contraction of cattle ranching, which led to the almost complete disappearance of the *tuiduk* genres. Only by the end of the century, with the revival of spiritual culture, did *tuiduk* performance begin to reappear on the professional scene.

The *bagshy* of the Mary region had a good command of the *dutar*, though their playing differed greatly from that of the musicians of the Akhal region. Most of the Mary *yoly dutar* pieces are based on sung prototypes. They are tuneful, simple in form and content, and make extensive use of repetitive structures. Some outstanding representatives of the southwestern school have been Nobat bagshy, Girman bagshy, Durdy Myradov, Durnazar Khudayberenov, Han Akyev, Ammannazar Atayev, Yazgeldy Kuvvadov and Odeniyaz Nobatov. Gurt Yakubov created a new style of performing epic poetry in Mary *yoly*. Taking the traditional structure of folk stories as his foundation, Yakubov's unhurried recitations would make use of the lower registers of his voice; his songs were distinguished by the tunefulness and slow enunciation characteristic of the Mary style. Yakubov's epic legacy includes about 60 *destans* and legends set to music, on lyric, religious and historical subjects. Among the most popular works were *Khatam tai*, *Gulnam* and *Ymam Khassayin*.

After 1924, Soviet cultural policy resulted in the opening up of the young Turkmen republic to the best musical achievements of Russia and the world, contributing to the radical transformation of local culture. Theaters and concert halls appeared in the capital and other big cities. The performance of folk music genres in such venues required modification of traditional instruments in order to widen their range and intensify their resonance. To bring the oral tradition in line with accepted systems of music notation, folk instruments were adjusted to fit the scale for all keys. The modified instruments were incorporated into the orchestras and folk ensembles of the State Philharmonic Society as well as into the new system of musical education establishments. Composers began to arrange traditional folk music for various types of ensemble.

In the 1970s and 1980s, Ashkabad was swept along on the wave of electronic music; new vocal-instrumental groups were created, the most popular being Gunesh, Destan and Firuza. These groups merged the Turkmen folk legacy with modern jazz-rock trends. Led by drummer Rishad Shafi, Gunesh was known throughout the Soviet Union and made recordings for the USSR state label Melodiya. These were reissued as *Rishad Shafi Presents Gunesh* in 1999.

The ever-expanding dissemination of popular forms of music began to obscure the primary characteristic of folk music, individual performance. Collective creativity simplified the oral tradition, completely eliminating improvisation and reducing the melodic ornamentation and complex rhythmical elements that had served as proof of the performer's skill.

After independence, Turkmenistan entered a new political, economic and cultural period. The government established a cultural program (*Rukhname*) whose aim was to revive the history, language and traditions of the people. Special folklore groups were created to collect and revive the musical folklore that was beginning to vanish from everyday life. Consequently, thanks to the performing activities of folk groups, grassroots musical creativity acquired a somewhat different incarnation on the stage.

The favorite music of the Turkmen people was always the oral-professional folk genre and, although complemented by new themes and instruments, the national tradition had remained largely unchanged at the turn of the millennium. The beginning of the twenty-first century had its own famous contemporary *bagshy*, such as Odeniyaz Nobatov, Oraznepes Dovletnazarov, Yagmyr Nurberdiyev, Chryar Jumayev, Ata Ablyyev, Akjagul Myradova and Jemal Saparova, whose work can be heard on the CD *Turkmenistan: The Music of the Bakhshy* (1995).

The focal point of all the regional performing traditions had, by then, become the National Conservatory of Turkmenistan, which alongside the generally accepted European system of music education, offered special courses in *bagshy* (folk singing) and *turkmen sary* (folk instruments) oriented towards oral instruction and learning. Transmitting the folk legacy orally not only promoted better acquisition by students of vocal and instrumental skills, but also gave them the opportunity to appreciate the traditions of a centuries-old culture.

Bibliography

Akhmedov, Azim. 1983. *Dutaryn ovazy – khalkymyn sazy*. Ashgabat: Turkmenistan.

Gulliyev, Shakhim. 1985. *Iskusstvo turkmenskikh bagshy* [The Art of the Turkmen *Bagshy*]. Ashgabat: Ylym.

Kurbanova, Jamilya. 2000. 'Pesennaya traditsiya turkmenskogo epicheskogo skazitel'stva' [The Singing Tradition of Turkmen Epic Poetry]. In *The Oral Epic: Performance and Music*, ed. Karl Reichl. Bamberg: *Intercultural Music Studies*, 12: 115–214.

Uspensky, V. and Beliayev, V. 1979. *Turkmenskaya muzyka* [Turkmen Music]. 2nd ed. Ashgabat: Turkmenistan.

Discographical References

Gunesh. *Rishad Shafi Presents Gunesh*. Boheme Music CD BMR 911107. *1999*: Czech Republic.

Turkmenistan: The Music of the Bakhshy. Gallo 651. *1995*: South Africa.

Discography

Instrumental Music of Turkmenistan. World Music Library WML 5175. *1994*: France.

Songs of Turkmenistan. World Music Library WML 5230. *1997*: France.

DZNAMILYA KURBANOVA (trans. ALISA LOCKWOOD)

Uzbekistan

Population: 25,981,647 (2003)

Uzbekistan is a landlocked country, sharing borders with Turkmenistan, Kazakhstan, Afghanistan, Tajikistan and Kyrgyzstan. Uzbekistan is the most populous of the newly independent (1991) former Soviet Central Asian republics. It is one of the world's leading cotton producers, and possesses significant mineral wealth. Uzbekistan's territory is mostly desert, punctuated by oases and river valleys which have supported large-scale irrigation agriculture and urban civilization since early antiquity.

The majority of citizens are Sunni Muslims. They are descendants of proto-Iranian agriculturalists who settled in the oases millennia ago, and of Turkic pastoral nomads from the northern steppes who came in several waves from the sixth to the sixteenth centuries to raid the rich oases and were absorbed into the sedentary population. A 1996 estimate of Uzbekistan's cultural composition lists the following – Uzbek 80 percent; Russian 5.5

percent; Tajik 5 percent; others 9.5 percent. Language preference is roughly parallel to these population subgroups, with Russian and Uzbek as lingua franca, and Tajik Persian standard in many locales. Literacy is universal; citizens across the country have absorbed a Soviet version of modernity. Nevertheless, two-thirds of the population live in rural areas, and most native Central Asians are socially conservative. Their expressive culture, including contemporary popular music, is rooted in oral tradition.

Uzbekistan's population is concentrated in the basins of the Amudarya and Syrdarya rivers, which descend from the Tien Shan-Pamir mountain system in the east, encircling the country on their way to the Aral Sea in Uzbekistan's northwest. The Syrdarya system waters the Fergana Valley, the major agricultural region, and Tashkent, Uzbekistan's capital. To the south, the Amudarya basin includes the Zerafshan Valley, with medieval imperial capitals Bukhara and Samarqand; and the Amudarya delta region, known since antiquity as Khorezm. Tashkent/Fergana, Bukhara and Khorezm have maintained separate classical music repertoires since late medieval times. These regional distinctions also characterize contemporary popular styles, with Tashkent/Fergana as the dominant voice. The Uzbek language also dominates. The following discussion will focus on Uzbek-language music, but is also relevant to the stylistically similar music of Uzbekistan's Tajik minority (concentrated in Samarqand and Bukhara), who share a centuries-old bilingual musical heritage with Uzbeks across Central Asia.

State-controlled broadcast media, recording studios and public concerts play an undeniable role in disseminating contemporary Uzbek music, but the ultimate influence of formal mass-market outlets is peripheral. Public sector music projects are severely hampered by red tape and scant resources; commercial activity is limited to makeshift dubbing operations. The primary venue for this music is at weddings and other life-cycle celebrations; such a celebration, known as a *to'y*, is conducted on a grand scale. Musicians earn their living as live performers; a select few achieve national media exposure. Thus Uzbekistan provides the interesting case of a dynamic mass-audience music scene that is usually experienced live at invitation-only events, and promoted by word of mouth.

Uzbek contemporary music is likewise noteworthy in its close relation to traditional genres. Uzbek wedding party performers tend to promote conservative Muslim values with artfully didactic songs, evoking themes such as loyalty to hearth and homeland, and the ephemerality of worldly concerns. Virtually all Uzbek song texts are cast in traditional verse forms. Rhythms are those used in folk music and light classical styles (adapted for the drum set). Songwriters simplify the arch-shaped melodies of the classical repertoire, eschewing the verse-chorus form of Western pop melodies. Ensemble textures are heterophonic, a characteristically Middle Eastern practice in which all voices simultaneously perform differing interpretations of a single melody. Western major scales are rare, and a form of modal harmony appears only in the most Westernized dance styles.

Contemporary Uzbek music began to take shape in the mid-1970s, concurrent with general acceptance of Western-style wedding receptions – as promoted by Soviet social engineers – and the use of public address systems at these events. Hosts in Tashkent began hiring *estrada* (pop) ensembles, which normally performed Western and Russian pop music in downtown restaurants, to liven up the entertainment at family events. The practice spread rapidly, and inspired traditional Uzbek musicians to adopt the *estrada* musicians' electric guitars, synthesizers and drum sets, combining them with local instruments like the Azerbaijani *tar* (a plucked lute), *doyra* (frame drum) and *gijjak* (spike fiddle or violin held vertically). Within 10 years, these Uzbek (or Tajik) *milliy estrada* (national/ethnic pop) ensembles and an updated native-language, traditional repertoire had become standard at wedding parties across Uzbekistan. Only in Khorezm did musicians retain their acoustic instrumentation, which features the Azerbaijani *tar*, *doyra* and accordion. Since weddings and other life-cycle events in Uzbekistan are celebrations of ethnicity and traditional values, once there was a native alternative, the Russian-speaking *estrada* ensembles returned to the restaurants.

There are two basic polarities in Uzbek popular music style; most performers have identified with one or the other, but are versatile enough to handle both when necessary. The more traditional and prestigious end of the spectrum is *og'ir* (weighty) music, sung exclusively by men, typically in the early stages of a wedding celebration. Stylistic conventions are best described as a simplification of light classical genres – elevated language, philosophical themes, slow to medium tempos, complex melodies, vocal virtuosity. Performers readily switch to acoustic accompaniment for concert performances and recordings. This style's most prominent exponent is Sherali Juraev (Fergana). Juraev and countless others, such as Nuriddin Haydarov (Fergana), Mardon Moulanov (Samarkand Tajik), Ortiq Otajonov (Khorazm) and film actor Baxtiyor Xolhujaev (Forish/Tashkent), may be considered mainstream popular artists. Dadahon Hasan (Fergana), whose lyrics feature sharp political criticism, reaches a large audience through the underground circulation of audiocassettes. Recordings of the above artists are largely unavailable outside Central Asia, although some are now accessible on the Internet.

The other end of the spectrum is *sho'x* (rowdy) music – simple music for dancing during the latter hours of the celebration. Many *sho'x* singers are women, who are often stigmatized as cheap entertainers. This music is the Uzbek analog of Middle East pop styles like Turkish arabesk, and is gradually elbowing other styles into the shadows. Song lyrics often contain traditional rhetorical devices and social commentary, but the percentage of formulaic love songs in a performer's repertoire is directly proportional to the degree of their stylistic simplicity and the adoption of Western pop elements. The father of Uzbek *sho'x* music is Farrukh Zakirov (Tashkent). His Yalla ensemble has been the official Uzbekistan national pop group since the mid-1970s. Zakirov performs only in concert, and much of his repertoire falls into the multilingual Soviet-era *estrada* category; however, his frequent Uzbek-language hits are covered by nearly everyone. Yulduz Usmanova (Fergana Valley), who draws heavily on Uzbek folk songs for inspiration, and Mavluda Asalhujaeva (Fergana Valley), with an ear for Turkish pop music, are more typical in their connection to the wedding party venue and predominance of Uzbek-language lyrics. The music of Yalla and Usmanova is easily available in the West on independent World Beat labels. Yulduz Usmanova in particular has developed a following in Western Europe. MP3-format downloads of current *sho'x* hits are available from a government Web site (http://www.umid.uz/Uzdessert/).

Bibliography

Allworth, Edward A. 1990. *The Modern Uzbeks: From the Fourteenth Century to the Present: A Cultural History*. Stanford, CA: Hoover Institution Press, Stanford University.

Karomatov, Faizullah. 1972. 'On the Regional Styles of Uzbek Music.' *Asian Music* 4(1): 48–58.

Levin, Theodore Craig. 1996. *The Hundred Thousand Fools of God: Musical Travels in Central Asia (and Queens, New York)*. Bloomington and Indianapolis: Indiana University Press.

Tyson, David. 1994. 'The Role of Unofficial Audio Media in Contemporary Uzbekistan.' *Central Asian Survey* 13(2): 283–93.

Discography

From Samarkand to Bukhara: A Musical Journey Through Uzbekistan. Long Distance/Womad Anthology *1996*: France. (Includes acoustic selections by Mardon Moulanov.)

Jo'raev (Juraev), Sherali. *Karvon*. Melodiya S30 24777 005. *1986*: Uzbekistan.

Otajonov, Ortiq. *Sening Kulishlaring*. Melodiya S30 25975 006. *1987*: Uzbekistan.

UMID Foundation Web site. MP3 format downloads of current Uzbek pop hits available. http://www.umid.uz/Uzdessert/

Usmanova, Yulduz. *Alma, Alma*. Blue Flame 09006-23050-2. *1994*: USA.

Yalla (Farrukh Zakirov). *Beard of the Camel*. Imagina 70950-11010-2-4. *1995*: USA.

Yalla (Farrukh Zakirov). *Jinouni*. Imagina 70950-11011-2-3. *2000*: USA.

CRAIG MACRAE

CITIES

Tashkent

Population: 4,000,000 (2003)

Tashkent is the capital of Uzbekistan, and the largest city in the former Soviet Central Asian republics. It is located on the Chirchik River, a tributary of the great Syrdar'ya. Although a market center of great antiquity, Tashkent achieved its present prominence following its occupation in 1865 by Russian forces, when it was transformed into the regional administrative hub for Russian colonial and Soviet regimes. Uzbekistan's broadcast media, recording studios and national conservatory are based in Tashkent, attracting aspiring artists from all corners of Uzbekistan.

Tashkent's own local musical traditions are linked to those of the Fergana Valley, whose musicians are the most influential in contemporary Uzbek music. The Ferghana Valley art music tradition, known as the Fergana or Chahar *maqom*, developed in the courts of the Uzbek Khanate at Kokand, and in the medieval Timurid center, Andijon. The repertoire of Sherali Juraev, leading exponent of the 'serious' (*og'ir*) style of Uzbek popular music, is rooted in a simplification of *maqom* melodies adapted to a mixed ensemble of native and amplified Western instruments. Yulduz Usmanova, the model for female singers in the 'rowdy' (*sho'x*) style of popular dance music, draws major inspiration from the melodies and formal structure of Uzbek folk songs of the Fergana Valley and Tashkent region.

Other important regional art music traditions in Uzbek music include the famous 'Shashmaqom' of Samarqand and Bukhara, and the 'Khorezm Maqom' ('Xorazm Maqomi') of Khiva. The corresponding folk music traditions of Samarqand and Bukhara reflect a strong Tajik (Persian) influence, while the folk traditions of Khorezm share a strong bond with the music of Azerbaijan. Song forms, poetic imagery, dance rhythms and melodic elements from all these regional traditions appear in the music of contemporary musicians across Uzbekistan, including those in the dominant Tashkent/Ferghana tradition.

The most eclectic of Uzbek pop musicians, and the musician most credited with bringing Western pop elements into Uzbek music is Farrukh Zakirov, leader since 1972 of the Tashkent based ensemble Yalla. His music can be said to reflect the Soviet internationalist vision of Tashkent as the modern Eurasian metropolis with its cosmopolitan mix of Uzbek, Arab, Turkish, Russian, Hindi and Western pop styles.

Bibliography

Allworth, Edward A. 1990. *The Modern Uzbeks: From the Fourteenth Century to the Present: A Cultural History*. Stanford, CA: Hoover Institution Press, Stanford University.

Karomatov, Faizullah. 1972. 'On the Regional Styles of Uzbek Music.' *Asian Music* 4(1): 48–58.

Levin, Theodore Craig. 1996. *The Hundred Thousand Fools of God: Musical Travels in Central Asia (and Queens, New York)*. Bloomington and Indianapolis: Indiana University Press.

Discography

Jo'raev (Juraev), Sherali. *Karvon*. Melodiya S30 24777 005. *1986*: Uzbekistan.

Usmanova, Yulduz. *Alma, Alma*. Blue Flame 09006-23050-2. *1994*: USA.

Yalla (Farrukh Zakirov). *Beard of the Camel*. Imagina 70950-11010-2-4. *1995*: USA.

Yalla (Farrukh Zakirov). *Jinouni*. Imagina 70950-11011-2-3. *2000*: USA.

CRAIG MACRAE

2. Indian Subcontinent

Bangladesh and West Bengal (India)

Population: Bangladesh: 138,448,210 (2003); West Bengal: 80,220,000 (2003)

The geographical area now called Bangladesh was in the Indian state of Bengal until partition in 1947, when it became part of the newly formed nation of Pakistan. Until 1971 present-day Bangladesh was known as East Pakistan. Following a war of independence in 1971, Bangladesh was established as a separate nation. The official religion of Bangladesh is Islam, in contrast to the predominantly Hindu culture of neighboring Indian West Bengal.

In many respects Bangladesh shares musical characteristics that are also common to Pakistan and India. Specifically, its musical heritage is closely related to that of the Indian state of West Bengal; in fact, it would be inaccurate to speak of the two areas as having different musical cultures. Hindustani or Northern Indian classical music is the major classical system in Bangladesh and *filmi* music (or *chaya chobir gan* as it is known in Bengali), music from popular Indian films, has the same omnipresent influence in Bangladesh as it does elsewhere in South Asia. However, the folk and popular genres of West Bengal and Bangladesh are unique in many important respects. In particular, the presence of a number of Bengali language-specific genres gives modern Bangladeshi music a distinctive identity. The centrality of the musician-songwriter is a constant feature of the Bengali cultural and musical life, the most famous twentieth-century exponents of popular and political Bengali song being Rabindranath Tagore (1861–1941) and Kazi Nazrul Islam (1899–1976). Any definition of Bengali popular music would be complex, as, in contrast to Western definitions of popular music, which may emphasize music disseminated primarily through the mass medium of recording, Bengali music has a long tradition of popular song styles that have adapted to changing media rather than being the result of them.

Musical and Cultural Background

The music of West Bengal and Bangladesh can be divided into several broad categories, which have had a direct influence on popular musical forms: devotional and folk genres, theater music and *adhunik gān* (modern song).

There is a large repertoire of devotional Bengali-language song (*gīt, gīti, gīta*) dating back to the ninth century and developing through to the twentieth century (Goswami 2000, 844–48). These genres of music such as *Carya gīti, Gīta Govinda, Sri Krishna Kirtan, Padavali Kirtan, Saktapada sangīt* and others have in common a devotional aesthetic, in particular themes of separation both human and spiritual, that has had a significant influence on many other genres of *adhunik*, or modern song. This music is distinguished by being linked to a number of specific composers, including Jayadeva (ca. 1178), Baru Chandidas, Narottama Thakur (1531–87), Kamalakanta Bhattacarya (1772–1821), Nidhu Babu (1741–1839) and Raja Rammohan Roy (1744–1833).

Forms of folk music such as that of the itinerant *baul* singers of West Bengal have also had a lasting influence on the development of popular forms, particularly in the compositions of Rabindranath Tagore.

Dating from the late nineteenth century, a

distinctive form of theater music emerged in Kolkata (Calcutta). This music drew influences from a number of classical, folk, regional and religious forms, and became a focus for the composition and dissemination of patriotic songs from 1875 to Indian independence in 1947. Theater music also incorporated Western influences through the widespread use of Western-style orchestras. This style of theater music in Bengal had a significant influence on the emerging *filmi* songs of the 1930s.

The broad term *adhunik gān* (modern song) refers to songs composed throughout the twentieth century. It covers the work of a number of urban composers but is generally considered to describe songwriting after Tagore. The term seeks to distinguish this body of music from older, traditional devotional and folk genres, although *adhunik gān* may draw extensively on these as part of its general musical language. The development of different types of modern song is closely linked to the rise of the recording and film industry in the early decades of the twentieth century. *Adhunik gān* may therefore refer to songs by composers such as Kazi Nazrul Islam, as well as film song and other popular genres.

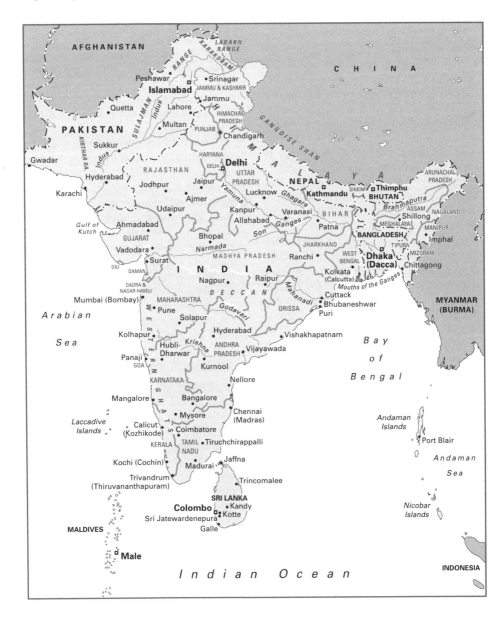

Composers

Several important composers contributed significantly to the development of modern song in the first decades of the twentieth century in Bengal. A central figure is Rabindranath Tagore, whose vast body of song compositions has become known as a musical genre in it own right: *Rabindrasangīt* (literally Rabindramusic). Tagore came from one of the most famous families of Calcutta, part of the burgeoning Western-educated intelligentsia who were central to the artistic and cultural movement known as 'The Bengal Renaissance.' He would later win the Nobel Prize for literature for his poetry (1913). Tagore received his early education in Britain. His elder brother Jyotirindranath Tagore (1849–1925) was well known as a composer and poet. He used Western compositional models and played the piano. His musical views had a significant influence on his younger brother. Rabindranath Tagore's songs drew on a number of musical sources, including classical forms such as *dhrūpad* and folk music, from *baul* song to Scottish and Irish folk music. His songs covered a wide range of themes that included nature, patriotism and love songs. Unlike some of the musical models he drew upon, Tagore eschewed improvisation in favor of stricter and more composer-controlled music. As the British musicologist A.H. Fox-Strangways, who visited Tagore at his ashram in Shantineketan in the first decade of the twentieth century, noted: 'These [Tagore] songs show a securer balance and stronger sense of rhythmical proportion than many Hindostani songs, and without doing violence to the principles of music, bind it in a closer grip' (1914, 99). The style of Tagore songs was highly influential on later composers of Bengali song. A Tagore composition became the Indian national anthem after independence, and another became the national anthem of the newly formed state of Bangladesh.

Unlike Tagore, Kazi Nazrul Islam did not come from the urban milieu of Calcutta, but was born into a poor rural family and received his musical education performing in folk music troupes (Goswami 2000, 853). He became a prolific composer, creating thousands of songs. His first compositions reflected his opposition to British rule in India and the *swadeshi* movement of the time. He was arrested for his political activities in 1922. In the mid-1920s he began using the *ghazal* form to compose songs in Bengali. This was an unusual and innovative step. *Ghazal* is a form of Persian poetry in rhyming couplets which became the basis for a widespread

light classical music form in North India from the eighteenth century, particularly in Lucknow. Significantly, it is primarily a product of Indo-Islamic culture and is usually sung in Urdu. With its themes of love and longing, often unrequited, it would later form a perfect basis for thousands of *filmi* songs in modern times. Until Nazrul's time, the *ghazal* had received little attention as a form of composition by Bengali composers. However, he made this form his own, composing new lyrics in Bengali, and his new songs received wide acclaim. He joined the Gramophone Company of India in 1928 and began to compose in a number of different styles, becoming a central exponent of *adhunik* song. His music was used extensively in films. The subject matter of his songs brings together Islamic and Hindu themes, and the fusion of these religious elements in his music is in many respects unique. More than any other composer Nazrul represented a strong cultural and music identity for the new state of Bangladesh, not least because of his strong connections with Islamic culture. He moved to Dhaka in 1972 after a long illness which had effectively ended his career as a composer in 1942. In Bangladesh he was honored by the state as the national poet of Bangladesh. He died there in 1976.

Although Tagore and Nazrul are towering figures in the history of twentieth-century Bengali music, many predecessors and contemporaries made important and lasting contributions to the development of modern Bengali music. In particular, Dwijendralal Ray (1863–1913) experimented with Indian and Western forms; Rajani Kanta (Rajanikanta) Sen (1865–1910) combined folk and classical musical elements; Atulprasad Sen (1871–1934) worked with a number of Indian classical forms including *khyāl*, *thumri* and *ghazal*.

Musical Form and Instrumentation

Although drawing largely on Indian music forms and instrumentation, much Bengali music is characterized by a more eclectic approach. The musical roots of *adhunik gān* lie in a number of classical folk and popular forms, but the nature of the songs allows for wide diversity of interpretation and instrumentation. As elsewhere in the northern area of the Indian subcontinent, the harmonium is ubiquitous and used to accompany a variety of songs, including *Nazrulgīt* and *Rabindrasangīt*, although Tagore himself loathed the instrument and called it 'that bane of Indian music' (Tagore 1961, 4). Similarly, the North Indian *tablā* is commonly used. However, the many musical aspects of *adhunik* song have allowed for broader musical interpretations. Western instruments such as guitar and piano are frequently used, and rather than being a purely solo song form, this type of song commonly involves group singing.

Modern Developments

After the separation of India and Pakistan in 1947, large-scale migration took place by Hindus from East Pakistan (now Bangladesh) to India, and by Muslims from West Bengal to East Pakistan. These demographic upheavals had far-reaching effects on musical culture. Dhaka, now with a predominantly Muslim population, became the cultural center of East Bengali music, whereas previously Calcutta had been the center for all Bengali culture. The division between Hindu and Muslim populations meant that new forms developed in the predominantly Islamic milieu of Dhaka, although this was complicated by the traditional suspicion of musical activity within some Muslim religious circles.

In parallel with the continuance of *adhunik* song as a central genre of music, a new repertoire of patriotic songs developed in response to perceived domination by East Pakistan. Tagore and Nazrul patriotic songs became prominent again but in a new political context. A central facet of this struggle was now to institute Bengali as the national language of East Pakistan, and in 1952 students demonstrating for this cause were shot and killed by police. From this point on agitation for independence was an important social and cultural movement, in which music played a central role. The struggle for independence resulted in the war of 1971 and the establishment of the state of Bangladesh.

Throughout this period *filmi* has been an important focus for popular music composition in Bangladesh, as it is throughout the Indian subcontinent. Although influenced by Hindi-language film music, there had been an indigenous Bengali film industry since the 1930s; it drew on a variety of music sources, notably theater music, as noted above. Through the channels of film music a number of popular and devotional Indian and Pakistani musical genres have been adapted to Bengali popular song, including *bhangra* and *qawwāli*. It is also common practice for cover versions of hit Hindi-language songs to be dubbed in Bengali for sale in West Bengal and Bangladesh.

Despite the popularity of indigenous musical forms in West Bengal and Bangladesh, Western popular music has had a significant impact in recent years. A new generation of urban youth sees Western pop as their reference point, and bands such as Ark, Souls, Jewel, and Generation 2000, although producing songs in both Bengali and English, draw almost exclusively on Western models of pop and rock in terms of instrumentation and musical form.

Bibliography
Fox-Strangways, A.H. 1914. *The Music of Hindonstan.* Oxford: Clarendon Press.
Goswami, K. 2000. 'West Bengal and Bangladesh.' In *The Garland Encyclopedia of World Music. Vol. 5: South Asia: The Indian Subcontinent*, ed. A. Arnold. New York: Garland, 842–63.
Tagore, R. 1961. 'Reminiscences.' In *Sangeet Natak Academy Bulletin: Rabindranath Tagore Centenary Number*. New Delhi: Sangeet Natak Academy.
GERRY FARRELL and JAYEETA BHOWMICK

India
Population: 1,029,991,145 (2001)

India has the world's second-largest population, which now exceeds one billion people. The neighboring countries of Pakistan, Bangladesh (part of India until 1947), Nepal and Sri Lanka share many aspects of Indian culture, together constituting a broader South Asian cultural entity. India's population, however, is extremely heterogeneous in terms of language, religion, music and other aspects of culture. Around 16 major languages and over 1,500 lesser languages and dialects are spoken; most North Indian languages, especially those in the Hindi family, are Indo-Aryan tongues, while the main South Indian languages belong to the Dravidian family. Around 80 percent of Indians are Hindu, 14 percent Muslim, and the remainder mostly Sikh, Christian, Buddhist and animist. Levels of socioeconomic development are particularly diverse, with the country hosting communities of technologically primitive hunter-gatherers, along with nuclear physicists. Around three-quarters of the population remain rural. India is sometimes characterized as constituting two countries, one of roughly the population and level of affluence of France, and another, constituting the remaining 95 percent of the population, which lives in moderate to abject poverty. Since the late 1970s the size, self-consciousness and cosmopolitan sophistication of the bourgeoisie have increased markedly. Since achieving independence from Great Britain in 1947, although beset by spasms of

2. Indian Subcontinent

regional, ethnic and religious tensions, the nation has been able to persist as a political entity, due largely to its practices, however deeply flawed, of democracy, civil liberty and cultural pluralism.

India has long hosted one of the world's richest music cultures, which has adapted quite well to the pressures and dislocations of modernity. The country's two classical music systems, North Indian or Hindustani music and South Indian or Karnatak music, thrive with considerable vigor. Many regional folk music traditions continue to flourish, whether menaced or stimulated by the mass media and other aspects of socioeconomic change. For their part, Indian popular music styles have evolved as remarkably vital entities, freely adopting elements from the West while retaining their own stylistically indigenous character. Indian film music, which has dominated the popular music scene since the 1930s, has also enjoyed considerable international popularity, being spread, especially via the films themselves, throughout much of Asia, Africa and elsewhere. In recent decades the popular music scene has been further invigorated, internally by the decentralization of the industry via cassettes, and abroad by the growth and increasing cultural vitality of diasporic communities, especially in Great Britain and North America.

North India

Popular Music Outside of Cinema

Indian popular music is often thought of as roughly synonymous with commercial film music, because of the predominance of that genre from the mid-1930s until the present. However, incipient forms of popular music existed independently of cinema for nearly three decades before the advent of sound film, and, after surviving marginally for the next half-century, reemerged with unprecedented vigor and diversity with the spread of cassettes in the 1980s.

Insofar as popular music can be conceived as music that evolves in connection with the commercial mass media, embryonic forms of Indian popular music can be said to have emerged in the first decade of the twentieth century. From 1902 the Gramophone Company of India (later absorbed by EMI, and using the logo 'His Master's Voice' or HMV) started energetically marketing recordings of diverse indigenous classical, light-classical and regional folk genres throughout the subcontinent. The market for these genres was largely restricted to the urban bourgeoisie who could afford phonographs and, from the 1920s, radios. For its part,

classical music did not enjoy mass popularity, and regional folk genres faced their own natural market limitations.

However, a few 'light' genres did enjoy pan-regional appeal and soon came to be marketed with special intensity by EMI and the handful of small indigenous competitors. The Urdu *ghazal*, or sung versions thereof, had enjoyed considerable popularity throughout urban North India as a light-classical genre, especially since Hindi-Urdu functioned as a pan-regional lingua franca. *Ghazals* constituted a considerable portion of recorded output during this period, with singers like Gauhar Jan coming to earn wide renown, as well as considerable wealth, through their recordings. *Ghazal* consists of a series of couplets (in the rhyme and melodic scheme AA BA CA, etc.) set to a fixed meter and employing a conventional vocabulary of images and metaphors. When sung in the light-classical style, improvisatory *bol banâo* passages (textual-melodic elaboration) would be performed on the non-rhyming lines, and the verses would be punctuated by *tablā* improvisations called *laggi*. Increasingly, however, the commercially marketed *ghazals* tended to eliminate improvisation, replacing the *laggi* passages with pre-composed ensemble interludes, and having the vocalist sing relatively fixed melodies instead of *bol banâo*. In coming to constitute a fixed song rather than a sample of improvisation, this variety of *ghazal* evolved in the direction of a commercial popular music, instead of a genteel light-classical genre informed by art music. Such tendencies could also be seen in other urban genres which evolved in tandem with music theater, such as Marathi *lâvni*.

With the advent of sound cinema in 1931, film music soon emerged as the dominant popular music genre throughout India. Many early film songs followed the conventions already established in the record industry, particularly, for example, in the case of *ghazals*. However, film songs rapidly developed their own conventions and aesthetics, which came to dominate the popular music scene as a whole. Popular music independent of cinema came to be thoroughly marginalized by the slick sounds emanating from the Bombay (now Mumbai) studios, and the largely derivative styles of regional-language cinema. Film music production itself came to be dominated by EMI's near monopoly, and by a small coterie of singers and composers. For its part, the *ghazal* evolved into a sub-style of film music, while continuing to survive in other contexts as a sophisticated light-classical genre. While

EMI continued to market a limited number of records of classical and, to a lesser extent, folk music, from the 1940s until the spread of cassettes around 1980, very little 'non-*filmi*' popular music was produced by the music industry.

From the late 1970s, the structure and output of the South Asian music industry came to be dramatically altered by the spread of cassette technology, which ended the monopolization of the music industry by EMI and the film world. Cassettes and cassette players were considerably cheaper and more durable than records and phonographs, and had simpler power requirements. As such, cassettes could be purchased by a much broader range of people, including lower-class consumers and villagers without access to electricity. Most importantly, commercial production of cassettes was exponentially cheaper than production of vinyl records, not to mention feature films. As such, the somewhat belated spread of cassette technology in India precipitated the emergence of an entire new sector of the music industry, which was free from HMV and cinematic dominance and could cater to the tastes of a wide diversity of consumers.

From the mid-1970s, much of the early cassette output was devoted, as it has continued to be, to film music, and cassettes have thus served to increase the dissemination of film music, especially beyond the urban middle classes. However, a new generation of 'non-*filmi*' popular musics – which had been marginalized for so many decades – soon made their appearance. The first of these genres to flourish was a stylized and simplified form of the *ghazal*, which could still enjoy enough pan-regional popularity to sustain a broad-based consumer audience in the days when cassette and cassette-player ownership was just beginning to spread. The new *ghazal* style, as popularized initially by Pakistani singers Mehdi Hasan and Ghulam Ali, appealed especially to middle-class listeners who, while generally uninterested in classical music, felt alienated by the increasing disco-style rowdiness of much film music and sought at least a facsimile of the refinement and sophistication of the light-classical *ghazal*. For their part, cassette producers, including local firms as well as EMI, sought to circumvent pirate cassette producers by offering a genre – the new pop *ghazal* – with smooth, silky timbres that would be poorly reproduced on the generally inferior pirate tapes. Especially as popularized by the subsequent generation of singers such as Jagjit and Chitra Singh, the pop *ghazal* came to

employ simple, accessible Urdu, relaxed vocal improvisation on the first line of each couplet, and catchy refrains, over a leisurely, languid rhythmic background. Critics note that it lacks the skillful improvisation and expressive intensity of the traditional light-classical *ghazal*, and serves very well as 'easy-listening' music in offices, elevators and, especially, restaurants.

In the wake of pop *ghazal* emerged a vogue of cassette-based Hindu devotional music styles. These have included a mainstream, *ghazal*-influenced, solo *bhajan* genre, as sung by vocalists like Anup Jalota and Pankaj Udhas, and a variety of stylized lesser genres associated with particular regional cults, deities, festivities and rituals. Many of these combine traditional elements with film-influenced melodies and instrumentation. Although the *ghazal* boom has waned somewhat at present, the vogue of cassette-based devotional musics has continued unabated, reflecting both the diversity of Hindu-oriented traditional musics and the lively resurgence of pop Hinduism in general.

By the early 1980s, commercial cassette producers in North India came to constitute not only large companies like EMI and T-Series, but also over 300 smaller producers. Many of these have been fledgling 'cottage cassette' enterprises which record and market diverse regional musics to local audiences. Much of this cassette output has consisted of recordings of folk music in purely traditional style. A significant proportion, however, has comprised relatively new subgenres explicitly associated with cassettes, often using film-style orchestration or other studio enhancements. In their evolutionary association with the mass media (especially cassettes), many such genres combine features of both folk music and commercial, syncretic popular music. Particularly popular among rural listeners are tapes of ribald songs, based on folk genres (e.g., Braj *rasiya*, Haryanvi *rāgini* and Maharashtrian *popat*), but produced especially to be marketed on cassette. In Gujerat, pop versions of indigenous *garbā* and *rās* have flourished in connection with the vogue of these social-dance genres. Punjabi popular music has been particularly dynamic, encompassing text-oriented songs of artists like Gurdas Maan, and more Westernized forms of pop *bhangra* (*bhangra* being a traditional Punjabi folk dance). The latter has evolved in a parallel fashion as a product of both South Asian Punjabis and Punjabi emigrant communities, especially in Great Britain. International renown also helped to boost the local popularity of a few artists, such as the late *qawwāli* superstar Nusrat Fateh Ali Khan. Along with reaching ethnic, linguistic and regional niches, much of the cassette output has consisted of topical songs, in various styles and languages, which address contemporary sociopolitical events, from dowry murders to the 1999 Kargill conflict with Pakistan.

The cassette revolution effectively decentralized and democratized the South Asian music industry, providing a new vehicle for music idioms that could respond to the tastes of diverse consumers rather than seeking simply to provide a common-denominator film music. Some critics deplore the lewdness and triviality of much of the cassette output, and it could be argued that some of the new mass-mediated popular musics appear to be flourishing at the expense of live performance. Nevertheless, there is no doubt that cassettes have revitalized regional-music traditions and have offered new mass-mediated alternatives to the otherwise hegemonic film music industry.

Since 1990 the 'non-*filmi*' popular music scene in North India has continued to thrive and diversify. Much of the most dynamic activity in the Indian popular music scene – including the most creative uses of new media technologies – has taken place in the 'upper end' of the market, that is, the proportionately small but in absolute size quite substantial urban bourgeois youth culture. Compact discs, although prohibitively expensive for most South Asians, have become a preferred format for upper-class consumers. Television has also become an influential medium for local and imported popular music. Television's expansion had commenced in the early 1980s, partly due to state policies of media modernization and economic deregulation. It was not until a decade later, however, that television blossomed as an independent medium for music. In this respect, its effects have been diverse. While television has served as an essential vehicle for Indian films and their music, the advent of satellite and cable television networks – which were reaching 10 million homes by 1996 – has led to the emergence of several music-oriented programs and channels, much of whose content is independent of cinema per se. In the wake of MTV International, locally produced music videos have now become established components of Indian music culture. Stylistically, these often represent a confluence of Western, MTV-type aesthetics and the largely indigenous conventions of the song-and-dance scenes in Indian commercial cinema. As elsewhere in the Third World, Indian music videos

are quickly developing their own clichés and formulae, and in some cases are becoming more sophisticated in production standards. Such music videos, as in the West, are only marginal commercial entities in themselves, and serve primarily – and even more transparently – as advertisements for films or non-*filmi* pop recordings, from *bhangra* to *ghazal*. Recapitulating the role of cassettes in the early 1980s, commercial music-video shows do not disseminate a cross section of Indian popular music, but only genres oriented toward the urban bourgeoisie, and especially those with pan-regional appeal such as Hindi pop or film music.

Television has made the complex Indian dialectic between local and imported musics more overtly visible. Music-video networks such as MTV have served to further promote Western pop music, helping to double its sales in the early 1990s alone. This trend, however, has been effectively offset by the broadcasting of Indian-produced videos promoting local music. Thus, while television was essential in boosting sales of foreign music to some 5 percent of the Indian market in 1996, it should be kept in mind that this figure represents a rather small amount in comparison to that of many countries, from Canada to Tunisia. If anything, the fact that some 95 percent of music purchased remains local illustrates the ongoing internal dynamism and resilience of the Indian popular music industry. There is no doubt that Westernization is increasingly conspicuous in the techno-pop styles favored in much film music, and in Hindi pop and other independent genres. However, these styles continue to draw from indigenous traditions (whether old or new), as in the disco-style remixes of old Hindi film songs and Punjabi folk tunes. Paralleling these developments has been the emergence of a lively discothèque scene in Mumbai and other cities, although social dancing per se (and especially couple dancing) remains rare outside the milieu of the Westernized elite.

The new media such as computer networks and cable and satellite television have considerably intensified the availability and popularity of Indian popular music outside India, especially but not only among diasporic communities. These communities are increasingly developing their own distinctive popular music cultures; paradoxically, as India itself becomes ever more remote to these third- and fourth-generation nonresident Indian citizens (NRIs), they are increasingly able and inclined to access Indian popular music through the mass media, from Web sites to music-video programs.

Popular Film Music

The predominant form of popular music in North India is *filmi gīt* (film song), which arose in conjunction with the Indian sound film industry in the 1930s. Virtually all Indian commercial feature films since this time have incorporated on-screen songs and dances to heighten their appeal to Indian audiences. Transmitted not only via cinema but also by radio, audio and video recordings, television and, most recently, the Internet, Indian film songs have prospered both as an essential cinematic element and as a popular music genre. Other forms of Indian music – rural and urban, devotional and secular – have enjoyed popularity prior to and alongside film songs, particularly on a local and regional level. Since the 1980s non-film popular music production has grown significantly, encompassing new genres such as *indipop, indirock, bhangrapop* and remix. Yet, as the rapid and wide-spread distribution and promotion of film songs continue, this genre remains India's primary mass-mediated popular music.

The Beginnings of Film Song   The three major North Indian centers of film production in the 1930s and 1940s were Mumbai (Bombay) and Pune in the west and Kolkata (Calcutta) in the east. Ardeshir Irani and his Imperial Film Company in Mumbai produced the nation's first 'talkie' feature film *Alam Ara* (Beauty of the World) in March 1931, based on a popular stage play of the same name, and incorporated seven songs within the narrative. The production proved so successful at the box office that sound filmmakers in all three centers rapidly followed with similar musical film productions, mostly on mythological and historical subjects. By combining music, dance and drama the early sound film producers were drawing on India's long and diverse history of theatrical entertainment – ancient classical Sanskrit drama, religious plays, regional theater (*jatra, tamasha, nautanki)* and urban stage traditions (Urdu and Parsi theater) – to create this new twentieth-century genre of popular musical cinema.

Film actors and actresses sang the film songs on camera in the early 1930s. Many came from the stage, and some had received classical vocal training. Musical accomplishment among singers was thus uneven. The songs were typically light-classical or devotional in style, consisting of a solo singer with harmonium and *tablā* accompaniment, and were interspersed throughout the narrative. Since few early sound film companies initially employed song composers (later known as music directors), actors and actresses had to draw on their own musical knowledge, talent and experience in singing lyrics provided by the producer, scriptwriter or director. In the Prabhat Film Company in Pune, for example, Master Krishnarao produced songs as he did for the Marathi stage, where 'music selectors' chose classical or light-classical *rāgas*, playwrights composed new lyrics to fit the meter and scansion of the original composition, and actor-singers performed the 'song' for at least 20 minutes. His early film songs were shorter in length but were still *rāga*-based performances generally approximating existing song structures (*thumri, bhajan*, etc.).

Instrumental accompaniment was one of the few stylistic traits that distinguished early film songs from non-film songs. To the *tablā* and harmonium commonly used for stage music and silent film accompaniment film music directors added the *sārangi* and the violin, and by the mid-1930s the ensemble included *sitār*, piano, cello, mandolin and clarinet. Western instruments were readily available in India, still under colonial rule until 1947, and especially in Mumbai and Pune Goan musicians were increasingly in demand for their Western musical training and their ability to read Western notation. Film music directors added folk instruments and regional musical styles to produce songs appropriate for bilingual and trilingual film versions common in the three regional centers. Prabhat's orchestra in Pune, for example, included *jaltarang, jhanjh, dholak* and *tuntun*, and its Marathi music directors drew on the *lāvni* and *tamāsha* styles of Maharashtra. The rapid adoption of Western instruments by the New Theatres Film Company in Calcutta led to early experiments by Rai Chand Boral (*Vidyapati* [1937], *Street Singer* [1938]), with harmonic arrangements and long instrumental interludes between vocal phrases.

Commercial disc recordings of film songs were not initially produced. The British-owned Gramophone Company (later the Gramophone Company of India and now Saregama India Ltd., with the logo EMI-India) had begun regularly recording a few songs from each film by 1934, but not until about 1937 were all film songs regularly recorded. The demand for gramophone records had already been established when cheap phonograph machines made in Japan invaded the Indian market in the late 1920s (Joshi 1988). Further media exposure came via the national broadcasting service All India Radio, which began transmitting film songs on a daily basis probably in the late 1930s.

The Establishment of Commercial Popular Film Music
In the 1940s the revolutionary advance to double-system cinematography with separate recording of sound and picture gave birth to the playback singer. Producers hired trained singers to record film songs for the film soundtrack, which was 'played back' during film shooting to allow the actors to lip-sync the lyrics. Heard but not seen, playback singers became the voices of India's popular music. Their renditions of film songs spread rapidly via radio and gramophone records in addition to cinema, earning them widespread fame and adulation. Among a variety of actress-singers and playback singers in the mid-1940s, Noor Jehan in Mumbai was awarded the title 'Mallika-e-Tarannum' (Queen of Melody) for her powerful, weighty voice. After she emigrated to Pakistan in 1947, the thinner, higher-pitched voice of playback singer Lata Mangeshkar attracted attention, and over the next three decades Lata and her sister Asha dominated the world of female playback singing. Following the extraordinary success and popularity of male actor-singer Kundan Lal Saigal in the 1930s and early 1940s, the best-known male playback singers were Manna Day, Mohammad Rafi, Mukesh, Talat Mahmood and Kishore Kumar.

When the major film studios in Mumbai, Pune and Kolkata collapsed in the 1940s, unable to compete financially with the rising number of independent filmmakers capitalizing on the war-time economy, film and film song production diverged along linguistic lines. Hindustani, a spoken dialect related to Hindi and Urdu, prevailed as the favored film language capable of reaching the widest possible audience in northern India, and Hindi film production (encompassing these languages) became centralized in the cosmopolitan port city of Mumbai. Regional-language production primarily in Bengali, Marathi and Gujarati split from the Hindi film industry, although it remained strongly influenced by it. An important development in song production, enhanced by the centralization of the Hindi film industry in Bollywood (the Bombay Hollywood), was the standardization of a mainstream film song style and sound.

The film song of the 1950s and 1960s, 'the golden age of melody,' was typically a three-and-a-half-minute composition for one or two singers and orchestra in refrain-verse form. The enduring box-office draw of the time was the romantic love story, and each production had at least eight to 10 songs. Song lyrics most commonly expressed the emotions of human relationships, the excitement of festivals and celebrations, or religious devotion, as portrayed by the actors on-screen. By the 1950s, music directors employed studio orchestras consisting of up to a hundred musicians, modeled on the Western symphony orchestra combined with Indian instrumentation. Western harmony was relatively simple when used, and orchestration was often in unison with the melody or a simple bass line support. Particularly distinctive was the vocal style, unlike that of any other Indian vocal music. The female vocal sound, established by Lata Mangeshkar and imitated by others, was high-pitched and thin; male singers crooned in a high or mid-range voice.

Cinema, radio and gramophone records remained the three forms of mass media disseminating film songs up to the 1960s. The Gramophone Company held a monopoly in the Indian recording industry, releasing the vast majority of film songs on LP and EP records. All India Radio started a weekly film song hit parade – *Binaca Geet Mala* – based on audience ratings and record sales in the early 1950s that became one of its most popular broadcasts of the time. Realizing the potential of these media, film producers began to release song recordings prior to a film's release as an enticement to Indian audiences. The demand for novelty increased, and in their efforts to achieve new effects in their song compositions film music directors drew on diverse sources, including classical Hindustani *rāgas*, regional folk songs, Western classical compositions, and Caribbean and Latin American tunes. Naushad, Vasant Desai and Madan Mohan, for example, frequently adopted classical or light-classical styles; Anil Biswas and O.P. Nayyar introduced Bengali and Punjabi musical traits, respectively; and C. Ramchandra experimented with various Latin American rhythms and forms.

New Trends and Competition In the 1970s romantic film melodramas gave way to themes of violence and revenge, and film songs accordingly decreased both in number per film and in stature. Popular cinema responded to the nation's political climate of widespread discontent, decreasing confidence in the modern state, and increasing poverty and unemployment. In a succession of extraordinarily popular action movies, the superhero Amitabh Bachchan played an angry young man who personally took on an enemy of the common people – a drug lord, mafia leader, smuggler, but never the system itself – sought revenge and restored order (Kazmi 1996). The films' songs were typically fast-paced and less lyrical than those of previous decades, accompanying wild dance scenes and allowing chase or fight episodes to occur during instrumental interludes. Music directors borrowed freely from pop styles in vogue elsewhere, such as Kalyanji-Anandji's disco dance songs in *Qurbani* (1980).

Film songs in the 1980s and 1990s continued to play an ancillary role in violent action movies, but made a significant resurgence in the latest love films that mixed emotional drama with violence. Music directors such as Anand Milind and Raam Laxman returned to romantic song melodies and met with phenomenal success in the films *Qayamat Se Qayamat Tak* (1988) and *Maine Pyar Kiya* (1989), respectively. Western beats and synthesized sounds became commonplace. Borrowing and adapting foreign styles and even songs was now a conventional approach to film song composition, as in Raam Laxman's version of the Stevie Wonder hit 'I Just Called to Say I Love You' in *Maine Pyar Kiya*. A host of new playback artists joined the industry, including Kavita Krishnamurty, Udit Narayan, Anuradha Paudwal, Sadhana Sargam, Suresh Wadkar and Alka Yagnik. Unlike their predecessors, these artists sought public exposure through live performance, and they gained popularity and success through international multi-star entertainment shows that have now become a regular engagement for playback artists.

The first genuine challenge to the recording industry monopoly held by the Gramophone Company of India came from the German-based Polydor record company in the late 1960s. Previous attempts by the National Record Company and foreign labels Columbia and Odeon had been thwarted by EMI (Joshi 1988). However, the introduction of cassette tape and the portable cassette recorder in the late 1970s proved an insurmountable challenge. New small-scale companies and individuals could afford the cheap technology to produce their own audiocassette recordings, which led not only to a vast increase in the amount and variety of Indian music recordings but also to 'an unprecedented degree of diversity and responsiveness in the popular-music scene' (Manuel 1993, 24).

The introduction of other new technologies has both enhanced and harmed the popular film music industry. The national television broadcasting service Doordarshan, whose limited broadcasting in the 1960s and 1970s increased dramatically in the early 1980s, found its Indian film and film song programs to be among its most popular broadcasts.

Initially beneficial to the film music industry, television proved detrimental to the industry both by attracting audiences away from the cinema and by opening the way for videocassette recording and viewing. Piracy plagued the videocassette industry as it did the audiocassette market, further threatening film and film music producers. Their collective complaints in the early to mid-1980s convinced the national government to legislate against the sale and exhibition of unauthorized films, and film producers simultaneously developed protective rights for the legal production and distribution of video prints. While video piracy has continued, the video market has nevertheless aided the global dissemination of Indian cinema and film song, which has most recently benefited from the latest technologies of satellite television and the Internet.

The growth of a non-film pop music market since the late 1980s encompassing such genres as *indipop*, *indirock* and *bhangrapop* has presented direct competition for the Indian film music industry and playback singers. Pop artists such as Alisha Chinai, the Colonial Cousins, Daler Mehndi and Shubha Mudgal have gained international recognition through live performance, compact disc recordings, music videos, television and the World Wide Web. However, since the 1990s the distinction between film and non-film music has begun to blur, increasing media attention for the film music industry; playback singers have released non-film song albums and non-film artists have been invited to record film songs. The start of the twenty-first century is witnessing healthy competition in the Indian popular music market and, as Indian film music circulates the globe via audio and video recordings, satellite television and the Internet, it remains a potent force within Indian popular culture.

South India

South Indian popular music is an increasing part of an Indian pop sound that now carries around the world. It is heard in the Middle East, Ukraine, North Africa, Malaysia and Indonesia, the Caribbean, and also in Indian communities in London, New York, Toronto and San Francisco. As South Indian sounds carry around the world, they retain important musical qualities from South Indian musical cultures. The South Indian states share a distinctly southern folk and classical culture, and also a linguistic heritage from the Dravidian language family. As in North India, film songs comprise the leading popular music genre. Other genres include popularized rural and urban folk songs and songs of Hindu religious devotion. Since the 1980s, the advent of affordable cassette players to the region has facilitated a greatly expanded range of non-film popular musics.

Film Song

South India's film industry is centered in Chennai, a city formerly known as Madras and the capital of Tamil Nadu. A handful of film companies produces most of the popular songs in the languages of Tamil, Telugu, Malayalam and Kannada. In South India, as in the North, virtually every film is a musical. Song and dance numbers are interspersed in the film narrative, and actors are shown dancing and singing from time to time. Films feature a syncretic dance style generally called disco, which fuses folk, classical and Western elements. Songs from films are continually played back over the radio and through cassette and compact disc players on buses, at general stores, at home, at tea shops and during religious festivals. It is almost impossible to walk through a South Indian village, town or city without hearing film songs. Dickey (1993) argues that, as South Indian filmgoers identify with film characters, they connect their own ways of life to those they see on the screen (67–68). This process of identification is taken beyond the walls of the cinema, for filmgoers re-work and re-perform film songs as folk songs in their own lives (Greene 1995, 239–49).

Film's cultural niche was originally occupied by classical and folk drama companies, which set tales from Hindu mythology to music and dance. These included the classical *kathakali* dramas of Kerala and the folk *terukkuttu* dramas of Tamil Nadu – performances that often lasted several hours. Perhaps the remarkable length of contemporary Indian films – typically three hours or more – can be traced to these drama performances.

The British arranged for the first film screenings in South India sometime during the early 1900s. When silent films were first produced in Chennai in 1916, musical variety acts were performed before and after screenings (Baskaran 1981, 99). Music was thus an important part of film events even before sound film technology. The first sound films in a South Indian language were *Kaalidaas*, produced in 1931, and *Galavarishi*, produced in 1932.

South Indian cinema followed the earlier musical drama traditions in its emphasis on mythologies, its combination of spoken dialog with songs, and its incorporation of dance. Film music, like its musical

theater antecedents, was rooted in Karnatak or South Indian classical music. Music directors such as S.V. Venkatraman and G. Ramanathan developed what has since been termed a 'light-classical' style: music performed on the traditional instruments of Karnatak music, including *vīnā*, *sarod*, *sitār*, *mridangam*, *tablā*, harmonium, flute and violin, based on simplified Karnatak forms, *rāgas*, *tālas* and performance techniques. The new style generally involved reduction of melodic variation and improvisation, and repetition of catchy tunes.

As in the earlier musical dramas, film actors were also singers and sang their own parts. But in the 1940s this began to change. Music directors hired playback singers to sing the original vocal lines, and actors then just mouthed the words. This had become standard practice by the 1950s. As specialists took over singing roles, the film singing style shifted from a loud, open-throated style to a less ornate, smoother, clearer and more nasal style typical of film songs today.

During the 1940s and 1950s, emphasis shifted from films based on mythology to social dramas. In the 1940s these dramas raised awareness of the issues of caste inequity and emerging Indian nationalism, despite attempts by British colonial administrators to censor films presenting potentially revolutionary themes. After Independence in 1947, the social dramas increasingly became flashy and escapist spectacles, such as the 1948 hit *Chandralekha*. Orchestras accompanying film songs became larger and included more Western instruments. Further, the orchestra became more important, increasingly reinforcing shifts in the unfolding dramas and 'transcend[ing] the conventional accompanying role ... by "re-stating" and complementing the lyrical sentiments' (Mohan 1994, 63).

During the 1960s and 1970s, South Indian film songs were strongly influenced by Hollywood and Western classical music. Film orchestras were expanded to include clarinet, cello, saxophone, piano, conga drum, xylophone, vibraphone and mandolin. Music directors such as M.S. Viswanathan and T.K. Ramamoorthy composed music in Western tempered tunings and chordal harmonies.

Starting in 1976 with his first successful film score for the movie *Annakkili* (1976), composer I. Ilaiyaraaja became the leading music director of South Indian films. He is a remarkably capable composer of several styles of music, including Karnatak, Western classical and South Indian folk music. Ilaiyaraaja was born in a farming household, and thus heard Tamil folk songs from a very young age (Mohan 1994, 106–

107). Perhaps because of his rural background, he was always able to compose scores that had an authentic folk flavor. He frequently incorporated folk instruments (Mohan 1994, 117). Ilaiyaraaja was also a master of Western compositional techniques (as demonstrated, for example, in *Priya* [1978]), and he studied and developed a strong command of Karnatak music, which he brought to bear in his score for *Salangai Oli* (1982).

In the 1990s, Ilaiyaraaja brought new music technologies, such as rhythm boxes, MIDI guitar, electronic keyboards and synthesizers, into film music (as, for example, in *Vīrā* [1994]). Throughout his career he has shown a talent for integrating many different styles of music. His syncretic pieces combine very different musical idioms into unified, coherent musical statements. For example, in his album *How to Name It* (1988), he masterfully fuses Karnatak *rāgas* and performance techniques with Western baroque musical textures, and Bach partitas and fugues with the Karnatak *pallavi-anupallavi* form. His music simultaneously appeals to villagers listening for folk rhythms, Karnatak music aficionados listening to the *rāga* and cosmopolitan urbanites listening for 'modern' electronic sounds.

Cassette Technology and the Diversification of Popular Music

The advent of cassettes had as great an impact in South India as in North India, leading to an explosion of new popular music genres starting in the 1980s (Greene 1995; Manuel 1993), including many genres of popularized folk and devotional music. Before audiocassette technology became commonplace, folk music was essentially absent from the South Indian commercial mass media except in the form of occasional borrowings into film music. Now folklore popularizers, such as Professor Vijayalakshmi Navan'thakrishnan of Madurai Kamaraj University and Pushpavanam Kuppuswamy, collect hundreds of genres of folk music and perform and produce them in sound studios, often adding new instruments.

The practice of marketing folk songs on cassette began as an extension of the performing and touring activities of professional folk musicians. Cassettes were marketed in cities and towns where the musicians typically performed. Popular genres include the Tamil *terukkuttu pāttu* – street dramas representing situations from village life that feature several voices to the accompaniment of drums, cymbals and rattles; and *temāngupāttu* – a nondramatic genre featuring a solo voice accompanied by folk percussion. Other folk genres include the Tamil bow song, *utukkuppāttu*, drum songs and *tālāttu* lullabies. Telugu folk singer Gaddar uses cassettes as sounding boards for political messages and socialist concerns, set to music.

During the 1990s, an urban folk music called *gānās* emerged in Tamil Nadu, and was recorded and marketed on cassette. *Gānā* musicians, who are mostly university students, borrow melodies from popular recordings of film, devotional and folk songs, and compose new words reflecting the concerns of student life. Thus, musical borrowings and influences go full circle from popular to folk and from folk to popular, and new musics emerge from this synergy.

The affordable cassette technology also facilitated the production and popularization of a variety of religious musics, and starting in the 1980s the Hindu devotional song could be said to be a genre of popular music. Devotional songs are in strophic or South Indian classical forms, sometimes addressing deities directly, and sometimes offering philosophical insights about religious life. A handful of highly popular devotional singers, notably Yesudas, S. Govindarajan and L.R. Eswari, have produced thousands of songs in several South Indian languages. The most common musical accompaniment is provided by the light-classical instruments *vīnā*, *tablā*, *mridangam*, *nadaswaram*, flute, violin and synthesizer. South Indians incorporate these commercial recordings into personal daily devotion and meditation. Early morning traditions in villages, towns and cities throughout the region are imbued with the music of these commercial recordings. In addition, devotional songs are continually played during religious festivals, weddings and other communal events (Greene 1999, 477).

The advent of audiocassette technology has also made possible the dissemination of devotional music of minority religions such as Islam and, especially in Kerala and Tamil Nadu, Christianity. Most of this music is in Indian languages and in South Indian classical and light-classical styles. Also fairly popular are recordings of instrumental music, which is believed to be *mangalam*: 'auspicious' or pleasing to the Hindu gods (Greene 1999, 465–67). *Mangalam* recordings are commonly played before important events, such as marriages, house openings, *pūjās* (formal rituals) and ear-piercing ceremonies.

Contemporary South Indian Popular Music

Contemporary South Indian popular music has again been influenced by Western popular culture and has become more high-tech, urban-oriented and cosmopolitan. Although rural villagers continue to constitute the leading market for popular music, middle and upper class city-dwellers, especially students, have also become an important market. Music directors such as A.R. Rahman and Karthik Raja produce film scores that are more eclectic, incorporating rap, jazz, reggae, hard rock and fast dance beats (as, for example, for *Duet* [1994], *Kadhalan* [1994] and *Bombay* [1995]). Movie characters are shown living in South Indian cities, sporting Indian and Western fashions and hairstyles, and performing Indian and Western dances. Actor Prabhu Deva is known as the 'Michael Jackson of South India' for his break-dancing talent, which he exhibits, for example, in *Merupu Kallalu* (1997). Also during the 1990s, the remix – a reworking of a familiar song against a shifting musical background with a fast dance beat – became a new pop genre throughout South Asia.

The new South Indian sound has also had an increasing influence on North India. Starting in 1993 with A.R. Rahman's score for *Roja*, South Indian films have been overdubbed in North Indian languages and screened in the North. As South Indian popular music has become an increasing part of the Indian pop influence on East and Southeast Asia, the Middle East, the Caribbean and North Africa, it has retained distinctively South Indian musical elements. In film songs and remixes one can still hear the smooth, clear singing style developed in film songs since the 1940s, the distinctive timbres of South Indian folk percussion and the Karnatak instruments *vīnā*, violin and *mridangam*.

Bibliography

Arnold, Alison. 1988. 'Popular Film Song in India: A Case of Mass Market Musical Eclecticism.' *Popular Music* 7(2): 177–88.

Arnold, Alison. 1991. *Hindi* Filmi Git: *On the History of Commercial Indian Popular Music*. Unpublished Ph.D. thesis, University of Illinois at Urbana-Champaign.

Barnouw, Eric, and Krishnaswamy, S. 1980. *Indian Film*. 2nd ed. New York: Oxford University Press.

Baskaran, Theodore. 1981. *The Message Bearers: The Nationalist Politics and the Entertainment Media in South India 1880–1945*. Chennai: Cre-A.

Bhimani, Harish. 1995. *In Search of Lata Mangeshkar*. New Delhi: HarperCollins Publishers India.

Dickey, Sara. 1993. *Cinema and the Urban Poor in South India*. New Delhi: Foundation Books.

Greene, Paul. 1995. *Cassettes in Culture: Emotion, Politics, and Performance in Rural Tamil Nadu*. Unpublished Ph.D. thesis, University of Pennsylvania.

Greene, Paul. 1999. 'Sound Engineering in a Tamil Village: Playing Audio Cassettes as Devotional Performance.' *Ethnomusicology* 43(3): 459–89.

Joshi, G.N. 1988. 'A Concise History of the Phonograph Industry in India.' *Popular Music* 7(2): 147–56.

Kazmi, Nikhat. 1996. *Ire in the Soul: Bollywood's Angry Years*. New Delhi: HarperCollins Publishers India.

Manuel, Peter. 1988. *Popular Musics of the Non-Western World*. New York: Oxford University Press.

Manuel, Peter. 1993. *Cassette Culture: Popular Music and Technology in North India*. Chicago: University of Chicago Press.

Mohan, Anuradha. 1994. *Ilaiyaraja: Composer as Phenomenon in Tamil Film Culture*. Unpublished M.A. thesis, Wesleyan University.

Discographical References

Ilaiyaraaja, I. *How to Name It*. Oriental Records ORI/AAMS CD 115. *1988*: India/USA.

Wonder, Stevie. 'I Just Called to Say I Love You.' Motown 1745. *1984*: USA.

Discography: North India

Amitabh Bachchan, Superstar of the Millennium. EMI-India CDF 132452/53. n.d.: India. (Songs sung by playback artists for Amitabh Bachchan's film characters.)

Best of 2000. T Series Gold SFCD 1/590. *2001*: India. (Various playback songs.)

Bhosle, Asha. *Legends: The Enchantress*. EMI-India CDF 132371/75. *1997*: India.

Dey, Manna. *Legends: The Maestro*. EMI-India CDF 132383/87. *1997*: India.

Evergreen Hits from Old Films. EMI-India PMLP 5831. *1994*: India. (Songs from Hindi films, 1936–49.)

Geetmala Hit Parade Vol. 2: Hits of 1955. EMI-India CDF 130057/58. n.d.: India.

Greatest Hits of the '50s, Vol. 3. EMI-India CDF 130121. *1997*: India. (Hindi film songs by music directors C. Ramchandra, Naushad, O.P. Nayyar, Shankar-Jaikishen and others.)

Greatest Hits of the '60s, Vol. 3. EMI-India CDF 130126. *1997*: India. (Hindi film songs by music directors Naushad, Shankar-Jaikishen, S.D. Burman, Lakshmikant-Pyarelal and others.)

Greatest Hits of the '70s, Vol. 3. EMI-India CDF 130136. *1997*: India. (Hindi film songs by music directors R.D Burman, Shankar-Jaikishen, Lakshmikant-Pyarelal, Kalyanji-Anandji and others.)

Greatest Hits of the '80s, Vol. 1. EMI-India CDF 130118. *1997*: India. (Hindi film songs by music directors Shiv Hari, Lakshmikant-Pyarelal, R.D. Burman, Khayyam and others.)

Jehan, Noor. *The Golden Collection: Noor Jehan.* EMI-India CDF 131117/18. *1998*: India.

Kumar, Kishore. *Legends: The Prodigy.* EMI-India CDF 132344/48. *1998*: India.

Mahmood, Talat. *Legends: The Silken Voice.* EMI-India CDF 132398/402. *1998*: India.

Mangeshkar, Lata. *Legends: The Nightingale.* EMI-India CDF 130111/15. *1997*: India. (5 CDs with accompanying 32-page booklet.)

Mukesh. *Legends.* EMI-India CDF 132351/55. *1998*: India.

Playback: The Exciting Era 1976–1986. EMI-India CDF 130027. *1991*: India.

Playback: The Fabulous Years 1946–1956. EMI-India CDF 130024. *1991*: India.

Playback: The Melodious Decade 1956–1966. EMI-India CDF 130025. *1991*: India.

Playback: The Sentimental Era 1936–1946. EMI-India CDF 130023. *1991*: India.

Rafi, Mohammad. *Legends: The Virtuoso.* EMI-India CDF 132336/40. *1997*: India.

Saigal, Kundan Lal. *Kundan Saigal: The Immortal.* Inreco-Pyramid IP 6041/43. *1997*: India.

The Golden Collection Duets of Lata Mangeshkar and Mohammad Rafi, Vol. 1. EMI-India CDF 131011/12. *1997*: India.

The New Generation – Alka Yagnik, Udit Narayan, Kavita Krishnamurty, Kumar Sanu. EMI-India CDF 132317. n.d.: India. (Playback artists of the 1980s and 1990s.)

Discography: South India

Golden Collections of A.R. Rahman (2 CDs). Pyramid CD PYR 8486. *1996*: India.

Gramiya Vaasanai (2 CDs). Pyramid CD PYR 8680. *1998*: India. (Folk songs incorporated into Tamil films.)

Greatest Remixes of A.R. Rahman. Pyramid CD PYR 8654. *1997*: India.

Kuppuswamy, Pushpavanam. *Mannu Manakkuthu* (audiocassette). Indu Musik IMR 1465. *1989*: India.

Kuppuswamy, Pushpavanam. *Man Vaasam* (audio-cassette). Indu Musik IMR 1545. *1990*: India.

Navaneethakrishnan, Vijayalakshmi. *Ammayee Paattukkal (Tamil Folk Songs, Vol. 6)* (audiocassette). Raaky VNK 909. *1994*: India.

Navaneethakrishnan, Vijayalakshmi. *Kiraamiya Paattukkal (Folk Songs)* (audiocassette). Raaky Audio VNK 099. *1990*: India.

Filmography: North India

Alam Ara, dir. Ardeshir Irani. 1931. Bombay, India. Costume Drama. Songs composed and arranged by Firozshah Mistry and B. Irani.

Maine Pyar Kiya, dir. Sooraj Barjatya. 1989. Bombay, India. Social Drama. Songs composed by Raam Laxman.

Qayamat Se Qayamat Tak, dir. Mansoor Khan. 1988. Bombay, India. Social Drama. Songs composed by Anand Milind.

Qurbani, dir. Feroz Khan. 1980. Bombay, India. Social Drama. Songs composed by Kalyanji-Anandji and Biddu.

Street Singer, dir. Phani Majumdar. 1938. Calcutta, India. Social Drama. Songs composed by Rai Chand Boral.

Vidyapati, dir. Debaki Bose. 1937. Calcutta, India. Biographical Film. Songs composed by Rai Chand Boral.

Filmography: South India

Annakkili, dir. Devaraj-Mohan. 1976. Chennai, India. Social Drama. Songs composed by I. Ilaiyaraaja.

Bombay, dir. Mani Rathnam. 1995. Chennai, India. Social Drama. Songs composed by A.R. Rahman.

Chandralekha, dir. S.S. Vasan. 1948. Chennai, India. Social Drama. Songs composed by S. Rajeswara Rao.

Duet, dir. K. Balachandar. 1994. Chennai, India. Social Drama. Songs composed by A.R. Rahman.

Galavarishi, dir. P.P. Rangachari. 1932. Chennai, India. Social Drama.

Kaalidaas, dir. H.M. Reddy. 1931. Chennai, India. Epic Drama. Songs composed based on South Indian classical music.

Kadhalan, dir. S. Shamkar. 1994. Chennai, India. Social Drama. Songs composed by A.R. Rahman.

Merupu Kallalu, dir. Rajiv Menon. 1997. Chennai, India. Social Drama. Songs composed by A.R. Rahman.

Priya, dir. S.P. Muthuraman. 1978. Chennai, India. Social Drama. Songs composed by I. Ilaiyaraaja.

Roja, dir. Mani Ratnam. 1993. Chennai, India. Social Drama. Songs composed by A.R. Rahman.

Salangai Oli, dir. K. Vishvanath. 1982. Chennai, India. Social Drama. Songs composed by I. Ilaiyaraaja.

Vīrā, dir. Suresh Krishna. 1994. Chennai, India. Social Drama. Songs composed by I. Ilaiyaraaja.

Representative Filmography: North India

Albela, dir. Bhagwan. 1951. Bombay, India. Social Drama. Songs composed by C. Ramchandra.

(Includes songs drawing on Latin American musical styles.)

Amar Akbar Anthony, dir. Manmohan Desai. 1977. Bombay, India. Social Drama. Songs composed by Laxmikant-Pyarelal. (Includes popular film *qawwāli* 'Parda hai parda.')

Anmol Ghadi, dir. Mehboob. 1946. Bombay, India. Social Drama. Songs composed by Naushad.

Anpadh, dir. Mohan Kumar. 1962. Bombay, India. Social Drama. Songs composed by Madan Mohan. (Includes film *ghazals*.)

Aurat, dir. Mehboob. 1940. Bombay, India. Social Drama. Songs composed by Anil Biswas. (Several songs based on Bengali folk songs.)

Baiju Bawra, dir. Vijay Bhatt. 1952. Bombay, India. Historical Film. Songs composed by Naushad. (Songs based on Hindustani classical music.)

Barsaat, dir. Raj Kapoor. 1949. Bombay, India. Social Drama. Songs composed by Shankar-Jaikishan.

Bhoot Bungla, dir. Mehmood. 1965. Bombay, India. Social Drama. Songs composed by R.D. Burman. (One song employs the Western pop dance style, the twist.)

Bobby, dir. Raj Kapoor. 1973. Bombay, India. Social Drama. Songs composed by Lakshmikant-Pyarelal.

Chhaya, dir. Hrishikesh Mukherji. 1961. Bombay, India. Social Drama. Songs composed by Salil Chaudhury. (Includes song based on first movement of Mozart's Symphony No. 40 in G Minor.)

Devdas, dir. Prem Chand Barua. 1935. Calcutta, India. Social Drama. Songs composed by Timir Baran.

Dil Se, dir. Mani Rathnam. 1998. Bombay, India. Social Drama. Songs composed by A.R. Rahman.

Dil To Pagal Hai, dir. Yash Chopra. 1997. Bombay, India. Social Drama. Songs composed by Uttam Singh.

Gopal Krishna, dir. V. Damle and S. Fatehlal. 1938. Pune, India. Mythological Film. Songs composed by Master Krishnarao.

Jhanak Jhanak Payal Baje, dir. V. Shantaram. 1955. Bombay, India. Social Drama. Songs composed by Vasant Desai. (Includes Indian classical-style songs and dances.)

Khazanchi, dir. Moti Gidwani. 1941. Lahore, India (before Partition). Social Drama. Songs composed by Ghulam Haider. (Introduced Punjabi music into Indian films.)

Kismet, dir. Gyan Mukerji. 1943. Bombay, India. Social Drama. Songs composed by Anil Biswas.

Mugal-e-Azam, dir. K. Asif. 1960. Bombay, India.

Legendary Tale. Songs composed by Naushad. (Songs based on Hindustani classical style.)

Mujhe Jeene Do, dir. Moni Bhattacharya. 1963. Bombay, India. Social Drama. Songs composed by Jaidev. (Composer used folk songs from Madhya Pradesh, where the film was set.)

Naya Daur, dir. B.R. Chopra. 1957. Bombay, India. Social Drama. Songs composed by O.P. Nayyar. (Songs show Punjabi musical influence.)

1942 A Love Story, dir. Vidhu Vinod Chopra. 1994. Bombay, India. Social Drama. Songs composed by R.D. Burman.

Pakeezah, dir. Kamal Amrohi. 1971. Bombay, India. Social Drama. Songs composed by Ghulam Mohammad and Naushad.

Pyaasa, dir. Guru Dutt. 1957. Bombay, India. Social Drama. Songs composed by S.D. Burman.

Ram Teri Ganga Maili, dir. Raj Kapoor. 1986. Bombay, India. Social Drama. Songs composed by Ravindra Jain.

Rangeela, dir. Ramgopal Varma. 1995. Bombay, India. Social Drama. Songs composed by A.R. Rahman.

Sholay, dir. Ramesh Sippy. 1975. Bombay, India. Social Drama. Songs composed by R.D. Burman.

Shree 420, dir. Raj Kapoor. 1955. Bombay, India. Social Drama. Songs composed by Shankar-Jaikishen.

Umrao Jaan, dir. Muzaffar Ali. 1982. Bombay, India. Social Drama. Songs composed by Khayyam.

PETER MANUEL, ALISON ARNOLD and PAUL D. GREENE

REGIONS

Andaman and Nicobar Islands

Population: Indigenous Andaman people – 500 (2000); Indigenous Nicobarese – 30,000 (2001); Settlers – 500,000 (2001)

The 570 or so tropical Andaman and Nicobar Islands lie in the Bay of Bengal, close to the Myanmar coast. First mentioned in texts attributed to Marco Polo, the islands were inhabited by several indigenous communities that had little contact with each other or the outside world until the early nineteenth century, when the British established an outpost on South Andaman. The Onge, Jarawa, Andamanese and North Sentinelese minorities are surviving in ever-dwindling numbers on the Andaman Islands. The origins of these isolated groups are still unclear. Their nearest relatives live in Central Africa. The Nicobarese and a smaller minority group called the Shompen continue to live on some of the Nicobar Islands.

Initially the British found it hard to utilize the islands. Malaria was rampant and the minorities were reluctant workers in coconut plantations. From the mid-nineteenth century until World War II, Port Blair, the islands' capital, served as a British prison colony for Indian independence fighters. Few of the inmates ever returned to the mainland. Some defected to the indigenous minorities in order to escape the brutal prison regime. After a brief Japanese occupation during World War II, the entire archipelago was incorporated into the Indian Union in 1947. In the 1960s and 1970s many Nicobarese moved to the Andaman Islands.

Since the 1980s, the population of settlers in the Andamans has risen from 50,000 to half a million, with the indigenous communities fast diminishing along with the rain forest and coral reefs. A ban on logging and the formulation of indigenous rights by India's Supreme Court in 2001 had yet to take effect in 2004. All statistics and information on the Nicobar Islands are sketchy at best. For strategic reasons, the Nicobar Islands are now off limits to both foreigners and Indian nationals, and little is known about the fate of the Shompen minority.

While the Nicobarese have converted to Christianity and number about 30,000, the remaining four minority population groups in the Andamans are facing extinction. The Nicobarese are the only indigenous community with a growing population. Their partial adaptation to Indian culture and their South East Asian origin has sustained the cultural invasion of their islands by mainland India. Nicobarese populist Christian songs (mostly written in the 1960s) can be heard on Sundays in their community churches on Little Andaman and the Nicobar Islands. The church songs, played during services, are usually accompanied by guitars. Melodies are often taken from the Protestant folk song genre of the 1960s and 1970s in the United States.

The settlers are refugees from Sri Lanka, and flood victims from Bengal and Andhra Pradesh. Each group has brought their own music traditions to the islands. Most settlers are Hindus, but Muslims, Christians, Buddhists and Sikhs have settled on the islands too.

Major Hindu festivals such as Sivaratri, Holi, Ramanvami and Diwali are celebrated, and processions are held in Port Blair, Diglipur (North Andaman) and Hut Bay (Little Andaman). The Hindu faithful sing *bhajans* (devotional prayers) in the temples, while brass bands are an integral part of any celebration.

In Port Blair, Hut Bay and on Neil Island, groups of Bengali settlers have set up informal music cooperatives. Bengali concerts are held at the The Ravindra Bengla Vidyalaya, a Bengali secondary school, and at the Atul Samiti Club, both in Port Blair. Tamil and Andhra settlers also have cultural community centers in the Port Blair area. On Neil Island, a *baul* (a wandering minstrel from West Bengal) regularly performs informally with friends at the Island Community Center.

All India Radio broadcasts on the Islands in seven Indian languages.

Bibliography

Das, S.T. 1982. *The Andaman and Nicobar Islands: A Study of Habitat, Economy and Society.* Delhi: Sagar Publications.

Lonely Islands: The Andamanese (an NGO documenting the history of the indigenous minorities in the island chain may furnish scholars with information related the islands' indigenous music). www.andaman.org

Tamta, B.R. 1991. *Andaman and Nicobar Islands.* New Delhi: National Book Trust.

Discography

The British Library National Sound Archive holds a collection of indigenous and populist music, including processions and informal concerts by Bengali and Andhra settlers, Christian songs of the Nicobarese and the music of the Onge, one of the indigenous Andamanese minorities, which can be accessed through their listening service. (For further information, please check at www.nsa.co.uk. Reference # Cat: C 799, rec 2000, Tom Vater.)

Filmography

Andaman, Les Isles Invisibles, dir. J. Cousteau. 1990. France. 60 mins. Documentary (features settlers' processions, rituals, festivals). Cousteau Society/ Amaya Films.

TOM VATER

Andhra Pradesh
Population: 75,700,000 (2001)

Andhra Pradesh epitomizes the confluence of North and South Indian cultures. The river Godavari separates the Indo-Germanic languages of the North and the Dravidian languages of the South, as well as the Hindustani style of music in northern India and the Carnatic style of South India.

The state was formed in 1952 out of the Telugu speaking districts of Madras (now called Tamil Nadu) after intense agitation, and in 1956 it merged with nine Telugu speaking districts of the erstwhile princely state of Hyderabad, a region known as Telengana. Andhra Pradesh was thus the first state of the Indian Union based on the principle of a common language: Telugu. Once part of the Satavahana Empire, the two parts of the new state had experienced different histories. The coastal region of Andhra became part of the Madras Presidency in stages between 1765–1801 and was directly ruled by the British, but Telengana had been the core area of the state of Hyderabad, ruled by a Muslim dynasty. Urdu is the second language in Andhra Pradesh, and both Hindustani and Carnatic music can be heard in and around the capital Hyderabad. In Andhra Pradesh a multi-cultural tradition coexists – and sometimes clashes – with an intense pride in Telugu culture.

The division between classical 'serious' music and 'popular' music is a Western concept; in South India classical and popular styles intermingle. Music is essentially a religious medium: classical rāgas are based on sacred texts, devotional songs abound, and even folk songs and folk theater convey stories about gods and goddesses, thus reinforcing the value system. Mystic poetry is popular and often needs to be understood at two levels: mundane love with its joys and pains becomes the symbol for intense devotion. Hindu and Muslim traditions merge in mysticism, and saints of both religions are invoked in qawwāli as well as in kirtana music styles. Ghazal, a north Indian form of song based on poetry, is even composed in Telugu.

Popular music takes several forms: burrakatha and harikatha, bommalata (shadowplay), folk songs, devotional songs (kirtana) and most recently film music.

Burrakatha is very popular in villages as well as in cities. It derives its name from burra, a one-headed finger drum, and katha which means 'story.' Burrakatha is of fairly recent origin; the Communist Party of India adopted this form derived from jangama katha, the music of itinerant shaivite minstrels, during World War II, and used it to propagate their message. There are usually three performers: a singer, who carries a tambūra (a string instrument) on his right shoulder and andelu (hollow brass rings filled with metal balls) on the left thumb and forefinger; and two accompanists who play the burra. All three wear colorful tunics and turbans. The village communities support them. In the early twenty-first century one finds Hindu, Muslim and even Christian singers, men and women, who express their political ideas, particularly during election campaigns. Quite a few have taken to historical themes with a strong social message, but based on contemporary texts.

Related to burrakatha is the older form of harikatha, originally with stories of God Vishnu, but more recently with themes that tell of modern heroes like Mahatma Gandhi or the revolutionary M. Maqdoom. The composer/performers of texts and music are often very learned men. They are accompanied by violin, harmonium and drum, while the singer plays a kind of castanets. Some of their stories and songs are translations of North Indian poets like Kabir, or even Omar Khayyam, the Persian poet, into Sanskrit or Telugu.

Shadowplay is unique to Andhra Pradesh and it is said that this art form traveled from here to the Malay world. Small traveling troupes perform at night, their stage a screen of white cloth illuminated from behind. The performers move their puppets – large flat brightly colored figures made of leather – with the help of strings, and thus their shadows fall on the screen. One or more puppeteers tell the story, imitating male, female, deer or bird voices, singing and interspersing their narratives with satirical comments on current affairs.

Andhra Pradesh is rich in folk songs. They too often deal with religious themes or with stories from the epics, which have a moral content. Devotional songs from the temples have trickled down to the villages. In addition, film songs become folk songs and vice versa. There are songs only women sing at the time of weddings or childbirth or at work, i.e., when fetching water or grinding grain. Some reflect domestic tensions:

A tiger's son is my husband.
A tigress is my mother-in-law.
I am a tender calf.

Devotional songs (kirtana), sung in temples in praise of the deity, are close to classical music and use the same instruments, such as the double-headed drum mridangam, flutes, violins, natuvangam (a cymbal), and the stringed vīnā, but are less complex. The kirtana are sung during ceremonies or to 'wake up' the idol in the early hours of the morning, and are relayed by loudspeaker to wake everybody else in the neighborhood. The artists are often classical singers, like Dr. M. Balamurli Krishna or the unforgettable M. S. Subbulakshmi. The Venkateshwara Temple at Thirupati, which draws millions of devotees per year, is the most important pilgrimage place of Andhra Pradesh and the center of this art form.

The most popular genre in Andhra Pradesh, as in most of India, is film music. Barring a few serious films, Indian commercial feature films in whatever language are like musicals and have to contain dances and five or six songs to be successful. The Telugu film industry started in 1942 in the city of Madras (now called Chennai). For about 12 years the music was based on classical rāgas and sung by actors, like Nagaya or Bhamuvati. In the mid-1950s light classical music was introduced, together with playback singers, many of them highly popular, such as Ghantasala or S. P. Balasubramaniam. They sang not only in Telugu but also in other South-Indian languages, some even in Hindi. In the 1960s the film studios moved to Hyderabad.

A large number of films are still based on themes and stories from the epics *Ramayana* and *Mahabharata*. Some voice social criticism, such as those written by the poets Sri Sri or C. Narayan Reddy. Love stories and action films dominate the 70–80 Telugu films produced per year, the Telugu film ranking third in number of productions in India (after Hindi and Tamil films).

Since the 1980s Telugu film music has absorbed elements of Hindi film music, as well as Western instruments and concepts of orchestration. Influences of rock and disco are obvious. Thus, even in films, Andhra Pradesh is true to its syncretic heritage.

Bibliography

Baskaran, S. Theodore. 1981. *The Message Bearers, The Nationalist Politics and the Entertainment Media in South India 1880–1945*. Madras: Cre-A.

Rama Raju, B. 1978. *Folklore of Andhra Pradesh*. New Delhi: National Book Trust.

Discography

Badri, Oke Okkadu. Aditya Music MID AM – 507. *2000*: India.

Krishna, M. Balamurli. *Bhaktha Ramadasa Keerthanalu, Telugu Devotional Songs, Vol. 2*. Magnasound (India) Ltd. C6-N2867. *2000*: India.

Sarma, Madugula Nagaphani. *Potana Bhagavata Kathagana Sudha (Bhagvata Purana), Vol. 2*. Avadhana Saraswathi Peetham. *1999*: India.

Subbulakshmi, M.S. *Sanskrit Devotional*. HMV SM 947001. *1963*: India.

Tattvaneetisaramu, Sri Venkateshwara Gita Malika. Annamacharya Project. Tirumala Thirupati Devasthanams. TTD SERIES. *2001*: India.

DAGMAR BERNSTORFF

Bihar

Population: 83,000,000 (2001)

The state of Bihar in eastern India takes its name from the Sanskrit word *vihara*, meaning monastery.

It borders Nepal to the north, and the Indian states Uttar Pradesh, Jharkhand and West Bengal to the west, south and east respectively. Carved from Bihar in 2000 after decades of struggle for its creation, the state of Jharkhand, meaning 'forest region,' was formerly part of its northern neighbor. Together with Orissa, both were part of Bengal during the British colonial era.

The major river Ganga (Ganges) bisects Bihar, flowing west to east. Bihar's mostly flat area of 67,134 sq miles (173,877 sq km) is intensively cultivated with rice, wheat, sugar cane, cotton and other crops. The state capital Patna encompasses the site of an ancient capital of the Magadha Empire (sixth century B.C.). Important historical places in Bihar include Rajgir, an earlier capital of the Magadhas; Gaya, a major Hindu pilgrimage center; Bodh Gaya, sacred place of the Buddha's enlightenment (ca. 530 B.C.) and home to Buddhist temples from many nations; Nalanda, site of a major university (fifth to twelfth centuries A.D.); and Sasaram, tomb of Afghan ruler Sher Shah Suri (sixth century A.D.).

Principal spoken languages of Bihar are Maithili, Bhojpuri, Magahi, Bihari, Urdu and Hindi. The population of 83 million people is approximately 82 percent Hindu, 14 percent Muslim, with the remainder of other religions. Poverty is widespread and literacy rates are low; about 13 percent of the population are urbanized. Many low-caste people identify themselves as *dalit*, meaning oppressed. Land reforms after Indian independence in 1947 were less equitable in Bihar than in other states, and great disparities in wealth persist. Other problems include caste-based conflicts, government corruption and violent conflict among groups such as Maoists and private militias. Many Biharis have migrated to other areas in India or abroad. Despite these problems, tourism to the state's significant historic and pilgrimage sites is a growing industry.

Bihar has a great wealth of music traditions. Music genres include *lok gīt* (folk songs), work songs, *chhat puja* songs (for the unique Sun festival), *sohar* songs (for a baby's birth), *samdaun* songs (for the departure of the bride from her home), and other forms such as *qawwāli, purvi, biraha* and *nirgun bhajan*. Examples of musical instruments are the drums *dhaal* (a very large drum), *dholak* (smaller, barrel-shaped) and *nagara* (kettle drum), and melodic instruments harmonium (reed organ) and *benjo* (amplified autoharp). Brass bands (with clarinet, valved horns, drums and amplified keyboards and vocalists) perform in processions for weddings and festivals. Music is found at celebrations, in homes, and as accompaniment for theater and dance (performed by men, women and *launda*, men impersonating women). The image of Bihar is not as clearly linked with its performing traditions as is the case elsewhere. Tamil Nadu state, for example, is known for *bharatanātyam* dance. This lack of clear linkage in Bihar is due in part to inadequate government and private support for the arts.

Some performers of Bihar's traditions have achieved commercial success. For example, Sharda Sinha (b. 1953) sings Bihari language folk songs in concerts throughout the world and has released many recordings. Another popular Bhojpuri singer from Bihar is Manoj Tiwari. Others come from neighboring Uttar Pradesh state, as the Bhojpuri language crosses the border. Folk dancer and theater company director Bhikhari Thakur (1887–1971) was a popular performer of dramas (staged stories with music and dance). Some of his productions focused on the phenomenon of '*bidesiya*,' a term – from the point of view of those still living in Bihar – for those who have migrated away. Dancer Hari Uppal (b. 1926) studied classical Indian dances and then became a well-known proponent of Bihari folk dances. In 1950 he established the dance school Bharatiya Nritya Kala Mandir in Patna. The Governors of India's prestigious Sangeet Natak Akademy (National Academy of Music, Dance and Drama) have recognized several performers from Bihar, including folk singer Bindhya Basini Devi (in 1991), Sharda Sinha (1999–2000) and Hari Uppal (2001).

The music of Bihar is broadcast on the Indian government networks Doordarshan (television) and All India Radio; for example, one may hear a folk song during a radio farm report. However, in India the chief source of mass-mediated popular music is the Bollywood film industry. Its musical movies with Hindi language *filmi gīt* songs are produced in far-away Mumbai. There are cinema halls all over Bihar, and radio and television broadcasts of film music now cover the state; private cable and satellite networks also exist. Recordings of film songs and other types of music are readily available for purchase, and are played back in homes, places of work and worship, tea and snack shops, transportation vehicles, and at festivals. The first local-language film was *Ganga Maiya Tohe Piyari Chadhaibo*, a Bhojpuri film released in 1962; since then several dozen films have been made in this language, and a handful more in Maitili and

Magahi. Film production in Bihar is growing, and in 2003 the Pataliputra Acting Institute and Studio was inaugurated in Patna.

Kalajatha (street theater) is employed by various groups to promote social movements. These plays have songs and dances as well as stories and empowering messages. The Ravi Bharati Institute for Communication Arts, Patna, organizes *kalajathas* on topics such as birth control, health and women's rights; the group also has a recording studio for broadcast production. The Notre Dame Communication Centre, Patna, a television-training institute, produces street plays as well as local language 'tele-serials' (soap operas), which in India have continuous melodramatic background music.

Bibliography

Babiracki, Carol M. 1990. 'Music and History of Mundari-Caste Interaction in Chotanagpur.' *Ethnomusicology and Modern Music History*, ed. Steve Blum, Philip Bohlman and Daniel Neuman. Urbana: University of Illinois Press, 207–28

Babiracki, Carol M. 1991. 'Tribal Music in the Study of Great and Little Traditions of Indian Music.' *Comparative Musicology and the Anthropology of Music: Essays in the History of Ethnomusicology*, ed. Bruno Nettl and Philip Bohlman. Chicago: University of Chicago Press, 69–90.

Booth, Gregory. 2000. 'Popular Artists and Their Audiences.' *The Garland Encyclopedia of World Music. Vol. 5: South Asia, The Indian Subcontinent*, ed. Arnold, Alison. New York: Garland, 418–29.

Gupta, Shaibal. 'Bihar: Identity and Development.' http://www.bihartimes.com/articles/shaibal/biharidentity.html

Henry, Edward O. 1988. *Chant the Names of God: Musical Culture in Bhojpuri-Speaking India*. San Diego, CA: San Diego State University Press.

Henry, Edward O. 2000. 'Maithila.' *The Garland Encyclopedia of World Music. Vol. 5: South Asia, The Indian Subcontinent*, ed. Arnold, Alison. New York: Garland, 677–79.

Henry, Edward O., and Lord, Maria. 2001. 'India: VII. Local Traditions.' *The New Grove Dictionary of Music and Musicians*, ed. S. Sadie and J. Tyrrell. London: Macmillan, vol. 12, 237–53.

Mahata, Pasupati Prasada. *The Performing Arts of Jharkhand*. B.B. Prakasan. *1987*: India.

Manuel, Peter. 1993. *Cassette Culture: Popular Music and Technology in North India*. Chicago: University of Chicago Press.

Tiwari, Badri Narayan. 'Bidesia: Migration, Change,

and Folk Culture.' *IIAS Newsletter* 30, March
2003. Leiden: International Institute for Asian
Studies. http://www.iias.nl/iiasn/30/
IIASNL30_12.pdf

Uppal, Hari. 1963. *Folk Dances of Bihar*. Patna:
Bharatiya Nritya Kala Mandir.

Discography

Adivasi Jhankara Adiwasi Jhankar. Satya Bharati.
ca.1980: India.

Chhau & Nagpuri Group. *Folksongs & Dances From
India*. ARC Music EUCD 1815. *1999*: UK.

Ganga: Les Musiques du Gange. Virgin Classics 7254 5
61532 2 6. *1998*: UK.

Henry, Edward O. *Women's Songs From India*.
Rounder 82161-5040-2. 2000: USA.

Jairazbhoy, Nazir Ali. *Musical Journey Through India:
1963–1964*. Los Angeles: Dept of Ethnomusicology, University of California. *1988*: USA.

Jha, Rekha, and Azim, Mohammad. *Rekha Jha ke
Maithila Gita*. Music India 2222 841. *1982*: India.

Najam, Yasina, et al. *Bhojapuri Lokagita*. Super
Cassettes SNMC 147, SNMC 211. *1983*: India.

Salema. *Salem's Preet Adhunik Nagpuri Geet*. Mirzur
Cassettes 1/2008. *1992*: India.

Salema. *Tusa Dippa Kudukh Bhajana*. Satya Bharati.
ca.1990: India.

Tirkey, Sushil Kumar. *Sushil Kumar Tirkey Presents
Dulara Gatinga Loka Priya Mundari Gita*. Minzur
Cassettes Pvt. Ltd. MC 005. *1999*: India.

Yadava, Kasi. *Bhojapuri Biraha Saharanapura Kanda
va Bharata se Bharata*. Super Cassettes Industries
SBJNC 01/149. *1990*: India.

JOSEPH GETTER

Jharkhand

Population: 26,909,428 (2001)

The state of Jharkhand is India's leading producer of
mineral wealth, ranking among its top three
producers of coal, iron ore, bauxite, copper ores,
uranium, kainite and asbestos, among other minerals. Nevertheless, some 84 percent of its people live
in rural areas as rice cultivators and artisans. In
2001, Jharkhand's average per capita income was
Rs. 4161 (about US$100), and its literacy rate was 54
percent. As participants in India's thriving parliamentary democracy, Jharkhand candidates in the
recent 2004 election represented some 19 political
parties; 54 percent of its eligible voters turned out to
vote. Jharkhand is a multilingual region, with nine
major languages representing all of India's major
language families (Austro-Asiatic, Indo-European
and Dravidian). In 2001, overall approximately 28
percent of Jharkhand's population was 'tribal'
(indigenous); in some districts that figure rose to
well over 50 percent.

On 15 November 2000, the Chotanagpur region
of southern Bihar became India's newest state,
Jharkhand, ending a 200-year struggle for autonomy. In its last decades, beginning in the mid-1970s,
that struggle was fueled by a cultural revival that
spread from the city of Ranchi into remote towns
and villages, carried by the voices – and cassettes –
of a newly emerging circle of itinerant, popular
stage singers. The revival rapidly coalesced around
the poetic and musical language of Nagpuri, the
most widely spoken lingua franca in Jharkhand.
Unlike Hindi, it was a language that could unite
diverse population groups while still remaining
grounded in the local culture. The new stage singers
and accompanists themselves reflected the diversity
of Nagpuri speakers. They were Hindu, Muslim and
'tribal' (indigenous); from dominant ('high') as well
as from marginal ('low') castes; of relative wealth
and of the migrant poor. The possibility of making a
living as a modern stage singer was particularly
attractive to the traditional village ceremonial and
ritual musicians, the *Ghasis*. As urbanization and
modernization spread out from Ranchi, consuming
towns and villages along the way, many of the
Ghasis' traditional performance opportunities at
weddings and festivals disappeared. The stage
offered a new source of livelihood for *Ghasi* men,
but only rarely for women. It was and is largely a
man's world, although the few professional female
singers (some from village 'courtesan' traditions)
who venture there are wildly popular.

During the first decades of the Nagpuri revival,
popular stage performances and the cassette market
were dominated by traditional musicians singing in
village song genres once associated with specific
seasons, times of night and gendered dances (men's,
women's). The new media – stage, cassettes, radio –
loosened those genres' associations of place, time
and gender. The live stage performances, whether in
cities, towns or villages, still went on all night, but
singers were now more concerned with maintaining
a good variety of songs and cultivating signature
hits. Without dance and participatory performance,
the songs and their musical accompaniment began
changing rapidly. Tempos became more upbeat, and
melodies became more varied, extended and intricate. Mass-produced, urban *dholaks*, harmoniums,
electric keyboards, snare-drum kits and accordions
joined the traditional drums (*dhulki*, *mandar*),
cymbals and clappers.

In these early years, the modern sounds carried texts that spoke about the social and political issues igniting the Jharkhand movement. The hit protest song of the early 1980s, 'Bucu,' (Brother) by Mukund Nayak, a *Ghasi* singer, drummer and dancer, is a good example. Nayak claims to have cast the song in a men's village song genre to make it both more Nagpuri and more powerful. When performed live, Nayak's *jhum*-ing (grooving) made the song virtually dance off the stage (excerpted here from a 1994 translation by Mukund Nayak and Carol Babiracki):

Refrain:
  Brother, run quickly to the village,
  Taking everyone along.
  Find out how to save the country.
Verses:
  Breaking the banks of the Ganges,
  A dangerous flood is coming.
  Snakes, insects, crocodiles are floating in it.
  Find out how to save the country.
  Beat the kettledrum,
  Wake up everyone.
  Our buried jewels should not be looted.
  Find out how to save the country.
  As our sleep was broken,
  Mukund [the poet] ran and joined,
  Holding the hoe, axe, bow and arrow
  Find out how to save the country.

By the early 1980s, competition and experimentation among singers had sparked a proliferation of new popular song styles, each niche promoted by its own stars and troupes. The Muslim poet, Mustaqim Ahmed, composed an original style of 'Nagpuri *qawwāli* songs,' localizing the pan-South Asian style of Sufi religious singing for Nagpuri audiences. His messages, too, concerned social reform:

  North, south, east and west, everything has changed.
  Bihar has changed, Orissa has changed.
  Guru has changed, disciple has changed.
  Uncle has changed, nephew has changed.
  Now film songs play in places of worship.

  Now people celebrate festivals carrying sticks.
  The food is ready in the houses, but the men eat in hotels [restaurants].
  They've left aside ghee and milk, their life is in the bottle.

('Diśā Baḍhail Gelak' [Everything Has Changed], recorded in live performance by Carol Babiracki, 11 February 1984; translation by Mukund Nayak and Carol Babiracki.)

Madhu Mansuri 'Hansmukh' (laughing face), 'the father of Nagpuri modern song,' composed his own idiosyncratic texts and tunes, first dubbed '*filmi*,' then 'disco,' and now 'modern.' His nostalgic, nationalist signature hit was 'Nagpur kar Kora' (In the Lap of Nagpur), recorded on locally distributed cassettes beginning in approximately 1981 (excerpted):

  In the lap of Nagpur,
  River, rain, boulders, large and small forests.
  Oh dear, decorate your hair with flowers,
  While you are unmarried, swing on the swing.

  The cymbals of the mind are ringing,
  And the smell of honey ['Madhu,' the poet] is spreading wonderfully.
  The Koel and Karo rivers are flowing here and there, back and forth.
  Oh, purify the Subarnarekha [river] and the Hundru, Dasham, and Jonha falls.

  Combing your hair with a bamboo comb,
  Please, dear girl, give me your word.
  The love of today is faltering,
  But tomorrow I will see you at this same time.

(Translation by Mukund Nayak and Carol Babiracki.)

Mansuri strategically and self-consciously offered Nagpuris an alternative to the ubiquitous pan-Indian commercial film music. By the mid-1980s, the sound systems of Ranchi shops, homes, processions, weddings and festivals were blaring *Nagpuri* popular songs rather than Hindi film songs. Singers and poets published and distributed small magazines filled with their song texts and stories, and people remarked on how the Nagpuri language was once again proudly spoken on the streets of Ranchi.

In the early 1990s, commercial interests began to overshadow the social. The tiny, dark, make-shift village stage with its single microphone gave way to a huge platform, brilliantly lit by fluorescent lights. Sponsors of programs erected boundaries around the concert space and charged admission, although the musicians still saw only a small percentage of the profits. Young female singers have become more prominent; young men have affected a smooth, crooning urban vocal style. Singers move, sway and dance around the stage, offering simple love songs in attractive packages to whooping, cheering crowds.

The production of the first Nagpuri feature film in 1993, *Sona kar Nagpur* (Golden Nagpur), a musical, of course, marked a high point and inevitability the growth of Nagpuri popular music. The music director, singer Mukund Nayak, presented a full range of traditional Nagpuri song forms with modern texts to underscore writer/director D. N. Tiwari's script, a love story laced with commentary on the virtues of literacy, social reform and political unity. Nayak and members of his troupe, Kunjban, recorded the playback soundtrack in 'Bollywood' (Bombay film industry) fashion, while the actors danced and lip-synced across the screen. The film's production quality may have been poor, but thousands cheered its message: Jharkhand was joining modern India, and on its own terms.

Nagpuri modern, popular songs have circulated primarily through live performances and locally produced and distributed cassette tapes, many of them pirated from live performances. In 1984, Ranchi city acquired its own radio transmission tower, from which the national All India Radio programming was broadcast. Village listeners, however, seemed most interested in the half-hour weekly program of local songs and singers.

Discographical References

Ahmed, Mustaqim. 'Diśā Baḍhail Gelak' [Everything has Changed]. Recorded in live performance by Carol Babiracki in Ganaloya, Jharkhand, 11 February 1984.

Mansuri, 'Hansmukh,' Madhu. 'Nagpur kar Kora.' *Nagpur kar Kora.* Chetana. *1981*: India.

Nayak, Mukund. 'Bucu.' Recorded in live performance by Carol Babiracki, 1983–84.

Filmography

Sona kar Nagpur, dir. D. N. Tiwari. 1993. India. 150 mins. Musical. Original music and music direction by Mukund Nayak.

CAROL M. BABIRACKI

Kashmir

Population: 5,000,000 (2001)

Although the Jammu and Kashmir State is divided between India and Pakistan, the valley of Kashmir (which is seven percent of the area of the undivided state), the region where the Kashmiri language is spoken, is fully a part of India. The Indian Jammu and Kashmir State has several other language and population areas: principally, Dogari in Jammu and Ladakhi in Ladakh. In the Indian Jammu and Kashmir State, Kashmir is the only region of the three (Kashmir, Jammu, Ladakh) that has a Muslim majority. While the Kashmiri language belongs to the Indo-Aryan

family, it has distinctive features and a rich tradition that make Kashmir a unique cultural area.

Kashmir has contributed a great deal to the Indian musical tradition. Some scholars have suggested that Bharata Muni, author of the *Natya Shastra* (The Science of Drama, Dance, and Music), was a Kashmiri. A commentary on the *Natya Shastra* was given by the philosopher Abhinavagupta (1000 A.D.) in his *Abhinava-Bharati.* Sharngadeva (1210–47), whose father went from Kashmir to Devagiri (later renamed Daulatabad) in Maharashtra, wrote the extremely influential *Sangita-Ratnakara* (The Mine of Jewels of Music), which lists 264 rāgas.

The *Rajatarangini,* authored by Kalhana (twelfth century), described the lute, the flute and the drum as common instruments. The Kashmiri sultans were also patrons of dance and music. Popular Kashmiri music goes back to the work of two women: the mystic sayings of Lalleshvari (fourteenth century), and the *lol* poetry of Habba Khatun (sixteenth century). Contemporary practice of these can be seen and heard through the following genres: *vanavun,* which is sung by groups of women at ceremonies and festivals; *chhakri,* sung with instrumental accompaniment in a responsorial style; *sufiyana* music, a classical tradition synthesizing of Indian and Persian elements that goes back to the seventeenth century; *bhand pather,* a dramatic musical form that fuses mythological themes with contemporary social satire; and light songs and *ghazals* popularized by Radio Kashmir starting in the 1930s.

Vanavun

Henzae is thought to be the oldest extant form of the *vanavun* genre of Kashmiri music. In its basic form it is a ceremonial song framed within a couplet, the second line of which is invariably shorter than the first, at least by two syllables. This and other forms of *vanavun* are sung by women at weddings and other ceremonies.

Chhakri

In this popular genre, vocal sections alternate with choral responses and instrumental interludes. The accompaniment is provided by the bowed lute (*sārang*), the plucked lute (*rabāb*), a goblet-shaped drum (*tumbaknari*), a clay pot (*nāt* or *ghātam*), a harmonium, the brass pot (*ghaghar*) and a *chumta* (a forked rod with attached cymbals).

Ruf

Sung by women at religious and social functions, *ruf* (dance song) uses the question and answer form. Arms interlocked round each other's waists and heaving forward and backward, the singers sing couplets in chorus.

Sufiyana Kalam

This is the Kashmiri version of the Indian classical music tradition. The repertoire consists of 54 suites (*maqām*), each of which can be sung over varying lengths of time. The lyrics may be of a *ghazal* or *ruba'i*. The instruments include the *santūr*, the *sāz*, the *setar* (the Kashmiri variant of the *sitār*), and *dokra* (*tablā*). The theory and philosophy behind this music is described in two books from the seventeenth and the eighteenth centuries, written in Persian: the anonymous *Karamat-e mujra* (The Flowering of Munificence), and Daya Ram Kachroo Khushdil's *Tarana-e-Sarur* (The Song of Joy), respectively. *Sufiyana* music is in a state of great decline due to the increasing popularity of lighter songs and *ghazals* influenced by Hindi film music.

Bhand Pather

The *Bhand* dance, to the tune of a specified *maqām* with orchestral accompaniment from the *svarnai*, *dhol*, *nagāra* and the *thalij*, is integral to the dramatic productions of *pather* (from the Sanskrit 'patra,' or 'actor'). These performances begin in the evening and continue until the early hours of the morning. The *svarnai* is a wind instrument like the *shehnai*, only a bit larger. It has a wooden pipe and a reed inside a copper disc, which makes a strong metallic sound. The *dhol* and the *nagāra* are drums; and the *thalij* are metal cymbals.

Popular Music

The music of everyday entertainment has been transformed since the 1950s by radio and television, which are both state-run and broadcast from Srinagar. In particular, light song and *ghazal* have become very popular at the expense of the *chhakri* and *sufiyana kalam*. Just a few commercial films have ever been made in Kashmir. Hindi film songs and Indian classical music broadcast over All India Radio have been influential in the transformation of Kashmiri music. Kashmiri songs are increasingly sung to the light *rāgas* of Hindustani music.

Bibliography

'Abhinava-bharati of Abhinavagupta.' In *Natyasastra of Bharata Muni, with the Commentary Abhinavabharati of Abhinavagupta*. 1964. ed. M. Ramakrishna Kaviand J. S. Pade. Gaekwad's Oriental Series, Vol. IV. Baroda: Oriental Institute.

Aima, Mohanlal. 1969. 'Music of Kashmir.' *Sangeet Natak* 11: 67–73.

Aziz, Sheikh Abdul. 1963–1965. *Koshur Sargam*. 3 vols. Srinagar: Jammu and Kashmir Academy of Arts, Culture and Language.

Bamzai, Prithvi Nath Kaul. 1962. *A History of Kashmir*. Delhi: Metropolitan Book Company.

Danielou, Alain. 1980. *The Ragas of Northern Indian Music*. Delhi: Munshiram Manoharlal.

Natya Shastra, Manomohan Ghosh (trans.). 1967. Calcutta: Manisha Granthalaya,

Pacholczyk, Jozef M. and Arnold, Gordon K. 2000. 'Kashmir.' In *The Garland Encyclopedia of World Music. Vol. 5: South Asia: The Indian Subcontinent*, ed. Alison Arnold. New York: Garland Publishing, 682–95.

Pushp, Prithvi Nath. 1996. 'Henzae: a Folk Genre Viewed Afresh.'*Koshur Samachar* 41. http://www.kashmir.org/KoshSam/Henzae.html

Raina, M.K. 1998. 'The Bhand Pather of Kashmir.' *Kashmir Overseas Association Essay*. http://www.koausa.org/BhandPather/

Shringy, R.K. and Lata Sharma, Prem (ed. and trans.). 1978/1989. *Sangita-Ratnakara of Sharngadeva*. Delhi/New Delhi: Motilal Banarsidass/Munshiram Manoharlal.

Subrahmanyam, Padma. 1979. *Karanas in Indian Dance and Sculpture*. Unpublished Ph.D. Dissertation, Annamalai University.

Discography

(Note: Kashmiri music was not commercially reproduced until the 1970s. The music of the great performers of the radio age is available in the archives of Radio Kashmir and some songs have been reproduced and made available on the Internet at the Web site http://www.Kashmir.org/ which has examples of traditional music also.)

Ensemble Sheikh Abdul Aziz. *Sufyana Musiqi: Classical Sufi Music of Kashmir, India*. New Samarkand Records, SAMCD9005. *2001*: The Netherlands.

Ganai, Gulzar Ahmed. *Maenzraat*. RaviMech, Srinagar. *1995*: India.

Janbaz, Jahanara. *Songs*. Vir House, Jammu. *1995*: India.

Kaul, Arti Tiku. *Lalleshwari Songs*. Lalleshwari International Trust, Delhi. *1993*: India.

Shah, Manzoor Ahmed. *Khaander*. RaviMech, Srinagar. *1996*: India.

Sharma, Shiv Kumar. *Raga Kedar*. Navras Records NRCD 0013. *1983*: UK.

Sharma, Shiv Kumar. *Rag Rageshri*. Moment Records MR 1010. *1993*: USA.

Sharma, Shiv Kumar and Chaurasia, Hari Prasad.

The Valley Recalls: Raga Bhoopali. Navras Records NRCD 0067: UK.

Sharma, Shiv Kumar. *Sampradaya.* Emd/Real World B0000018BC. *1999*: India.

Sopori, Bhajan. *Jugalbandi: Sitar and Santoor.* Music India. *1993*: India.

SUBHASH KAK

Kerala

Population: 31,800,000 (2001)

Kerala, a small state on the southwest coast of India, is one of the most densely populated regions in the world. Its lush terrain is adorned with mountains, forests, plains, the Arabian Sea coast, backwaters and numerous rivers. The region is connected to the rest of the country by roads, waterways, railways and three airports. The population consists of Hindus, Christians, Muslims and a small number of Jews and Jains. Kerala has the highest literacy rate in India. Besides the state-owned radio stations and a television channel, there are five privately owned television stations that provide programs in Malayalam, the local language. Kerala claims the largest regional film industry in the country, and the recording industry is equally active. The monsoon season – June through August – is the busiest time for recording activities.

In common parlance people use two terms to distinguish two broad categories of music: *sangatīm* (music) and *pāttu* or *gānam* (song). The first – derived from the Sanskrit word *sangīt* – denotes the abstract concept of music as well as the cultivated, disciplined art music that has the support of an established theory. Thus, Indian classical music, and compositions for classical and ritual dances such as *bharatanātyam, mohiniattam, kuttiyātam* and *kathakali*, fall within this category. Every other genre of music, including film, folk and devotional song as well as song for stage plays, belongs to the second category.

As elsewhere in India, film is the most popular form of entertainment in Kerala. Over 100 films in Malayalam are released annually. Each film contains three to six songs. What makes these songs popular, besides their dissemination through pre-recorded cassettes and compact discs, is the extensive airplay they receive from radio and television stations. The emergence of a new form of entertainment, known as *gānamēla* (literally, 'song ensemble'), since the 1970s is yet another reason for the vast popularity of film songs. A

performance of *gānamēla* consists of about 20 film songs. A troupe consists of two (a male and a female) to six singers, and an all-male ensemble of performers of traditional and modern musical instruments similar to those played in the original recording. Church and temple festivals, wedding celebrations and even political party conventions are among the occasions that call for a *gānamēla*. At the beginning of the twenty-first century, there were approximately 50 touring ensembles in Kerala. The most popular among them performed also for the expatriate Keralites in the Middle East, Europe and North America.

As well as for movies, song and dance sequences are essential elements for stage plays (*nātakam*). Around 30 professional drama troupes tour within the state, and these troupes produce one new play in Malayalam every one or two years. The Kerala Sangeetha Nātaka Academy promotes new productions by organizing competitions annually. Until the 1980s, drama songs maintained a distinctive character in both melody and orchestration. Melodies showed closer affinity to classical and folk styles, depending on the theme of the play. The orchestra consisted of a small ensemble led by a harmonium player. Often actors themselves sang the songs. Beginning in the 1980s, electronic keyboards replaced the hand-pumped harmonium. Songs have become stylistically similar to film songs. Most troupes employ professional playback singers and orchestral ensembles to prepare pre-recorded songs for the actors to lip-sync on the stage, as in the movies.

The cassette culture became prevalent in Kerala in the early 1980s. Advanced sound recording and copying technologies became available in the cities at about the same time. This led to an unprecedented increase in the number of commercial releases of devotional songs. These releases often coincided with the Hindu, Christian and Muslim religious festivals. For example, there were about 50 releases of prerecorded cassettes of Christian devotional songs in Malayalam during the Christmas season of 1999. Like the songs for stage plays, devotional songs are stylistically similar to film songs. Although consumers of these songs restrict their choice to their respective religious themes, the lyricists, composers and singers cross over religious boundaries. Thus a devout Hindu singer may perform Christian and Muslim devotional songs for their respective audiences.

In general, the soundscape of Kerala's popular music changed considerably during the last quarter of the twentieth century, partly due to the availability of electronic musical instruments and advanced recording technologies. It appeared that the mass media gave far more attention to film and film-style songs than to the numerous local and regional genres and their sonorities.

Bibliography

Groesbeck, Rolf, and Palackal, Joseph. 2000. 'Kerala.' In *The Garland Encyclopedia of World Music. Vol. 5: South Asia*, ed. Alison Arnold. New York and London: Garland Publishing, Inc., 929–51.

Manorama Yearbook. 1999. Kottayam: Malayala Manorama.

JOSEPH J. PALACKAL

Mizoram
Population: 891,058 (2001)

Mizoram is a state in the southern tip of northeast India; Aizawl is its capital. During British rule the region was known as Lushai Hills, and was included in the Assam administration. In post-Independence India, Lusei, a local dialect, known as Huolngo in Burma, became Mizo, the state's lingua franca. The major ethnic clans in the state are Lusei, Chongthu, Thadou and Ralte; the main groups, comprising a mix of the various clans, include Hmar, Paite and Poi. They are a part of a wider community broadly identified as Mizo and Kuki. 'Kuki' refers to the people north of Mizoram, while 'Mizo' is a general appellation for the people of Mizoram. This wider community is concentrated along a contiguous terrain in northeast India, northwest Myanmar (Burma) and the Chittagong Hill tracts in Bangladesh.

In contrast to other regional folk music in India that incorporates elements of Hindi film music (Manuel 1993), Mizo popular tunes are distinctively influenced by Western popular music. The beginnings of this overt influence can be traced to the Welsh Presbyterian Mission, which introduced the Protestant variety of Christianity into the Lushai Hills in the nineteenth century. This brought with it some Western cultural elements, marking the onset of social norms and practices that have ever since made the people receptive to a Westernized lifestyle. From the 1950s, the spread of Hollywood films and Western magazines that markedly increased this identification prepared the grounds for Western popular music to be fused with local Mizo styles.

A notable distinction between the types of indigenous Christian religious music and secular popular music is their accompanying musical instrumentation: the former mainly relies on the traditional drum (*khoung*) made out of animal hide; the latter has adopted the ubiquitous synthesizer, electric guitar and drumset. These instruments are usually the main accompaniments for performances held at social functions.

A similar pattern follows in the local recordings that are broadcast from the government-owned All India Radio station in Aizawl. Western popular music from the 1960s – especially the songs of Jim Reeves and Elvis Presley – disseminated through vinyl, cassettes, shortwave radio, together with the accessibility of Western musical instruments, have served to influence these local recordings of popular music by Mizo artists, who include Lalsangzuali Sailo, Lalrindiki Khiangte and Vanlalsailoa.

The popular music of the Kuki, who are predominantly in the neighboring state of Manipur situated to the north of Mizoram, is marked by melodic characteristics that are unique in comparison to those of other clans. The popular music of the Kuki is often accompanied by an acoustic guitar. An unusual admixture, however, has had increasing influence: Hindi film music that borrows from 'Western musical culture' (Arnold 1988), the 'incorporation of film-music melodies into regional folk music' (Manuel 1993), and ornamental Burmese-style vocals. This adaptation of Kuki music is nearly indistinguishable from Burmese popular music. In addition to this syncretic genre are earlier versions of studio recordings by vocalists such as Jangkholam and Hoinuat made in the All India Radio studio in Imphal, Manipur's capital. These compositions of the 1970s rely essentially on the acoustic guitar for accompaniment and so minimize external influences and maintain a degree of originality that is characteristically Kuki. A fusion of Kuki popular music and *lakoila* (traditional folk music), incorporating the indigenous *goshem* (woodwind instrument made from the shell of gourd and bamboo pipes) began in the 1980s.

Bibliography

Arnold, Alison. 1988. 'Popular Film Song in India – A Case of Mass Market Musical Eclecticism.' *Popular Music* 7(2): 177–88.

Manuel, Peter. 1988. *Popular Music in India: 1901–1986*. Cambridge: Cambridge University Press.

Manuel, Peter. 1993. *Cassette Culture: Popular Culture and Technology in North India*. Chicago: University of Chicago Press.

Discography

Haokip, Jangkholam and Khongsai, Hoinu. Recordings in late 1960s at the All India Radio station, Imphal, Manipur.

SEILEN HAOKIP

Nagaland

Population: 1,209,546 (2001)

Nagaland is a state in northeast India, of which the capital city is Kohima. Nagaland is comprised of a disparate group of tribes, the major ones being Angami, Ao, Sema, Lotha, Konyak and Chakhesang. Each of these tribes has a distinct language, culture and tradition. Nagamese – a derivative of colloquial phrases and terms taken from the Assamese, Hindustani and Bengali languages – serves as the common medium of communication, and is developing into the state's lingua franca.

An early Western influence on Naga popular music was Christian church music. This type of music, especially hymns and choruses, translated from English into various Naga languages, could be categorized as gospel pop. In addition, from the 1950s onwards, there was a widespread following of country and western music in Nagaland. The recordings of Jim Reeves and Cliff Richard (who also sang Christian songs) popularized this genre. Besides these influences, Hollywood films and the media at large have contributed to the general Naga identification with Western popular music. In some ways this style of music and its contemporary counterpart in Nagaland, influenced by what Mitchell (1996) refers to as 'Anglo-American rock hegemony,' expresses Naga cultural identity.

Many would view Naga nationalism as having come about under the influence of British colonialists and Western Christian missionaries (Gray 1986; Jacobs 1990). Certainly, the nineteenth-century Christian missionaries, in setting themselves and their culture as the archetype to be emulated by 'model' converts, induced among Nagas a taste for things Western, including music.

Bollywood films and Hindi music are the preferred genres of non-English speaking Nagas. The regional music of this category has incorporated certain elements and melodies from Hindi film music that Manuel (1993) has noted in other regions of India. This trend has grown with the prevalence of Westernized Hindi popular music on television. A new development has been the launch in the late 1990s of a cable television music channel in Dimapur town, complete with VJing in Nagamese.

Most Naga tribes have groups that play their own renditions of popular music. Performances are usually held at social functions such as weddings and birthday celebrations. For accompaniment, virtually all of the groups play a combination of musical instruments comprising mainly synthesizer, guitar and drumset; the local drum, made out of a wooden log, is mostly utilized during festivals, solemn occasions and church services.

Several well-known Naga vocalists have used Nagamese in their music. Methaneilie Jütakhrie, an Angami, had a big hit with the song 'Nagaland City Kuribole.' The title, which is also the name of the album, 'skewers' the stereotypical Naga clannish characteristics.

Naga popular music has been recorded and distributed locally on cassette tape in Nagaland. The government-owned All India Radio station at Kohima has also made studio recordings that are broadcast as a part of their cultural program. There is as yet no fusion of Naga traditional and popular music.

Bibliography

Gray, Andrew. 1986. 'The British in Nagaland – Their Anthropology and Their Legacy.' In *The Naga Nation and its Struggle against Genocide*. A report compiled by IWGIA, Document 56, Copenhagen, July.

Jacobs, Julian, et al. 1990. *The Nagas*. Stuttgart: Hansjörg Mayer.

Manuel, Peter. 1993. *Cassette Culture: Popular Culture and Technology in North India*. Chicago: University of Chicago Press.

Mitchell, Tony. 1996. *Popular Music and Local Identity*. London: Leicester University Press.

SEILEN HAOKIP

Orissa

Population: 31,659,736 (1991)

Orissa, an eastern coastal state of India situated below West Bengal on the Indian Ocean, has been the site of many famous ancient Hindu kingdoms. When the Emperor Ashoka came to Orissa in the third century B.C. it was called Kalinga, a part of the larger Mauryan Empire and the place where he had his famous conversion to Buddhism. This empire later peacefully influenced the Indianization of the greater portion of Southeast Asia, including Cambodia, Thailand, Jawa (Java) and Sumatra, during medieval times. The celebrated temple complex at Angkor Wat in Cambodia is a splendid example of Orissan architecture, and the name 'Siam' for premodern Thailand is a modification of Shyama Desa, the land of the deity of Krishna. The ancient coastal town of Puri in Orissa is home to the famous Vaishnava temple of Lord Jagannath that attracts millions of pilgrims every year, especially during the annual chariot festival Ratha Yatra in July.

With 37 million people scattered over 103 cities and towns in 30 districts, Orissa comprises a diverse cultural ethnicity that displays a variety of folk and classical music and dance traditions. Often referred to as Odissi, which means simply 'Orissan,' the cultural matrix of the state's art and music traditions is in many ways the result of a unique blend of southern and northern Indian sources. The folk and classical music of Orissa reflects the state's geographical position between the Hindustani classical music of the north and the Karnatic music of the south, such that many forms of popular and devotional song have always drawn from the rhythms and scales of both traditions. Moreover, a newer more vibrant popular music has emerged in recent years due in part to the Odissi film industry, which is less influenced by the European themes that appear in other urban areas of India.

Prior to the development of the film industry in Orissa in the 1930s (first film in 1934, *Seeta Bibaha* [Sita's Wedding], produced by Mohan Sundar Dev Goswami), the musical culture of Orissa was dominated by the religious music and dance associated with the Jagannath Temple in Puri. Odissi, as the dance was called, was a pure classical form originally performed by Devdasis (young women who 'married' the deity for life) called Maharis (from *mahat naris*, 'great women'), and has been recently revived using young boys. The temple music was of classical style set to and inspired by the poems of Jayadeva in his twelfth-century *Gita-Govinda*, a story about the love between Radha and Krishna. Other folk dances such as *chau, dalkhai, ghumra, dhangada-dhangidi, oshakothi* and *pala*, employed various forms of percussive music, even using kettledrums, which provided a cultural source from which some very lively popular music has derived. *Janana* is a popular genre of folk music of the area.

The most famous name in Orissa's modern song, of the decades leading up to the end of the twentieth century, is the late Akshaya Mohanty, who has numerous albums to his credit. Other famous artists include Trupti Das, Arati Basu (folk songs), Chita Jena, Fakir Patnaik, Geeta Patnaik, Gopala Krushna, Raghunath Panigrahi (husband of dancer Sanjukta Panigrahi), Shyamamani Devi,

Bhubaneswari Mishra, Indira Pratihari, Balkrishna Das, Prafulla Kar, Pranab Patnaik, Sikandar Alam and Sushree Sangeeta Mahapatra. In addition to millions of cassette recordings by these and many other popular artists, the presence of popular music on All India Radio (AIR) in Cuttack, and in the capital city of Bhubaneshwar (since 1947), as well as on local programming of the national TV network (Doordarshan), has insured a steady growth of popular and devotional music throughout Orissa.

Bibliography

Ray, Sukumar. 1985. *Music of Eastern India: Vocal Music in Bengali, Oriya, Assamese and Manipuri with Special Emphasis on Bengali.* Calcutta: Firma KLM.

Discography

Alam, Sikandar. *Sikandar Alam.* S/7LPE 149, 183. HMV. n.d.: India.
Das,Trupti and Patnaik, Geeta. *Trupti Das & Geeta Patnaik.* 7EPE. HMV. n.d.: India.
Mohanty, Akshaya. *Akshaya Mohanty.* S/7LPE 148. HMV. n.d.: India.

Filmography

Seeta Bibaha, dir. Mohan Sunder Dev Goswami. 1934. India. Original music by Haricharan Mohanty.

GUY L. BECK

Punjab

'Punjab,' aside from denoting states in India and Pakistan, refers to the corresponding geographic region where the Punjabi language, in its 'standard' or dialect forms, dominates. Traditionally populated by Hindus, Muslims and Sikhs, in 1947 the region was divided between the two new nations, with most Muslims relocating to Pakistan, and Hindu and Sikh Punjabis shifting to the Indian Punjab, Delhi and elsewhere. The combined Punjabi population numbers around one hundred million and, since the 1960s, has come to include a large diaspora in the UK and North America. Despite the divisions created by Partition and the Khalistan (Sikh nationalist) movement of the 1980s, most aspects of Punjabi traditional culture, including music, evolved as, and to some extent remain, the shared patrimony of all three religious communities.

Punjabis have generated one of the most dynamic popular music cultures in South Asia, invigorated, from inception, by the region's rich folk music traditions. These traditions include narrative strophic ballads (*kissa*); devotional genres like *Multani kafi*, (Urdu-language) *qawwāli*, and Sikh *kirtan* and *shabd gurbani*; and a variety of secular genres more influential on modern popular music. Prominent in the latter category are such genres as: women's wedding songs; specific folk songs like *jindua* and *jugni*; *bhangra* and *giddha*, which are regional folk dances traditionally performed at weddings and occasions like the vernal Baisakhi festival; *boli*, which is a form of sung/recited poetry, consisting of a string of (often improvised) one or two-line strophes, sung in a narrow melodic range by a solo singer, perhaps with a responsorial choral refrain, as a brief interlude in a dance-setting like *bhangra* or *giddha*; and *tappa*, a short self-contained song, or one verse of a longer song, typically in the form of an impromptu dialogue between two performers. Forms like *bhangra* might be accompanied by the *dhol*, a large barrel-drum. A distinctive feature of much traditional Punjabi singing is the use of zigzag ornamental patterns, especially at cadential points.

Many commercial recordings (especially cassettes) are made of traditional genres like *tappa*, *jugni* and wedding songs, often with enhanced studio instrumentation, and many performers move back and forth between folk and pop milieus. Further, many specific features of such traditional genres, including melodies, rhythms, modes, instrumentation, ornamentation styles and text themes, persist in recordings that are otherwise clearly in the realm of commercial popular music.

From the emergence of sound cinema in the early 1930s in India, regional popular music styles developed largely in the shadow of the Bombay-based Hindi film-song style. Punjabi music producers such as Ghulam Haider contributed to mainstream Hindi film song, while often interjecting Punjabi features. In the 1930s–1950s, recordings began to be produced of Punjabi-language songs, predominantly in mainstream Hindi film-song style.

The 1960s–1970s saw the evolution and marketing – via radio, records and live performances – of more distinctive forms of Punjabi popular music. Most of these were studio-produced versions of folk songs, perhaps fitted with new lyrics and modernized instrumentation; others were new compositions – especially male-female duets – more or less in folk style. The recording scene was dominated by singers Asa Singh Mastana, Surinder Kaur, and her younger sister Prakash Kaur, whose styles were quite distinct from the shrill film-song norm associated with Lata Mangeshkar.

Although in the 1980s the Indian state of Punjab was wracked by violence, the decade proved to be dynamic for music. In the UK, Punjabi immigrant groups like Alaap cultivated a lively, dance-oriented music which came to be called *bhangra*, fusing disco-style rhythms and timbres with heavy *dhol* drumming and traditional-style melodic fragments. In South Asia, Punjabi popular music evolved in a somewhat parallel rather than derivative fashion, retaining greater emphasis on the Punjabi-language texts, but often incorporating in a similar fashion the vigorous *dhol* rhythms, familiar *bolis*, and the distinctive vocal style of folk music. Influential artists of this period were Mohammed Siddiqi, Sardool Sikander, Kuldip Manak, Malkit Singh (who migrated to the UK in 1984) and especially Gurdas Maan. While Maan modernized the music with Western-style instrumentation, rhythms and other features, he perpetuated many core Punjabi stylistic traits. With an appeal transcending generational, class and religious boundaries, he was particularly celebrated for his fine voice, attractive melodies, tasteful arrangements, dynamic stage demeanor and engaging lyrics. The boom of audio-cassettes precipitated the marketing of a prodigious amount of Punjabi popular music, ranging from neo-traditional women's songs – often generically referred to as *giddha* – to truck-drivers' ditties disparaged for their lewdness.

The period since 1990 has been marked by a number of trends. Singers like Daler Mehndi have extended their popularity beyond the Punjab, often singing in Hindi as well as Punjabi. Links between the diaspora and South Asia have also intensified, via collaborative recordings, international tours and media exchanges. As fusions and remixes abound, musicians freely incorporate aspects of rap, reggae, R&B and techno, while others self-consciously foreground folk roots. With the spread of televisions, music videos have become important aspects of the music scene. Live music continues to be performed at private clubs, stage programs, and free concerts at festivals. In India, as in the diaspora, competitive *bhangra* dance groups, typically accompanied by recorded popular music, have proliferated in college circuits. Aspiring singers are innumerable, with several hundred albums – many self-financed – released in India each year.

Bibliography
Bedi, Sohinder S. 1968. *Punjabi Lok Dhara Vishwa Kosh* [Encyclopedia of Punjabi Folk Tradition]. New Delhi: National Book Shop.

Manuel, Peter. 1988. *Popular Musics of the Non-Western World: An Introductory Survey*. Oxford: Oxford University Press.

Manuel, Peter. 1993. *Cassette Culture: Popular Music and Technology in North India*. Chicago: University of Chicago Press.

Paintal, Geeta. 1988. *Panjab ki Sangeet Parampara*. New Delhi: Radha Publications.

Pande, Alka. 1999. *From Mustard Fields to Disco Lights: Folk Music & Musical Instruments of Punjab*. Ahmedabad: Mapin Publishing.

Schreffler, Gibb. 2002. *Out of the* Dhol *Drums: The Rhythmic 'System' of Punjabi* Bhangra. Unpublished M.A. thesis, University of California, Santa Barbara.

Zuberi, Nabeel. 2002. 'India Song: Popular Music Genres Since Economic Liberalization.' In *Popular Music Studies*, ed. David Hesmondhalgh and Keith Negus. London: Arnold, 238–50.

PETER MANUEL and JOYCE HUGHES

Tamil Nadu
Population: 62,110,839 (2001)

Tamil Nadu is a state in southeastern India. Its leading pop genre is the film song, a syncretic fusion of South Indian classical, Tamil folk and Western music incorporated into feature films. The state capital, Chennai, is the center of Tamil film production, and it is also a vital center for the entire South Indian film industry. Beginning in 1976, music director Iliyaraaja cultivated, in his hundreds of film songs, a leading Tamil film song style that integrates Karnatak, Western classical and Tamil folk music. More recently, music directors such as A.R. Rahman have also incorporated other Western and non-Indian influences into film songs, including rap, reggae and jazz. In the 1990s, remixes became popular among urban young people – familiar film and pop songs reworked to include a fast dance beat and elements of many world musical styles.

Due to the recent advent of affordable audiocassette technology, several traditional and new music genres have entered the mass media, and the Tamil popular music market has become considerably more diverse. Numerous Hindu devotional songs are now commercially marketed and available, set to light classical music and accompanied by traditional and Western instruments. Also, starting in the 1980s, folklore popularizers such as Pushpavanam Kuppuswamy and Prof. Vijayalakshmi Navaneethakrishnan have produced a wide variety of Tamil folk music genres on cassette, including street

dramas, folk devotional songs, lullabies and transplantation songs, bringing these into Tamil Nadu's popular music market (Greene 2001). The Tamil popular music market also includes devotional songs for minority religious groups such as Christians and Muslims, and also urban folk music traditions such as *gānās*. The advent of the Internet has further enhanced the diversity of the popular music market, opening up new channels for music distribution, in particular to Tamil Nadu's middle and upper classes.

Bibliography
Greene, Paul. 2001. 'Authoring the Folk: The Crafting of a Rural Popular Music in South India.' *Journal of Intercultural Studies* 22(2): 161–72.

Discography
Golden Collections of A. R. Rahman. Pyramid CD PYR 8486. 2 CDs. *1996*: India.

Kuppuswamy, Pushpavanam. *Man Vaasam*. Indu Musik IMR 1545. Audiocassette. *1990*: India.

Navaneethakrishnan, Vijayalakshmi. *Kiraamiya Paattukkal (Folk Songs)*. Raaky Audio VNK 099. Audiocassette. *1990*: India.

PAUL D. GREENE

Uttar Pradesh
Population: 166,100,000 (2001)

Uttar Pradesh is India's most populous state, with approximately 79 percent of its 166.1 million residents living in rural areas. Popular musics performed in the Hindi dialects of Bhojpuri, Braj and Awadhi reflect this rural base, while classical and semi-classical musics sung in Urdu and Hindi flourish in the cities of Lucknow, Varanasi (formerly Benaras) and Allahabad. Though much of Uttar Pradesh's popular music is intended for local audiences, some styles have gained national popularity through the work of the region's Hindi film music composers and Hindustani art musicians.

The history of mass-mediated music in Uttar Pradesh begins in 1906–1907, when Fred Gaisberg of the Gramophone Company first recorded courtesan singers from Allahabad, Lucknow, Banaras and Agra. These singers, who included the famous Janki Bai of Allahabad, as well as Malka Jan of Agra and Kurshaid Jan of Kanpur, were best known as proponents of *thumri* and *ghazal*, but their recorded repertoire also included local seasonal genres such as *holi*, *kajri* and *chaiti* (Kinnear 1994, 238–53). Though commercially produced, their recordings did not represent a truly 'popular' music since they were enjoyed only by the upper classes and were not significantly different from live performance (Manuel 1993, 353). The Gramophone Company emerged in India at a time of transition, when elites were beginning to withdraw patronage from a variety of folk and popular art forms and the reformist tendencies of nationalism were leading to the demise of courtesan culture. The Gaisberg recordings bolstered singers' popularity and assisted some of them in negotiating a transition from courtesan to concert performer (Manuel 1987, 15).

The next major event in the history of popular music in Uttar Pradesh was the birth of the Hindi film song, an eclectic genre that emerged in the 1940s from a blending of Western and Indian musical styles and instrumentation. Though the Hindi film industry was based in Mumbai (Bombay), a few prominent Hindi film music composers from Uttar Pradesh have turned to the music of their native state for inspiration. Naushad Ali, a Lucknow-born composer, used elements of Bhojpuri folk music in his score for *Ganga Jamuna* (1961) and drew on Lucknow salon music in his songs for *Pakeezah* (1971). Film music has in turn inspired changes in the performance of folk music in Uttar Pradesh. By the 1950s, film music began replacing or supplementing live performance at weddings in the region, and served as a source of new melodies for performers and composers of *birhā, nautanki, qawwāli* and *kajli* (Manuel 1988, 186; Marcus 1992–93, 103).

As discussed by Manuel, the advent of cassette technology in the 1980s transformed the popular music scene in Uttar Pradesh by providing regional alternatives to Hindi film music. The music of Mumbai films is created in studios and disseminated almost entirely through recordings, while regional cassette musics of Uttar Pradesh are studio versions of genres with active live performance traditions (Manuel 1993, 176–77). In a case study of 'cassette culture,' Manuel discusses how cassette versions of erotic *Braj rasiya* are musically and culturally distinct from their live performance counterparts. *Rasiya* was formerly sung by women in sex-segregated home environments, but has acquired a distinctly male orientation through cassette technology. Since 'respectable' women do not sing *rasiya* in public, the singers on cassettes are either courtesans or men, and the scantily clad women on the cassette covers are there for the male gaze. In cassette recordings, songs tend to be shorter than in live performances: microphones enable singers to sing more quietly, and synthesizers are sometimes used in musical interludes (Manuel 1993, 196–230).

More recently, a few classical musicians from Uttar Pradesh have made recordings that reacquaint national audiences with music from the region. Shubha Mudgal, a classically trained crossover singer from Allahabad, was the music director and lead vocalist for a set of two cassettes entitled *Wedding Songs of Uttar Pradesh* (1994) produced by Music Today, a subsidiary of the national conglomerate Living Media. Mudgal recreates the sparse textures of folk music but adds synthesized sounds and uses classically trained singers whose voices are augmented by artificial reverberation. Though informed by the overall sound of Hindi film, this new popularized 'folk' music is not mediated through films, and unlike most cassettes by smaller companies in Uttar Pradesh and Delhi, these cassettes have English-language covers and are marketed to a middle-class, all-India audience.

From the courtesan singers of early recordings to the classical musicians and film song composers of later years, recording personalities of Uttar Pradesh have been introducing their native music to national audiences for almost a century. In return, Hindi film music has helped shape the landscape of popular music in Uttar Pradesh, and local musicians have both appropriated film music in creative ways and resisted its hegemony through cassettes of local popular genres.

Bibliography

Kinnear, Michael. 1994. *The Gramophone Company's First Indian Recordings: 1899–1908*. Bombay: Popular Prakashan.

Kumar, Nita. 1988. *The Artisans of Banaras: Popular Culture and Identity, 1880–1986*. Princeton, NJ: Princeton University Press.

Manuel, Peter. 1987. 'Courtesans and Hindustani Music.' *Asian Review* (Spring): 12–17.

Manuel, Peter. 1988. *Popular Musics of the Non-Western World: An Introductory Survey*. New York: Oxford University Press.

Manuel, Peter. 1993. *Cassette Culture: Popular Music and Technology in North India*. Chicago: University of Chicago Press.

Marcus, Scott. 1992–93. 'Recycling Indian Film Songs: Popular Music as a Source of Melodies for North Indian Folk Musicians.' *Asian Music* 24 (1): 101–109.

'Provisional Population Totals: India.' *Census of India 2001*. 4 April 2001. http://www.censusindia.net

Discographical Reference

Mudgal, Shubha. *Wedding Songs of Uttar Pradesh, Vols. 1 and 2*. Music Today. *1994*: India.

Discography

Chaurasia, Hariprasad. 'Marriage Song from Uttar Pradesh.' *Rag Ahir Bhairav; Marriage Song.* Nimbus NI 5111. *1987*: United Kingdom.

Filmography

Ganga Jamuna, dir. Nitin Bose. 1961. India. 170 mins. Musical. Original music by Naushad Ali.

Pakeezah, dir. Kamal Amrohi. 1971. India. 148 mins. Musical. Original music by Naushad Ali, Ghulam Mohammed.

ANNA SCHULTZ

CITIES

Ahmadabad

Population: 4,500,000 (2003)

This capital of Gujarat State is the largest urban center located between Mumbai and Delhi; it has a growing international presence in commerce and is the center of Gujarati culture. Although dominated by the products of Mumbai's pop and film music industries and the Western pop music filtered into the city by the large number of Gujaratis living overseas, Ahmedabad has a distinctive traditional popular music culture centered largely on the yearly festival of Navaratri (usually September/October). Primarily a folk music form of group circle dance, the musics associated with this festival, *dandia* and *ras garba*, are distinctively Gujarati popular forms, well represented in locally and regionally produced cassettes.

Contemporary popular *ras garba* singers include Mridula Desai, Uday Mazumdar and Karsan Sagathia, and Veena Mehta. Singer Falguni Pathak, who leads his own *garba* group, is one of many that tour internationally during Navaratri. More recently, disco-style rhythms and electronic effects have been added to recorded *dandiya* tracks (in consonance with the general trend toward remix in India) to attract younger audiences to this community-based music. This style has been relabeled 'disco dandiya.'

Other traditional forms of Gujarati popular music, all available in cassette form, are Gujarati variants on regional forms. Wedding song (*lagana geet*) and Gujarati Ghazal (sometimes labeled *sugam sangeet*) singers include the late Avinash Vyas, as well as Ninu Mazmudar, Kadmudi Munshi and Kshemu Divetiya.

Recordings of distinctively Gujarati popular music are also derived from *bhavai* music drama. Historically, popular artists include Jayshankar Nayak, Prabhakar Kirti and Ghanshyam Nayak.

Djing and and Dj-dominated dance parties appeared in Ahmedabad in the 1990s. These are especially prevalent during the period from December to February.

Ahmadabad is also a distribution point for the small amount of locally produced popular music from Kutch, in far western Gujarat.

GREGORY BOOTH

Chennai (Madras)

Population: 4,216,268 (2001)

Chennai, capital city of the State of Tamil Nadu, is a metropolis located on India's southeastern coast by the Indian Ocean. The city is India's fourth-largest, with an area of 67 sq miles (174 sq km) and a population of 4.2 million people. Formerly known as Madras, the area once contained fishing villages, long since subsumed into the urban sprawl, and some significant Hindu temples that survive to the present. An early British trading post was established there in 1640, and Madras was incorporated in 1688. It became the capital of British-ruled south India and was their most important colonial Indian city until Calcutta was later developed.

Like all of India, Chennai has changed significantly in the past few decades, experiencing the achievement of national independence in 1947, the pressures of increasing urbanization, and more recently the effects of governmental policies of economic liberalization and globalization. The city is a national center of education, industry, technology and the arts. The culture and lifestyle of Chennai is regarded by many as more traditional than that of other Indian cities. The main local language is Tamil; other Indian languages and English are also spoken. The Tamil language has an ancient literature and is greatly loved by its speakers, who primarily live in Tamil Nadu, Sri Lanka, Malaysia and other communities in Southeast Asia, North America, Europe and elsewhere.

Popular music in Chennai encompasses many genres: film music, pop music, advertisement jingles for television and radio, brass band music at weddings and festivals, stage show concerts by light music troupes, rock, jazz, fusion, Indian and Western choral groups, Western classical guitar and orchestra ensembles, music for theater and drama productions and background music for television programs.

Film Music

Chennai is one of India's major producers of films and film music, the most important form of popular music throughout the nation. The city's film industry is often called 'Kollywood,' for Hollywood with the 'K' representing Kodambakkam, a locale with many studios. The output of the Chennai film studios rivals that of the more well-known Hindi-language Bollywood industry of Mumbai. Tamil folk music and Hindu, Muslim and Christian devotional music performances and recordings are part of the city's musical life. Chennai is also the most important center in India for the southern Indian classical traditions of Karnatak (or Carnatic) music and Bharatanatyam dance. The city is home to many writers, visual artists, actors, filmmakers, craft artisans, dancers and musicians.

Music has always been a vitally important ingredient in Indian movies. Early films usually portrayed a mythological story or saint's biography, while later film genres include social, patriotic, action, family and romance films. Beginning with the first Tamil talkie *Kalidas* in 1931, early sound films often had dozens of short songs. The forms, styles and instruments used in songs and background music were developed from precedents of the silent film era (in India, 1898–1931), as well as urban theater drama productions, traditional theatrical and folk performances and storytelling traditions. South Indian film music makes use of a wide range of stylistic influences, including Karnatak and Hindustani classical music, bands and orchestras of the colonial British rulers and Indian Maharajas, foreign popular music, Western classical music and many genres of religious, popular and folk music from all over the India.

Vocal melodies lie at the heart of Tamil film songs, and listeners appreciate beautiful melodies, the particular voices of star singers and the poetics of the lyrics. Others enjoy beats and rhythms, instrumental timbres and textures, or arrangements and song forms. Instrumental sounds are not insignificant, and may be used to signal important ideas to the movie audience, such as sounding a *rāga* (melodic mode) to set a certain mood, or a folk rhythm to establish a rural scene. There is no single typical ensemble for film music, but instruments utilized include: synthesizer, sampled sounds, violin, string ensemble, trumpet, saxophone, clarinet, acoustic guitar, electric guitar, bass guitar, drumset, vibraphone, Indian percussion such as *mridangam* and *tavil* (double-headed barrel drums), *urumi* (folk friction drum), *tablā* (north Indian pair of drums), *ghātam* (clay pot), Indian bamboo flute, *nāgasvaram* (double-reed horn) and *vīnā* (string instrument similar to the *sitār*).

Composers of film songs are known as 'music directors' or simply 'MDs' and, if successful, they may become internationally famous. The duo M.S. Viswanathan and T.K. Ramamoorthy were the leading MDs of the 1960s and 1970s, while Iliyaraaja dominated the 1980s and A.R. Rahman the 1990s. Viswanathan-Ramamoorthy produced many hit songs with beautiful vocal melodies; Viswanathan has continued to sing, compose and perform concerts well into the first decade of the twenty-first century. Iliyaraaja's hit debut film score was for *Annakilli* (1976); since then he has composed for over 800 films. He was born poor in a small remote village, receiving no formal education, but with many early musical experiences and his well-known self-discipline, he managed to become probably the best-loved Tamil film music director. Iliyaraaja's music is noted for its complex instrumental arrangements and his unique blend of Tamil folk, Indian classical, and Western classical and pop music genres. Film scholar Theodore Baskaran described Iliyaraaja's music as both 'innovative' and 'authentically folk' (Baskaran 2002), thus neatly summarizing how it can be challenging and interesting while remaining tied to local styles and traditions. In 2004, Illiyaraaja undertook the 'Thiruvasakam in Symphony' project, composing a piece for Western orchestra inspired by an ancient Tamil philosophical poem. His goal was to use performances, recordings, and Western notation to make available – to the world – an Indian 'musical masterpiece in an universally accepted format which others can read and play' (Thiruvasakam in Symphony 2004). He toured the world visiting associations of Tamil people to raise funds for the work and an envisioned music education center which he will direct in Chennai.

A.R. Rahman began his career as a keyboard performer and composer of some 300 jingles for television ads. His debut film score, for *Roja* (released in 1992), was very popular and won him many awards, including the Government of India's National Film Award for best music director. He was born Dilip Kumar as a Hindu, converting to Islam after a Muslim saint saved the life of his sister. He is known to be very devout and studious about his religion – he has completed a *hajj* (pilgrimage) to Mecca – and he possesses a somewhat mystical personal nature. Rahman's music has been very influential in part due to his early use of advanced studio technologies like sampling. Hallmarks of his music include lush orchestrations, unusual voices and a melodic and rhythmic style that was quite different from others. In 2003–2004, Rahman's music was featured in the Andrew Lloyd Webber musical *Bollywood Dreams*, produced in London and on Broadway in New York. Some other significant composers of South Indian film music include: Karthik Raja, Yuvan Shankar Raja, Bhavatarini (the preceeding are children of Iliyaraaja), Adithyan, Deva, Dina, Harris Jeyaraj, K.V. Mahadevan, S.A. Rajkumar, G. Ramanathan, Mani Sharma, S.M. Subbaiah Naidu, G.K. Venkatesh and Vidyasagar.

There are only a small number of artists who create the large corpus of film music for the hundreds of movies produced annually. Singers are deeply loved by fans, and may enjoy popularity greater than that of film stars. Some vocalists are: S.P. Balasubramaniam, M.K. Thyagaraja Bhagavatar, Chitra, Vasundara Das, L.R. Eswari, Hariharan, S. Janaki, Kavita Krishnamurthy, Shankar Mahadevan, T.M. Soundarajan, P.B. Srinivasa, K.B. Sundarambal, P. Susheela, P. Unnikrishnan and K.J. Yesudas. Well-known lyricists for Tamil film songs are even fewer in number, and include Gangai Amaran, Kannadasan, Papanasam Sivan, Vairamuthu and Vali.

Musicians trained in various genres reside in Chennai and are available for recording sessions and live performances or stage shows. Music schools and private teachers in town teach Western music or, much more commonly, Indian classical music. There are many modern digital audio recording studios throughout Chennai, such as Audio Media, AVM Audio and Pallavi Digital Audio Studio. The process of creating a film song is a lengthy team effort that attempts to fulfill the needs of the movie's narrative as well as the requirements of song form and style. Typically, the film director and music director begin with a discussion of the film's story and overall style. The music director, alone or with assistants, develops appropriate songs that are then shared with the film's producers in a 'composing session.' Next, instrumental tracks are recorded in a studio, using temporary vocal tracks. Star singers are later brought in to re-record the vocal tracks, and then the song is ready for release to the public, perhaps ahead of the film itself.

Songs for films are then 'picturized,' a process in which scenes are filmed to fit the song. As the pre-recorded song plays, the actors mouth the lyrics (hence the term 'playback' singing) and dance, often with a number of choreographed dancers in the background. The finished song sequence then becomes part of a film, but can also circulate widely outside of movie theaters. Songs from a single film are released on audiocassette and compact disc, and may be compiled into packages of hits by a particular singer, music director or actor. Video compact discs are similarly marketed. Television became very widely available in the early years of the twenty-first century in Chennai, and many satellite and cable channels broadcast entire films as well as programs of songs. Lyrics are of particular interest to audiences, and booklets of lyrics are available near cinema halls; nowadays lyrics are posted online. Fans use such resources to learn to sing film songs, and may share their renditions as karaoke, or in games that test one's knowledge of the repertoire. Other elements of the film music culture of Chennai include giant hoardings (billboards for current films) that line certain major streets, with huge hand-painted depictions of stars. Shops ranging from small stalls to mega-stores sell music recordings; major public holidays commemorate the lives of famous actors of the past; and film and music reviews are published in magazines and newspapers.

Pop and Rock Music

Tamil pop music is also produced in Chennai, and the recordings are sometimes known as 'private albums' to differentiate them from film music. Artists of this genre include Suresh Peters, Aruradha Sriram, Subha and Aslam Mustafa. They sing in the Tamil language and utilize many styles, from Western rock and pop to Indian film and folk music. Because film music is produced by a group and must adhere to a film, it cannot express the personal point of view of a singer or composer; however, in Tamil pop there is the possibility of an individual expression. For example, a review of music director Mahesh Shankar and vocalist Anita Chandrasekaran's pop album *Mugangal* (2002) noted that '[t]he album is an effort to portray some of emotions encountered in our daily lives' (Ram n.d.). These two artists were raised in India but now reside in the United States and, interestingly, they are not the only Indians of the diaspora to produce a Tamil pop album: another is US based composer-singer Sampath, whose *Sam's Pops Pops* (2001) was recorded in Chennai. Some film music directors have released private albums, such as A.R. Rahman's pop revival of the national anthem, *Vande Mataram* (1997), and Iliyaraaja's *How to Name It?* (1987), a fusion of Western and Indian classical styles featuring violinist V.S. Narasimhan.

Rock music thrives in Chennai as well. Some bands active at the turn of the millennium include:

Another Page, the Banned, Burn, Grasshopper Green, Mercury Rising, Moksha, Molotov Cocktail, Mystique, Nemesis Avenue (which included A.R. Rahman on keyboards), Octane, Rare Junk and the Revelations. Many bands play covers of songs by US and British rock groups like Pink Floyd, Santana, Metallica and the Eagles, while others perform originals influenced by genres such as metal, funk, classic rock and Indian classical music. Rock bands are often comprised of college students, and thus may disband when the members graduate, while other groups consist of professional musicians and have a longer life. The rock scene is active, yet has not achieved a level of commercial success comparable to that of film music. The band Moksha states on its website (http://www.mokshaonline.com/index.htm) that rock in India has not fared well due to a lack of support from Indian record labels and broadcasters, and the failure of many bands to develop a distinctive identity and a repertoire of original compositions.

There is an informal circuit of colleges and music festivals at which rock music is performed all over India. In Chennai, there are many college campuses that host rock shows, among them Madras Christian College, the University of Madras, Indian Institute of Technology Madras, Loyola College and Stella Maris College. Other venues for rock include the Vineyard Center. Event management companies such as Boardwalkers produce concerts, musicals and shows in Chennai. An article about this company noted that the past decade has seen so much growth in Chennai's non-film popular music scene that some people now proclaim the city as 'happening,' replacing its previous image as the 'sleepy city' (Kumar 2000).

Bibliography

Baskaran, S. Theodore. 1996. *The Eye of the Serpent: An Introduction to Tamil Cinema*. Madras, India: East-West Books, 38–61.

Baskaran, S. Theodore. 'Music for the People.' *The Hindu*, online edition. January 6, 2002. http://www.hindu.com/thehindu/mag/2002/01/06/stories/2002010600150500.htm [Accessed May 20, 2004].

Booth, Gregory. 1996/97. 'The Madras Corporation Band: A Story of Social Change and Indigenization.' *Asian Music* 28(1): 61–87.

Greene, Paul. 2000. 'Pop Music and Audio-Cassette Technology: Southern Area.' In *The Garland Encyclopedia of World Music. Vol. 5: South Asia, The Indian Subcontinent*, ed. Alison Arnold. New York: Garland, 554–59.

Greene, Paul. 2000. 'Film Music: Southern Area.' In *The Garland Encyclopedia of World Music. Vol. 5: South Asia, The Indian Subcontinent*, ed. Alison Arnold. New York: Garland, 542–46.

Dickey, Sara. 1993. *Cinema and the Urban Poor in South India*. Cambridge: Cambridge University Press.

Kumar, Rajat. 2000. 'From Staid to Swing – with the Boardwalkers.' Chennaionline.com. http://www.chennaionline.com/bandstand/boardwalkers.asp [Accessed May 31, 2004].

L'Armand, Kathleen and Adrian L'Armand. 1983. 'One Hundred Years of Music in Madras: A Case Study in Secondary Urbanization.' *Ethnomusicology* 27(3): 411–38.

Manuel, Peter. 1993. *Cassette Culture: Popular Music and Technology in North India*. Chicago: University of Chicago Press.

Mohan, Anuradha. 1994. *Ilaiyaraja: Composer as Phenomenon in Tamil Film Culture*. Unpublished M.A. thesis. Middletown, Connecticut: Wesleyan University.

Moksha. 'Moksha's Official Site: Rock in India.' http://www.mokshaonline.com/index.htm [Accessed February 1, 2004].

Narayan, R. K. 1990. 'On Films.' In *A Story-Teller's World*. New Delhi: Penguin Books, 110–112.

Rajadhyaksha, Ashish, and Paul Willemen, eds. 1995. *Encyclopaedia of Indian Cinema*. Oxford: University Press.

Ram, Vignesh. 'Mugangal – Music Review.' Nilacharal.com, a Tamil ezine. http://www.nilacharal.com/enter/review/mugangal.html [Accessed May 29, 2004].

Scott, Iain. 1997 'Rahman Empire.' *Folk Roots* 18: 25–27.

Thiruvasakam in Symphony. 'The Project Plan.' http://www.thiruvasakaminsymphony.com/v_eng.htm#8a [Accessed May 8, 2004].

Discographical References

Iliyaraaja. *How to Name It?*. Oriental Records. ORI CD 115 1987. *1987*: USA.

Rahman, A.R. *Vande Mataram* Columbia Records/Sony Music Entertainment India CK 68525. *1997*: USA.

Shankar, Mahesh and Chandrasekaran, Anita. *Mugangal*. Dreams Audio. *2002*: India.

Discography

50 Glorious Playback Years, Independent India's Greatest Hits: Tamil. The Gramophone Company of India SFHV 849415-849419. *1997*: India.

Iliyaraaja. *Super Hits of Iliyaraaja*. AVM Audio Sony Music AV 5108 4. *2000*: India.

Legends: Mellisai Mannargal Viswanathan Rama-moorthy. The Gramophone Company of India STHV 858573-858577. *1997*: India.

Mustafa, Aslam. *Excuse Me, Tamil Pop.* The Gramophone Company of India SCHVS 849385. *1997*: India.

Peter, Suresh. *Minnal.* Aruna Records. *1996*: India.

Rahman, A.R. *Roja.* Lahari Recording. *1994*: India.

Sampath. *Sam's Pops Pops.* Meta Audio Sam 001. *2001*: India.

Sriram, Anoorada. *Chennai Girl, Tamil Pop.* Magnasound C6-P2417. *1997*: India.

Subha. *Vaalparai Vattaparai, Tamil Techno Folk Songs.* Super Recording SR 115. *2000*: India.

Vidyasagar. *Snehithiye.* BGM Crescendo India 10356. *2000*: India.

Filmography

Annakilli, dir. Devaraj-Mohan. 1976. Chennai, India. Social Drama. Songs composed by I. Iliyaraaja.

Kalidas, dir. H.M. Reddy. 1931. Chennai, India. Epic Drama. Songs composed based on South Indian classical music.

Roja, dir. Mani Ratnam. 1993. Chennai, India. Social Drama. Songs composed by A.R. Rahman.

JOSEPH GETTER

Delhi

Population: 13,800,000 (2001)

The National Capital Territory of Delhi sits on a plain in North India and incorporates New Delhi (the capital of India) as well as Old Delhi and numerous villages. These areas have merged into a sprawling metropolis with a rich history, diverse population, and thriving culture and economy. Delhi is the third-largest city in India, with a fast-growing population of 13.8 million (2001 census) and an area of 573 sq miles (1,483 sq km). It borders the states Uttar Pradesh to the east and Haryana in other directions; the Yamuna River, a tributary of the Ganga (Ganges River), flows through the city. Delhi's long recorded history begins in the first century B.C.; from the twelfth through eighteenth centuries A.D. a succession of Turkish, Mughal, Persian and Maratha rulers left seven cities, including Tughlakabad and Shahjahabanad. The British ruled from the early 1800s and, in 1911, moved the colonial Indian capital from Calcutta (now Kolkata) to their new, planned city of New Delhi. It subsequently became the capital of India when the nation achieved independence in 1947.

Delhi has long been a cultural crossroads, and continues to draw people from throughout India and around the world. The city's main institutions are numerous industries, universities, government bureaucracies, non-governmental organizations, diplomatic missions and multi-national companies. Hindi, Punjabi, Urdu and English are the city's primary languages, and there are sizeable populations of speakers of India's many regional languages, such as Bengali and Tamil. Delhi is the base for many significant national cultural organizations, including the Sangeet Natak Akademi (National Academy of Music, Dance and Drama), the Indira Gandhi National Center for the Arts, Natrang Pratishthan (Theater Resource Center) and the Archives and Research Center for Ethnomusicology. The Delhi government's cultural organizations include the Sahitya Kala Parishad (for music, dance, drama and visual art). Dilli Haat, a model village in South Delhi with workshops and vendors of crafts and folk arts, creates both jobs for artisans and a destination for Delhi's many tourists. Numerous trade, book, film, holiday and religious festivals are held in Delhi throughout the year. Republic Day (26 January) is a major public event with a televised parade of state cultures, musicians and dancers, and military hardware through the main governmental area. Weddings and religious festivals such as Diwali (the Hindu festival of light) include processions of brass bands (with clarinet, valved brass horns, percussion, and amplified keyboards and vocalists) playing Bollywood film songs and other repertoire.

Delhi has many forms of mass media, and is home to several national newspapers, government radio and television broadcasters, and private broadcast and cable networks. Internet access is rapidly growing. The city has modern audio recording studios (e.g., Studio Synthesis India, Neelam Recordings, Simran Audio Studio, BPM Studio and Alfa Sound Studios), and a small film and television production industry. Many shops around the city sell recordings of a variety of music genres. In India, the music and film industries have suffered decreased earnings in recent years due to the growing phenomenon of piracy, the unlicensed production of media such as audiocassettes, CDs and MP3s. Some production and distribution of pirated music occurs in Delhi, and occasional news accounts of police raids on factories and warehouses relate the seizure of thousands of illegal copies.

Indipop is a term for various styles of music that combine Indian instruments, melodies and rhythms with international pop and rock music styles. Delhi-based Shubha Mudgal is a classically trained Hindustani singer who has released several pop albums, including her 1999 debut hit *Ab ke Sawan*. Her music features a powerful voice, and a mix of rock, pop, classical *rāgas*, and Indian regional and folk musics. The band Euphoria began as a college band in Delhi and has released three albums of '*Hindrock*,' blending rock, pop and Indian styles such as *ghazal* and Punjabi folk music. The band RockNRaga, led by Raja Bhattacharya, term themselves as 'Delhi's hot pop band.' They are a cover band that performs a large repertoire of disco, Latin, jazz standards, US pop and rock, reggae, and old Hindi film music at venues such as corporate events and college campuses.

Daler Mehndi, the self-styled 'Pasha of Pop,' is considered to be the most popular international star of *bhangra*. He is also Delhi's most prominent popular musician, having moved to the city in his youth and maintained his base there. *Bhangra* is a musical style based on Punjabi harvest festival folk music, and is characterized by its dance moves and an insistent rhythm played on the *dhol* (a large barrel-drum). The music was transformed from rural folk to urban electronic dance music in the 1980s by South Asians in the United Kingdom, and now has a global audience. *Bhangra* is found in live concerts, music videos, studio recordings, at informal '*bhangra* parties' at universities and nightclubs, and as staged, choreographed dance routines performed by troupes in costume. In 2003, police accused Mehndi of smuggling people to the West by disguising them as crew members for his international tours; the charges were found to be false and the high-profile case was dropped. Mehndi has spearheaded civic initiatives such as the Daler Mehndi Green Drive, which has planted thousands of trees in Delhi. His album *Mojaan Laen Do* (2003) is a move away from *bhangra* towards a new sound that revives *rabāb* music, an old style of Sikh religious music with Sufi and Arabic musical influences; he released it on his own music label: Daler Mehndi Music Company.

Delhi has a lively rock music scene. Indian rock musicians usually form bands, rather than launching solo careers, as is the norm in film and pop music. Many rock bands play original Indian rock; some exclusively perform their own compositions, while others play a mix of originals and covers of American rock songs. Various forms of metal are common, as well as blues, funk, electronica, and fusions with Indian, jazz and global influences. Many rock fans and musicians voice an extreme

distaste for other genres of Indian popular music such as film music and *Indipop*. Rock bands based in Delhi include After Dark, Anupam, Envision, the Karmic Circle, Orange Street, Parikrama and Them Clones; the online *Rock Street Journal* lists almost 50 rock bands based in Delhi. The group Parikrama also runs a music school with courses in guitar, bass and drums. The rock concert circuit consists primarily of university shows, in settings such as parties, festivals and battle-of-the-bands competitions, such as the Avalanche festival at the Netaji Subhas Institute of Technology, Quest at Delhi College of Engineering, and Utopia at the School of Planning and Architecture. The multinational clothing company Levi's sponsors the festival Great Indian Rock, and in 2004 held its eighth annual event in both Mumbai and Delhi with two days of outdoor concerts by rocks bands from around the country.

Throughout Delhi there are many discos, pubs, nightclubs, bars and banquet facilities with music and dancing (for example, www.wanabuzz.com lists over 100 such establishments). These trendy, often expensive, and popular clubs host local, national and international DJs spinning a variety of genres of dance music. A venue or event might be devoted to a particular style, such as rock, techno, Latin, hip-hop or Punjabi. Some electronic dance music is produced locally: Delhi-based Midival Punditz, a duo of Gaurav Raina and Tapan Raj, record techno music in their own studio and perform internationally. Their music is computer and synthesizer-based, with Indian vocals, percussion and melodic instruments contributed by guest artists. They are part of the international Asian Massive movement, connecting them to artists such as Talvin Singh of London and Karsh Kale of San Francisco.

Bibliography

Arnold, Alison. 2000. 'Film Music: Northern Area.' In *The Garland Encyclopedia of World Music. Vol. 5: South Asia, The Indian Subcontinent*, ed. Alison Arnold. New York: Garland Pub, 531–41.

Arnold, Alison, et al. 2001. 'India. VIII. Film and popular musics.' *The New Grove Dictionary of Music and Musicians*, ed. S. Sadie and J. Tyrrell. London: Macmillan, Vol. 12, 253–60.

Booth, Gregory. 1990. 'Brass Bands: Tradition, Change, and the Mass Media in Indian Wedding Music.' *Ethnomusicology* 34/2, 245–62.

Booth, Gregory. 2000. 'Popular Artists and Their Audiences.' *The Garland Encyclopedia of World Music. Vol. 5: South Asia, The Indian Subcontinent*, ed. Alison Arnold. New York: Garland, 418–29.

Daler Mehndi. Official site.
   http://www.dalermehndi.com
Joshi, G.N. 1988. 'A Concise History of the Phonograph Industry in India.' *Popular Music* 7(2), 147–56.
Manuel, Peter. 1988. 'Popular Music in India, 1901–1986.' *Popular Music* 7(2), 157–76.
Midival Punditz. Official site.
   http://www.punditz.com
Parikrama. Band and school site.
   http://www.parikrama.com
RockNRaga. Band's site. http://hotdelhiband.
   tripod.com/roadhouseblooz/index.html
RSJ Online. Online edition of *RSJ* (*Rock Street Journal*), with links to many bands and events.
   http://www.rsjonline.com
Wanabuzz. Delhi club and DJ listings.
   http://www.wanabuzz.com

Discographical References

Mehndi, Daler. *Mojaan Laen Do*. Daler Mehndi Music Company DM03. *2003*: India.
Mudgal, Shubha. *Ab ke Sawan*. Virgin Records 7243 847641 2 8. *1999*: India.

Discography

Envision. *Patterns & Moodswings*. RSJ Records. *2003*: India.
Euphoria. *Dhoom*. Archies Music. *1998*: India.
Euphoria. *Phir Dhoom*. Archies Music A-136. *2000*: India.
Euphoria. *Gully*. Super Cassettes Industries SNCD 01/3317. *2002*: India.
Levi's. *Great Indian Rock, Vol. 4*. RSJ Records. n.d.: India.
Mehndi, Daler. *Bolo Ta Ra Ra*. Magnasound 1679. *1995*: India.
Mehndi, Daler. *Dardi Rab Rab*. Magnasound 2296. *1996*: India.
Mehndi, Daler. *Mojaan Laen Do*. Daler Mehndi Music Company DM03. *2003*: India.
Midival Punditz. *Midival Punditz*. Six Degrees 657036 1079-2. *2002*: USA.
Mudgal, Shubha. *Ab ke Sawan*. Virgin Records (India) 7243 847641 2 8. *1999*: India.
Orange Street. *Drive Carefully for Our Shake*. RSJ Records. *2003*: India.

JOSEPH GETTER

Jammu

Population: City – 378,431 (2001)

Jammu is the capital city of the Jammu region of the Jammu and Kashmir State. The main language of the region is Dogari, but a large number of Kashmiri-speaking refugees settled here in the 1990s due to the ongoing insurgency in the Kashmir valley. Punjabi and Hindi are other languages that are commonly spoken. Jammu is the winter capital of the Jammu and Kashmir State and its economy is based largely on tourism to the nearby Vaishno Devi shrine.

Dogari folk music, which belongs to the Hindustani Pahari music tradition, popular in the hills of Jammu and Himachal Pradesh, is also popular in urban Jammu. The musical accompaniment to these songs is simple, consisting usually of a drum (*dholaki*) and often a flute. The tunes, however, are rich in beauty and variety. In addition, there are many schools that teach Hindustani classical music. Hindi film music is popular here as elsewhere in the Jammu and Kashmir State. An important force in the cultural life of Jammu are the local stations of the state-run Radio Kashmir and Doordarshan television network, which provides patronage to the local artists.

Kundan Lal Saigal (1904–47), actor and singer (and perhaps the greatest name in the early Hindi film-music era) and Malika Pukhraj (1920–2004), the famous singer of *ghazals* in classical Hindustani style and of Dogari songs who later lived in Pakistan, were both from Jammu.

Shiv Kumar Sharma, the great classical instrumentalist, is also from Jammu. Born in 1938, he had his training from his father, Uma Dutt Sharma, a state musician of Jammu and Kashmir.

Sharma is known for elevating the *santūr* to a major concert hall instrument through his innovations and characteristic style. An ancient instrument (in Sanskrit, *shatatantri vina*, 'a hundred-stringed lute'), it has steel strings on a trapezoidal frame that are struck with small wooden hammers. He modified the *santūr* by increasing the number of bridges to get a wider range of octaves, and changed the system of tuning and the structural configuration of the strings to allow for more precision on note reproduction. His album *The Call of the Valley* (1995) is one of the most successful hits in the history of Indian classical music.

Discographical Reference

Sharma, Shiv Kumar. *The Call of the Valley*. Blue Note Records B000005H0H. *1995*: USA.

SUBHASH KAK

Kochi

Population: city area – 564,589 (1991)

Kochi (Cochin), a port city on the southwest coast of central Kerala, is known as the 'Queen of the

Arabian Sea.' For many centuries the city has been the commercial center for the spice trade between India and the Middle East. Settlement by Portuguese traders and missionaries in the early sixteenth century strengthened its ties with the Western world. Kochi became an industrial center at the turn of the twentieth century. The city houses the Southern Command of the Indian Navy. The new international airport (built in 1999) connects Kochi to other major cities in the country, to the Middle East and to Europe. There are 18 arts and science colleges, besides the Cochin University of Science and Technology and the Sri Sankara University of Sanskrit. A relay station of All India Radio, an FM station and three television stations serve the metropolitan area; 10 daily newspapers (nine in Malayalam and one in English) have their local editions from Kochi. There are four performance halls and two open-air stadiums.

Among the prominent music institutions located in the center of the city are Rama Laxmi Vilasam (RLV) Music Academy, Kalabhavan, and Christian Arts and Communications (CAC). The RLV Music Academy offers four- and six-year diploma courses (equivalent to bachelor's and master's degrees, respectively) in South Indian classical music. These diplomas are often prerequisites for playback singers for films and stage plays. Kalabhavan and CAC offer preliminary training in South Indian classical music and advanced training in Western instrumental music.

Among the cultural institutions in Kochi, Kalabhavan (established in 1969) contributed considerably to the popular entertainment and recording industry in Kerala. In the 1970s, Kalabhavan ushered in a new movement in popular music by promoting *gānamēla* as a form of musical entertainment. To meet the ever-growing need for artists in *gānamēla* troupes, Kalabhavan initiated programs for training professional singers and instrumentalists. Fr. Abel Periyappuram, C.M.I., the founder of Kalabhavan, in collaboration with its first music director, K.K. Anthony Master, created a new genre of Christian devotional songs based on biblical themes for commercial release. The first recording of its kind took place in 1971 at the HMV studio in Madras (now Chennai), and the long-playing record *Christian Devotional Songs (Malayalam)* was produced by the Gramophone Company of India in Calcutta (now Kolkata) in 1972. Until the early 1980s, Kerala relied on the recording industry of Madras, in the neighboring state of Tamil Nadu, to prepare the master tapes for commercial reproduction of Malayalam songs. Kalabhavan established the first recording studio in Kerala in 1981 and laid the foundation for a recording industry that continued to be very active into the twenty-first century.

Kochi's contact with European culture through traders and missionaries from Portugal, Spain and Italy facilitated the formation of a unique musical theater, called *cavittunātakam* (foot-stamping drama), mostly among the Latin Christians (descendants of Portuguese settlers and local converts to Roman Catholicism). The theatrical form probably developed in the seventeenth century. The lives of Western Christian heroes and the legends and stories associated with them became the exclusive themes for *cavittunātakam*. The first and the most popular *cavittunātakam* celebrates the chivalrous exploits of the Emperor Charlemagne (*Kāralsmān*) and his nephew, Roland (*Rōldōn*). The actors sing and dance their roles to the accompaniment of instrumental music. The ensemble consists of Indian and Western instruments such as pedal organ, violin and bass drum. Colorful costumes and elaborate stage settings make this theatrical form quite similar to an opera (Palackal 1995, 45–47; Rafi 1980).

The commercial climate in Kochi has a direct impact on the entertainment industry in Kerala. There are over 10 *gānamāla* troupes and nine sound recording studios in the city, with advanced sound recording and copying facilities. At the end of the twentieth century, about 90 percent of the commercial releases of Malayalam songs were produced in Kochi.

Bibliography

Kunnappally, Mathukutty, ed. 1990. *Kalabhavan silpavum silpiyum* [Kalabhavan: The Sculpture and the Sculptor]. Thiruvananthapuram: Apsara Promotions.

Palackal, Joseph J. 1995. *Puthen Pāna: A Musical Study*. Unpublished M.A. thesis, Hunter College of the City University of New York.

Rafi, Sabeena. 1980 (1964). *Cavittunātakam* [Foot-Stamping Drama]. Kottayam: Sahitya Pravarthaka Co-operative Society.

Discography

Christian Devotional Songs (Malayalam). The Gramophone Company of India Ltd. ESCD 3210. *1972*: India.

JOSEPH J. PALACKAL

Kolkata (Calcutta)

Population: city – 3,305,000 (1998); metropolitan area – 12,000,000 (2000)

Calcutta, renamed Kolkata in 2000, is the capital of the state of West Bengal, and India's largest city and port. Located 80 miles (130 km) from the Bay of Bengal on the Houghly River (tributary of the Ganga [Ganges River]), Kolkata is the leading transportation, industrial, financial, and commercial center of eastern India, with road and rail links with the whole of north India, and an international airport. The main raw exports are tea, jute, iron, manganese and mica, with factories producing steel, textiles, shoes, rubber, leather, glass and cement. Ethnically, Kolkata is extremely diverse, yet is composed primarily of Bengali-speaking people from both West Bengal and Bangladesh. There are many migrants from Orissa, Tamil Nadu and other parts of India, including a large community of Hindi-speaking Marwaris from Rajasthan, who engage in industry and trade. There are also sizeable communities of Muslims, Parsees, Christians, Jews, Tibetans and Chinese.

Originally founded in 1690 by the British East India Company, and eventually with a military base at Fort William, Kolkata became the center of English political and intellectual life in India as well as the colonial capital from 1757 until 1911, when the capital was shifted to New Delhi. However, during the entire colonial period, which included the emergence of modernity in the nineteenth century, Kolkata formed the most important cultural nexus, not only of the multiple regions of India, but also of European civilization in Asia. English language and culture were most prevalent, and the development of popular music came under their influence. Kolkata came to represent one of the richest and most vibrant cities in the history of the development of popular music in India, which took definitive shape during roughly the same time period as the so-called Golden Age of popular 'standards' in the United States, 1920–60.

The Emergence of Popular Music

The vernacular term for popular music in eastern India (West Bengal, Assam, Orissa) is *adhunik gān*, or 'modern song,' which is the same concept as *geet* in Hindi-speaking regions as well as other parts of India. Modern songs are primarily vocal music, songs with lyrics, though the term can also refer to instrumental pieces, which in most cases are simply modern songs rendered without the lyrics, played on guitar or piano, for example.

One of the key features of the modern era in Indian music was the ultimate break from a former religious culture in which saint-musicians composed songs in rural areas or in sovereign courts and passed them along to disciples through oral transmission. The themes of the songs of these earlier times were primarily religious and mythological and intended for worship and religious reflection. They were termed *kirtan* or *bhajan*, and were often composed spontaneously in praise of a deity in the Hindu pantheon, such as Krishna or Shiva, and usually contained descriptions or expressions of personal religious experiences.

Breaking from this trend, modern songs in both their lyrics and melody were closely bound up with the everyday experiences of life in modern times and with issues of secularism and progressive urbanization in cosmopolitan environments. The most prevalent theme of modern songs, as in the West, was romantic love rather than love of God or the divine love shared between spiritual beings. The social context for changes in music also included some modern freedoms and the gradual erosion of caste and gender restrictions.

The eventual production of modern songs followed a pattern of a threefold division of labor that included a professional lyricist, musician and performer, and involved the publication of written musical compositions. This system was more suitable than former improvisational methods to the placing of songs in the newly emerging commercial media such as radio, film and recordings, with their specific time limitations. The composer and lyricist were rarely the same person as the performer who, as the most important of these three individuals, was bound more strictly to the finished composition and thus not at liberty to engage in extended improvisation, as in former classical-based genres. Several modern composers in Bengal initially composed and published songs that were based on the models of the old genres of *dhrupad*, *khyāl*, *thumri* and *tappa*, yet were more firmly fixed melodically and had lyrics in Bengali instead of Hindi. Newer types of modern song were also influenced to some degree by Western harmonization and chords.

Development from Classical Genres

The Hindustani classical form of *dhrupad* was introduced into Bengal society chiefly during the late seventeenth century, when a school or *gharāna* was established at Vishnupur. *Dhrupad*, as a rigid classical style that allowed for improvisation under strict guidelines, was the preferred genre for serious religious music in North India, especially among Vaishnava followers of Krishna in Vrindavan and Mathura (Uttar Pradesh). Vaishnava devotees from Bengal quickly adopted *dhrūpad* styles and formulated their own genre known as *padavali kirtan* by the mid-seventeenth century. Through the agency of a new, elite religious movement in Kolkata known as the Brahmo Samaj, founded in 1828 by Raja Rammohan Roy, new Bengali *dhrūpad* compositions were created by classically trained Bengali musicians and circulated among Bengali intelligentsia during Brahmo Samaj worship services, thus beginning what became known as *brahmo sangit*.

Following Rammohan Roy, pivotal figures in the transition from former times of religious or court musicians to the modern professional composer or lyricist used the example of the Bengali *dhrūpad* to enlarge the stock of Bengali songs by drawing upon other genres. These persons, including Brahmo Samaj leaders and members of the important Tagore family in the late nineteenth century, sought to formally 'fix' the lyrics with melody in order to inhibit the improvisatory freedom of the performer, and to give a finished result to the compositional effort. In Bengal, and in eastern India generally, there had always been a preference for the integrity of the lyrics over and above melody, the reverse of the Hindi or Hindustani traditions in the north and central parts of India, which gave more importance to the melodic or raga dimension. There is even a saying in Bengal that the melody is like an obedient husband who serves the lyric-wife. This principle can be said to have guided the production of popular music in this entire region.

Jyotirindranath Tagore (1849–1925) is considered the main pioneer with regard to the emergence of the 'fixed composition,' and was the forerunner of the five so-called great Bengali poet-composers including Rabindranath Tagore (1861–1941), D.L. Ray (1863–1913), Rajani Kanta Sen (1865–1910), Atulprasad Sen (1871–1934) and Kazi Nazrul Islam (1899–1976). Each of these figures made contributions to the ways in which Bengali compositions became fixed from former improvisational genres such as *dhrūpad*, *khyāl*, *thumri*, *tappa* and *ghazal*. They also created new genres of patriotic and romantic songs.

Modern Genres and Song Types

Patriotic songs were part of the emerging catalog of many modern composers. While first articulated by Ishwar Gupta (1812–59), patriotic music or

swadeshi gān grew in popularity at the turn of the twentieth century during the struggle for independence, and especially during the protest surrounding the issue of partition of Bengal by Lord Curzon, 1905–11.

The light Hindustani genre of *tappa* was originally modified and developed with Bengali lyrics by Ramnidhi Gupta (1741–1839), known affectionately as 'Nidhu Babu' or 'Master Nidhu,' derivative of *'nidhi'* which means 'treasure.' This style of Bengali music was very influential in the later creation of the new genre of *rāg-pradhān*, songs with non-religious themes yet structured according to classical *rāgas*. This led then to modern song, as artists experimented with Bengali *tappa* and also *thumri*, another Hindustani love song genre that was originally religious but lent itself very easily to human romantic themes. The Persian *ghazal* song form is an Urdu secular poem that found its way into Bengali language mostly through Kazi Nazrul Islam, the famous national poet-singer of Bangladesh.

Rabindranath Tagore (1861–1941) contributed over 2,500 original songs, composing lyrics and then setting them to melodies based upon classical *rāgas*, while maintaining the modern preference for 'finished compositions.' This genre is known as *Rabindra sangīt*, and though not classed as *adhunik gān*, is nonetheless widely performed and extremely influential in the realm of popular music. The fourfold method he used for dividing his song catalog (*gīta bitan*) into worship (*puja*), patriotic songs (*swadeshi*), celebrations of nature (*prakriti*) and love songs (*prem*) has influenced many of the modern composers. Originally taught at the university he founded in Shantineketan – Visvabharati University – Tagore songs are part of the repertoire of nearly all modern Bengali musicians.

The Influence of Recording and Broadcasting Technologies

The Gramophone Company of India (later to become HMV) was established as early as 1901 in Shantineketan Kolkata, followed by a record factory in 1908 in northern Kolkata. This was contemporary with the establishment of the first record factories in England, as India was considered a major market for popular music from the beginning. The first catalog of recordings in Kolkata included songs in many regional languages, for example Bengali, Hindi, Urdu and Burmese.

Following an era of silent films in India, Indian film music began in 1931 with the first talkies made in Bombay (now Mumbai) in the Hindi language. Kolkata soon developed several productions of its own which included many new songs sung in Bengali that drew upon existing styles of Bengali music. During this period there was a close connection between film music in Bengal and recorded popular music, though many other folk genres of Bengali music such as *baul*, *kirtan*, *bhatiyāli* and *jhoomra* also found their way into film scores and performances. Names associated with these times include Dilip Kumar Ray (1897–1980), Rai Chand Boral (1903–81), Pankaj Mullik (1905–78) and Hemanta Mukherjee (1920–89).

The various, clearly defined roles in modern song are best exemplified by Ajoy Bhattacharrya (lyricist), Himanshu Dutta (melodist), and Sachin Dev Burman and Rahul Dev Burman (singers/performers). These artists worked as a professional team to produce the first major body of work that might be firmly denoted as *adhunik gān*. Paralleling these artists, scores of other singers and composers have flooded the market with recordings and concerts: Juthika Roy, Dwijen Mukherjee, Vishmadev Chatterjee, Bhupen Hazarika, Arati Mukherjee, Sandhya Mukherjee, Anup Ghosal, Kishore Kumar, Satinath Mukherjee, Manna De, Shyamal Mitra, Sudhin Sarkar, Arundhati Holme Choudhury, Tarun Banerjee, Pratima Banerjee, Runa Laila, Pintoo Bhattacharjee, Biswajit and Bhupinder.

Several famous modern singers have also succeeded in crossing over into Bengali from other languages, especially Hindi, by recording entire albums of hit songs. Examples include Kundan Lal Saigal (songs of Rai Chand Boral), Asha Bhosle, Lata Mangeshkar, Talat Mahmood, Begum Akhtar and Vani Jairam. By the same token, a number of originally Bengali artists, besides becoming prominent singers in Bengali, have made a definitive contribution toward Hindi film songs, including Hemanta Mukherjee, Manna De, Salil Chaudhury, Kishore Kumar and Sandhya Mukherjee.

Kolkata, due to the strong colonial presence, was one of the leading urban areas where Western musical influences took hold. While Western harmony and chord structure did not figure centrally in modern songs until the mid-twentieth century, the use of piano, violin, clarinet and other symphonic instruments in Indian popular music began in the late nineteenth century. Jyotirindranath Tagore and his circle had already started experimenting with these and the use of small-scale orchestral music in theater productions. These trends continued into the twentieth century in

Hindi and Bengali film making. While Ravi Shankar exemplifies the way classical artists have employed Western orchestral accompaniments for *sitār* music, the use of light orchestral music, particularly strings, continues to be carefully used in Bengali film music and modern song.

Other Influences

North American jazz and swing music had a strong colonial presence in Kolkata, with many local enthusiasts reacting by creating fusion genres, right up to the present. Several of the big hotels and clubs had regular jazz and dance bands that performed for social occasions where Indians were in attendance. Teddy Weatherford, an important Chicago jazz pianist, performed regularly with his band at the Grand Hotel in Kolkata well into the 1940s. Many other giants of jazz including Duke Ellington have toured to enthusiastic audiences. Since the 1970s and 1980s, Western-style popular music has penetrated the youth markets, with stars like Michael Jackson and Madonna playing to sell-out crowds. In the early years of the twenty-first century, an annual jazz festival was started called 'Congo Square,' inspired by the New Orleans Jazz Fest, and native Bengali rock bands have performed at Kolkata clubs and studios, including Cactus, Paraspathar, Miles, Chandrabindoo and Bhumi. In addition, *bangla* remix groups such as Britain 2 Bangladesh have gained in popularity.

Kolkata is thus saturated with the songs and sounds of the most varied popular musical climate in all of India, and remains an ever-burgeoning region of continual musical exploration and invention, both drawing from older traditions and creating new ones. In the early years of the twenty-first century, Music World, a chain of music stores associated with HMV Gramophone originally based in Kolkata, and Planet M, another chain with headquarters in Mumbai (Bombay), consolidated most of the popular music distribution in India. Their stores in Kolkata remain the central outlets for all Bengali music, of which new interpretations of Tagore songs continue to lead the charts.

Bibliography

Banerjee, Jayasri (ed). 1988. *The Music of Bengal: Essays in Contemporary Perspective.* Bombay and Baroda: Indian Musicological Society.

Goswami, Karunamaya. 2000. 'West Bengal and Bangladesh.' In *The Garland Encyclopedia of World Music. Vol. 5: South Asia: The Indian Subcontinent*, ed. Alison Arnold. New York and London: Garland Publishing, 844–63.

Manuel, Peter. 1993. *Cassette Culture: Popular Music and Technology in North India*. Chicago: University of Chicago Press.

Ray, Sukumar. 1985. *Music of Eastern India: Vocal Music in Bengali, Oriya, Assamese and Manipuri with Special Emphasis on Bengali*. Calcutta: Firma KLM Private Ltd.

Discography

Burman, Sachin Dev. *The Incomparable Sachin Dev Burman*. ECLP 2327 HMV. n.d.: India.

Calcutta Youth Choir. *Bengali Choral Songs*. S/45NLP 2008 HMV. n.d.: India.

De, Manna. *Hits of Manna De*. ECLP 2518 HMV. n.d.: India.

Down Memory Lane, Vols. 1 & 2. ECLP 2493 and ECSD 2526 HMV. n.d.: India.

Islam, Kazi Nazrul. *The Best Loved Songs of Kazi Nazrul*. EALP 1300 HMV. n.d.: India.

Kumar, Kishore. *Kishore Kumar*. ECLP 259 HMV. n.d.: India.

Memorable Puja Hits. ECLP 2379 HMV. n.d.: India.

Mukherjee, Hemanta. *Songs to Remember*. 33ESX 4255 HMV. n.d.: India.

Mullik, Pankaj. *The Greatest Hits of Pankaj Mullik*. EAHA 1003 HMV. n.d.: India.

Sen, Atul Prasad. *Songs of Atul Prasad*. ECLP 2279 HMV. n.d.: India.

Sen, Rajani Kanta. *Songs of Rajanikanta*. EALP 1392 HMV. n.d.: India.

Tagore, Jyotirindranath. *Songs of Jyotirindra Nath Tagore*. ECSD 2535 HMV. n.d.: India.

Tagore, Rabindranath. *Gems From Tagore*. ECLP 2552 HMV. n.d.: India.

GUY L. BECK

Lucknow
Population: 2,000,000 (2002)

Lucknow is the capital of India's most populous state, Uttar Pradesh. It is in many ways an ordinary city where, as with most Indian conurbations, one can hear strains of Bollywood hits past and present seeping from storefronts and houses amid the cacophony of street noises. By the mid-1990s, MTV and the Indian television channels that mimicked it had penetrated deeply into the living rooms of the rich and even the not-so-rich where, just 10 years prior, only All India Radio and the sole state television station had reigned supreme. What makes Lucknow special is not its present but its past: an era when this city of 'palaces, minars, domes azure and golden' (Russell 1957, entry dated 3 March 1858) was the hub of the Hindustani music

world, and the locus of many of its most profound changes.

From 1775 Lucknow became the capital of the province of Awadh. Massive building and urban beautification projects were undertaken by its rulers, known as Nawabs (i.e., viceroys of the Mughal Emperor), who lavished resources on the arts to the extent that Lucknow quickly became a magnet for dancers, musicians and poets, particularly from the crumbling imperial capital of Delhi. Evidence suggests too that groups of folk performers entered the city in search of patronage. It was in this vibrant, competitive atmosphere of the early nineteenth century that the more austere, 'classical' genres began to be shunted aside in favor of a mélange of more popular vocal and instrumental forms. The now ubiquitous *sitār* was at that time a vehicle for music considered comparatively light and easy to understand: it had become all the rage by the mid-nineteenth century, and the mischievous player Ghulam Raza wheedled his way into a position of considerable ministerial power in the court of Awadh's last Nawab, Wajid Ali Shah (reigning 1847–56), a ruler for whom the arts held particular importance. Ghulam Raza created a unique style and a type of composition known as the *razākhani gat* (Miner 1993, 112–17), which is now a standard form in classical instrumental music.

Popular legend has it that Wajid Ali Shah invented *thumri*: a genre of vocal music that synthesized 'some of the most vital aspects of folk and classical music' and which developed 'to a degree of exquisite refinement the technique of elaborating text through melody' (Manuel 1989, ix). *Thumri*'s history goes considerably deeper than the mid-nineteenth century, but Wajid Ali was certainly responsible for both popularizing and refining the form. Among his many artistic accomplishments he was known, primarily, as a *thumri* composer and singer and the poignant metaphor he is said to have uttered on being deposed and exiled from Lucknow by the British in 1856 has become one of the most popular and frequently performed *thumris*:

Baabul moraa naihar chhuuto jaae
chaar kahaaar mili doliyaan uthaae
apnaa bigaanaa chhuuto jaae

Father, my maternal home is being left behind.
Four water-carriers together lift up my palanquin;
what's mine, what's not, it's all being left behind.
(Trans. du Perron 2000, 250)

Set in the intensely expressive and plaintive mode

109

of *Bhairavi* (basically the Phrygian mode, but accidental notes are permitted), this *thumri* recalls the vulnerability and sense of loss of a young woman as she is borne away from the security and familiarity of her father's house, destined to marry into a new life with her groom's family. The palanquin also evokes a funeral procession: a final journey from which there is no return. Wajid Ali never saw his beloved Lucknow again.

Thumri texts, commonly in the Braj dialect and mostly surrounding the divine figure of Lord Krishna as lover, always take a female perspective and speak predominantly of longing for union – sexual and spiritual – with the mischievous, philandering, yet irresistible god. Other texts are plainly romantic or erotic. *Thumris* were sung by women of the courtesan tradition; these *Baijis*, as they were known, added gesture and dance to intensify or reinterpret the meanings of the poetry. In the climate of the early years of the British Raj (post 1858), *thumri* continued to prosper because the nobility had both the financial means and the aesthetic desire to support courtesans; yet, with increasing British influence and the growing code of Victorian moral values, courtesan culture began to decline rapidly from around 1900, and with it the popularity and prevalence of the *thumri*. Nevertheless, the doyens of Hindustani classical vocal music in the early to mid-twentieth century, women and men alike, all knew and performed *thumris*. In many senses, the *thumri* style liberated classical music, infusing it with more flexibility, responsiveness and emotion.

Purists will argue that the female torchbearers of *thumri* in the twentieth century were Rasoolan Bai, Siddeshwari Devi and Girija Devi of Benares (Varanasi); but Lucknow's prominent representative was the courtesan Akhtari Bai of Faizabad (1914–74), who married 'respectably' in Lucknow and was latterly known as Begum Akhtar. Her penchant for the lighter, popular *ghazal*, a Persian-Urdu poetic form set to simple, embellished tunes, made her *thumris* correspondingly lighter and thus more widely accessible to a vast, adoring public. A beguiling prima donna, whose seductive charm could quickly turn to caustic wit or even withdrawn depression, she captured the public imagination with her many superb performances and recordings (Dhar 1996; Ollikkala 1997).

The sung *ghazal* has fared better than the *thumri* in that, though it too was once the domain of courtesans and feudal patronage, it was transformed through bourgeois patronage into a respect-

able form of modern public entertainment (Manuel 1993, 91). It has spread from the confines of Urdu-speaking courts like Delhi and Lucknow to the entire subcontinent and to South Asian diasporic communities everywhere. The Pakistani singer Mehdi Hassan is considered a pioneer of the modern form, as are the Punjabi husband-wife duo Jagjit and Chitra Singh (Ollikkala 1997, 285–91).

The culture of Lucknow, particularly at its zenith around 1850, has frequently been described as frivolous, superficial and pandering to popular tastes. Yet, so far-reaching were its influences that many scholars believe the popular vocal and instrumental genres that titillated the Nawabs have had a profound, though largely unacknowledged, effect on the style of modern classical, light-classical and popular genres in North India.

Bibliography

Dhar, Sheila. 1996. *'Here's Someone I'd Like You to Meet': Tales of Innocents, Musicians and Bureau-crats*. Delhi: Oxford University Press.

du Perron, Lalita. 2000. *The Lyrics of Thumri: Hindi Poetry in a Musical Genre*. Unpublished Ph.D. dissertation, University of London.

Manuel, Peter. 1989. *Thumri in Historical and Stylistic Perspectives*. Delhi: Motilal Banarasidass.

Manuel, Peter. 1993. *Cassette Culture: Popular Music and Technology in North India*. Chicago: University of Chicago Press.

Miner, Allyn. 1993. *Sitar and Sarod in the 18th and 19th Centuries*. Wilhelmshaven: F. Noetzel.

Ollikkala, Robert. 1997. *Concerning Begum Akhtar, 'Queen of Ghazal'*. Unpublished Ph.D. dissertation, University of Illinois at Urbana-Champaign.

Russell, William. 1957. *My Indian Mutiny Diary*, ed. Michael Edwardes. London: Cassell.

Sharar, Abdul Halim. 1975. *Lucknow: The Phase of an Oriental Culture*, trans. and ed. E.S. Harcourt and Fakhir Hussein. London: Paul Elek.

Discography

Devi, Siddeshwari et al. *Chairman's Choice–Great Thumris*. EMI/The Gramaphone Company of India CD CMC 1 82515-16. *1994*: India.

JAMES KIPPEN

Mumbai (Bombay)
Population 18,100,000 (2000)

Bombay (renamed Mumbai in the mid-1990s) is the capital of Maharashtra, and is also considered the financial capital of India. It is a major port situated on the Arabian Sea on India's west coast, and ranks as the most populous city in the country. Ptolemy, the Greek historian, reportedly referred to it in 150 A.D., but Bombay/Mumbai is mainly a product of British rule and, as such, reflects many facets of the complex Indo-British cultural history.

Originally, Mumbai was a group of seven islets, and its early inhabitants were probably engaged in fishing and agriculture. The area was settled by Hindu castes which worshipped a deity called Mumbadevi, or Mumbamai, from which the settlement's name was derived. In 1348 A.D., Muslims from Gujarat defeated the reigning Hindu King Nagardeva, and a large number of Muslims from Konkan – the coastal area of Maharashtra – settled in Mumbai. Muslims controlled the area for the next two centuries, before the arrival of the Portuguese in 1534. The Portuguese forcibly converted many native residents to Christianity but, in an important sense, their intolerant attitude paved the way for the next, and more fruitful, East-West encounter with the British who proved – comparatively speaking – to be more tolerant. However, the Portuguese also built a good, all-seasons harbor and, according to some, the name Bombay was derived from the Portuguese formation 'bom' = good + 'behiya' = port, or bom baia (good bay).

The career of the city really began when the British Crown handed over the group of islands to the trading East India Company in 1668 for an annual rent of 10 pounds. The religious tolerance of the British rulers proved an inviting feature for people of all kinds and creeds. Followers of different religions chose to settle in Mumbai. In the case of the Parsis, followers of Zoroastrianism, who had migrated to India from Persia in the seventh century to avoid persecution in their homeland, the community in Mumbai eagerly welcomed the input of Western culture that arrived with the British, and this feature has influenced the city's cultural composition and its increasingly cosmopolitan character. The Parsis' own melodramatic music theater, an 'eclectic amalgam of song, dance and dramatic passages meant to please all kinds of audiences' (Gupta 1991, 16), was an important form in the city, and a forerunner of the Hindi cinema. An immense variety of performance culture with a religious bias prospered – and has continued to prosper – in Mumbai.

After 1800, the city grew apace. Railways, telegraph, reclamation of land and the joining of the seven islets to make one linear city successfully turned Mumbai into a beehive of activity, featuring people of varied nationalities, races, religious faiths and castes, all off whom have contributed to its nature and stature.

Alongside the diversity of religions, another factor that proved conducive to the growth of performing arts in general and of popular music in particular has been linguistic plurality. Marathi, Hindi, Gujarati, Sindhi, Urdu, Parsi-Gujarati, Konkani and Tamil are spoken, a sign of the ongoing sense of identity among minority groups. To such groups, popular music and music making has offered a major avenue of expression.

The Young City

Mumbai emerged in the nineteenth century as an energetic, relatively young metropolitan city, one not heavily weighed down by deep-rooted cultural traditions. Being a young trading center meant two things: firstly, the inhabitants – whether Indians, British, or Portuguese – placed a great premium on communication systems; secondly, they strove to ensure that the city was easily accessible. By 1853, railways had begun a new era of communication, one consequence of which was that music, musicians and musical ideas circulated at an unprecedented pace. Drama troupes traveled to and from Mumbai, and individuals visiting the city from elsewhere in India could gather inspiration from the foreign formats/genres in the performing and entertainment arts, as well as in recreational activities in general, and would naturally take these home – sometimes a good distance from Mumbai – and begin experimenting with them.

A number of influential new developments occurred in the city as a result of its particular cultural composition. One was band music. For example, the Governor's Band gave free public performances of band music every evening. Professional bands such as the Noor Mohammad Band, reportedly established in 1840s, were hired by wealthy citizens to play at marriage functions and similar occasions. By 1889, band music in specially constructed bandstands had become a regular feature of the cityscape. Its influence spread beyond the city, as all princely states in the country took their cue from Mumbai and strove to have bands of their own.

Another use of band music – and one that contributed to the expanding category of popular music – was in the circus. In 1878, the first performance of an 'Indian circus' owned by a Mr. Chatre took place in Mumbai. A feature of his presentations was the spirit of 'nascent nationalism' with which the presentations were imbued – even though the inspiration for the nationalistic spirit was non-Indian. Chatre emphasized in his advertisements and publicity that his use of band music was nationalistic because all the major performers were Indian.

Another important development was Sokar Bapuji Trilokekar's staging (1878–79) of the 'new vogue music drama,' which came to be known as *Sangit Natak*. In this music drama, the older format of entrusting the *sutradhara* (stage manager/director) to do all 'talking and singing' was replaced for the first time. All his characters talked and sang. The format was soon to be perfected by Annasaheb Kirloskar in Pune.

Industrialization, Migrant Labor and the Emerging Middle Class

Various factors in the climate and geography of Mumbai encouraged the growth of industrialization as distinct from an agricultural economy. This created a demand for both labor and entrepreneurs from different parts of India and from abroad. In the social strata that formed during this process, many people were eager to try out new ideas. At the same time, the migrants also brought their 'own' culture with them. These factors were instrumental in creating new combinations of performing genres, something that happened in Mumbai with telling effect.

For example, the establishment of the first cotton mill in 1854 led to the migration of cheap labor to Mumbai from other parts of Maharashtra, notably Konkan, the coastal area. This class enthusiastically welcomed religious festivals such as that of Lord Ganesha, or festivals with political/nationalistic leanings such as that of the birthday of King Shivaji. This same class would later patronize new genres of songs such as *powāda* (ballads) on mill strikes, *mela*-performances (a musico-dramatic form noted for its use of dance and costumes) devoted to patriotic and reformist themes, *prabhatpheri* (morning march) songs, and also other 'variety presentations' staged as public festivals.

The emerging new middle class also accepted new recreational modes, partly out of a desire to imitate the British ruling class. Thus, by 1890, dance-music and acting performances of professional female dancers known to the colonizing British as 'nautch-girls' had become a feature of elite life in cities, including Mumbai. Yet another instance was of the new genre called '*bhavgeet*' – a marriage between concepts of 'lyric' in English literary

studies and the indigenous '*pada*' (song) tradition in Maharashtra. In 1932, the first recording of Marathi *bhavgeet* was made by G.N. Joshi at the Gramophone Company's studio on Rampart Row in Mumbai. It proved a trendsetter in Marathi popular music. (Joshi went on to work as a recording executive for the company in Mumbai for over 30 years (Joshi 1988, 151).)

Readiness to Use New Media

In 1905, electricity was introduced for the first time to light the city's roads. Theaters soon abandoned gaslights, and the way was paved for new kinds of theater – with music – appropriate to the changed presentational environment. This ability of the city to respond creatively to new developments was characteristic also of its response to new media. With its multi-strata society, industrialization and the availability of energy sources, all of which generated ideal conditions for effective media-operations, Mumbai was to prove fertile ground for the new media – especially the mass media, so intertwined with the phenomenon of popular music.

Radio broadcasting in India began on an experimental basis in 1925. The Indian Broadcasting Company opened its Bombay station in 1927 and began India's first regular radio service. The transmission reached only about 30 miles (48 km) beyond the city. When IBC went into liquidation in 1930, the government of India took it over and renamed it the 'Indian State Broadcasting Service.' ISBS set up a station in Delhi in 1936, the year the name was changed to All India Radio. One of the items broadcast on the first day was classical vocal music by Ustad Faiyaz Khan. Music has remained a staple diet of Indian broadcasting. In 1972, telecasting began in Mumbai with dance, drama and music playing a prominent part.

Although Kolkata (formerly Calcutta) has always been the main center for recording in India, Mumbai has played a significant role. During the first 50 or so years of the early twentieth century, during which the Gramophone Company Ltd (GCL, later EMI) exercised a monopoly in the country, small record companies were set up in Mumbai, as in other cities, to act as subsidiary sister companies. In the case of Mumbai, the companies were Jai-Bharat and King (Joshi 1988, 149). The first challenge to the Gramophone Company occurred when the National Record Company was set up in 1938, and V. Shantaram was lured away from directing an associate company of GCL in Pune to run the new company's label, Young India. This was at a time when the nationalist movement was growing fast. Although the new company had some successes, it was hindered by poor technical quality and eventually folded (Joshi 1988, 150). Efforts by other overseas companies to break the GCL monopoly came to nothing until the establishment of Polydor in Mumbai in 1969. Backed by Mumbai businessmen with experience in the cinema, the company introduced improvements in recording quality and became strong enough to engage in successful competition with the Gramophone Company (151, 154).

Important though radio and record companies have been to the development and consumption of popular music in Mumbai, the major contribution by the new media has been that of cinema. The first experiments with silent film production in India began in Mumbai and Kolkata at the turn of the twentieth century, and the first full-length silent feature film, *Raja Harishchandra*, was screened in Mumbai in 1913. Produced by Dhundiraj Govind Phalke (commonly known as Dadasaheb Phalke), it was based on Hindu mythology, as was common in Parsi theater of the time. Mumbai audiences – mixed as they were – could easily relate to the new medium and also to the live musical accompaniment, typically played on harmonium and *tablā*, which served to drown out the projection and other noises as well as to provide music, songs and sound effects familiar to theater audiences. Indian films, with their characteristic accent on mythology and music, have continued to attract and bring together diverse audiences. In 1931, *Alam Ara* (Beauty of the World), the first 'talkie,' was shown in the Novelty theater in the city. Adapted from Parsi theater, it contained numerous songs. Songs from films soon began to enjoy life outside the cinema, via radio and audio recordings, and actor-singers enjoyed a special iconic status – a vogue that has continued in the personae of film actors and playback singers.

Popular Film Music

As a component of Indian popular cinema since the beginning of sound films in 1931, music became increasingly important both in film as a medium and in the cinema as an industry. In the 1930s, the phenomenon of 'playback singing' was introduced, a practice using trained vocalists to record the songs that were lip-synched by film actors. Scholars do not agree on the precise film and date in which this first occurred but *Dhoop Chhaon* (The Sun's Shadow) (1935) is a leading contender

(Arnold 1991, 102–106). Soon Mumbai – as one of three northern centers of filmmaking (the others were Pune and Kolkata, with Madras producing South Indian films) – took to it with enthusiasm. It was no longer necessary to limit film roles to actors who could sing (at least tolerably!). Consequently, actors/actresses began to have two voices – their own speaking voice and a singing-voice provided for them by 'playback singers.'

From the late 1940s through the 1970s, the playback vocalists of Mumbai's film industry were the dominant popular singers in India. Most famous were the sisters Lata Mangeshkar and Asha Bhosle whose father, Dinanath Mangeshkar, had been a popular Marathi music-drama actor, singer and composer. In 1947, Lata Mangeshkar sang her first Hindi playback song for the film industry in Mumbai, beginning a period of immense popularity that saw her earn a place in the *Guinness Book of Records* as the singer who had sung the most songs (reportedly, 30,000 songs in 2,000 films). Lata has continued to live in Mumbai, spending her entire career as a playback artist recording in Mumbai's studios. Other early playback 'stars,' all based in Mumbai, included singers Shamshad Begum, Mohammed Rafi, Kishore Kumar, Geeta Dutt, Talat Mehmood, Mukesh and Suraiya. A small handful of popular instrumentalists made careers out of interpreting film songs for independent recordings. These included clarinetist Master Ibrahim and accordionists Goodi Servai and Enoch Daniel. In this period, the Hindi film song industry established a hegemonic position with a cultural depth and historical longevity that has been unrivaled in the history of world popular music.

A new generation of playback singers (including Anuradha Paudwal, Suresh Wadkar, Alka Yagnik, Vinod Rathole, Nithin Mukesh, Anuradha Paudwal and Kavita Krishnamurthi, Sonu Nigam and Mohammed Aziz) gradually took over from the Mangeshkar sisters and their male contemporaries beginning in the 1980s. However, changes in the film music industry's position and structure has meant that none of these newcomers has achieved the levels of star-status of the 1950s–1970s generation.

The essential nature of music's contribution to films in India can hardly be overestimated. When, in 1937, the Wadia Brothers produced the film *Naujavan* without a single song, it led to so many protests that they had to screen a trailer with an explanation. It took until 1954, when K.A. Abbas produced the film *Munna* without a song, for the industry to get away without tendering an apology for deliberate 'songlessness.'

In the 1950s, Mumbai became the unrivaled center of the Hindi film industry, and has seen that industry go from strength to strength. Hindi is India's official national language (together with English), and this enabled Mumbai-based Hindi film production to establish the widest distribution in the country's multilingual film industry. Its rise to pre-eminence was one consequence of the break-up of the studio system, under which actors and musicians were on the permanent staff of the company, and the move to independent film making. With independent film making came competition. Music was central to that competition and music directors were hired independently for each film production. As songs proved to be a major selling point for a film, music directors were able to make a name for themselves, and as their success grew, some became 'stars' along with the film actors; their names were prominently placed in the film credits, and they began to demand high salaries. Employing huge, 100-piece orchestras became commonplace – a status symbol as well as an avenue of experimentation. In the process, songs were recorded with more tonal color and a greater body of sound. By 1983, the number of songs per film was on the decrease but the number of commercial Hindi films was on the increase.

The money to allow this growth in the film industry came in part from the black market that flourished at the time of World War II and India's Independence (1947). Industrial growth (especially iron and steel) supporting the war effort (despite the Indian government's war boycott) led to shortages and a black market for essential goods, which in turn led to speculation and illicit profits. As Barnouw and Krishnaswamy have written, 'the film industry became an increasingly attractive investment opportunity for black marketeer and profiteer' (1980, 128), since artists' and directors' fees could be paid partly in cash without written record.

While music was establishing itself as a central feature of Hindi films, the popular dance music of Britain and (more importantly) the United States, especially jazz, was beginning to have an Indian presence. Anglo-Indian, Parsi and (most importantly) Goan musicians began performing jazz in Mumbai's elite clubs and restaurants such as Green's, and in the smaller nightclubs along what is now Veer Nariman Road. One of the earliest who has remained famous is trumpeter Antonio Xavier

Vaz, better known as Chic Chocolate who, with his band the Music Makers, had a powerful impact on popular music in the city. In the 1940s and 1950s, Rudy Cotton (a Mumbai-based Parsi who had been born Cawasji Khatau) led a largely Goan dance band in many residencies at the Taj, as well as at other popular hotels in Mumbai and throughout India and South/Southeast Asia. Chris Perry (born Pereira) was another important jazz musician in Mumbai in the 1960s and 1970s. By the early 1940s at the latest, some of these jazz musicians were finding work in the film music studios in Mumbai. Film composer Chitalkar Ramchandra and Mumbai's dance-band musicians were collectively crucial in establishing African-American popular styles in Mumbai's growing film music industry.

The other major contributors to Mumbai's (and thus India's) popular film music scene have been the film music composers (called music directors) and lyricists. Notable among music directors of the 1950s to 1970s were Naushad Ali, Sachin Dev Burman, Shankar-Jaikishan, O.P. Nayyar, Usha Khanna, Kalyanji-Anandji, Rahul Dev Burman and Laxmikant-Pyarelal. The hyphenated names show the importance of teams of composers in this period.

By the 1970s, the impact of the cassette revolution heightened the accessibility of US popular music in Mumbai, and improved the dynamics of indigenous production and consumption. New film composers in the 1980s who took full advantage of the ease of access to US sounds afforded by cassettes included Bappi Lahiri, Anu Malik, Rajesh Roshan and Anand-Milind. More recently, music director A.R. Rahman has been notable for his compositions that integrate the Bollywood sound (a shortening of 'Bombay's Hollywood') with the sound and style of MTV. Other popular film composers in early twenty-first century Mumbai include Himesh Reshamiya, Vishal-Shankar and Shankar-Ehsaan-Loy. Contemporary Hindi film song – that has continued to be produced in Mumbai – takes full advantage of the entire range of Indian and foreign popular styles: rap, hip-hop, pop ballad, Indian classical and folk ideas, all combined in an eclectic blend. Hindi commercial films are exported to about one hundred countries and, thanks to the Internet, Hindi film songs are now exported around the world.

The impact that the Indian film industry and film music has had on traditional music and theater forms has ranged from compromise with to the disappearance of the latter (Manuel 1993, 55–58;

Marre and Charlton 1985). The role of Indian film in integrating the ethnically diverse population of India has thus been achieved at the expense of local and regional musical and theatrical forms. As Aziz (2003, 2–3) observes:

> The Hindustani film-song and its associated melodramatic singing-dancing *masala* genre film deeply influenced the social organization of South Asian society. The movie and its peculiar soundtrack joined the railway, the telegraph, the radio, shipping and aerial transport, to unify Southern Asia in ways not previously achieved. Despite several fissions, South Asia is united in its appreciation of the *masala* Indian film – especially its songs. So ubiquitous is the Hindustani film-song (and associated popular music) that it has become a signature of the geographical region … More recently, the young visionary composer A.R. Rahman has succeeded in removing the 'Dravidian divide' to create a unified musical culture in India itself.

Independent Popular Music

The hegemonic position of the film-music industry helps explain the fragmented history and sometimes anonymous nature of non-film popular music in Mumbai. Simultaneously, however, the industry's presence in Mumbai meant that the majority of popular musicians, arrangers, composers and recording studios were located there. The first stylistic, industrial and generic crack in film-song's hegemony came from within. The 1980 film song, 'Aap jaisa koi,' from *Qurbani* was sung in a Western pop style by London-based Nazia Hassan. Hassan was able to follow the film song's success with an independent (non-film-based) cassette of Hindi-language pop, *Disco Deewane* (Disco Madness), marking a clear departure from the film-based cassettes that dominated Mumbai's popular output. 'Disco' became a generic and highly popular label for the adoption of pop and rock US dance-music styles.

Taking advantage of cassette technology's ease of production, a host of new popular music companies gradually appeared in Mumbai (e.g., Venus, Times-Music, Tips, MagnaSound and T-Series). Their products were popular music cassettes. Most concentrated initially on film music. Milestone Dance became the first Indian music company to start a purely dance label in 1997.

Two of the most visible products of Mumbai's popular-music industry are produced by largely anonymous musicians at industry behest. Recording companies routinely respond to the seasonal holidays of all types by releasing cassettes and CDs of appropriate music. These range from recordings of devotional songs celebrating the Muslim New Year (*Eid*) to compilations of romantic ballads songs packaged in hearts and flowers for Valentine's Day.

Another phenomenon that began in the mid-1980s – which has grown to occupy a dominant place in Mumbai's contemporary music scene – is 'remix.' In contemporary Mumbai, Hindi film music as such is far outsold by 'remix,' in which old and new film songs are remixed with new rhythm and accompaniment tracks, and usually new arrangements and singers. The paradox of remix is that while discs become quite popular, the singers and musicians are almost completely interchangeable and so cannot be said to be popular in their own right. The host of young aspiring popular singers, attracted to Mumbai by the film industry, provides a large talent pool of singers who are willing to record whatever songs are offered to them by record industry producers.

Disco Deewane was the height of Nazia Hassan's career; but she was followed by other popular artists from outside the film world. The Goan musician Remo Fernandes formed his first English language rock-band, the Savages, in 1965, and later shifted to Mumbai in the 1970s, producing rock-based popular music sung in English that attracted considerable attention. His group is called Microwave Papadums. Vocalists Sharon Prabhakar and Bally Sagoo were other successful and early entrants in the popular-music field during the 1980s. Vocalist Alisha Chinoy had perhaps the biggest success as an independent Indi-pop singer with her adoption of the Western vocalist Madonna's image and musical style, beginning in the late 1980s.

In the 1990s, successful popular-music acts included the Colonial Cousins (*Sa Re Ga Ma*, 1996), Lucky Ali (*Get Lucky*, 2001), Devang Patel (*Patelscope*, 2001) and Stereo Nation (*Oh Laila*, 2001), all of whom combine Indo-Western fusion with the outright adoption of Western styles. From the early 1990s, vocalist Altaf Raja has been one of Mumbai's most successful traditional popular singers, concentrating in large part on Muslim devotional releases such as the 1998 *qawwl* release *Mujhe Apna Bana Lo*, but also on *ghazals* and other light romantic song styles. More recently Abhijeet, the Bombay Vikings, Shaan and Bagheshree stand out as acts whose music has had distinctive impact.

Bibliography

Arnold, Alison. 1991. *Hindi Filmi Git: On the History*

of Commercial Indian Popular Music. Unpublished Ph.D. dissertation, University of Illinois at Urbana-Champaign.

Aziz, Ashraf. 2003. *Light of the Universe: Essays on Hindustani Film Music*. New Delhi: Three Essays Collective.

Barnouw, Erik, and S. Krishnaswamy. 1980. *Indian Film*. 2nd ed. New York: Oxford University Press.

Booth, Gregory. 1990. 'Brass Bands: Tradition, Change, and the Mass Media in Indian Wedding Music.' *Ethnomusicology* 34(2): 245–62.

Gupta, Chidananda . 1991. *The Painted Face: Studies in India's Popular Cinema*. New Delhi: Roli Books.

Joshi, G.N. 1988. 'A Concise History of the Phonograph Industry in India.' *Popular Music* 7(2): 147–56.

Kinikar, Shashikant. 2003. *Notes of Naushad*. Mumbai: English Edition Publishers & Distributors.

Manto, Saadat Hasan. 1998. *Stars from Another Sky*. Delhi: Penguin Books India.

Manuel, Peter. 1993. *Cassette Culture: Popular Music and Technology in North India*. Chicago: University of Chicago Press.

Marre, Jeremy, and Charlton, Hannah. 1985. 'There'll Always Be Stars in the Sky: The Indian Film Music Phenomenon.' In *Beats of the Heart: Popular Music of the World*, ed. Jeremy Marre and Hannah Charlton. New York: Pantheon, 137–54.

Mullick, K.S. 1974. *Tangled Tapes: The Inside Story of Indian Broadcasting*. New Delhi: Sterling.

Pinto, Jerry and Fernandes, Naresh, eds. 2003. *Bombay, Meri Jaan*. Delhi: Penguin Books India.

Premchand, Manek. 2003. *Yesterday's Melodies, Today's Memories*. Mumbai: Jharna Books.

Ranade, Ashok. 1986. *Stage Music of Maharashtra*. New Delhi: Sangeet Natak Akademi.

Discographical References

Colonial Cousins. *Sa Re Ga Ma*. Magnasound/OMI 1573. *1996*: India.

Hassan, Nazia and Hassan, Zoheb. *Disco Deewane*. EMI India 5077. n.d.: India.

Filmography

Alam Ara, dir. Ardeshir Irani. 1931. Mumbai. Costume Drama. Songs composed and arranged by Firozshah Mistry and B. Irani.

Dhoop Chhaon (The Sun's Shadow), dir. Nitin Bose. 1935. Kolkata. Music directors Rai Chand Boral and Pankaj Mullick.

Munna, dir. Khwaja Ahmad Abbas. 1954. Mumbai. 139 mins. Music director Anil Biswas.

Qurbani, dir. Firoze Khan. 1980. Mumbai. Music directors Kalyanji-Anandji and Biddu.

Raja Harishchandra, dir. Dhundiraj Govind Phalke. 1913. Mumbai. Silent movie.

Visual Recording

Marre, Jeremy, prod. 1992. *There'll Always Be Stars in the Sky: The Indian Film Music Phenomenon*. Video. Shanachie 1209.

ASHOK RANADE, ALISON ARNOLD and
GREGORY BOOTH

Puri

Population: 125,199 (1991)

The eastern coastal town of Puri is located in the modern state of Orissa in India. Home to one of the most famous Hindu temples – to Lord Jagannath – Puri is an important pilgrimage site for Hindus from all over the world. Though mentioned in the more ancient *Puranas*, Puri in its present form dates back to King Yayati in the eighth century A.D., when ancient Orissa was known as Kalinga, once part of the great Mauryan Empire. During the annual Ratha Yatra ('Chariot Festival') in July, millions of pilgrims from all over India gather to participate in what is perhaps the largest religious procession in the world. The huge wooden deities of Jagannath (a form of Lord Krishna), Balarama (Krishna's brother), and Subhadra (Krishna's sister) are taken out on giant carts and pulled through the town.

The musical culture of Puri had, until the twentieth century, been dominated by the temple dance and music associated with the worship of Lord Jagannath. Odissi, as the most important dance, was a pure classical form originally performed by Devdasis (young women who 'married' the deity for life) called *Maharis* (from *mahat naris*, 'great women'), a tradition revived since independence using young men. The temple music was of classical style similar to northern *dhrūpad*, but also influenced by southern Karnatic styles. The lyrics were often drawn from or inspired by the poems of Jayadeva in his twelfth-century *Gita-Govinda*, a story about the love between Radha and Krishna. The Naga dance was a very virile folk dance performed by young men in the religious procession. While the popular music of Puri has been controlled primarily by the religious inspiration directly derived from the temple complex, which includes many types of *bhajan* (religious song), newer forms of popular music set to known rhythms and variations of classical *rāgas* from both northern Hindustani and southern Karnatic traditions continue to thrive.

Puri is home to hundreds of religious ashrams or

compounds containing religious devotees of spiritual teachers and gurus of many doctrinal persuasions. Thus, there is a strong concentration of religious and devotional music that is popular throughout the township. Besides the daily live performances of religious *bhajans* and *kirtans* by musicians affiliated with the compounds, many of these religious groups have released cassettes of specific songs that are aired in the streets over loudspeakers. In addition, the All India Radio branch in Puri specializes in religious songs for the enjoyment of the ubiquitous crowds that gather locally for purposes of pilgrimage and purification.

The most famous of modern exponents of the devotional Puri tradition have blended classical traditions with mass media production. Raghunath Panigrahi, classical singer, and his wife Sanjukta, a famous name in Odissi dance, are the most notable names in this regard. Raghunath's recordings have sold millions as he was a prominent radio artist. The songs of the late Akshaya Mohanty are also extremely popular. In Orissa, and especially in Puri, there is much less of a Western influence on music and culture than in the rest of India, and thus there is an uninhibited tendency to create a uniquely vibrant type of popular music.

Bibliography

Ray, Sukumar. 1985. *Music of Eastern India: Vocal Music in Bengali, Oriya, Assamese and Manipuri with Special Emphasis on Bengali.* Kolkata: Firma KLM.

Discography

Raghunath Panigrahi. *Selections from Sree Jayadeva's Gita-Govindam* EASD 1416 HMV. n.d.: India.
Songs from the Land of Jagannath. (Sung by Akshaya Mohanty, Trupti Das, Geeta Patnaik, Binoy Patra & Dhananjaya Satpathi.) ECLP 2508 HMV. n.d.: India.

GUY L. BECK

Srinagar
Population: 894,940 (2001)

Srinagar, in Kashmir, is the capital of the Jammu and Kashmir State, which consists of different ethnic, linguistic, and religious groups. The three broad regions of the State are Jammu, which has a Hindu majority, Kashmir with a Muslim majority, and Ladakh and Kargil, which is split between Buddhists and Muslims. Situated at the crossroads of Central Asian trade routes, Kashmir has absorbed diverse cultural influences. Srinagar is a tourist destination and well-known for its crafts and the carpet industry. Radio Kashmir in Srinagar has played a major role in sponsoring innovations in Kashmiri music. In 1948, the musician and musicologist Mohanlal Aima introduced the custom of coupling *chhakri* with *ruf* on radio shows. Radio Kashmir has also tried to popularize *sufiyana kalam*, the classical music of Kashmir and *bhand pather*, a dramatic musical form that fuses mythological themes with contemporary social satire.

Although Hindi music, films, and television influenced popular tastes in the region, Kashmiri music was able to hold its own in popularity in the years leading up to 1990, when an insurgency broke out in the region. In the 1990s, Islamist groups made Kashmiri Hindus a target of their violence and, as a result, Hindus were forced to leave their homes to take refuge in Jammu and other parts of India. The Islamists also issued decrees against television and films, leading to a closure of cinemas and video-rental shops for most of the 1990s. Lassa Kaul, a well-known station director of Kashmir Television, was murdered in 1990. The *bhands*, although they are Muslim, felt too insecure to perform because their themes were declared to have un-Islamic components. This affected the vitality of the music being performed in Srinagar for over a decade. The Islamists have, since 2001, softened their opposition to secular music and films, and cinemas have reopened.

Popular singers since 1950 include Raj Begum, Shameema Dev, Naseem Akhtar, Arati Tikku, Kailash Mehra, Surinder Kaur, Ghulam Nabi Dolwal, Ghulam Hassan Sofi, Ghulam Mohammad Sheikh, Ghulam Nabi Sheikh and Vijay Malla. Bhajan Sopori has received acclaim for his playing of the *santūr*, a trapezoidal stringed instrument played with wooden hammers, and he has composed music for Hindi films and television serials. With the formation of the popular government in 2001, life in Srinagar has become increasingly normal and music shops have begun marketing popular songs in cassette and CD format, and a black market exists for these items.

SUBHASH KAK

Trivandrum (Thiruvananthapuram)
Population: city area – 744,739 (2001)

Trivandrum (Thiruvananthapuram), the capital city of Kerala, is located in the southern district bordering Tamil Nadu. Two features of the city are an international airport, and the famous tourist attraction Kovalam beach. The government-owned television station Doordarshan and All-India Radio have their regional headquarters in the city. Three other private television stations, the Kerala State Film Development Corporation and Kerala University also have their headquarters here. Trivandrum has 10 *gānamēla* troupes and eight performance halls. There are nine recording studios in the city: the two most popular are Chitranjali of the Cultural Department of the state government and Tharangini, owned by the famous recording artist K.J. Jesudas.

Trivandrum is a city of temples, and temples promote music and dance. The city has a long-standing cultural tradition, especially from the time of King Swati Tirunal (1813–47), who was a great patron of music, dance and painting. Besides the Sri Swati Tirunal College of Music, three other colleges provide degree courses in South Indian classical music. Since 1985, the state government's Department for Education has played a significant role in promoting popular music by organizing annual competitions for school and college students in the state. The annual dance and music festivals and the talent search organized by Soorya, one of the leading cultural organizations in the city, have also become extremely popular events.

Bibliography

Ravindranath, A.K. 1989 (1970). *Dakshinendyan sangeetham* [South Indian Music]. Trivandrum: Department of Cultural Publications, Government of Kerala.

JOSEPH J. PALACKAL

The Maldives

Population: 309,000 (2002)

The Islamic republic of the Maldives consists of an archipelago of more than 1,000 coral islands (land area: 180 sq miles [300 sq km]) in the Indian Ocean southwest of India and Sri Lanka, and either side of the equator. Less than 200 islands are inhabited. The capital is Male, with a population of 72,000 (1999). The principal industries have been fishing and the production of coconut oil but, since the 1990s, tourism has become vital to the economy of the Maldives.

From the fifteenth century the main islands were a staging post for shipping from Europe and Africa to the Far East. In the late nineteenth century the hereditary ruler, the Sultan of the Maldives, accepted the military protection of the British, who later set up a naval base on Gan island. They

assisted the Sultan to defeat rebellions in the 1950s before the Maldives achieved independence in 1965. In 1968, the islanders voted to establish a republic and the Sultan was deposed.

The traditional culture of the country shows influences from southern India, East Africa, the Middle East and Malaysia/Indonesia. Typical percussion instruments include *onugandu* (a grooved bamboo that is scraped), *thaara* ('tambourine' in the national language Dhiveli), *kadhaa* (a copper plate struck with a rod) and a metal pot on which young women beat time in the *bandiyaa jehun*, a dance originating in South India. *Thaara* is also the name of a wedding song and dance performed by men and brought to the Maldives by Gulf Arabs. Other songs and associated dances were performed for the Sultan by men (*gaa odilava*) and women whose *bolimarlaafath neshun* dance involved offering gifts to the Sultan on special occasions. The *fathidandu jehun* is a genre of epic songs accompanied by drums and dancing.

The most widely performed traditional form is *boduberu*, also known as 'vibrating the island.' The *boduberu* ensemble consists of some 15 performers, including three drummers and a solo singer. It is a central feature of festivals and celebrations as well as of entertainment provided for tourists. Tourist shows are also vital to the income of most modern popular music bands and singers. These perform cover versions of Western pop hits, calypso songs and some local material using the big drums from *boduberu*.

Recording facilities were available in Male at the start of the twenty-first century at Maar Studios. Maar Studios also had a label for pop artists, such as Ahmed Amir. Other popular Maldivian acts were Munko (Mohammed Muthasir) and Theater Mirage, progressive rock band Zero Degree Atoll, the Hindi-music influenced Ali Rameez, and Dandana, a boy band from the far south of the archipelago.

Discography

Amir, Ahmed. *Fanvaiy*. Maar Studios. *1999*: The Maldives.
Zero Degree Atoll. *Island Pulse*. *1993*: The Maldives.

DAVE LAING

Nepal

Population: 24,702,119 (2000)

Nepal is a country located in the Himalayan Mountains, to the north and east of India and to the south of Xizang Zizhiqu (Tibet) and the People's Republic of China. Its primary religion is Hinduism although many groups are Buddhist, and in many contexts elements of Hinduism and Buddhism are mixed together. The country contains over a dozen distinct ethnic groups, and the country's native languages include several Tibeto-Burman languages as well as Sanskrit-derived ones. Growing public and private education programs have the effect of drawing diverse Nepalis together, and most people have become at least conversant in the national language of Nepali. Popular music also frequently functions as a vehicle of national unity, although many genres celebrate the country's rich cultural and musical diversity as well.

The leading genres of popular music are *adhunik gīt* (modern song), *lok gīt* (folk song), film song and Nepali pop. Each of Nepal's popular genres, in one way or another, is caught in a tension between the drive toward national unity and the celebration of cultural diversity. Also, all have undergone waves of influence from Nepali folk, North Indian and Western musics, although these influences take many different forms. North Indian film songs, *ghazals* and remixes are also popular in Nepal, especially since there is considerable overlap between the languages of Nepali and Hindi.

Adhunik Gīt

Adhunik gīt, 'modern song,' is a melodious, poetic song with an orchestral accompaniment, including a Western string section, brass instruments, guitar, piano, flute, percussion and, since the 1980s, electric guitar, bass and synthesizer. For many, it is a musical symbol of the new, modern Nepal. Melodies draw on North Indian *rāgas* and also distinctive melodic turns, phrases and scales from Nepali folk melodies. Songs are based on alternations of two musical units: the *sthāi* (refrain) and the *antarā* (verse) (Grandin 1989, 119). As *sthāi* and *antarā* recur, the chordal accompaniments are repeated exactly, but the melodies are varied each time. Secondary instrumental melodies often accompany the vocal melody and fill in gaps in the line. *Adhunik gīt* is simultaneously heard as having *Nepālipān* (Nepaliness) and as being *adhunik* (modern). As Nepalis describe the music, its 'Nepaliness' lies in the melody, and its modern quality lies in the timbres. Folk-inspired melodies are said to have *Nepālipān* even if they are performed on Western instruments and set to Western harmonies.

Ingemar Grandin, in his history of *adhunik gīt* (1989, 116–19), draws the key distinction that, in India, popular music was cultivated through film, but in Nepal it was cultivated through radio (1989,

116). In 1951, just a few months after the Rana regime was overpowered, the first, government-controlled radio station, Radio Nepal, went on the air. In 1961, the first Nepali recording company, the Ratna Recording Trust (later reorganized as the Sri Ratna Recording Corporation) formed and produced phonograph records of the music produced at Radio Nepal. When Nepal's film industry emerged in 1973, *adhunik gīt* was already a well-established popular genre, as was *lok gīt*.

In the 1950s and 1960s, Master Ratna Das Prakash, Nati Kazi, Shiva Shankar and Amber Gurung established the *adhunik gīt* idiom as a new integration of Nepali melodies, Indian *rāgas* and Western polyphony. Over the decades Prem Dhoj, Narayan Gopal, Tara Devi, Aruna Lama, Arun Thapa and Shanbhujeet Baskota have added stylistic breadth to the *adhunik gīt* genre. *Adhunīk gīt* has remained popular among people of all age groups, and recordings of Shanbhujeet Baskota and Ram Krishna Dhakal were among Nepal's best-selling albums at the end of the twentieth century.

Most *adhunik gīt* songs are love songs, but some take on social issues. Songs of Nepali patriotism, or *rastriya gīt*, comprise a significant sub-category of *adhunik gīt*. Other songs call for social change, drawing attention to poverty and social hardships. These 'songs of the people' (*janatākā gīt*) are less well represented in the media, and in some cases have even been banned by the government (Grandin 1989, 126–29).

Lok Gīt

Lok gīt, 'folk song,' also emerged in Nepal's popular music media in the 1950s. *Lok gīt* mixes elements of Nepal's many diverse folk musics, and sets them to Western- and Indian-influenced instrumental accompaniments similar to those of *adhunik gīt*. Some folk instruments are included, such as *sārangi* (a fiddle), *bānsuri* (a flute), mandolin and *mādal* (a double-headed barrel drum). *Lok gīt* is always sung in Nepali, regardless of the primary language of the ethnic group from which the song comes. Many *lok gīt* songs are *jhyāures*, songs based on folk dance rhythms. *Lok gīt* comprises primarily love songs and songs about village ways of life. As in *adhunik gīt*, subsets of *lok gīt* songs are patriotic songs (*rastriya gīt*) and social songs (*janatākā gīt*).

Popular *lok gīt* began with folk song collector-singer Dharma Raj Thapa, who traveled throughout Nepal collecting and learning folk songs in the 1950s. He reworked the folk songs and performed them in live radio broadcasts. He soon became head of a folk music division at Radio Nepal. Starting in 1965, Jhalakman Gandharwa also began to sing for Radio Nepal. He sang songs from his own caste community, the Gandharwas, formerly known as the Gaines, one of the traditionally low-ranking communities of Nepal's caste system. He accompanied himself on the *sārangi*, a small, four-string fiddle common to several peoples of northern South Asia and especially to the Gandharwas in Nepal.

Folk song collector-singer Kumar Basnet began to sing at Radio Nepal in 1961. He became especially famous for popularizing songs of the Tamangs, and also collected songs from several other 'ethnic' groups in Nepal. His early recordings were quite commercially successful, and he continues to be one of Nepal's most popular musicians. He has brought many new sounds into *lok gīt*, including distorted electric guitar and synthesizers (Henderson 2003).

Film Song

Starting almost immediately in 1951 with the end of Rana rule, North Indian film songs became a prominent part of Nepal's soundscapes. The first Nepali films were made in 1962, supported by government agencies (Grandin 1989, 113). In 1971, the government initiated the National Communication Service Plan to promote national unity and pride through the mass media under the Ministry of Communications. Accordingly, the Royal Nepal Film Corporation was established and began to produce Nepali films and film songs in 1973 to compete with Indian films. Several of the pioneers of Nepali film were Nepalis, like producer Prakash Thapa, who had trained and worked in the Bombay (now Mumbai) film industry for many years, and who then brought their talents back to Nepal. Indian studios continue to be important sites for the production of Nepali film songs. Music directors commonly take their featured singers to India to produce songs, drawing on the more powerful technologies and extensive musical resources available there. This is beginning to change, as Nepali sound studios have begun to compete more seriously with Indian ones.

Like Indian films, Nepali films are typically at least three hours long. Each film is a musical, and features four to six song and dance numbers, for which the film's plot is temporarily suspended and actors are shown dancing and mouthing the words. Nepali film songs often incorporate elements of Nepal's diverse alpine musical cultures, particularly when film characters are shown journeying to mountainous settings. The leading Nepali film music director at the beginning of the twenty-first century was Shanbhujeet Baskota, a famous *adhunik gīt* singer whose film songs incorporate influences from a wide variety of folk, classical, Western and modern Nepali styles.

Nepali Pop

Nepali pop is urban, youth-oriented music deeply influenced by Western pop. With roots in the 1970s, it became prominent in the 1980s and increasingly during the 1990s, stimulated by accelerating processes of Western influence. Nepali pop musicians use contemporary electronic sound technologies to accurately reproduce the timbres and production techniques of rap, reggae, disco and heavy metal, while also retaining important Nepali musical elements. Nepali pop is played at parties, picnics and discothèques, contexts in which young Nepali men and women dance together, and sometimes even pair up. This practice breaks with long-standing Nepali custom, by which parents arrange partners for their children.

Nepali pop is the music of an increasingly distinct culture of middle- and upper-class urban *ketāketi-haru*, 'young people' (Liechty 1995, 179). This culture is centered on urban schools and tourist areas like Kathmandu's Thamel district, where young Nepalis encounter and increasingly contemplate Western ideas, people and popular music. The recent advent of satellite television and MTV, and the expansion of FM radio stations, also accelerated the influence of Western pop. In the 1980s and 1990s, a growing number of Nepali students trained themselves to play Western rock instruments, formed Western cover bands and covered Western pop songs.

Some bands, such as the Elegance, the Classical Guitar Society and the Influence, began to compose and perform original, Nepali-language songs with strong, contemporary Western pop and rock influences. The Influence produced the first Nepali pop songs in 1983, and Sunil Parajuli and Kishor Gurung of the Classical Guitar Society produced the first Nepali pop album, *Sunsān Rātma*, in 1985. Bhim Tuladhar of the Influence says that his band's name reflects the fact that they were among the first to sing in Nepali and, at the same time, openly embrace Western pop music influences. The Influence became a symbol of a new, inescapable Western influence that young Nepalis have increasingly been experiencing (Greene and Henderson 2001). Western influences are evident in the instruments, singing style and melodies of these early Nepali pop bands.

Starting in 1993, Pokhara-based band Nepathya popularized a new kind of Nepali pop that incorporated important elements of various local folk music. They came to be known as the 'Village Pop Singers,' and this new sound came to be known as *lok pop* ('folk pop'). *Lok pop* bands also incorporated descriptions of local folk customs and words from local languages and dialects. Following the rise of Nepathya, many other Pokhara-based *lok pop* bands became popular, including Peace Hankey, Pokhareli, Madhyana, Kandara, Deurali, Nizzer, Vagabond, Bro-Sis and Manoj Shrestha. An eastern branch of *lok pop* also emerged through Mongolian Hearts and Gloomy Guys (Greene 2003).

Nepali pop also developed other musical dimensions, as it was been influenced by other Western popular musics. Cobweb, Heartbreaker, Stash, Mile Stone, Grease and Dristhy incorporate heavy metal in Nepali pop, specifically the heavily distorted electric guitar, virtuosic guitar solos and imagery of Western heavy metal. A band called 1974 A.D. features Nepali music influenced by Western pop from around 1974. Robin 'n' Looza are celebrated for a Nepali pop that features rhythm and blues guitar and vocal styles. In the late 1990s, 'mix music' became popular. 'Mix music' is music that includes sudden juxtapositions of reggae, rap, disco, heavy metal guitar and/or Nepali folk music. The most common genre is the remix: a reworking of a familiar song against a shifting musical background with a danceable beat. Nepali remixes are influenced by Indian remixes, and are made possible by the advent of affordable multitrack recording technology to the Kathmandu Valley in 1993 (Greene 2001).

Although more and more Western musical styles, instruments, performing styles and production techniques are borrowed and reproduced in Nepali pop, the genre also retains important elements of *Nepālipān* (Nepaliness). Young people value the fact that Nepali pop addresses new concerns of dating, technology and Western influences, articulated in the Nepali language, in a musical genre that is Nepali. Finally, there is something distinctively Nepali in the ways that musicians and listeners select Western sounds to incorporate into their lives. Nepali pop borrows from rap, disco, reggae, rhythm and blues, and heavy metal, but not so much from country and western, gospel or punk.

This selection process suggests that Nepali pop is not simply an imitation of Western pop. Instead, Nepali musicians and listeners are borrowing and reworking those selected elements that fit their cultural needs.

Bibliography

Grandin, Ingemar. 1989. *Music and Media in Local Life: Music Practice in a Newar Neighbourhood in Nepal*. Linköping, Sweden: Linköping University Department of Communication Studies.

Greene, Paul, D. 2001. 'Mixed Messages: Unsettled Cosmopolitanisms in Nepali Pop.' *Popular Music* 20(2): 169–87.

Greene, Paul, D. 2003. 'Nepal's Lok Pop Music: Representations of the Folk, Tropes of Memory, and Studio Technologies.' *Asian Music* 34(1): 43–65.

Greene, Paul, D., and Henderson, David. 2001. 'At the Crossroads of Languages, Musics, and Emotions in Kathmandu.' *Popular Music and Society* 24(3): 95–116.

Henderson, David. 2003. ' "Who Needs 'The Folk'?" A Nepali Remodeling Project.' *Asian Music* 34(1): 19–42.

Liechty, Mark. 1995. 'Media, Markets, and Modernization: Youth Identities and the Experience of Modernity in Kathmandu, Nepal.' In *Youth Cultures: A Cross-Cultural Perspective*, ed. Vered Amit-Talai and Helena Wulff. New York: Routledge, 166–201.

Discographical Reference

Parajuli, Sunil and Gurung, Kishor of the Classical Guitar Society. *Sunsan Ratma*. Music Nepal (Audio cassette). *1985*: Nepal.

PAUL D. GREENE

Pakistan
Population: 150,000,000 (2003)

Pakistan is an independent Islamic republic that came into being in 1947 upon the partition of British India. Culturally and geographically, it occupies a strategic cultural position between South Asia (India and Nepal) and West and Central Asia (Iran and Afghanistan). It is home to one of the planet's oldest urban cultures (beginning roughly in 3000 B.C.), centered most famously on Harrapa and Mohenjo Daro, located along the Indus River. The city of Lahore first appears in written history as 'Labokla' in Ptolemy's *Geographia* (ca. 150 A.D.). From roughly 1100 A.D. through 1500 A.D., Lahore often served as an interim capital for Central Asian rulers (such as the early Mughal rulers) who had military and political designs on the Indian plains. In the mid-nineteenth century it was the capital of the emergent Sikh Kingdom. After the 'Sikh Wars' of 1844–49, the British extended their control throughout what is now Pakistan. British control continued until 1947, when Pakistan was created as a homeland for South Asian Muslims who chose not to remain in the more secular (but predominantly Hindu) India. The Punjab region (named after the five tributaries of the Indus River, the Ravi, Jhelum, Chenab, Beas and Sutlej) was divided between the two new nations, generating political and religious tensions that have persisted. Increasing cultural differences, exacerbated by Partition, have continued to play an important role in the direction of music and other performing arts.

Pakistan is divided into four provinces (Sindh, Balochistan, Punjab and the North West Frontier), a federal capital district (Islamabad) and a series of federally administered Northern Tribal Areas (Gilgit, Baltistan, Diamar, Ghanche and Ghizar). The largest urban center is the southern port city of Karachi, also capital of Sindh province. This city of 14 million people is the economic and business heart of the country and a production center for music recording and videos made by the country's rock and pop artists. Lahore, capital of Punjab province (Pakistan's most densely populated province), is the nation's second-largest city, but has long occupied a place as the center of Pakistani music culture. This region is home to most of the traditional classical musicians in the country and the nation's film (and film music) industry. The Lahore branch of Radio Pakistan is the most active in recording and broadcasting music of all kinds. Lahore is also home to many of Pakistan's leading rock bands. Karachi and Lahore collectively produce the bulk of popular music in the country. The national capital, Islamabad, and its larger neighbor Rawalpindi have an important political and commercial presence, but little cultural leadership. Smaller cities, such as Hyderabad and Peshawar, have still less influence on popular culture.

Pakistan contains extreme geographical contrasts, from low-altitude salt marshes and deserts rising to desert plateaus, such as areas in parts of Sindh and Balochistan, and the central riverine plains of the Punjab and adjacent regions in neighboring Sindh and the Northwest Frontier. The latter collectively form the agricultural heart of the nation. The country's industrial centers are found also in the Punjab and in the regions surrounding Karachi and Rawalpindi. Further north, the country becomes extremely mountainous. A limited agricultural industry (primarily in fruits and nuts), subsistence farming, and wool and meat production are the major occupations in the far north (Gilgit, Chitral, Hunza and so on). Pakistan shares three major mountain ranges with its neighbors: the Karakorams, Himalayas and Hindu Kush.

Geographical and historical regionalism is reflected in Pakistan's linguistic and cultural makeup. Urdu is the national language, but each province has its own dominant language. Pakistan's popular music reflects its geography and history, and is related to, but distinct from, the sounds of its neighbors. The strongest musical influence comes from India; popular theater melodies and (increasingly after the mid-1930s) popular film melodies from the larger Indian centers dominated both before and after Partition. In the 1930s Lahore, together with Kolkata and Mumbai, became an important film and music production center (especially Pancholi Studios), a distinction it has retained despite overwhelming competition from India's huge cinematic output. Film music influenced stylistically more traditional musical and narrative styles, such as *sher*, an oral poetry form now sometimes accompanied by electronic instruments and mediated melodies.

West of Sindh and Punjab, West and Central Asian musical content and styles become much stronger, as does the influence of a more fundamental version of Islam, in which music occupies a marginal place at best. As an important element in the West's opposition to Soviet military presence in Afghanistan, Pakistan experienced an influx of European and US popular musical styles. North American pop and rock styles thus figure prominently in Pakistani popular culture. A relaxed approach to international copyright concerns has aided the rapid spread of foreign popular styles.

Popular Devotional Music

Islamic fundamentalism (however defined) has an undetermined number of adherents in Pakistan; recent events in Afghanistan may actually have increased the importance of Islamic fundamentalism in the country. Regardless of actual numbers, the fundamentalist voice is an especially powerful influence on how music is produced and represented. Consequently, devotional music is a significant component of traditional and popular culture. What is more, Sindh and Punjab are home to a number of major shrines of the Sufi sects of Islam. These mystical sects use music and dance in worship. They are responsible for *qawwāli*, a pan-regional popular devotional style that is Pakistan's most important musical national symbol and international export.

Qawwāli has a distinguished history that began in the thirteenth century, but it is now widely distributed via popular commercial media. Pakistan's national radio and television stations have been influential in promoting a range of popular devotional styles, including *qawwāli*. The country's leading *qawwāls* (singers of *qawwāli*) are national and regional stars.

Two family groups have dominated Pakistani *qawwāli*. The family of the late Ustad Fateh Ali Khan includes his son, the late Nusrat Fateh Ali Khan (1951–97), who achieved a high level of global prominence through collaborative work with Western artists, appearances at international festivals and a highly accessible virtuosity. Comprised largely of hereditary singers and musicians (including his brother and primary accompanist, Farrukh Fateh Ali Khan), this group is an exponent of the northern, Punjabi style. Rahat Nusrat Fateh Ali Khan (b. 1974 in Faisalabad), the nephew of Nusrat Fateh Ali Khan, has assumed musical leadership of the group following the death of his uncle, from whom he received instruction. A second *qawwāli* group, once led by the brothers Ghulam Farid and Maqbool Ahmed Sabri, also enjoys national and international stardom. The Sabri style is typical of the southern Sindh province. Although the brothers were also vocal virtuosos, their recordings and performances emphasize text, composition and group performance. Although both groups employ the traditional harmonium, *tablā* and *dholak*, along with solo-chorus singing and clapping, the Sabris frequently record songs using large film-style orchestras, electronic keyboards and other imported instruments, and even heavy-metal guitar bands. Since the death of both brothers in the 1990s, younger members of the hereditary group have assumed its leadership. Rizwan Muazam, Aziz Mian and Farid Sabri are other contemporary Pakistani *qawwāls* with popular recordings. In any measure of popularity, however, these artists lag well behind the two family groups described here.

Sufiyana kalam is a devotional style associated primarily with the Kashmir region. It combines elements of South Asian and Persian music in which the *santūr* and a version of the *tablā* specific to the Kashmir region figure prominently as accompanimental instruments. Abida Parveen is a popular artist who specializes in *sufiyana kalam*. Pathana Khan and the late Ustad Manzoor Ali Khan are other important singers in this style.

Other Muslim devotional genres, such as *hamd*, *nāth* and *marsiya*, are popular in Pakistan, although these generally do not have specific musical styles associated with them. All are strophic song-forms sung in praise of God/Allah and his Holy Prophet Muhammad, traditionally rendered as solo vocal forms with no instrumental accompaniment. Despite the traditional avoidance of instrumentation, some artists use orchestrated arrangements and vocal styles that combine the minute ornamentation of South Asian light-classical music with the crooning film-music style. Syed Muhammad Fasih Uddin, Qari Waheed Zafar and Alhaaj Khurshid Ahmed are some of the contemporary artists who specialize in devotional music. But many of the bestselling devotional recordings at the beginning of the twenty-first century are by artists associated with other styles. Recordings by the late Noor Jehan, whose primary career was as a singer of *ghazals* and film songs, remain very popular.

In the Punjab and in Sindh *kāfi*, a vernacular poetic form with mystic devotional content, forms the basis for popular music performances and recordings of the same name. Abida Parveen and Allan Faqir are two contemporary vocalists with many popular recordings of *kāfis*. Shahida Parveen (d. 1975) is especially well remembered for her recordings of *kāfis*, as are Saeen Marna (d. 1961) and Hamid Ali Khan Bela, who both sang exclusively in Punjabi. Popular dance musics such as *roff*, originally performed by women on Muslim holidays, and *dhamāl*, originally a folk dance associated with the religious practices of Sufi dervishes, have since become part of popular culture. Recordings maintain their devotional texts, but musical accompaniment is subjected to remix through the addition of electronic keyboard and drum machine tracks. These recordings are marketed under such titles as 'non-stop *dhamāl*,' a clear attempt to associate them with other popular dance musics of the region.

These and other musical styles were distinctive, locally produced and popular enough to be marketed to large audiences and elite patrons even before the advent of sound recording. With regard to the early recording industry, Columbia, HMV and Jain-o-phone Records were active players in the popular music industry prior to 1947. EMI-Pakistan is the only major label remaining. A host of small, often short-lived labels produce popular music.

With the advent of cassettes many folk genres have been transferred to this medium, often with input from Western and local popular musical features. Music piracy continues to impose significant difficulties on the growth of local record labels.

When considering the history of musical styles anywhere in South Asia, it must be recalled that poetic form and content are often the basis on which names are given to musical style or performance and vice versa. The term 'qawwali,' for example, can refer to performances of devotional texts in the familiar rhythmic, choral and responsorial musical style, but it can also describe romantic texts sung in that style. Similarly, one of Pakistan's most important and prestigious popular genres, ghazal, identifies not musical content but poetic content. Consequently, ghazal poetry can be heard in a range of musical styles from qawwali to the dominant style of commercial film songs. In both cases, the resulting musical performance is identified as ghazal.

Traditional Popular Songs

'Traditional' is used here only to identify songs sung in forms and styles that do not reflect the influence of mediated Western popular music. Many such forms nevertheless use Western musical instruments. This category includes songs that are largely or totally composed and sung in a range of poetic styles and languages. Some have connections to the world of classical South Asian music; others are connected to folk styles. Preeminent among Pakistan's popular-song genres are settings of ghazal poetry. 'Ghazal' most properly identifies a poetic structure and rhyme scheme, but it is also used to refer to musical settings of such poems. Ghazals have come to occupy a special place in the national musical consciousness of Pakistan because of their perceptibly Turko-Persian, and often Islamic, poetic content. Begum Akhtar Fiazabadi is the most famous popular ghazal singer of the pre-Partition era, but Barkat Ali Khan (d. 1963) is more distinctively a Pakistani master from this period. Other stars who sang and recorded ghazals in the mid- and later twentieth century include: Ijaz Hussain Hazarvi, Noor Jehan, Iqbal Bano, Farida Khanum, Nayyara Nur, Amanat Ali Khan and Malika Pukhraj.

The first and still most famous ghazal artists of the Independence era are Ghulam Ali and Mehdi Hasan, both of whom have released hundreds of recordings, mostly on audiotapes. Both came to national and, later, international attention in the mid-1960s. Like their predecessors, these artists participated actively in the recording and film industries, composing and singing film soundtracks in addition to making commercial recordings. Their coincident rise to prominence alongside the cassette revolution, however, made their impact outside the film industry much broader than that of earlier ghazal singers. The musical style developed in the ghazal recordings of Hasan and Ali has remained dominant. This standardized format uses a base of light-classical musical content to construct repetitive melodic compositions, sung in a crooning vocal style in medium to slow tempos with a somewhat simplified Urdu vocabulary. Tabla and harmonium provide accompaniment, with semi-improvised instrumental interludes performed on a variety of instruments including guitar, santur, sitar and flute. Ghazals are typically romantic and rather melancholy, although in Pakistan instructive, religious or nationalist texts are not unknown.

The success of Hasan and Ali prompted a host of followers. During the latter part of the twentieth century these included Shaukat Ali, Nahid Akhter, Shahida Parveen, Masood Malik and Munawar Sultana. Two contemporary and popular ghazal specialists are Munni Begum and Ata'ullah Khan.

Popular songs in regional languages have relatively small audience bases. Few artists can survive by singing only to such small audiences. Rahim Shah, who also records songs in Urdu, sings mostly in Pakhtu, one of the languages spoken by increasing numbers of Pakistanis toward the Afghani border. His release, Peera, has been a regional hit. Almost the only well-known artist singing in Sindhi is the popular Shazia Khushk.

Some singers and recordings of folk songs might also be mentioned in a discussion of popular music, since the most successful of these recordings receive heavy media attention. Lahore artist Asif Bhatti, who comes from a hereditary musical caste, sings popularized folk-song repertoire in Punjabi. Karachi artist Mussarat Nazir records a wide variety of material, including a recent and popular album of wedding songs.

Popular Film Song

Film songs have been well-documented mainstays of South Asian popular music since the inception of sound films on the subcontinent in 1931. Shortly thereafter, Lahore became an important center for the production of films in Punjabi and in Urdu. A generation of Punjabi and other musicians from what is now Pakistan made enormous contributions to South Asian cinema from the late 1940s through the 1960s. This is especially true of composers such as Ghulam Haider (1906–53), Khurshid Anwar (1912–84), Feroze'uddin Ahmad (Feroze Nizami) (d. 1975), Jhandhey Khan, Inayat Hussain, Rashid Attray, Mian Shahryar (b. 1927), Ghulam Ahmad Chishti, and brothers Saleem and Iqbal Hussain. Many of these men belonged to hereditary musician castes (Mirasi and Rababi). Singers Shamshad Begum and Noor Jehan are especially associated with the early Lahore film industry. The Hindu-owned film studios in Lahore did not survive the riots of Partition, but the industry revived in the 1950s, with many of the same personnel. Saleem Raza and Mala (real name, Naseem) were both extremely popular film singers beginning in the 1960s, as was Ahmed Rushdi. Lahore's contemporary Mirasi community has continued to contribute to the so-called 'Lollywood' film industry (Lollywood being an imitation of the term 'Bollywood' – coined for the film industry in what was then Bombay – and thus the original, Hollywood). However, the domination of the West (often via Mumbai) has erased the region's earlier distinctive film music culture.

Rock and Pop Music in Pakistan

Pakistan's history of relative openness to Western culture led to developments in Western-style pop and rock in non-cinematic contexts that are significant and that are at the forefront of subcontinental popular music. Like *ghazals*, however, the style began in the cinema, with a recording by Nazia Hassan (1955–2000) and her brother Zohaib, who pioneered the use of modern rock content in South Asia. The pair's first success was in the 1980 film *Qurbani*. This film was produced in India as a Hindi-language film. The song 'Aap jaisa koi' led to the inclusion of more Western rock and pop in Indian and Pakistani soundtracks, but also encouraged Hassan and her brother to embark on careers as pop musicians outside the film world. Although they worked for much of their careers in India, their Islamic identity helped them influence Pakistani musicians. Early pop vocalists in Pakistan included Runa Laila and Alamghir. Both were influenced by Hindi film music's infatuation with disco. Muhammad Ali Sheikhi was yet another vocalist quite popular in Pakistan, although he was of Persian (Irani) origin. Hassan Jehangir is another pop vocalist in the disco style, releasing his first single, 'Hawa Hawa,' in 1989. Solo vocalists have continued to generate popular songs in a studio production mode that uses Western models. The majority of singers sing in Urdu or Punjabi. Solo vocalists in popular styles include Ali Haider, Bunny, Hadiqa Kiyani (*Roshni* being her 1999 hit), Sajjad Ali and Uzma Shah. Song texts are predominantly romantic, musical styles combine Western and local content, but electronic instrumentation and heavily orchestrated arrangements are the norm. Uzma Shah's 1994 patriotic song 'Hayat' represents another lyrical trend in Pakistani pop songs, one slightly more common among vocalists than among rock guitar bands. Fariha Pervaiz has made two highly successful pop albums: Her *Naughty and Nice*, featuring the hit single 'Patangbaaz Sajna,' was followed by *Jhumka*. Two more very successful solo vocalists are Ahmad Jehanzeb and Ali Zafar.

The major Pakistani rock bands of the early twenty-first century were Vital Signs and Junoon. String Fellows was initially quite influential but broke up in the 1990s. Other bands include Fuzon (whose 2002 debut was very well received), Aaroh, EP and Noori, a more alternative, punk- or grunge-style band. The appearance of these and other guitar bands, beginning in the mid-1980s, was associated with the expansion of satellite television broadcasts into South Asia and the consequent broad-scale access to music video culture for young South Asians. The rapid growth of programming aimed at the South Asian market offered models and avenues for aspiring Pakistani popular musicians, among others. Generally, Pakistani rock bands draw both their members and their audience from the nation's secondary and tertiary educational institutions. The bands mentioned here have all been formed by upper-middle-class college students from Lahore. Although String Fellows, established in 1985, was one of the earliest full-blown guitar bands to appear on the Pakistani music scene, Vital Signs was initially the most popular and influential of Pakistan's rock bands. The band's first major music video, 'Dil dil Pakistan,' provoked considerable political debate, into which even the nation's prime minister entered. This centered on matters of image (long hair, jeans and denim jackets as opposed to the traditional *shalwar kamiz*) rather than directly addressing the issue of music in Islamic culture. The nationalist content of the song's text seems not to have been seen by the Establishment as a redeeming feature.

Both the musical content and cultural images of US and British rock and heavy metal bands are dominant in Pakistani rock music. As noted, long hair, jeans and denim jackets are important aspects of most bands' image. Musically, however, even bands labeled heavy metal would seem rather inoffensive by Western standards. As in the West, rock music in Pakistan offers a potential forum for social and political comment. Thus, the Western model of youth music as a vehicle for social comment is applied in a uniquely Pakistani formula that expresses protest and concern for the future as well as respect for religion and traditional cultural ways.

Although Pakistani rock and pop styles sound very much like their foreign models, local musical elements do also make an appearance. Saleem Javed, originally from Multan (near Lahore), incorporates folk music styles into pop productions. His 1997 release *Kiraya* blends traditional, cultural songs with modern, Western rhythms. Hits included on this album were 'Dil Ne,' 'Randana,' 'Kiraya' and 'Abb Se Kal.' The recently formed Karavan is another rock band active in Pakistan, as was the now defunct Awaz.

Sajjad Ali, mentioned above as a pop vocalist, includes folk and classical elements in his songs and performances. Ali began his career singing *ghazals*. Traces of classical music can also be heard in the songs of Hadiqa Kiyani, who studied South Asian classical music in her youth.

Many younger popular musicians mix traditional musical elements (especially Punjabi *bhangra*) with Western elements. Junoon routinely includes a *tablā* player in its recordings and live concerts.

One of the most popular mixes of traditional and Western popular musics is *bhangra*, which began as a Punjabi folk dance. *Bhangra* is common to Punjabis of all religious and national affiliations, and its dominant rhythms have blended well with contemporary pop in Pakistan, in India, and in Britain among expatriate Punjabis. Abrar-ul-Haq is one of the important Punjabi pop musicians who plays what is sometimes called *bhangra* rock.

The styles associated with rap, hip-hop and house all make their appearance in Pakistani popular music. Among the early leaders in this type of music were the Lahore duo Yatagaan. Their first video, 'Bhangara Rap' (1993), indicates the complex overlapping of musical styles and style labels in much popular music. The song became a major headliner on Pakistani music charts.

Pakistan's geographical and political identity has caused difficulties for some classical musicians, who have turned also to popular music as a means of making a living. Even younger members of heredi- tary musical families, such as vocalists Rafaqat Ali Khan and Shafqat Ali Khan, both of whom use their classical training to good effect in recordings of *ghazal*-style pop and global fusion, have been affected.

Conclusion

Pakistan's popular music is distinctive in a number of ways. First is the juxtaposition of South and West-Central Asian styles within its national borders. Although not combined in any individual genre, both cultural orientations are present, to a greater or lesser extent, throughout the country. Second, Pakistani music culture has had to develop an intentional emphasis on a number of regional devotional styles and has elevated these to popular status through heavy media saturation. *Sufiyana kalam* and *kāfi* are examples of this trend, but *qawwāli* epitomizes and exceeds the notion of a devotional style transformed into a national musi- cal icon. Initially, Pakistan's international musical profile was generated almost exclusively by its major *qawwāli* stars, but within South Asia and across the South Asian diaspora rock bands and solo pop vocalists are becoming more visible. Finally, and in contrast to this devotional trend, Western and Western-style pop and rock musics have a stronger foothold and a higher profile in Pakistan than in neighboring countries. The overall result is a highly variegated musical package.

Bibliography

Broughton, Simon, and Ellingham, Mark, eds. 2000. *World Music – The Rough Guide. Vol. 2: Latin & North America, Caribbean, India, Asia and Pacific.* London: Rough Guides.

Malik, Saeed. 1998. *Lahore, Its Music Culture.* Lahore: Sang-e-Meel Publications.

Discographical References

Javed, Saleem. *Kiraya.* SoundMaster. *1997*: Pakistan.

Jehangir, Hassan. 'Hawa Hawa.' T Series 5000 Series. *1989*: Pakistan.

Kiyani, Hadiqa. *Roshni.* SoundMaster. *1999*: Pakistan.

Pervaiz, Fariha. 'Patangbaaz Sajna.' *Naughty and Nice.*

Vital Signs. 'Dil dil Pakistan.' *Vital Signs.* EMI. *1989*: Pakistan.

Yatagaan. 'Bhangara Rap.' Tips Exclusive TC 2374. *1993*: Pakistan.

Discography

Music Pakistan. http://www.netpakistani.com/music
MuziqPakistan. http://www.muziqpakistan.com
Pakistani Music. http://www.pakistanimusic.com
Pakistani Pop Music. http://www.pakipop.com

Filmography

Qurbani, dir. Feroz Khan. 1980. India. 157 mins. Drama. Original music by Anandji Veerji Shah, Kalyanji Veerji Shah.

GREGORY BOOTH

CITIES

Karachi

Population: 14,000,000 (2004)

Karachi is the capital of Pakistan's southernmost province, Sindh, and the nation's major seaport. Although originally Sindhi in language and culture, Karachi's importance as a destination for Bihari, Afghani and Indian Muslims after Partition in 1947 has resulted in the city becoming Pakistan's largest and most heterogeneous city. Many immigrants (*mohajir*) contributed to the city's popular music profile.

Haji Ghulam Farid Sabri (1930–94) and Haji Maqbool Ahmed Sabri (b. 1945), members of one of the most popular *qawwāli* families to perform in this devotional genre, settled in Karachi in 1947. They first recorded for EMI-Pakistan in 1958, scoring a popular hit with 'Hera Koi Nahin Hai Teray Siwa.' Farid Sabri's son, Amjid, has carried on the Sabri Brothers' name. Other popular music immigrants who settled in Karachi are Mehdi Hasan, the extremely popular *ghazal* singer whose post-Partition career began in 1952 at Radio Pakistan (Karachi); Noor Jehan (1926–2000), Pakistan's 'Mallika-e-Tarannum' (Queen of Melody), who sang *ghazals*, devotional songs and film songs; and Sohail Rahana (b. 1938), Pakistan's foremost film music director in the period 1960–80 and Director General at the Ministry of Culture from 1976 to 1978. Rahana is also associated with the Pakistan television corporation and a number of popular national songs, especially 'Allah-o-Akbar.'

Like other metropolises that developed under nineteenth-century colonial rule, Karachi has a long history of exposure to contemporary Western music and culture, and was a regular stop on the tours of local and international dance and jazz bands. The city was the original home of Pakistan's film and music industries, including the country's only pre-Partition recording label, originally the Gramophone Company of Pakistan, but now EMI-Pakistan. Although Lahore's film industry rapidly became dominant, Karachi remained the center for music audio and video production until well into the 1990s. Major recording production has been inhibited by Pakistan's historical and contemporary inability to solve rampant recording piracy.

Pakistan's first music channel, Indus Music, is located in Karachi, as well as more modern multimedia production houses such as Indus Vision and VCI Music. Singers and bands routinely travel to Karachi for live performances and recordings.

Karachi is also home to a number of professional and semiprofessional pop bands performing in various styles, which grew in number through the 1990s. Groups include the duo Fringe Benefits, Rixan, Wireless and Just In Case, as well as vocalists Najam Sheraz and Ahmed Jehanzeb.

Discographical Reference

Sabri Brothers, The. 'Hera Koi Nahin Hai Teray Siwa.' EMI-Pakistan. *1958*: Pakistan.

GREGORY BOOTH

Lahore

Population: 5,452,000 (2000)

Lahore is Pakistan's second-largest city and the capital of Punjab province. Since roughly 1100 A.D., the city has been a center (or regional center) for Afghan, Mughal, Sikh and British polities. The city consequently has a long history of involvement with the arts, and is popularly described as Pakistan's artistic and educational capital. Lahore is home to the nation's largest concentration of hereditary classical and light-classical music families (Mirasis), who participate actively in popular music of all sorts as well as in the film music industry. In addition, the female performers of Lahore's red-light district, Hira Mandi, have had a connection with traditional forms of popular music performed in private and public venues, including the city's many *takiyahs* (travelers' inns located just outside the city walls). In the early twentieth century, under British rule, Lahore's many European-style hotels featured regular performances of Western popular music by European, Goan and Anglo-Indian dance bands. Finally, Lahore Radio, the regional station of the national network and the most musically active nationally, has been a key factor in the careers of many musicians, broadcasting live and recorded performances of *ghazals*, *geet*, *qawwāli*, *sufiyana kalam* and other traditional forms of popular music.

Within the city, the Sufi shrines of Hazrat Ali Hajveri (aka Data Ganj Baksh) and Shah Hussain have long been sites for traditional popular music performances, especially *qawwāli*. Lahore is home to a number of popular *qawwāli* families, especially the family of the late Nusrat Fateh Ali Khan (1951–97). Rahat Nusrat Fateh Ali Khan (b. 1974 in Faisalabad), the nephew of Nusrat Fateh Ali Khan, has assumed musical leadership of the original group following the death of his uncle. However, two other nephews, the brothers Rizwan and Muazzam Ali Khan, have also made an impact internationally, especially in their fusion recordings as Temple of Sound.

Lahore is the center of Pakistan's popular film industry, and its musicians have produced the majority of the popular film songs – sung in Punjabi and Urdu – found therein. Popular composers include: Ghulam Haider (1906–53), Khurshid Anwar (1912–84), Feroze'uddin Ahmad (Feroze Nizami) (d. 1975), Jhandhey Khan, Master Tasadduq, Rafiq Ghaznavi, Master Abdullah, Tufail Farooqi, Ustad Nazar, Inayat Hussain, Rashid Attray, Mian Shahryar (b. 1927), Ghulam Ahmad Chishti, and brothers Saleem and Iqbal Hussain. Many of these men belonged to hereditary musician castes (Mirasi and Rababi). Saleem Raza and Mala (real name, Naseem) were both extremely popular film singers beginning in the 1960s, as was Ahmed Rushdi.

Lahore's many colleges and schools have produced a thriving youth culture, which has in turn produced many popular bands and vocalists. Singing mostly in Punjabi, but sometimes in Urdu, these include early pioneer bands Junoon, Yatagaan, Vital Signs and String Fellows. More recent entries onto the pop music scene include EP, Junaid Jamshed Aaroh, Awaz and Noori. Solo vocalists include: Abrar-ul-Haq, Ali Haider, Faiz, Hadiqa Kiyani, Danish Rahi, Komal Rizvi, Sajjad Ali, Shehzad Roy and Tahira Syed. These artists produce everything from punk and grunge styles to *bhangra* rock and contemporary ballad styles.

GREGORY BOOTH

Sri Lanka

Population: 18,700,000 (2001)

The Democratic Socialist Republic of Sri Lanka, formerly know as Ceylon, is an island nation located in South Asia. While it shares much with its neighbors, Sri Lanka has a unique culture, including musical styles distinct from others in the region. Sri Lanka has long been a trading crossroads in the sea; to the east is the Bay of Bengal, to the west the Arabian sea, and close by to the northwest, across the Gulf of Mannar and the Palk Strait, is the southern tip of India. The island has a distinctive teardrop shape, and is often called

the 'resplendent land' – its old name, 'serendib,' is the root of the word 'serendipity.' It is 270 miles (435 km) from north to south and 140 miles (225 km) from east to west, with a total land area of 25,332 sq miles (65,610 sq km). The landscape consists of palm trees, beautiful beaches, rolling hills and flat plains, aside from some peaks of about 8,000 ft (2,400 m) in the south. The climate is subtropical, with monsoon rains, an average temperature of 80° F (27° C) and high humidity.

Sri Lanka is a multiethnic society with an estimated population of 18.7 million people (Census of 2001), comprising groups of Sinhalese (13,815,500 people, or about three-quarters of the total population), Sri Lankan Tamil (emigrated in the past; 730,200), India Tamil (arrived in the nineteenth century as plantation laborers; 855,900), Sri Lankan Moor (Muslims; 1,351,400), Malay (47,600), Burgher (descendants of Portuguese and Dutch), Eurasian (descendants of British; together, 34,600), and others (29,500). Languages include Sinhala, Tamil and English. The main religions are Theravada Buddhism (practiced by the Sinhalese), Hinduism (by the Tamils), Islam and Christianity. Education from primary through university levels is free, and over 90 percent are literate. Life expectancy is 72 years (2004 figure; Department of Census and Statistics). Social problems include the generally lower status of women, poverty and malnutrition. The main agricultural product is rice, the staple of the country's diet; cassava, potato, sugar cane and coconut are also widely grown. Tea, rubber, coconut products and textiles are the economy's main export industries; in addition, some three-quarters of a million Sri Lankans send home remittances from their jobs in the Middle East. Important cities include the major commercial city Colombo (population 642,163), Dehiwala-Mount Lavinia (209,787), Kandy (110,049), Negombo (121,933), Moratuwa (177,190), the national administrative capital Sri Jayawardenepura Kotte (115,826) (all previous figures from the Census of 2001), and Jaffna (118,224; Census of 1991).

The earliest humans to reside in Sri Lanka were aboriginal people thought to have arrived perhaps 18 millennia ago. Today, their descendants are known as the Vedda, or Wanniya-laeto (forest-dwellers), of whom only about 3,000 survive as a distinct group; many others have assimilated over time. In about the sixth century B.C., the Indo-Aryan ancestors of the Sinhalese arrived from northern India. Dravidian Tamils then emigrated from southern India between about the third century B.C. and the fourteenth century A.D. Indian Tamil and local Sinhalese rulers exchanged control of the island over the centuries. Rule by Portuguese, Dutch, and British traders and colonialists began in 1505 and ended when Ceylon entered the Commonwealth of Nations as an independent nation in 1948; the name Sri Lanka was adopted in 1972.

Civil war between Tamil and Sinhalese factions has raged since 1983, aside from some periods of cease-fire and occasional negotiations. An estimated 65,000 people have died in the conflict (as of 2001), which has had a devastating effect on the nation. Upon achieving independence the two groups initially co-existed, but gradually the more numerous Sinhalese came to dominate the government and society. As a result, many Tamils felt excluded, voicing the complaint that their Tamil language had been suppressed. Tamil people live primarily in the northern portions of the island, where some such as the Liberation Tigers of Tamil Eelam seek to establish a separate state. Tamil groups have frequently used terrorism and suicide bombing, including a presidential assassination in 1993. Several hundred thousand Sri Lankan Tamils have sought refuge in the West and India, where refugee camps provide shelter for some.

Music in Sri Lanka presents a wide variety of fascinating genres, contexts and histories. Local styles of music include religious, classical, old and new pop, film, folk and *baila*. According to Sheeran, the music of Sri Lankan has not received a great deal of scholarly attention, in part because it does not fit paradigms established in the colonial era for understanding the music of India, which has canonical Sanskrit texts and codified theories. In contrast, Sri Lankan traditional chanted prose music of the Sinhalese people lacks a central authority and thus has many separate styles, lineages, performance practices and musical theories that do not necessarily conform to one another (Sheeran 2001, 231). Some other genres unique to Sri Lanka include religious chants performed by Theravada Buddhist monks, and many drumming genres that exist to accompany ritual dances. Among the Tamil people, traditional musical styles include chanting of the Qur'an by Muslims, and *nagaswaram* (double-reed horn) and *tāvil* (barrel drum) music at Hindu temples.

An early popular music genre is a theatrical music called *nurthi*, typically consisting of vocals with harmonium and other instruments. This North Indian-influenced music accompanied shows in urban theaters such as Colombo's Tower Hall throughout the late nineteenth and early twentieth centuries. The earliest gramophone recordings of Sri Lanka music date from 1903 and feature this theatrical music. *Baila* music originated with the Portuguese, who brought their musical instruments (such as the guitar, violin and mandolin) and song forms, as well as enslaved African people. The genre is sometimes termed 'Afro-Portuguese,' while it is also uniquely Sri Lankan – thus it is an example of African creole music formed in a colonial South Asian context (Sheeran 2000, 955). It has evolved from a simple ensemble of voice, guitar, violin and conga drums to a version with synthesizers and electric guitars. Some stars of the genre include Desmond de Silva, M.S. Fernando, Paul Fernando, Saman de Silva, Joseph Wisidagama and Voli Bastian. In the 1960s, a calypso-influenced style of *baila* became popular, produced by groups such the Hummingbirds and the Moonstones.

Indian film music – the dominant form of popular music in India since the 1930s – has long been popular in Sri Lanka as well. For a time in the mid-twentieth century, Indian radio stations excluded film music in favor of classical Indian music. However, Sri Lanka's Radio Ceylon (established in 1925) programmed Indian film music in its broadcasts, which were able to reach audiences in both nations; many in India acknowledge the role played by the Sri Lankan station in popularizing Indian film music within India itself. Film and other pop music from India has continued to have a place in the Sri Lankan market.

The Sri Lankan film industry, based in Colombo, has produced many movies with songs, which may then circulate independently of the films. Some film composers are Mohammad Gauss, Premasiri Kemadasa and W.D. Amaradeva, also well known as a singer. The separate category of Sinhalese pop has evolved from the mid-twentieth century, and may resemble Indian film music or Western pop. Its instrumentation features electric guitar, drum machine and synthesizer; the genre is often considered to be in opposition to *baila*, even though one may enjoy both (Sheeran 2000, 971). Some singers cross these genre borders and are known to sing folk, pop, national and film music. For example, vocalist Sunil Shantha has remained popular years after his death in 1981. The lyrics of his songs often had a nationalistic meaning, and were said to transcend the many social, religious, economic and political divisions of Sri Lankan society: '. . . when it comes to appreciating the musical prowess of Visharada Sunil

Shantha, all stand united under one banner' ('A Salute to the Legends,' paragraph 3). Vocalist and actor Rukmani Devi has been called the 'queen of the silver screen and nightingale of song' ('A Salute to the Legends,' paragraph 5). The popular vocalist Milton Mallawarachchi performed as a playback singer for over 100 films and was known for his romantic songs. Other popular Sinhalese singers include Mahagama Sekara, Wally Bastiansz, Angeline Gunatilleka, Clarence Wijewardan, Annesley Malawana, Surya Shankar Molligoda, Ananda Samarakoon, Indrani Perera and Eddie Jayamanne.

The government ended its broadcasting monopoly in the 1990s, opening the airwaves to private stations. Music is broadcast on several state and private television and radio stations, such as Sirasa, TNL, Yes, Sooriyan, Sun and Hiru. Some play English-language US and British pop music; for example, the playlist for Yes FM radio in June 2004 included US and British artists Beyonce, Sting, George Michael, Chingy and Blink 182 (see: http://www.yesfmonline.com). Other stations, such as Sirasu FM, focus on Sinhalese pop, while some, such as TNL FM, play a mix of music. Dance clubs and radio stations may feature local and Western rock music. In a socially conservative society such as Sri Lanka, rock can represent risk and rebellion to its youthful audiences, according to anthropologist Dan Bass. Of a night spent dancing in a Colombo club to a live metal band and a DJ spinning US rock music, he writes that, against a backdrop in which informal contact between men and women can be discouraged or limited, '[r]ock music provides a real alternative for young … Sri Lankans' (Bass 1996, paragraph 11).

Sri Lankan popular music continues to absorb new sounds as a result of the contemporary transnational flows of music genres, audio recordings, instruments, music technology and people. Keyboardist, sequencer programmer and vocalist Ranidu Lankage achieved great success in the first years of the twenty-first century with his blend of pop and techno music. He was once a member of the popular youth-oriented pop group Bathiya and Santhush, until he departed for studies at Yale University in the US in 2001. He has composed music for the opening ceremony of the Asian Athletic Championships in 2002 and, in 2003, released a hit techno pop album, *Oba Magemai*, with vocalist Ashanthi.

Bibliography

Ariyaratna, Sunil. 1986. *The Gramophone Era in Sinhala Music.* Maradana, Sri Lanka: Samayawardena.

'A Salute to the Legends.' *The Sunday Leader*, online edition. http://www.thesundayleader.lk/20030907/arts.htm

Bass, Dan. 'Rock and Rebellion in South Asia.' WCBN Program Guide, Ann Arbor, Fall 1996. http://www.wcbn.org/sos/article.dan.html

Benaim, Lexy. 2002. 'Electronica Sensation in Pierson.' *The Yale Herald*, online edition, 18 October. http://www.yaleherald.com/article.php?Article=1222

Ganhewa, Lalith. 2000. 'Sri Lanka: Sounds of Serendipity.' In *World Music: The Rough Guide, Vol. 2: Latin and North America, Caribbean, India, Asia and Pacific*, ed. Simon Broughton and Mark Ellingham. London: Rough Guides, 230–34.

Department of Census and Statistics, Sri Lanka. 'Social Conditions.' http://www.statistics.gov.lk/social/index.htm

Karunanayake, Nandana. 1990. *Radio Broadcasting in Sri Lanka: Potential and Performance*. Moratuwa, Sri Lanka: Centre for Media and Policy Studies.

Kulatillake, Cyril de Silva. 1976. *Metre, Melody, and Rhythm in Sinhala Music*. Colombo: Sinhala Music Research Unit, Sri Lanka Broadcasting Corp.

Kulatillake, Cyril de Silva. 1993. 'Sri Lanka.' In *Ethnomusicology: Historical and Regional Studies*, ed. Helen Myers. New York: W.W. Norton, 297–99.

Mel, Vasana K. de. 1998. *A History of the Sacred, the Devotional, and the Secular in Sri Lankan Buddhist Music*. Unpublished M.A. thesis. Los Angeles: University of California,

Myers, Charles. 1911. *Vedda Music*. Cambridge: Cambridge University Press.

Sabin, Jennifer. 2003. 'Spotlight on Ranidu Lankage: Sri Lankan idol in our midst.' *Yale Daily News*, online edition, April 24. http://www.yaledailynews.com/article.asp?AID=22764

Sheeran, Anne. 1997. *White Noise: European Modernity, Sinhala Musical Nationalism, and the Practice of a Creole Popular Music in Modern Sri Lanka*. Unpublished Ph.D. dissertation. Seattle: University of Washington.

Sheeran, Anne. 2000. 'Sri Lanka.' In *The Garland Encyclopedia of World Music. Vol. 5: South Asia, The Indian Subcontinent*, ed. Alison Arnold. New York: Garland, 952–74.

Sheeran, Anne. 2001. 'Sri Lanka.' In *The New Grove Dictionary of Music and Musicians*, vol. 24, ed. Stanley Sadie. 2nd ed. New York: Grove, 229–32.

Discographical Reference

Ashanthi and Ranidu Lankage. *Oba Magemai*: Sony Music India. *2003*: India.

Discography

Baila Session in Sri Lanka. Torana Music Box SPSK 1028. *ca.1999*: Sri Lanka.

Bathiya and Santhush. *Tharunyay*. Sony Music India. *2002*: India.

Best of the Light Classics. Wickremesooriya & Co. GDNU 20. *1992*: Sri Lanka.

Celvaraja, M.S., and Aruna Cellatturai. *A.V.A. Presents Oli Thenral*. AVA Limited. *1994*: Sri Lanka.

Gypsies. *Singyore*. Gypsy Enterprises Limited. *ca.1999*: Sri Lanka.

Mahesan, Niranjini Ananda. *Paktip pamalar Ilankai alayankal mel patappatta paktip patalkal*. Tamil Cevai, Ilankai Oliparappuk Kuttuttapanam. *2000*: Sri Lanka. (Tamil devotional songs, brought out on the occasion of 75th year of Sri Lanka Broadcasting Corporation, Tamil Service.)

Malini, Nanda. *Gramophone Songs of Sri Lanka*. Singlanka SLCD 013095. *1995*: Sri Lanka.

Mallawarachchi, Milton. *Milton Pranama*. Torana Music Box SPSK 1042. n.d.: Sri Lanka.

Peiris, Stanley and the Fortunes. *Golden Melodies of Sri Lanka*. Torana Music Box SPSK 1009. n.d.: Sri Lanka.

The Star-Spangled Sooriya Show. Torana Music Box SPSK 1017. n.d.: Sri Lanka.

Wijewardena, Clarence. *Unforgettable Melodies*. Torana Music Box SPSK 1011. n.d.: Sri Lanka.

JOSEPH GETTER

3. Japan

Japan

Population: 127,620,000 (2003)

Japan, called Nippon or Nihon domestically, is located off the east coast of the Asian continent, and consists of an archipelago extending from northeast to southwest, with its size slightly larger than that of Finland.

A national reunification in Japan was accomplished in the modern period when Tokugawa Iéyasu won a victory over pro-Toyotomi Hideyoshi warriors and assumed the title of shogun in 1603. In the late 1630s, under his rule, Japan closed its doors to all foreigners, eradicating Christianity and controlling contacts with overseas countries. It was not until the mid-1850s that the country was finally forced to open its ports to the United States (as a result of repeated visits by Commodore Perry with his intimidating squadrons) and then to some dominant European countries. The ensuing unequal trade treaties eventually led to the Meiji Revolution in the late 1860s. Conscious of Japan's relative underdevelopment in terms of industrialization and democratization, the new post-revolutionary government accelerated the Westernization of Japan.

A Brief Outline of Musics

Government policy led to a growing appreciation of alien Western music. The historical development of this process of Japanese musical acculturation, conspicuous in the field of popular music, and its relationship with the music industry as a whole are sketched out in chronological order below. It should be kept in mind, however, that the various stylized forms of indigenous music have never been seriously threatened per se by the impulse of Westernization. Despite the active introduction of Western music, many stylized forms of indigenous music have survived with established repertoires, coexisting with Western music as well as with manifold combinations of Western and Japanese musical elements. The conventional forms of Japanese music include *gagaku*, an ancient upper-class art music; *shômyô*, the Buddhist vocal music; *nagauta*, the accompaniment to *kabuki* and *kabuki* dances; and the professional singing of folk songs, which was developed many years after the Meiji Revolution. This conventional indigenous music, generically called *hôgaku*, has been enjoyed more as live performance than in recorded form, but its tenacity is witnessed in the number of new record releases of the music: for example, 570 out of 10,689, the sum total of all domestic recordings released in 1998. This is comparable to the number of new releases by Japanese artists of Western classical music, which was 386 during the same period (RIAJ 1999, 11).

Out of the remainder of the 1998 new releases recorded by Japanese performers, 7,752 were recordings of popular music and 1,767 were 'educational and children's songs,' 'music for animation films' and others. All of these displayed Western influences to some degree, though many of the Western elements had been absorbed for so long that they were not always felt to be particularly Western. On the other hand, the huge number of foreign recordings released in Japan, that is, compact discs and cassettes of foreign origin, should be noted as a reflection of the continuing Japanese infatuation with Western musical culture. The sum total of the releases of such foreign recordings in 1998 amounted to 10,265 in comparison to the 10,689 released by domestic performers. Out of the 10,265 releases, 7,061 were of popular music, including film scores, and 2,986 were categorized as classical music (RIAJ 1999, 11).

The Reception of Western Culture and the Taishô Democracy

In terms of the Japanese music industry, attempts to adapt Western musical elements to Japanese taste were first noticeable in the linkage of theater and gramophone recording, when Matsui Sumako sang 'Katyusha-no Uta' (Katyusha's Song) in 1914.

There had already been quite a few recordings by Japanese performers, ever since the days of the cylinder in the late nineteenth century, but most of the music recorded was the stylized indigenous music mentioned above. The rest were mostly *hayari-uta* (fashionable ditties) and *shosei-bushi* (student ditties), which were first recorded in the years following 1910. These were topical, satirical and humorous songs in the tradition of *enka*, which

were political protest songs in the mid-Meiji era, though this *enka* should not be confused with a hard-core type of modern *kayôkyoku* with the same appellation. Musically, this genre, whose heyday lasted until the late 1920s, was characterized by Japanese traditional pentatonic (five-note) modes, a traditional vocal style, which sounds rustic to modern ears, and a violin accompaniment in unison, the performing style of which was raucous. The violin was a new adoption from the West, as was the piano, which was sometimes used along with the violin at recording sessions, but its performance style by people who were musically untrained self-accompanists was anything but refined. The whole rustic effect engendered by these musical characteristics can be compared to such Anglo-American folk music as is heard in the 1923 recordings of Fiddlin' John Carson from Atlanta, Georgia.

Meanwhile, *naniwa-bushi*, or *rôkyoku*, was very popular from the late 1870s to the end of World

War II. The popular narrative with *shamisen* accompaniment, rooted in street singing, was characterized by a deep chanting voice and melismatic ornamentation of melodies, which were later inherited by such postwar *kayôkyoku* singers as Minami Haruo.

The Birth of a Hit Song

A newer kind of song with much more appeal first appeared in one particular theatrical presentation. The play was *Fukkatsu* (Resurrection), adapted from Tolstoy's novel and performed by Geijutsuza (The Art Company), one of the troupes in the theatrical new wave that in the late 1900s began performances under the influence of European drama, in opposition to the indigenous forms of drama. Songs had been used in plays before 1910 but had been of a more conventional type (Kurata 1979, 170). The innovative 'Katyusha-no Uta' from *Fukkatsu*, sung by Matsui Sumako (who already enjoyed a good reputation as an actress), attained popularity in the course of a month and a half after Geijutsuza began touring in March 1914.

The lyrics, about the pain of a lovesick parting, written by Sôma Gyofû, were a precursor of poetry in a colloquial style, and were set to an original melody composed by Nakayama Shimpei. The latter was a young graduate of the Tôkyô College of Music, a national institution oriented to Western music. According to Nakayama, when Shimamura Hôgetsu, the leader of Geijutsuza, was interviewed by a Tôkyô newspaper reporter in 1935 (Nishizawa 1990a, 3003–3004), he made a comment on musical composition to the effect that Japanese musicians should make music that is identifiably Japanese, instead of imitating Western ways. He suggested that Nakayama should aim at a hybrid between a Japanese indigenous ditty and a Western Lied as a song to be sung by a housemaid in the play. The result was an enjoyable tune in a compromised pentatonic major scale (the fourth and seventh notes 'lacking'). Nevertheless, the unaccompanied singing of the song, recorded in May in Kyôto during the tour for the Orient label, sounds utterly amateurish to modern ears (though truly realistic as a casual performance by a housemaid). But this musically underdeveloped Westernization of pitch and vocalization, along with the song itself, must have sounded refreshing to the contemporary audience as a blend that retained an identifiably Japanese substance.

The record, entitled 'Fukkatsu Shôka' (Resurrection Song) but later known as 'Katyusha-no Uta,'

increased the song's popularity, particularly since Shimamura played it at a lecture meeting that preceded a run of performances in each city during the tour, thus boosting the audience's anticipation (Kurata 1979, 176). The record sold some 20,000 copies, making it the first hit in the history of the Japanese recording industry. This was before the invention of electronic recording, when the price of a record was high (¥1.5, when the initial monthly salary of an elementary-school teacher was ¥12–¥20 (Nishizawa 1990a, 3007)). Meanwhile, the Geijutsuza tour ran on well into 1915. A Tôkyô cosmetics manufacturer parodied the song lyrics in a newspaper advertisement, making it one of the earliest advertising jingles (Kurata 1979, 173).

The Taishô Democracy

That the core of the audience was students is apparent from various quotes from contemporary newspapers, such as 'Students are singing this song enthusiastically. Those who are not singing aloud are singing under their breath' (Kurata 1979, 173). These students were obviously attracted in the beginning by the new age suggested by the name of the play's original author and his latest novel, which had been translated into Japanese in 1905, six years after its original publication. Behind this intellectual thirst was a certain zeitgeist, which, long afterward, became known as the Taishô Democracy (the Taishô period began in 1912, when the newly crowned Emperor Taishô succeeded the deceased Emperor Meiji, and lasted until 1926). The Taishô Democracy, which approximately covered the Taishô period, refers to a growing democratic and liberal tendency in Japanese politics, society and culture in general. It was fostered by, among other things, an easing of strained relations between Asian nations following the termination of the Russo-Japanese war in 1905, and the wakening to political and civil liberty of the urban middle and non-propertied class, which grew up in association with the rapid development of capitalism after the same war (Heibonsha 1985, Vol. 8, 1267). It was this period that produced the first commoner premier in Japan, Hara Takashi, who promoted Japanese–US cooperation in foreign transactions before he was assassinated in 1921, three years after assuming office. On the other hand, in this period many poets ardently admired Walt Whitman, whose work was first introduced in 1892.

Nakayama wrote more hits that were recorded by Matsui thereafter, elaborating his compositions in pentatonic major and minor scales. Even after

Matsui committed suicide following the death of Shimamura, her lover, from sickness, Nakayama's songs continued to be successful, making him a leading composer of popular songs in the Taishô period and in the early Shôwa period. 'Sendô Kouta' (Boatman's Ditty) was particularly successful, with its mood of despair and pessimism (lyrics by Noguchi Ujô) emphasized by the typical minor-inclined pentatonic scale, which touched the heart-strings of the Japanese more intimately than had Nakayama's melodies in the similarly typical major-inclined pentatonic scale. The song was not only recorded by several singers, including Tottori Shun'yô, in 1922, but was also featured as the theme song of a successful film, which further increased its popularity – an early example of the mutual benefits from interrelated media.

The Asakusa Opera

The period of the Taishô Democracy was also characterized in musical terms by an adaptation of Italian opera, which gained favor in the show-business field as a new popular theatrical art. The first performance of opera in Japan took place in 1903, when the graduates and students of the Tôkyô College of Music performed Gluck's *Orfeo ed Euridice* in Japanese translation under the direction of European instructors (Masui 1990, 47–49). And in 1912 Giovanni Vittorio Rossi from Italy began giving lessons at a newly formed theater. After this proved unsuccessful, some of his pupils formed troupes of their own to perform in several theaters in Asakusa, an old entertainment district in Tôkyô.

The age of the Asakusa Opera began in 1917, and its success was due to its transformation of such operas as Verdi's *Aida*, Bizet's *Carmen* and Suppé's *Boccaccio* into the style of Japanese entertainment. The original works were invariably reduced to operettas by being abbreviated, and the arbitrari-ness of the abbreviation was reflected in the way in which the lyrics were loosely translated. Thus the Asakusa Opera was a popular entertainment in which 'the stage and audience were happily united' (Miyazawa 1990, 1). It should also be noted that this was a nationwide phenomenon, because the troupes often toured the country. It can be argued, therefore, that the Asakusa Opera contributed to the modification of the musical sensibility of the Japanese by exposing them to refined musical idioms from the West. On the other hand, skill in adapting Japanese lyrics to occidental melodies was honed by those involved in the performance of the operettas.

The Asakusa Opera – which put on everybody's lips such songs as 'Hab' ich nur deine Liebe' (translated into Japanese) from *Boccaccio*, sung by Taya Rikizô – came to an end in 1925 due to the effects of the great Kantô earthquake two years before. However, the Opera served as a breeding ground for many talented people, including Fuji-wara Yoshié, who led a full-scale opera company, Futamura Tei'ichi, a successful recording artist, Enomoto Ken'ichi, a high-spirited comedian, Sasa Kôka, a proficient songwriter, and Iba Takashi, a popular playwright.

The Takarazuka Revue

Around the time when the Asakusa Opera was coming into vogue, the show-business field saw the emergence of a musical revue that was again a Japanese adaptation of a European model. With its first show in 1914 and the establishment a decade later of Japan's largest theater (with a seating capacity of 3,000), the Takarazuka Kagekidan (Takarazuka Revue Company) was formed by Hankyû, an electric train company, as the chief attraction in Takarazuka, a hot-spring resort town near Ôsaka, the second-largest city in Japan. The all-female Takarazuka Kagekidan has been character-ized by its luxurious spectacle and girlish romanti-cism, featuring male protagonists played by star members to create an image of idealized men or safe male beauty. Significantly, the Takarazuka is still going strong as a theater that 'presents a pastiche of styles derived from European and American musi-cals and juxtaposes these against a variety of Japanese theater and dance traditions' (Brau 1990, 80), and many of the foremost accomplished actresses in Japan graduated from the company, which has its own training school of dancing, singing and playing for girls.

Dance Band Music and Jazz

Jazz was also introduced to Japan during the period of the Taishô Democracy. In fact, it seems to have been introduced to Japanese audiences before 1917, when the first recognized recordings of jazz music were released in the United States by a white quintet, the Original Dixieland Jass (or Jazz) Band, for Victor and Columbia. Japan participated in World War I on the side of the Allied forces and established diplomatic relations with the United States. Passenger and cargo liners crossed back and forth over the Pacific Ocean, importing and export-ing commodities – including records – in abun-dance. A veteran music journalist recalled that North American gramophone records by white dance bands were often played in modish, namely Western-style, coffeehouses, which were called 'milk halls' (Noguchi 1976, 7). Moreover, the five graduates of the Tôyô College of Music who made up the Hatano Orchestra used to buy the scores of popular dance music in San Francisco between 1912 and 1918, when they were employed by a Japanese steamship company to perform for the passengers on its regular liner. After leaving the liner, this orchestra, led by Hatano Fukutarô, worked as an intermission band in theaters that featured North American silent films, playing short classical pieces, pre-jazz dance music and some jazz. They then performed at Kagétsuén in Yokohama, which was the first commercial dance hall ever opened in Japan (1920). Conversely, in the 1920s, some US house bands on passenger liners, with some jazz orientation, often performed in hotels in Yokohama and Kôbé, the two largest international seaports, when their ships were lying in harbor (Uchida 1976, 16).

The Flowering of the Record Industry

In 1923 the great Kantô earthquake had badly affected show business in general, as well as the record industry in particular. However, the first Japanese broadcasting station, JOAK, began operating in 1925. This Tôkyô station and two more in other large cities were combined to form NHK, the Japanese equivalent to the BBC, in the following year (which marked the end of the Taishô period and the beginning of the long Shôwa period). The popularity of broadcasting can be inferred from the rapid increase in the number of receiving sets: in just one year, ownership rose from 5,455 sets to 338,204 (Kawabata 1990, 26). Although the record industry initially feared the competition from this new entertainment medium, the two industries eventually proved to be mutually beneficial.

The Formation of Joint Ventures

To improve economic conditions, the government encouraged the production of domestic goods by passing a bill in 1924 to impose customs duties on imported luxury goods. Imported gramophone records, considered luxury items at that time, were liable to a 10 percent tax (Morimoto 1975, 15). The record companies and dealers that owned the selling rights of specified foreign records were thus obliged to find a means of pressing records in Japan rather than importing them. Japanese companies therefore began to enter into joint ventures with foreign firms. Japan's oldest and largest record dealer, Nicchiku (Nippon Chikuonki), formed a

subsidiary, Japan Columbia, first with Columbia (UK) and then also with Columbia (US), in early 1928. In May 1927 the Anan Company formed Japan Polydor with German Gramophone, with which Anan had had a sales agreement. Japan Victor was formed in July 1927 as a joint venture with the Fraser Company in Tôkyô and Victor (US). Surprisingly, records domestically pressed and produced by these joint-venture companies were priced at one-half to one-sixth of the amount charged for imported discs (Kurata 1979, 315).

At the same time, the new companies set about producing records by Japanese artists with the newly introduced technique of electronic recording. The first such hit by a Japanese artist was, however, a disc recorded overseas originally for overseas audiences. Pressed anew in Japan in the same year, 1928, this record was a coupling of 'Debuné-no Minato' (Seaport) and 'Debune' (Outgoing Ship) sung, with a piano accompaniment, by Fujiwara Yoshié, a tenor trained in the Asakusa Opera. Fujiwara, born to a Scottish father and a Japanese mother, had been invited to record the songs for Victor's prestigious 'Red Label' in 1928 at Victor's studio in Camden, New Jersey (Spottswood 1990, Vol. 5, 2545). While he waited for his session, a renowned violinist, Fritz Kreisler, was recording (Daicel 1990, 4). The song-poems Fujiwara recorded were born out of a movement to create new 'folk songs' among a new generation of poets, and the equally pseudo-traditional music was composed by Nakayama Shimpei, whose first success had been in composing songs for Matsui Sumako.

Encouraged by the success of the record, Japan Victor pressed and released another song in the same vein by Fujiwara, 'Habu-no Minato' (Port of Habu), recorded in Oakland, California in March 1928. The song was also recorded in Tôkyô by Satô Chiyako, a female soprano who was also trained in Western vocals, and the two versions, released in May 1928, sold some 160,000 copies, to the surprise of the Japan Victor staff: 'We little dreamed that a record would have such a great sale' (Daicel 1990, 5).

The newly formed firms also undertook to make domestic versions of US songs, including such hits as 'Valencia,' 'Barcelona' and 'Ramona.' The most successful was the domestic version of 'My Blue Heaven' (Gene Austin and Paul Whiteman, 1927; Nick Lucas and others, 1928 (Whitburn 1986, 39, 450, 284, etc.)), titled 'Aozora,' released in March 1928 by Nipponophone and in September by Japan Victor. The first version was sung by Futamura Tei'ichi, a former Asakusa Opera singer whose vocal style was characterized, to modern ears, by straight-forward, unsophisticated delivery, and by Amano Kikuyo, while the second version was sung only by Futamura. The lyrics were translated by Hori'uchi Keizô, one of the first to translate jazz lyrics, who was also in charge of arranging the music for the Japan Columbia Jazz Band. The arrangement for the Japan Victor Jazz Band was made by Ida Ichirô, a pioneering Japanese jazz band leader. Both records were coupled with 'Sing Me a Song of Araby,' translated by Hori'uchi as 'Arabia-no Uta' and sung by Futamura and Amano in the first version and by Futamura alone in the second version, which also became very popular on its own in contrast to the total obscurity of the song in the United States.

Hits Produced by Newly Formed Companies

Aside from cover versions, the first successful popular song conceived and produced by a Japanese record company was 'Kimi Koishi' (Yearning for You), released by Japan Victor in January 1929. It was one of the songs released in response to a comment made by Japan Victor's first president, Benjamin Gardener, that in the United States popular songs were produced monthly and placed on the market (Morimoto 1975, 27). The light-hearted music composed by Sasa Kôka in the minor scale, tinted with a hint of jazz or US contemporary popular music, was combined with the languish-in-love lyrics written by Shiguré Otowa and sung gaily, again by Futamura Tei'ichi, with an arrangement by Ida Ichirô and accompaniment by the Japan Victor Jazz Band. This great hit was also a precursor of what came to be called 'jazz songs' – newly composed and performed songs that were composites of Japanese sentiments and North American modernism.

'Kimi Koishi' was soon followed by another hit released by Japan Victor, 'Tôkyô Kôshinkyoku' (Tôkyô March), composed by Nakayama Shimpei, with lyrics by Saijô Yaso, professor of French at a Tôkyô university, who, in his own words, 'verbally caricatured some scenes of "modern" Tôkyô life' (Morimoto 1975, 28). The song (actually not a 'march'), in the conventional minor pentatonic scale, was sung by Satô Chiyako and released in May 1929 with backing arranged by Ida Ichirô, whose work was characterized by its jazzy flavor. It is noteworthy that, while 'Kimi Koishi' was followed by a film of the same title in March 1929, 'Tôkyô March' was produced from the outset as the theme song for a film version of a novel, *Tôkyô March*. It was, however, still in the days of silent films, and

theme songs were performed during the intermission. Following the introduction of talking pictures, of course, theme songs for films were far more widely heard and sung.

Thus, record companies established themselves as business enterprises to produce as many hit songs as possible while they introduced a new type of Japanese popular song called *ryûkôka* (fashionable songs), a hybrid of modified vernacular expressions and adapted occidental and North American idioms that mirrored social and cultural changes in Japan. To systematize their hit-making machinery, the record companies entered into exclusive contracts with lyricists, composers and singers. Whereas singers were given royalties, payment to lyricists and composers was made on a non-royalty basis until the early 1960s, when the exclusive contract practice was invalidated. At the same time, many domestically financed record companies were emerging, such as Taihei, Nittô and Tsuru, and these stimulated the entire industry.

The Widening Spectrum of *Ryûkôka*

In 1931 'Paris-no Yané-no Shita,' a Japanese cover version of 'Sous les toits de Paris' by Taya Rikizô, a former star of the Asakusa Opera, became a hit. The song was taken from a talkie with the same title directed by René Clair, which had become popular among students and young urban intellectuals. October of the same year saw the release of an epoch-making song entitled 'Saké-wa Namida-ka Taméiki-ka' (Is Wine Tears or a Sigh?), with which the composer, lyricist and singer all made their debut. The guitarist-composer, Koga Masao, who was soon to displace Nakayama Shimpei, composed it with the intention of creating 'something that is intermediate between "jazz song" and *dodoitsu*' (Morimoto 1975, 46), and the record became an instant hit, reflecting the despondency felt by people in those hard times. (*Dodoitsu* is an old colloquial love ditty form perfected in the mid-nineteenth century.) The song, with its violin, cello, guitar and ukulele accompaniment, was sung in a trained but crooning voice by Fujiyama Ichirô. The singer thereafter enjoyed a happy collaboration with Koga, producing continual hits – not only in the conventional gloomy minor pentatonic scale, but also in the conventional lively major pentatonic one.

The flip side of the record was also a success: Awaya Noriko made her debut with 'Watashi Konogoro Yû'utsuyo' (I'm Feeling So Down These Days), although she was severely reproached, as

Fujiwara had been, by the authorities of the institute from which she had graduated, for singing *ryûkôka*. From this woeful song of self-abandonment she went on to develop her career, the first successful period of which was in the late 1930s when she became 'the queen of the blues' with such compositions as 'Wakaré-no Blues' (Farewell Blues, 1937), 'Amé-no Blues' (Rainy Blues, 1938) and 'Tôkyô Blues' (1939), written by Hattori Ryôichi, who was well acquainted with jazz idioms. Established as a loose genre of *ryûkôka*, these were slow-tempo songs in minor keys with melancholic lyrics, and had no musical affinity with the blues proper.

At the same time, the hard times popularized a rollicking dance song, 'Tôkyô Ondo' (Saijô Yaso and Nakayama Shimpei), sung by Katsutarô (later Ko-uta Katsutarô) and Mishima Issei, and released in July 1933. Originally a kind of collective Japanese folk dance and song, with indigenous rhythm emphasized by a response refrain sung in chorus, *ondo* was reinvigorated with a new melody and lyrics in traditional style performed with Western orchestration featuring traditional drums and *shamisen*. Since this big hit, many occasional and regional *ondo* have been produced successfully, establishing a solid genre in Japanese popular songs. Meanwhile, Katsutarô was the first of many geisha (traditional song-and-dance female entertainers for customers at a feast) to become popular recording artists. They contributed especially to *ryûkôka* by incorporating *ko-uta*, a short piece of *shamisen* song standardized in the mid-nineteenth century. On recordings, new *ko-uta* was performed with an orchestral accompaniment, but the arrangement retained the traditional elements, which were complemented by the typical murmur-like vocalizing in which geisha were trained, along with their own *shamisen* accompaniment.

While the domestic song-forms *ondo* and *ko-uta* were adapted for use in the field of recorded popular song, early 1934 saw the emergence of a new song type featuring lyrics about popular historical heroes or tales about life before the Meiji period or Westernization. The first hit of this kind, 'Akagi-no Komoriuta' (Lullaby of Akagi), which was the theme song of a film based on a well-known story of a wandering gambler who died in 1850, and was sung by the pioneer of this song type, Shôji Tarô, sold as many as 400,000 copies. The combination of a clear, modulated voice, conventional minor pentatonic scale and 'Japanized' orchestration with heroic or tragic tales of domestic legendary figures was successfully repeated in many songs in the 1930s and the early 1940s. As has been conjectured by one historian, the appearance of these romanticized retrospective songs might well have been designed by record companies as a counter to governmental censorship of recorded songs (Nishizawa 1990b, 10). Indeed, in August 1934 the Ministry of Home Affairs began to impose censorship on records.

Censorship, Jingoistic Songs and Wartime Pressure

The instability of social conditions caused by the international disturbance stemming from the Manchurian Incident, which began in September 1931, and the Shanghai Incident in January 1932 led to enhanced activity by both extreme rightists and leftists. This triggered action by the special political police, who later in 1932 set out to suppress political offenders. Accordingly, they kept a close watch on various publications, as well as broadcasting and films, and eventually found that extreme leftists had begun to use gramophone records for propaganda purposes. This prompted the Ministry of Home Affairs to begin to regard records, for legal purposes, as another kind of publication (Kurata 1979, 408). In a newspaper article in the following year, it was made clear that the authorities also took offense at excessive amorous expression (Kurata 1979, 408), as had the organization of music teachers educated in Western classical tradition. Three years before, the organization, presided over by the head of the Tôyô College of Music, had offered to both the Ministry of Education and that of Home Affairs a proposal for legislating censorship on sheet music and records to eliminate 'indecent' and 'decadent' popular songs (Nishizawa 1990b, 8).

An amendment of the publication law to place censorship within the legal framework was passed in March 1934 and put into operation in August (Kurata 1979, 409). It emerged that the recordings affected were those that included allegedly sexy and erotic lyrics and those that contained critical references to the government or the military authorities.

Then, the Sino-Japanese Incident in July 1937 caused the government to issue orders for 'nationwide mobilization,' which required citizens to be engaged in the war even on the home front and affected every aspect of civilian life. Thereupon, in conformity with state policy, record companies began releasing such songs as 'Sen'ninbari' (Thousand-Stitch Belt) by Seki Tanéko and 'Jûgo-no

'Tsuma' (Wife on the Home Front) by Asakusa Soméchiyo to raise the morale of civilians, and others like 'Shingun-no Uta' (Marching Song) by the Toyama Army School Military Band and 'Kôkû Kesshitai' (Air Force Suicide Squad) by Matsubara Sô to give encouragement to soldiers. The production of these songs was possibly designed to take the edge off censorship, but the constant release of amorous songs resulted in more stringent censorship.

Meanwhile, in September 1937 the Public Information Section of the Cabinet invited the public to enter a contest for writing a patriotic marching song in order to foster a sense of unity (Kurata 1979, 443). Through this governmental adoption of the kind of contest favored by newspapers since 1932, record companies, willingly or not, were urged to give more priority to the morale-raising policy, and numerous martial and jingoistic songs were produced. Their orchestrated music was either heroically major pentatonic or sentimentally minor pentatonic, with public preference for the latter.

In 1940, the Ministry of Home Affairs issued orders for singers with such stage names as Dick Miné, Miss Columbia and Ama Ryllis to change them to appropriate Japanese ones on the grounds that their stage names were words used in hostile countries. Furthermore, after Japan entered the Pacific War in late 1941, even record companies with such foreign names as Columbia, Victor and King were forced to have their names replaced with Japanese phrasing (Kurata 1979, 437, 457–58). The joint ventures had not been run under joint management since 1938, when foreign parent companies had withdrawn from the business (Kawabata 1990, 27).

Immediately after the beginning of the Pacific War, the Public Information Section of the Cabinet and the Ministry of Home Affairs gave instructions to the public that US and British music should not be performed either live or in recorded form. Then in 1943, vexed at the general failure to follow these instructions, the Public Information Section listed in its official weekly bulletin the catalog numbers of all records that should not be played, asserting that they were 'a disclosure of nationalities characterized by frivolity, materialism and paying high regard to sensuality.' Arbitrarily, the songs included not only such Tin Pan Alley songs as 'My Blue Heaven' and 'Alexander's Ragtime Band,' but also 'Annie Laurie,' 'Home on the Range' and all the Stephen Foster songs (PIDC 1943). It should also be noted that, in October 1940, the government had ordered all

dance halls to be closed – 52 on the four main islands – throwing the dancers and musicians out of work (Nishizawa 1990b, 16).

Needless to say, the quota of such material as shellac for record companies had been cut because of its indispensability for the manufacture of weapons. Steel, which was even more indispensable, had ceased to be allocated to gramophone manufacturers in 1938 (Kawabata 1990, 27).

The Postwar Resuscitation of the Music Industry

The New Development of Ryûkôka or Kayôkyoku

In August 1945, the war ended in the defeat of Japan, with the result that people suffered from hunger and despondency in their destroyed land under US occupation.

The first postwar hit song, 'Ringo-no Uta' (Song of an Apple), appeared late in 1945 as a theme song for a film, *Soyokaze* (Breeze), sung by Namiki Michiko. The song has left an indelible impression in the memory of those who lived in the postwar period. First sung on stage, broadcast live on radio, and finally recorded for Japan Columbia in late December and released in January 1946, this carefree ditty about a symbolic red apple served to raise the spirits of disheartened people all over Japan. The melodious tune had an appealing gaiety despite its minor scale, and the fact that the scale was fully diatonic saved the song from possible gloominess and crassness caused by the conventional pentatonic minor.

Six months later, the fortunes of King Records were revived by a great hit, 'Tôkyô-no Hanauri Musumé' (Flower Girl of Tôkyô). Sweetly sung by Oka Haruo in medium tempo and backed by an orchestra playing with syncopated rhythm, this depiction of a postwar street scene in Tôkyô was also cheerful enough to offer people a diversion. 'Asawa Dokokara' (Where Does the Morning Come From?), released at the same time by Japan Columbia, was similar in its high-spirited feel, though more homely. The mixed duo of Anzai Aiko and Okamoto Atsuo, backed by a female chorus, contributed to the innovative and positive qualities of the performance.

While melancholic songs in the conventional pentatonic minor mode made a comeback, especially early in 1947 with King Records' 'Nakuna Kobato-yo' (Don't Cry, Little Dove) sung by Oka Haruo, more characteristic of the postwar period were morale-boosting songs. This tendency was underlined by a series of songs in boogie-woogie rhythm sung by a sprightly female singer, Kasagi

Shizuko. Composed by Hattori Ryôichi, who had tried his hand at boogie-woogie tunes in the late 1930s before the time was ripe for them, the first of the hits to burst on the postwar scene was 'Tôkyô Boogie-Woogie,' released in December 1947 by Japan Columbia. The lyrics, by Suzuki Masaru, were also vivacious, with *ukiuki* (buoyant) and *zukizuki* (throbbing) rhyming with 'boogie-woogie.' Thus, the prevailing feeling of depression and sense of humiliation under US occupation were swept away, if only temporarily, by the adoption of an African-American rhythm imported as a jazz element. Meanwhile, the monthly output of five existing record companies in late 1947 amounted to about 900,000, which was one-third of the average monthly production before the war (Kurata 1979, 481).

The Korean War, which began in June 1950, brought economic benefits to Japan through a munitions boom, while the United States concluded a treaty with Japan in 1951 that ended the occupation, though a certain number of US bases remained in operation. The consequent easing of social conditions made the public more receptive to lyrical songs. At the same time, a singing prodigy, Misora Hibari, was developing her extraordinary talent. The 12-year-old girl had her first big hit, 'Kanashiki Kuchibué' (Plaintive Whistle), released as her second single in September 1949, and she followed this up with a succession of hits, including 'Tôkyô Kid' and 'Watashi-wa Machino-ko' (I'm a City Girl). Her stardom, consolidated by 'Ringo Oiwaké' (Apple Oiwaké) (*oiwaké* is traditionally a packhorse-driver's song), a release in June 1952, continued until her death in 1989 (Tansman 1996).

From the mid-1950s on, there emerged a large group of successful songs about homesickness, reflecting the mood of the great number of young rural workers who had moved to large cities as a result of the general switch to heavy and chemical industries in Japan. Examples of hits of this kind are: 'Gokigensan-yo Tasshakané' (How Are You, Are You All Right?), sung by Mihashi Michiya in a nasal tenor reminiscent of his background in professional folk singing; 'Wakaré-no Ipponsugi' (Solitary Cedar by Which We Parted), sung by Kasuga Hachirô, who had made himself extremely popular with 'Otomi-san' (Miss Tomi), a convivial song about a character in a well-known kabuki play; and 'Tôkyô-dayo Okkasan' (Here We Are in Tôkyô, Mama), sung with grief-stricken crying by Shimakura Chiyoko. Conversely, along with these nostalgic songs, invariably in the conventional pentatonic minor scale, sometimes with the addition of the passing

sixth note, the late 1950s saw quite a few hit songs that affirmed urban life. These songs, in full-minor melodies performed with sophisticated orchestration and crooning, included such self-explanatory titles as 'Tôkyô Gozen-sanji' (Tôkyô, 3:00 a.m.) and 'Yûrakuchô-de Aimashô' (Let's Meet in Yûrakuchô), sung by Frank Nagai, who had made his debut as a jazz singer.

Broadcasting and Popular Music

It should be noted that those popular postwar songs were disseminated to a majority of people mainly by means of radio, which was the predominant audio entertainment for people with restricted life styles and no gramophone.

When it was formed in 1926, NHK, or the Japanese Broadcasting Corporation, was supposed to play the role of cultural leader, and the music broadcast was classically oriented, with refined Western and Western-style music as well as stylized indigenous music. The popularity of recorded *ryûkôka*, however, made it increasingly difficult for NHK to avoid playing these records. Then, in 1936 it started, under governmental control, a program entitled *Shin-kayôkyoku* (New *Kayôkyoku*), in which 'wholesome' *ryûkôka* were deliberately selected and the use of the word '*ryûkôka*' avoided (Sanseidô 1991, 924–25). The use of '*kayôkyoku*' as the term referring to *ryûkôka* began with this program before being popularized through liberated postwar programming. It gradually superseded '*ryûkôka*' with its less respectable connotations, although the term continued to be used for some time.

The postwar contribution of radio to the popularity of *ryûkôka* records was largely made through the *Nodojiman Shirôto Ongakukai* (Amateur Singing Contest), which NHK started in January 1946 as a weekend live show. The way in which the program was of use to record companies was illustrated from the beginning by the fact that, in February 1946, 'Ringo-no Uta' proved to be the favorite song among the contestants (Kurata 1979, 480), boosting the popularity of the record, which had been released a couple of weeks before and played on the radio. This barometer effect long characterized the program, and hit songs were inadvertently publicized to the benefit of record companies. The long-lived *Nodojiman* was eclipsed by the rise of other entertainments in parallel with the increase in general affluence, but the phenomenon of amateur singers gleefully imitating their favorite recording artists in public was a harbinger of the emergence and popularity of karaoke in the 1970s.

140

With the opening of commercial broadcasting stations in 1951 and the inauguration of the television service in 1953, more record-playing programs and amateur singing shows appeared, as well as live performances by popular singers. The television shows, using such techniques as panning and zooming, showed not only the facial expressions and gestures of singers during their delivery, but also the reaction of the audience. This transformed the ways in which artists performed popular songs and, consequently, the ways in which audiences responded.

The year 1953 was also when the annual New Year Eve's show *Kôhaku Utagassen* (Singing Battle Between 'Red' and 'White') started concurrently on radio and television as a remodeled version of a program that used to be broadcast on New Year's Day. This show, featuring an array of exclusively domestic stars of popular song, became a national event, boasting an extremely high audience rating. Even when its popularity finally began to decline in the late 1980s for various reasons, including generational changes in musical taste, its rating was more than 50 percent. As a result, the whole music industry has taken note of the annual lists of participants in *Kôhaku*, which reflect the popularity of singers.

It was in the late 1950s too that the first music publisher was established. Shortly thereafter, the practice of paying songwriters who were under exclusive contract to a specific record company on a non-royalty basis was discontinued. The Japanese Society for Rights of Authors, Composers and Publishers (JASRAC) had just become operational domestically after a long period of instability since its formation in early 1940.

Infatuation with US/European Music

By means of radio, people were also exposed to a great amount of recorded Western music, largely US popular music, especially after the opening of commercial stations in 1951. In fact, Japanese interest in Western popular music was rekindled with the overnight introduction of US democracy and the exclusion of militarism. Newly introduced democracy looked dazzling, with images of freedom, positiveness and affluence, and this encouraged an infatuation with music from the West among the young Japanese, which overlapped with the postwar development of *kayôkyoku*.

It was in August 1948 that US hit records began to be pressed from the original masters imported under a royalty contract between Japan Columbia and Columbia (US). This was done with the permission of the General Headquarters (GHQ) of the occupation forces, to which application had been made by Columbia (US). In the following year another international contract was concluded between Japan Victor and Victor (US) (Kawabata 1990, 30). Indeed, the Japanese preoccupation with North American popular music was inseparable from the presence of US occupation forces. Significantly, a station, FEN (Far East Network), was started in September 1945 for these 400,000 soldiers. The service, with playlists of the latest releases of popular music, was easily accessible to Japanese people living in the vicinity of the many US bases located all over Japan. The first song to be aired was 'Smoke Gets in Your Eyes,' presumably the 1941 recording by Artie Shaw, which gave the defeated Japanese a refreshing surprise with its bright and sweet melody, initiating a yearning for North American culture among younger people (Sanseidô 1991, 792).

Furthermore, the demand for live music to be performed at recreational facilities on US bases led the GHQ to employ many Japanese musicians, who honed their skill in playing US popular music to cater to the tastes of the soldiers. The musicians, including those who had been active since prewar days, former military band members and music school students, played mostly contemporary jazz band music, although there was a limited number of younger performers who formed country and western bands. This kind of self-apprenticeship produced talented jazz musicians, who became active in the newly evolved Japanese jazz scene in the 1950s – for example, Matsumoto Hidehiko, George Kawaguchi, Nakamura Hachidai, Shiraki Hideo and Ono Mitsuru. Akiyoshi Toshiko and Watanabé Sadao were involved in more progressive trends and later studied in the United States, but they were also schooled on the bases.

The GHQ also contributed to the development of a Japanese entertainment agency by ordering the government to supply a variety of entertainment, including not only music, plays and some sports but also exhibitions of such Japanese martial arts as judo, kendo and karate. To cope with this order, many new agencies were organized, and these would eventually form the basis for the subsequent expansion of the agency industry that accompanied the growth of television and the reinvigoration of show business. Additionally, dance halls were reopened in 1945 to entertain the US troops, and their doors were subsequently opened to the

3. Japan

Japanese public in 1947 (Sanseidô 1991, 590). This led to the later developments of go-go clubs and discothèques.

The most favored form of imported popular music that the Japanese listened to and performed themselves was what was called jazz, although it was in fact mainstream popular music. The popularity of country music, which had been called hillbilly music until the early 1950s, was largely due to the tastes of the US troops stationed locally, among whom even non-Southerners enjoyed the music because of its nostalgic quality. The Japanese interest in Hawaiian music dated back to the 1920s, when a strong sense of affinity had been engendered by Japanese-Hawaiian performers who were active in Japan (for example, Haida Katsuhiko and Bucky Shirakata). Tango, having also been imported before the Pacific War (Savigliano 1992), was revived with Fujisawa Ranko as the female leading spirit, and *chansons* (*variétés*) made a comeback with conservatory-trained Japanese chanteurs and chanteuses, who emphasized a romanticized image of Paris. In the mid- and late 1950s, Afro-Cuban mambo and cha-cha merrily reverberated from the records of Perez Prado and performances by Japanese Latin bands. In addition, rock 'n' roll songs were sung against a background of strummed guitar by late-teen country and western stars, who were invariably called rockabilly singers and posed as Elvis Presley, Gene Vincent and Paul Anka, among others.

In the meantime, beginning with the Gene Krupa Trio in April 1952, a handful of foreign artists/groups visited Japan every year throughout the 1950s, in addition to those who were sent from the United States to perform exclusively on the bases. The former included such a variety of acts as the Xavier Cugat Band, Louis Armstrong (1953), Joséphine Baker (1954), Johnnie Ray, Perez Prado, Yvette Giraud (1955), Benny Goodman and His Orchestra (1957), Paul Anka (1958), the Jack Teagarden Sextet, Charles Trenet, Carlos Montoya and the Golden Gate Quartet (1959) (Nakamura 1988, 454–56). From 1962 on, the number of visiting artists/groups – particularly jazz musicians at first and, later, rock musicians – continually increased in proportion to Japan's economic growth.

The Assimilation of Imported Music and New Domestic Music

The 1950s can be labeled as a period of adoration and imitation for those who were involved in performing cover versions of imported music, both on television and on record. Whereas the lyrics of prewar covers were exclusively Japanese, these covers sandwiched original verses between translated ones and were sung in a style closer to that of the original, as can be heard in such successful records as Eri Chiemi's 'Tennessee Waltz' and Koshiji Fubuki's 'C'est Si Bon.' This practice of performing covers, which was in vogue until the early 1960s, has survived in the field of musicals, as exemplified in the Japanese version of *Cats* in the mid-1980s.

Japanese composition in the idiom of imported music was also attempted, as in the case of successful boogie-woogie tunes by Hattori Ryôichi, quite a few tango songs in both the prewar and postwar periods, some *chansons*, and a couple of country and western songs (for example, 'Wagon Master' by Kosaka Kazuya). However, such undertakings were not sufficiently enduring or supported to establish genres.

On the other hand, quite a few performers who started their careers as imitators of imported music tried their hand at, or often converted to, Japanese music, especially *kayôkyoku* with the introduction of some foreign elements. The Dark Ducks, the Duke Aces and the Bonny Jacks are longstanding male quartets, all dressed in tuxedos, who have been strong in Russian folk songs, African-American spirituals and children's songs, respectively. They have an additional repertoire of school-taught Japanese songs, as well as some jazz songs, in which they specialized when they were formed in the mid-1950s. Some Hawaiian bands and Latin bands became successful with *kayôkyoku* composed for their musical format, in which a male chorus and the steel or *requinto* guitar were featured.

Likewise, jazz singers won renown by singing successful *kayôkyoku*, as was the case with Frank Nagai and with Peggy Hayama, whose name has been closely associated with 'Nangoku Tosao Atonishité' (Leaving Tosa, My Southern Home). Even the 'rockabilly' singers who achieved success were those who were provided with *kayôkyoku* songs. The most distinguished example is Mizuhara Hiroshi, whose 'Kuroi Hanabira' (Black Petals) was widely enjoyed. The songwriting team responsible for this song, Nakamura Hachidai and Ei Rokusuke, also composed 'Ueo-muite Arukô' (I Look Up When I Walk) for another converted 'rockabilly' singer, Sakamoto Kyû. This record was later released in the United States and became an international hit as 'Sukiyaki.' Although the record retained some of the indigenous feel of *kayôkyoku*, it represented a move away from the confines of the genre, but this innovative sound failed to catch on.

The Mid-1960s Onward

Rock Music

As an extension of the 'rockabilly' craze, the Ventures, who visited Japan from the United States in May 1962, sparked off among young people what was called an 'elec boom,' which was characterized by a display of electric guitar performance. This instrumental-oriented music was combined with vocals influenced by the Beatles and other British beat groups. Promoted by evolving artist agencies, beat groups consisting of four to seven male singers who played electric guitars and drums, wore uniforms and had long hair became a phenomenon called 'group sounds.' They initially modeled their own compositions on those of the British groups as well as copying them, but songs composed by professional songwriters as a compromise with *kayôkyoku* were successfully released. The fad intensified with the Spiders' 'No No Boy,' followed by the Blue Comets' 'Aoi Hitomi' (Blue Eyes) in 1966, the year when the Beatles performed in Tôkyô. In the following year, when the Blue Comets succeeded with another great hit, 'Blue Chateau,' many more groups, including the Tigers, the Golden Cups, the Jaguars, the Carnabeats and the Tempters, emerged, expanding the genre in different directions.

It is perhaps significant that, in late 1967, the annual consumption rate of imported music (records pressed from imported masters) – 46.2 percent – was less than that of Japanese music (records originally recorded by Japanese artists) – 53.8 percent. The corresponding figures for the preceding year had been 50.8 percent and 49.2 percent (Kawabata 1991, 335). Since 1948, when the GHQ had permitted international dealings, imported music had dominated sales; now, for the first time in 20 years, domestic music outsold imported music, reflecting a change in the market and the popularity of 'group sounds.' This year (1967), four years after Japan had joined the OECD, was also when the Japanese government decided to ease restrictions on foreign investment, and in the following year CBS-Sony was formed. It was the first of several powerful joint ventures formed in the record industry, including Tôshiba-EMI, Nippon-Phonogram, Warner-Pioneer and RVC. It should also be noted that, in the late 1960s and early 1970s, quite a few music publishers, as well as firms that produced records for record companies, were formed.

Manipulated by the music industry, which was basically interested in promoting the groups' pretty-boy image for teeny-boppers, 'group sounds' rapidly died away in 1970. However, the phenomenon contributed to the musical sensibility of young Japanese with music that emphasized beat and vocal harmony, and the idea of music 'for youth by youth' which was first conveyed by 'rockabilly' was further underscored.

Some talented former members turned to what were called art-rock and psychedelic music, a couple of years or so after they became popular in the United States, forming such bands as the Flower Traveling Band, the Power House and the Blues Creation. The most influential band in the early 1970s was Happy End, which contributed to the expansion of the scope of Japanese rock with experiments in sound and style, including, among others, adherence to Japanese lyrics. In terms of resistance to the Establishment, the Zunô Keisatsu (Brain Police) and the Murahachibu (Ostracism) were more representative of hard-rock bands that spoke for disaffected youth. The commercial success of Japanese rock bands, first achieved in the mid-1970s by the Godiego singing in English to a Japanese sound and the Sadistic Mika Band singing in Japanese to a British sound, was reinforced in the late 1970s by the Carol, who specialized in early rock 'n' roll, and the Downtown Boogie-Woogie Band, which performed Japanese boogie-woogie songs. However, while the Yellow Magic Orchestra succeeded with its electronic instrumentation and the Southern All Stars with 'Itoshi-no Ellie' (Ellie, My Love), later successfully covered by Ray Charles, the early 1980s saw the appearance of many indie labels for obscure bands which emerged under the influence of imported punk and new wave music.

Contemporary Folk

Running parallel with 'group sounds,' Japanese contemporary 'folk' music (which had nothing whatsoever to do with indigenous folk music) evolved when the North American folk revival was introduced to Japan. In the early and mid-1960s an interest in such pop-folk groups as the Kingston Trio, the Brothers Four and Peter, Paul and Mary produced 'college folk.' This vogue for sing-it-yourself acoustic music was not commercially remarkable except for 'Bara-ga Saita' (Roses Are Out), a gentle song composed by Hamaguchi Kuranosuké and sung by Mike Maki in 1966.

What was more durable was the tendency, engendered among the followers of Bob Dylan and other singer-songwriters, to perform to one's own guitar accompaniment songs of a socially and politically committed nature. Although the songs were in the style of US models, the words, which were often ill-fitted to Western melodies, were a deviation from the conventional *kayôkyoku* tradition in their rhythms and vocabulary, and therefore to compose one's own songs was in itself a positive aspect of this movement. This somewhat underground school of amateurish singers surfaced commercially when 'Kaéttekita Yopparai' (Drunkard Returning from Heaven) sold a million discs in 1967. Sung and independently produced by the Folk Crusaders, a group of Kyôto students, this humorous and ironic song about a drunkard who died in a car accident opened the door to socially and politically oriented singers, including Taka'ishi Tomoya, Okabayashi Nobuyasu, Nakagawa Gorô and Takada Wataru. This school then led in the early 1970s to the emergence of a more cultivated group, whose introspective style was typified by songs of daily life, as exemplified by Yoshida Takurô, Garo, Kaguyahimé and Tulip.

'New Music'

Developing out of the music of singer-songwriters as well as early 1970s rock, a loosely defined 'new music' arose, with Arai Yumi (later Mattôya Yumi) as its instigator. Her first album, *Hikôki-gumo* (Vapor Trail), displayed her urbane sophistication and eclecticism, causing the critics to hail her as a neo-sensualist. Supported by other 'Tin Pan Alley' musicians, her kind of music became popular among young audiences. It was soon grouped together with the newly developed music of such singer-songwriters as Yoshida Takurô and Inoué Yôsui, whose careers slightly preceded hers, and also with that of newcomers, including Nakajima Miyuki, a gifted poet who made her debut in 1975. Hence, the appellation 'new music,' which appeared in the same year, was originally given to music that was difficult to categorize under the existing terms 'folk' and 'rock,' but eventually the lines became blurred and the term 'new music' fell out of use. In fact, its usage was in direct opposition to *kayôkyoku*, a conservative music produced within a hit-making system in which the singer, lyricist, composer and recording orchestra are separate; in 'new music,' all these roles were combined for fuller self-expression.

It should be noted here that this interest in composing and performing one's own material, which was first encouraged by beat groups and then by contemporary folk singers, had much to do with the growth of the Japanese manufacturing industry for musical instruments. The manufacture of such musical instruments as piano, harmonica, acoustic and electric guitar, electric organ and synthesizer has long flourished in Japan, popularizing these instruments among many Japanese. This prosperity has involved an amazing expansion of music lessons. Yamaha and Kawai, the two largest manufacturers, made Japan the world's leading piano producer in the 1970s (Kôbundô 1991, 636). They formed their nationwide network of music classes in 1954 and 1956, respectively, which expanded to accept more than a million students in the 1970s (Kôbundô 1991, 121). These classes provided early training for those aspiring to a musical career, and to encourage them the manufacturers sponsored talent scout contests. These contests included the Yamaha Popular Music Contest, which launched the careers of such folk groups as the Akai Tori and Off Course in 1969, as well as such solo singers as Nakajima Miyuki. Meanwhile, the Yamaha Corporation soon became the largest musical instrument manufacturer in the world in sales volume, with the number of overseas subsidiaries reaching more than 40 in 1989 and 85 in early 2002. Kawai Musical Instruments, which also has subsidiaries all over the world, exports to over 80 countries.

The relative sophistication of 'new music' can be explained partly by the fact that advertising agencies cooperated with record companies from the mid-1970s onward in making many 'new music' songs successful. They did this by using them as the soundtracks for television commercials in which manufacturers of such goods as cosmetics, whiskey and coffee invested.

In 1980 the percentage of sales of 'new music' singles (50 percent) finally exceeded that of *kayôkyoku* (42 percent) (Kôbundô 1991, 589). It should also be noted that, from the mid-1970s, the record and tape sales figures of the Japanese record industry exceeded those of the industries of other capitalist nations, except the United States. However, the ratio of domestic records to overseas records, which were pressed by Japanese companies from masters recorded by overseas companies primarily for their own customers, was about three to two (Kawabata 1982, 199). A good many of these overseas records were of US and British popular music.

'Idol kayô'

In the meantime, there appeared in the early 1970s a type of *kayôkyoku* for young people who found it difficult to identify with music based on imported idioms, such as adapted rock and folk. With three young male singers from the early 1960s – including Funaki Kazuo, who first succeeded with 'Kôkô San'nen-sei' (The Twelfth Grade) – as its precursors, 'idol *kayô*' arose out of the popularity of another three young male singers among teeny-boppers: Noguchi Gorô, Saijô Hideki and Gô Hiromi. It soon, however, developed a more feminine aspect with the advent of three girl singers, Minami Saori, Mori Masako and Koyanagi Rumiko, who made their debuts at around the same time and established an image of purity and innocence. The success of this image was instantly proved by another trio of female singers who, independently of each other, had won a television talent scout show, *Star Tanjô* (A Star Is Born), which had begun in 1971 and was followed by two similar shows.

In the mid- to late 1970s 'idol *kayô*' underwent changes when Yamaguchi Momoé and the elaborately choreographed performances of two girl groups, the Candies and Pink Lady, added an element of sexuality. Moreover, Matsuda Seiko, who replaced Yamaguchi as the leading star in the 1980s, stressed her feminist life style by challenging the conservative concept of wife and mother while retaining her assumed innocence. At the same time, the popularity of boy idols was revived with the emergence of groups such as the Tanokin Trio and the Hikaru Genji. These changes occurred in parallel with musical deviation from *kayôkyoku* conventions, as significantly suggested by a book entitled *Dorobô Kayôkyoku* (Stealing *Kayôkyoku*). This fully annotated list of 190 songs, alleged to be partly copied from North American and European originals, consists of 'compositions' of 'new music,' folk, rock and 'group sounds,' as well as many 'idol *kayô*,' although all are categorized under the umbrella of *kayôkyoku* (Datahouse 1987).

Enka

In the early 1970s *kayôkyoku* was given fresh impetus. Mainstream *kayôkyoku* had remained vigorous during the 1960s with Record Awards, which were founded after the Grammy Awards in 1959, and with some television shows that emphasized conventional singers and songs in contrast to others that catered for younger and urban tastes. However, it was also true that many people who were not young enough to feel comfortable with rock, folk or 'idol *kayô*' demanded their own type of music. What filled this void was a series of hits in

the early 1970s, beginning with Fuji Keiko's 'Keiko-no Yume-wa Yoru-hiraku' (Keiko's Dream Unfolds at Night), that were labeled *enka*. The despairing sadness and self-denying forbearance that permeated these songs harked back, in terms of both lyrical and musical characteristics, to 'Sendô Ko-uta,' the extremely popular song of the early 1920s.

Enka has been connected closely with drinking, as is suggested by the emergence of karaoke in bars in the early 1970s where *enka* provided the main repertoire, and also by the fact that *enka* was popularized by cable radio. The music programs of this new medium, which began service in the early 1960s, were so enjoyed by bar customers that record companies eventually linked up with cable companies to boost their new *enka* singles. Thus, *enka* became the mainstream version of *kayôkyoku*, even though the popularity of *kayôkyoku* began to be eclipsed by the pervasive 'new music' after the mid-1980s. This reversal was also reflected in the changing preferences of karaoke customers as generations moved on and as the 'karaoke box' was introduced. The box is essentially a separately constructed small room that is hired out to small groups. This allows karaoke singing to be available exclusively to an intimate group, as well as easily accessible to women and teenagers (Mitsui and Hosokawa 1998; Yano 1995).

The 1990s and Beyond

New Ethnic Music

Meanwhile, the 'world music' phenomenon (which blossomed in the early 1990s) indirectly awakened the younger generation in Japan to the popular and folk music of Southeast Asian countries and, on a smaller scale, to the indigenous music of their own land. This arose out of interest in 'ethnic' music, particularly African popular music, which was in itself another fad imported from the West. However, along with the Japanese economic 'invasion' of Southeast Asian countries, it helped to give impetus to young Japanese interest in the music of, for example, Indonesia and Singapore. In the 1990s, for the first time, foreign popular music began to be imported from places other than Europe or the United States.

Largely as an extension of this interest, many young Japanese enjoy the modernized music of Okinawa, a Japanese prefecture consisting of numerous small islands located far from the mainland in the subtropical zones. This 'exotic' music is performed in the local dialect by a limited number of bands, including the Rinken Band, with synthesizer and electric guitar as well as *sanshin* (a three-string instrument with a snakeskin membrane across the resonator) and local drums. The music emerged recently as a revitalization of the kind of music experimented with in the mid-1970s by the Champroos, who can be compared to Fairport Convention in the United Kingdom or, more closely, to Alan Stivell and his band in Brittany. As to mainland musicians, the Shang Shang Typhoon is popular with its hybrid of Asian, Japanese and Western elements, and Itô Takio and the Takio Band with a mixture of tradition and innovation in their lively performance of Japanese folk songs. The limited but growing interest among young Japanese in the forms of stylized indigenous music, as well as in such musical experiments as combining *shakuhachi* with Western idioms, will possibly generate more musicians who are less Westernized in the twenty-first century (Mitsui 1998).

It is uncertain how much this kind of music will be appreciated overseas, but a few critics believe that the twenty-first century will be the century of the East as a final reaction to the domination of the West. Anyhow, this new ethnic music will probably be exported, along with other kinds of domestic music, to Western countries particularly through such companies as Sony and Matsushita, which now own CBS and MCA, respectively. It should be pointed out that the international market for domestic artists has already been opened up by more than a dozen New Age musicians, such as Tomita Isao and Kitarô.

J-Pop

In the late 1990s a new appellation, 'J-pop,' emerged in music journalism to denote contemporary Japanese pop in globalized musical idioms, and it became popular among young audiences. 'J-pop,' with the alphabetical abbreviation of 'Japan' to 'J' in English, is particularly appealing in its sound and spelling to younger Japanese, and the 'J-' itself was adopted by other media, which concocted such labels as J-*bungaku* (Japanese literature) and J-Phone (the brand name of a cellular phone).

Obviously deriving from 'J-rock,' the term used as the title of a small Kansai rock magazine that was started in the mid-1990s, 'J-pop' has turned out to be a convenient umbrella term to cover a new trend that is characterized by its seemingly nationless sound and the almost indispensable accompaniment of choreographed dancing. The dancing is by a fashionably dressed singer or group of singers with the support of other proficient dancers. The new trend was first evidenced by Komuro Tetsuya, a prolific producer-performer, and Amuro Namié, his young protégée, and was highlighted in 1999 by the appearance of 16-year-old Utada Hikaru, daughter of Fuji Keiko who debuted in 1970 as a popular *enka* singer. Utada Hikaru was born and raised in New York, listening to the latest African-American music. Her first album, *First Love*, was released in March 1999 and sold 650 million copies in two months. The visual image of J-pop is well illustrated in a recent book on Japanese popular music, written in English for a general readership by a North American journalist (McClure 1998).

The appearance of J-pop roughly coincided with the increasing interest in the study of popular music in Japan. A couple of years after the formation of the Japanese Association for the Study of Popular Music (JASPM) in 1990, its first chair, Tôru Mitsui, began to get involved in a postgraduate program at Kanazawa University that encourages the academic study of popular music. In the late 1990s a handful of undergraduate classes on popular music were introduced at some other institutions, while the number of students with an interest in engaging in popular music studies began to increase.

Bibliography

Brau, Lorie. 1990. 'The Women's Theater of Takarazuka.' *TDR: The Drama Review* 34(4): 79–95.

Daicel. 1990. *Nihonno Ryûkokashi Taikei* [A Chronological Collection of Japanese Popular Songs] (A book that accompanies a 66-CD set with the same title). Tôkyô: Daicel Chemical Industries.

Datahouse. 1987. *Dorobô Kayôkyoku* [Stealing *Kayôkyoku*]. Tôkyô: Datahouse.

Heibonsha. 1985. *Heibonsha Daihyakkajiten* [Encyclopedia Heibonsha]. 16 vols. Tôkyô: Heibonsha.

Kawabata, Shigéru. 1982. *Record Sangyô-kai* [The Record Industry]. Tôkyô: Kyôiku-sha.

Kawabata, Shigéru. 1990. *Record Gyôkai* [The Record Industry]. 6th ed. Tôkyô: Kyôiku-sha.

Kawabata, Shigéru. 1991. 'The Japanese Record Industry.' *Popular Music* 10(3): 327–45.

Kôbundô. 1991. *Taishûbunka Jiten* [Encyclopedia of Popular Culture]. Tôkyô: Kôbundô.

Kurata, Yoshihiro. 1979. *Nihon Record Bunka-shi* [A Cultural History of Records in Japan]. Tôkyô: Tôkyô Shoseki.

Masui, Keiji. 1990. *Asakusa Opera Monogatari* [A Story of the Asakusa Opera]. Tôkyô: Geijutsugendai-sha.

McClure, Steve. 1998. *Nipponpop*. Tôkyô: Charles E. Tuttle.

Mitsui, Tôru. 1998. 'Domestic Exoticism: A Recent Trend in Japanese Popular Music.' *Perfect Beat: The Pacific Journal of Research into Contemporary Music and Popular Culture* 3(4): 1–12.

Mitsui, Tôru, and Hosokawa, Shûhei, eds. 1998. *Karaoke Around the World: Global Technology, Local Singing*. London: Routledge.

Miyazawa, Jûichi. 1990. 'Foreword.' In Keiji Masui, *Asakusa Opera Monogatari* [A Story of the Asakusa Opera]. Tôkyô: Geijutsugendai-sha, 1–3.

Morimoto, Toshikatsu. 1975. *Onban Kayôshi* [A History of *Kayôkyoku* on Records]. Kyôto: Shirakawa-shoin.

Nakamura, Tôyô. 1988. 'Rainichishita artisttachino sokuseki' [Visiting Foreign Artists]. *Music Guidebook* 88: 454–61.

Nishizawa, Sô. 1990a. *Nihon Kindai Kayôshi* [A History of Modern Japanese Songs]. Tôkyô: Ôfûsha.

Nishizawa, Sô. 1990b. *Nihon Ryûkôka Taikei: Ryakushi* [A Chronology of Japanese Popular Songs] (Supplement to Nishizawa 1990a). Tôkyô: Ôfûsha.

Noguchi, Hisamitsu. 1976. 'Nippon-no jazz popular-no ayumi' [A Historical Sketch of Japanese Jazz and Popular Music]. Liner notes to *Nihon-no Jazz-Song* (5-LP set). Nippon Columbia SZ7011-15: 6–9.

PIDC. 1943. 'The Expatriation of American and British Music.' *Weekly Bulletin* (The Public Information Section of the Cabinet), No. 328 (27 January). (Reproduced in *Nihon Ongaku Chosaku-ken-shi* [A History of Rights of Authors, Composers and Publishers in Japan], Vol. 2. Tôkyô: JASRAC, 1990, 97–102.)

Recording Industry Association of Japan (RIAJ). 1999. *A Brief Description of the Japanese Recording Industry*. Tôkyô: RIAJ.

Sanseidô. 1991. *Sengoshi Daijiten 1945–1990* [Encyclopedia of Postwar Japan 1945–1990]. Tôkyô: Sanseidô.

Savigliano, Marta E. 1992. 'Tango in Japan and the World Economy of Passion.' In *Re-Made in Japan: Everyday Life and Consumer Taste in a Changing Society*, ed. Joseph J. Tobin. New Haven, CT: Yale University Press, 235–52.

Spottswood, Richard, ed. 1990. *Ethnic Music on Records*. 7 vols. Urbana, IL: University of Illinois Press.

Tansman, Alan M. 1996. 'Mournful Tears and *Sake*: The Postwar Myth of Misora Hibari.' In *Contemporary Japan and Popular Culture*, ed. John Whittier Treat. Richmond, Surrey: Curzon, 103–36.

Uchida, Kôichi. 1976. *Nihonno Jazz-shi* [A History of Jazz in Japan]. Tôkyô: SwingJournal.

Whitburn, Joel, ed. 1986. *Pop Memories 1890–1954: The History of American Popular Music*. Menomonee Falls, WI: Record Research.

Yano, Christine. 1995. *Shaping Tears of a Nation: An Ethnography of Emotion in Japanese Popular Song*. Unpublished Ph.D. thesis, University of Hawaii. (Revised and published as *Tears of Longing: Nostalgia and the Nation in Japanese Popular Song*. Cambridge, MA: Harvard University Asia Center, 2002.)

Discographical References

Anzai, Aiko, and Okamoto, Atsuo. 'Asawa Dokokara.' Columbia A97. 1946: Japan.

Arai, Yumi. *Hikôki-gumo*. Alfa ALCA5241. *1973*: Japan.

Asakusa, Soméchiyo. 'Jûgo-no Tsuma.' Polydor 2565. 1937: Japan.

Austin, Gene. 'My Blue Heaven.' Victor 20964. 1927: USA.

Awaya, Noriko. 'Amé-no Blues.' Columbia 29761. 1938: Japan.

Awaya, Noriko. 'Tôkyô Blues.' Columbia 30291. 1939: Japan.

Awaya, Noriko. 'Wakaré-no Blues.' Columbia 29384. 1937: Japan.

Awaya, Noriko. 'Watashi Konogoro Yû'utsuyo.' Victor 26486. 1931: Japan.

Blue Comets. 'Aoi Hitomi.' CBS Columbia LL902. *1966*: Japan.

Blue Comets. 'Blue Chateau.' CBS Columbia LL10022. *1967*: Japan.

Charles, Ray. 'Itoshi-no Ellie.' Victor VDPS-1050. *1989*: Japan.

Crosby, Bing, with the Jimmie Grier Orchestra. 'Home on the Range.' Brunswick 6663. 1934: USA.

Eri, Chiemi. 'Tennessee Waltz.' King CL101. 1952: Japan.

Folk Crusaders. 'Kaéttekita Yopparai.' Tôshiba Capitol Records CP-1014. *1967*: Japan.

Fuji, Keiko. 'Keiko-no Yume-wa Yoru-hiraku.' RCA JRT-1077. *1970*: Japan.

Fujiwara, Yoshié. 'Debuné-no Minato'/'Debune.' Victor 1230. 1928: USA/Japan.

Fujiwara, Yoshié. 'Habu-no Minato.' Victor 4042. 1928: USA/Japan.

Fujiyama, Ichirô. 'Saké-wa Namida-ka Taméiki-ka.' Victor 26486. 1931: Japan.

Funaki, Kazuo. 'Kôkô San'nen-sei.' Columbia SAS-60. *1963*: Japan.

Futamura, Tei'ichi. 'Arabia-no Uta'/'Aozora.' Victor 50460. 1928 (October): Japan.

Futamura, Tei'ichi. 'Kimi Koishi.' Victor 50559. 1929: Japan.

Futamura, Tei'ichi, and Amano, Kikuyo. 'Aozora'/'Arabia-no Uta.' Nipponophone 16855. 1928 (May): Japan. Reissue: Futamura, Tei'ichi, and Amano, Kikuyo. 'Aozora'/'Arabia-no Uta.' Columbia 25033. 1928 (November): Japan.

Hayama, Peggy. 'Nangoku Tosao Atoni-shité.' King C1716. *1958*: Japan.

Kasagi, Shizuko. 'Tôkyô Boogie-Woogie.' Columbia A339. 1947: Japan.

Kasuga, Hachirô. 'Otomi-san.' King C1086. 1953: Japan.

Kasuga, Hachirô. 'Wakaré-no Ipponsugi.' King C1277. *1956*: Japan.

Katsutarô and Mishima, Issei. 'Tôkyô Ondo.' Victor 52793. 1933: Japan.

Kosaka, Kazuya. 'Wagon Master.' Columbia JL123. 1954: Japan.

Koshiji, Fubuki. 'C'est Si Bon.' Columbia JL10. 1952: Japan.

Lucas, Nick. 'My Blue Heaven.' Brunswick 3684. 1928: USA.

Maki, Mike. 'Bara-ga Saita.' Philips SFL-105. *1966*: Japan.

Matsubara, Sô. 'Kôkû Kesshitai.' Columbia 29584. 1937: Japan.

Matsui, Sumako. 'Fukkatsu Shôka' (Katyusha-no Uta). Orient A757. 1914: Japan.

Mihashi, Michiya. 'Gokigensan-yo Tasshakané.' King C1221. 1955: Japan.

Miller, Reed. 'Annie Laurie.' Victor 16675. 1910: USA.

Misora, Hibari. 'Kanashiki Kuchibué.' Columbia A622. 1949: Japan.

Misora, Hibari. 'Ringo Oiwaké.' Columbia A1420. 1952: Japan.

Misora, Hibari. 'Tôkyô Kid.' Columbia A857. 1950: Japan.

Misora, Hibari. 'Watashi-wa Machino-ko.' Columbia A1077. 1951: Japan.

Mizuhara, Hiroshi. 'Kuroi Hanabira.' Tôshiba JP-1070. *1959*: Japan.

Nagai, Frank. 'Tôkyô Gozen-sanji.' Victor V41646. *1957*: Japan.

Nagai, Frank. 'Yûrakuchô-de Aimashô.' Victor V41744. *1957*: Japan.

Namiki, Michiko. 'Ringo-no Uta.' Columbia A59. 1946: Japan.

Oka, Haruo. 'Nakuna Kobato-yo.' King C166. 1947: Japan.

Oka, Haruo. 'Tôkyô-no Hanauri Musumé.' King C123. 1946: Japan.

Sakamoto, Kyû. 'Ueo-muite Arukô.' Tôshiba JP5083. *1961*: Japan. Released in the United States as: 'Sukiyaki.' Capitol 4945. *1963*: USA.

Satô, Chiyako. 'Habu-no Minato.' Japan Victor. 1928: Japan.

Satô, Chiyako. 'Tôkyô Kôshinkyoku.' Japan Victor. 1929: Japan.

Seki, Tanéko. 'Sen'ninbari.' Polydor 2548. 1938: Japan.

Shaw, Artie, and His Orchestra. 'Smoke Gets in Your Eyes.' Victor 27335. 1941: USA.

Shimakura, Chiyoko. 'Tôkyô-dayo Okkasan.' Columbia A2710. *1957*: Japan.

Shôji, Tarô. 'Akagi-no Komoriuta.' Polydor S65. 1934: Japan.

Southern All Stars. 'Itoshi-no Ellie.' Victor VIHX-1652. *1979*: Japan.

Spiders. 'No No Boy.' Crown SFL-1034. *1966*: Japan.

Taya, Rikizô. 'Paris-no Yané-no Shita.' Victor 51774. 1931: Japan.

Tottori, Shun'yô. 'Sendô Ko-uta.' Hikôki 1059. 1922: Japan.

Toyama Army School Military Band. 'Shingun-no Uta.' Columbia 29530. 1937: Japan.

Utada, Hikaru. *First Love*. Tôshiba-EMI TOCT-24067. *1999*: Japan.

Victor Military Band. 'Alexander's Ragtime Band.' Victor 17006. 1911: USA.

Whiteman, Paul. 'My Blue Heaven.' Victor 20828. 1927: USA.

Filmography

Kimi Koishi, dir. Shôzô Makino. 1929. Japan.

Sous les toits de Paris, dir. René Clair. 1930. France/Germany. 95 mins. Romantic Drama. Original music by Raoul Moretti.

Soyokazé, dir. Kô Sasaki. 1945. Japan.

Tôkyô Kôshinkyoku, dir. Kenji Mizoguchi. 1929. Japan.

TÔRU MITSUI

REGIONS

Okinawa

Population: 1,329,000 (2003)

Okinawa Prefecture consists of numerous small islands, which are located in the far southwest corner of Kyûshû. The capital city, Naha, on the main island, Okinawa, was a trading port of the

Ryûkyû kingdom from early times until 1879, when Okinawa was incorporated along with other adjacent islands into the Japanese prefectural system. After World War II, Okinawa Prefecture was under US administration until 1972, and the main island still remains the location of US military bases.

In Okinawa, vernacular music, which has a distinctive scale that approximates to the first, third, fourth, fifth, seventh and eighth notes of the Western major scale, remains intertwined with the daily cultural life of the people. An identifiable Okinawan popular music appeared in the mid-1970s, when Kina Shôkichi (1944–) debuted with his band, the Champroos, featuring Kina's bouncing *sanshin* (a three-string instrument with a snakeskin membrane across the resonator – a variant of the mainland *shamisen*) and his vigorous vocals. Rising to national prominence in 1977 with his single 'Haisai Ojisan' (Uncle Haisai), Kina announced a further blend of indigenous music and rock-electrification by other Okinawan musicians, in which mainland people showed a gradual interest. However, the framework of 'world music' was apparently needed to make Okinawan pop enjoy nationwide popularity, and it was in the early 1990s that two more Okinawan groups, the Rinken Band and the Nênês, became nationally popular. Both of these groups were associated with another prominent Okinawan musician, China Sadao (1950–), who debuted in the mainland with the 1978 album *Akabana* (Red Flowers), which incorporated rock and reggae idioms into Okinawan folk music. His backing band became independent in 1982 as the Rinken Band. Its music is characterized by a lively combination of traditional Okinawan idioms with new instrumentation, featuring the *sanshin* by the leader Teruya Rinken (1949–) and a female vocalist backed by a male chorus, who play Okinawan drums on certain pieces. China Sadao produced a significant album, *Ikawaû*, in 1991, recorded by the Nênês, a female vocal quartet formed in the preceding year. The distinctively Okinawan vocal style of the four sisters, who grew up playing the *sanshin* and singing domestic folk songs, was modernized by incorporating some contemporary instruments, including the synthesizer. Later Kina Shôkichi became internationally known through the success of 'Hana' (Flowers), originally 'Subéte-no Hito-no Kokoro-ni Hana-o' (Flowers to the Heart of Everybody), which he performed with his band, upon invitation, at the Olympic Games in Atlanta in 1996.

The presence of an audience of US servicemen in entertainment venues outside military bases prompted a growth in the number of domestic rock bands, particularly during the period of the Vietnam War. The music they played was exclusively hard rock sung in English. Among allegedly 50 to 100 bands, Mary with Medusa, which was formed in 1974, reigned over the Okinawa rock scene, outshining such prominent senior bands as the Condition Green and the Murasaki. The lead vocalist, Kiyan Mary, one of quite a few Okinawan residents with mixed Japanese (mother) and US (father) parentage, was known as 'Janis in Okinawa,' and her life was made into a film, *A Sign Days*, in 1989.

Bibliography
Fujita, Tadashi, ed. 1998. *Uchinâ-no Uta: Meikyoku 101-sen CD Guide* [Songs of Uchina: Guide to Select 101 Songs]. Tôkyô: Ongakunotomo-sha.

Fujita, Tadashi. 2000. *Okinawa-wa Uta-no Shima: Uchinâ Ongku-no 500-nen* [Okinawa Is an Island of Songs: 500 Years of Okinawan Music]. Tôkyô: Shôbun-sha.

Haisai, K., and Takarajima, T., eds. 1991. *Kina Shôkichi Champroo Book* (Collected essays on Kina and Okinawan music). Tôkyô: JICC.

Discographical References
China, Sadao. *Akabana*. Canyon FX8002. *1978*: Japan.

Kina, Shôkichi, and Champroos. 'Haisai Ojisan.' *Kina Shôkichi & Champroos*. Nippon Phonogram S-7025. *1977*: Japan.

Kina, Shôkichi, and Champroos. 'Hana.' *Blood Line*. Mercury PHCL-3034. *1980*: Japan.

Nênês. *Ikawaû*. Disc Akabana APCD-1001. *1991*: Japan.

Discography
Murasaki. *Murasaki*. Tokuma BMC-3004. *1976*: Japan.

Rinken Band. *Qing-dahmi: Rinken Band Best*. Daiki RINKEN-2088. *2000*: Japan.

Filmography
A Sign Days, dir. Yoichi Sai. 1989. Japan. 111 mins. Drama. Original music by Kiyan Mary.

TÔRU MITSUI

Shônan
Population: 1,325,000 (2000)

The Shônan region is the name given to the coastal area of Sagami Bay in central Japan, covering – from east to west – Kamakura, Fujisawa, Chigasaki, Hiratsuka, Ôiso, Ninomiya and Odawara. Zushi and Hayama in the northern Miura peninsula are often included as well. The warm climate and beautiful scenery have made the area popular for sightseeing and sea bathing since the beginning of the twentieth century. While it has developed as a residential and industrial area, it has also continued to attract people as both a holiday and a health resort.

In the 1930s Haida Katsuhiko (1909–82), who was born and raised in Hawaii, began playing Hawaiian music with his band in a resort venue in Zushi, providing the resort with appropriate live background music. His later activities in the 1940s and 1950s helped develop and extend the range of Japanese popular music with his appearance in films and many recordings of new, urbane *kayôkyoku* songs. In the period after World War II, a number of the sons of former hereditary peers, whose villas abounded in this region, got involved in playing country and western music while attending colleges in Tôkyô, forming bands with other rich college students. Starting with appearances at clubs in US military bases, they enjoyed popularity at live spots in downtown Tôkyô and eventually led the way to the rockabilly movement of the late 1950s.

Meanwhile, the image of the Shônan region as an urbane resort first became familiar nationwide after a series of successful films depicting the newly developed youth culture of the postwar years. These featured in particular Ishihara Yûjirô (1934–87), who grew up and resided in Zushi with his well-to-do family. Production of the series of films was itself initially inspired by a movie version of *Taiyô-no Kisetsu* (The Season of the Sun), a 1956 prize-winning novel by his elder brother, Ishihara Shintarô, then a college student and more recently the governor of Tôkyô from 1999. The amateurish singing of the younger brother, Ishihara Yûjirô, with his ukulele accompaniment as well as his performance on drums in a later film, which were combined with his nihilistic coolness, prompted him before long to set about recording *kayôkyoku* songs with great success, while his popularity as an actor kept rising. At the same time, Ishihara Shintarô, whose sexually uninhibited fiction invited frowns of disapproval even from contemporary college students, used to cruise in a yacht in fashionable attire, helping to construct the Shônan image.

The slightly younger Kayama Yûzô (b. 1937), son of a good-looking film star, Uehara Kenji, became popular through a series of films (1961–70) celebrating youth culture, in which there was an unrelentingly cheerful emphasis on the sunny side of Shônan life. Kayama sang in the films, playing the electric guitar with his band, the Wild Ones, performing songs he had composed under the influence of US pop in the late 1950s and early 1960s. The success of these films coincided with the time of the Tôkyô Olympics, when the image of Shônan as a popular resort was made widely known through the 1964 construction in Ôiso of athletes' quarters for participants in the yachting races at Enoshima. In terms of its music, Kuwata Keisuke (b. 1956) from Chigasaki, leader of Southern All Stars, strengthened Shônan's image from the late 1970s with his great success as a rock singer. A series of his compositions made the charts, including 'Itoshi-no Ellie' (Ellie, My Love) (1979), which was covered by Ray Charles (1989). The smaller-scale success of a jaunty older duo, Bread & Butter, formed by the Iwamisawa brothers, has also helped the Shônan image since the late 1970s. Without any remarkable new faces appearing, both Kayama Yûzô and Kuwata Keisuké keep alive music romantically associated with the Shônan region.

Bibliography

Ishihara, Shintarô. 1956. *Taiyô-no Kisetsu* [The Season of the Sun]. Tôkyô: Shinchô-sha.

Kiuchi, Yasushi. 1995. *Shônan Sound-to Taishû Resort Bunka-no Hassei* [Shônan Sound and the Emergence of Popular Resort Culture]. Unpublished M.A. thesis (music), Kanazawa University.

Discographical References

Charles, Ray. 'Itoshi-no Ellie.' Victor VDPS-1050. *1989*: Japan.

Southern All Stars. 'Itoshi-no Ellie.' Victor VIHX-1652. *1979*: Japan.

Discography

Bread & Butter. *Super Best 200*. Funhouse FHCF-9602. *1995*: Japan.

Haida, Katsuhiko. *Nangoku-no Yoru: Haida Katsuhiko Early Days 1936–1944*. Victor VICG-60408. *2000*: Japan.

Ishihara, Yûjirô. *Eién-no Utagoé: Ishihara Yûjirô-no Subété*. Teichiku TECE-28471-6. *2004*: Japan.

Kayama, Yûzô. *Kayama Yûzô-no Subété: The Ranchers-to Tomoni*. Tôshiba TP7100. *1966*: Japan.

Southern All Stars. *Tiny Bubbles*. Victor VOR-7003. *1980*: Japan.

Filmography

Taiyô-no Kisetsu, dir. Furukawa Takumi. 1956. Japan. 89 mins. Drama.

TÔRU MITSUI

Tôhoku and Hokkaidô

Population: Sendai: 1,024,000 (2003); Sapporo: 1,858,000 (2003)

Hokkaidô, which was inhabited by the aboriginal people Ainu, is the second-largest of the four major islands in Japan, being located at the northern end of the country, with the coldest climate and with unspoiled scenery. The government established after the Meiji Restoration in 1868 encouraged people from other islands to settle Hokkaidô, which became one prefecture in 1886 with Sapporo as its capital. This prefecture's gross area amounts to 20 percent of that of Japan, but its population is less than 1 percent of the national population. The Tôhoku region, which is adjacent to Hokkaidô and was also inhabited by the Ainu, encompasses the northern area of Honshû, which consists of six prefectures: Aomori, Iwaté, Miyagi, Akita, Yamagata and Fukushima. The largest city in this region is Sendai in Miyagi Prefecture.

The image of the north has long permeated *enka* songs, which are characterized by unrequited love, desolation and endurance. Their protagonists invariably wish to head north for anywhere in Tôhoku and Hokkaidô, where the climate reflects their inconsolable desolation. While there are many songs with nonspecific references to 'the north' in their titles, such as 'Kita-no Hotaru' (Fireflies in the North), 'Kita-no Yado-kara' (From an Inn in the North) and 'Kita-é Kaerô' (I'll Go Back to the North), there are quite a few with proper place names in the titles: 'Erimo Misaki' (Erimo Point), 'Hakodaté Honsen' (The Hakodaté Main Line) and 'Tsugaru-kaikyô Fuyu-geshiki' (The Wintry Scene of Tsugaru Channel).

An explicit link was made between the north and a specific singer when Satô Munéyuki (b. 1949) made his recording debut in 1978 with 'Aobajô Koi-uta' (Aoba Castle Love Song), singing his own lyrics with his own acoustic guitar accompaniment. This song makes reference to the castle in Sendai where he had spent his college days, and was a national hit, selling 1,200,000 copies. The popular music scene in Sendai, a university town, had been led by students in the same way as in other cities such as Kyôto and Fukuoka. Around the time when Satô first began singing 'Aobajô Koi-uta' on his local FM radio program – but before it was recorded – another local musician, Ôtomo Kôhei (b. 1956), had formed a rock band, Hound Dog, while a student, and was gigging around the Tôhoku region. The band won the first prize in a local contest and debuted in 1980 in Tôkyô

with 'Arashi-no Kin'yôbi' (Stormy Friday). Ôtomo went on to gain more national fame when 'ff' (pronounced 'fortissimo') from the band's album *Spirits!* was successfully used in a television commercial. Other successful artists from the Tôhoku region include Inaba Akira (b. 1954), a singer-songwriter from Ôdate, Akita, where he worked as a mining engineer, and Himékami (b. 1946) from Morioka, Iwaté. Inaba, whose 'Wakatté-kudasai' (I Hope You'll Understand) became a big hit in 1976, was one of the first artists to continue living in his native town rather than moving to Tôkyô. Himékami has been known internationally since the early 1980s for his 'new age' sound, produced with full use of synthesizers. He also stays close to the provinces (Morioka, Iwaté).

Hokkaidô began to attract the attention of the music industry when Fukinotô, a 'folk' duo formed by Yamaki Kôsei (b. 1950) and Hosotsubo Motoyoshi (b. 1952), returned to their native Sapporo after residing briefly in Tôkyô. This residency was prompted by the success of 'Shiroi Fuyu' (White Winter) in 1974. In the following year Nakajima Miyuki (b. 1952), a female singer-songwriter from Sapporo, won the grand prix at the 10th Yamaha Popular Song Contest with 'Jidai' (The Times). She eventually moved to Tôkyô, becoming one of the two queens of 'new music' (the other being Arai Yumi, later renamed Mattôya Yumi) with a series of hits including 'Wakaré Uta' (Farewell Song). Meanwhile, Matsuyama Chiharu (b. 1955), whose 'Kisétsu-no Naka-dé' (In the Midst of the Season) became a big hit in 1978, has maintained his success without leaving Hokkaidô. More recently, another act in which Hokkaidô has also taken pride is Glay, a rock band originally consisting of high-school students in Hakodaté, with an impressive ability to draw an audience.

Bibliography

Maéda, Yoshitaké, and Hirahara, Kôji, eds. 1993. *New Music-no Jidai* [The Age of New Music]. Tôkyô: Shinkô Music.

Nichigai Associates, ed. 2001. *Popular Ongaku Jinmei Jiten* [Who's Who of Popular Music]. Tôkyô: Nichigai Associates.

Discographical References

Fukinotô. 'Shiroi Fuyu.' CBS Sony SRCL2512. *1974*: Japan.

Hound Dog. 'Arashi-no Kin'yôbi.' CBS Sony 06SH 726. *1980*: Japan.

Hound Dog. 'ff.' *Spirits!*. CBS Sony 25(07SH1676). *1985*: Japan.

Inaba, Akira. 'Wakatté-kudasai.' Disco Mate DSF-1.
  1976: Japan.
Matsuyama, Chiharu. 'Kisétsu-no Naka-dé.' Canyon
  F-216. *1978*: Japan.
Nakajima, Miyuki. 'Jidai.' Canyon AV-74. *1975*:
  Japan.
Nakajima, Miyuki. 'Wakaré Uta.' Canyon V-22.
  1977: Japan.
Satô, Munéyuki. 'Aobajô Koi-uta.' King GK-201.
  1978: Japan.

Discography
Himékami. *Shinrabanshô*. Pony Canyon PCCA-
  01207. *1998*: Japan.

Visual Recording
Glay. 2001. 'Glay Best Video Clips 1994–1998.'
  Universal Japan POBE-8500/1 (DVD).

TÔRU MITSUI AND YASUSHI OGASAWARA

CITIES

Fukuoka
Population: 1,341,489 (2000)

Fukuoka, the capital of Fukuoka Prefecture and the
largest city on the southern island of Kyûshû, has
been important as the political, economic and
cultural center of northern Kyûshû since the
seventh century because of its adjacency to the
Chinese continent.

Fukuoka was perhaps first recognized nationally in
1973 as being a rich vein of contemporary popular
music when Takéda Tetsuya (b. 1949), a singer-
songwriter, and his band Kaiéntai rose in popularity
with the great success of 'Haha-ni Sasageru Ballad'
(Ballad Dedicated to Mother), a song characterized
by a narration in the local dialect. In the same year
Inoué Yôsui (b. 1948), a talented singer-songwriter
who was also under the influence of the Japanese
'folk' movement, saw his album *Kôri-no Sekai* (The
World of Ice) sell more than a million copies and
become the first million-selling album in Japan. It
was also in 1973 that Zaitsu Kazuo (b. 1948) made
the charts, leading his band, Tulip, in playing music
strongly influenced by the Beatles. All these pioneers
went on to national success in Tôkyô. They were
soon followed (1975–80) first by Kai Yoshihiro (b.
1953) and his Kai Band, and then by Chagé & Asuka,
Christal King and Nagabuchi Tsuyoshi (b. 1956).
What these bands had in common with the pioneers
was that they were popular attractions at Shôwa –
now a legendary venue for live performances in
downtown Fukuoka – before going on to Tôkyô.

Shôwa served as a cradle of Japanese pop, fostering
other bands such as Sheena & the Rockets (formerly
Son House) led by Ayukawa Makoto (b. 1958), a
group that has continued to enjoy national popularity and longevity without achieving any major
hits. The late 1990s and the early years of the
twenty-first century were characterized in particular
by the emergence of two vivacious female singers,
Misia (b. 1978) and Shîna Ringo (b. 1978). Someone
once called Fukuoka the 'Liverpool of Japan.'
However, no one has ever conceived of producing
an album with the representative artists who would
substantiate this claim.

Historically, the source of the musical environment in which artists and groups such as these were
fostered can be traced back to the postwar years
when local Japanese jazz bands supplied the music
at the clubs attached to the handful of US military
camps that were scattered around Fukuoka and its
vicinity. It is also traceable to the late 1950s and
early 1960s, when newly formed colleges and
universities, established as part of the postwar
reform of the educational system in Japan – and
in a period of general infatuation with North
American music – provided a context for the
emergence of student bands playing jazz, Hawaiian
and country and western music.

Bibliography
Nichigai Associates, ed. 2001. *Popular Ongaku Jinmei
  Jiten* [Who's Who of Popular Music]. Tôkyô:
  Nichigai Associates.
Q-Music FM Fukuoka and Planning Shûkô-sha.
  2002. *Fukuoka Ongaku-bon* [Book on Music in
  Fukuoka]. Fukuoka: Planning Shûkô-sha.

Discographical References
Inoué, Yôsui. *Kôri-no Sekai*. Polydor MR-5038. *1973*:
  Japan.
Kaiéntai. 'Haha-ni Sasageru Ballad.' Elec B-1016.
  1973: Japan.

Discography
Chagé & Asuka. *Neppû*. Warner Pioneer L12017.
  1981: Japan.
Kai Band. *Glass-no Dôbutsuen*. Tôshiba ETP-72206.
  1976: Japan.
Kaiéntai. *Bôkyô-hen*. ELEC ELEC-2022. *1973*: Japan.
Misia. *Misia Single Collection 5th Anniversary*. BMG
  Fun House BVCS-21035. *2003*: Japan.
Nagabuchi, Tsuyoshi. *Kazé-wa Minami-kara*. Tôshi-
  ba ETP-80065. *1979*: Japan.
Sheena & the Rockets. *Shinkû Pack*. Alfa ALR-6023.
  1979: Japan.

Shîna, Ringo. *Muzai Moratorium*. Tôshiba EMI
TOCT-24065. *1999*: Japan.
Shîna, Ringo. *Shôso Strip*. Tôshiba EMI TOCT-24321.
2000: Japan.
Tulip. *Kokoro-no Tabi*. Tôshiba ETP-9078. *1973*:
Japan.

TÔRU MITSUI

Hamamatsu

Population: 582,120 (2000)

Hamamatsu, the second-largest city in Shizuoka
Prefecture, is situated on the west bank of the
Tenryû River in the center of Japan's major island,
Honshû, near the Pacific Ocean. It developed as a
town on the major highway along this long,
southern coastline.

The city is best known for the manufacture of
motorcycles by the Yamaha and Suzuki companies,
and for the production of musical instruments,
including the brand names Yamaha and Kawai.
Ninety percent of all pianos produced in Japan are
made in Hamamatsu. Nippon Gakki, which expanded later to become the Yamaha Corporation,
was originally formed by Yamaha Torakusu in 1889
as a firm manufacturing organs. The company
produced the first upright piano in Japan in 1900
before extending its activities to the production of
harmonicas in 1914 and pipe organs in 1932. Later
the company added guitars and accordions to its
product list, and soon became the largest manufacturer of musical instruments in Japan. By the
beginning of the twenty-first century, not only
pianos and other instruments, but various pieces of
audio equipment were being exported worldwide,
with more than 40 overseas subsidiaries having
been established since 1958. (The company began
producing motorcycles in 1954, a year before
Yamaha Motor was formed.) Kawai Gakki, which
was established in 1927 as a manufacturer of
pianos, also expanded its operations by undertaking
the production of harmonicas and, later, guitars.

Both companies are known nationwide for the
fact that they employ local instructors all over Japan
to give music lessons, particularly to children
learning the piano. These music lessons, which have
operated outside official schools since the mid-1950s
as part of the sales promotion of musical instruments, have helped foster musical literacy among
the people and have encouraged young people,
including some prominent female singer-songwriters
such as Nakajima Miyuki (b. 1952) and Mattôya
Yumi (b. 1954), to become professional musicians.

Bibliography

Kawai Corporation. http://www.kawai.co.jp (in Ja-
panese).
Maema, Takanori, and Iwano, Yûichirô. 2001. *Piano
Hyaku-nen: Piano-zukuri-ni Kaketa hitobito* [A Hun-
dred Years of the Piano: Those Who Committed
Themselves to Manufacturing the Piano]. Tôkyô:
Sôshi-sha.
Sumikura, Ichirô, and Tsuchida, Eisaburô. 1985.
'Piano.' In *Heibon-sha Dai-hyakka Jiten* [Heibon-
sha Encyclopedia], Vol. 12. Tôkyô: Heibon-sha,
323–27.
Yamaha Corporation. http://www.yamaha.co.jp (in
Japanese).

TÔRU MITSUI

Kyôto, Ôsaka and Kôbé

Population: Kyôto: 1,465,000 (2003); Ôsaka:
2,627,000 (2003); Kôbé: 1,517,000 (2003)

Kyôto, situated some 320 miles (510 km) west of
Tôkyô, is the capital of Kyôto Prefecture. From 794
to 1868 it was the capital of Japan and home of the
imperial court, being rich in historical sites and
relics, including several palaces and castles as well
as innumerable temples. Recently, the name of the
city entered the limelight of environmental affairs
through the Kyôto Accord, an international treaty
whereby countries agree to reduce the amount of
greenhouse gases they emit. Ôsaka, the capital of
Ôsaka Prefecture, situated southwest of Kyôto at a
distance of 30 minutes by fast train, is the third-
largest city next to Tôkyô and Yokohama, and the
financial center of western Japan as well as the
center of the Hanshin industrial zone. Kôbé, the
capital of Kôbé Prefecture, is situated west of Ôsaka
at a distance of 20 minutes by fast train, and it ranks
as Japan's second international seaport, after Yokohama, with its importance going back to the eighth
century. These three neighboring metropolises
constitute the core of the Kansai region with its
own local speech patterns, manners and customs,
which form a pronounced contrast with those in
the eastern metropolitan area that surrounds Tôkyô
and Yokohama. As a common metaphorical comparison of these three neighboring cities has it:
'Kyôto is the graceful eldest sister, and Kôbé is the
stylish youngest sister, while Ôsaka, the second
sister, is somehow looked upon as inferior, though
she is in fact a belle and clever.'

In the early 1920s North American seamen
introduced New Orleans-style jazz to the city of
Kôbé, a prosperous international trading port, and

the music inspired those who worked for organizations such as department stores and fire stations to form their own bands. Meanwhile, house bands, consisting of Japanese musicians, on luxury liners brought the latest music scores from San Francisco and Los Angeles. The first professional jazz band in Japan was formed in Kôbé in 1923 by Ida Ichirô. Ida recruited members from the band for the Takarazuka Revue Company, a musical revue founded in 1914 on a European model, and later developed his career further as a pioneering jazz musician in Tôkyô.

Fascination with North American music spread to Ôsaka along with the large-scale influx of musicians and entertainers who left Tôkyô after 1923, following the city's devastation by the great Kantô earthquake. The lively character of the music scene that developed in Ôsaka was also due in part to the fact that the military band that belonged to the divisional headquarters in Ôsaka ceased to exist and its members went looking for musical opportunities in the private sector. Among them, Hattori Ryôichi was exceptionally talented in arranging big band music, and later moved to Tôkyô to become one of the most prolific and successful composers of kayôkyoku.

Another significant movement, and one that attracted more national attention, emerged in the mid- and late 1960s when the singing of self-penned songs after the fashion of the folk revival movement in the United States became popular among young Japanese. In the Kansai area the social protest aspect of the folk revival movement had a particular appeal to young audiences, many of whose members soon began forming their own bands or composing their own songs with guitars. The Underground Record Club (URC), formed initially as a mail-order system, supported the 'folk' scene in the Kansai area and evolved into an influential record label, eventually releasing the debut albums of many popular singer-songwriters/groups such as Takaishi Tomoya, Okabayashi Nobuyasu, Nakagawa Gorô, Takada Wataru, Endô Kenji, Tomobé Masato, the Itsutsu-no Akai Fûsen, the Happy End and the Dylan II. Commercially, the most successful record was 'Kaéttekita Yopparai' (Drunkard Returning from Heaven) by the Folk Crusaders, a home-taped recording that created a sensation when first played on cable radio. This tongue-in-cheek million-seller by college students in Kyôto was not explicitly a protest, but innovative in many respects, including the consistent use of Kansai dialect in the lyrics and narrative of the song and the comical effect caused by the double-speed revolution of vocals recorded on reel-to-reel tape.

Meanwhile, the Kansai area also served as one of the important cradles of Japanese rock music. Apart from the deep-rooted sense of rivalry with Tôkyô or the Kantô area, the rise of the rock scene in the Kansai area had something to do with the gradual arrival of an increasing number of residents from the United States and Europe. This was partly caused by the attraction of overseas tourists to the Ôsaka International Exposition in 1970. Another factor was the ancient city of Kyôto, which drew many hippies and others on spiritual journeys from the United States and Europe in the early 1970s. The West Auditorium of Kyôto University and two live spots, Juttoku and Takutaku, which were huge converted warehouses, were nationally known in the 1970s as regular venues for rock bands as well as for Japanese blues and R&B bands, which were more active here than in Tôkyô. Ueda Masaki and his band presided over the R&B scene, while Yûkadan was a prominent blues band.

Among numerous bands produced in Kôbé, Ôsaka and Kyôto in the late 1970s and early 1980s, which ranged through punk, new wave, electronic, progressive and heavy metal, the Ôsaka-based Loudness was distinguished by its international appeal, which it gained by signing to the Atlantic label in 1984. Ôsaka received international attention again in the early 1990s when an exuberant female trio, Shônen Knife, unknown to most Japanese audiences, succeeded in Europe and the United States. Following a solo tour of the United States in 1989, the band toured Europe and the United States with Nirvana and Sonic Youth. Its success prompted other Kansai bands, the Boredoms and S.O.B., to make successful inroads into overseas markets.

Bibliography

Hanshin-kan Modernism-ten Jikkô-iinkai. 1997. *Hanshin-kan Modernism* [Modernism in Ôsaka-Kôbé]. Kyôto: Tankô-sha.

Kitanaka, Masakazu. 1995. *Sengo Kayôkyoku-shi* [A History of Postwar *Kayôkyoku*]. Tôkyô: Shinchô-sha.

Kurata, Yoshihiro. 1979. *Nihon Record Bunka-shi* [A Cultural History of Records in Japan]. Tôkyô: Tôkyô Shoseki.

Maéda, Yoshitaké, and Hirahara, Kôji, eds. 1993. *New Music-no Jidai* [The Age of New Music]. Tôkyô: Shinkô Music.

Discographical Reference

Folk Crusaders. 'Kaéttekita Yopparai.' Tôshiba Capitol Records CP-1014. *1967*: Japan.

Discography

Boredoms. *SUPER ae*. Warner WPC6-8433. *1998*: Japan.

Endô, Kenji. *nyago*. URC MD33-4134. *1970*: Japan.

Happy End. *Happy End*. King OFL-8. *1973*: Japan.

Itsutsu-no Akai Fûsen. *Folk Album Dai 1-shû*. Victor SV-430. *1969*: Japan.

Loudness. *Thunder in the East*. Nippon Columbia CA-4084. *1985*: Japan.

Nakagawa, Gorô. *Owari Hajimaru*. URC URL-1010. *1969*: Japan.

Okabayashi, Nobuyasu. 'San'ya Blues.' Victor SV-1028. *1968*: Japan.

Shônen Knife. *Millennium Edition*. Universal Japan UUCH-1029. *2001*: Japan.

S.O.B. *Gate of Doom*. Toys Factory TFCC88028. *1993*: Japan.

Takada, Wataru. 'Jieitai-ni Hairô.' URC URC0827. *1968*: Japan.

Takaishi, Tomoya. 'Jukensei Blues.' Victor SV-681. *1968*: Japan.

Tomobé, Masato. *Ôsaka-é Yattekita*. SMS (URC) D38-4138. *1972*: Japan.

Ueda, Masaki, and Ariyama, Junji. *Bochi-bochi Ikoka*. Tokuma BMC-3003. *1975*: Japan.

Yûkadan. *Second Hand*. Torio 3A2021. *1976*: Japan.

TÔRU MITSUI AND HIDEKO HAGUCHI

Tôkyô

Population: 12,380,000 (2003)

Tôkyô, which is home to some 10 percent of the population of Japan and is located on the Pacific side of central Honshû with Tôkyô Bay on the southeast, has been the capital of Japan since 1868. The larger Tôkyô area comprises 23 wards of urban Tôkyô, 27 cities, one county and four island administrative units. Kyôto had been the capital of Japan as the residence of the Emperor, but central Tôkyô, previously called Edo, had remained the largest city with the establishment of the Tokugawa Shôgunate there in 1603.

Tôkyô, as the seat of government, is the political, commercial, financial, information, cultural and transportation center of Japan. Most large corporations, the national press and mass media, a majority of publishers, important libraries and museums, nearly 200 universities and colleges, and all the main railway lines are concentrated there.

Most record companies, both large and small, operate in Tôkyô. At the time of the introduction of electronic recording, the modern Japanese recording industry began with the establishment in Tôkyô of Nippon Columbia, Polydor and Nippon Victor in 1927 and Teichiku in 1934. After World War II, King was founded in 1951, Tôshiba in 1960, Tokuma in 1965 and Pony Canyon in 1966. These were followed by the formation of such new joint ventures as CBS-Sony, Tôshiba-EMI, Warner-Pioneer, Nippon-Phonogram and RVC in the late 1960s and early 1970s, prompted by the government's easing of restrictions on foreign investment. Most of the record companies that were registered in 2003 as the regular members (21), associate members (4) and supporting members (15) of the Recording Industry Association of Japan are located in Tôkyô. Meanwhile, a number of commercial broadcasting stations came into existence all over Japan after 1951, following the long monopolization of the airwaves by NHK, a Japanese equivalent of the BBC, but national broadcasting networks, particularly television networks, are based on such key Tôkyô-centered stations as TBS, Nippon, Fuji and Asahi. Consequently, numerous production companies and talent agencies have also become based in Tôkyô, among which Watanabé Production (established in 1959) and Hori Production (started in 1963) have dominated the entertainment industry. As for the promoters of overseas musicians, Kyôdô Tôkyô has remained predominant since its organization in 1950.

Roughly 2,400 monthly and weekly magazines of all kinds are published in Tôykô according to an early 1990s estimate. Music publishers and publishers of periodicals and books on music are also centered, for the most part, in Tôkyô. Seno'o Gakufu was established in the second decade of the twentieth century as the first successful publisher of music scores. Shinkô Gakufu, which was established in 1932, has continued to specialize in publishing popular song scores, and it also started *Music Life*, a longstanding monthly magazine that covers Western-oriented popular music, in 1951. Shinkô Gakufu was renamed Shinkô Music in 1983, and it has become known as the most successful publisher of fan-oriented books on music. Ongaku-notomo-sha was set up in 1941 as a publisher of serious music, but began to expand its activities to popular music in the early 1960s; since the late 1980s it has boasted a comprehensive catalog of books on popular music while giving priority to art music. The first jazz periodical, *Swing Journal*, was published in the early 1960s. At the beginning of the twenty-first century this monthly is still going strong, as is *New Music Magazine* (later renamed *Music Magazine*), which was started in 1969 as a monthly review of rock music and covers various aspects of contemporary music.

With Tôkyô abounding in concert halls and various kinds of clubs for live music, a majority of musicians, songwriters, producers, managers, promoters and journalists involved in the popular music business reside in the city. The only substantial change to this situation occurred in the days before the flowering of the record industry, in 1923, when the great Kantô earthquake violently shook Tôkyô. As a result of this, many musicians lost their jobs and moved to Ôsaka and its environs. It should be noted, however, that a majority of those who attained musical fame in Tôkyô came, as in many other fields, from the provinces. These musicians ranged from Nakayama Shinpei (from Nakano, Nagano), the prewar hit composer, and Awaya Noriko (from Aomori), who was known as the queen of the Japanese 'blues,' to Hamazaki Ayumi (from Fukuoka), one of the most prominent female J-pop (contemporary Japanese pop) stars in the new century.

TÔRU MITSUI

4. North Asia

Mongolia

Population: 2,740,000 (2000)

Mongolia, a democratic country located at the heart of Inner Asia, is situated between the Russian Federation lying to the north and China to the east, west and south. It is the size of Western Europe, and in 2000 78.8 percent of its population were classified as Khalkha Mongols. Other Mongol groups within Mongolia include Altai Urianghais, Bargas, Baits, Buryats, Chahars, Darhats, Darigangas, Dörbets, Hamnigans, Harchins, Horchins, Hoshuts, Hotogoids, Mingats, Ölöts, Sünits, Torguts, Üzemchins and Zakchins. Turkic minorities within Mongolia include Kazakhs (5.9 percent) and small numbers of Tyvans, Üzbeks (Chantous), Uighur and Soyot Urianghais, Tsaatans and Hotons. Approximately 3 million Mongols also live in Inner Mongolia, in the People's Republic of China, and there are Mongols in other areas of China – for instance, in the autonomous region of Xinjiang and in Qinghai and Gansu provinces. Buryat Mongols are located primarily in Buryatia, part of the Russian Federation, and Kalmyk Mongols live close to the River Volga in European Russia, as well as in West Mongolia. Traditionally, Mongols express in their music the culture and practices of nomadic pastoralism, ranging from herding and hunting to domestic celebrations, sport and play, their identities in terms of ethnicity and gender, and their overlapping folk-religious, shamanic and Buddhist spiritual beliefs.

Music in Early History

Mongols emerged as a distinct group during the eleventh and twelfth centuries. Chinggis (Genghis) Khan established the first Mongol Uls (Mongolian Nation) in 1206, a nomadic empire that united the Mongol tribes and, at its height, reached from the Pacific Ocean to the Black Sea (1206–1368). *The Secret History of the Mongols*, a thirteenth-century epic chronicle of Chinggis' imperial Borjigin clan, refers to Chinggis' *huur* (fiddle) player, to skin-headed drums beaten before battle, and to a round, stamping dance, performed around a 'branching tree' (Cleaves 1982).

From that time, a division developed between Eastern and Western (Oirat) Mongols, two confederations that have periodically opposed each other in war, with each having periods of supremacy over the other. Chinggis' Borjigin clan was part of the Eastern Mongol confederation, but a powerful Western Mongol Jungar state held sway from 1630 until the 1750s. Eastern Mongols swore allegiance to the Manchu emperor K'ang Hsi in 1691, while Western Mongols resisted Manchu domination for another 70 years. Mongol subordination to the Manchu dynasty (until 1911) did not impinge on culture at the local level, provided that the annual tribute was paid. Traditional styles of song, music and dance continued, therefore, to express confederative, clan and tribal differences. While all Mongols performed *urtyn duu* (long-song), for instance, a broad division in styles expressed membership of Eastern (melismatic, highly ornamented, through-composed melodies) and Western (angular contours, little ornamentation, repeated verses) confederations, and smaller stylistic differences expressed 'tribal' and 'clan' identities within that division. Similarly, while members of both confederations played the two-string spike fiddle (*huur*), there was a difference in function: Eastern Mongols used it to accompany *urtyn duu* and

Western Mongols to accompany the *biy*-dance (performed using predominantly the top half of the body). Difference was also expressed in the distribution of certain vocal genres and instruments. For instance, *höömii* (overtone-singing), *tuul'* (heroic epics) and the *tsuur* (end-blown pipe) were performed or played only by Western Mongols, while *bengsen-ü üliger* (narrative tales set to music), *holboo* (connected verse), *dörvön chihtei huur* (four-string spike tube fiddle) and *limbe* (side-blown flute) were performed or played only by Eastern Mongols.

There were also musical practices specific to folk religion (e.g., *tuul'* heroic epics, *magtaal* praise-songs, *biy*-dance), shamanism (e.g., 'walking' or 'riding' songs, *aman huur* jew's-harp, *hets* frame drum) and Buddhism (e.g., *bishgüür* trumpets, *büree* horns, masked *tsam* dance).

'National' Music During the 'People's Republic' (1924–90)

The first major changes came during the twentieth century. During the Communist period, a systematic homogenization of ethnicity prohibited the expression of ethnic diversity through musical styles and genres. The music of the largest ethnic group, the Khalkhas, was chosen as the basis for a 'national' music, created for a new nation with a single socialist national identity. Any music that could be labeled 'traditional,' rather than 'new,' was considered reactionary and therefore bad. Although the new music adapted the forms of Khalkha traditional music, its musical content was changed so that it could be played together with Western instruments in folk ensembles, the construction and tunings of instruments were adapted, and its lyrical content was rewritten to express national and socialist ideals. Throughout the first half of the twentieth century, national music was disseminated through national and regional theaters (the ubiquitous State Folksong and Dance Ensembles), schools and the media. Mongolia's musical history was reinvented. Religious instruments and songs became secularized, as all religious beliefs and practices were squashed. And there was obliteration from public memory of Chinggis Khan, who had previously been worshiped, about whom many long-songs and melodies had been written, and to whom connections were made in performance (Pegg 2001). Although restructured from the center and above, this music was called *ardyn högjim*, the 'music of the people.'

In the mid-twentieth century, when commercial rock and pop music began to grip Western Europe,

the Mongolian People's Revolutionary Party decreed that pop music was ideologically unsound because it contained elements of capitalism. During the late 1960s, however, recordings of a few key Western pop groups were smuggled in, and young musicians began to experiment. The Party eventually allowed two state bands to be formed. Soyol Erdene (Precious Culture), named after a revolutionary song of the 1920s and 1930s, was founded in 1967 when it took part in the first Mongolian television transmission to celebrate the 50th anniversary of the October Revolution. Bayan Mongol (Rich Mongolia) was based in the state center of music, the Philharmonic, until the end of the 1970s, and continued to produce vinyl records until the early 1980s. Both played a genre known in Mongolia as *estrad* (from the French *estrade*, meaning 'platform' or 'stage'), found in all countries of the former Soviet Union. Given the English translation 'variety,' it consisted of a mixture of popular and folk songs. These were arranged in regular rhythm for brass, electric organ, bass and drums to produce bland middle-of-the-road sounds, and covered the accepted Communist themes of glorifying the homeland and praising parents. The groups were affiliated with the state-sponsored Philharmonic, which acted as manager, booking agent and censor, and played in the auditoria of houses of culture. Musicians received salaries from the state. It was impossible to be a pop or variety musician without having formal musical training, or to appear in concert without possessing a diploma in music. Unhaa, the founder of Soyol Erdene, spent six years training in the Conservatoire in Bulgaria. He became a 'state-merited artist' (*gavyat*), 'Conductor of Variety' and director of the Mongolian Philharmonic Orchestra. Jazz, considered the music of the exploited blacks of the United States, was also acceptable in orchestral form.

Contemporary Mongolia

In contemporary Mongolia, rock and pop groups are able to develop their own sounds and repertoires and are no longer employed by the state. Some draw inspiration from their ethnic origins and religious traditions; some react to the influx of new sounds and global influences by cross-fertilizing their music with that of the West; and some, deterred from producing anything traditional by the doctored music of the former regime, play solely Western sounds, though sometimes with Mongolian themes.

Hünd rock (hard rock), *höngön rock* (soft rock), *pop*

högjim (pop music) and rap bands form part of a vibrant music scene. They have the freedom to choose their own names, produce their own sounds and write their own lyrics. There is a band called Chinggis Khan, and others with religious or traditional connotations, such as Haranga (a gong used in Buddhist rituals) and Aizam (a traditional long-song style). Haranga, which was formed in 1989 in the capital, Ulaanbaatar, introduced hard rock to Mongolian youth and throughout the late 1990s was considered to produce 'classic' rock. With heavy-metal wailing lead guitar and raunchy vocals, Haranga's song 'Our Mongolia' pleads: 'Let us develop at the speed of light now that we are set free into the vast world.' The members of rap-influenced Black Rose sport sunglasses and ancient Mongol outfits, and inject into their performances English terms such as 'East-West, East-West' and 'drumscapes' (*Great and Destroy* [1996]). The members of the six-piece pop group Niciton, led by vocalist and keyboard player Batchuluun, cite their influences as Billy Joel, Elton John, the Beatles and the Rolling Stones in a song called 'Niciton Is Singing.'

There are many 'boy bands' in Mongolia, of which Camerton – four teenagers who produce sweet harmonies and Swingle-type arrangements – was the most highly rated in the closing decade of the twentieth century. There are also a number of 'girl bands,' including the trio Spike. The pop singer Sarantuya, or Saara, who had a hit in the mid-1990s with the feminist song 'Chi Heregui' (I Don't Need You), describes her music as Mongolian folk songs combined with US soul, gospel and R&B (Waugh 1996). And Ariunaa, a member of Soyol Erdene and singer of the title track of the Mongolian film *Bi Chamd Hairtai* (I Love You), recently declared: 'I am the Mongolian Madonna.' The male vocalist Chingghis imitates Elvis Presley.

A hybrid Mongol-Western music has also developed that falls somewhere between folk-rock and world music. The female vocalist with Chinggis Khan, for example, wearing a traditional gown, hair in 'winged' style, and holding a ritual scarf in outstretched hands, performs a long-song, accompanied by *höömii* (overtone-singing), *morin huur* (horse-head fiddle), *topshuur* (two-string lute), electric piano, synthesizer and full drumkit.

The first field recordings of Mongol music made available to the West were two LPs from the

Indigenous People of Siberia

A. Ob-Ugrian: Mansis and Khantys
B. Selkup Samoyed: Selkups, Sym Kets
C. Northern Samoyed: Nenets and Nganasans
D. Southern Altai: Altai Kizhis and Telengits
E. Northern Altai
F. Khakas
G. Sayan Turkic
H. Buryats
I. Amur Tungus
J. Northern Turkic: Sakhas
K. Northern Tungus: Evenkis
L. Chukchis, Koryaks, Yukagirs

159

Hungarian Lajos Vargyas, published in 1967 by Hungaroton with the help of UNESCO. The French ethnologist and sociologist Roberte Hamayon's LP followed in 1973, and then, in 1977, two LPs came from the English Jean Jenkins, one of which was devoted to Mongolian vocal music, the other to instrumental music. The profile of Mongol music has been raised since the late 1980s by the release of a number of traditional music compilations from Mongolia – for example, *Mongolie: Musique et chants de l'Altai* (1986), *Mongolie: Musique vocale et instrumentale* (1989), *Mongolia: Musics and Musicians of the World* (1991), *Musiques de Mongolie* (1993), *Mongolie: Chants Kazakhs et tradition épique de l'Ouest* (1993) and *Mongolia: Chamanes et lamas* (1994) – as well as one including music from Inner Mongolia (*Mongolia: Living Music of the Steppes* [1997]). Its profile has also been raised by the promotion in the West of a few bands, such as Altai-Hangai and Egschiglen, and singers, such as Una Chahartugchi. The latter, from a herding family in Ordos, Inner Mongolia, is one of the few Inner Mongolian musicians to emerge. She experiments with cross-fertilization, performing traditional Ordos songs that are accompanied by Robert Zollitsch on the Bavarian zither and Oliver Kälberer on the classical guitar.

Mongolian *höömii*, the extraordinary vocal technique in which a single performer produces a simultaneous vocal drone and reinforced harmonics that form a melody above it, has been slower to establish itself on the world music circuit than the throat-singing of musicians from neighboring Tuva, such as Huun-Huur Tu (*60 Horses in My Herd* [1993]) and Yat-kha (*Yenesei-Punk* [1995]). This is the case even though *höömii* is well developed as an art form within Mongolia, being classified into seven different types (Pegg 1992). The Mongolian Amra, from the Germany-based band Egschiglen, produces deep, rich *höömii* vocal textures, but his recognition has been hampered by the band's arranged 'ensemble' sounds, as illustrated on the band's *Sounds of Mongolia* (2001).

Bibliography

Cleaves, Francis W., trans. 1982. *The Secret History of the Mongols*. Cambridge, MA: Harvard University Press for the Harvard-Yenching Institute.

Pegg, Carole. 1992. 'Mongolian Conceptualisations of Overtone-Singing (*xöömii*).' *The British Journal of Ethnomusicology* 1: 31–55.

Pegg, Carole. 2001. *Mongolian Music, Dance and Oral Narrative: Performing Diverse Identities* (with CD).

Seattle and London: University of Washington Press.

Waugh, L. 1996. 'Dreaming of Monte Carlo.' *Ulaanbaatar Post* (9 July).

Discographical References

Ariunaa. 'Bi Chamd Hairtai.' *1992*: Mongolia.

Black Rose. *Great and Destroy*. Sonor Records. *1996*: Germany.

Chants mongols et bouriates (rec. Roberte Hamayon). Collection Musée de l'Homme. Vogue LDM 30138. *1973*: France.

Egschiglen. *Sounds of Mongolia*. ARC Music EUCD 1652. *2001*: Germany.

Haranga. 'Our Mongolia.' *Best of Haranga*. Stonehenge Productions. *1997*: Austria.

Huun-Huur Tu. *60 Horses in My Herd*. Shanachie 64050. *1993*: USA.

Instrumental Music of Mongolia (rec. Jean Jenkins). Topic Records TGS 127. *1977*: UK. Reissue: *Vocal and Instrumental Music of Mongolia* (rec. Jean Jenkins). Topic Records TSCD909. *1994*: UK.

Mongolia: Chamanes et lamas (rec. Alain Desjacques). Ocora C560059. *1994*: France.

Mongolia: Living Music of the Steppes (rec. Haruo Hasumi). Multicultural Media MCM 3002. *1997*: USA.

Mongolia: Musics and Musicians of the World (rec. Alain Desjacques). Auvidis-UNESCO D8207. *1991*: France.

Mongolie: Chants Kazakhs et tradition épique de l'Ouest (rec. Alain Desjacques). Ocora C580051. *1993*: France.

Mongolie: Musique et chants de l'Altai (rec. Alain Desjacques). ORSTOM SELAF Cero 811. *1986*: France.

Mongolie: Musique vocale et instrumentale. Inédit MCM W 260009. *1989*: France.

Mongol Nepzene (Mongolian Folk Music). Hungaroton LPX 18013-14. 1967; *1990*: Hungary.

Musiques de Mongolie (rec. P. Chesneau and Henri Lecomte). Buda Records SACEM 92591-2. *1993*: France.

Niciton. 'Niciton Is Singing.' *Tsamtai Tail (Please, Take Off Your Shirt Darling)*. Sonor Records. *1997*: Mongolia.

Sarantuya (Saara). 'Chi Heregui.' *1995*: Mongolia.

Vocal Music of Mongolia (rec. Jean Jenkins). Topic Records TGS 126. *1977*: UK. Reissue: *Vocal and Instrumental Music of Mongolia* (rec. Jean Jenkins). Topic Records TSCD909. *1994*: UK.

Yat-kha. *Yenesei-Punk*. Global Music Center GMCD 9504. *1995*: Finland.

Discography

Altai-Hangai. *Naarits biilye: Let's Dance!*. Pan 2061. *1999*: The Netherlands.

Bayan Mongol. *Estradyn 'Bayan Mongol' Chuulga (The 'Bayan Mongol' Variety Group)*. Melodiya C90-15959-60. *1981*: USSR.

Camerton. *18 Years*. Sonor Records. *1996*: Germany.

Chahartugchi, Una. *Tal Nutag. Lieder aus dem mongolischen Grasland*. Klangräume 30200. *1995*: Germany.

Folk Music from Mongolia. Internationales Institut für Traditionelle Musik. *1993*: Germany.

Mongolia: Höömii and Urtiin Duu: The Folk Music Traditions, 1. JVC World Sounds V1CG-5211. *1992*: Japan.

Music and Dance of Mongolia (audiocassette). Global Arts GA001. *1988*: UK.

Sarantuya, B., and Gankhugyag, N. *Dreaming in Gobi*. MCB93-6868. n.d.: Mongolia.

Filmography

Bi Chamd Hairtai, dir. B. Baljinnyam. 1986. Mongolia. 91 mins. Drama.

CAROLE PEGG

Siberia (Region of Russia)

Population: ca. 2,200,000 (2000)

Siberia is a vast area of arctic and subarctic zones, occupying approximately one-quarter of the continent of Asia. It is bordered by the Ural Mountains in the west (marking the division from European Russia), the Pacific Ocean in the east and the Arctic regions in the north. Its southern border sits on a line roughly coinciding with the 50° north latitude. Siberian peoples traditionally hunt, fish or breed cattle.

A range of indigenous peoples lives in Siberia, including Tungus, Samoyed, Turkic and Mongol peoples, each with their own musics. Northern cultures are influenced by reindeer husbandry and fishing; southern cultures by herding and hunting in the mountains and steppes. Information about the music traditions from these regions came first from travelers in the seventeenth century and then from Russian ethnographers at the turn of the nineteenth century: V.G. Bogorazz-Tan and V.I. Iokhelson worked with peoples of northeastern Siberia; S.M. Shirokogorov with the Tungus peoples; L.Ya. Shternberg with the Nivkhs; F.Ya. Kon with the Turkic peoples of central Siberia; and A.A. Dunin-Gorkavich with the peoples of the Ob' region. Beginning in the 1960s, the Russian ethnomusicologist Igor Bogdanov made field recordings

published between the 1970s and 1990s. Researchers from the Novosibirsk Conservatory have carried out extensive fieldwork with various Siberian peoples since the 1980s, especially in central and eastern Siberia (Sheikin 2001).

The Twentieth-Century Sovietization of Music

All Siberian peoples endured cultural colonization during the implementation of Soviet nationality policies in the twentieth century. Local musical traditions were changed and incorporated into the Western art music forms and institutions, for instance, opera and ballet companies (in the republics of Buryatia and Sakha), musical theaters (in the southern republics of Altai, Khakassia and Tyva), and music and dance ensembles (in the northern regions of the Koryak, Chuchki, Khanty, Mansi and Evenki peoples). More than 1,000 primary music schools were established together with more than 30 music colleges and four higher music institutions (in Novbosibirsk, Krasnoyarsk, Yakutsk and Vladivostok).

Spiritual activities and associated ritual musics were brutally oppressed. Throughout Siberia, shamans were purged or had their instruments destroyed or removed. In Tyva, Altai and Buryatia, where Tibetan Buddhism had become established, lamas were murdered, monks made to join the army, and monasteries – together with their instruments and books – were destroyed. Traditional music, songs and dances were taken from different groups and synthesized in order to eradicate differences in status, ethnicity and religion. They were also adapted to the European scale system. Performances were relocated from traditional contexts to the theatrical stage. Instruments were standardized and modified to enable production of the new European scales and sounds that could fill a concert hall or that were banned from public performance. Traditional instruments, formerly used as accompaniment for vocal sounds, were developed for solo performance.

Since the collapse of the Soviet Union (1991), diversity has once again become possible, and the indigenous peoples of Siberia are expressing identity and difference through music. Some field recordings have been issued on CDs. But groups from southern Siberia have also emerged onto the international stage through live and recorded performances.

Late Twentieth and Early Twenty-First Musical Characteristics and Diversity

There are some similarities between the music of all indigenous Siberians, for instance, an emphasis on mimesis in song, an intonation based on timbres rather than pitch, melodies with a small ambitus but large intervallic leaps, and lullabies comprising vocables or mostly non-semantic sounds. A wide range of vocal sounds is deployed, including gravelly textures during epic performance, rapid delivery during 'hurried speech' and throbbing glottal stops during long laments. Each Siberian group interacts with and embodies sounds of the natural world. They produce sounds to lure, decoy and imitate animals and birds during hunting and to control animals when hunting and herding. All perform epics and other forms of songs and music that are influenced by spiritual beliefs associated with shamanism. These are often performed using a hoarse vocal timbre. Shaman songs are accompanied by a single-headed frame drum, creating patterns that activate rattling metal bells, pendants or animal figures attached to the shaman's costume and inside the drum (Lecomte 1992, 6). Whirling and rotating aerophones are also used, and musical instruments are often used as non-tonal sound or signal instruments. Rattles are the most representative idiophone. Sakhas are well-known for their technically accomplished jew's-harp (*khomus*) playing in solo performance, duos and quintets. Samoyodic peoples and a few other groups – for instance, Yukagirs – use the musical bow instead, an instrument which is called a 'women's jew's-harp' by Ob-Ugrian, Selkup, Ket, northern and Amur Tungus, Chukchi-Koryak, Yupik-Aleut and Kamchatka peoples (Sheiken 2000).

These underlying features take on regional and ethnic characteristics. Although a range of fiddles is used, for instance, their construction and function varies, as with the birch-bark and salmon-skin one-string *julanku* fiddle of the Oroc, the four-string *krympa* fiddle of the Sakhas (Vertkov et al. 1975), and the two-string horse-hair fiddles (e.g. Khakas *yykh*, Tyvan *igil*) of southern pastoralist groups. Similarly, bear ceremony traditions (in which the bear is the subject of rituals because of its totemic status) occur among the peoples who live along the River Amur, on the island of Sakhalin, and also among the Ob-Ugrian peoples. However, in the Amur region women use the musical log as accompaniment for these ceremonies, while in Sakhalin the men play the lyre, harp or lute (Sheikin 2001).

Siberian musics are predominantly vocal, including the dance musics. Perhaps best-known are Siberian 'throat-singing' and 'overtone-singing' vocal techniques. 'Throat-singing' has been used

to describe the extraordinary inhalation-exhalation sounds produced by eastern and northeastern groups such as the Chukchis, Evens, Evenks, Koryaks and Jukagirs. These may be incorporated into drum-dances or sung independently and are similar to the sounds used during throat-games by the Inuits of Canada (*katajjaq*) (Nattiez 1999) and the *Kraft Ainu* of Hokkaido island, northern Japan (*rekutkar*). The Sakha singing technique *kolerach* – used by a *tayuk* performer – in which there is a rapid passage from the chest to falsetto, accompanied by glottal jerking, is a related genre.

Characteristic of Arctic nomads and hunters, such as the Nenets, Nganasans, Yukagirs and Chuchkis, are pitch sets of melodies that change and expand during performance. Among the Nenets, this gradual widening of the interval size of melodic intonations may eventually exceed an octave (Abramovich-Gomon 1999). Also fundamental to Arctic music cultures are songs composed for individuals as children that become a means of self-identification equivalent to the singer's personal name. These are often, but not always, executed during drum-dances.

The music cultures of the peoples of southern Siberia, such as Altaians, Khakasses, Tyvans and Mongolian Buryats, connect to those of the nomadic pastoralists of Inner Asia and, in some cases, Central Asia. These peoples have become noted for their use of another kind of 'throat-singing,' often referred to as 'overtone-singing' (Pegg 2001a, 2001b; Van Tongeren 2002). In this vocal technique, a single performer simultaneously produces two or three vocal lines by selectively amplifying harmonics. Because the top line is often an ethereal, shimmering melody, this complicated vocal technique has been referred to as 'overtone-singing,' although technically there is usually no singing – the sounds are without lyrics. The melodies, formed by harmonics or partials, are made louder than the fundamental drone from which they derive and are produced by means of precise movements of the lips, tongue, larynx, and a range of chest and stomach muscles.

'Overtone-singing' first emerged in the West on a field recording from Mongolia made by the Hungarian Vargyas Lajos in 1967. Mongols call it *höömii* and the Tyvan term '*xöömej*' is a variant of this. The Russian researcher Aksenov (1973 [1964]) identified four basic Tyvan styles: *kargiraa* (*kargyraa*), *sygyt*, *borbannadir* (*borbangnadyr*) and *ezengileer*, and noted that in some regions *xöömej* (*khöömii*, *höömii*) was used to refer to *borbannadir* (*borbangnadyr*). In 1987, a Soviet-American musical-ethnographic expedition (Eduard Alekseev and Ted Levin) arrived in Tyva, where they worked with the Head of the Music Section of the Institute of Language, Literature and History in Kyzyl, Zoya Kyrgyz. The resulting CD, *Tuva: Voices from the Center of Asia* (1994), introduced to the Western public Aksenov's five overtone-singing styles. Since then, styles and sub-styles have proliferated, such as steppe *kargyraa*, *tespeng höömei* and *Oidupaa* (Pegg 2000a, 2001b), which may be heard on the CD *Hörekteer*, produced by Zoya Kyrgyz (2002). Overtone-singing is also performed by the Altai Kizhi (*karkiraa*) and the Sakhas (*khabarga*). It has connection with certain types of epic performance, as among the Khakasses (*khai*), Altai Urianghais (*hailah*) and Altai Teleuts (*kay chörchök*).

The musics of southern Siberian peoples are influenced by practices of Buddhism and shamanism. Monodic singing with instrumental accompaniment is a tradition of the Ob-Ugrain peoples, Altais, Khakasses, Sayan Turks, Buryats and their southern neighbors, the Mongols. Buryats, Tyvans and Altais, also like their Mongolian neighbors, play melodies to encourage animals to feed their newborn or orphan young.

Tyvans, Buryats, Khakasses and Altaians share instruments with other Inner Asian groups. The four-string fiddle, for instance, is called *pyzanchy* by Tyvans and *dörvön chihtei huur* by Mongols and is played by men in southern Mongolia and Inner Mongolia (China) to accompany praise-songs and tales. The two-string horse-hair fiddle, in which the body and neck are carved from a single piece of wood (Tyvan *igil*, Khakas *yykh*) is also found in West Mongolia, as is the two-string plucked lute (Tyvan *toshpuluur*, Khakas *khomys*, Altai Urianghai *topshuur*) and three-string plucked lute (Tyvan *chanzy*, Mongolian *shanz* or *shudraga*). The ancient three-holed end-blown pipe is called *shöör* by the Tofalars of Tyva, *tsuur* by the Altai Urianghais, *syylys* by the Khakasses and *sibizgi* by the Kazakhs of West Mongolia. The Khakas zither *chatkhan*, formerly played by epic bards and in ritual contexts, was promoted to the status of 'national' instrument with the fall of communism in 1991 and has become a prime symbol of their ethnicity. It is also played by Tyvans (*yatkha*) and Mongols (*yatga*).

World Music

Siberian musicians that have emerged into the world music arena have looked to the 'deep past' of the pre-Soviet traditions to recreate or reinvent their identities in the post-Soviet era. The remarkable 'overtone-singing' of Tyva and Mongolia has fascinated and puzzled world music audiences since the early 1990s. With the increasing popularization of overtone-singing, musical fusions and neo-shamanism, some Tyvan artists and groups have become internationally successful.

First to emerge was Huun-Huur Tu ('the vertical separation of light rays that you see out on the grasslands just after sunrise or just before sunset'). Formed in 1992, the combination of Albert Kuvezin's deep bass *kargyraa* throat-singing and the timbral emphasis of the music on the classic CD *60 Horses in my Herd* (1993) and subsequent *The Orphan's Lament* (1997) startled and intrigued Western audiences. They went on to pioneer Tyvan fusion music, first by producing popular Tyvan songs with Russian musicians on their third CD *If I'd Been Born an Eagle* (1997), and then by collaborating with the Bulgarian female choir Angelite, the Moscow Art Trio, US rockers Frank Zappa and Ry Cooder, the Chieftains Celtic folk band, and the US classical music Kronos Quartet. They won a BBC Radio 3 World Music Award in 2004. During the process of recording old Tyvan singers and copying their nuances and melodic orientations, their music became more subtle.

In 1996, Alexander 'Sasha' Bapa, a founding member and producer of Huun Huur Tu, gathered up a group of young Tyvan musicians to form Chirgilchin, ('mirage' or 'dance of the air in the heat of the day'). Bapa played guitar, arranged the songs and produced their first CD, *The Wolf and the Kid*, which although competent, remained in the shadow of Huun Huur Tu. The contemporary lineup, including Igor Oshenkendey, a champion overtone-singer performing in the contemporary *Oidupaa* style, appeared at the San Francisco World Music Festival in 2000.

Formed in 1992 by Boris Salchak, and Alexei and Nadezhda Shoigu, Shu-De was a more distinctive band. Having appeared in the same year in Wales at the Eisteddfodd, they were invited to perform at the WOMAD Festival in Reading, UK and from there were taken into Peter Gabriel's studio to record *Voices from the Distant Steppe* (1994). Three overtone-singers – Mergen Mongush, Leonid Oorzhak and Oleg Kuular – performed an impressive range of styles in differing combinations and a gritty female singer provided further diversity. From lullaby to tongue-twister, shaman ritual to overtone-wrapped Buddhist mantra, Shu-De's music expressed the essence of the Tyvan musical universe. Mergen Mongush and Leonid Oorzhak then left the group to be replaced by the renowned overtone-singer Ondar Monguun-Ool. Their second CD *Kongurei* (1996), recorded for an Italian label, showed an ability to integrate into the world music scene without sacrificing their traditional sounds. In 1997, they collaborated with the English group Telepathy, and Oleg Kuular played on a CD *Tammze* recorded by the Russian psychedelic rock group Ole Lukkoye. The premature departure of Oleg Kuular brought the career of Shu-De to an end. Boris Salchak used brooding layers of sustained ambient sounds to fuse Tyvan music with Christy Doran's electric guitars and Airto Moreira's percussion on the CD *Shaman* (2000).

Recognized at the Voices of Asia festival competition in Alma-Ata in 1990 by a panel of international judges including Brian Eno, Yat-kha brought driving rhythms and a punk sensibility to Tyvan music. The distinctive *khanzak kargyraa* throat singing style of Albert Kuvezin, founding member of Huun-Huur-Tu, reached its zenith with Yat-kha's first CD, *Yenesei Punk* (1995). The bands Deep Purple and Sonic Youth had influenced Kuvezin as a boy. The resulting fusion caused a stir in Europe and their CD stayed at the top of the world music play lists for several months. Coming from the Tyvan/Khakassian border, Kuvezin's style has affinity with Khakas epic performance (*khai*). Just a bit odd that, although it was recorded in 1994, some of their lyrics still praised their 'beautiful Soviet country' and the 'powerful USSR giving a happy life to us,' although these may be intended to be ironic. A smoother, more electronic production, with perhaps too many foreign 'guest' musicians, ensured that *Dalai Beldiri* (1999), released on Paddy Maloney of the Chieftains' Wicklow label, failed to live up to the promise of their first. However, it won the German Critics Prize in 1999. Soviet-style songs about industrious people and road building sit uncomfortably amid the more traditional themes of rivers, mountains and love, but intriguing is the inclusion of Zhenya Tkach's 'Old Believers' chant. *Aldyn Dashka*, released on the band's own label, followed. Their 2003 release, *Tyva Rock*, saw them returning to a harder edge but with English and French lyrics that sometimes fall flat. Yat-kha provided live music to accompany an uncensored version of the great Soviet director Pudovkin's 1928 silent classic *Storm Over Asia: The Heir of Genghis Khan* ('*Potomok Chingis Khana*'), incorporating riffs from the well-known rock repertoire, such as Pink Floyd's 'Money' (1988) and Deep Purple's 'Smoke on the Water' (1981). Premiering at London's National Film Theatre in 2002, they then toured the United States with it (including the Chicago World Music Festival, the Kennedy Center and the Harvard University Sanders Theater). Following this tour, Yat-kha won the Asia/Pacific category of the BBC Radio 3 World Music Awards.

Although overtone-singing was traditionally the province of men, during the 1990s the Tyvans Sainkho Namchylak and Tyva Kyzy began to challenge this gender divide. Having trained musically in Moscow and toured internationally with the Tyvan State Folk Ensemble *Sayani*, Sainkho left for Moscow in the mid-1980s. Her first CD for CramWorld, *Out of Tyva* (1993), includes recordings from these periods ('arranged' traditional sounds of the ensemble in Kyzyl, experiments with large Russian orchestras in Moscow, with French composer/producer Hector Zazou, and on the Moscow free-jazz scene) as well as her later improvised vocal wailings (incorporating overtone-singing and natural sounds). Her fusions of experimental jazz, electronic music, hip-hop, and drum 'n' bass make for dissonant, disorientating and challenging listening. Her later recorded output includes the entirely improvised *Lost Rivers* (1991) and the more melodic *Naked Spirit* (1998), recorded with Armenian *duduk* oboe-player Djivan Gasparan. In 2000, she released *Stepmother City*. The three-piece band Tyva Kyzy has met with some opposition from traditionally minded Tyvans, particularly men.

Although Tyvans have dominated the world music scene, a few bands from other areas have also produced CDs. The three-piece Khakas group Sabjilar ('The Messengers'), formed in 1997, have released CDs that try to perpetuate 'authentic' Khakas music, such as *Syr Chome* (1999) with its nomadic songs of the steppes, hunting songs of the mountain taiga, and epics that connect their peoples to the Kyrgyz Khanate of the sixth to twelfth centuries. *Khai* performer Sergei Charkov, who makes and plays the Khakas zither (*chatkhan*), fiddle (*yykh*), pipe (*khobyrakh*) and shaman's drum (*tüür*) for his own group (Sabjilar) and for others, works closely with traditional musicians but is also active on the international stage. The Tyvan shaman Ai-Churek and the Altaian musician and singer Sarymai have also reached an international audience through the California-based label, management and touring agency, Pure Nature Music.

Bibliography

Abramovich-Gomon, Alla. 1999. *The Nenets' Song: A Microcosm of a Vanishing Culture*. Aldershot: Ashgate.

Aksenov, A.N. 1973 [1964]. 'Tuvin Folk Music.' *Asian Music* 4(2): 7–18.

Bours, Etienne. 1991. *Musiques des peuples de l'arctique: analyse discographie* [Musics of Arctic Peoples: Discographical Analysis]. Belgium: Médiathèque de la Communauté française de Belgique.

Cornwall, Jane. 2000. 'Sainkho Namtchulak: In a World of Her Own.' *Songlines* (Autumn/Winter): 22.

Lecomte, Henri. 1992–96. Sleeve notes to *Sibérie*. 5 vols. Buda Records: Musique du Monde.

Nattiez, Jean Jacques. 1999. 'Inuit Throat-games and Siberian Throat-singing.' *Ethnomusicology* 43(3): 399–418.

Pegg, Carole. 2000a. 'Mongolia and Tuva: Sixty Horses in My Herd.' *World Music: The Rough Guide*, Vol. 2. London: Rough Guides Ltd., 189–97.

Pegg, Carole. 2000b. 'Music of Siberian Peoples.' Review article. *British Journal of Ethnomusicology* 9(2): 159–64.

Pegg, Carole. 2001a. *Mongolian Music, Dance and Oral Narrative: Performing Diverse Identities*. Washington and London: University of Washington Press.

Pegg, Carole. 2001b. 'Overtone-singing.' In *The New Grove Dictionary of Music and Musicians*, Vol. 18, ed. Stanley Sadie. 2nd ed. London: Macmillan, 821–24.

Sheikin, Yuri. 2001. 'Russian Federation, §II, 3: Siberian Peoples.' In *The New Grove Dictionary of Music and Musicians*, Vol. 22, ed. Stanley Sadie. 2nd ed. London: Macmillan, 17–33.

Van Tongeren, Mark C. 2002. *Overtone-Singing: Physics and Metaphysics of Harmonics in East and West*. The Netherlands: Fusica.

Vertkov, K., et al. 1975 [1963]. 'Musical Instruments of the Peoples Inhabiting the USSR.' *Atlas muzikal'nikh instrumentov naradov SSR*. Four floppy disks and English summary. Moscow: State Publishers.

Discographical References

Chirgilchin. *The Wolf and the Kid*. Shanachie 64070. *1996*: USA.

Deep Purple. 'Smoke on the Water.' *Deep Purple in Concert*. Portrait 38050. *1981*: UK.

Hörekteer. 2002: Tyva.

Huun-Huur-Tu. *If I'd Been Born an Eagle*. Shanachie 64080. *1997*: USA.

Huun-Huur-Tu. *60 Horses in My Herd: Old Songs and Tunes of Tuva*. Shanachie 64050. *1993*: USA.

Huun-Huur-Tu. *The Orphan's Lament*. Jaro 4204-2. 1994; *1997*: Germany.

Pink Floyd. 'Money.' *Delicate Sound of Thunder*. Columbia 44484. *1988*: USA.

Sabiljar. *Syr Chome*. Pure Nature Music PNM CD003. *1999*: Russia/USA.

Sainkho Namtchylak. *Lost Rivers*. FMP CD 42. *1991*: Germany.

Sainkho Namtchylak. *Naked Spirit*. Amiata ARNR 2298. *1998*: Italy/UK.

Sainkho Namtchylak. *Out of Tyva*. CramWord/Crammed Discs CRAW 6. *1993*: Belgium.

Sainkho Namtchylak. *Stepmother City*. Ponderosa CD003. *2000*: Italy.

Salchak, Boris et al. *Shaman*. Meltdown BW2112. *2000*: South Africa.

Shu-De. *Kongurei*. Dunya Records. *1996*: Italy.

Shu-De. *Voices from the Distant Steppe*. Real World RW41. *1994*: The Netherlands.

Tuva: Voices from the Centre of Asia. Smithsonian Folkways 40017. *1990*: USA.

Vargyas, Lajos. *Mongolian Folk Music*. Hungaroton LPX18013-14. *1967*: Hungary.

Yat-kha. *Dalai Beldiri*. BMG/Wicklow 09026 63351-2. *1999*: UK/Ireland.

Yat-kha. *Tuva.rock*. Yat-kha Recordings YAT 003. *2003*: UK.

Yat-kha. *Yenesei-Punk*. Global Music Centre GMCD 9504. *1995*: Finland.

Discography

Ai-Churek. Pure Nature Music PNM 005. *2003*: USA.

Deep in the Heart of Tuva: Cowboy Music from the Wild East. Ellipsis Arts 4080. *1996*: USA.

Musiques de la toundra et de la taiga. URSS: Bouriates, Yacoutes, Toungouses, Nenets et Nganasan. Inédit: Maison des Cultures du Monde. 1987; *1990*: USA.

The Spirit of the Steppes: Throat Singing from Tuva and Beyond. Nascente NSCD 058. *2000*: UK.

Filmography

Storm Over Asia: The Heir of Genghis Khan ('Potomok Chingis Khana'), dir. Vsevolod I. Pudovkin. 1928. USSR. 82 mins.

CAROLE PEGG

5. Southeast Asia

Brunei

Population: 358,098 (2003)

The Sultanate of Brunei is a small, wealthy country that lies on the northwest coast of the island of Borneo. It has a land area of 2,252 sq miles (5,765 sq km) and a coastline of approximately 100 miles (161 km) along the South China Sea. Brunei shares a common border with the east Malaysian state, Sarawak. Lying just four degrees north of the equator, Brunei has a tropical climate with high temperatures, high humidity and heavy rainfall. The full name of the country is 'Negara Brunei Darussalam.'

Brunei is a constitutional monarchy that has been ruled by the same family for over six centuries. Its influence over other regions (most notably the Philippines) peaked in the sixteenth and seventeenth centuries. In 1888, Brunei officially became a British protectorate. It later achieved independence, in 1984. Its economy is mainly dependent on gas and oil, which are the country's primary natural resources. His Majesty the Sultan Haji Hassanal Bolkiah Mu'izzaddin Waddaulah has been both the chief of state and head of the government since 5 October 1967. The capital of Brunei is Bandar Seri Begawan, which is also the nation's center of education, culture and administration. The official language of Brunei is Malay, although English and some Chinese dialects are also widely spoken. Islam is the state's official religion, with his Majesty the Sultan and Yang Di-Pertuan as the head of the Islamic faith in the country. Christianity and Buddhism are also practiced in Brunei.

Since the sixteenth century Brunei Darussalam has been and continues to be a country of 'Melayu Islam Berjaya' (Malay Islamic Monarchy). 'Melayu Islam Berjaya' is often referred to within Brunei as simply 'MIB,' and can be regarded as an ideology, as a set of values, and even as a way of life within the country. Brunei's culture is derived from and based on Malay culture. This is true historically and in contemporary society, and is officially acknowledged as the guideline and motivation for the country.

Social life in Brunei is often described as being wholesome, with almost no nightlife similar to that which is found in urban areas of many other countries. There are no nightclubs, discos or pubs. Alcohol is not sold in Brunei, although non-Muslim visitors are allowed to bring a small amount of alcoholic beverages into the country for personal consumption. Although not actually nightclubs, some hotels feature live performances by bands in coffee houses or lobby lounges.

As a small country with virtually no nightlife it is very difficult for musicians in Brunei to survive unless they can develop a following in one or both of its two nearest geographic and linguistic neighbors, Malaysia and Indonesia. As a result, the few existing commercial recordings which feature performing artists from Brunei have generally been produced and recorded in Malaysia or Indonesia. For example, in 2001, Bruneian singer Dayangku Rofeza released a recording, *Kuserahkan*, of *dangdut* music that was produced and recorded in Indonesia. The music on this recording, like music performed by other Bruneian musicians who primarily take part in live stage shows, shares stylistic characteristics with popular music in Malaysia and Indonesia.

One of the principle venues for music performance in Brunei is the concert program broadcast on Radio Television Brunei (RTB). The station works closely with, and periodically hosts joint performances with, the Radio Television Malaysia (RTM) Orchestra, which further enhances the close cultural connections between these two countries.

Live concert performances by local and foreign musicians are also frequently arranged in the Jerudong Park Playground, a large amusement center with rides, polo and golf facilities, in addition to an amphitheater used for the concerts. As well as the live performances at this venue by well known US and European popular musicians, residents of Brunei have ready access to popular music from Malaysia, Indonesia, the Philippines and other Asian countries through similar concerts and recordings.

Although Bruneian musicians and critics talk about the need to develop a unique style of popular music for Brunei, the factors mentioned above make this very difficult. In the early years of the twenty-first century, young musicians from Brunei formed hip-hop bands that gained popularity and were being promoted by way of web sites such as http://www.bruscene.com/

Bibliography

BRUscene. http://www.bruscene.com/

Borneo Bulletin Brunei Yearbook. 2001. Brunei Darussalam: Brunei Press Sdn. Bhd.

Gorlinski, Virginia. 2001. 'Brunei.' In *The New Grove Dictionary of Music and Musicians*, Vol. 4, ed. John Tyrell and Stanley Sadie. London: Macmillan, 503–505.

Leake, David Jr. 1989. *Brunei: The Modern Southeast-Asian Islamic Sultanate*. London: McFarland & Co. Inc.

Saunders, Graham E. 2002. *History of Brunei*. 2nd ed. London: Routledge Curzon.

Discographical Reference

Dayangku Rofeza. *Kuserahkan*. Irama Konsortium. *2001*: Indonesia.

JIM CHOPYAK

Cambodia

Population: 13,124,764 (2003)

Cambodia is bordered by Laos to the north, Vietnam to the east, the Gulf of Thailand to the south and Thailand to the north and west. Its

population is mainly Khmer (more than 90 percent), but also includes smaller numbers of Vietnamese, Chinese, Khmer Leu (Highland Khmer) and Cham (Muslim). The capital of Cambodia is Phnom Penh.

By the beginning of the Christian era (first century A.D.), Kaundinya (believed to be a Brahman) had set to sea from India to conquer and defeat the indigenous Queen Soma of Cambodia, whom he wedded. He was crowned as the first King of Funan (Founan), the center of which was situated on the lower Mekong delta with its territory covering the southern part of present-day Vietnam, the middle Mekong and large parts of the Menam valley and the Malay Peninsula.

At the beginning of the eighth century, the country was divided into two states, Chenla Kok in the north and Chenla Toeuk in the south. In 802, Jayavarman II, having taken refuge in Java at the confutation of succession, liberated and unified Chenla, founding the kingdom of Angkor. This was the most glorious period of Khmer history in terms of military power, territorial expansion, health care, educational achievement, agricultural development and cultural expression. On the walls of the great temples constructed during this period in the Angkor vicinity are carved *apsara* (celestial dancers), figures with musical instruments: *pinn* (harp), *khse muoy* (musical bow), *sralai* (quadruple-reed oboe), *korng vung* (semicircular gong chime), *chhing* (small hand cymbals), *sampho* (small double-headed barrel drum), *skor yol* (suspended barrel drum) and *skor thomm* (large double-headed barrel drum). The similarity between the carvings and present-day Khmer instruments suggests strong musical links between the two periods.

During the twelfth century, Mahayana Buddhism had strong royal support and consequently became the state religion; by the beginning of the fourteenth century, the Khmers had converted to Theravada Buddhism, which has been practiced up to the present. The death of Jayavarman VII in 1219 (1181–1219) ended this period. Under his successor, Khmer power began to decline; in 1432, Angkor was abandoned to the Siamese. After the fall of Angkor, the country was unstable and unable to resist foreign invasions. Finally, with the help of the Siamese in 1842, Ang Duong ascended the throne and reigned until 1860; during this period Khmer arts saw a revival.

On 11 August 1863, three years after King Ang Duong's death, the Khmer kingdom became a French protectorate. Independence from the French

was proclaimed on 9 November 1953 by Prince Norodom Sihanouk, who then gave up his throne in 1955 and became Head of State. On 18 March 1970, Prince Sihanouk was overthrown in a military coup and Marshal Lon Nol created the Khmer Republic. On 17 April 1975, the Khmer Rouge took over; in their reign of terror (1975–79), during which some 2 million Khmers were killed, classical dancers were enemies of the state and revolutionary propaganda was the only recognized form of art. The Khmer Rouge were deposed on 7 January 1979, and national elections in May 1993 resulted in a national constitution, a coalition government and the reinstallation of the monarchy.

Cambodia under the Khmer Rouge was devastated, its inhabitants left in extreme poverty and with deteriorated health. Illiteracy was widespread, as was a sense of mistrust and hopelessness. Among the millions of lives lost in this period were those of 80–90 percent of Cambodia's artists – dancers, musicians, instrument-makers, painters and sculptors. Schools, libraries and theaters were systematically closed and demolished. As a result, artists afterwards lacked venues to present their works. As people were poor, they could not afford to pay for any entertainment. Artists themselves had to spend time earning extra income to make ends meet.

Introduction of Western Music and the Birth and Development of Popular Music in Cambodia

Western music first came to Cambodia during the sixteenth century with the Portuguese spice trade in Asia. However, recorded accounts only point to a twentieth-century European presence and the introduction of Western classical music, including chamber music and symphonic works. By the 1950s, with the establishment of l'Ecole Nationale de Musique (National School of Music), Khmer musicians were learning Western classical music, its harmonies and musical notations.

Western popular music and dances were introduced to Khmers by the Filipinos and the French. In the early 1900s, the Khmer court received the gift of a large band in residence from the Philippines. The Filipino musicians taught marching music to Khmer royal symphonic bands, participated in court ensembles and performed in jazz bands at nightclubs. The musicians introduced Latin rhythms – cha-cha, bolero, tango, bossa nova, rumba as well as the waltz, fox trot, madison, twist and other slow dances into Khmer dance, forming big bands that played at ballroom dances. Their music came to be called *phleng Manil* or 'Manila music.'

Western music was also disseminated by French high school teachers; and in some military academies, high-ranking officers received formal training in European-derived dances. The madison, for instance, was in vogue by the 1950s, and the twist was introduced by the popular entertainer Kem Chum upon his return from France in the early 1960s (Chen et al. 1993, 67).

The growth and development of urban popular music in Cambodia from the 1950s were influenced by the protectionism of the few individuals who controlled popular music in Cambodia, namely, Has Salan, Mer Bun, Peou Sipho and Voy Ho. Popular music was very difficult to get into for those who were not part of this scene. The country's most popular artists were Sin Sisamouth, Sos Math, Ros Serey Sothea, Pen Ran, Mao Sareth and Huoy Meas.

Sin Sisamouth has been regarded by the Khmers, both musicians and listeners, as the best Khmer popular singer of all time. The height of his popularity occurred during the pre-Khmer Rouge period (pre-1970s). He embraced all styles of popular music during this period, from Latin to European, from adapted Khmer to adapted Asian and Western. Sisamouth was referred to as the 'King of Golden Voice' (Sar 2000, 22). Even at the start of the twenty-first century, he was every musician's mentor and inspiration, his great voice just as popular as it was during the 1960s and 1970s. Many of his old recordings continue to be re-mastered, improving the overall sound quality or with the addition of some instruments. Others write new lyrics to his old melodies. He had more best-selling recordings than any other Khmer musician, such as 'Champey Siem Reap,' 'Champa Phsar Leu,' 'Pravah Sre Praing' and 'Kamrang Phka Phuong.'

Robaim pracheaprey (popular dance) is ubiquitous in Cambodia, involving people of all ages and both genders. Included in all social events, it is accompanied by a modern popular band made up of electric guitars, electric basses, keyboards, drumsets and vocals (latterly, there has been a move toward replacing the electric guitar with a second keyboard). Larger bands also include wind and string sections. Songs are often based on rhythms borrowed from Latin American music (e.g., cha-cha, bolero and bossa nova), with Khmer melodies and lyrics written anew. Cover versions of Western popular music are also performed. However, the most popular songs employ Khmer rhythms, including *roam vung, roam kbach, saravane* and *laim*

Leav. What makes them particularly Khmer is the melody and performing style.

Khmer musicians have retained imported rhythms and composed Khmer melodies and lyrics to each song. Borrowed foreign melodies have also been set with Khmer lyrics, including 'I Don't Want to Sleep Alone,' and 'My Heart Will Go On' from the soundtrack to the movie *Titanic* (1997). Straight cover versions of well-known songs are also popular. Throughout the 1990s and beyond, new rhythms and dances infused Khmer community dance events, including the *macarena* and the electric slide dances.

At parties, musicians usually perform dances in pairs, one in slow tempo, the other fast. *Roam vung* is always the first dance at any social event. Khmer traditional dances (*roam vung, roam kbach, saravane* and *laim Leav*) are all couple dances, danced in a circle with the men behind and the women moving in an anticlockwise direction; the host or some other prominent person leads. The woman leads the man, moving from side to side and seeking eye contact; these dances are an important part of courtship.

Themes of Khmer popular music have changed according to the moods of the time in Cambodia. During times of peace, for instance, songs are of love, separation, jealousy, or the everyday life of the Khmer people. These themes are easily understood, and touch the hearts of millions of listeners across age and gender. During times of war, music is more concerned with political ideologies and struggles and revolutionary activities. Oftentimes, in such situations, songs are used as a means of political propaganda.

Khmer Music Companies in Cambodia and Abroad

In the 1960s and 1970s, only a handful of music companies existed in Cambodia, exclusively in its capital city of Phnum Penh. Those few companies were Chan Chhaya, Heng Heng, Vann Chann, Wat Phnom, Chab Meas and Nokor Reach (Sar 2000, 22). The production of Khmer popular music continued to grow rapidly, thanks to technology that facilitated the production and dissemination of affordable recordings. Catering mainly for the overseas Khmer market at the turn of the century (the overseas market offers far greater profits than the home market), Khmer-language CDs were being produced in great numbers by several companies, two of the biggest being Chlangden Productions (owned by Thoeung Son) and Angkor Wat Music

Productions (owned by Yvette Sam). The majority of sales are in Western countries with large Khmer populations, primarily the United States, Australia, Canada and France. The audiocassette, which costs a fraction of the price of a CD, is the most popular and affordable medium for the Khmers in Cambodia. In deciding what will be the next release, music companies in Cambodia assign people to scout nightclubs to see which Khmer or foreign songs prompt the most reaction. The next hit song is the one that produces a stampede toward the dance floor.

Popular Music in Cambodia at the Turn of the Millennium

Popular Khmer musicians of the twenty-first century include those who were stars of the 1950s–1970s, as well as fresh new talent. Popular singers of a younger and new generation include Meng Keo Pichda (aka Meng Keo Pich Chenda), Him Sivorn, Touch Sun Nich, Khath Sokhim, Kim Leakhena, Noy Vanneth, Nou Sip, Chhoeun Uddam, Kong Sodina and Lo Sarith.

By the beginning of the twenty-first century, almost every large restaurant in Cambodia employed a live band. Some even employed up to a dozen singers, who could earn a good living in restaurants and nightclubs. However, some performers – such as Meng Keo Pichda, Touch Sun Nich and Noy Vanneth – were able to make enough money simply by recording and singing for special events, in this way polishing their image and reputation.

Conclusion

Cambodia is endowed with a rich culture. Functioning within an agrarian society, year-round ceremonies and festivals are organized involving customs and traditions that call for theater, dance and music. Since the late twentieth century, there have been approximately two dozen music ensembles functioning within the contexts of ceremonies and festivals. However, the Khmer traditional music they have been performing seems to be catering to the old, whereas young Khmers overwhelmingly enjoy so-called 'popular music.'

While Khmer traditional music struggles to survive, therefore, the music most popular in Cambodia in the twenty-first century is largely of Western origin. This is particularly the case among young people, who are willing to pay for this kind of entertainment. As a consequence, Khmer language rock or popular music produced by the Khmer music industry is in great demand and is easily available for purchase both in the home market and in the stores of Asian communities worldwide. Increased wealth and freedom among the general population have led to a liberalization of the music market, with far less protectionism than in the early years of popular music. The market remains fiercely competitive.

Among Khmer communities worldwide, social dancing helps bring individuals and families together at celebrations and fundraising activities. Many Khmers reminisce about dancing the *roam vung*, *roam kbach*, *saravane* and *laim Leav* to the accompaniment of the *tror* (two-string fiddle), *skor dey* (goblet drum) and *chamrieng* (vocals) in the Cambodian rice fields at the completion of planting and harvest in days long gone.

Bibliography

Cambodia. 1994. Phnom Penh: Ministry of Tourism.

Chap, Pin. 1964. *Danses populaires au Cambodge* [Popular Dances in Cambodia]. Phnom Penh: Iditions de l'Institut Bouddhique.

Chen, Vivian, et al. 1993. 'Sharing Common Ground: Social Dancing in the USA.' *1993 Festival of American Folklife*. Washington, DC: Smithsonian Institution, 63–68.

Sar, Rumanea. 2000. 'Peou Sipho: A Song Writer.' *Popular Magazine* (October): 22.

Discographical References

Meng, Keo Pichda. 'My Heart Will Go On.' *Samut Moha Alai*. Chlangden Productions 300. *1999*: USA.

Sin, Sisamouth. 'Champa Phsar Leu.' *Ar Sach Choun Mday*. Preah Chan Penh Vung Productions 2. *1996*: USA.

Sin, Sisamouth. 'Champey Siem Reap.' *Siklo*. Chan Chhaya 9. *1974*: Cambodia.

Sin, Sisamouth. 'Cheung Phnom Sampeou.' *Chamrieng Sin Sisamouth*. Golden Snake Productions 1. n.d.: Cambodia.

Sin, Sisamouth. 'Kamrang Phka Phuong.' *Ramvong*. Apsara Productions n.s. *n.d.*: Cambodia.

Sin, Sisamouth. 'Pravah Sre Praing.' *Phka Srah Krapum*. Golden Butterfly Productions 6. n.d.: USA.

Van, Vath Theany. 'I Don't Like to Sleep Alone.' *Chev Touk Rork Sne*. Preah Chan Penh Vung Productions. n.d.: USA.

Discography

Chheam Anatha. Stoeung Sangke Productions 731. n.d.: USA.

Lo, Sarith. *Muoy Meun Alai*. Rasmey Hang Meas 43.

n.d.: USA. (Dedication album in memory of Lo Sarith.)

Sam, Sam-Ang. *Hang Khnhomm-Saum Bang Vill Vinh.* Sen Monorom Productions SMP NCD001. *1999*: USA.

Sam, Sam-Ang. *Patriotic and Traditional Khmer Songs.* Cambodian Business Corporation International PTKS90-SS-NT001. *1990*: USA.

Sam, Sam-Ang. *Spean Yol.* Amarin-Rangsey Productions ARP NCD001. *2001*: USA.

Sin, Sisamouth. *Chamrieng Roam Vung Chamrauh.* Chlangden Productions 066. n.d.: USA.

Sin, Sisamouth. *Rasmey Kampuchea, Vol. 3.* SM Productions. *2001*: Cambodia.

Filmography

Titanic, dir. James Cameron. 1997. USA. 195 mins. Romantic epic. Original music by James Horner.

SAM-ANG SAM

Indonesia

Population: 234,893,453 (2003)

Upon the collapse of Japanese occupation of the Dutch East Indies during World War II, the Republic of Indonesia, under the leadership of Sukarno, declared its independence in August 1945, but several years of fighting between the colonial and native powers ensued before the United Nations succeeded in bringing the parties to agree on independence in 1949. Factional struggles over the form the independent government was to take pitted various groups against one another; these ranged from those wanting a socialist government to those wanting an Islamic republic. A compromise was reached in which five basic principles (Pancasila) of the state, first formulated by Sukarno in 1945, were adopted as the foundation of government in the provisional constitutions of 1949 and 1950; in the latter year, the various federal units existing at the time were collapsed into the Republic of Indonesia. The principles of Pancasila are: (a) monotheistic belief; (b) just and civilized humanitarianism; (c) Indonesian unity; (d) democracy guided by wise policy arising from deliberation and representation; and (e) social justice for all the people of Indonesia.

Sukarno, whose anti-colonialism had made him suspicious of the West and sympathetic to socialism, led Indonesia as president from 1945 until 1966, when he was dismissed by the People's Consultative Assembly, which had three years earlier appointed him president for life. In 1959 he had declared martial law and a policy of so-called Guided Democracy, appointing himself prime minister and replacing the provisional constitution of 1950 with the original one of 1945 because factionalism made it impossible for parliament to agree on one. His last significant act was in 1966, when he signed a letter transferring executive authority to General Suharto, who had put down an abortive coup on 30 September 1965. There followed a massacre of hundreds of thousands of Indonesians accused of having Communist sympathies – how many hundreds remains a matter of uncertainty; among them was a disproportionate number of Chinese, an ethnic group resented for its control of native commerce and its alleged links with Chinese Communism.

Upon Suharto's rise to power – he became Acting President in March 1967, and was elected to the position by the People's Consultative Assembly a year later – there began a 30-year period of developing social stability, political conservatism and openness to foreign investment known as the New Order. During this time, the general standard of living in Indonesia improved significantly for a sizable portion of the population, while Suharto became one of the richest people in the world. Because of endemic corruption, which benefited primarily the Suharto family and its associates, the Southeast Asian economic collapse of 1998 hit Indonesia most severely, reducing the rupiah, the unit of currency, to a fifth of its value a year earlier and virtually wiping out many gains of the previous 30 years. As a result of pressure brought to bear by popular demonstrations, led initially by students of Javanese universities but taken up by rioting mobs in the capital city Jakarta, Suharto was advised by senior army officers to resign the presidency, and on 21 May 1998 he stepped down in favor of B.J. Habibie, a German-trained aeronautical engineer who had been Suharto's protégé from his youth and one of the benefactors of his nepotistic financial policies. Habibie kept his promise to hold popular elections in 1999 and, as a result, Abdurrahman Wahid, leader of the nation's most populous organization, became president until he was forced to relinquish office less than a year later in favor of Vice President Megawati Soekarnoputri, daughter of the founder of the Republic.

An archipelago of more than 13,000 islands stretching across 3,000 miles eastward from the Indian Ocean, Indonesia has numerous ethnic and linguistic groups which are united by a single national language, Bahasa Indonesia. A variety of Malay (native to the islands of the Riau archipelago and the nearby shores of the Strait of Malacca which separates Indonesian Sumatera (Sumatra) from the nation of Malaysia), it is the medium of school instruction and has come to be widely understood throughout the country. Another variety of Malay, Bahasa Melayu, has become the national language of Malaysia and is one of the four languages of Singapore.

With a population of over 200 million, the Republic of Indonesia is the fourth most populous country in the world, and more than half the population is concentrated on its third-largest island, Jawa (Java). Despite its population density and the historical importance of the literature of the Javanese-speaking people on the eastern two-thirds of the island, Malay (Bahasa Indonesia) has been fostered as the national tongue because it has long served as a lingua franca of trade in the area and it is more egalitarian than Javanese, whose intricate distinctions of vocabulary and syntax reflect and support traditional social stratification.

As between 85 and 90 percent of its inhabitants consider themselves Muslims, Indonesia has a larger Islamic community than any other nation in the world. Two major Islamic organizations have a profound impact on the populace. Muhammadiyah, a Protestant return-to-the-scripture movement, has its origins in late nineteenth-century Egyptian reform movements, and it has continued to have a cosmopolitan outlook. Nahdlatul Ulama, more accommodating to native influences on Islam, was long under the leadership of Abdurrahman Wahid, who was briefly president. Well known for his love of music, Wahid's eclectic tastes include the music of Beethoven and Umm Kulthūm as well as that of performers such as Jimmy Page and Robert Plant. While he may not have been a fan or approved of the infamous Inul Daratista, who took Indonesia by storm in 2003 when she accompanied her *dangdut* singing with a local version of the 'bump and grind' known as '*ngebor*' or 'drilling,' he was among those who defended her right to perform against those such as the pop superstar Rhoma Irama, who thought that her act sullied the pop song style he had striven to make a medium for Islamic predication.

The complex colonial history of Indonesia has left its mark on the musical culture of the archipelago, and in the realm of popular music the well-known genre *kroncong* evolved from seeds planted by the Portuguese. The Portuguese first established themselves in the area in 1511 by capturing the important entrepôt of Melaka (Ma-

laysia), which had been founded a century earlier by a Hindu Sumatran prince whose descendants had converted to Islam. Near the extremity of the Portuguese trade routes, the area received 'Portuguese,' who were a diverse group of native and miscegenated peoples from the Iberian peninsula and from other Portuguese ports in Africa, India and Ceylon, and who undoubtedly added some elements of their own to the Portuguese tunes they transmitted. The community of *mardijkers*, Catholic slaves of 'Portuguese' heritage in Batavia who were freed by the Dutch upon converting to Protestantism, was particularly associated with *kroncong* in the late nineteenth and early twentieth centuries. The *mardijkers*' small ensembles of Western-type plucked lutes included a ukulele-like instrument onomatopoeically called *kroncong*.

'Kroncong Morisko,' the tune that might be considered emblematic of the *kroncong* genre, refers in its title to this mixed heritage. At the end of the twentieth century, well-to-do Jakartans were singing it to the accompaniment of laser discs in karaoke parlors, and the ordinary citizen heard it from serenading buskers while grabbing a quick lunch at a curbside foodstall or while commuting on a crowded bus. With its meandering melody, it typifies an older, traditional and anonymous style. 'Bengawan Solo,' on the other hand, by the composer Gesang, with its romantic nationalistic text and AABA, 32-bar form, represents a newer style from the period of Japanese occupation that became a nostalgic classic in Indonesia and much of Southeast Asia, as well as in Japan.

Although strongly associated with Java, *kroncong* is widely spread throughout Indonesia, but it may elsewhere be known by other names – as among the Makassarese of South Sulawesi, who call it *losquin*. *Kroncong*-style songs appear in many new transformations, illustrating how varied the musical resources of Indonesia are. It is possible, for example, to hear *kroncong* mixed with the Sundanese (West Java) style known as *jaipongan* or even to hear covers of Elvis Presley hits like 'Can't Help Falling in Love' or 'Love Me Tender' rendered in English with a *kroncong* accompaniment.

Sundanese *jaipongan* often combines gamelan-accompanied vocals in regional seven-tone scales with a pentatonic *slendro saron* (bronze slab-key instrument) of Java; it derives from an itinerant dancing girl tradition and has become popular in clubs and other venues in Bandung, the major city of the region, as well in other parts of the country. The popularity of *jaipongan*, the first regionally based music to have achieved popularity outside its own area, is largely due to the efforts of its creator Gugum Gumbira and his Jugala group, who presented formalized stage shows beginning in the mid-1970s and distributed cassettes under their own Jugala label. Having been inspired in his youth by the nationalistic agenda of the late Old Order period, Gugum found inspiration for *jaipongan* in Sundanese musical styles and instrumentation and avoided reference to Western sources.

Western musical influences are by no means the only ones of importance to fertilize the popular music of Indonesia. The fact that the country is overwhelmingly Islamic in religious orientation means that it has long been receptive to various cultural influences from Arabic-speaking peoples. Since Islam has an ambivalent attitude toward musical performance, debate over the propriety of music forms part of the Islamic discourse in Indonesia, as elsewhere in the Islamic world. Most acceptable in a continuum of acceptability is the unaccompanied cantillation of the Qur'an in Arabic musical modes. Although a very demanding vocal art, it is not classified as singing, and while far from any generally accepted concept of the 'popular,' its practice in Indonesia was popularized through nationally sponsored competitions, instructional cassettes, call-in radio shows and the growing prominence of female reciters of great artistry, the latter a phenomenon quite contrary to the principles of male Egyptian cantillators, who are the models.

In the continuum of acceptability beginning with Qur'anic recitation, genres derived from Arabic models and modernized with the addition of Western instruments are suspect to some but quite respectable to the great majority in Indonesia. *Qasidah*, which originally used Arabic texts and tunes and was accompanied solely by frame drums, began to adopt modernized instrumentation and Indonesian language in the 1970s and became popular in this form with a more conservative and traditional public who find the music, with its occasional Arabic tinge, an acceptable vehicle for moralizing texts. At the same time, the fact that one of the most popular groups, Nasida Ria, is an all-female band is evidence that a pious aesthetic is not the only factor ensuring its appeal.

While history records the presence of Arabic traders and princes in the area from the period of early European contact (see reference to Melaka above), a great influx of Yemenis during the nineteenth and twentieth centuries had a particular impact in introducing a regional variant of popular

Arabic culture. *Gambus* is the name of both a musical genre and an instrument, now commonly the Egyptian *'ūd* but originally a narrower, shallower lute from the Arabian peninsula. The genre, closely associated with Yemeni Arabs, spread throughout the archipelago in varying forms and became, along with *zapin*, its accompanying Yemeni-derived dance, an element of popular Islamic culture. The dance, usually performed at wedding parties by male couples among Arabo-Indonesians, became folkloricized to include mixed couples in large choreographed ensembles, particularly associated with the Malay cultural areas of Sumatra and Malaysia.

At the far end of the continuum of acceptability in the narrow Islamic view, *dangdut* is nevertheless the most universally popular indigenous genre of popular music. It too, however, lays claim to Islamic credentials by often being a vehicle for homiletic texts. Growing out of an earlier form of indigenous pop, *orkes Melayu*, which had a somewhat sleazy reputation, *dangdut* attained popularity in the mid-1970s when Rhoma Irama and Elvy Sukaesih teamed up to perform songs in which Rhoma combined the vocal quality and style of tunes familiar to Indonesians from Hindi films with rock instrumentation and the tabla and flute of his Indian models. Once famously vilified as 'dog turds,' *dangdut* was given its less insulting but nonetheless derogatory onomatopoeic name by those who found the strong upbeat-downbeat strokes on the tabla objectionable because of their inducement to physical movement. The early audiences for public performances of *dangdut* (consisting almost exclusively of young males) often caused concern about rowdiness, but Rhoma Irama's Islamic piety ensured that problems at such venues were less likely than at other types of pop concerts. Originally suspect to the respectable and associated with lower socioeconomic classes, *dangdut* induced its admirers among the well-to-do to join a general approbation, and even high government officials have begun to compose songs and perform them in public. As a consequence, *dangdut* lost some of its Islamic associations in favor of more romantic lyrics.

Western popular music on cassette and disc, as well as live concerts ranging from Chicago jazz groups to alternative rock bands, have a considerable impact on urban youth, but overall the popular music industry is dominated by local forces:

Of all the cultural industries, [the music industry] is the only one which can withstand the invasion of foreign pop cultures ... The Indonesian public may prefer Hollywood films and TV series to local ones, but they still listen to the local music ... [B]etween seven and eight million cassettes circulate here every month, 80 percent of which is local music. No Western music has outsold local music in terms of sales. (Simbolon 1995)

Like much other local entrepreneurship, that of the manufacturing and distribution of music cassettes – CDs have been uncommon for the local music because they are prohibitively expensive – is largely in the hands of the Indonesian Chinese. Since the late 1990s, VCDs (videodiscs) have become a widespread medium for popular music. VCDs make karaoke more easily available, as the discs and the players are much cheaper than the earlier technology of laser discs which were confined to the wealthier classes. Although a few composers may be able to negotiate royalty payments for their songs, most receive a single payment. At the end of the twentieth century, the half-dozen transnational media giants were prohibited from operating in Indonesia, but it was hoped that they would be allowed to do so in the future, a prospect many composers welcomed because of their eagerness for royalty contracts.

Aside from widely available cassettes, by the beginning of the twenty-first century popular music was heard everywhere on the broadcast media. The state-owned broadcast service, continuing policies begun in the colonial period, had the rather staid quality of most such non-commercial enterprises, and the yearly performance competition it sponsored to find new singing stars continued to use the long-established categories of 'seriosa,' 'kroncong' and 'lagu hiburan' (the first category is somewhat like operetta tunes; the last are like popular ballads). Livelier fare entered the media with the advent of private commercial stations which broadcast live performances and music videos by the most popular groups, both local and foreign. Among urban youth, current international styles like metal, alternative and grunge gained an increasing following, as their association with protest against the status quo appealed to feelings of frustration and anger against the government. Iwan Fals, a protest rocker, and Kantata Takwa, an Islamically oriented metal group led by the millionaire businessman Setiawan Djody, had devoted followers, but Slank, with gritty music and cynical lyrics, was among the most commercially successful bands of the 1990s,

and benefited from the growing awareness of and interest in current trends in international pop.

From an older, Beatles-inspired generation, the group Koes Plus was noteworthy as an example of Golden Oldies nostalgia as it reappeared on the scene to considerable popular interest in the 1990s. Other musicians, like the acoustic guitar-based group Bimbo or the rock singer Achmad Albar of the groups God Bless and Gong 2000, had a fairly continuous career over the last two decades of the twentieth century. Albar's father, as his Arabic name might suggest, had been a performer of the sedate gambus, but with the advent of commercial television Achmad's flashy rock star image enabled him to become the focus of an advertising campaign for a leading cigarette brand. Another father-son pair of musicians illustrate a quite different heritage in Indonesian popular music: Jack Lesmana, a well-known jazz pianist during the early national period, has a successor in his son Indra. Indra's pop jazz ballads and instrumentals appeal to urban sophisticates, as does the music of other jazz groups such as Karimata or Krakatau, and all are among the comparatively rare producers of CDs, which can be purchased only by the relatively wealthy (a CD can cost about as much as three weeks' salary for a minimum-wage laborer; even cassettes range from about one to three days' wages).

Traditionally, the only venue for social dancing was a celebratory occasion when male guests would be invited to dance in order of social precedence with a professional singing/dancing girl. With the advent of jaipongan and dangdut, public dancing became more accepted, and young people in cities who had the means might frequent clubs where recorded music was usually played, although the sale of alcohol and the possibilities for promiscuity gave them a salacious reputation. A club like Jamz in Jakarta, where patrons sit at tables to drink and snack while listening to jazz pop groups like Krakatau or visiting foreigners, was rarer.

While much of the rest of the world is relatively unaware of Indonesia, it has been the crossroads of diverse cultures for centuries, and that diversity is apparent in its popular music. Indonesian popular music consumers, in fact, may have a greater variety of musical styles to choose from than their Euro-American counterparts, even with the advent of worldbeat fusions. With the collapse of the economy and the growing mistreatment of ethnic Chinese entrepreneurs in the late twentieth century, the market was in danger of shrinking but the diversity of styles continued.

Bibliography

Baulch, Emma. 1996. 'Punks, Rastas and Head-bangers: Bali's Generation X.' *Inside Indonesia* 48 (October–December). http://serve.com/inside/edit48/emma.htm

Becker, Judith. 1975. 'Kroncong, Indonesian Popular Music.' *Asian Music* 7(1): 14–19.

Frederick, William. 1982. 'Rhoma Irama and the Dangdut Style: Aspects of Contemporary Indonesian Popular Culture.' *Indonesia* 34 (October): 103–30.

Hatch, Martin. 1989. 'Popular Music in Indonesia.' In *World Music, Politics and Social Change: Papers from the International Association for the Study of Popular Music*, ed. Simon Frith. Manchester: Manchester University Press, 49–68.

Heins, Ernst. 1975 'Kroncong and Tanjidor: Two Case Studies of Urban Folk Music in Jakarta.' *Asian Music* 7(1): 20–32.

Hill, David, and Sen, Krishna. 1997. 'Rock 'n' Roll Radicals.' *Inside Indonesia* 52 (October–December).

Kornhauser, Bronia. 1978. 'In Defence of Kroncong.' In *Monash Papers on Southeast Asia No. 7: Studies in Indonesian Music*, ed. Margaret J. Kartomi. Clayton, Victoria: Centre for Southeast Asian Studies, Monash University.

'Malam Final Anugerah Musik Indonesia' [Final Night of Indonesian Music Awards]. 1997. *Kompas* (29 November). http://www.kompas.com/9711/29/HIBURAN/mala.htm

Manuel, Peter. 1988. *Popular Musics of the Non-Western World: An Introductory Survey*. New York: Oxford University Press.

Manuel, Peter, and Baier, Randall. 1986. 'Jaipongan: Indigenous Popular Music of West Java.' *Asian Music* 18(1): 91–110.

Mutsaers, Lutgard. 1990. 'Indorock: An Early Euro-rock Style.' *Popular Music* 9(3): 307–20.

Piper, Suzan, and Jabo, Sawung. 1987. 'Indonesian Music from the 50s to the 80s.' *Prisma* (March): 25–37.

'Pop dan Dangdut Bersaing Merebut Anugerah Musik' [Pop and Dangdut Compete to Snatch the Music Award]. *Suara Pembaruan* (16 November). http://www.suarapembaruan.com/News/1997/11/161197/Musik/ms02.html

Simbolon, Johannes. 1995. 'Indonesian Music Industry Survives Foreign Invasion.' *Jakarta Post* (3 December).

Williams, Sean. 1989-90. 'Current Developments in Sundanese Popular Music.' *Asian Music* 11(1): 105–36.

Yampolsky, Philip. 1987. Notes for *Tonggeret*. Icon Explorer Series 9 79173-2.

Yampolsky, Philip. 1989. 'Hati Yang Luka: An Indonesian Hit.' *Indonesia* (April): 1–17.

Yampolsky, Philip. 1991. Notes for *Music of Indonesia 2: Indonesian Popular Music: Kroncong, Dangdut, and Langgam Jawa*. Smithsonian/Folkways CDSF 40056.

Yampolsky, Philip. 1991. Notes for *Music of Indonesia 3: Music from the Outskirts of Jakarta: Gambang Kromong*. Smithsonian/Folkways CDSF 40057.

Yampolsky, Philip. 1996. Notes for *Music of Indonesia 11: Melayu Music of Sumatra and the Riau Islands*. Smithsonian/Folkways CDSF 40427.

Discographical References

Presley, Elvis. 'Can't Help Falling in Love.' RCA 47-7968. *1961*: USA.

Presley, Elvis. 'Love Me Tender.' RCA 47-6643. *1956*: USA.

Discography

AB Three. *Cintailah Aku*. Program-PT Virgo Ramayana. Cassette 04/96. n.d.: Indonesia.

Bimbo. *24 Karat Golden Album*. Cassette Gema GR-234. n.d.: Indonesia.

Fals, Iwan. *20 Golden Hits*. Cassette Harpa.

Gesang. *Lagu-Lagu Kroncong Asli*. Cassette Pertiwi P039. *1988*: Indonesia.

Gong 2000. *Gong 2000 Live in Jakarta*. Ariesta PCC-002. *1991*: Indonesia.

Hadijdah, Idjah. *Tonggeret*. Icon Explorer Series 9 79173-2. *1987*: USA.

Irama, Rhoma. *Music of Indonesia 2: Indonesian Popular Music: Kroncong, Dangdut, and Langgam Jawa*. Smithsonian/Folkways CDSF 40056. *1991*: USA.

Irama, Rhoma. *22 Seleksi Dangdut*. Cassette Metrotama. *1993*: Indonesia.

Karimata. *Jézz*. Aquarius Ind. CD1935. Indonesia.

Koes Endang, Hetty, and Mulyadi, Mus. *Pop Keroncong Terbaru*. Musica 7722. *1993*: Indonesia.

Koes Plus. *Success of Koes Plus 4*. Cassette Gema GR-187. *1994*: Indonesia.

Krakatau. *Mystical Mist*. Aquarius. Cassette APC AQM16-4 P9603. n.d.: Indonesia.

Latul, Yopie. *Hot Mania: 'Emen,' Reggae, Disco Dangdut Mix*. Cassette Blackboard Ind 313. *1995*: Indonesia.

Lesmana, Indra. *Indra Lesmana: Cerita Lalu*. Musica MSCD 025. n.d.: Indonesia.

Lia, Alex. *Western Hits in Kroncong (Can't Help Falling in Love)*. Cassette AA Records AAR 169. *1995*: Indonesia.

Likumahuwa, Utha. *Single Hit*. Cassette Team 035. n.d.: Indonesia.

Mansyur, S., and Sukaesih, Elvy. *Dangdut Nostalgia*.
Cassette Dian. *1997*: Indonesia.

Siahaan, Rhien. *Batak Dang-dut*. Cassette Flower
Sound.

Trio Libels. *Jangan Kau Pergi*. Cassette Musica 7993.
1996: Indonesia.

CHARLES CAPWELL

REGIONS

Bali

Population: ca. 3,000,000 (2003)

The dense population of this small island in the
Republic of Indonesia off the east coast of Jawa (Java)
maintains a Hindu religious and cultural life in an
overwhelmingly Islamic republic. Renowned in the
West for the artistic abilities of its population, Bali
has attracted tourists in increasing numbers – among
them prominent artists like the German Walter Spies
and the Mexican Miguel Covarrubias, musicians like
the Canadian-born Colin McPhee, and ethnologists
like the North Americans Margaret Mead and Jane
Belo – since a Dutch invasion during 1906–08
established colonial control of the whole island.
After the local princes lost political power and
income, the performing arts formerly supported at
the courts became 'popular' in that they depended
for their continuity largely on village cooperatives.
These bought the instruments and hired teachers to
maintain their villages' needs for celebratory and
ceremonial music and to compete with the ensembles of other villages. In addition to preserving the
music, they have reshaped and developed it as well,
sometimes with the help of foreigners like Spies, who
was involved with the creation of *kecak*, the so-called
'Monkey Dance,' now so widely known.

Since an international airport was opened at the
capital city Denpasar in 1969, tourists have come in
ever larger numbers – 2 million annually in the
1990s, although the bombing of a nightclub in
Denpasar in 2002 by Islamic terrorists sharply
affected this vital part of Bali's economy. Tourism
has created a need to continue the 'exotic' performances rooted in tradition, as well as to provide
common international fare at the tourist enclaves.
While *kreasi baru* (new compositions) for gamelan
orchestras are a conduit for innovation, popular
music is that of the rest of Indonesia, dominated
largely by *dangdut*. At the tourist-oriented sites
along Kuta and Sanur beaches, local bands can be
heard playing reggae and other covers. Among local
youth, however, there is evidence of a growing

interest in the punk, metal and alternative bands
that are showcased at 'Sunday Hot Music,' a
biweekly venue at Padang Galak for local groups
that have few commercial prospects because they
do not appeal to the tourist crowd and have no
local opportunities to record.

Indicative of Bali's continuing international
cosmopolitanism is the 1994 *dangdut* hit 'Denpasar
Moon,' written and recorded for the Puspita label,
an Indonesian Chinese firm in Jakarta. Composer
Colin Bass, aka Sabah Habas Mustapha, formerly of
3 Mustaphas 3, was named best composer of an
Indonesian traditional song for the year.

Bibliography

Baulch, Emma. 1996. 'Punks, Rastas and Head-
bangers: Bali's Generation X.' *Inside Indonesia* 48
(October–December). http://serve.com/inside/
edit48/emma.htm

Baulch, Emma. 2003. 'Gesturing Elsewhere: The
Identity Politics of the Balinese Death/Thrash
Metal Scene.' *Popular Music* 22 (2): 195–216.

MustaphaWeb Discography. http://kartini-music.com/
home/ColinBass/?mainm1

Discographical Reference

'Denpasar Moon.' Puspita. *1994*: Indonesia.

CHARLES CAPWELL

Jawa (Java)

Population: ca. 110,000,000 (1998)

Although it is fifth-largest in area of the islands of
Indonesia, Jawa (Java) has more than half the
country's total population, a fact that has instigated
a government policy of transmigration – sending
Javanese to cultivate land on other, less densely
populated islands such as Borneo, Sumatera (Sumatra) and Sulawesi. The island is divided into several
provinces: West, Central and East Java. West Java is
also known as Sunda, a region with linguistic and
cultural elements distinct from those of the rest of
the island; located on the northwest coast of this
area, though administratively and culturally separate, is Jakarta, the national capital.

From about the sixth century A.D. the island came
under the cultural dominance of India. Writing
based on a South Indian script was adapted for Kawi,
the classical Javanese language, which, in turn,
inspired other scripts in the area. The elite were
profoundly influenced by Hinduism and Buddhism,
and these continued to flavor philosophical and
religious traditions even after the spread of Islam in
the sixteenth and seventeenth centuries, at about the

same time as Europeans began to arrive. However, their influence was mainly outside the religious realm. Major state-sponsored universities, originating at the end of the colonial period during World War II, exist in each of the provinces: the University of Indonesia in Jakarta; the Bandung Institute of Technology in Bandung, West Java; Gadjah Mada University in Yogyakarta, Central Java; and Airlangga University in Surabaya, East Java. There are also numerous private and religious universities.

To the world outside Indonesia, Javanese music is essentially known for the classical repertoire of the Central Javanese courts in the cities of Solo and Yogyakarta, which is played on ensembles of bronze idiophones called gamelan. In the realm of popular music, it is prominent within the nation as the center whence styles like *kroncong, dangdut* and *jaipongan* have originated and spread to other areas; *dangdut* has made some impact in Japan as well. In the big cities, numerous singers and musical groups perform versions of Western pop styles, ranging from blues and country to death metal, as well as more locally oriented styles of rock and pop ballads. The Yogyakarta-based Kyai Kanjeng, led by the Islamic poet, playwright and essayist Emha Ainun Nadjib, originally of East Java, attempts to meld gamelan instruments with Western orchestral instruments in art pop ensembles, and the jazz group Krakatau, under the leadership of Dwiki Dharmawan and with other members from the Bandung music academy (ASTI), has made recordings with Sundanese and other musical components in an effective and original mix.

At the end of the 1990s, however, one of the most popular groups in terms of general recognition within the country and a growing recognition internationally was the female vocal trio AB Three, whose English and Indonesian repertoire consisted of slickly arranged covers and original tunes in a generally sweet style. They were chosen Best Vocal Group of 1997 for their song 'Suaramu' (Your Voice) in the Anugerah Musik Indonesia (AMI) competition. This competition originated in 1997 with the backing of various music groups, such as the Indonesian Recording Industry Association (ASIRI), the Association of Indonesian Song Writers and Recorded Music Arrangers (PAPPRI) and the Indonesian Creative Work Foundation (YKCI). It is modeled on the North American Grammy Awards and is a response to the BASF awards, which were initiated the year before with the top award going to the alternative group Slank. There were 11 categories in the AMI competition: pop, rock,

alternative, *dangdut*, traditional, children's songs, *kroncong*, rhythm and blues, disco/house/rap, country/ballad and jazz/fusion.

Bibliography

Becker, Judith. 1975. 'Kroncong, Indonesian Popular Music.' *Asian Music* 7(1): 14–19.

Frederick, William. 1982. 'Rhoma Irama and the Dangdut Style: Aspects of Contemporary Indonesian Popular Culture.' *Indonesia* 34 (October): 103–30.

Hatch, Martin. 1989. 'Popular Music in Indonesia.' In *World Music, Politics and Social Change: Papers from the International Association for the Study of Popular Music*, ed. Simon Frith. Manchester: Manchester University Press, 49–68.

Heins, Ernst. 1975. 'Kroncong and Tanjidor – Two Case Studies of Urban Folk Music in Jakarta.' *Asian Music* 7(1): 20–32.

Kornhauser, Bronia. 1978. 'In Defence of Kroncong.' In *Monash Papers on Southeast Asia No. 7: Studies in Indonesian Music*, ed. Margaret J. Kartomi. Clayton, Victoria: Centre for Southeast Asian Studies, Monash University.

'Malam Final Anugerah Musik Indonesia' [Final Night of Indonesian Music Award]. 1997. *Kompas* (29 November). http://www.kompas.com/9711/29/HIBURAN/mala.htm

Piper, Suzan, and Jabo, Sawung. 1987. 'Indonesian Music from the 50s to the 80s.' *Prisma* (March): 25–37.

'Pop dan Dangdut Bersaing Merebut Anugerah Musik' [Pop and Dangdut Compete to Snatch the Music Award]. 1997. *Suara Pembaruan* (16 November).

Simbolon, Johannes. 1995. 'Indonesian Music Industry Survives Foreign Invasion.' *Jakarta Post* (3 December).

Yampolsky, Philip. 1989. 'Hati Yang Luka: An Indonesian Hit.' *Indonesia* (April): 1–17.

Yampolsky, Philip. 1991. Notes for *Music of Indonesia 2: Indonesian Popular Music: Kroncong, Dangdut, and Langgam Jawa*. Smithsonian/Folkways CDSF 40056.

Yampolsky, Philip. 1991. Notes for *Music of Indonesia 3: Music from the Outskirts of Jakarta: Gambang Kromong*. Smithsonian/Folkways CDSF 40057.

Discographical Reference

AB Three. 'Suaramu.' *1997*: Indonesia.

Discography

AB Three. *Cintailah Aku*. Program-PT Virgo Ramayana. Cassette 04/96. n.d.: Indonesia.

Fals, Iwan. *20 Golden Hits*. Cassette Harpa.

Gong 2000. *Gong 2000 Live in Jakarta*. Ariesta PCC-002. *1991*: Indonesia.

Irama, Rhoma. *Music of Indonesia 2: Indonesian Popular Music: Kroncong, Dangdut, and Langgam Jawa*. Smithsonian/Folkways CDSF 40056. *1991*: USA.

Irama, Rhoma. *22 Seleksi Dangdut*. Cassette Metrotama. *1993*: Indonesia.

Karimata. *Jézz*. Aquarius Ind. CD1935. n.d.: Indonesia.

Koes Plus. *Success of Koes Plus 4*. Cassette Gema GR-187. *1994*: Indonesia.

Krakatau. *Mystical Mist*. Aquarius. Cassette APC AQM16-4 P9603. n.d.: Indonesia.

Lesmana, Indra. *Indra Lesmana: Cerita Lalu*. Musica MSCD 025. n.d.: Indonesia.

Mansyur, S., and Sukaesih, Elvy. *Dangdut Nostalgia*. Cassette Dian. *1997*: Indonesia.

Music of Indonesia 2: Indonesian Popular Music: Kroncong, Dangdut, and Langgam Jawa. Smithsonian/Folkways CDSF 40056. *1991*: USA.

Music of Indonesia 3: Music from the Outskirts of Jakarta: Gambang Kromong. Smithsonian/Folkways CDSF 40057. *1991*: USA.

Trio Libels. *Jangan Kau Pergi*. Cassette Musica 7993. *1996*: Indonesia.

CHARLES CAPWELL

Kalimantan (Indonesian Borneo)
Population: 10,900,000 (2000)

Borneo, the third-largest island in the world, sits squarely on the equator. Two of the 13 states of Malaysia, Sarawak and Sabah, and one sovereign nation, the Sultanate of Brunei Darussalam, occupy the northern quarter of the island, while the rest belongs to Indonesia and is known as 'Kalimantan.' Indonesians often use that name for the entire island, including Brunei and the Malaysian states, but it is more common to define Kalimantan as 'Indonesian Borneo.'

Kalimantan has never been a unified political entity. During the nineteenth century its several small Sultanates were gradually brought under Dutch colonial authority. After Indonesia declared independence in 1945, Kalimantan became part of the new republic. It is divided into four provinces, with (according to the government census of 2000) approximately 3.7 million inhabitants in Kalimantan Barat (West), 1.8 million in Kalimantan Tengah (Central), 3.0 million in Kalimantan Selatan (South), and 2.4 million in Kalimantan Timur (East). The population density is remarkably low for Indonesia: 20 persons per square kilometer, whereas for the country as a whole it is 109, and for the most densely populated island, Java, it is 951. The main reasons for this low density are ecological and geographical. Though rainfall is abundant, the soil is generally poor and cannot support extensive settled agriculture. The interior terrain is hilly with heavy forest cover (albeit now greatly depleted by logging) and overland travel is difficult. The primary mode of transportation is by way of the island's innumerable rivers.

The people of Kalimantan (in fact, of Borneo as a whole) are often classified in two main groups: Dayak and Melayu (Malays). The traditional homeland of the Dayak is in the interior. Aside from a small number of nomadic forest-dwelling groups, rural Dayak commonly live from shifting cultivation, which they may supplement with hunting, fishing, gathering, and the sale of forest products. Some Dayak follow the traditional religion now called Kaharingan, while many others have converted to one or another form of Christianity. For a Dayak to convert to Islam, on the other hand, is often seen as tantamount to renouncing Dayak identity, for Islam is considered the defining trait of the other main population group, the Melayu. The Melayu are typically Muslims who live in the cities or along the coasts and rivers and speak some dialect of Malay (essentially the same as Indonesian) as their primary language. As the name suggests, the Melayu of Kalimantan share traits, including musical ones, with other groups in the vast Melayu culture area of Southeast Asia.

One difficulty with this two-group analysis is that it leaves out other significant groups: the 'Chinese' (so-called, despite their having resided in Indonesia for generations and often centuries) and the many long- and short-term immigrants from other parts of Indonesia (especially Java, Bali, Madura, and Sulawesi). Another is that it implies, incorrectly, that Dayak and Melayu are unified cultural categories. In fact there are striking linguistic and cultural differences among Dayak groups in different parts of Kalimantan. Regional variation among Melayu groups, though less marked, is also significant.

Music
Specific types of music in Kalimantan may be placed along a continuum running from music showing no obvious foreign (extra-Indonesian) influence in its structure, idiom and repertoire, to

music that is wholly foreign in those respects. In Indonesia these poles are often called 'traditional' and 'modern.' Music lying at the 'traditional' end of the continuum is commonly performed live among Dayak groups living in the interior. Ceremonial music in those communities often centers on gongs. A typical ensemble involves a row of kettle gongs played melodically and a second group of gongs playing one or more ostinato patterns; drums and other instruments (flute, plucked lute) may also be present. Another form features the gong ostinato, without the melodic gong-row. Stringed instruments are also important in Dayak traditional music: plucked lutes may be played solo or in duos and trios to accompany dance or just as instrumental pieces, and they may accompany singing. The Ngaju of Central Kalimantan have a string ensemble with plucked lutes, a bowed lute, and optional flute and voice. Ensembles of bamboo concussion idiophones play metrically complex rhythmic compositions in the southern part of West Kalimantan. Dayak solo instruments, in addition to the lutes, are the mouth organ (nearly extinct), flute, jew's harp, and xylophone (often played in pairs). Finally, solo singing is heard in sung narratives; solo and choral singing occurs in ritual observances; and among the Kenyah of East Kalimantan choral singing accompanies social dance.

What is considered the traditional music of the Melayu groups often shows some influence from the Middle East in scales or idiom. The *gambus*, a plucked lute that originated in Yemen, and the *zapin* (or *jepen*) dance, featuring *gambus* and interlocking drumming played on small frame drums, are strongly associated with the Middle East and therefore with Islam. The *joget* ensemble, with violin and sometimes accordion as the main melody instruments and a rhythmic cycle maintained by frame drums, mixes European and apparently indigenous Melayu elements. These Melayu genres are heard live in many Melayu communities, including the cities.

The Banjar, a Muslim people in South Kalimantan, had cultural ties with Central Java and developed idiosyncratic forms of genres originally imported from Java: gamelan music, masked dance (*topeng*), and shadow puppetry (*wayang kulit*). These genres – along with local versions of Melayu and Islamic music – are still performed live in rural areas and small cities of South Kalimantan.

At the 'modern' end of the continuum are the genres of national popular music: *pop Indonesia*,

rock, reggae and other genres – all in an essentially Euro-American popular idiom depending on Western scales and harmony – and *dangdut*, which adds timbres and melodic touches from Indian film music and Middle Eastern popular music to the Euro-American base. They are national rather than regional in character if they are sung in the national language, Indonesian. Their performers may be based in Java (most commonly Jakarta), or they may be based in Kalimantan but take the repertoire and style of the 'national' bands as their model and standard. National popular music reaches Kalimantan mainly in the form of recordings and television broadcasts; live performance by Kalimantan musicians is usually in frank imitation of the national bands. Regional adaptations of national popular genres, on the other hand, are sung in local languages and may involve attempts to add tokens of local culture (such as a characteristic instrumental timbre or figuration) to the prevailing national idioms.

It should be noted that the presence of national popular music in Kalimantan is not a new phenomenon. There is scant documentation from before independence, but it is certain that the forms of popular music known in the big colonial cities of Java – *kroncong*, 'Hawaiian' music, swing, European and US (as well as Egyptian, Turkish, Indian, Latin American and Chinese) popular tunes, marches, waltzes – were also known at least among the well-to-do inhabitants of cities of Kalimantan. They were disseminated by gramophone records and, from 1934 on, by radio broadcasts over the Java-based Nederlands-Indische Radio Omroep Maatschappij (NIROM) network. One of the few items of hard information on popular music in Kalimantan from this period is that the Sultan of Kutai in East Kalimantan led his own jazz band in the 1930s.

Religious Music

Islamic religious music (as distinguished from Qur'anic recitation) is of two types: singing (usually in Arabic) clearly based on Middle Eastern devotional models, with a soloist answered by a unison chorus, often accompanied by frame drums; and singing (usually in Indonesian) in idioms much closer to national popular music, especially *dangdut*. The latter type, called *qasidah*, is essentially a religious popular music, disseminated in the same way as secular varieties. Equivalent religious popular musics cast in the national *pop Indonesia* idiom have developed among Catholics and Protestants. Catholics also sing and listen to a body of

Indonesian-language church music produced by the Pusat Musik Liturgi (Center for Liturgical Music) in Yogyakarta; this music includes Western hymns and newly-composed 'inculturation songs' that incorporate or approximate elements of traditional Dayak music (and also the music of Indonesian Chinese living in Kalimantan). Protestant churches rely mainly on translated versions of Western hymns.

The Recording Industry

Gramophone records (78 rpm) were produced for the Dutch East Indies market from 1903 onwards. They presented mainly Indonesian popular music, Qur'anic recitation, and some prominent regional traditions such as Javanese *gamelan* and Sundanese *tembang*, but nothing from Kalimantan. Kalimantan did not appear on commercial recordings until 1961, when the government-owned recording company, Lokananta, issued two 10″ (25 cm) LPs of *hiburan daerah* ('regional entertainment') performed by Kalimantan bands. Promoted by Lokananta for many parts of Indonesia, the *hiburan daerah* genre featured songs with regional associations, played in the style of a Western nightclub combo plus crooner. A few field recordings of traditional music were issued on European LPs in the 1950s, and a few more on European and US CDs in the 1990s. As of 2004, none of these field recordings had been republished in Indonesia; and none of the other recordings discussed in this section has ever been available outside Indonesia.

With the introduction of audiocassettes at the beginning of the 1970s, small local producers emerged who recorded whatever they thought local audiences might want: regional versions of national popular music, but also a few genres from the traditional end of the continuum: Banjar shadow-plays (*wayang Banjar*), Melayu and Banjar *gambus* or *panting*, Banjar sung poetry with frame-drums (*madihin*), solo plucked-lute (*sampeq*) music of the Kenyah, the *karungut* string-and-vocal ensemble of the Ngaju. In the early 2000s VCDs (video compact discs) began to appear. Although most VCDs for sale in Kalimantan feature national popular music, there are a few VCDs of regional adaptations of such music (*dangdut* from Banjarmasin and Melayu groups; pop from the Iban and Kanayatn of West Kalimantan; pop arrangements of 'nostalgic' Melayu songs).

A Growing Trend: The *Sanggar*

In the context of music and dance, *sanggar* – initially a workshop or artist's studio – typically designates a semi-professional group of performers presenting a distinctive style or program. In Kalimantan (and elsewhere in Indonesia) *sanggar* have sprung up in response to the recognition that traditional arts will die out if they are not passed on to young performers and audiences. This threat is itself a consequence of social and economic changes, particularly urbanization, the general devaluation of rural life, and the concomitant fact that many young people find urban, modern, national (and international) arts much more attractive than rural, local, traditional arts. *Sanggar* attempt to deal with this threat by adapting traditional dances and music to the changed social and aesthetic conditions. The adaptations may entail anything from simply shortening the length of the performance and presenting it to an urban audience to rearranging the music for Western (or a combination of Western and traditional) instruments, increasing the number of dancers so as to be more impressive, or staging ritual performance in a secular context. *Sanggar* perform for tourists, in stage shows, on television, or as the entertainment at domestic or official celebrations. Increasingly, they also produce VCDs, which are sometimes the closest one can get, in a recorded medium, to traditional Dayak or Melayu performance. The national popular forms and their regional adaptations flourish in Kalimantan, and while the traditionalist will surely regret the shift to an urban, youth-oriented aesthetic, this accommodation with the popular forms may be the only way to ensure any involvement of young people in the traditional arts.

Bibliography

General

Avé, Jan B., and King, Victor T. 1986. *Borneo: The People of the Weeping Forest: Tradition and Change in Borneo*. Leiden: Rijksmuseum voor Volkenkunde.

King, Victor T. 1993. *The Peoples of Borneo*. Oxford: Blackwell

Maunati, Yekti. 2004 *Identitas Dayak: Komodifikasi dan Politik Kebudayaan* [Dayak Identity: Commodification and Cultural Politics]. Yogyakarta: LKiS.

Rousseau, Jérôme. 1990. *Central Borneo: Ethnic Identity and Social Life in a Stratified Society*. Oxford: Clarendon Press.

Sellato, Bernard. 1989. *Hornbill and Dragon: Naga dan Burung Enggang: Kalimantan, Sarawak, Sabah, Brunei*. Jakarta & Kuala Lumpur: Elf Aquitaine.

Traditional Music

Gorlinski, Virginia K. 1988. 'Some Insights into the Art of *Sape'* Playing.' *Sarawak Museum Journal* 39(60 n.s.): 77–104.

Gorlinski, Virginia K. 1995. *Songs of Honor, Words of Respect: Social Contours of Kenyah Lepo' Tau Versification, Sarawak, Malaysia.* Unpublished Ph.D. dissertation, University of Wisconsin–Madison.

Saleh, M. Idwar. 1983/1984. *Wayang Banjar dan Gamelannya* [*Wayang Banjar* and its Gamelan]. Banjarbaru, Kalimantan Selatan: Museum Negeri Lambung Mangkurat, Departemen P&K.

Sukanda, Al. Yan. 1994. 'Tradisi Musikal Dalam Kebudayaan Dayak' [Musical Traditions in Dayak Culture]. In *Kebudayaan Dayak: Aktualisasi dan Transformasi*, ed. Paulus Florus et al. Jakarta: Grasindo, 133–46.

Sukanda, Al. Yan. 1993. 'Musik Besenggayung Dalam Masyarakat Dayak Kabupaten Ketapang, Kalimantan Barat' [*Besenggayung* Music among the Dayak of Kabupaten Ketapang, West Kalimantan]. *Seni Pertunjukan Indonesia* 4: 122–38.

Discography

Bornéo: Musiques des Dayaks et des Punans. (Musique du Monde Series). Buda 92718-2. 1997–98: France.

Kalimantan: Dayak Ritual and Festival Music. (Music of Indonesia Series, 17). Smithsonian Folkways SF 40444. 1995–96; 1998: USA.

Kalimantan Strings. (Music of Indonesia Series, 13). Smithsonian Folkways SF 40429. 1995; 1997: USA.

Lombok, Kalimantan, Banyumas: Little-Known Forms of Gamelan and Wayang. (Music of Indonesia series, 14). Smithsonian Folkways SF 40441. 1996; *1997*: USA.

Musique dayak: Bornéo (Kalimantan). Disques Vogue LDM 30108. *1972*: France.

The Kenyah of Kalimantan (Indonesia). Musicaphon M 52576. *1995*: Germany.

PHILIP YAMPOLSKY

Sulawesi

Population: ca. 12,500,000 (1998)

Separated from Borneo to the west by the Makassar Strait, Sulawesi (formerly Celebes) is an island near the center of the Indonesian archipelago. Its four long peninsulas give it an exceptionally long coastline as they stretch into the Celebes Sea to the north and the Flores Sea to the south. The Bugis and Makassarese, who are Muslim, are the predominant groups in the south; the Minahasa in the north and the Toraja of the south central highlands are mostly Christian. The island comprises four Indonesian provinces: North, South, Central and Southeast Sulawesi. Manado is the chief city at the tip of the northern peninsula, while Makassar (Ujung Pandang) is the chief city near the southern tip of South Sulawesi. Hasanuddin University is situated in the latter city.

Popular trends in the music of Sulawesi have to do with the attempts to 'folkloricize' performing arts from traditional cultures and to make them part of the national multiethnic heritage. Thus, for example, *pakarena*, a dance of the former Makassarese court, has become a standard form of entertainment for visiting dignitaries, culture festival audiences and tourists. This elegant and restrained dance for women is accompanied by ecstatically frenzied drumming and double reed melodies. Even the religious rituals associated with the Bugis *bissu*, a transvestite priest and shaman, have been presented at folkloric competitions in an attempt to highlight and revalorize local traditions among the populace.

Among the Minahasa, the religious proselytizing of Dutch missionaries in the colonial period brought with it the pervasive influence of Western music-making. As brass bands were often the vehicle of this influence, a local imitation of them in bamboo became well established, although newer versions in zinc and copper began to replace these in the late twentieth century. Later, distinct forms of these amateur bands included versions of clarinets and saxophones. The tunes they play derive largely from the social dance repertoire of old, such as mazurkas, quadrilles, polkas and waltzes.

A local variant of the widely popular Indonesian song form *kroncong*, which uses Makassarese rather than the national language Bahasa Indonesia, is known in the area as *losquin*. It is available on cassettes from ethnic Chinese producers and distributors in Makassar, who offer other varieties of local music as well. Among these, for example, is a type of *gambus*, an Arabic-derived genre that differs considerably from the types heard in Java or Sumatra.

Bibliography

Flaes, Robert Boonzajer. 1994. 'Bamboo Brass in the Minahassa.' *Experimental Musical Instruments* 9(4): 10–15.

Grunden, Amanda. 1995. *Multiple Narratives in the Construction of Identity: A Continuum of Self-Other, Case Study of a Cultural Festival in South Sulawesi.* Unpublished M.A. thesis, University of Illinois at Urbana-Champaign.

Sutton, R. Anderson. 1998. 'From Ritual Enactment

to Stage Entertainment: Andi Nurhani Sapada and the Aestheticization of South Sulawesi's Music and Dance.' *Asian Music* 29(2): 1–30.

Discography

'Gambus Tunggal Makassar, v. 2.' Irama Baru Cassette, Makassar. n.d.: Indonesia.
'Losquin Mandar.' Irama Baru cassette, Makassar. n.d.: Indonesia.

CHARLES CAPWELL

Sumatera (Sumatra)
Population: ca. 87,000,000 (1998)

Second-largest of the islands constituting the Republic of Indonesia, Sumatera (Sumatra) lies at the republic's northwestern extremity, forming part of an archipelago that concludes in the Nicobar and Andaman islands just south of the Bay of Bengal. The Indonesian province of Aceh, one of several special administrative areas in Indonesia, is at its northernmost tip, the other provinces on the island being North Sumatra, West Sumatra, Riau, Jambi, Bengkulu, South Sumatra, and Lampung at the southern end, which is separated from Java by the Sunda Strait. Because of its strategic position at the entrance to the Strait of Malacca, Aceh was for a while in the sixteenth century a powerful Islamic commercial port, rivaling that of Portuguese Melaka across the strait and further south on the Malay peninsula. Its tendency to look toward the west to Islamic India and Arabia, and its history of feisty military and religious traditions, have garnered it a degree of autonomy in its fraught relationship with the Indonesian republic. Medan, in North Sumatra province, is the island's largest city (population about 1.75 million) and is the site of a major university (the University of North Sumatra). Like other Indonesian cities, it has a considerable number of Chinese.

Riau province, which includes the Riau Archipelago stretching from the east Sumatran coast and Singapore, is the heartland of Malay culture, along with its opposite shore on the Malay peninsula. Malay peoples are noted for a delicate sensuality in their arts, so that, for example, *zapin*, a dance imported by Yemeni Arabs that has a vigorous, masculine nature, is modified in the Malay area to exhibit a more flowing and sinuous style for mixed groups of young people. *Gambus*, the music associated with this dance, is a traditional style of popular music for festivities, but *orkes Melayu* ('Malay orchestra') is more truly a popular music associated with secular entertainments and early

twentieth-century theatrical traditions, as well as with life-cycle celebrations. No doubt as a result of their lyrics being in the Malay language, which in Indonesia has become the national lingua franca, these songs have spread throughout the nation. They usually have a simple accompaniment of guitars and violin, although they had more elaborate accompanying ensembles in early twentieth-century *komedi stamboul* and *bangsawan* theaters. It was from the seed of *orkes Melayu* that *dangdut*, an extremely popular Indonesian song style, was developed in the 1970s, with the technological development of electric guitars and the stylistic development of Hindi film song.

In contrast to the mainly Malay population of the eastern littoral region, the interior highlands are noteworthy because they are home to the Batak people. Although the latter were notorious until the end of the nineteenth century as fierce resistors to outside interference, Christian missionaries succeeded in converting many, who took readily to hymn singing. This has had an interesting side effect. They have become the itinerant bards of Indonesia, and may be encountered in hotels and cafés throughout the country.

Bibliography

Rodgers, Susan. 1986. 'Batak Tape Cassette Kinship: Constructing Kinship through the Indonesian National Media.' *American Ethnologist* 13(1): 23–42.
Simon, Artur. 1984. 'Functional Changes in Batak Traditional Music and Its Role in Modern Indonesian Society.' *Asian Music* 15(2): 58–66.
Yampolsky, Philip. 1996. Notes for *Music of Indonesia 11: Melayu Music of Sumatra and the Riau Islands*. Smithsonian/Folkways CDSF 40427.

Discography

Music of Indonesia 11: Melayu Music of Sumatra and the Riau Islands. Smithsonian/Folkways CDSF 40427. *1996*: USA.
Siahaan, Rhien. *Batak Dang-dut*. Cassette Flower Sound.
12 Seleksi Pop Sumsel. Cassette Palapa. n.d.: Indonesia.

CHARLES CAPWELL

CITIES

Jakarta
Population: city – 9,500,000 (1999); metropolitan area – ca. 18,000,000 (1999)

Commemorating a 1527 victory against the Portuguese in the port of Sunda Kelapa on the northwest coast of Jawa (Java), Fatahillah, ruler of Banten, renamed the place Jayakarta (Sanskrit). This event has continued to be celebrated yearly. In 1601, the Dutch defeated another Iberian fleet in the harbor and began their trading presence in the area; they renamed Jayakarta as Batavia when it was made regional headquarters of the Dutch East India Company in 1619. Thereafter many Chinese merchants and Balinese slaves added to the ethnic mix that later shaped the local Malay dialect and culture known as Betawi. The city was renamed Jakarta in 1943 and became the capital of the independent Republic of Indonesia in 1945; it was designated a special administrative area in 1957.

Remains of the seventeenth-century town continue to be found in the old city near the port, but the newer commercial and business area starts inland to the south, while residential suburbs spread further still to the south. The metropolitan area encompasses the satellite towns of Bogor, Tanggerang and Bekasi, and is referred to as 'Jabotabek.'

Traditional Betawi popular entertainments include *lenong*, improvised theater with songs and instrumentals provided by a *gambang kromong* ensemble which includes Chinese fiddles. *Cokek* is the local variant, among the Chinese, of a dance form widespread in Indonesia that has a professional female take turns dancing with males in the audience, and it, too, uses Chinese instruments with Malay ones.

Contemporary popular music exists in every form in this city. Clubs and restaurants may feature up-to-date recorded Western rock, as in the Hard Rock Café, which also has live concerts by local and foreign groups, string bands of Bataks from Sumatra playing sentimental ballads and show tunes, or *dangdut* stars. The latter may also play to audiences of 200,000 at the Ancol amusement park near the port area.

Bibliography

Becker, Judith. 1975. 'Kroncong, Indonesian Popular Music.' *Asian Music* 7(1): 14–19.

Frederick, William. 1982. 'Rhoma Irama and the Dangdut Style: Aspects of Contemporary Indonesian Popular Culture.' *Indonesia* 34 (October): 103–30.

Hatch, Martin. 1989. 'Popular Music in Indonesia.' In *World Music, Politics and Social Change: Papers from the International Association for the Study of Popular Music*, ed. Simon Frith. Manchester: Manchester University Press, 49–68.

Heins, Ernst. 1975. 'Kroncong and Tanjidor – Two Case Studies of Urban Folk Music in Jakarta.' *Asian Music* 7(1): 20–32.

Kornhauser, Bronia. 1978. 'In Defence of Kroncong.' In *Monash Papers on Southeast Asia No. 7: Studies in Indonesian Music*, ed. Margaret J. Kartomi. Clayton, Victoria: Centre for Southeast Asian Studies, Monash University.

Piper, Suzan, and Jabo, Sawung. 1987. 'Indonesian Music from the 50s to the 80s.' *Prisma* (March): 25–37.

Simbolon, Johannes. 1995. 'Indonesian Music Industry Survives Foreign Invasion.' *Jakarta Post* (3 December).

Yampolsky, Philip. 1989. 'Hati Yang Luka: An Indonesian Hit.' *Indonesia* (April): 1–17.

Yampolsky, Philip. 1991. Notes for *Music of Indonesia 2: Indonesian Popular Music: Kroncong, Dangdut, and Langgam Jawa*. Smithsonian/Folkways CDSF 40056.

Yampolsky, Philip. 1991. Notes for *Music of Indonesia 3: Music from the Outskirts of Jakarta: Gambang Kromong*. Smithsonian/Folkways CDSF 40057.

Discography

AB Three. *Cintailah Aku*. Program-PT Virgo Ramayana. Cassette 04/96. n.d.: Indonesia.

Fals, Iwan. *20 Golden Hits*. Cassette Harpa.

Gong 2000. *Gong 2000 Live in Jakarta*. Ariesta PCC-002. *1991*: Indonesia.

Irama, Rhoma. *Music of Indonesia 2: Indonesian Popular Music: Kroncong, Dangdut, and Langgam Jawa*. Smithsonian/Folkways CDSF 40056. *1991*: USA.

Irama, Rhoma. *22 Seleksi Dangdut*. Cassette Metrotama. *1993*: Indonesia.

Karimata. *Jézz*. Aquarius Ind. CD1935. n.d.: Indonesia.

Koes Plus. *Success of Koes Plus 4*. Cassette Gema GR-187. *1994*: Indonesia.

Krakatau. *Mystical Mist*. Aquarius. Cassette APC AQM16-4 P9603. n.d.: Indonesia.

Lesmana, Indra. *Indra Lesmana: Cerita Lalu*. Musica MSCD 025. n.d.: Indonesia.

Mansyur, S., and Sukaesih, Elvy. *Dangdut Nostalgia*. Cassette Dian. *1997*: Indonesia.

Music of Indonesia 2: Indonesian Popular Music: Kroncong, Dangdut, and Langgam Jawa. Smithsonian/Folkways CDSF 40056. *1991*: USA.

Music of Indonesia 3: Music from the Outskirts of Jakarta: Gambang Kromong. Smithsonian/Folkways CDSF 40057. *1991*: USA.

Trio Libels. *Jangan Kau Pergi*. Cassette Musica 7993. *1996*: Indonesia.

CHARLES CAPWELL

Laos

Population: 5,500,000 (2002)

Laos, or the Lao People's Democratic Republic, is located in the northern part of Southeast Asia, sharing common borders with China, Myanmar, Cambodia and Vietnam; it also shares a major part of the Mènam Khong (Mekong) River as a border with Thailand. It is one of the last remaining Communist states in the world and is one of the poorest and least developed countries in Asia; nearly 80 percent of the population is involved in subsistence agriculture.

The Republic (formerly part of France) was formed, with Viangchan (Vientiane) as the capital, in 1975 from three major geographical areas that corresponded to three ancient kingdoms – Luang Prabang in the north, Vientiane in Central Laos, and Champasak in the south. Moreover, in terms of culture, Laos extends over much of the Khorat Plateau into present-day Thailand and, as a consequence, more Laotian speakers live in northeastern Thailand (18 million) than in Laos (5.5 million).

Music is an important part of Laotian life, accompanying many major social events like courtship, New Year celebrations, births, sicknesses, funerals and harvesting. Every village has its own musicians and singers, many of whom make their own instruments. In many highland towns and villages, brass gongs are included in many ceremonies. In terms of folk music, there are distinctive differences between regions and also between the 47 different population subgroups in the country, which the government classifies as: 56 percent Lao Lum (lowlanders), 34 percent Lao Thueng (uplanders) and 9 percent Lao Soung (hill tribes).

Common to nearly all groups in Laos is singing, particularly the singing of poetic verse, which is a legacy of the pre-Buddhist era. The term for this is *lam*, or *khap* in the north and central regions, which means 'to sing,' as well as 'song.' *Lam* can also be used to describe a melody that comes from the tonal inflections of the lyrics (Laotian is a tonal language) and a rhythm derived from rhyming verse.

Popular styles of *lam* and *khap* include: *khap thum* and *khap Samneua* in the north; *lam Khonsavan*, *lam toei* and *lam long* (Viangchan) in the central region; and *lam Siphadone* and *lam Saravane* in the south. Nearly all the towns of the Mekong basin have a regional *lam* or *khap* style. But the most well-known term used for all the styles is *mawlam*, which actually means 'skilled singer of *lam*.' One of the oldest types is *lam phun* in which the *mawlam*

(usually male) sings and acts out the life of Buddha (*jataka*), history, local legends and contemporary news, performing a role similar to that of West African praise singers. The *mawlam* is accompanied by a bamboo reed pipe, the *khaen*, played by a *maw khaen* The *khaen* is a direct descendent of the Chinese *sheng* but it is the most complicated of all the reed pipes of Asia, and is used in acoustic village-level performance, in classical ensembles (*dontri lao derm*) and in modern bands playing *mawlam* where the *khaen* is played alongside Western instruments; it is promoted as the national symbol of Laos by the Laotian Government.

Lam phun was popular in the early part of the twentieth century across the Mekong basin area and, by the 1930s, more elaborate presentations with multiple singers began to emerge, particularly in Thailand. From the 1940s, this new theatrical style was called *lam mou* (*mou* means 'props'). These presentations were to be influenced in part by the *likay* troupes from Thailand that had been traveling and performing in Laos around this time. But by the end of the 1940s, the term *lam luang* (*luang* means 'story,' 'myth' or 'epic') had replaced *lam mou*, and the style had become a folk operetta in which ancient myths and modern narratives were presented. In the 1970s, the Laotian cultural authorities actively encouraged a more song-and-dance oriented form, *lakhon lam* (*lakhon* means 'drama'), with the aim of presenting revolutionary narratives to the masses.

After World War II, radio and recorded music brought Western music and Westernized Thai songs to Laos, and Laotian composers began to develop Westernized Laotian songs, in particular utilizing French influences (the tango remains a much requested dance in Laos). The circular dance, the *ram wong* (*lam vong* in Laotian), promoted by the then nationalistic Thai government, also became popular at this time and remains an integral part of many temple fairs, or *bouns*.

Rock and pop became popular in the 1960s and 1970s, particularly during the Vietnam War, but the Communist takeover in 1975 led to tight controls on entertainment and the movement of musicians. Many musicians and artists left Laos for the United States and Europe and, as a result, more Laotian-language albums have since been produced by the Laotian diaspora in the United States and Europe every year than in Laos (even more are produced in Thailand).

The close proximity of Laotians in northeast Thailand has spurred the electrification of *mawlam*, a process that began in the 1960s, with many top Laotian acts recording in northeast Thai studios and releasing albums heavily influenced by the latest *mawlam* trends in Thailand. Indeed, Thai country music, or *luk thung*, is enormously popular in Laos and has influenced a more pop-oriented form of *mawlam*, *lam luang* and Western pop, known as *lam luang samay*. Laotian singer Taobuangern Chapoo-wong had an enormous hit album of Laotian 'golden oldies' (*samay*) and Thai *luk thung*, entitled *Kookwam Fang Khong* (A Couple Sings From Both Sides of the Mekong), in Thailand in 1992 with leading Thai *luk thung* star Sunaree Ratchasima.

In 1986, the government began a policy of economic liberalization, which brought more exposure to Thai popular culture as a result of increased trade with Thailand; Thai consumer goods, television and radio have since become easily accessible in Laos, particularly along the Mènam Khong (Mekong) River. Thai rock, pop and 'songs for life' styles are all popular with Laotian youth in towns and cities across the country, particularly as audiocassettes, and more recently CDs, have penetrated rural towns and villages. Concern over the growing influence of Thai popular culture prompted the Ministry of Information and Culture to ban Thai television from public places in May 2004. Nonetheless, Laotians can still enjoy Thai television soap opera and Thai radio stations in their homes. Radio, from northeastern Thai stations, is hugely popular; Laos has only state-run radio and just two staid national television channels. The main record companies include Soon Ruam Phleng Lao, Sunny Promotion, BK Promotion and Lao Entertainment.

Despite having to register with the authorities and sign an agreement to use promotional materials in line with official cultural policy, different kinds of pop and rock bands have slowly begun to emerge in Laos since the 1980s. In 1994, the heavy rock band Sapphire released *Heavy Lao* in Thailand, only to be banned, although the songwriter Daowieng Budnakho has written songs for US-based Laotian bands and the Thai *luk thung* star Mike Phiromporn. Increasing interchange between US-based Laotian communities and Laos has also exposed a new generation to Lao-language rock and rap from the United States, which has encouraged urban Lao youth to create their own music, while the US market offers substantially greater financial rewards via overseas recordings and tours for the more established Laotian musicians.

Bibliography

Bond, Katherine and Pathammavong, Kingsavanh. 1992. 'Contexts of *Dontrii Lao Deum* (Traditional Lao Music).' In *Selected Reports in Ethnomusicology. Vol IX. Text, Context and Performance in Cambodia, Laos and Vietnam*, ed. Amy Catlin, Eran Fraenkel and Therese Mahoney. Los Angeles, CA: University of California at Los Angeles, 131–36.

Compton, Carol J. 1992. 'Traditional Verbal Arts in Laos: Functions, Forms, Continuities, and Changes in Texts, Contexts, and Performances.' In *Selected Reports in Ethnomusicology. Vol IX. Text, Context and Performance in Cambodia, Laos and Vietnam*, ed. Amy Catlin, Eran Fraenkel and Therese Mahoney. Los Angeles, CA: University of California at Los Angeles, 150–88.

Mansfield, Stephen. 2000. *Lao Hill Tribes, Traditions and Patterns of Existence*. Oxford: Oxford University Press.

Rattanavong, Houmphanh. 1992. 'The *Lam Luang*, A Popular Lao Entertainment.' In *Selected Reports in Ethnomusicology. Vol IX. Text, Context and Performance in Cambodia, Laos and Vietnam*, ed. Amy Catlin, Eran Fraenkel and Therese Mahoney. Los Angeles, CA: University of California at Los Angeles, 189–91.

Stuart-Fox, Martin. 1986. *Laos: Politics, Economics and Society*. London: Pinter.

Stuart-Fox, Martin. 1997. *A History of Laos*. Cambridge: Cambridge University Press.

Discographical References

Chapoowong, Taobuangern and Ratchasima, Sunaree. *Kookwan Fang Khong*. Sure Audio. *1992*: Thailand.

Sapphire. *Heavy Lao*. *1994*: Thailand.

Discography

Anthology of World Music. The Music of Laos. Rounder Records 5119. *1999*: USA.

Fanshawe, David. *Music From Thailand and Laos: Southeast Asia Recordings*. Arc Music 1425. *1994*: UK

Kmhmu Highlanders. *Bamboo in the Mountains*. Smithsonian Folkways Recordings 40456. *1999*: USA.

Laos Lam Saravane/Musique Pour le Khene. Ocora C 559 958. *1989*: France.

Molam Lao. *Music From Southern Laos*. Nimbus Records NI 5401. *1994*: UK.

Music of Laos. The Buddhist Tradition. Celestial Harmonies 13218-2. *2003*: Germany.

JOHN CLEWLEY

Malaysia

Population: 23,092,940 (2003)

Malaysia was formed in 1963 from the Federation of Malaya, Singapore, and the two Borneo states of Sarawak and Sabah. Singapore opted out to become an independent country in 1965. Malaysia has a multicultural population comprising 63 percent Bumiputera (Malays and other indigenous groups such as the Iban, Bidayuh, Melanau, Kadazan, Bajau, Murut, Orang Asli), 26 percent Chinese (of different dialect groups), 7 percent Indians (originating from different parts of India), and 3 percent others (including Arabs, Eurasians and Indonesians). Malaysia encompasses a great diversity of folk music from the various local communities, as well as jazz and Western classical music (Matusky and Tan 2004).

Different population subgroups in peninsular Malaysia tend to listen to different varieties of popular music. The Malays and other indigenous people who form the majority of the population favor pop/rock with Malay lyrics from Malaysia and Indonesia, as well as various types of heavy metal and rap music sung in English and Malay. The Chinese community, especially those from Chinese schools, is attracted to Mandarin/Canto/Japanese pop from Taiwan, Hong Kong and Japan; while Hindustani/Tamil film songs mesmerize the Indian population. Chinese, Indians and Malays who are English-educated prefer Anglo-American transnational pop, country and western, rap, soft R&B and other forms of pop, rock, metal and hip-hop in the English language. Local mainstream pop songs are sung in Malay, Chinese, Tamil/Hindustani or English and follow transnational trends.

Malay pop is, therefore the predominant local pop music in Malaysia and is aimed mainly at Malay and other Bumiputera audiences. It encompasses syncretic music with varying degrees of acculturation, ranging from pop that is derived from local folk music, to pop and rock derived from Anglo-American mainstream styles. Chinese, Arabic and Indian elements are often added to attract other cultural groups.

Popular Music of the Pre-World War II Era

Popular music developed in the early twentieth century when socioeconomic and political changes were taking place in Malaya as a consequence of British intervention. It was performed live in *bangsawan* (literally 'of the aristocratic class') theaters, dance halls and amusement parks in new urban centers such as Singapore, Pinang, Ipoh and Kuala Lumpur. Popular music was disseminated by foreign recording companies such as The Gramophone Company or His Master's Voice (HMV), Columbia, Pathé, Beka, Hindenburg and Odeon, and local labels such as Chap Kuching (Cat Label) and Chap Singa (Lion Label), which were established by local dealers of The Gramophone Company. Popular music was also broadcast by amateur radio societies set up in the main towns. Urban popular music audiences were multicultural, comprising Malays and immigrants engaged in government services, trade, mining, plantations and construction. During the colonial period, Singapore was the center for Malay popular music but the center shifted to Kuala Lumpur after Singapore opted out of Malaysia (Tan 1993, Ch. 2; Tan 1997).

Approximately half of the prewar gramophone pieces were derived from Malay folk social dance and entertainment music, such as *asli, inang, joget, dondang sayang, zapin (gambos)* and *masri*, which were performed at social occasions such as weddings and at amusement parks in various parts of Malaya. These song genres combined Malay, Western and other foreign instruments and musical elements. *Asli, inang, joget* and *dondang sayang* were accompanied by a violin or accordion, together with one or two Malay frame drums called *rebana*, and a Malay gong. Musical instruments used in early recordings of *zapin* and *masri* included the *'ūd* or *gambos* (originating from the Middle East), a violin, three or four *marwas* hand-drums, and a *dok* (cylindrical drum). Each song genre was associated with a specific local or foreign-derived rhythmic pattern. Syncretism made the music accessible and helped to attract multicultural audiences (Chopyak 1986; Matusky and Tan 2004, Ch. 5).

Asli, inang, joget, dondang sayang, zapin and *masri* were gradually transformed into modern popular genres by *bangsawan* musicians in the prewar period. They substituted piano for the accordion and the Western drum kit for the frame drum. The ensemble was enlarged with a plucked bass, extra violins and other instruments of the Western dance band. However, the newly arranged songs retained their local folk character by using the rhythmic patterns associated with each dance song, topical texts, alternating witty exchange of Malay *pantun* (poetry) verses, fairly independent vocal and instrumental lines, and a singing style with a narrow and tense vocal timbre (Tan 1993, Ch.6). Famous singers such as Temah, Tijah and Dean often incorporated Chinese, Middle Eastern and Indian elements.

Popular music based on Anglo-American and Latin American dance music sung in Malay formed the other half of the recorded repertoire of the pre-World War II period. Compared to the modern versions of Malay folk social dance music recorded, Anglo-American pop elements predominated in this category of song, with catchy melodies superimposed on the waltz, fox trot, tango and rumba rhythms. These songs were accompanied by Western dance bands known locally as the *orkes Melayu* ('Malay orchestras') comprising the violin, trumpet, trombone, flute, clarinet, piano, double bass, guitar, saxophone, drums, maracas, claves and wood block. Well-known musicians included Soliano, D'Cruz and Martinez, who were in fact Filipinos brought to Malaya in the early twentieth century by the British to form the Selangor State Band. The *orkes Melayu* performed at dance halls in the amusement parks, *bangsawan* shows and other festivities. Besides Latin American dance music, the *orkes Melayu* also played sub styles of *kroncong* such as *kroncong rumba*, *kroncong slowfox* and *kroncong Hawaii*, which were popularized by Indonesian singers.

Local flavor was maintained in the *orkes Melayu* repertoire through the song texts. In keeping with the spirit of nationalism came songs such as 'Malaya' (Ahmad C.B., ca.1940s), which instilled the spirit of harmony and love of one's motherland. A number of the recorded songs had topical texts. 'Taxi Rumba' and 'Apik Tukang Becha' (The Old Trishaw Puller) (Tarminah and Piet S. ca.1930s) identified with the common people such as the taxi driver and the trishaw man who had to work very hard to earn a living. These songs had elements of humor added, incorporated different local dialects, portrayed the sentiments of the people and provided an insight into significant social changes in Malaya. They formed a tradition that prevailed in the songs of P. Ramlee (1950s) and Hang Mokhtar (1990s).

Film Music of the 1950s and Early 1960s

During the Japanese occupation of Malaya in 1942, record production stopped. Only a few labels such as HMV, Parlophone, Columbia and Pathé survived after the war in 1945. During this period, popular music developed in close association with Malay film, which reached its peak in the 1950s. Malay films were produced by Chinese-owned companies such as Malay Film Productions (Shaw Brothers) and Cathay-Keris Productions (Ho Ah Loke and Loke Wan Tho). These companies employed Indian directors who relied on local actors

and choreographers from the *bangsawan* theater. Legends and folk tales from *bangsawan* as well as new contemporary stories with social themes were filmed. *Bangsawan* musicians such as Zubir Said, Osman Ahmad, Wandi Yazid, Yusoff B., Ahmad Wan Yet and Ahmad Jaafar composed and performed music for the song and dance sequences (Baharudin Latif 1989a).

Outstanding film stars who recorded their songs included Asiah, R. Azmi, Lena, Salmah Ismail or Saloma, Momo, Jamaliah Shariff and Jasni. Most of the film music was, however, sung by P. Ramlee who began his film career as a playback singer, slowly taking on small supporting roles to become the leading actor of the 1950s. He is said to have appeared in 63 films and sung more than 200 songs (Baharudin Latif 1989b, 63). His films and songs attracted both Malay and non-Malay audiences as they portrayed the lives and problems of ordinary people (*Penarik Beca* [The Trishaw Puller] 1955; *Bujang Lapok* [Unmarried Trio] 1957).

As with *bangsawan*, Malay films of the 1950s drew on the Malay *asli*, *inang*, *joget*, *masri* and *zapin*, as well as the modern Latin American and Anglo-American dances for their repertoire. There was, however, greater stylistic homogeneity with film music as this was composed and arranged by just a few studio musicians who also played in the studio orchestra. Film songs were sung by just a few film stars such as P. Ramlee, Asiah, Momo and Saloma.

Film songs, which derived from Malay social dance music, increasingly used more Western musical elements. Terms such as *joget baru* (new *joget*) and *masri moden* (modern *masri*) were often employed by recording companies to differentiate such songs from the prewar ones. Band leaders expanded traditional linear arrangements with brass and reed instruments such as the trumpet, trombone, saxophone and clarinet, as well as the Western trap set. There was also a tendency toward Western instrumentation replacing all traditional instruments. Singers used the crooning style and added more vibrato as they adapted to the microphone. 'Rintihan Jiwaku' (Lament of My Soul) sung by P. Ramlee and Saloma in the 1950s and 'Serampang Lapan' (referring to a type of malay dance) performed by Asiah and Abd. Chik in the 1950s) were examples of *asli* and *joget* songs that exemplified the film style.

New Latin American dances such as the *kaparinyo*, *pasodoble*, bolero, samba, beguine, conga, cha-cha, *baion* and mambo were popularized through film. Swing numbers were also recorded. The *orkes*

Melayu began adding more instruments than had been used before the war. Besides the trumpet, trombone, clarinet, saxophone, flute, violin, accordion, piano, plucked bass, drum and other percussion instruments, the electric guitar was introduced at the end of the 1950s. There also began a trend toward orchestration and less improvisation. Contrasting instrumental timbres and long instrumental interludes were often employed.

Despite greater stylistic homogeneity, the film style was eclectic. The *asli* song 'Tudong Periok' (referring to a kind of sea fish), by P. Ramlee and Saloma in the 1950s, incorporated characteristic phrases using minor third intervals in a typical Chinese pentatonic scale. Rhythmic patterns derived from Middle Eastern musics, such as *zapin* and *masri*, were employed in 'Maafkan Kami' (Pardon Us) and 'Nasib Si Miskin' (The Fate of the Poor) by P. Ramlee during the 1950s. Songs with a Hindustani flavor (*irama* Hindustan) also became popular in film. 'Tidorlah Nanda' (Sleep Nanda) by Noormadiah (1950s) began with an unmetered introduction like an *alap* and used typical Indian vocal ornamentations. *Ghazal* melodies sung to Malay *pantun* and accompanied by the Indian harmonium and tabla, Middle Eastern *gambos* and Western violin, guitar, maracas and tambourine, were also recorded.

Singers continued to add humor to their songs. They used colloquial Malay, English, Tamil, Hindustani and even some Chinese dialects to comment on personal, ethnic and social problems, or to appeal to the social conscience of the audience. Comical songs such as 'Yam Choi Chow' (Drink Alcohol) (Mohd. Yatim 1950s), 'Kling Mabok' (The Drunken Indian) (Aman Ballon and Leiman S.S. 1940s) and 'Dalam Masa Nipon' (During the Japanese Occupation) (Mohd. Yatim 1950s) incorporated Cantonese, Tamil and Japanese texts, and commented on drinking and hardships faced during the Japanese occupation.

Pop-Yeh-Yeh, Ballads and Rock (Late 1960s–80s)

In the late 1960s, Anglo-American derived pop began to dominate the music scene in Malaysia. Only a few singers such as Orchid Abdullah, Rafeah Buang and Rosiah Chik continued to record *asli* songs. Paralleling the Beatles craze, a phenomenon called *pop-yeh-yeh* emerged. Bands called *kugiran* (*kumpulan gitar rancak* literally meaning 'lively guitar groups'), comprising three guitars and a drum, gradually replaced the *orkes Melayu* that had accompanied *bangsawan* and social dancing in the 1940s and 1950s. Jeffridin and the Siglap 5, the Hooks,

Nirwana, Mutiara Timur, Roziah Latiff and the Jay Hawkers, Les Flingers, Ramlie and the Rhythm Boys, and Ahmad Daud and the Swallows were some of the popular bands of the 1960s. Dressed in colorful jackets and ties (or bow ties), dark glasses and cowboy boots, band singers with outrageous hairstyles delivered songs in the style of the Rolling Stones and Cliff Richard and the Shadows. They played the twist, shake and a go-go at live concerts. Lyrics of *pop-yeh-yeh* songs were about romantic love or invited audiences to dance. EMI and Philips recorded some of the famous bands' singles. Some groups also appeared on local television (*Bintang dan Lagu*, August 1966, October 1967).

In the 1970s and 1980s, a type of transnational music by pop stars such as Michael Jackson, Boney M. and ABBA was marketed throughout Malaysia by giant conglomerates like CBS, EMI, Polygram-Philips, and WEA (Sony and BMG entered Malaysia in the 1990s). This music became accessible even to those in remote villages through the introduction of cheaper transistor radios and cassette pirating. In the wake of the invasion of transnational pop, local pop concentrated on versions of chart-oriented and easy listening songs. Central figures such as Sharifah Aini, Khatijah Ibrahim, Latif Ibrahim, Uji Rashid, Noorkumalasari, Azlina Aziz, DJ Dave, Zalipah Ibrahim, and prominent groups such as the Alleycats, Sweet Charity and Sweet September were known for their formulaic soft rock and sentimental ballads (*balada*), dominated by minor chords. The disco beat became hip after *Saturday Night Fever* was released in 1977. Although *joget* and *asli* rhythms were incorporated by some of the singers of the time, the music was so heavily synthesized that the *asli* flavor was lost.

Nevertheless, some innovation took place. Sharifah Aini, Zaleha Hamid and other EMI singers popularized a form of Hindustani-influenced pop called *dangdut*, which first emerged in Indonesia in the 1960s. *Dangdut* fused the Indian tabla and the Hindustani film vocal style with electric guitars, synthesizers and drums. Sudirman and Kembara who recorded for EMI and Philips respectively, included lyrics about the problems of rural–urban migration and the problems faced by Malay youths in the city. Asiabeat, a prominent group advocating jazz fusion in Malaysia, combined Malay gamelan and Japanese *shakuhachi* with Western electric guitars and drums on their CBS albums.

Smaller independent local record companies such as Warnada, Sinar, Suara Cipta Sempurna (SCS), and Suria Records promoted music on the fringe, which was disregarded by big foreign companies. The availability of cassettes provided new means for the distribution of songs, especially underground ones. Hang Mokhtar and Rampa incorporated comments on poverty, corruption and even complaints against the government in their lyrics. There was a rash of songs that parodied the problems in Malaysian society such as excessive drinking, gambling, motorbike racing, womanizing and the plight of taxi drivers. Taking after P. Ramlee, these singers invigorated their songs with humor in the tone of voice and lyrics, and started a trend called *lucu* ('comical') songs. In 'Tampal Korek' (Patching Up Digging, 1987), Hang Mokhtar employed a Chinese popular tune and the Chinese language syntax to sing about the perpetual digging of roads to the frustration of commuters. Rampa showed how working people of all cultural groups in Malaysia (such as Malay shoemakers and Chinese and Indian street hawkers) shared the same fate and aspirations in 'Senasib' (Of the Same Fate) (Tan 1995).

A Malaysian brand of heavy metal emerged in the 1980s. Rock bands such as Search, Lefthanded, Bumiputera Rockers, Bloodshed and Wings attracted thousands of fans to their live rock concerts. A youth subculture comprising mainly Malays who called themselves 'rockers' or *mat/minah rok* emerged – Mat (short for Ahmad) and Minah are common names for Malay men and women respectively. The rockers wore long hair, corduroy jeans and T-shirts, rode motorbikes, spoke their own language and hung out at shopping complexes. The rock groups promoted two main styles. The first, known as slow rock, resembled the core of mainstream *balada*, except that it was amplified and hardened. The second style, which rockers referred to as heavy metal, featured heavily amplified drums and electric bass juxtaposed with electric guitar riffs. Although singers shouted in hoarse (*serak*) voices, the melodic component was still prominent. Lyrics invited the audience to 'fight' (*berjuang*) against injustice, greed, power, money and drugs and for rockers' rights. 'Hukum Karma' (Condemn Fate) by Wings (1988) and 'Ringgit' (Money) by Ababil (1989) were two examples. Above all, heavy metal music helped young people to dance and to release frustrations arising from everyday problems (Tan 1995).

World Beat, Metal and Hip-hop in the 1990s and at the Turn of the Millennium

Mainstream singers of the 1990s such as Nora, Jesslina Hashim, Siti Nurhaliza, Amy Mastura, Fauziah Latiff, Sheila Majid, Siti Sarah, Ning

Baizura, Camelia, Anita Sarawak and KRU continued to favor easy-listening pop such as the Malay *balada*, soft versions of R&B and soft rock (Tan 2003).

However, there was a resurgent interest in the use of indigenous elements in mainstream pop due to the exposure of local musicians to world beat and the increased circulation of diverse musics through satellite TV, Internet, VCDs and CDs. Local musicians initiated new types of syncretic music in which local instruments, musical elements and concerns were combined with global musical idioms (Tan 2002, 2003). Manan Ngah and Sheqal initiated the *balada nusantara* ('ballad of the archipelago'), which combined traditional instruments such as *caklempung, angklung, gamelan, gendang, seruling*, tabla, *gambus, sitar* and *kompang* with electric guitars and synthesizers (e.g., Sheqal's 1990 release, *Balada Nusantara Menampilkan Sheqal*).

Zainal Abidin blended different Malay, Indian, Latin American and African drums, as heard on the album *Zainal Abidin* (1990). His music emphasized African rhythms, syncopated phrasing, and call-and-response singing style. *Gamal* (Images, 1994) began with a sample of a live recording of the gong chime ensemble (*engkerumong*) of the Iban of Sarawak, evoking images of the activities of the Iban longhouse. M. Nasir experimented with the Sarawakian *sape* and the Malay *seruling, rebab, gong, serunai* and drums such as *gendang* and *kompang* on *Canggong Mendonan* (Deserted Strangers, 1993).

World beat also influenced devotional music – namely *nasyid*, a type of Islamic devotional song previously sung without musical accompaniment. Groups like Raihan, Hijjaz, Rabbani, In-Team, Unic, Saujana, Nowseeheart, Brothers, Hawa and Solehah sang *nasyid pop* in two or three-part harmony. They were accompanied by the *masri* rhythm played by percussion instruments such as the Malay *kompang* and *rebana*, cowbells and congo drums.

The 1990s witnessed the emergence of *irama Malaysia* (Malaysian beat), pop music that combined Malay social syncretic music such as *asli, inang, joget, zapin* and *ghazal* with the Anglo-American pop idiom. The composer Suhaimi Md. Zain (better known as Pak Ngah) and singers such as Noraniza Idris, Jamal Abdillah and Siti Nurhaliza were associated with this genre. *Irama Malaysia* differed from earlier synthesized versions as the songs stressed the mixture of traditional drums such as the *rebana, kompang, tar rodat, jidor, marwas*, *gendang dikir* and tabla. The *gambus* and accordion were often added. The lyrics were written in Malay verse form.

World beat also made an impact on local Chinese pop musicians. To forge a new Chinese-Malaysian identity, Chinese groups such as the BM Boys combined Malay, Chinese and Indian drums and incorporated Malay folk songs such as 'Lenggang Lenggang Kangkong' and *dikir barat* in their Mandarin songs such as 'Tong Nian Xiong' (Song for Childhood, 1998).

World beat cut 'n' mix soundscapes were employed to communicate social concerns and responses to modernity. Zainal Abidin expressed concerns about the environment in 'Hijau' (Green, 1990). M. Nasir sang about the meaning of life and enlightenment in 'Apokalips' (Apocalypse) and 'Di Balik Cermin Mimpi' (Behind the Dream Mirror) in Canggung Mendonan (1993). *Nasyid pop* singers encouraged youths to praise Allah, to stay away from social ills, and prescribed universal brotherhood in Islam. *Irama Malaysia* singers were concerned about revitalizing traditional Malay music. The BM Boys used Teochew and other Chinese dialects to sing about the concerns of the Malaysian Chinese, such as living in harmony with other ethnic groups (as in 'Nang Si Chit Keh Nang' [We Are a Family] from 1998) (Tan 2002).

Through the world beat idiom, indigenous peoples were also able to articulate their anxieties as aggressive development agendas impacted on their survival in the forest. *Akar umbi* (meaning 'tap root') featured the ceremonial songs of Mak Minah Anggung, a *temuan* ceremonial singer, in their album *Songs of the Dragon* (2002). They combined traditional *temuan* bamboo stampers with the guitar, synthesizer and other instruments. The lyrics portrayed the dependence of the *temuan* on the forest, rivers and mountains.

Besides interest in local elements and instrumentation, the 1990s also saw the advent of new types of heavy metal music. A new generation of heavy metal fans dismissed the rock singers of the 1980s (such as Wings, Ellie, Amy and Awie) as conformists – they had contracts with transnational companies and sang commercial rock ballads. The critics dedicated themselves to punk, thrash metal and other subgenres of heavy metal such as black/death metal with their high decibel count, pace, discordant chords, guitar riffs and non-pitched melodies. Under the banner of non-commercialism, these groups went underground (*bawah tanah*). They emphasized the DIY (Do-It-Yourself) spirit, orga-

nized gigs that brought different bands together, produced their own magazines (fanzines), often simply photocopied, and informed fans about their gigs through flyers. Unknown groups produced their own demo tapes for sale, while the more established ones were recorded by independent companies such as Psychic Scream Entertainment and Strange Culture Records.

Thrash metal groups such as FTG (Freedom That's Gone), Koffin Kanser and Samurai highlighted the alienation of Malay youths from the materialistic and controlled world in which they lived. Black metal music (As Sahar, Koma, Vrykolakas, Sil Khannaz), punk (Carburetor Dung) and alternative (Butterfingers, Subculture) helped Malay youths to release tension at gigs through headbanging and moshing.

Beginning in the mid-1990s, hip-hop and rap (mainly in the English language) began to make some impact among the Malay youths. Except for a few groups such as Poetic Ammo, Ruffedge, Teh Tarik Crew and Too Phat that became mainstream, most hip-hop groups such as Project and Phlowtron operated the underground DIY way. Clad in oversized T-shirts, baggy pants or jumpsuits, sneakers and baseball/ski caps, they rapped and break danced at outdoor venues for teenage audiences too young to enter clubs. Some groups began to create their own distinct style. Poetic Ammo's album *It's a Nice Day to be Alive* (1998) encompassed Malay, Tamil and Cantonese raps and local-flavored samples. In 'Anak Ayam,' Too Phat rapped over the folk song 'Kuda Ku Lari' using the *zapin* beat.

Conclusion

Throughout the history of popular music in Malaysia, there has been a continuous dialog between the local, the national and the global, resulting in tensions between homogeneity and heterogeneity. Malay pop musicians have not broken into the international scene but there is an emerging market for Malay pop in Singapore, Indonesia and Japan. *Nasyid pop* singers are trying to make inroads in the Islamic countries of the Middle East. Some Chinese singers are becoming well known in Hong Kong, Taiwan and Japan.

Bibliography

Baharudin Latif. 1989a. 'The Beginning.' In *Cintai Filem Malaysia*. Kuala Lumpur: Perbadanan Kemajuan Filem Nasional Malaysia, 45–48.

Baharudin Latif. 1989b. 'P. Ramlee: The Living Legend.' In *Cintai Filem Malaysia*. Kuala Lumpur:

Perbadanan Kemajuan Filem Nasional Malaysia, 63–65.

Bintang dan Lagu. August 1966 (2), October 1967 (15).

Chopyak, James. 1986. 'Music in Modern Malaysia: A Survey of the Musics Affecting the Development of Malaysian Popular Music.' *Asian Music* 18(1): 111–38.

Lockard, Craig. 1996. 'From Folk to Computer Songs: The Evolution of Malaysian Popular Music, 1930–1990.' *Journal of Popular Culture* 30(3): 1–26.

Matusky, Patricia, and Tan Sooi Beng. 2004. *The Music of Malaysia: The Classical, Syncretic and Folk Traditions*, SOAS Musicology Series. Aldershot: Ashgate Publishing Company.

Tan Sooi Beng. 1990. 'The Performing Arts in Malaysia: State and Society.' *Asian Music* 21(1): 137–71.

Tan Sooi Beng. 1993. *Bangsawan: A Social and Stylistic History of Malay Opera.* Singapore: Oxford University Press.

Tan Sooi Beng. 1995. 'Popular Music in Multi-Ethnic Malaysia: Diversity Despite Control.' In *Intercultural Music,* Vol. 1, ed. Cynthia Kimberlin and Akin Euba. Bayreuth: Bayreuth African Studies 29, 143–63.

Tan Sooi Beng. 1997. 'The 78 rpm Record Industry in Malaya Prior to World War II.' *Asian Music* 28(1): 1–42.

Tan Sooi Beng. 2002. 'Negotiating Identities: Reconstructing the Local in Malaysia Through World Beat.' *Perfect Beat*, 5 (4): 3–20.

Tan Sooi Beng. 2003. 'Musical Exotica and Nostalgia: Localizing Malaysian Music Video?' *Wacana Seni: Journal of Arts Discourse*, 2: 91–108.

Discographical References

78 rpm
Ahmad C.B. 'Malaya' (nationalistic song). Chap Singa QF 87. *1940s*: India.

Aman Ballon, and Leiman S.S. 'Kling Mabok' (comic song). HMV P 22900. *1940s*: India.

Asiah and Abd. Chik. 'Serampang Lapan' (*joget*). Composers: Q. Jaafar and S. Rahman. A. Jaafar Orchestra. Pathé PTH 173. *1950*: India.

Mohd. Yatim. 'Dalam Masa Nipon' (comic song). HMV P 22945. *1950s*: India.

Mohd. Yatim. 'Yam Choi Chow' (comic song). HMV NAM 13. *1950s*: India.

Noormadiah. 'Tidorlah Nanda' (*irama Hindustan*). Osman Ahmad Orchestra. Film: *Merana.* HMV NAM 206. *1950s*: India.

P. Ramlee. 'Maafkan Kami' (*zapin*). P. Ramlee Orchestra. Film: *Pendekar Bujang Lapok.* Parlophone DPE 8093. *1950s*: India.

P. Ramlee. 'Nasib Si Miskin' (*masri*). A. Jaafar Orchestra. Film: *Antara Senyum dan Tangis.* Parlophone DPE 8050. *1950s*: India.

P. Ramlee and Saloma. 'Rintihan Jiwaku' (*asli*). Composers: Osman Ahmad and Sudarmadji. P. Ramlee Orchestra. Film: *Batu Belah Batu Bertangkup.* Parlophone DPE 8103. *1950s*: India.

P. Ramlee and Saloma. 'Tudong Periok' (*asli*). P. Ramlee Orchestra. Film: *Sumpah Orang Minyak.* Parlophone DPE 8073. *1950s*: India.

Tarminah and Piet S. 'Apik Tukang Becha.' HMV P 13171. *1930s*: India.

Tarminah and Piet S. 'Taxi Rumba' (rumba). HMV P 13172. *1930s*: India.

Cassettes and CDs
Ababil. *Ababil.* Target Records TRC 8002. *1989*: Malaysia.

Akar Umbi. *Songs of The Dragon.* Magick River. *2003*: Malaysia.

Asiabeat. *Bamboo Groove.* CBS MC 111. *1983*: Malaysia.

BM Boys. 'Nang Si Chit Keh Nang.' *Shi Nian Hao Ge.* Follow Me Records FMC 8064. *1998*: Malaysia.

BM Boys. 'Tong Nian Xiong.' *Shi Nian Hao Ge.* Follow Me Records FMC 8064. *1998*: Malaysia.

Hang Mokhtar. 'Tampal Korek.' *Kocik-kocik Jago Kobau.* Segar CL 1001. *1987*: Malaysia.

Kembara. *Perjuangan.* Polygram-Philips 7179159. *1982*: Malaysia.

M. Nasir. 'Apokalips.' *Canggong Mendonan.* Luncai Emas, distributed by BMG-Pacific 74321 170124. *1993*: Malaysia.

M. Nasir. 'Di Balik Cermin Mimpi.' *Canggong Mendonan.* Luncai Emas, distributed by BMG-Pacific 74321 170124. *1993*: Malaysia.

Noraniza Idris. *Berkaba.* Suria Records SRCD 99-23475. *1999*: Malaysia.

Poetic Ammo. *It's a Nice Day to be Alive.* Positive Tone PT 3008 CS, distributed by Sony. *1998*: Malaysia.

Raihan. *Puji-Pujian.* Warner 0630-17715-4. *1997*: Malaysia.

Rampa. 'Senasib.' *Koleksi Emas Rampa.* Warnada WA 1520. *1988*: Malaysia.

Sharifah Aini. 'Masih Ingat Masih Setia.' *Dangdut-Dangdut.* EMI TC-BM 32521. *1988*: Malaysia.

Sheqal. *Balada Nusantara Menampilkan Sheqal.* Ciku Records, distributed by BMG BMG/CM 01190. *1990*: Malaysia.

Sudirman. *Lagu Anak Desa*. EMI TC-EMGS 5554. *1980*: Malaysia.

Sudirman. *Orang Baru*. EMI TC-EMGS 5626. *1984*: Malaysia.

Too Phat. *Plan B*. Positive Tone 07243532771 47, distributed by EMI. *2001*: Malaysia.

Wings. *Hukum Karma*. Antarctic Sound Production ASP 0048. *1988*: Malaysia.

Zainal Abidin. 'Hijau.' *Zainal Abidin*. Roslan Aziz Productions, distributed by Warner WEA 9031-74404-4. *1990*: Malaysia.

Zainal Abidin. *Gamal*. Roslan Aziz Productions, distributed by Warner WEA 4509-97377-4. *1994*: Malaysia.

Discography

78 rpm

Ahmad C. B. 'Anak Koe' (*kroncong*). Chap Singa QF 89. *1930s*: India.

Asiah. 'Lihatlah' (swing). A. Jaafar Orchestra. Pathé, PTH 181. *1950s*: India.

Che Norlia. 'Linggang Mak Inang' (*inang*). HMV 15980. *1930s*: India.

City Opera. 'Aladom' (*masri*). Beka 26408. *1930s*: India.

Ismael. 'Lagu Djalak Lintang' (*asli*). The Gramophone Co. 2-120008. *1904*: India.

Jacoba Regar. 'Kawin Paksaan' (*kroncong* fox trot). HMV NS 587. *1930s*: India.

Lena. 'Nasib Di Bunga' (cha-cha). Yusof B. Orchestra. Columbia GEM 201. *1950s*: India.

Temah. 'Mas Merah' (*asli*). HMV GC-12-13169. *1920s*: India.

Tijah. 'Tandi-Tandi' (*lagu Hindustan*). HMV P 16489. *1940s*: India.

Tijah and Dean. 'Dondang Sayang.' Chap Kuching NG 2. *1930s*: India.

45 rpm

Abdullah, Orchid. 'Bertemu Di Dalam Mimpi' (*ghazal*). EMI/Parlophone. *1966*: Singapore.

Flingers, Les. 'Sa Hati Sa Jiwa' (*pop-yeh-yeh*). Philips 437816 PE. *1967*: Singapore.

Hussein, Maimun and the Dulcet Boys. 'Gerhana, Pemergian' (*pop-yeh-yeh*). Philips 437811 PE. *1967*: Singapore.

Roziah Latiff and the Jay Hawkers. 'Aku Ingat Pada Mu' (*pop-yeh-yeh*). Philips 437812 PE. *1967*: Singapore.

Cassettes and CDs

Ella. 'Dunia Kehidupan.' *Pengemis Cinta*. Warner WEA M40-93565. *1989*: Malaysia.

FTG (Freedom That's Gone). *Aku Tak Peduli*. Pony Canyon *1998*: Malaysia.

Koma. *Aftermath*. Muzik Box Production. *2001*: Malaysia.

KRU. *Relax*. KRU Music Group. *2003*: Malaysia.

M. Nasir. *Saudagar Mimpi*. Luncai Emas, distributed by BMG-Pacific PMC/MAL 1101. *1992*: Malaysia.

Rabbani. *Intifada*. EMI 07243 5313724 3. *2000*: Malaysia.

Raihan. *Allahu*. Warner. *2004*: Malaysia.

Samurai. *Pendekar Belantara*. Pony Canyon. *2000*: Malaysia.

Siti Nurhaliza. *Sahmura*. Suria Records. *2000*: Malaysia.

Vrykolakas. *Aftermath*. Muzik Box Production. *2001*: Malaysia.

Zaleha Hamid. 'Dangdut Reggae.' *Dangdut*-Dangdut. EMI TC-BM 32521. *1988*: Malaysia.

Filmography

Antara Senyum dan Tangis, dir. L. Krishnan. 1952. Singapore. Musical Drama. Original music by Yusuf.B.

Batu Belah Batu Bertangkup, dir. Jamil Sulong. 1958. Singapore. Musical Drama. Original music by Osman Ahmad, Sudarmadji.

Bujang Lapok, dir. P.Ramlee. 1957. Singapore. Musical Drama. Original music by P. Ramlee.

Merana, dir. B.N. Rao. 1954. Singapore. Musical Drama. Original music by M.F.P. Studio Orkes.

Penarik Beca, dir. P. Ramlee. 1955. Singapore. Musical Drama. Original music by P. Ramlee.

Pendekar Bujang Lapok, dir. P. Ramlee. 1959. Musical Drama. Original music by P. Ramlee.

Saturday Night Fever, dir. John Badham. 1977. USA. 119 mins. Musical Drama. Original music by Barry Gibb, Maurice Gibb, Robin Gibb, David Shire.

Sumpah Orang Minyak, dir. P. Ramlee, 1958. Singapore. Musical Drama. Original Music by Yusram.

TAN SOOI BENG

REGIONS

Sarawak and Sabah

Population: Sarawak – 2,012,616 (2000); Sabah – 2,444,398 (2000)

Sarawak and Sabah are the two states of Malaysia located on the northern coast of the island of Borneo. The larger of the pair, Sarawak, embraces an area of 48,050 sq miles (124,450 sq km), while neighboring Sabah to the east spans 28,424 sq miles (73,619 sq km). Both states were British protectorates from 1888 until Japanese occupation in 1942. After World War II, Sarawak and Sabah became official

British crown colonies, until they joined the independent Federation of Malaysia in 1963. The major business and administrative centers of the two states are seated on or near the coasts, alongside and in contrast to numerous small fishing communities. Multinational oil companies also conduct onshore and offshore operations from the coastal regions. Moderate-sized towns dot the interior lowlands, where rice, oil palm, pepper, and in Sabah, tea cultivation are among the principal industries or occupations. Smaller villages of subsistence rice farmers are scattered along the riverbanks of the rain-forested mountains in the southern interior, recently linked to downriver urban centers by the roads of timber companies logging the upriver areas.

The population of Sarawak and Sabah is remarkably diverse. Although some groups span the political border, the two states are demographically, culturally, linguistically and musically distinct. In Sarawak, Malays, Chinese and Iban make up the majority of the population, followed by the Bidayuh and Melanau, all of whom are primarily coastal or lowland dwellers. The numerous peoples inhabiting the highland areas are usually designated by the blanket term Orang Ulu ('Upriver People'), largely for administrative purposes. Malays and Iban are also settled in the coastal regions of Sabah, along with Bajau peoples of Philippine descent. Dusun and Kadazan populations are dominant on the western coast and in the inland plains and hinterlands, while the Murut (known as Lun Bawang in Sarawak, an Orang Ulu group) predominate in the mountains and highland plateaus. Islam is the primary religion of the coastal Malays and Bajau, as well as many Melanau, Dusun and Kadazan. The Chinese are usually Buddhist, Taoist or Christian. The further one travels to the interior, the more Christianity predominates, alongside various local religions.

General Trends in Popular Music

Despite the diversity of the population of Sarawak and Sabah, several distinct trends are recognizable in the realm of popular music production. For the most part, groups work within transnational music styles, most of which originated beyond the island of Borneo. The musics are localized primarily through the lyrics, which are usually sung in the regional languages and dialects of their performers, and often address group-specific celebrations and customs. Many album covers depict the artists or others dressed in the traditional attire of their particular communities. The most common prototypes of the popular musics of Sarawak and Sabah are Malay *joget*, and Western-style rock and light pop. Sporadic releases of translations, translated remixes, or new compositions in the styles of Chinese pop, Indian Bollywood and reggae may also season the shelves of cassette and CD shops. Especially since the late 1990s, a number of groups have begun to move in a new direction, incorporating unique local instruments and melodies in a quest for a distinctly Sarawakian or Sabahan sound.

Regardless of ethnic affiliation, many popular bands perform a type of *joget*, a quick-paced music and dance associated primarily with the Malay communities of Southeast Asia. *Joget* is a blend of Malay and European elements, some of which can be traced back to a dance brought to Melaka (Malacca) by the Portuguese in the sixteenth century. The older-style acoustic forms highlight frame drum, flute, violin or accordion. The quintessential contemporary *joget* pop songs, however, use flute or accordion (usually synthesized) as the main melody instrument, while a drumset and electric bass carry a repetitive rhythmic figure in duple or triple throughout the song. Vocal lines are typically rendered in paired couplets or quatrains spanning four bars, often with light ornamentation reminiscent of Muslim vocalization. Harmonically, the music generally adheres to a straightforward I-IV-V-I pattern, which frequently underscores modal melodic passages that outline pentatonic scales (with semitones). If multiple vocalists sing simultaneously, they normally do so in unison (or at the octave). The term *joget* often appears in the titles of songs that follow this style.

Light pop songs enjoy an appeal in Sarawak and Sabah comparable to that of *joget*. Like *joget*, these pop songs are usually founded on a solid I-IV-V-I harmonic structure. The phrases, however, do not adhere so strictly to a four-square couplet or quatrain arrangement. A 'light' ensemble supports clearly articulated, sometimes crooner-like, vocal lines with an electronic keyboard usually performing most, if not all, of the parts. The drumset and bass (or their synthesized equivalents) regularly accentuate the backbeats, often with short flourishes to mark the ends of stanzas. Electric guitars, when present, serve a predominantly rhythmic function, although they may occasionally take solos, sounding the melody, like the vocalist, in a clear and undistorted fashion. Many groups perform a repertoire in both light pop and *joget* styles.

While significant, rock music is less abundant in Sarawak and Sabah as a local production. Usually more slickly produced than *joget* or light pop releases, both hard and soft rock styles generally rely on an ensemble of live musicians, arrangers and sound technicians, who are credited by name in the liner notes of the recordings. Vocal lines often span the timbral gamut both within and between numbers on a given album. Some passages might be breathy, others crisp and clear, others coarse and semi-articulate, punctuated with shouts, screams, moans or wails. Phrase length varies. The harmonic structure of rock songs can be quite intricate, weaving through several tonal centers in the course of one piece. Choral singing with harmonization is not uncommon.

A smattering of other popular styles may also be encountered in the bins of local record shops. Some bands have released albums of anhemitonic pentatonic flavored Chinese light pop tunes. Others have experimented with Bollywood-style songs with alternating, ornamented male and high-pitched female vocals, synthesized orchestral instruments, and hand-drums. Yet others have worked with reggae remixes. All of these productions are rendered in Sarawakian or Sabahan languages.

Especially since the advent of the Rainforest World Music Festival, held annually in Kuching, Sarawak since 1998, more bands, such as Tu-ku'Kame', are beginning to work with self-consciously hybrid forms, blending elements of local traditional musics with transnational popular styles. These world music ensembles usually combine any of an array of indigenous instruments including gongs, drums, xylophones, plucked lutes, flutes, mouth organs and assorted rattles and shakers with electric guitars, bass, drumset and keyboard to create a broadly popular, yet unique, local musical style. Some groups also use African drums and gourd-resonated xylophones, which mark much of the global pop sound. The bands often draw their melodic material from local songs, and may sing in several regional languages. Unlike some of the more commercially successful rock and pop artists, who sing primarily in the national language of Malay, and sometimes move to peninsular Malaysia for better access to 'cutting-edge' recording studios and the transnational music industry, most Sarawak and Sabah-based world music ensembles have continued strongly to associate themselves and their music with the diversity of their home states.

Industry and Artists

The commercial recording industries in Sarawak and Sabah work primarily within a cassette and VCD (video compact disc) culture. VCDs, which usually contain a series of music videos subtitled for optional karaoke performance, are generally preferred by consumers of local music over sound-only compact discs. Some communities are more active in the industry than others. In Sarawak, the Iban and Bidayuh are the most prominent producers of local popular music, with some artists, such as Bidayuh musician, Mike Rantai and his group, Spitfire setting up their own record labels (e.g., Spitfire). A few Orang Ulu artists have made light pop or Christian pop recordings, such as *UR Lovely* by Fragrance. These recordings, however, are not readily available through the commercial channels. Similarly, local Malay, Melanau and Chinese popular musicians do not have a strong presence in the commercial circuit. In Sabah, the Dusun/Kadazan are the most established in the pop music market, although some Bajau, local Malay and Murut recordings are also available. The most visible record labels specializing in local music are Sabah Records and Kinabalu Cassettes. These labels handle not only original artists such as Roslin Ginsuak, but also those who do covers and remixes of pop songs and styles from Asia to the Caribbean to Europe. A good example of the latter would be Vengaboom Dusun's *The Party Album*, a Dusun-language remake of the Dutch group Vengaboys' 1998 album of the same name. In both Sarawak and Sabah, availability of recordings varies substantially from region to region, according to local demographics. Bidayuh pop, for instance, is accessible in Kuching and the surrounding areas, but in Miri, where there is no substantial Bidayuh population, recordings are scarce. By the same token, Bajau pop, which is local to Sabah, is virtually non-existent in Sarawak.

Conclusion

Popular musics in Sarawak and Sabah take a variety of forms and are performed in an array of local languages. Many groups work within Malay-based *joget*, light pop or, less frequently, Bollywood styles that circulate broadly through Southeast Asia. Others adopt globally popular rock, or more recently, self-consciously eclectic world music formats. Especially on account of the regionally shifting character of local popular music production and consumption, Sarawak and Sabah offer a provocative call to researchers.

Discographical References

Fragrance. *UR Lovely*. Petros Ministries PMF 01-CD. N.d.: Malaysia.

Vengaboom Dusun. *The Party Album*. Sabah Records. *2000*: Malaysia.

Discography

Acid Rain. *Acid Rain*. Spitfire SF 2001. n.d.: Malaysia.

Bollywood Dusun: Kano Gompio Piginawaan To. Sabah Records SRT2129. *2000*: Malaysia.

Camelia. *Mimpi*. Abadi (Universal) 515515-4. *2001*: Malaysia.

Ginsuak, Roslin. *Dapat Bini No. 2*. Sabah Records SR 2074. n.d.: Malaysia.

Jogit Dusun 3. Kinabalu Cassette SH9351. n.d.: Malyasia.

Karaoke Sabah: The Land Below the Wind. Skyline/Kinabalu Cassette SK VCD 100. n.d.: Malaysia.

Impira, Alim and Gek, Felicia. *Kang Kang Kuk*. Spitfire 2003. n.d.: Malaysia.

Lagu Lagu Murut 1. SECA Stereo 0001. n.d.: Malaysia.

Lupeng, Alon. *Spitfire MTV Vol. 2: Koleski 5 MTV*. Spitfire SFVCD 2002. n.d.: Malaysia.

Mega Sumazau. Kinabalu Cassette SHK-714. n.d.: Malaysia.

Nurfaizah, Dayang. *Seandainya Masih Ada Cinta*. Broadway Entertainment (EMI) 7243 5316774 5. *2001*: Malaysia.

Pop Mandarin: Igitai Tadat Pogulu. Sabah Records SR 2103. *1998*: Malaysia.

Ralmaya, Koyong. *Top Bajau*. Asia Baru BJ5064. n.d.: Malaysia.

Rantai, Mike and Spitfire. *Mike Rantai and Spifire*. Spitfire SF 1022. n.d.: Malaysia.

Sanggam, Johnnycal. *Karung Surat Bebungai*. Tiew Brothers Company TBC CHB 1150. n.d.: Malaysia.

Selamat Ngintu Gawai. Luh Productions Sdn. Bhd. LUH 64. *2000*: Malaysia.

Sinding Reggae Remixes, Vol. 1. Kinabalu Cassette SHK 673. n.d.: Malaysia.

Spitfire 2000. *Terima Kasih Babeh*. Spitfire SF 1026. *ca. 2000*: Malaysia.

Tuku'Kame.' *Tuku'Kame'*. Sarawak Cultural Village. n.d.: Malaysia.

VIRGINIA GORLINSKI

CITIES

Kuala Lumpur

Population: 1,800,000 (2003)

Located midway along the west coast of the Malay Peninsular, Kuala Lumpur is the capital and largest city of Malaysia. It is the administrative, commercial and financial center of the country. Kuala Lumpur is the site of massive development with some of the world's tallest buildings and a multimedia industry that symbolizes Malaysia's modernity. Major recording companies, radio and television stations are based there.

The city has a vibrant live music scene catering to the varied tastes of the multicultural residents who come from different Malaysian states, as well as overseas, to seek employment. Show promoters in Kuala Lumpur organize international jazz festivals and commercial pop/rock concerts featuring transnational stars from the United States, Europe, Hong Kong, Taiwan and India. Local and foreign bands perform light-and-easy pop, country and western and folk/blues and jazz at hotel lounges and pubs. Pop, soft rock and R&B divas such as Ning Baizura, Siti Nurhaliza, Anita Sarawak, Camelia and Sheila Majid sing at special functions at hotels and other entertainment venues.

Kuala Lumpur has become an international venue for clubbing (rivaling Singapore, Hong Kong and Japan). Foreign DJs such as Roger Sanchez, David Morales, Judge Jules, Sister Bliss and King BT perform at dance clubs such as Embassy, Emporium, the Grand Café, Viva, the Backroom, Movement and Scandals. They are supported by local DJs such as Gabriel, Callen, Ben Katana, DJ Love, Jungle Jerry and Rabbit. Modern foreign genres of club music like house, trance, progressive, techno, garage and drum 'n' bass provide lively dance music. Young Malays and Indonesians also gyrate to the pulsating and hypnotic *dangdut* beat in *dangdut* clubs such as Tiara Dangdut, Mawar Biru, Istana Dangdut, Sun Dangdut and Yasmin Dangdut.

Underground groups, such as As Sahar, Chaotic Mass, Silent Death, Carburetor Dung, Karatz, Butterfingers, Koffin Kanser and Mandatory, play hardcore, punk, alternative and various types of metal at clubs such as the Fire Disco and Piccadilly, pubs and open-air venues. Hip-hop performers (Too Phat, Ruffedge, Teh Tarik Crew, Phlowtron, Project) rap and break dance at open spaces such as the Sunway Lagoon, Bintang Walk and at the Sungai Wang Plaza shopping complex before teenage audiences who are too young to enter clubs.

Mandarin-based Chinese rock bands (such as Chong Yang, Moxuan, KRMA) perform at the clubhouse run by the Huang Huo (Yellow Flame), an organization which is independent of the state and music companies, and at various pubs and

195

community halls. Tamil rock bands such as Lock-Up, the Keys, Darkkey, Apachean and Vyrus contest mainstream foreign Hindustani/Tamil film stars and playback singers through their own gigs.

Fringe singers (namely Rafique Rashid, Amir Yusof and Julian Mokhtar) showcase an alternative flow of music in pubs, cafés and restaurants. They go for the unplugged acoustic sound and songs with social concerns. Rafique Rashid's songs take pot-shots at Malaysian society. He is known for his slapstick parody and biting commentary.

The Halo Café has championed local Chinese music with regular folk-pop evenings and mini-showcases for unsigned acts. Several of Malaysia's Chinese singers who have made it big, such as Michael and Victor, Ah Gu and the BM Boys, first performed in the café.

Discography

Ah Gu/Ah Niu. *Chang Ge Gei Ni Ting*. Rock Records and Tapes. *1998*: Taiwan.

Amir Yusof. *Altered Native*. Ragtime and Warner Chapell Music. *1998*: Malaysia.

Amir Yusof. *Some of This is Real*. Ragtime. *2003*: Malaysia.

Anita Sarawak. *Seksis*. KRU Music Group. *2004*: Malaysia.

BM Boys. *Tong Nian Xiong*. Follow Me Records. *1995*: Malaysia.

BM Boys. *Fang Yen Chuan Zhuo*. Follow Me Records. *1997*: Malaysia.

Jamal Abdillah. *Raja Pop*. Warner Music. *2003*: Malaysia.

Ning Baizura. *Selagi Ada ... Ning*. Warner Music. *2004*: Malaysia.

Sheila Majid. *Cinta Kita*. Warner. *2003*: Malaysia.

Siti Nurhaliza. *Emas*. Suria Records. *2003*: Malaysia.

Rock the World, The Malaysian Rock Festival. Unic Sound Production. *2004*: Malaysia. (16 tracks by local bands such as False Opus, Prana, Love Me Butch, Butterfingers, Subculture, Disagree etc.)

Sembunyi, Hidden Sounds of Malaysia. Pyretta Records. *2001*: Malaysia. (Compilation of Electronica Music by groups such as Strangedays, Urban XS, Joyless, Dead Star, Herb Vendors, Nightlife Camera, etc.)

Teh Tarik Crew. *How's the Level?*. Positive Tone. *2003*: Malaysia.

Too Phat. *360 Degrees*. Positive Tone and EMI. *2003*: Malaysia.

V.E. and Ruffedge. *Extreme Pleasure Extra*. Positive Tone and EMI. *2003*: Malaysia.

TAN SOOI BENG

Myanmar (Burma)

Population: 42,510,537 (2003)

Myanmar (formerly Burma) is located in mainland Southeast Asia bordering India, China, Laos and Thailand. The country is naturally divided into highland forest, mountain areas and the lowland valley of the Irrawaddy River. The upland areas are home to many ethnic minorities groups (Shan, Kachin, Chin, Rakhine, Karen and others), while the Burmese majority comprising approximately two-thirds of the population inhabits the lowland river valley. The less-developed areas of the minority population subgroups have few urban centers and, with marginal economic development and communications technology, they play a minimal role in the nation's popular music. The urban areas of Mandalay, set on the Irrawaddy River, and the capital Rangoon (renamed Yangôn in 1989) in the delta, have been the centers of modernization and, subsequently, of popular music production and consumption. Myanmar's nineteenth- and twentieth-century political history – from royal kingdom to British colony to military dictatorship – has had an immense influence on the development, practice and distribution of popular musics. In 1989, the State Law and Order Restoration Council (SLORC), the ruling junta, changed the country's official name from the Union of Burma to the Union of Myanmar, and the capital from Rangoon to Yangôn (many other name changes also occurred throughout the country). Throughout the global community these name changes are contested.

While some genres of popular music mimic various international models, several traditions have combined with the indigenous folk and classical styles to a significant degree. As Garfias writes, 'there are in Burma today a number of traditional music styles, and even the line of demarcation between the traditional styles and modern popular music seems to merge into a kind of grey area in which these different traditions are mixed' (1975, 4). Western instruments such as the guitar, violin and piano were absorbed into the classical court music by the end of the nineteenth century. New avenues of expression, as well as new compositional possibilities, were discovered as this music was performed on these Western instruments, and they eventually came to influence the tuning systems used throughout the country and presented opportunities for the introduction of Western-style harmonies and chordal accompaniments. The arrival of recording technology and radio broadcasting soon after the turn of the twentieth century quickly spread many of these new musical ideas throughout the country. In the twenty-first century, the advent of the World Wide Web is also furthering the development of a Burmese popular music in unique ways.

Pre-Colonial Antecedents

The last Burmese dynasty, the Konbaung dynasty (1752–1885), patronized the classical music and theatrical arts of the country to a much greater degree than previous dynasties. Theater troops, radiating out from the Mandalay courts, traveled up and down the Irrawaddy River and throughout the countryside during the dry season. The productions of these theatrical troupes were based on historical stories of previous Burmese kings or, after the turn of the century, morality plays portraying the previous lives of the Buddha. These popular plays included songs and dances both as part of the drama and as intermissions between scenes and acts. These theatrical performances or *pwes* (*zat pwe* [classical] or *pya zat* [contemporary]) continued as a viable form of popular entertainment after the fall of the dynasty and are localized up country in the Mandalay region. Traditionally, these events were accompanied by a *saing waing* orchestra consisting of a *patt waing* (drum circle), *hne* (oboe) and *kyi waing* (gong circle). However, early in the twentieth century they began to incorporate new instruments including electronic keyboards, guitars, bass and trap set into their accompaniments. Since the 1970s and 1980s, *pwes* have utilized two orchestras: a traditional *saing waing* on one side of the stage and a modern pop band (guitar, keyboard, bass and drums) on the other.

One popular theatrical genre that began in the nineteenth century and is still popular is called *anyeint*. In the days of the Burmese kings, this was exclusively royal entertainment but in modern times it is patronized by civilians throughout the country. *Anyeint* is considered to be light entertainment compared with the more serious theatrical traditions of the classical *pwe* (*zat pwe*). *Anyeint* makes use of a small group of players dominated by a female dancer/singer known as the *anyeint*. The *anyeint* alternates dances or songs with a group of two, three or four clowns who entertain with skits, jokes and physical comedy. The performances of both the *anyeint* and the clowns are accompanied by a small ensemble of *pattala* (xylophone) and *chauk lone batt* (tuned drums) (see Garfias 1975, 7–8).

Anyeint, as with many theatrical traditions, can be found in religious contexts such as temple festivals and monk initiations as well as secular celebrations. Many of these theatrical performances run the entire night. *Anyeint* performances are regularly broadcast on state television and in the late twentieth century the government began national competitions. Traditionally the role of comic characters in Burmese theater has been to interject commentary (often social or political) throughout the performance. These comics have been largely responsible for the popularity of Burmese theater. The increased censorship by the government after 1962 led to a decline in popularity of the genre.

Though the roots of these theatrical traditions can be found in the artistic traditions of the Burmese court, the popular support of the theater maintained the tradition after the patronage of the royal court ceased. With the arrival of the British in the nineteenth century and the subsequent takeover of the country in three successive wars (1824, 1852 and 1885), colonial governance and the increased introduction of foreign ideas gradually changed the social and musical landscape of the society. After the third Anglo-Burmese war, Burma was annexed to India and operated as a province of that colony. Under British control Burma's economy grew rapidly, and the steady stream of Indian migrants greatly increased the population, particularly in the new British-designated capital of Rangoon. After the fall of the dynasty and the subsequent loss of patronage, musicians moved throughout the country seeking public patronage. These musicians landed primarily in the urban centers of Mandalay and Rangoon.

Western instruments such as the piano and guitar have been used in Myanmar since the end of the nineteenth century. In the early 1880s the Italian ambassador to Burma gave a piano as a gift to King Thibaw, who immediately set his court musicians to adapting the classical canon to the new instrument. Though the piano was certainly in Burma prior to this time (the British were in occupation of lower Burma by 1852), this endorsement by the reigning king encouraged many of the leading musicians to compose on the piano and adopt it into their performances. A branch of J.C. Misquith & Sons opened in Rangoon in 1889, making pianos available in the urban centers. Misquith's pianos were specially made in European factories with extra specifications for the hot damp climate of Burma (Wright 1910, 351).

Traditional Burmese music consists of a seven-tone scale. The tuning of this scale is roughly equidistant, with a slightly raised fourth and slightly lowered seventh scale degree. Turn-of-the-century approaches to the piano thus disregarded the black keys and included a two-part style that mimicked traditional techniques: the two-mallet or two-hand technique of the *pattala* (xylophone) and *patt waing* (drum circle) and the two-finger technique of the *saung gauk* (arched harp). As the piano allows for greater flexibility and virtuosity than the above traditional instruments, performers soon developed great virtuosity, though the basic two-part style remained. This two-part style, which can also be found in the approaches to guitar and mandolin playing, is a distinctive feature of early Burmese popular music. Up until the 1930s, pianos were often retuned to the traditional Burmese scale; however, with the introduction in the 1920s and 1930s of imported fixed-pitch instruments such as the saxophone, clarinet and trumpet, this practice gradually disappeared. Early performances in keys other than C (and its related modes) involved tuning the entire piano up as much as a step and a half to match with the E♭ of a saxophone or clarinet, or to conform to the comfortable pitch range of a singer. Recent pitch-flexible electronic keyboards have allowed players to conceptually remain in C (and closely related keys), with minimal use of the black keys.

The Recording Industry

The introduction of the recording industry began with Fred Gaisberg's exploration of South and Southeast Asian markets for the Gramophone - Company. As early as 1903, the Gramophone Company had made recordings of local artists in Burma and, by 1910, over 500 Burmese recordings had been pressed (Gronow 1981, 258). These recording sessions were drawn from short trips from India on rushed schedules, after which master tapes were taken back to Calcutta for pressing. Recordings were then returned to Burma for sale on the local market. It was not until 1952 that recording studios were built in Burma. In the 1960s, pressing plants were finally constructed in the country, and Burmese locals engineered the recordings. The recording industry was primarily centralized around Rangoon and occasionally Mandalay. Very little music of the minority populations was recorded.

Columbia Records, HMV (known as the 'Dog Brand'), and the A-1 Film and Recording Company were the largest companies working in prewar Burma. These companies catered to two different, yet overlapping, markets. Columbia and HMV recorded many of the more traditional classical/court-related styles, including much of the theatrical *pwe* repertoire, and A-1 recorded a more modernized international style. Columbia Records recorded performers and composers such as Shwe Pyi Aye, Shwe Dien Nyunt and Nandaw She Saya Tin, as well as Sein Be Da, the last court *saing* player. The leading stage actors, notably the Great Po Sein (1880–1952) and later Shwe Man Tin Maung (1919–69), were early favorites of HMV's Burmese catalog (Sein and Withey 1965, 60). The modern sound documented by A-1 included greater degrees of Western chromaticism, chordal harmonizations of melodies and Burmanized cover versions of North American and British popular songs. A-1's roster included such artists as Kitaya Aye, Tekatho Soe and Daw Mae Shin.

Throughout the 1930s, 1940s and early 1950s Rangoon, with its large British and Indian population, developed a growing interest in US big band jazz. Several nightclubs were established, catering to these musical interests and hiring musicians from outside the country (often from the Philippines) to perform. Visits from jazz greats such as Count Basie, Duke Ellington and Benny Goodman reinforced an interest in big band jazz and the Tin Pan Alley repertoire. Small orchestras modeled on these large bands soon became part of the musical landscape. Though a limited nightclub scene existed (and virtually died in the 1960s and 1970s), these small orchestras, led by notables such as Shwe Pyi Aye, Saya Myein and Aye One Khin Maung, continued to work, primarily in the film industry but also in the growing commercial arena of weddings.

The repertoire of this prewar period was known as *kalabaw*. *Kalabaw*, 'the music of our times,' was distinct from the classical *thachin gyi*, 'great song,' repertoire yet retained a characteristically Burmese style. These numbers are recognized as being 'oldies' of the popular music scene, set apart from the classical repertoire through the combination of Western instruments with Burmese and, to varying degrees, the use of harmonic and chromatic elements. Many of these oldies are, however, still very close to the classical Burmese style, drawing from classical melodies and traditional modes, and utilizing the two-part accompaniment style.

The 1930s and 1940s were a time of great political unrest in the country. A rising anti-colonial movement capitalized on the modern sound and the growing opportunities for distribution with an immense number of nationalistic songs. In 1937 the country gained partial independence, as Burma was separated from India and administration of key civil positions returned to Burmese hands. The *Dobama* ('Our Burma') movement of the 1930 and 1940s, a movement that eventually led to independence, generated many popular songs that were still being sung many decades later. One such famous song – 'Dobama' (lyrics by YMB Sayatin, music by Thakin Ba Thaung) – was designated as the national anthem after independence in 1948. Throughout much of India the Gramophone Company, though a British company, freely recorded many of the national songs that were making a significant contribution to the national movement.

Movies

Films naturally evolved out of the popular theatrical tradition. The rise of the film industry in the 1930s and 1940s drew an increasingly large number of actors from the theater stage. Though film, compared to the theater tradition, was considered low art, the opportunities for financial and popular success were much greater. As with traditional theater (as well as models for films coming from India), many of these early films were musicals. Silent films, popular in Burma into the 1940s, provided full orchestras or single pianists with opportunities for composition and accompaniment in a fast-growing popular medium. By the 1950s, film was much more popular than traditional theater and the success of the Burmese film industry peaked in this decade, with well over 100 pictures per year coming out of Rangoon alone. Preferences for film and newer urban styles encouraged a relocation of sorts for many musicians from the former center of Burmese culture, Mandalay, to the more cosmopolitan Rangoon. Until the 1960s and 1970s, male and female actors were expected to sing, dance and act, though vocal tracks were eventually performed by professional playback singers, with an increasingly small number of singers covering many films. Economic struggles in the latter half of the 1990s greatly diminished the output of the industry; fewer than 10 films were made in the 1999 season. At the beginning of the twenty-first century there was an increase in low-budget video production; however, most of the soundtracks for these productions were drawn from prerecorded music and no musicians were hired for original compositions or recordings. In addition to the Burmese industry, imported Hindi films from Mumbai (formerly Bombay) and Chinese action films were shown regularly in Yangôn and Mandalay theaters.

Independence

After independence on 4 January 1948, Burma moved into a period of troubled democracy, which suffered from insurgent movements (primarily from minority population groups), political factioning and an unstable economy. Coupled with this was a growing emphasis on national unity, which sought to preserve elements of Burmese culture vis-à-vis Western infiltration. Various agencies of the state, including the Ministry of Union Culture and the Burma Broadcasting Service, reinforced certain ideas of national unity with state funding and broadcasting of officially sanctioned cultural products. A fear of losing traditional culture to the modernizing and Westernizing ideas carried through music, film and popular culture, and ultimately became a national agenda. As U Khin Zaw, head of the Burma Broadcasting Corporation during the 1950s, writes: 'The implacability of business so far as gramophone records are concerned, the rapid deterioration of public taste pandered to by cinema and gramophone, the invasion of Western instruments and instrumentation, the ephemeral catchiness of jazz tunes, who but the Government can save Burmese music from the combined assault of these powerful forces?' (1961, 200).

General Ne Win's military government, after its coup of 1962, proceeded to limit relations with the international community. Access to international popular musics was increasingly restricted and often available only through the black market distribution of cassettes. State-endorsed musics included limited amounts of Western-influenced sound (though the piano, guitar, banjo and other instruments had by this time been accepted as a part of Burmese culture). The leading composers and performers of postwar Burma, such as U Ko Ko (see *Piano Birman/Burmese Piano*, Ko Ko, 1995), U Hla Htut, Sandaya Chit Swe, Ma Ma Aye and Tin Tin Myat, remained successful and available in the media due to their apolitical positioning. Shortly after the coup, censorship of popular music increased and lyrical content was subjected to a scrutiny board. Other popular music images, from long hairstyles to Western clothes, were labeled decadent and immoral and occasionally were outlawed.

By the mid-1960s, state-censorship boards were set in place that would review the content of books, periodicals and magazines as well as films and popular songs. This board, originally under the control of the Ministry of Information (transferred in 1970 to the Ministry of Home and Religious Affairs) had the power to forbid distribution of any material that was potentially state-threatening or subversive (Allott 1993, 7–12).

The 1970s to 1980s and Stereo Songs

In the 1970s, fusion between Western styles and Burmese modern traditional music slowed significantly. This was the result of several factors, which included the increased role of the censors, a stronger emphasis by the state on the decadence of Western culture and a general economic decline during the tenure of Ne Win's government. One successful recording by the *saing waing* troupe led by Sein Ba Maw involved a full cassette of US and British popular songs rearranged for traditional (*saing waing*) orchestra, entitled *Burma Disco*. Songs on this recording included the Rolling Stones' 'Paint it Black,' and Boney M's 'Rasputin,' among others. Though the tape had significant success, Sein Ba Maw was reluctant to repeat the project, and returned instead to more traditional performances. Such fusions have tended to be more the exception than the rule, and such endeavors are more often found in live settings than in mass-distributed cassette projects. Precedents for performing US hits on traditional instruments were made many years earlier with Sein Beda (the last court *saing waing* player), famous for his version of 'Colonel Bogie' in 1932 (Lintner 1989, 40). However, the socialist regime of 1962–88, as well as the post-1988 regime, strongly discouraged such musical behavior.

Throughout the 1960s and 1970s, with Western instruments and styles deemed decadent and highly censored, a popular underground culture known as 'stereo' music developed. 'Stereo' music was not only a reflection of technological advances but also a contrast to the stylized, officially sanctioned 'mono' music played on state radio. Despite frequent bans on their material, one group that broke through to popular acclaim was the Thabawa Yinthwenge (the Wild Ones), a band of Mandalay University students formed in 1973 by a young Shan (notably one of the ethnic minorities) named Sain Hti Hsaing. Their songs, which had a carefully veiled social message, became nationwide hits, and Sain Hti Hsaing and his band were the leading popular artists during the 1970s. Though performing on Western instruments (gui-

tar, bass and drums) and drawing influence from such musicians as Bob Dylan and the Beatles, Sain Hti Hsaing's original lyric content reflected on locally significant topics such as life in rural Burma, racial tensions and subtly veiled political commentary with resolute hope for change (Lintner 1989, 40).

1988 and the Pro-Democracy Uprising

In the late summer of 1988, economic and political hardship led to mass pro-democracy demonstrations throughout the country. Many popular musicians joined the events, either as demonstrators or as entertainers on makeshift stages. Events of the 'democracy summer' included a short-lived free press and the formation of labor unions. Sain Hti Hsaing was elected chairman of the Musicians' Union of Burma (the first of its kind), comprised of an independent and informal body of musicians. The union, however, only lasted a month, as it was again outlawed with every other newly formed union by late September of that year. The 1988 demonstrations had their roots in the student movements and were brutally crushed in several massacres of August and September. Though General Ne Win had stepped down, control of the state was taken over by the newly formed State Law and Order Restoration Council (SLORC), a committee of high-ranking generals, many of whom worked directly under the former leader. Despite a free election in May of 1990 (in which Aung San Suu Kyi and her National League for Democracy won the large majority of the vote), the dictatorship refused to relinquish power. As the events of 1988 were partially due to economic mismanagement over the previous decades, the regime was forced to abandon their xenophobic, socialist platform and open up the borders for trade and tourism, and the inevitable increase in foreign influences that accompanied this move.

Following the 1988 events, the State Law and Order Restoration Council (SLORC) came to power, with increasingly draconian censorship laws that directly affected popular musicians. By June 1991 an additional censorship board had been set up under the Ministry of Home and Religious Affairs to scrutinize not only the lyrics, but also the rendition and the musical arrangement of songs, and to protect Burmese cassette tapes against foreign influences, which the SLORC alleged were 'undermining national spirit and patriotism and making Myanmar culture extinct' (Smith 1991, 54). Musicians, filmmakers and artists of all varieties were compelled by Military Intelligence Chief Lt. Gen. Khin Nyunt to work, as their patriotic duty, with the state-controlled Myanmar Music Organization. Since 'music is an effective public relations instrument,' he claimed that 'the public could be organized with the strength of music' (quoted from Smith 1991, 54).

1990s and the Twenty-First Century

In the late 1990s Burma's popular music was dominated by a very few bands. The industry was driven almost entirely by cassette distribution, as few concerts were allowed by the state except in highly controlled environments. The nationalist agenda of the state-controlled radio offered no support to the foreign-influenced styles. Dominating the scene throughout the 1980s and early 1990s were bands highly influenced by heavy metal. Groups such as Emperor and Iron Cross drew their influence from North American and British heavy metal groups from late 1970s to mid-1980s era, including Van Halen, Judas Priest and Metallica. Emperor and Iron Cross were also regularly hired as backing bands for singers wishing to put out an album of their own songs or Burmese-language 'copy songs' of Western and Asian pop songs. These two bands, in addition to frequent releases of their own material, regularly backed-up singers on 30–50 albums per year, which amounted to a large majority of the market. Many of the albums did not have a heavy edge to them, but rather mimicked many softer Asian pop styles. All albums were distributed via cassette after careful self-scrutiny and clearance by the censor board.

As copyright protection was virtually non-existent in the country, performers and their recording companies earned their keep by operating tape duplication stores. Income was earned directly through cassette sales rather than through any royalty distribution system. Many of these tape duplication enterprises also created small booklets of song lyrics and guitar chords of all the popular albums. These 10-page booklets/pamphlets were sold at the duplication shops and on the downtown sidewalks of Yangôn and Mandalay.

Several artists with greater economic means have recorded albums in Bangkok for redistribution in Myanmar. The payoff of the higher-quality recordings is seemingly negligible, as few in the country can afford CD versions of these recordings. One album by the group Big V, entitled *Chit Thaw Kibya Mye*, a collection of five of the country's leading singer-songwriters (Saw Win Htut [of Emperor],

Htoo Ein Thin, Myo Kyaw Myein, Si Thu Lwin and Bo Bo), was released with sponsorship by Thai Airways and London Cigarettes (1998). Though available in Thailand, these projects have had very limited success outside of Myanmar itself.

One additional genre that deserves mention is a style of antiphonal improvised group/leader singing known as *than gyat*. *Than gyat* is found prominently in the Water Festival New Year festivities of mid-April. *Than gyat* is known historically as a politically flavored recitation of the year's events, which greatly amuses the festival crowds gathering on the street to wash away the old year and bring in the new. Given the highly repetitive rhythmic vocal style, often accompanied by drums, Burmese themselves often refer to *than gyat* as Burmese rap, another style that, since the mid 1990s, has become increasingly popular in Myanmar (see Irrawaddy 2002).

The World Wide Web and Burmese Popular Music

Burma's contribution to global pop was, at the beginning of the twenty-first century, quite limited, and little representation of this music could be found even in neighboring countries. The growing political consciousness and anti-dictatorship movement outside the country has become increasingly visible on the World Wide Web in the form of resistance pop. Musicians who were forced to leave the country after the 1988 demonstrations fuel much of this new virtual music scene. Strangely, this Burmese popular music cannot be consumed or purchased within the country due to censorship and the political nature of the material. Government control over fax machines and modems restricts access to the Internet by those inside the country.

An increasing number of political and economic refugees outside the country have capitalized on the distribution potential of the World Wide Web to disseminate Burmese popular music, primarily to other refugees, unrestricted by the government censors. Many of these Web pages are personal home pages, though several pro-democracy organizations have developed their own music pages. Many of these sites contain popular songs by artists inside the country that, likewise, are difficult to obtain while living outside of the country. The reliability and permanence of these web sites is, however, inconsistent.

Discography

At the beginning of the twenty-first century, no Burmese popular recordings were widely available outside of the country, with only small and occasional distribution in Thailand. The classical tradition has been superficially represented outside the country with a handful of CDs marketed internationally by the Shanachie, King and Ocora labels. On these 'traditional' recordings there are, however, several tracks of the early *kalabaw* and modern traditional songs now accessible to the international listener. These albums include U Ko Ko's *Burmese Piano* (1995), Shanachie's *White Elephants and Golden Ducks* (1997) and *Sandaya: The Spellbinding Piano of Burma Featuring U Yee Nwe* (1998).

Bibliography

Allott, Anna J. 1993. *Inked Over, Ripped Out: Burmese Storytellers and the Censors*. Chiang Mai: Silkworm Books.
Aung Zaw, ed. 2002. *Sound Effects: Politics and Popular Music in Burma*. Special volume of *The Irrawaddy* Vol. 10 No. 7. Chiang Mai, Thailand. www.irrawaddy.org.
Becker, Alton J. 1974. 'Journey Through the Night: Some Reflections on Burmese Traditional Theatre.' In *Traditional Drama and Music of Southeast Asia*, ed. Mohd. Taib Osman. Kuala Lumpur: Dewan Bahasa dan Pustaka, 154–64.
Garfias, Robert. 1975. 'A Musical Visit to Burma.' *World of Music* 17(1): 3–13.
Gronow, Pekka. 1981. 'The Record Industry Comes to the Orient.' *Ethnomusicology* 25(2): 251–84.
Keeler, Ward. 1998. 'Burma.' In *The Garland Encyclopedia of World Music. Vol. 4: Southeast Asia*, ed. Terry E. Miller and Sean Williams. New York and London: Garland Publishing, 363–400.
Khin Zaw, U. 1961. *Burmese Culture General and Particular*. Yangôn: Sarpay Beikman Printing and Publishing Corp.
Khin Zaw, U. 1981. 'Burmese Music.' *Open Mind* 2(12): 175–214.
Lintner, Bertil. 1989. 'Politics of Pop.' *Far Eastern Economic Review* (22 June): 40.
Sein, Kenneth (Maung Khe), and Withey, J.A. 1965. *The Great Po Sein: A Chronicle of Burmese Theatre*. Bloomington and London: Indiana University Press.
Smith, Martin. 1991. *State of Fear: Censorship in Burma (Myanmar): An Article 19 Country Report*. London: Article 19.
Wright, Arnold, ed. 1910. 'Misquith & Co.' In *Twentieth Century Impressions of Burma: Its History, People, Commerce, Industries and Resources*. London: Lloyd's Greater Britain Publishing Company, 351.

Discographical References

Big V. *Chit Thaw Kibya Mye*. BEC-TERO Entertainment Co., Ltd. N. n.d.: Myanmar.
Boney M. 'Rasputin.' *Nightflight to Venus*. Sire 6062. *1978*: UK.
Ko Ko, U. *Piano Birman/Burmese Piano*. UMMUS UMM 203. *1995*: Canada.
Rolling Stones. 'Paint it Black.' *Hot Rocks 1964–1971*. ABKCO 6667. *1972*: UK.
Sein Ba Maw. *Burma Disco*. Karaweik Records. *1979*: Myanmar.
White Elephants and Golden Ducks. Shanachie 64087. *1997*: USA.
Yee Nwe, U. *Sandaya: The Spellbinding Piano of Burma Featuring U Yee Nwe*. Shanachie 66007. *1998*: USA.

GAVIN D. DOUGLAS

REGIONS

Chin
Population: 480,000 (2001)

The Chin state (also known as the Chin Hills) is located in the northwestern part of Myanmar (formerly Burma). It borders India in the west (Mizoram and Manipur states) and Bangladesh (in particular, the Chittagong Hill Tracks) to the southwest. Within Myanmar, it meets the Sagaing and Magwe divisions to the east and Arakan state to the south. The mountainous country spreads over an area of 13,902 sq miles (36,000 sq km), inhabited by many different Chin tribes (Myanmar Socialist Lanzin Party 1969). It can be divided into three regions, the northern, central and southern, containing nine townships (northern: Tonzang, Tedim, Falam, Haka, Thanthlang; central: Matupi, Mindat; southern: Kanpalet, Paletwa). There is no common language; instead there are more than 40 dialects. Chin people belong to the Mongoloid race, more specifically to the Tibeto-Burman group, as do a number of other tribes of Myanmar. It is thought that they originated from the eastern part of Central Asia (Lewis 1910). They came into Myanmar from the northwest and the northeast in A.D. 750 and reached their present location around A.D. 1374 (Myanmar Socialist Lanzin Party 1969). The majority live in the Chin and Mizoram states. However, more have settled in Manipur state, the northern Cachar Hills in India and the Chittagong Hill Tracks of Bangladesh. Due to the underdevelopment of the area and an increasing population, many are migrating to India proper, Myanmar proper and abroad.

In 1892, the British annexed the Chin Hills and, two years later, the Chin Hills Battalion was founded by the British Army. In 1948, the Chin Hills became the Chin Special Division and it was transformed by Act of Parliament into the Chin State (with a new constitution) in 1974. The capital city of the Chin State, was moved from Falam to Haka in 1966. Presumably, the first experiences people of the region had with Western music were while serving in the Battalion, although this was probably limited to marching music and standard dances such as the fox trot (Za Tawn Eng 1999). People started to use these dances for social gatherings and so further modified their traditional dances, such as the *che raw kan* (bamboo dance) and the *sar lam* (funeral dance), with freer movement. Increasingly, indigenous music was transformed into the style of North American folk music by adding keyboards and guitars, or by swapping these instruments for gongs, horns and traditional drums.

After the army, Western missionaries entered the Chin Hills: two missionaries, Rev. J.H. Lorrain and Rev. F.W. Savidge from England, reached Mizoram in 1894 (Sangkhuma 1995). Other, North American missionaries (for example Arthur E. Carson and his wife Laura) reached Chin state in 1899 (Chin Evangel Centenary 1998). The Chin (people of the Chin state) had been animists up to this time, believing in evil spirits. A hundred years later, about 80 percent had adopted Christianity. With the arrival of Western hymns (Chin Evangel Centenary 1999) four-part singing became popular. Some young people started to replace the Christian lyrics with secular love lyrics for courting (Za Tawn Eng 1999). However, these songs were never recorded due to the disapproval of the Christian community.

Later, a system for bridging the gap (Ward Keeler 1998) between indigenous music and Western music was developed. An early pioneer of this, Rev. Bawka (a Hualngo, one of the Chin tribes) of the Falam area, adapted further the traditional speech tone and two to three-tone musical scale to the pentatonic scale. His first songs, 'Hawi vel i la zan thim hnuai ah' (Longing for Friends, 1924) and 'Hun leh kum te an ral zel' (Our Eternal Home, 1930) were accompanied only by a drum and sung in the traditional slurring style. The songs of the eighteenth-century Methodist Wesley brothers influenced his lyrics. Even before the songs composed by Rev. Bawka were published in *Mizo Kristian Hla Thar Bu* (New Mizo Christian Hymn Book), their popularity spread all over the Mizo-speaking areas (formerly known as the Duhlian and the Lushai

dialect of the Hualngo and the Mizo people of Mizoram). In the 1980s, singers in Myanmar and in Mizoram recorded some of Rev. Bawka's songs on cassette tapes with Western instruments, for example, 'Hawi vel I la zan thim hnuai ah' (1997) and 'Hun leh kum te an ral ze' (1997).

In 1945, the Burma Broadcasting Service (BBS) began to broadcast Western secular music on a frequent basis (personal communication, Henny Co Htwe 2001). All kinds of Western music, including pop, country, rock 'n' roll and classical, were listened to in private houses. In the 1950s, the Western six-string guitar was introduced. Other instruments, such as the mandolin, the banjo, the accordion, the trumpet and the violin, were also introduced, but rarely employed. By the end of the twentieth century, no brass band, jazz band or classical orchestra had been formed. Rather, the North American country music style had had a major impact on Chin popular music.

Around the mid-1930s, Za Nei Sum of the Falam area composed 'Kan lai tlang ih ca zir mi' (Encouragement to Develop) in the style of the hymns which had been popular in local schools for many years (personal communication, Rev. Lal Biak Lian, 2001). This song was later recorded by Mai Thang Nguri in 1997. From the late 1960s, indigenous singers were given a platform to sing on the radio in Yangôn (Rangoon). Chan Er, of the Thantlang area, composed 'La mawt bang dawt nak hri fek lo cun' (Fragility of Love) in the late 1960s, a romantic love song, recorded by Tin Tin Htun in 1971. It was the first to be discovered by a Bamar (one of the Burman, the majority people of Myanmar), translated into Burmese and broadcast on the radio. This occurred during the early 1970s.

The first local guitar-based groups playing popular Western music were: Vulmawi (Flourishing for Ever) (1976–82) and ABC (Amawi Ber Chinram [Most Beautiful Chin Land]) (1982–89). They played music in the Western pop, country and rock styles. Although both groups recorded cassette tapes of their own songs with native lyrics, only after the ABC recorded their songs in Burmese (the official language) – some of which were written by Salai Tawna – were they broadcast on Burmese radio and television in Myanmar. Many other groups followed in their footsteps.

From the late 1970s, popular Burmese and Western music was played mainly from cassette tapes with large loudspeakers or sound boxes in city tea shops. Salai Thauh Aung was the first to compose ballads in Burmese, such as 'Myaing nan san pan ta pwit,' recorded in 1973 in a native dialect (Laizo) (personal communication, Salai Thuah Aung, 2001). Salai Thauh Aung was followed by Salai Sun Ceu, of the Falam area (personal communication, Salai Sun Ceu, 2001), who became very popular with songs such as 'An mawi sin sin ding lai rawn' (Encouragement to Develop, 1978). Later, in 1979 Za Tawn Eng, known as Salai Tawna, a songwriter, composer, arranger and guitarist (Chin National Day Golden Jubilee Commemorative Magazine 1998), also of the Falam area, wrote 'Chin tawng dan hmah kyu shu liat' (Welcome to the Chin Hills) in Burmese – it was a song of praise, a paean to the area. This song acted like an anthem of the Chin State. The songs 'Tlai tla eng' (Beauty of Sunset' 1979) and 'Tlawmngaihna hlu' (Unselfish, Stouthearted, 1983) in the Mizo language also became very popular in the diaspora of Mizoram and Manipur state. The song 'Tlawmngaihna hlu' acted like the Mizo national anthem. Salai K. Ling Maung, of the southern regions of the Chin state (the Mindat area), was the first to release the title 'Shwe pyidaw hmiau dai wui' in Burmese (Longing for Home) in 1983.

All the above artists and songs became popular in the Chin state as well as the diaspora. However, due to lack of copyright, and production and distribution facilities, recordings were made at the musicians' own expense. In a very few cases, master tapes would be sold to a distributor. At the turn of the twenty-first century, there were no radio stations or recording studios in the Chin Hills. Since there was only one radio station in Yangôn, most radio singers had to go to Yangôn to record. Other musicians used recording studios in Mandalay. Later, in the early 1980s, more and better studios were available, mainly in Yangôn. After 2000, Chin musicians were able to record at the Music Ministry for Christ (MMC) in the neighboring town of Tahan, in the Sagaing division, only 76 miles (120 km) from Falam.

In the Tedim area, in the northern part of the Chin State, the two bands, the Lengtong (1985–1995) and the Zomi Artist Society (ZAS), formed in 2000, have remained popular. Sizang (Kam Za Tual) wrote Burmese songs and recorded in 1993, and Thawnkham recorded his Chin songs in 1999.

At the beginning of the twenty-first century, no music school had been established in the region. Other than in churches, there are no concert halls, clubs or theaters in which to perform. Owing to long-term underdevelopment, transportation is arduous and time-consuming; however, once popular, songs remain popular for some time.

Important Chin Musicians and their Bands

ABC (*Amawi Ber Chinram*) 1982–89:	Za Tawn Eng – Guitar, Bass, Vocals
	Zara – Drums, Vocals
	Hmuaka – Guitar
	Lawma – Drums
	Wyne – Keyboards
	Thuama – Bass, Vocals
	Kyaw Swe Htoo – Vocals
Access, 1973–87:	Salai Za Lian, bass guitarist
Iron Cross, formed in the early 1990s:	Salai Khin Maung Thant – bass guitarist
Emperor, formed in the early 1990s:	Cin Khan Pum – bass guitarist
Vul Mawi, 1976–82:	Lal Ruanga – Vocals
	Siama – Vocals
	Buta – Guitar, Vocals
	Hming Liana – Vocals, Guitar
	Za Tawn Eng – Bass
	Zara – Drums
	Thawng noa – Bass
	Zo Thana – Drums

Bibliography

Chin Evangel Centenary 1899–1999. 1998. Yangôn: Yangôn Press.

Eng, Za Tawn. 1999. *The Impact of Christian Mission Work on the Hualngo People's Music and Culture in Myanmar (Burma)*. Unpublished M.A.thesis, Anglia Polytechnic University, UK.

Keeler, Ward. 1998. 'Burma.' *The Garland Encyclopedia of World Music. Vol. 4: Southeast Asia*, ed.

Terry E. Miller and Sean Williams. New York and London: Garland Publishing, 363–400.

Lewis, C.C. 1910. *The Tribes of Burma*. Yangôn: Government Printing Press.

Magazine Committee. 1998. *Chin National Day Golden Jubilee Commemorative Magazine (1948–1998)*. Yangôn: U Kyaw Sein Press.

Myanmar Socialist Lanzin Party. 1969. *Taiyintha Yinkyihmuh Yuya Dalih Thungsan Mia (Chin)* [The Culture of Ethnic Groups of Myanmar (Chin)]. Yangôn: Sapay Beikman Press.

Sangkhuma, Z.T. Rev. 1995. *Missionary te Hnuhma* [The Work of Missionaries]. Aizawl, Mizoram: Lengchhawn Press.

Personal Communications

Henny Co Htwe, Program Officer (Chin), Myanmar Radio Service. Yangôn, Myanmar. 1 January 2001.

Rev. Lal Biak Lian, Rit. High School Headmaster. Yangôn, Myanmar. 14 December 2000

Molly Muan, Immigration Officer. Yangôn, Myanmar. 19 November 2001.

Salai Sun Ceu, songwriter and singer. Pathein, Myanmar. 14 January 2001.

Salai Thuah Aung, songwriter and singer. USA. 11 December 2001.

Rev. Van Lal Ding. Yangôn, Myanmar. 16 January 2001.

Clifford Van Thang, singer. Yangôn, Myanmar. 29 December 2000.

Discographical References

ABC. 'Tlawmngaihna.' Lynn Studio. *1983*: Myanmar.

C. Luri. 'Tlai tla eng.' Lynn Studio. *1983*: Myanmar.

Mai Seni and Salai Tawna. 'Chin tawng dan hmah kyu shu liat.' Kuat Cia Moe Tah 880. *1982*: Myanmar.

Mai Thang Nguri. 'Hun leh kum te an ral zel.' Logos Studio. *1997*: Myanmar.

Mai Thang Nguri. 'Kan lai tlang ih ca zir mi.' Logos Studio. *1997*: Myanmar.

Mai Van Lal Muani. 'Hawi vel i la zan thim hnuai ah.' Logos Studio. *1997*: Myanmar.

Salai K. Ling Maung. 'Shwe pyidaw hmiau dai wui.' May Studio. *1983*: Myanmar.

Salai Sun Ceu. 'An mawi sin sin ding lai rawn.' May Studio. *1978*: Myanmar.

Salai Thuah Aung. 'Lung thli tum par dawh.' BBS Radio Studio, Yangôn. *1974*: Myanmar.

Sizang (Kam Za Tual). 'A yik ih miu sih.' Lynn Studio Tah 25. *1993*: Myanmar.

Thawnkham. 'It na ngaih na.' December Studio 261 / 99 (6). *1999*: Myanmar.

Tin Tin Htun. 'La mawt bang dawt nak hri fek lo cun.' BBS Radio Studio. *1971*: Myanmar.

Yangôn Hualngo Singers. 'Hawi vel i la zan thim hnuai ah.' Logos Studio. *1997*: Myanmar.

Yangôn Hualngo Singers. 'Hun leh kum te an ral zel'. Logos Studio. *1997*: Myanmar.

Discography

ABC. 'A hla ka ba nging si tha.' May Studio. Tah 959. *1984*: Myanmar.

ABC. 'Chit tu Nu Nu.' *Kuat cia moe*. Lynn Studio. Tah 880. *1982*: Myanmar

Salai Thuah Aung. 'Myaing nan san pan ta pwit.' St. Paul Studio. *1973*: Myanmar.

Vulmawi. 'Lalruanga duh ai sam.' *Raldawna leh Tumchhingi*. Myo That Studio. *1976*: Myanmar.

Vulmawi. 'Rem ang maw.' *Parmawi rimtui*. Oasis Studio. *1980*: Myanmar.

ZA TAWN ENG (SALAI TAWNA)

The Philippines

Population: 84,619,974 (2003)

The Philippines is an archipelago of about 7,107 islands located to the south of China and at the northern tip of Borneo, within the tropical region of Southeast Asia. Its economy is largely agricultural, with rice, corn, various tropical fruits, coconut and sugar cane as its principal crops. In past decades, an upsurge in transnational timber and mining production caused many problems of forest denudation and soil erosion. These once dense forests have been home to a number of minority groups of people who practice a 'traditional' Southeast Asian culture that has almost if not totally withstood 300 years of Spanish colonization, beginning in the sixteenth century, and North American subjugation at the turn of the twentieth century. In its urban and suburban areas a strong 'Westernized' Christian population resides, while in the island of Mindanao in the south are peoples who practice the Islamic religion. The seat of government is located in Metro Manila in the National Capital Region.

Ferdinand Magellan incorporated the Philippines into territory held by the Spanish crown in 1521. Three centuries of subsequent Spanish rule transformed the relatively isolated subsistence economies into a feudal system made up of *encomiendas* (land grants to the Spanish elite), later transformed into the *haciendas* (big plantations owned by the elite) (Constantino 1992). The nineteenth century marked the opening of trade routes through the Suez Canal and the emergence of a privileged class of *illustrados* among the local ('*indio*') population.

Liberal ideas that now found their way into the intelligentsia gave rise to a reform movement, which developed into a revolutionary sentiment in the late nineteenth century. A revolution culminated in 1898 in a brief period of independence from Spain. Months later, however, Spain sold the Philippines to the United States in the Treaty of Paris, ushering in a new regime of social and cultural domination. Japanese invasion during World War II did not have much cultural influence, especially as liberation came quickly when the United States reoccupied the country and gave the Philippines its 'independence' in 1946. From that time on, the Philippines was under a democratic rule, up until the declaration of martial law by the Marcos dictatorship in 1972. Democratic institutions returned only after the Marcos regime was toppled by the so-called 'peaceful revolution' that ushered in the regime of Corazon Aquino.

The Spanish and US colonial regimes had strong cultural and social influences on the majority of the Philippine population. These colonial experiences created a society whose social institutions were modeled after the colonizer's respective societal structures. It was the practice of Roman Catholicism and the establishment of Spanish political rule that created and shaped a mainstream Philippine culture. This mainstream culture would subsequently be alienated from that of traditional Southeast Asia, cultivated by those who rejected Spanish rule by retreating into the hinterlands. But while much influence may still be traced from the Spanish colonial regime, it was the US regime that established institutions that make up most of the structures of modern Philippine society. The creation of modern institutions and the absorption of the Philippines into the global political economy likewise created a need for forms of leisure that would fit such a society. These changing social conditions, shaped by both colonial regimes, gave rise to the development of Filipino popular music in the forms that are known in the twenty-first century.

Folk and Popular Forms up to the Nineteenth Century

The changes introduced by Spanish colonization to the Philippine social, political and physical landscapes produced hybrid forms of music that may be rooted in Asian traditions but have strong musical influence from Spain. It was out of these conditions that a Westernized music culture in the Philippines had crystallized by about the nineteenth century.

A major part of the cultural experience of the people centered on religious or Christian subjects. At the beginning, Western music was introduced by way of the Spanish friars who taught Gregorian chant for masses and other liturgical celebrations. In Lumbang, Laguna, the southern part of the island of Luzon, Fray (friar) Juan de Santa Maria in 1606 gathered about 400 boys from various places and trained them in singing and instrumental playing. In 1742, a singing school was established at the Manila Cathedral (J. Maceda 1979). At about this period, baroque pipe organs were constructed in various parts of the country, including Luzon and Bohol in the central islands of the Visayas. Among the pipe organs built during this period, the one in the San Agustin church in Manila (restored in 1998) and the famous Bamboo Organ of Las Pinas have survived until the twenty-first century.

Folk music of a religious nature, but outside the Roman Catholic liturgy, developed as indigenous traditions were transformed to utilize Christian symbols (Baes 1998b; Santos 1994, 1998). Music in these rites became widely popular; it utilized Westernized forms of Hispanic origin for indigenous rites and/or the veneration of spirits, now symbolized by Roman Catholic saints. The *sanghiyang* in the province of Cavite, the *subli* in the province of Batangas and the *turumba* in the town of Pakil in Laguna are examples of such folk rites combined with Christian symbolism in the Southern Tagalog region. The Catholic church had incorporated some of these para-liturgical rites into the liturgy in the form of feasts and devotions to the Virgin Mary, or to other saints. These include the *flores de Mayo* (May flower devotions), the *panunuluyan* (a rite performed on Christmas Eve depicting Joseph and Mary searching for a room in Bethlehem), the *salubong* (performed at dawn during Easter) and the *pangangaluluwa* (performed during All Saint's Day in November). The *villancicos* became popular Christmas songs by the nineteenth century, adapted directly from the Spanish form. In the Visayan islands, these Christmas songs are referred to as the *daigon*.

Perhaps the most widespread among these rites is the *pasyon*, a form of chanted poetry on the life of Christ performed during the Lenten season. The *pasyon* was still popular at the beginning of the twenty-first century in both urban and rural areas and is widespread among the lowland Christians in the entire Luzon as well as the Visayan islands. The text takes the form of a long narrative poem of epic proportions. Versions of the *pasyon* emerged before the nineteenth century, but the one published in 1814 as the *Casaysayan nang Pasiong Mahal ni Jesucristong Panginoon* (Account of the Sacred Passion of Our Lord Jesus Christ) became popular among the rural folk in the nineteenth century. This version's authorship was attributed to a native priest by the name of Mariano Pilapil, hence known as the *Pasyong Pilapil* (Ileto 1989 [1979]). Other versions of the *pasyon* have existed in other regions as well, utilizing regional languages such as Bicolano or Ilocano.

Secular entertainment and theatrical forms would also have Christian elements and served as a medium of Spanish religious propaganda (Santos 1998). These include the *moro-moro*, which depicted the Muslim-Christian wars; the *cenaculo*, a play on the passion of Christ; as well as the *awit at corrido* and the *comedia*, adapted from the Spanish forms of metrical romances. Other forms include the *duplo*, a literary musical form associated with a nine-day series of prayers; the *zarzuela*, a kind of popular music theater; and the *carillo*, a shadow play.

Song genres that may have developed from older 'native' forms include the *dalit*, a long prayer or litany to the Virgin Mary; the *tagulaylay*, a recitative lament used also in the context of the *pasyon*; and the *awit*, a slow song in triple meter. The word *awit* in modern Filipino language means 'song.'

The *kumintang* was originally a war song (*canto guerrero*) but developed into a song and dance form associated with love and courtship during the colonial period (Dioquino 1994). In the early 1800s, travelogues describe the *kumintang* as a seductive love dance in triple time, performed to a melancholy song accompanied by the guitar and the *bajo de unas* (string bass).

The *kundiman* is another type of song that may have developed from older forms but became associated with love and courtship in the nineteenth century. This also developed into songs that symbolized the revolutionary sentiment of the late nineteenth century, during the fight for independence against Spain. Perhaps the most popular of these is the song 'Joselynang Baliwag' (Joselina of Baliwag), which has been referred to as the *kundiman ng himagsikan* (*kundiman* of the revolution) and was said to have inspired the *katipuneros* (revolutionaries). Originally, 'Joselynang Baliwag' was a love song dedicated to a certain Joselina Tiongson of Baliwag in the province of Bulacan. The expression of revolutionary sentiments is made possible because the woman symbolizes the mother country (Hila and Santos 1994). Other *kundiman* songs

popular among the revolutionaries were 'Kundiman de 1800' (which adapted the folk song 'Doon Po sa Amin') by Bonifacio Abdon, and 'Sa Dalampasigan,' which dealt with the death of national heroes Jose Rizal and Jose Burgos (T. Maceda 1994b). In the early twentieth century, with the emergence of Filipino composers such as Bonifacio Abdon, Nicanor Abelardo and Francisco Santiago, the *kumintang* and the *kundiman* developed into what might be considered a counterpart of the German lied.

Filipino dance music was patterned after Spanish and European dance forms. These include the *carinosa*, *balitao*, *pandanggo*, polka, *dansa*, habanera, *jota* and the *rigodon*.

Along with these musical developments were the emergence of musical groups, the most popular of which were the *rondalla*, an ensemble of plucked stringed instruments that included the *bandurria*, *laud*, *octavina*, *gitarra* and the *bajo*. These are adapted from Spanish stringed instruments. The *rondalla* is said to have evolved from the Spanish-organized string ensembles known as the *estudiantina* and the *comparza*, which performed popular pieces and more formal repertoire, respectively (Culig 1994).

Another instrumental group popular for celebrations and theater performances is the marching band, known as the *banda* or the *mosiko*. In certain regions in Luzon, band instruments have been made out of bamboo, hence the term *mosikong bumbong*, while the *banda boka* is a group that simulates band instruments using voices (Santos 1994).

The emergence of the Filipino privileged class saw the cultivation of a Euro-Hispanic culture that bred concert artists and composers. These included composers Marcelo Adonay (1848–1928), Jose Canseco, Jr. (1843–1912), Simplicio Solis (1864–1903), Fugencio Tolentino (flourished ca. 1887) and Bonifacio Abdon (1876–1944). At the same time, musical theater and 'folk' music continued to be cultivated among the people.

'Seditious' Forms Under the US Regime

The revolutionary sentiment that brought the Philippines independence from Spain continued even when the United States invaded the country at the turn of the twentieth century. This was met with harsh treatment, and eventually war broke out against the US forces, who tortured and imprisoned those suspected of aiding the revolutionaries. Those who continued to resist US rule were considered bandits and insurrectionists (*tulisanes* or *ladrones*).

By 1901, the United States resorted to 'hamleting,' in which entire communities were restricted to small 'reconcentration camps' to prevent them from aiding the revolutionary forces and causing the rest of the people anxiety and apprehension (Constantino 1992). By November of that year, the state passed the *Sedition Law*, which punished by long imprisonment or even death any sentiments of independence from the United States either by armed revolt or by peaceful means. Any expression of nationalism was suppressed and the law was used against journalists, writers or anyone who expressed nationalist sentiments 'even in the most veiled manner' (Constantino 1992).

While US rule began building structures of control and domination among the entire Philippine population, a number of artists and playwrights dared to express themselves using symbols that communicated sentiments of independence from the United States to Filipino audiences (Cervantes 1976). This move capitalized on the continued popularity of theatrical forms like the *zarzuela* or musical theater.

One of the most notable among the so-called 'seditious' playwrights was Aurelio Tolentino, who was arrested and sentenced to life imprisonment in 1905 but was pardoned in 1912 (Constantino 1992). *Kahapon, Ngayon at Bukas* (Yesterday, Today and Tommorow) (ca. 1902) is the best-known drama by Tolentino, and utilized such symbols as the Philippine flag and the singing of the *Hymno Nacional* (the Philippine National Anthem), which were then prohibited under the *Sedition Law* (Fernandez 1994). It was clear that plays like *Kahapon, Ngayon at Bukas* as well as other theatrical forms became important genres that transmitted the Filipino aspiration for independence and self-determination, so powerful that the United States considered them seditious.

The struggle for independence continued up to the 1920s, a period that produced the song 'Bayan Ko' (My Country), which is perhaps the most popular song of nationalist struggle right up to the twenty-first century. Constancio de Guzman composed the song in 1928.

In the 1930s, when the Filipino elite class proved to be collaborating with US rule, songs transmitting sentiments of independence were created along with the rise of mass movements. This period was also marked by the organization of the *Partido Komunista ng Pilipinas* (Communist Party of the Philippines) and the *Partido Sosyalista ng Pilipinas* (Socialist Party of the Philippines), with their respective unions forming their labor and peasant arms. Songs popularized in mass movements of the period include 'Gumising ka, kabataan' (Wake Up, Youth) and 'Babaeng walang kibo' (Passive Woman), which symbolized the struggle for change. The plaintive *kundiman* and the *danza* now became rallying calls that symbolized the long struggle for Filipino nationalism (T. Maceda 1994b). Such a wave of protest music culture continued into the guerrilla movement during the Japanese invasion and the subsequent re-entry of US forces after World War II.

Anglo-American Popular Music in the Twentieth Century

By building structures of social, political and economic control, the United States was able to pacify the mainstream of Philippine society into acceptance of the supremacy of the US system. Collaboration with the native elite produced what has been referred to as an 'erosion of [nationalist] consciousness' (Constantino and Constantino 1990), as educational institutions were shaped according to the US system along with the introduction of the English language. Earlier in the twentieth century, forms of Philippine entertainment were still hewn out of traditional 'Filipino-Hispanic' forms like the *kundiman*, *balitao* and the *zarzuela* (T. Maceda 1994a). But Anglo-American popular music became widely heard as a result of the opening of dance halls and cabaret, and the advent of vaudeville shows. This was perhaps where forms like the fox trot, ragtime and the cakewalk were first heard, as played by Filipino dance bands. Vaudeville shows (*bodabil*) consisted of a variety of acts, which included slapstick comedy routines and dance numbers. Filipino folk songs were also arranged into dance rhythms that would suit the US taste.

In the 1920s, Victor Records and Columbia Records took an interest in recording popular *kundiman* and *zarzuela* songs as well as those by well-known Filipino composers, notably Nicanor Abelardo (*Mutya ng Pasig* 1924), Francisco Santiago (*Anak Dalita* 1917) or even *Bayan Ko* by Constancio de Guzman (T. Maceda 1994a). With the introduction of radio, sheet music, live entertainment, movies and records, commercial popular music from the United States had found its place in mainstream Philippine society.

During the Japanese invasion of 1942 to 1944 during World War II, popular entertainment like the *bodabil* shows continued, but other forms of US entertainment were banned and US values were suppressed. The Japanese branded US culture as decadent, while concealing its own agenda of economic and cultural expansionism in what was termed the 'Greater Asia-Pacific Co-Prosperity Sphere.' In this way, pro-Filipino virtues were promoted side by side with pro-Japanese virtues, with emphasis on the latter; songs were one medium through which to disseminate these values.

The late 1940s saw the re-entry of US forces and the granting of Philippine 'independence' in 1946. As the world was rebuilding itself after the turmoil of World War II, US forms of entertainment resurfaced in the Philippines. The US military presence exposed the Filipinos to swing music through the continued proliferation of the *bodabil* type of variety shows.

In the 1950s, a Latin American influence on Filipino popular music grew out of the popularity of famous Latin American artists, among them Xavier Cugat (Roman 1998). Cugat visited the Philippines in 1953, and since then has served as an icon for dance band artists who saw the potential in cultivating music with Latin rhythms such as the rumba or the samba. One important development was the sprouting of instrumental groups called the *cumbachero*, which played in town gatherings such as fiestas. Filipino folk songs were arranged in Latin American rhythmic modes and played on guitars, harmonica, a *bajo* (one-stringed bass made of an empty gasoline tank) and an assortment of percussion instruments such as the *güiro*, maracas, congas and bongos.

The 1950s and the 1960s were marked by the entry of recent trends in the United States via the medium of radio, television and phonograph records. Country music, rock 'n' roll and the blues carried on as 'standards,' shaping Filipino popular taste. Local artists patterned their acts after popular US artists. Eddie Mesa was dubbed the 'Elvis Presley of the Philippines,' Anita Valenzuela the 'Doris Day of the Philippines,' Diomedes Maturan the 'Perry Como of the Philippines' and Nora Aunor the 'Timi Yuro of the Philippines' (T. Maceda 1994a). While all of this was taking place, the *kundiman* in its more popularized form continued to be cultivated, especially in the rural areas during amateur singing contests. Artists like Rick Manrique and Ruben Tagalog, both dubbed the 'Kings of Kundiman,' made recordings and had their own following among sectors of the population.

In the 1960s, Beatlemania swept the country

until the unfortunate incident in 1966 when, during their scheduled concert in Manila, the group was literally 'thrown out of the Manila airport' after a misunderstanding with the Marcos government. Even then, such groups as the Moonstrucks, the Highjacks, RJ and the Riots, the Tilt Down Men, the Bad Habits and the Electromaniacs were clearly patterned after such famous groups as the Ventures, the Dave Clark Five, the Monkees and the Rolling Stones, as well as the Beatles (Roman 1998).

From the late 1960s until about the mid-1970s, some groups such as the Circus Band and the Ambivalent Crowd brought more 'sophisticated' trends like 'R&B and/or 'Joe Cocker's Mad Dogs and Englishmen' type of vocal ensemble arrangements, which were relatively uncommon, to the Filipino popular music scene. After they disbanded, members of both these groups were to become major artists toward the end of the 1970s, when Filipino popular music had reached a point of relatively strong development. Moreover, a few radio stations, such as DZRJ, gave the Filipinos a taste of such groups as Blind Faith, Cream, Traffic, Jethro Tull, Steely Dan and Return to Forever. All these groups were almost unheard of, and their recordings were 'unavailable' in local record stores and unknown to the mainstream who, during that time, appreciated ballad and pop, rock 'n' roll and the latest dance crazes such as salsa (Baes 1999).

Counter-Trends from the 1970s to the 1990s

From the 1970s to the 1990s, popular music in the Philippines reached a period of significant development, in what could be described as 'various degrees of Filipino consciousness.' In the early 1970s, the radio station DZRJ was instrumental in the proliferation of *pinoy rock* (Filipino rock). Their daily program, called *Pinoy Rock and Rhythm*, featured commercially produced recordings of bands such as the Juan de la Cruz Band and Maria Cafra. It also gave playing time to songs by upcoming artists such as the group Aunt Irma, the folk singers Florante, and Charlie Brown. By the mid-1970s, DZRJ's *Battle of the Bands* bred even more artists and promoted *pinoy rock* to even more audiences. DZRJ did not confine its promotion of *pinoy rock* to rock music. The radio station also featured bands like Heber Bartolome's Banyuhay, which utilized the folk-rock genre to communicate messages of social significance, or Bong Penera's Batucada, which was a major exponent of Latin jazz.

At about the same time, the 'Manila sound' flourished as a genre of Filipino popular music, with the groups Hotdog and Cinderella as its main exponents. The 'Manila sound' was a fad made up of the 'bubblegum' type of pop ballad with lyrics that dealt mostly, if not solely, with love. Toward the 1980s, when John Travolta's *Saturday Night Fever* and the Bee Gees rose to popularity, disco groups like VST and Company as well as the Boyfriends recorded songs in the same discothèque genre, but with Filipino texts.

The late 1970s also saw the flowering of the Filipino pop genre, with the institution by both government and private sectors of the Metro Manila Popular Music Festival (Metropop). This annual songwriting competition was geared toward discovering new Filipino talent in popular music, and produced a rich repertoire of Filipino music ranging from pop ballads to folk and folk-rock songs. Ryan Cayabyab's 'Kay ganda ng ating musika' (How Beautiful our Music) won the top prize in the first Metropop competition and gained instant commercial success. Meanwhile, Freddie Aguilar's 'Anak,' which did not garner any prize during the 1978 Metropop, eventually earned commercial success in the international pop music scene.

The 1970s were significant also because, for the first time, the state showed its support for Filipino popular artists, with its decree to allot radio airtime to Filipino pop singers as well as local compositions every hour. Such conditions enabled Filipino commercial music to flourish on its own and Filipino artists to gain national recognition. This continued into the 1990s.

While these musical activities were going on in the commercial sphere, another type of popular music resulted from the growing militancy and the rise of student activism against the Marcos regime. In 1977, a group of students from a university in southern Luzon grouped together to form the Tulisanes, which created music based on socially relevant texts that were used by popular social movements throughout the country. During the Marcos dictatorship, one cassette album was recorded by the Tulisanes in utmost secrecy, and was distributed to communities through various advocacy groups. Composed of original music and adaptations of Latin American *nueva canción*, with texts dealing mainly with the plight of the poor, the album inspired other groups in the country to produce new protest songs. This, along with groups such as Asin, Banyuhay, Inang Laya and the singer Jess Santiago in Metro Manila, created a musical counter-culture that was critical of the political situation in the country. Later in the 1980s, groups

such as the Patatag in Manila, the Salidummay in northern Philippines, the Balitaw in the Visayan islands and Joey Ayala's Bagong Lumad in the southern island of Mindanao added the flavor of local culture to protest music, with the incorporation of traditional ('ethnic') instruments and appropriation of Asian singing styles. Protest music took another significant step when, at the height of the EDSA (Epiphania de los Santos Avenue) uprising – which toppled the Marcos dictatorship – commercial artists like Freddie Aguilar and the pop-music group Apo Hiking Society joined the 'parliament of the streets.' On this occasion, Aguilar's rendition of the 1920s song 'Bayan Ko' became a rallying call.

The relatively democratic situation during the post-Marcos era allowed the popularization of protest music, particularly since independently produced cassette albums flourished during this period, as during other popular social movements. Later in the 1990s, such songs, which contained vital social commentaries, were lumped together by enthusiasts as 'Filipino alternative music.' However, while a clear ideological base characterized protest music of the 1980s, those musicians dubbed 'alternative' in the 1990s were not very clear about issues such as 'imperialism' or 'colonization,' a fact that hindered the development of what might otherwise have become a modern popular protest music movement in the Philippines.

Picking up from the trends of the times, especially with the appropriation of indigenous musical elements, artists from the commercial music industry attempted to create a type of Filipino popular music that was identifiable as 'Filipino.' In the late 1980s, Cayabyab created a set of songs under the title of 'Brown Music.' This was seen as a counterpart to African-American 'black music,' and combined indigenous rhythms with the beats of commercial music. Similar to Cayabyab's music was Francis Magallona's localized rap, which appropriated indigenous elements as well. With the emergence of 'world beat,' Cayabyab attempted to penetrate the international market, but his hopes were unfulfilled as no international record company shared his vision (Baes and Baes 1998).

Conclusion

Popular music in the Philippines emerged from the colonial experience of the Filipinos, which created a mainstream society that could cultivate such a form of entertainment. While the idioms and the medium have been predominantly patterned after the cultures of Spain and the United States, Filipino musicians have integrated such forms into their own cultural expressions. This integration took the form either of syncretic music in the nineteenth century, of localized versions of Western trends from the 1950s to the 1970s, or of self-exoticized versions of Anglo-American music that appropriated indigenous rhythms and other musical elements in the 1990s.

While Filipino popular music has developed into a unique form of expression for the Filipinos, one has yet to see how significant these developments would be to the current state of popular music. How could Filipino popular music contribute to a music industry that is still predominantly Western? How could the Philippines contribute significantly when the world market, dominated by certain forces, seemingly cancels out any probable contributions by default? While more recent trends like 'world beat' appear to have opened the doors of the global market to local music cultures, one has yet to see the entry into this market of any Filipino artist comparable to the likes of Shankar of India.

Bibliography

Baes, Jonas. 1998a. *Popular Music in the Philippines*. www.ncca.gov.ph

Baes, Jonas. 1998b. *Westernized Musical Traditions in the Philippines*. www.ncca.gov.ph

Baes, Jonas. 1999. 'Broadcasting Ethnicity: On the Synergy Between Composer and Broadcaster in the Philippine Context.' Paper read at the First Asia-Pacific Regional Meeting on Radio Programming Traditional Cultures. Solo and Bali, Indonesia: KOMSENI Group.

Baes, Jonas, and Baes, Amapola. 1998. 'East-West Synthesis or Cultural Hegemony? Questions on the Use of Indigenous Elements in Philippine Popular Music.' *Perfect Beat* 4(1): 47–55.

Cervantes, Behn. 1976. 'Seditious Theater.' In *Filipino Heritage*, Vol. 9, ed. A. Roces. Manila: Vera-Reyes Inc., 2284-90.

Constantino, Renato. 1992 (1975). *The Philippines: A Past Revisited*. Quezon City: The Foundation for Nationalist Studies.

Constantino, Renato, and Constantino, Letizia R. 1990 (1978). *The Philippines: A Continuing Past*. Quezon City: The Foundation for Nationalist Studies.

Culig, Edna. 1994. *The Philippine Banduria: A Study of Its Educational and Artistic Possibilities*. Unpublished M.A. thesis, University of the Philippines.

Dioquino, Corazon. 1994. 'The Kumintang.' In *The CCP Encyclopedia of Philippine Art*, Vol. 6 (Music), ed. N. Tiongson. Manila: Cultural Center of the Philippines, 92.

Fernandez, Doreen. 1994. 'Kahapon, Ngayon at Bukas' [Yesterday, Today and Tomorrow]. In *The CCP Encyclopedia of Philippine Art*, Vol. 7 (Theater), ed. N. Tiongson. Manila: Cultural Center of the Philippines, 205–206.

Hila, Antonio, and Santos, Ramon P. 1994. 'Joselynang Baliwag' [Joselina of Baliwag]. In *The CCP Encyclopedia of Philippine Art*, Vol. 6 (Music), ed. N. Tiongson. Manila: Cultural Center of the Philippines, 242.

Ileto, Reynaldo. 1989 (1979). *Pasyon and Revolution: Popular Movements in the Philippines, 1840–1910*. Quezon City: Ateneo de Manila University Press.

Maceda, Jose. 1979 (1972). 'Ang Musika sa Pilipinas noong ika-19 Daangtaon' [Music in the Philippines in the Nineteenth Century]. *Musika Jornal* 3: 1–67.

Maceda, Teresita G. 1994a. 'Pinoy Pop.' In *The CCP Encyclopedia of Philippine Art*, Vol. 6 (Music), ed. N. Tiongson. Manila: Cultural Center of the Philippines, 107–113.

Maceda, Teresita G. 1994b. 'Protest SONGS.' In *The CCP Encyclopedia of Philippine Art*, Vol. 6 (Music), ed. N. Tiongson. Manila: Cultural Center of the Philippines, 114–121.

Roman, Nancy. 1998. 'Popular Music in the Philippines.' In *Compendium of the Humanities of the Philippines*, ed. C.C. Dioquino. Manila: The National Research Council of the Philippines, 190–200.

Santos, Ramon P. 1994. 'Sources and Influences.' In *The CCP Encyclopedia of Philippine Art*, Vol. 6 (Music), ed. N. Tiongson. Manila: Cultural Center of the Philippines, 70–77.

Santos, Ramon P. 1998.'Philippine Music: Pluralism and Change.' In *Compendium of the Humanities of the Philippines*, ed. C.C. Dioquino. Manila: The National Research Council of the Philippines, 1–17.

JONAS BAES

CITIES

Metro Manila
Population: 10,818,000 (2000)

Metro Manila is the seat of the Philippine government, and consists of several cities combined to form the National Capital Region. The region is served by an international airport and is located on the island of Luzon, midway between the central provinces of Bulacan and Nueva Ecija, and the southern provinces of Laguna, Cavite and Batangas. The center of economic development, Metro Manila has been an important concert destination for a number of popular artists, ranging from Michael Jackson and Thalia to James Taylor and Chick Corea, reflecting the variety of popular music audiences. At the height of Beatlemania in 1966, Manila made the news when security men in the international airport harassed the Liverpool group after a misunderstanding with then President Marcos. The charm of the rustic modern Southeast Asian city inspired Jim Chappell to issue the album *Manila Nights* (1994).

Metro Manila is also the birthplace of important developments in Filipino popular music, namely, the 'Manila sound,' a type of 'bubblegum love ballad' genre that swept the airwaves in the 1970s. At about the same time, it was on radio station DZRJ, the 'rock of Manila,' that *pinoy rock* (Filipino Rock) was first heard over the airwaves (Baes 1999). Manila is also the birthplace of the Metro Manila Popular Music Festival (Metropop), which since 1978 has bred new artists and composers and enriched the repertoire of Filipino popular songs (see Baes 1998; Maceda 1994; Roman 1998). Important artists and composers in pop music such as Ryan Cayabyab, Freddie Aguilar and Jose Marie Chan, and groups like the Apo Hiking Society, are all based in Metro Manila. The importance of place in the construction of a musical identity was seen when the Filipino artist Joey Ayala, known to have been based in the city of Davao in southern Philippines, moved his base to the National Capital Region to enter into the mainstream of the commercial music industry.

Bibliography

Baes, Jonas. 1998. *Popular Music in the Philippines*. www.ncca.gov.ph

Baes, Jonas. 1999. 'Broadcasting Ethnicity: Towards a Synergy between Composer and Broadcaster in the Philippine Context.' Paper read at the First Asia-Pacific Regional Meeting on Radio Programming of Traditional Cultures. Solo and Bali, Indonesia: KOMSENI Group.

Maceda, Teresita G. 1994. 'Pinoy Pop.' In *The CCP Encyclopedia of Philippine Art*, Vol. 6 (Music), ed. N. Tiongson. Manila: Cultural Center of the Philippines, 107–113.

Roman, Nancy. 1998. 'Popular Music in the Philippines.' In *Compendium of the Humanities of the Philippines*, ed. C.C. Dioquino. Manila: The National Research Council of the Philippines, 190–200.

Discographical Reference

Chappell, Jim & Hearsay. *Manila Nights*. Real Music 138. *1994*: USA.

JONAS BAES

Singapore

Population: 4,188,000 (2003)

The Republic of Singapore consists of one large island and over 50 nearby islets. It is situated to the south of the Malay Peninsula to which it is connected by a causeway across the Johore Strait. It is effectively a city-state, with the city of Singapore accounting for more than 80 percent of the nation's population. The city is a major international commercial center and has textiles, electronics and oil refining industries. The population is 76 percent Chinese, 15 percent Malay and 6 percent Indian and Sri Lankan.

In 1819 the city became the Asian headquarters of the British East India Company and was later incorporated into the British colony of the Straits Settlements. Singapore was occupied by the Japanese during World War II. It gained independence in 1959 and in 1963 formed the Federation of Malaysia with Malaya. Because of tensions between the Malays and Singapore's majority Chinese population, the federation was dissolved in 1965. The authoritarian Lee Kwan Yew was prime minister of the Republic of Singapore until 1991.

Various communal organizations have maintained a range of traditional music and dance in Singapore. In the late twentieth century, *dikir barut* groups such as Sri Mahligai performed such Malay styles as *dondang sayang*, *inang* and *ronggeng*. There was also a Singapore Malay Orchestra. The Kathakali arts organization maintained the city's tradition of classical Hindu dance. The Chinese community celebrated the New Year with the Lion Dance, and Chinese music was played on the *er hu* and *gao hu* stringed instruments.

In the nineteenth century European colonialists and missionaries introduced choral music and, later, choirs. These were taken up by the Chinese community, which formed vocal ensembles in the 1920s and 1930s to perform four-part folk song arrangements and patriotic anti-Japanese songs from the Chinese mainland. These groups went underground during the Japanese occupation but were reestablished after 1945. Leading figures in the Chinese choral movement were Leong Yoon Pin with his Rediffusion Youth Choir, and the composer Lee Yuk Chuan, leader of the Melo Art Choir. Youth choirs were encouraged by the Ministry of Education after independence. Many performed at the Singapore Youth Festival, launched in 1966. The televised biannual *Sing Singapore* campaign was launched in 1988, when almost 200 choral groups performed patriotic songs.

The Singaporean interest in choral music found an outlet after World War II in barbershop quartets such as the Benny Singers (led by Benjamin Khoo) and Harry Tan's The Gospel Melody. Later in the twentieth century Singapore produced a cappella and pop vocal group ensembles like Vocaluptuous, Octmented and Baduk Pantai with their Beach Boys–style harmonies.

Other European influences were evident in the music of imported Filipino and Goan bands which played dance music in hotels and accompanied silent films in cinemas, and in the activities of the Singapore Music Society which sponsored light music and jazz events. In the 1950s hotel bands led by Ahmad Jaafar and Gerry Soliano performed for the British, Chinese and Eurasian middle class (Kong 1998, 454–55). The first Singaporean singer to create an international reputation was the Chinese actress S.K. Poon, who made films and recordings in Hong Kong in the 1950s.

Singapore's preeminence as a trading port made it an early center of the Asian recording industry. The British Gramophone Company, later part of EMI, opened a record manufacturing plant in the 1920s. The Gramophone Company's agent, T. Hemsley and Co., had its own label, Chap Singa (*singa* means 'lion' in Sanskrit), which recorded Indonesian *kronkong* as well as Malay and Chinese music. Singapore was the regional hub of the Malay music business until it separated from Malaysia in 1965.

In the 1960s, English-language pop came to dominate the Singapore scene. The British group Cliff Richard and the Shadows played in Singapore in 1961, and numerous beat groups were formed in imitation of this and other Anglo-American acts. These included the Shadows copyists the Quests, the Cyclones (Beatles) and Wilson David (Elvis Presley) (Kong 1998, 455).

This scene was curtailed in 1973 when a government anti-drugs campaign led to the closure of clubs, and groups disbanded or moved abroad. In the 1980s a more liberal attitude prevailed when the police force sponsored annual rock concerts, and new clubs and discothèques were opened. Nevertheless, the Singapore government remained vigilant about censoring foreign popular music on moral grounds. Tracks by Madonna, Sinead O'Connor and others were banned by the Controller of Undesirable Publications in the 1990s.

In the late 1970s singer-songwriters such as Liang Wern Foo and Eric Moo (born in Malaysia in 1963) established the Mandarin language *xinyao* pop genre in Singapore. Moo was the first Singaporean singer to reach regional Chinese audiences, notably in Taiwan. In the 1990s the young female singers Kit Chan and Stefanie Sun (b. 1978) emulated his international success.

Composer, singer and actor Dick Lee was a leading figure in the Singapore music scene for several decades. His most renowned album was *The Mad Chinaman* (1990), and in 2002 he wrote the musical show *Forbidden City: Portrait of an Empress*, with Kit Chan in the title role. He was later appointed as Asian regional head of A&R (artist and repertoire) for Sony Music.

Despite the government's suspicion of youth music trends, Singapore had its own reggae (Bushmen, No Names), R&B (Asha), techno (Club Ecstacy) and rap artists in the 1990s.

Singapore has a well-established media and music industry infrastructure. In the 1930s, popular music was broadcast by amateur radio societies set up in the main towns. Singapore has numerous broadcasting channels. Founded in 1936, by the start of the twenty-first century the Chinese-owned Media Corp group operated six television channels and 10 radio stations. In 1995 MTV International chose Singapore as the base for the relaunch of its MTV Asia service.

The Singapore Phonogram and Video Association was set up in 1976 and had about 40 members by the early twenty-first century. Much of its activity concerned piracy, and the International Federation of the Phonographic Industry opened a Singapore office in 1981 to lobby the government. While the local pirate retail business was curbed in the following decade, Singapore became a major exporter of pirate cassettes, mainly to Africa and Latin America. A copyright collection society, COMPASS, was formed in 1987 to exercise songwriters' and composers' rights to be paid by music users such as broadcasters, karaoke parlors and concert promoters.

Bibliography

Kong, Lily L.L. 1998. 'The Invention of Heritage: Popular Music in Singapore.' In *Popular Music:*

Intercultural Interpretations, ed. Tôru Mitsui. Kanazawa: Graduate Program in Music, Kanazawa University, 448–60.

Lockard, Craig A. 1998. *Dance of Life: Popular Music and Politics in Southeast Asia*. Hawaii: University of Hawaii Press.

Pereira, Joseph C. 2000. *Legends of the Golden Venus: Bands That Rocked Singapore from the '60s to the '90s*. Singapore: Times Editions.

Discographical Reference

Lee, Dick. *The Mad Chinaman*. WEA. *1989*: Singapore.

Discography

Chan, Kit. *Lola*. What's Music. *2000*: Singapore.

Club Ecstacy. 'Technohead Sex Education.' Valentine Music. *1996*: Singapore.

Moo, Eric, and Zhang Yu. *The Best Collection*. EMI 724359435121. *2002*: Singapore.

Sun, Stefanie. *I Am Sun Yanzi*. Warner Music. *2000*: Singapore.

DAVE LAING

Thailand

Population: 62.300,000 (2002).

The kingdom of Thailand, located in Southeast Asia on the Gulf of Thailand and the Andaman Sea, shares boundaries with Myanmar (Burma) to the west and northwest, Laos to the east and northeast, Cambodia to the southeast and Malaysia to the south. Although rich in natural resources, Thailand was never colonized by Europeans and has had a unified monarchy since 1350. Until the abolition of absolute monarchy in 1932, the country was known as 'Siam.'

The first Thai kingdom was established in Sukhothai in 1238, but this was replaced with the Ayuthaya dynasty. The sacking of Ayuthaya by Burmese troops in 1767 led to the creation of a new capital in Bangkok in 1782 under the new Chakri dynasty, of which the reigning monarch King Bumibhol Adulyadej is the ninth king.

Until the twentieth century, travel within Thailand was mainly via the kingdom's extensive river systems. As a result, the four main regions – central, north, northeast and south – remained socially and culturally separate; each region developed distinctive popular cultural forms, such as *fon* dancing from the north, *mawlam* music from the northeast, *lam tad* music from the central region, and *dikir* music from the south. Many of these folk music styles continue to be performed at festivals, funerals, weddings, harvests and, increasingly, at tourism events. Moreover, it is these folk music styles that migrants began to bring to Bangkok from around 1850 onwards that helped shape some of the most important urban song styles in the twentieth century.

Thailand is an ethnically diverse country; within each region there are many different ethnic groups speaking more than 80 languages and dialects.

Music Origins

Spirit and ancestor worship, animistic dances and epic story telling, and other early proto-theatrical performances formed the basis for subsequent theatrical styles. Sung poetry, courting songs and healing rituals (*main puteri* in the south, *lam phi fah* in the northeast) have continued to be an important part of rural life.

The Thai classical tradition has developed over the past millennium, with distinct differences in presentation and performance in the four regions. Royal patronage brought into the court-music system the best folk musicians from the provinces; in the north and south, classical court music strongly influenced the folk music traditions of the two regions. In contrast, both the central and northeastern regions have strong folk traditions that existed prior to classical music. Indeed, central and northeastern folk music have greatly influenced the development of popular urban styles like *pleng luk thung*, or Thai country music, in the twentieth century.

What is clear from the 50 or so instruments used in Thai classical (and much folk music) is that Indian (via the Angkor and Javanese empires) and Chinese influences have been assimilated into a cultural mix that includes Mon, Cambodian, Burmese, Laotian, Javanese and Malay elements.

The Thai Music System and the Importance of Folk Music

Thai music probably developed initially from the pentatonic Javanese music system. The Thai tonal system divides an octave into seven equidistant intervals, in contrast to the Western chromatic scale of 12 intervals. Classical music is polyphonic; typically, one instrument plays the principal melody, usually a circle set of gongs or a fiddle, while the other instruments embellish or make variations around the principal melody.

Much of the folk music of central and northeast Thailand is pentatonic, and music from these two regions remains an active part of rural life, although less so as industrialization progresses. As in Laos and Cambodia, rituals to propitiate the spirits and the chanting of stories written on palm-leaf manuscripts (*an nangsur*, or 'reading a book') were the initial forms of entertainment across the central plains of Thailand, the Korat plateau and the Mekong sub-basin. Gradually, various styles of singing emerged that derived their melodies from word tones (both Thai and Laotian are tonal languages).

In the central region, the main singing style is in the form of a dialogue between performers, often male-female, known as *pleng* (song). Typically, a performance centers around groups of men and women (or man/woman teams) verbally jousting through the improvised (or memorized) repartee of the main singers. *Lam tad* is the most popular style around Bangkok and the central region; usually two male and female groups of two or three members sing rhyming verse full of double entendres to a basic percussion accompaniment. Of the many forms that once existed in the central region, only *lam tad*, *pleng choi* and *pleng i-saw* were still being performed regularly in the early years of the twenty-first century.

The northeastern region, known in Thai as Isaan, developed initially under Laotian sovereignty, and the five million Laotians in Laos and the 18 million ethnic Laotians in Isaan share a common culture and language that bridges the Mekong river, the de facto border between Laos and Thailand. As in Laos, the main folk genre is the sung poetry and verbal tone trickery of *lam*; as many as 15 kinds of non-theatrical and three kinds of theatrical *lam* remain popular and many are widely performed today. The non-theatrical styles can be traced back many centuries but the theatrical styles are a modern phenomenon; in fact, *lam*, or *mawlam* (literally, 'skilled singer of *lam*') as it more widely known, exists in its traditional, acoustic forms like *lam glawn*, as well as the more modern, electrified forms like *lam mu* (large theatrical troupes) and *lam sing* (small, electrified combos) that use electrified and Western instruments.

The above folk styles have greatly influenced urban music like *pleng luk thung*, particularly singing styles. An indication of the strong influence *mawlam* had on what was then known as Siamese music can be seen from an 1865 royal decree banning '*Laokaen*' music (Laotian music), as it was called, across the country. King Mongkut was apparently concerned that the more rhythmically exciting Laotian music was causing Thais to abandon their own music.

The Beginning of the Modern Era: 1880–1932

During the nineteenth century, Siam, as Thailand was then known, came under constant threat from the expansion of European colonialists. Despite being forced to cede some territory in the south to the British and to sign a co-operation treaty with Britain in 1865, Siam remained independent. This was largely due to the modernizing efforts of King Mongkut (1851–68) and his son, King Chulalongkorn (1868–1910), as well as a foreign policy that played the major powers, in this case Britain and France, against each other.

Royal tours to Europe and a growing expatriate community in Bangkok brought Western technology to Siam. Electricity, telephony, photography and cinema all arrived in the latter part of the nineteenth century, during a period of rapid economic growth, bureaucratic reform and greater public access to education; Thomas Edison's phonograph technology arrived in Siam some ten years after its invention in 1877. New forms of technology were introduced by a small elite comprising mainly of royalty, wealthy Chinese traders and some important families.

One of the first forms of Western music to arrive in Thailand was Western military marching music, as was the case for Japan, followed shortly after by Western classical music. Phra Jenduriyang (1883–1968), is often referred to as the 'father of contemporary Thai music'; as a conductor, composer and teacher, he developed marching music for military bands. He also wrote the kingdom's national anthem as part of the process of developing Thailand's first constitution after the end of absolute monarchy in 1932. He was also instrumental in collecting Thai tunes and melodies and in devising a system, around 1910, to write down Thai tunes in Western notation, one of the first moves that led to development of modern Thai music. At the same time, one of King Chulalongkorn's most musically gifted sons, Prince Paribatra, composed what is often claimed as the first Thai Western song, 'Pleum Chit Waltz' (Happy Heart Waltz).

Many new popular theater styles began to emerge across Southeast Asia in the latter half of the nineteenth century as urban populations grew dramatically. Visiting Malaysian *Bangsawan* theater was an important forerunner of Thai popular theater; and in northern Malaysia at this time, a form of Islamic chanting (set to hand percussion) called *dikir* or *dikay*, was rapidly gaining prominence. After *dikir* performers were invited to Bangkok by royalty, the form became enormously popular and, combined with the Buddhist funeral chant, the *suat phramalai*, developed into Thai popular theater, *likay* (*yike* in Cambodia), which has remained popular, particularly in the provinces. *Likay* is similar to an operetta, as it is presented in Western style with wing-drop scenery and musical accompaniment from a small ensemble that plays both Thai traditional and modern instruments. Itinerant *likay* troupes paved the way for the traveling *luk thung/mor lam mu* revue shows that would emerge after World War II.

During the reign of King Vajiravudh (1910–25) support for the dramatic arts in general increased. Traditional Thai operatic drama, *lakhon rong*, from the Ayuthaya period, was revived and spoken drama, or *lakhon phut*, was introduced. Efforts to adapt Western plays and operas into Thai (perhaps the most successful was Prince Narathipprapanpong's adaptation of Puccini's *Madame Butterfly* as *Sao Khruah Fah*) encouraged composers to combine Thai lyrics and melodies with Western song styles. The King himself was also instrumental in this as he wrote many plays as well as songs to accompany dramas. Poems, some from classical poets like Sunthorn Phu, were adapted into song form, creating the foundation for *pleng Thai sakol*, or modern Thai songs.

At the same time, more migrants were arriving in Bangkok, bringing their own music and entertainment from different regions, particularly from the Central region. The folk music that immigrants brought to Bangkok led to urban song styles like *pleng talat* (market songs) and *pleng chiwit* (life songs), which were the roots of later important syncretic urban styles like *luk thung*. Often cited by Thai commentators as the first *luk thung* song, 'Oh Jow Sow Chai Rai' (Oh, the Vegetable Daughter's Bride) was composed by Kamrot Samboonanon, who enjoyed great popularity in the 1940s. Other *pleng talat* composers and singers included Saengnapha Bunrasi and Saneh Komarachun.

The endorsement of Western music and entertainment by royalty led to the development of a curriculum for music (including the use of Western musical instruments) and drama at various selected schools, and the first important graduates began to emerge towards the end of King Vajiravudh's reign. The most important musician to leave music school was the young 'Khru' (Teacher) Euah Sunthornsanan, the founder and leader of the Sunthraporn Band of the Government Public Relations Department, who went on over a 50 year career to become Thailand's most revered contemporary composer and band leader. The band is often referred to as Thailand's first Western music band.

Early influences on Sunthornsanan included Thai classical and various Western styles, particularly ballroom music. As a youth he was fascinated by jazz – then sweeping across Asia – particularly from Nart Tavornbutr, who was already combining Western music with Thai tunes. In 1934, he set up a band for hotel concerts; it proved so popular that the Thai Film Company, one of the first local movie production companies, invited the band to create movie soundtracks. One of Thailand's first 'talkies' was the 1936 release *Thaan Fai Kao* (Old Flame), and the soundtrack, which included Sunthornsanan singing in the song 'Nai Fan' (Dreaming), catapulted the band leader to national fame. In 1939, the band was named the Sunthraporn band and attached to the newly created Department of Advertisement (later renamed the Public Relations Department).

Radio was introduced in 1930 by the government, and Sunthraporn's music was the first to be broadcast nationally. During the military-dominated administration of Field Marshall Pibulsongkram, the band was used to promote nationalist policies, as typified by the song 'Rak Sa-ngob' (Peace Loving). Sunthornsanan created some 2,000 songs in a style that is often called *luk grung* (literally, 'child of the city'), writing poetic lyrics for many of them, as well as performing songs by Kaew Atchariyakul and Earb Prapaipleangprasom. When the movie industry was closed after the 1941 invasion by Japanese troops, the Sunthraporn band played concerts and gave stage shows around Bangkok, cementing its position as the kingdom's most famous band. Despite the rise of pop music in the 1950s and 1960s, the band's popularity continued; with the advent of television in 1955, the band was regularly featured playing concerts and providing soundtracks. Radio plays in the 1950s also featured the band's music.

Besides radio and movies, songbooks were a popular method of media transmission, dating back to the 1880s. Companies like Sri Krung and T. Ngek Chuan dominated the songbook and recorded music markets in the 1930s and 1940s. *Lam tad* was one of the first popular songbook styles, popular with the urban working classes because it touched on topical events and current affairs with bawdy humor. This was soon followed by the 'international songs' of *lakhon rong* musicals, as well as compilations of cinema, radio and musical songs. Interestingly, the post-World War II Pibulsongkhram administration promoted patriotic songs and *ramwong* from the late 1930s, mainly through songbooks and radio. *Ramwong*, based on the *ramthone* circle folk dance, has remained part of many temple fairs in Thailand and is still very popular in Laos and Cambodia.

Popular Music after World War II

After World War II, three trends can be discerned in popular music: *luk grung*, Thai pop and rock, and *luk thung*.

Western popular music became very popular in the 1950s as vinyl records started to arrive from UK-based companies like Decca, often via Malaysia and Singapore, and radio stations started to play international pop music. Ballroom dance bands, swing, soundtracks to Hollywood movies, Broadway shows, crooners, jazz, Latin (mambo, cha-cha) and music from Malayu orchestras began to appear at record stores and markets. Rock 'n' roll also arrived at this time. A second radio network, commercial but government controlled, was set up in the 1950s, enabling radio coverage in the provinces.

Thai musicians, mainly in Bangkok, began to play covers of Western pop in the late 1950s, although under the Sarit Thanarat administration (1957–63), censorship meant that anything deemed risqué was banned. The Southeast Asian tour of Cliff Richard and the Shadows in 1961 influenced popular music in the region as the basic set-up of an instrumental band, fronted by a singer, became the norm for pop groups. 'Beat' music from the UK proved as popular in Thailand as it was in Malaysia and Singapore, and copy bands like the Cats began to release singles and EPs. Bands who played this 'new' pop were called *wong Shadow* (*wong* means 'band') to differentiate them from *luk grung* bands.

The increasing involvement of the United States in Vietnam influenced pop music in the 1960s, and several key military bases were set up in the provinces, particularly in the northeastern towns of Nakorn Ratchasima, Udon Thani and Ubon Ratchathani, as well as on the eastern seaboard. With great demand for R&R, many Thai musicians learnt their music in the bases, where they were exposed to pop, rock 'n' roll, Chicago R&B, Latin rock and psychedelia.

Various bands emerged in the 1960s with the aim of developing Thai-language pop and rock. (A similar process of localization was also occurring in Japan [Hosono Haruomi, Shoukichi Kina] and the Philippines [*pinoy rock*]). One of the first bands was PM7, but it was the Impossibles, formed in 1967, who gained greatest popularity. The band released movie soundtracks for films like *Thone* (1970), as well as a key album from this period, *Ben Bai Mai Dai* (I Can't Go), released in 1971 on the Metro label. The Impossibles recorded what is probably the most sought after international release ever by a Thai band, *Hot Pepper* (1979), a collection of mainly funk covers.

The Impossibles' lead singer/guitarist Rewat Buddhinan emerged from the Impossibles as one of the key producers of Thai pop music. He formed Grammy in 1984 (since renamed as GMM Grammy) with consumer products marketer Paiboon Damrongchaitham. His creative savvy helped launch the careers of Thongchai McIntyre (the biggest star in the music business), Nantida Asawahame, Tata Young (the pop singer with the highest profile overseas) and Got Jakkrapun Arbkornburi (a middling rock singer who switched careers to become the top *luk thung* singer).

Songs for Life

Another rock genre emerged in the 1970s, *pleng phua chiwit* (songs for life), during a period of great political uncertainty. Between 1973 and 1976, Thailand had its first democratically elected government. Clashes between the authorities and students' and workers' groups in 1973 and 1976 encouraged students to take up protest rock and, after a brutal military coup in 1976, many students took refuge in jungles and mountain retreats.

Pleng phua chiwit became something of a symbol of the peaceful fight against dictatorial power. It was headed by Caravan, a band formed from two socially conscious bands, Tor Sen and Sunjorn, and the Bangladesh band. Using a musical soundtrack culled from Western folk rock, West Coast rock and the protest music of Bob Dylan (the musical base of the genre has not developed much since this period), Caravan added stirring lyrics by intellectuals like Jit Poumisak, and broadcast some of their music from jungle radio stations. An amnesty in 1980 brought students out of the jungle, and Caravan joined the Concert for Unicef at Thammasat University (scene of the worst atrocities in the 1976 coup) in 1982, as part of the process of reconciliation.

Carabao was another band to emerge from the turmoil of the late 1970s; the name means 'buffalo' in Tagalog, the majority language of the Philippines. Several key Carabao members studied in the Philippines, borrowing heavily from pioneering '*pinoy rock*' Filipino groups like Juan de la Cruz band. Carabao's fourth album, *Made in Thailand* (1984), catapulted the band to national fame, as did by *Ameri-Koi*. Socially conscious lyrics brought bans for some songs. In 2000, Caraboa's leader Ad Carabao (Yuenyong Ophhakul) used the band's name for a tonic beverage called Carabao Daeng (Red Buffalo).

Luk Thung, Country Music

Luk thung came of age in the 1950s when, in 1953, Suraphon Sombatjalern made his debut with the hit song, 'Nam Da Sow Vienne' (Tears of the Vientiane Girl). A talented singer and songwriter, Sombatjalern's influence is such that Thais call him the 'King of *Luk Thung*.'

Luk thung means literally 'child of the fields,' and refers to the music's origins among the rural poor. Lyrics typically speak of rural hardships and the tough conditions of life for poor urban migrants; this is often contrasted with the idealistic and romantic themes of *luk grung*, the music of Bangkok's elite, but there are also musical differences. *Luk thung* singers feature glissando and wavering ornamentation (initially in the Supanburi central region accent, where many of the first *luk thung* singers came from), in contrast to *luk grung*'s clearly enunciated diction.

Initially, *luk thung* was based on folk music, but external influences, ranging from Malay strings (from Malayu orchestras) to Latin rhythms (called *sam cha*, or '*three chas*'), and brass instrumentation (Xavier Cougat, who toured in the 1950s, was a big influence with his music and spectacular stage shows) and Hollywood musicals to US country music (Hank Williams and Gene Autry) were absorbed along with elements of *likay*. Some of the early stars like Sombatjalern and Toon Tongjai were skilled folk singers.

Typically, *luk thung* shows feature a lineup of singers led by the star of the show, a comedy team, band and a chorus of dancers called *hang kruang*. A glitzy stage show, often set at a temple fair or festival held on the grounds of a district office, features dances, comedy skits, duets, solo singing and may last four or five hours. These kinds of shows really took off in the 1960s and 1970s as the national road system developed, enabling touring to all the provinces. The music was further promoted by the wide availability of transistor radios in the 1960s and cassette technology in the 1970s.

New stars like Sayan Sanya and Pumpuang Duangjan from Supanburi emerged in the 1970s and 1980s, but the popularity of *luk thung* declined as new singers from the northeast brought *mawlam* into the music and Thai pop began to spread to the provinces. The first nationally prominent *mawlam* singer was Banyen Rakkaen, who emerged in the late 1970s. Large *mawlam* troupes (*mawlam mu*) declined in the 1980s as smaller electrified combos emerged, called *mawlam sing*. At the same time, Thai-Cambodians in the lower northeast started recording *kantrum rock*, the electrified version of *jariang* traditional music.

Following the death of Pumpuang in 1992, there was a revival in *luk thung*, and a new generation of stars emerged led by Got Jakkrapun, Sunaree Ratchasima, Dao Mayuri, Mongsit Khamsoi, Ekachai Srivichai, Arpaporn Nakornsawan and Yuyee Yadyar. New FM stations in Bangkok began to broadcast *luk thung* and the major record companies, such as GMM Grammy and RS Promotion, created *luk thung* labels. Moreover, *luk thung* singers have no longer been confined to Supanburi and the central region, as northeasterners have made inroads into the music – as have southern singers; *luk thung* has remained the most popular style across the kingdom.

The 1980s Onwards: Consolidation and Hybridization

From the mid-1980s until the Asian economic crisis of 1997, Thailand posted some of the world's highest economic growth; as a result, the entertainment industry expanded exponentially. Founded in 1983, GMM Grammy (then Grammy), has gone from an organization producing 'bubblegum' pop stars like Amata Tata Young and pop icons like Thongchai McIntyre to a stock-listed horizontally integrated entertainment corporation with interests in production, broadcast media (radio, television, mobile phone songs, movies) and distribution (retail and wholesale). In the early years of the twenty-first century, GMM Grammy claimed to have 50 percent of the recorded music market; its nearest competitor has been RS Promotion, followed by Sony-BEC-Tero and Bakery/BMG.

Thai pop, locally called 'string,' was dominated by Grammy pop stars until the emergence of the independent label, Bakery, in the early 1990s. This label broke the mold of Grammy's cute pop singers with the debut of Thailand's first 'indie' band, Modern Dog. Inspired by British indie bands, Modern Dog's DIY approach to music and witty street-smart lyrics have enabled the band to become one of the most successful Thai rock bands, and certainly one of the most influential. Bakery also set up a J-pop (Japanese pop music) label, Dojo, to release Thai versions of J-pop, and the company's marketing of different music under different label names proved so successful that GMM Grammy reorganized using a similar method. But, despite the initial success, which included pioneering Thai rap with Joey Boy, Bakery was forced to set up a joint-venture with BMG. The other major label, Sony-BEC-Tero became a joint-venture between the Japanese major and the television company BEC and its music production arm, Tero. Sony-BEC-Tero's biggest act has been Amita Tata Young, Thailand's most well-known international singer.

Bibliography

Barkin, Gary Bryden. 1984. *Likay: The Thai Popular Theatre Form and Its Function Within Thai Society.* Bangkok: National Research Council of Thailand.
Clewley, John. 2002. 'Thailand: Songs For Living.' In *World Music: The Rough Guide –Volume 2: Latin and North America, Caribbean, India, Asia and Pacific,* ed. Simon Broughton and Mark Ellingham. London: Rough Guides, 241–53.
Duriyang, Phra Jen. 1990. *Thai Music.* Bangkok: Fine Arts Department, Royal Thai Government.
Fine Arts Department, Royal Thai Government. 1960. *Ramwong.* Bangkok: Fine Arts Department, Royal Thai Government.
Kurusupa Business Organisation. 1982. *Rattanakosin Bicentennial: An Illustrated Book on Historical Events.* Kurusupa Business Organisation: Bangkok.
Kusalasaya, Ruengurai. 1992. *Bot Pleng Haeng Kwam Lang* [Songs of the Past]. Chon Niyom: Bangkok.
Miller, Terry E. 1985. *Traditional Music of the Lao: Kaen Playing and Mawlum Singing in Northeast Thailand.* Westport, CT: Greenwood Press.
Morton, David. 1976. *The Traditional Music of Thailand.* Berkeley, CA: University of California Press.
Pongpaichit, Pasuk and Baker, Chris. 1995. *Thailand: Economy and Politics.* Kuala Lumpur: Oxford University Press.
Rutnin, Mojdarra Mattani. 1993. *Dance, Drama and Theatre in Thailand: The Process of Development and Modernization.* Chiang Mai, Thailand: Silkworm Books.
Siriseriwan, W. 1984. *Jak Pleng Thai Tang Pleng Luktoong.* [From Thai Music to Luktoong]. Soon Sangkit Silp: Bangkok.
Siriyuvasak, Ubonrat. 1990. 'Commercialising the Sound of the People: Pleng Luktoong and the Thai Pop Music Industry.' *Popular Music* 9(1): 61–77.
Siriyuvasak, Ubonrat. 1998. 'Thai Pop Music And Cultural Negotiation In Everyday Politics.' In *Trajectories: Inter-Asian Cultural Studies.* London: Routledge, 206–27.
Nawikamoon, A. 1986. *Pleng Punmuang Tung Pleng Luktoong* [From Folk Music to LukToong]. Karawek: Bangkok.

Discographical References

Carabao. *Made in Thailand.* Krabue 04. *1984*: Thailand.
Impossibles. *Ben Bai Mai Dai.* Bangkok Cassette 128. *1971*: Thailand.

Discography

Damnoen, Chaweewan. *Mo Lam Singing of Northeast Thailand.* King Records KICC 5124. n.d.: Japan.
Duangjan, Pumpuang. *Keow Raw Pi.* Bangkok Cassette 108. *2003*: Thailand.
Modern Dog. *Modern Dog.* Bakery Music 01. *1994*: Thailand.
Mon Rak Luk Thung Soundtrack. Krung Thai Audio 043. n.d.: Thailand.
Prasit Thawon Ensemble. *Thai Classical Music.* Nimbus NI5412. *1994*: UK.
Sanya, Sayan. *Khwam Rak Meua Ya Comb (Bitter Love).* Bangkok Cassette 576. *2003*: Thailand.
Sombatcharoen, Surapon. *Luam Pleng.* Vols. 1–4. Bangkok Cassette S0467-70. *1994*: Thailand.
Suntaraporn, Euah. *Chabab Derm.* Vols. 1–5, 6–10. Bangkok Cassette S0109, S0110. *2002*: Thailand.
The Rough Guide to the Music of Thailand: Lukthung and Morlam: The Hidden Sounds of Asia. World Music Network RGNET1095. *2003*: UK.
Two Faces of Thailand: A Musical Portrait. Shanachi Entertainment Corp 1214. *2003*: USA.

JOHN CLEWLEY

CITIES

Bangkok
Population: 5,700,000 (2002)

Bangkok, the capital city of Thailand, is situated on the banks of the Chao Phraya River, 40 miles (64 km) from the sea. It was founded in 1782 by the first monarch of the current Chakri dynasty, Rama I (King Phra Phutthayotfa), following the fall of the previous capital, Ayuthaya, to the Burmese in 1767. Originally a small trading port dominated by Chinese merchants, Bangkok has developed into the kingdom's preeminent urban center (50 times bigger than the

219

next largest city, at 626 sq miles [1,565 sq km]), which dominates all political, commercial, religious and cultural activity in Thailand.

At the beginning of the Bangkok era, in 1782, there was a renaissance of Thai arts, particularly in classical (court) music and drama. Rules restricting commoners from playing classical music were relaxed, increasing the popularity of classical music and infusing it with folk music elements. European expansion into southeast Asia in the mid-1880s prompted a modernization program during the reign of Rama V (King Chulalongkorn). Military bands and Western instruments arrived. Western classical music was introduced in the late nineteenth century and Thai composers (many of them members of royalty) began to blend Thai music with Western orchestration. Rama VI (King Vajiravudh) continued the trend when he set up the Department of Royal Entertainments, which led in 1932 (following the end of absolute monarchy) to the establishment of the Department of Fine Arts, including a Thai classical music section headed by Luang Pradit Phayrau and a Western orchestra led by Phra Chen Duriyang.

Throughout the nineteenth century and into the twentieth century, new popular musical forms emerged along with the rapid modernization of the city; phonographs appeared around 1890. Folk music from Bangkok's ethnically diverse population (*lam tad* from the central region and *mawlam* from the northeast) eventually coalesced into what by the 1930s were known as *pleng talat* ('market songs'), while Western-style comedic operettas like *likay*, utilizing both Thai classical and Western music, entertained Bangkokians at temple fairs.

Between 1890 and 1932 modernization brought Western media technologies – photography, cinema and radio. Radio disseminated popular music widely, and westernized Thai songs, or *pleng Thai sakon*, developed. Songwriter Eua Sunthornsanan became the most famous *pleng sakon* composer; between 1940 and 1970 he composed hundreds of songs using Thai classical/folk and Western jazz and popular music, creating what is now known as *luk grung* (child of the city) music. *Luk grung* is often considered the romantic music of Bangkok's elite, and is contrasted with *luk thung*, the music of the urban working class and rural peasantry.

Rapid industrialization in the 1960s brought thousands of immigrants to the capital, along with their music. A national road network brought performers from Bangkok to the provinces, and the availability of cheap radios in the 1960s as well

as the development of a music cassette industry spurred Thai country music or *luk thung* (child of the fields) – an acculturated style based on folk music, *pleng talat* – as well as US dance bands, Latin rhythms, US country music and Hollywood musicals. Western pop music became popular from the 1950s and local bands copied the styles of the day. The presence of US servicemen during the Vietnam War in the 1960s and 1970s furthered the popularity of Western-style pop bands, dubbed *wong shadow* (named after the UK band, the Shadows).

Further economic growth from the mid-1980s led to the consolidation of the popular music industry, which in the twenty-first century is roughly divided into *luk grung*, string, songs for life (originally a form of protest folk rock), *luk thung* and international genres. Rock and pop are known as string music and include a wide range of hybrid pop styles from rock to rap to boy bands to indie to J-pop (Japanese-influenced), most of which are sung in Thai. The influence of Japanese popular culture is as important as Western popular culture among Thai youth.

The Thai entertainment industry is the largest in Southeast Asia, boasting one of the world's top 20 music companies in GMM Grammy. Moreover, Bangkok is renowned for the varied entertainment of its clubs (Bangkok is a major dance music center), temple fairs, festivals and cultural shows.

Bibliography

La-iad, Herabat. 1977. 'Development of Thai Music.' In *Asian Musics in an Asian Perspective*. Japan: Heibonsha.

Phongpaichit, Pasuk and Baker, Chris. 1995. *Thailand: Economy and Politics*. Oxford: Oxford University Press.

Rutnin, Mattani Mojdara. 1993. *Dance, Drama, and Theatre in Thailand*. Chiang Mai, Thailand: Silkworm Books.

Smithies, Michael. 1986. *Old Bangkok*. Singapore: Oxford University Press.

Wyatt, David, K. 1982. *Thailand, A Short History*. Chiang Mai, Thailand: Silkworm Books.

Discography

Impossibles. *Ben Bai Mai Dai*. Bangkok Cassette 128. n.d.: Thailand.

Kangsadan. *The Golden Jubilee Overture*. Pisces Music SCD0004. 1996: Thailand.

Prasit Thawon Ensemble. *Thai Classical Music*. Nimbus NI5412. 1994: UK.

Sombatcharcon, Surapon. *Luam Pleng*. Vols. 1–4. Bangkok Cassette S0467-70. 1994: Thailand.

Suntaraporn, Euah. *Chabab Derm*. Volumes 1–5, 6–10. Bangkok Cassette S0109, S0110. *2002*: Thailand.

The Rough Guide to the Music of Thailand: Lukthung and Morlam: The Hidden Sounds of Asia. World Music Network RGNET1095. *2003*: UK.

JOHN CLEWLEY

Vietnam

Population: ca. 79,000,000 (2000)

Vietnam is located in mainland Southeast Asia along the eastern coast of the Indochinese peninsula, bordered by China to the north, Laos and Cambodia to the west, the Gulf of Tongking and the South China Sea to the east, and the Gulf of Siam to the south. The Vietnamese describe their country's form as 'two rice baskets connected by a pole.' The two baskets are the Red River basin in the north and the Mekong River delta in the south, densely populated regions that support Vietnam's traditional rice economy. The pole is the Annamite Cordillera, a region of mountains and highland plateaus skirting the South China Sea. Though it contains a number of smaller river valleys that support rice agriculture, most of this region is rugged and sparsely populated. While the Việt (or Kinh) people make up nearly 90 percent of the population, Vietnam is also home to more than 50 ethnic groups. There are sizeable Chinese and Khmer minorities, and a variety of highland ethnic groups live along the Annamite Cordillera and in the mountains bordering China and Laos.

The origins of the Vietnamese people extend as far back as the Đồng Sơn culture, present in the Red River basin for several hundred years B.C. This region was captured by the Chinese in 111 B.C. and, despite continuous resistance, remained under Chinese control until 938 A.D. Upon achieving independence, Vietnam maintained a tributary relationship with its powerful neighbor to the north. Vietnam's rulers were strongly influenced by Chinese civilization, adopting its examination system and civil service bureaucracy. From the fifteenth century, Vietnam began its southern advance, over several centuries seizing and settling in the kingdom of Champa (located along the coastline of the Annamite Cordillera) and later in the Khmer territories of the Mekong delta.

In the sixteenth century, Vietnam came into contact with European culture through Catholic missionaries. France began exploring the possibility of colonizing Vietnam in the nineteenth century, in 1858 beginning a military campaign that would eventually seize all of Indochina. During the early twentieth century the French constructed a commercial and administrative infrastructure to consolidate their control of the colony. Though Vietnam continued to resist the French, they also sought to learn from the West in order to modernize their nation. The August Revolution in 1945 was the prelude to a war of resistance that led to France's defeat and exit from Vietnam in 1954. From that time Vietnam was split into two nations – the Socialist Republic of Vietnam in the north and the Republic of Vietnam in the south. During this period Vietnam became a hot spot in the global Cold War, with the United States intervening on behalf of South Vietnam, and North Vietnam receiving assistance from the Soviet Union and China. After the withdrawal of US armed forces South Vietnam was defeated in 1975, uniting the country. Despite the fall of communism in the Soviet Union and the Eastern bloc, the Socialist Republic of Vietnam remains a communist nation.

Vietnamese music is influenced by both Chinese and South Asian elements, the latter through long-term contact with the Cham and Khmer kingdoms. Prior to colonization, popular musical entertainments included *hát tuồng*, a court-supported musical theater with origins in Chinese opera; *hát chèo*, a folk theater, the ritual and entertainment music of the court and ceremonial music used in local festivals; *ca trù*, a form of chamber music featuring the musical recitation of poetry; and *nhạc tài tử* (or 'music of talented amateurs'), a style of chamber music emphasizing instrumental creativity and virtuosity. Vietnam also had a rich variety of regional folk song styles.

Popular Music Under French Colonial Rule

From around 1910, a new syncretic musical theater form developed in the Mekong delta that used elements of *hát bội* and *nhạc tài tử* as well as folk songs and the music of that region's ethnic Chinese. First known as *ca ra bộ*, (literally, 'gesture coming out of song'), it developed into a popular new theatrical genre called *cải lương*. Originally, plots were based on Chinese stories used in *hát bội*, but soon there were also stories influenced and adapted from French literature and from motion pictures. Vietnamese also composed new songs in the style of *nhạc tài tử*, most notably 'Dạ cổ hoài lang' (At the Night Drum Thinking of Him, 1918) by Cao Văn Lầu, which developed into the extremely popular aria type, *vọng cổ* (Lament for the Past).

During the mid-1920s, *cải lương* playwrights also began to utilize French song in their productions. By the 1930s, a movement in which Vietnamese lyrics were added to popular Western melodies gained popularity. At the same time, many young Vietnamese taught themselves how to read music and play Western instruments such as mandolins, banjos and guitars. Some musicians began to earn a living playing in dance halls or in military bands. This involvement in Western music served as a prelude to the first songs composed in the Western popular idiom. Songs were performed among friends, at school gatherings, before movie screenings or during theatrical productions. Among the dozens of fledgling songwriters of the 1930s and 1940s, one emblematic figure was Đặng Thế Phong, who composed the well-known songs 'Con thuyền không bến' (A Boat Without a Dock, 1938) and 'Giọt mưa thu' (Autumn Raindrops, ca. 1940). He lived a bohemian life, studying for a time at the Collège des Beaux Arts in the capital city Ha Nôi, and wandering throughout Indochina both giving music lessons and performing his songs on the guitar, before succumbing to tuberculosis at the age of 24 in 1942. His songs, while written in a Western diatonic idiom, retained the pentatonic flavor of the traditional music of northern Vietnam and expressed a drifting, sad romanticism that resonated with Vietnamese who felt powerless as second-class citizens in their own land.

Between 1941 and 1945, at the time of Nazi German occupation in France, Indochina was ruled by a Vichy administration under the supervision of the Japanese. Concerned that their colonial subjects might become sympathetic to the Japanese, the French promoted Scouting and physical education to channel the energies of Vietnamese youth. Songwriters like Lưu Hữu Phước, a student at Ha Nôi University, and Hoàng Quý, who wrote many songs for the Scouting movement, wrote patriotic songs in martial idiom that celebrated a rugged outdoor life and urged young people to remember the glory and sacrifices of their nation's heroes. Later, by the time the Japanese ultimately overthrew the French in March 1945, songs of this type were being popularized by the communist movement, such as Văn Cao's 'Tiến quân ca' (Advancing Army Song) (Thụy Loan 1993, 106–7), Vietnam's national anthem, and Nguyễn Đình Thi's 'Diệt Phát xít' (Wipe Out the Fascists) (Thụy Loan 1993, 108–9), an anti-Japanese song that provided a soundtrack to the August Revolution in 1945.

As a prelude to their war of resistance against the French, the communists formed a coalition of patriotic organizations called the Việt Minh. When war broke out in 1945 and 1946, urban Vietnamese of all backgrounds entered resistance zones in the rural and mountainous regions of the country. This was a heady time for Vietnamese youth, who composed many songs extolling a life of bravery and risk. Vietnam's communist leader, Hồ Chí Minh, told creative artists that the arts were a battlefield and that they were all warriors in the struggle for liberation. Artists were encouraged to create works that would instill a spirit of resistance among the people. Cultural and propaganda squads traveled the countryside singing and putting on skits. The Việt Minh also established radio stations and published songs in small quantities.

Communist China, especially after the victory over nationalist forces in 1949, supplied material and advisors to Vietnam. One emphasis of the Maoist cultural program had been to utilize folk music in composing resistance and revolutionary music in order to help win the hearts of the majority peasant population. One of the first songwriters to succeed in this vein was Phạm Duy with songs like 'Nhớ người thương binh' (Remembering the Wounded Soldier, 1947). Later songs that effectively utilized folk materials were Đỗ Nhuận's 'Hành quân xa' (Marching Far, 1953) (1994, 15), a march with a *hát chèo* flavor, and Hoàng Vân's 'Hò kéo pháo' (Heave Ho, Haul the Artillery, 1954) (*Tập nhạc được giải Đại Hội Văn Công Toàn Quốc* 1955, n.p.), a work song sung by the porters who transported the artillery that insured the Việt Minh's victory at Điện Biên Phủ.

Along with Chinese aid came pressure to adhere to a Maoist/Marxist doctrine. A combination of physical hardship and dislike of this growing political orthodoxy caused many intellectuals, among them songwriters and performers, to return to the French-occupied cities during the years 1947–51. The return of these musicians and an economy flush with military spending helped popular music flourish in cities under French control. While *cải luong* remained the dominant popular music of the south, songs composed in a Western idiom became prevalent in Ha Nôi and Huê. Each of these cities had radio stations with live bands that performed the latest songs written both in the French-defended cities and the resistance zones. Music publishing flourished and hundreds of songs were recorded on 78 rpm discs.

The songs written from the 1930s through 1954 became collectively known as *nhạc tiền chiến* or 'prewar songs.' Songs of this period both utilized elements of traditional music and absorbed outside influences like blues, jazz and Latin dance rhythms. 'Tiếng xưa' (Sounds of Old, 1948) by Dương Thiệu Tước utilized melodic patterns from southern traditional music. On the other hand 'Nỗi lòng' (Feelings, 1950) by Nguyễn Văn Khánh had a light jazz-like feel, combined with lyrics expressing love's heartaches.

The Partition of Vietnam

When the war of resistance with France ended in 1954, the Geneva Accords divided Vietnam at the seventeenth parallel into a communist north and a nationalist south until elections could be held. There was an exodus of combatants from both sides, as well as an evacuation of many northerners who feared reprisals from the communists. The influx of northern composers and musicians invigorated the popular music of South Vietnam. In the years immediately following the nation's division, many popular songs on both sides dealt with the yearning of those separated from the homeland. 'Giấc mơ hồi hương' (Dreams of Repatriation) written by northerner Vũ Thành in South Vietnam in 1956 expressed a longing for his home Ha Nôi, addressed as a distant lover. The southerner Hoàng Việt, now in Ha Nôi, wrote 'Tình ca' (Love Song) in 1957 (Lê Hùng and Văn Huyên 2001, 52–53) to a lover in South Vietnam imagined to be living under dark clouds in an enemy land.

The scheduled elections were never held and the musics of North and South Vietnam continued developing in opposite directions. In the North all performance, musical training, composition, publishing, recording and broadcast were controlled by the government. Music was encouraged that served the party, the consolidation of communism and the struggle against South Vietnam and the United States. All music that had previously circulated in the urban areas of North Vietnam, including *nhạc tiền chiến*, was banned. The Association of Vietnamese Musicians (*Hội Nhạc sĩ Việt Nam*) was established by the government in 1957 to supervise musical activity. Many musicians studied overseas in other communist bloc nations, or at a national school of music. Orchestra-like ensembles of traditional instruments played composed music that infused folk music styles with virtuosity.

Once the conflict in South Vietnam resumed, songs were written as propaganda urging everyone to sacrifice for the struggle. To compensate for comparative military and economic inferiority, the government stressed the importance of uniting everyone in the struggle. Songs were cast in images of socialist realism, depicting all participants in the war as resolute heroes destined for an ultimate victory, and leaving no possibility of pessimism or doubt. 'Việt Nam quê hương tôi' (Vietnam My Homeland, 1963) by Đỗ Nhuận (1994, 21–22) was a hymn of praise to the land and its people. 'Quảng Bình quê ta ơi' (My Native Land Quảng Bình, 1964) by Hoàng Việt (Dane and Silber 1969, 204–209) sang of the people of Quảng Bình, living just to the north of the border at the seventeenth parallel, who were in the thick of the struggle. Huy Du's setting of the poem 'Đường chúng ta đi' (The Road We're Taking, 1968) by Xuân Sách (Lê Hùng and Van Huyền 187–9) appealed to young recruits to join the war in South Vietnam. 'Bài ca năm tấn' (The Song of Five Tons, 1967) by Nguyễn Văn Tý (Xuân Giao 1971, 253–55) encouraged peasants to try to outdo each other producing rice to feed the soldiers sent south. Phó Đức Phương's 'Những cô gái quan họ' (Young Quan Ho Women, 1966) (Xuân Giao 1971, 188–89), influenced by northern *quan họ* folk song, celebrated the village women who took responsibility for the harvest while the young men were at the battlefield.

Songs were written in response to every advance, every victory. Many musicians active in composing and performing in the communist-controlled areas of the South were involved in attracting peasants to the cause. Songs were also written to celebrate those who were engaged in support activities, such as digging tunnels or sharpening spikes for booby-traps. Hoàng Hiệp's 'Trường Sơn đông, Trường Sơn tây' (East Trường Sơn, West Trường Sơn, 1971) (Lê Hùng and Văn Huyên 2000, 189–91), a setting of a Phạm Tiền Duật poem, is a song about a truck driver on the western branch of the Hồ Chí Minh trail (known as the Trường Sơn Road by the Vietnamese) and a woman porter he loves who is transporting supplies by foot on the trail's eastern branch. The poem addresses the dangers and hardships of their respective routes; Hoàng Hiệp's setting is lyrical and evocative of southern folk music.

In South Vietnam, while the army and the war played an important role, popular music was largely left to the free market. Throughout the period of 1954–75 the music industry operated like a Tin Pan Alley with a division of labor among song composers, publishers, arrangers, bands and record labels. In order to avoid conscription as foot soldiers, many musicians also worked for cultural and propaganda troupes of the various armed forces. An influx of US troops and money brought about major changes in southern life. The most lucrative gigs for many singers and musicians were in cover bands to entertain GIs and other foreigners. Those who found work serving Americans as secretaries, translators, housekeepers, or even prostitutes, suddenly had large disposable incomes that upset the traditional class structure. Songs were written to appeal to these new urban wage earners. Promoters organized *Đại nhạc hội* (Grand Music Festivals), variety shows with plays, dancers, magicians and a rotation of several singers that performed in urban theaters and toured the countryside. In Saigon (now Hồ Chi Minh) popular singers would travel a circuit of *phòng trà* (tea rooms), singing at several in a single evening.

Sheet music sold tens of thousands of copies, often to non-musicians who bought the music for its lyrics. During the *nhạc tiền chiến* era the songs used a florid, literary language. While some songwriters continued to write in that idiom, many new songs in South Vietnam used direct language to describe the circumstances of city life, reflecting the realities of Saigon's growing refugee populations. Lam Phương's 'Kiếp nghèo' (The Fate of the Poor, 1955) (*Hát cho tình yêu* n.d., 34–35) described a search for love among the urban poor. Other songs like 'Gạo trắng trăng thanh' (White Rice, Clear Moonlight, 1956) by Hoàng Thi Thơ celebrated the joys of country living lost to these refugees. The folk-like rhythms of this and other songs were transformed by some entertainers into what became derisively known as 'mambo-folk songs.' Such rhythms softened into slower tempos like the bolero that provided a base for ornamented melodies in the style of *cải lương* and southern folk music. Two of the more popular boleros of the early 1960s were 'Chuyện tình Lan và Điệp' (The Love Story of Lan and Điệp, 1965) by Anh Bằng, Lê Dinh and Minh Kỳ, and 'Những đồi hoa sim' (Hills of Purple Flowers, 1964) by Dzũng Chinh. The former was based on Nguyễn Công Hoan's novel of unrequited love, *Tắt lửa lòng* (Putting Out Love's Flames). The latter was based on a poem by Hữu Loan written during the resistance against France and tells of the tragedy of a young soldier's wife who died at home while he was at the front.

As the war intensified, there was growing pressure to compose music for the troops. A style of music called *nhạc kích động* (or 'action music') was popularized by the male/female duet of Hùng Cường and Mai Lệ Huyền, which performed songs portraying fun-loving soldiers and the young women attracted to them. However, the most popular songs for the military audience were sad boleros with lyrics that spoke of soldiers' dreams and longings. Typical of this type was the song '24 giờ phép' (24-Hour Leave, 1967) by Trúc Phương describing the joys and awkwardness of the brief conjugal visits. The bolero-style song reached a new level of simplicity and frank portrayal of poverty and separation, as in 'Nhẫn cỏ cho em' (A Ring of Grass for You, 1971) by Vinh Sử about a poor young man who cannot afford a real wedding ring so crafts one out of grass. The withdrawal of US armed forces from around 1970 caused a downturn in the southern economy. This, along with the introduction of audiocassettes, took a heavy toll on music publishing and record production.

There was also a current of music in opposition to the war. Trịnh Công Sơn, already well known for his poetic love songs, wrote a collection of songs entitled *Ca khúc da vàng* (Songs of the Golden-Skinned, n.d. [1967]), with lyrics that described the absurd brutality inflicted upon ordinary people by the war. Another movement called *du ca*, or 'roving songs,' was modeled after US protest song and Vietnamese folk song. The most radical songs came from a student song movement called *hát cho đồng bào tôi nghe* (Sing for My Compatriots) that directly opposed the war and condemned the US presence in Vietnam (Hội Sinh Viên 1970).

Cải lương remained a popular entertainment with a few hundred troupes performing throughout the South, on stage, radio and television. Owing to intense competition, plots became more sensational and exotic. The music also incorporated more Western elements. In 1963, a new form of music was invented by Viễn Châu, a *cải lương* playwright, that alternated popular songs with the *vọng cổ* aria to create a genre called *tân cổ giao duyên* (new and old pre-ordained love) that fleshed out the subject matter of the song into short melodramas, fitting one side of an extended 45 rpm record.

Reunification

On 30 April 1975 the southern government surrendered. One of the first acts of the communist victors was to ban and confiscate all cultural vestiges of the former Republic of Vietnam, which were condemned under a blanket rubric of 'American neocolonialism.' Southerners were instead fed a musical diet of the songs used to sustain North Vietnam during the long war. Many singers and songwriters fled Vietnam, moving primarily to France, Australia and especially the United States.

Songs were composed that reflected the enthusiasm of victory such as 'Như có Bác trong ngày đại thắng' (It's As If Uncle [Hồ Chí Minh] Were Here at This Major Victory, 1975) by Phạm Tuyên (*Tiếng hát Việt Nam* 1977, 401–402) and 'Mùa xuân trên Thành phố Hồ Chí Minh' (Spring in Hồ Chí Minh City, 1975) by Xuân Hồng (Vương Tâm 2000, 76–77). Reflecting the postwar mission of developing the state-controlled economy, a song like 'Tình đất đỏ miền Đông' (Love of the Red Lands of the East, 1979) by Trần Long Ẩn (Lê Hùng and Văn Huyên 2001, 227–28) encouraged the cultivation of the previously marginal land along the eastern border with Cambodia. However, Vietnam could not translate its success on the battlefield into economic prosperity. In 'Bài ca không quên' (A Song Not Forgotten, 1981), by Phạm Mạnh Tuấn (Lê Hùng and Văn Huyên 2001, 240–41), the composer reminds himself not to forget the hardships of the war – and the joys that came from having a common purpose.

Despite the efforts of the government, the banned songs of the former southern regime continued to circulate widely. Cafés clandestinely played cassettes, itinerant singers on the trains sang the songs, and soldiers returning to their home villages in the north brought back recordings. By the middle of the 1980s, in light of the move toward glasnost in the Soviet Union, Vietnam's government began to relax its control on culture and the economy. This allowed for the resuscitation of *nhạc tiền chiến* as well as a limited number of songs from the former southern regime. When overseas Vietnamese returned to visit their families they secretly brought back recordings and videotapes of Vietnamese music produced among the diaspora communities. This music was copied and smuggled throughout the country and proved more popular than the relatively unexciting music produced by state-controlled companies. It also introduced the Vietnamese to karaoke, which became so popular that the government at times feared it as a 'social evil.'

By the late 1980s, songwriters began to respond to the new openness. Trần Tiến formed a Soviet-influenced rock group called the Black and White Group. His song 'Sao em nỡ vội lấy chồng' (How You Could Hurry to Get Married, ca. 1989) (Trần Tiến 1995, 25–27), based on a poem by the former dissident poet Hoàng Cầm, became popular in Vietnam and overseas. Another popular song from that time, 'Em đi Chùa Hương' (I'm Going to the Perfume Pagoda, ca. 1990) by Trung Đức (Vương Tâm 2000, 68), was based on a well-known colonial era poem by Nguyễn Nhược Pháp and used a folk-style melody to suggest nostalgia for a traditional Vietnam. The early 1990s brought a reemergence of many songwriters who were active in Saigon before 1975, as well as younger singers who performed songs in a pre-1975 style. Noteworthy were a series of videos entitled *Mưa bụi* (Rain Dust) that presented songs and dialog depicting innocent courtship in the countryside.

The government-controlled music industry was slow in catching up with the smuggled overseas product – the first domestically produced compact discs and karaoke videos were released around 1995. By the mid-1990s, *nhạc nhẹ* (light music) became the dominant popular style with love songs in a light rock idiom, such as: 'Em ơi Hà Nội phố' (My Dear, Hanoi's Streets, ca. 1990 music by Phú Quang, words by Phan Vũ (Vương Tâm 2000, 162–163), 'Thì thầm mùa xuân' (Springtime Whispers, 1992) by Ngọc Châu (Vương Tâm 2000, 43) and 'Dòng sông lơ đãng' (Absent-Minded River, 1998) by Việt Anh (Vương Tâm 2000, 18). Another popular song style known as *rock rừng* (jungle rock) was developed by the songwriter Nguyễn Cường (1994) and featured ethnic minority performers from Vietnam's highlands.

Since the late 1990s, Vietnamese commentators have expressed concern about the undue influence and popularity of overseas Vietnamese music, then Hong Kong music, US music and, in the early years of the twenty-first century, Thai music on the music marketplace. A considerable factor weakening domestically produced music is persistent smuggling and illegal copying of music. While playing a negligible role in music commerce, Internet use in Vietnam is growing. There are chat rooms for music fans, and some government-controlled Web sites allow low bandwidth downloads of popular songs.

At the turn of the twenty-first century, more than half the population in Vietnam was under 25, suggesting that a youth culture would continue to grow. There was a growing subculture receptive to Western rock and rap music. During the 1990s, a new generation of well-trained singers achieved stardom. Another new craze has been boy-groups and girl-groups, often modeled after groups popular in Europe and the United States. Since the mid-1990s, some overseas Vietnamese singers have performed in Vietnam, and some Vietnamese have performed overseas. In contrast to many years of hostility between the Vietnamese diaspora and those residing in Vietnam following 1975, this suggests a growing interaction between the native and diaspora musics and music industries.

Bibliography

Arana, Miranda. 1999. 'Neotraditional Music in Vietnam.' *Nhạc Việt*: 1–152.

Blackburn, Philip. 2000. 'Vietnam.' In *World Music: The Rough Guide*, ed. Simon Broughton and Mark Ellingham. New York: Rough Guides, 262–69.

Dao Trong Tu. 1984. 'Renaissance of Vietnamese Music.' In *Essays on Vietnamese Music*. Ha Nôi: Foreign Languages Publishing House, 96–161.

Gibbs, Jason. 1997a. 'Reform and Tradition in Early Vietnam Popular Song.' *Nhạc Việt* 6 (Fall): 5–33.

Gibbs, Jason. 1998. 'Nhac Tien Chien: The Origins of Vietnamese Popular Song.' *Destination Vietnam online*. http://www.thingsasian.com/goto_article/article.801.html

Gibbs, Jason. 2000. 'Spoken Theater, *La Scène Tonkinois*, and the First Modern Vietnamese Songs.' *Asian Music* 31(2) (Spring–Summer): 1–34.

Gibbs, Jason. 2003. 'Rumba on the Mekong: Bolero as a Vietnamese Popular Song Form.' Paper presented at the annual meeting of the International Association for the Study of Popular Music, September 21, in Los Angeles, CA.

Gibbs, Jason. 2003–2004. 'The West's Songs, Our Songs: The Introduction of Western Popular Song in Vietnam.' *Asian Music* 35(1) (Fall/Winter), 57–83.

Gibbs, Jason. 2004. 'Love and Longing at the Border: Songs on Both Sides of the 17th Parallel.' Paper presented at the annual meeting of the Popular Culture Association, April 8, San Antonio, TX.

Hồ Trường An. 1998. *Theo chân những tiếng hát* [Following the Footsteps of Those Voices]. Arlington, VA: Tổ hợp Xuất bản Đông Hoa kỳ.

Jamieson, Neil L. 1993. *Understanding Vietnam*. Berkeley, CA: University of California Press.

Lê Thương. 1971. 'Thời tiền chiến trong tân nhạc (1939–1945)' [The Prewar Era in New Music]. In *Tuyển tập nhạc tiền chiến*, Đỗ Kim Bảng, compiler. Saigon: Kẻ sĩ xuất bản, 62–70.

Miller, Terry E. 1991. 'Music and Theater in Saigon – 1970: An American Soldier's Observations Revisited.' In *New Perspectives on Vietnamese Music: Six Essays*, ed. Phong T. Nguyen. n.p.: Council on Southeast Asian Studies, Yale Center for International Studies, 21–35.

Nguyễn, Phong T. 1998. 'Vietnam.' In *Garland Encyclopedia of World Music. Vol. 4: Southeast Asia*, ed. Terry E. Miller and Sean Williams. New York: Garland: 444–517.

Nguyên Sa. 1993. *Nghệ sĩ Việt Nam ở hải ngoại* [Vietnamese Artists Living Overseas]. Irvine, CA: Đời.

Nguyễn Thị Minh Châu. 1999. 'Một số vấn đề thị hiếu đại chúng và ca khúc đang thịnh hành tại Thành phố Hồ Chí Minh' [Some Problems of Mass Taste and Songs Currently Popular in Hồ Chí Minh City]. *Viện Âm nhạc – Thông báo Khoa học* [Bulletin of the Vietnam Musicology Institute] 1, 31–65.

Nguyen Tri Binh. 1995. 'Vietnam Wants to Cut Its Own Discs,' *Vietnam News* (1 October): 1–2.

Phạm Đình Sáu. 1990. 'Thực chất nhạc "hải ngoạ" là gì?' ['What is the Substance of "Overseas" Music']. *Nhân dân* (7 October): 14.

Phạm Duy. 1975. *Musics of Vietnam*, ed. Dale R. Whiteside. Carbondale, IL: Southern Illinois University Press.

Phạm Duy. 1989. *Hồi ký: Thời cách mạng kháng chiến* [Memoirs: Times of Revolution and Resistance]. Midway City, CA: Pham Duy Cuong Productions.

Phạm Duy. 1990. *Hồi ký: Thời thơ ấu – vào đời* [Memoirs: Times of Youth – Coming of Age]. Midway City, CA: Pham Duy Cuong Productions.

Phạm Duy. 1991. *Hồi ký: Thời phân chia quốc cộng* [Memoirs: Times of a Divided Nation]. Midway City, CA: Pham Duy Cuong Productions.

Phạm Duy. c. 1996. *Viet Nam Pham Duy*. http://209.172.66.143/phamduy/ [viewed April 25, 2004].

Phi Sơn. 1995. 'Viễn Châu (Bảy Bá): Gần nửa thế kỷ viết tuồng cải lương và vọng cổ [Viễn Châu (Bảy Bá): Nearly a Half Century Writing Cải Lương and Vọng Cổ]. *Van hóa Nguyệt san* 2: 28–29.

Taylor, Philip. 2000. 'Music as a "Neocolonial Poison" in Post-war Southern Vietnam.' *Crossroads: An Interdisciplinary Journal of Southeast Asian Studies* 14(1): 99–131.

Thái Bảo. 2000. 'Ca khúc trong nước đang "lên ngồi"' [Songs Inside the Country Are 'Taking the Throne']. *Nhân dân* (29 August). http://www.nhandan.org.vn/Vietnamese/08292000/bai-vh3.htm

Thái Hà. 1992. 'Báo động về dịch ca-ra-ô-kê đen' [Alarm Over an Epidemic of Black-Market Karaoke]. *Nhân dân* (31 October): 3.

Thụy Loan. 1993. *Lược sử âm nhạc Việt Nam: Giáo trình cho bậc đại học* [A Historical Sketch of Vietnam Music: Teaching Material at the University Level]. Ha Nôi: Nhạc Viện Hà Nội; Nhà xuất bản Âm nhạc. Includes 'Diệt Phát xít' and 'Tiến quân ca.'

Trainor, John P. 1975. 'Significance and Development in the Vọng Cổ of South Vietnam.' *Asian Music* 7(1): 50–56.

Trần Minh Phi. 1998. 'Rap Việt Nam' [Vietnamese Rap]. *Sống nhạc* 2: 6–7.

Trường Kỳ. 1995. *Tuyển tập Nghệ sĩ, tập 1* [A Selection of Performing Artists, Vol. 1]. Montréal, Canada: Trường Kỳ.

Trường Kỳ. 1997. *Tuyển tập Nghệ sĩ, tập 3* [A Selection of Performing Artists, Vol. 3]. Montréal, Canada: Trường Kỳ.

Trường Kỳ. 2002. *Một thời nhạc trẻ: Bút ký* [A Time of Youth Music: Sketches]. Montréal, Canada: Trường Kỳ.

Tú Ngọc et al. 2000. *Âm nhạc mới Việt Nam: Tiến trình và thành tựu* [Vietnam's New Music: Evolution and Achievement]. Ha Nôi: Viện Âm Nhạc.

V.N. 1988. 'Về những nhạc phẩm Sài Gòn trước năm 1975' [About Musical Works From Saigon Before 1975]. *Sài Gòn giải phóng* (27 November): 3.

Văn Hà Luận. 1993. 'Làm thế nào để chống nhạc hải ngoại' [How to Resist Overseas Music] *Văn hóa* (10 October): 1, 5.

Vương Hồng Sển. 1968. *Hồi ký 50 năm mê hát* [50 Years of Passion for the Theater]. Saigon: Cơ sở Xuất bản Phạm Quang Khai.

Xuân Hồng, ed. 1997. *Hồi ức 50 năm âm nhạc cách mạng miền Nam* [Recollections of 50 Years of Southern Revolutionary Music]. Hồ Chi Minh: Nhà xuất bản Văn nghệ TP. Hồ Chí Minh: Hội Âm Nhạc TP.

Sheet Music

Dương Thiệu Tước, comp. and lyr. 1949. 'Tiếng xưa' [Sounds of Old]. Ha Nôi: Thế Giới.

Dzung Chính, comp. and lyr. 1964. 'Những đồi hoa sim' [Hills of Sim Flowers]. Saigon: 1001 Bài Ca Hay.

Đặng Thế Phong, comp. and Bùi Công Kỳ, lyr. 1964. 'Giọt mưa thu' [Autumn Raindrops]. Saigon: Diên Hồng.

Hoàng Thi Thơ, comp. and lyr. 1956. 'Gạo trắng thanh' [White Rice, Clear Moon]. Huê: Tinh Hoa.

Mạc Phong Linh and Mai Thiết Lĩnh [Anh Bằng, Lê Dinh and Minh Kỳ], comp. and lyr. 1965. 'Chuyện tình Lan và Điệp' [The Love Story of Lan and Điệp]. Saigon: Minh Phát.

Nguyễn Văn Khánh, comp. and lyr. 1968. 'Nỗi lòng' [Feelings]. Saigon: Minh Phát.

Phạm Duy, comp. and lyr. 1950. 'Nhớ người thương binh' [Remembering the Wounded Soldier]. Ha Nôi: Nhà xuất bản Thế Giới.

Trúc Phương, comp. and lyr. 1967. '24 giờ phép' [24-Hour Leave]. Saigon: Việt Nam Nhạc Tuyển.

Vinh Sử, comp. and lyr. 1971. 'Nhẫn cỏ cho em' [A Ring of Grass for You]. Saigon: Vinh Sử.

Vũ Thành, comp. and lyr. 1956. 'Giấc mơ hồi hương' [Dreams of Repatriation]. Huê: Tinh Hoa.

Song Collections

14 khuôn mặt du ca với những điều trông thấy [14 Faces of Roving Songs and Those Things Seen]. 1973. Saigon: Sống xuất bản.

Đỗ Nhuận. 1994. *Tuyển chọn ca khúc Đỗ Nhuận* [A Selection of Songs by Do Nhuan]. Ha Nôi: Hội Nhạc sĩ Việt Nam; Nhà xuất bản Âm nhạc.

Dane, Barbara, and Silber, Irwin, compilers and editors. 1969. *The Vietnam Songbook*. New York: The Guardian. Includes 'Quảng Bình quê ta ơi.'

Hát cho tình yêu [Sing for Love]. n.d. n.p.: Nhạc Hay của Bạn. Includes 'Kiếp nghèo.'

Hội Sinh Viên. [Student Association]. 1970. *Hát cho đồng bào tôi nghe: Chúng ta đã đứng dậy, tập 1* [Sing for my Compatriots: We Have Awakened, Vol. 1I]. Saigon: Tổng Hội Sinh Viên.

Lê Hùng and Văn Huyên, eds. 2001. *100 ca khúc chào thế kỷ* [100 Songs to Greet the Century]. 2001. Ha Nôi: Nhà xuất bản Thanh niên. Includes 'Bài ca không quên,' 'Đường chúng ta đi,' 'Tình ca,' and 'Tình đất đỏ miền đông,' and 'Trường Sơn đông, Trường Sơn tây.'

Lưu Hữu Phước. 1945. *Tráng sĩ ca* [Songs for Heroes]. Ha Nôi: Lửa hồng.

Nguyễn Cường. 1994. *Tuyển chọn ca khúc Nguyễn Cường* [A Selection of Songs by Nguyen Cuong]. Ha Nôi: Hội Nhạc sĩ Việt Nam; Nhà xuất bản Âm nhạc.

Phòng chính trị Bộ Thương binh Cựu Binh [Political Office of the Ministry for Wounded and Retired Soldiers]. 1948. *Thương binh ca hát, tập 1* [Songs for Wounded Soldiers, vol. 1]. n.p.: Tủ sách Thương binh.

Tập nhạc được giải Đại Hội Văn Công Toàn Quốc [Collection of Songs Awarded at the National Song and Dance Festival]. 1955. Ha Nôi: Nhà xuất bản Văn Nghệ. 'Hò kéo pháo.'

Tiếng hát Việt Nam (1964–1975), tập 2 [The Songs of Vietnam (1964–1975), vol. 2]. 1977. Ha Nôi: Nhà xuất bản Văn hóa. Includes 'Như có Bác trong ngày đại thắng,'

Trần Tiến. 1995. *Tuyển chọn ca khúc Trần Tiến* [A Selection of Songs by Tran Tien]. Ha Nôi: Hội Nhạc sĩ Việt Nam; Nhà xuất bản Âm nhạc.

Trịnh Công Sơn. n.d. *Ca khúc da vàng* [Songs of the Golden Skinned]. Glendale, CA: Đại Nam.

Vương Tâm, comp. *99 bài hát được nhiều người ưa thích* [99 Songs Loved by Many]. 2000. Ha Nôi: Nhà xuất bản Thanh Niên, Báo Hà Nội Mới. Includes 'Dòng sông lơ đãng,' 'Em đi Chùa Hương' 'Em ơi Hà Nội phố,' 'Mùa xuân trên Thành Phố Hồ Chí Minh,' 'Thì thầm mùa xuân,' and 'Tình ca.'

Xuân Giao, ed. 1971. *Tiếng hát chống Mỹ cứu nước* [Songs Combatting America, Saving the Nation]. Ha Nôi: Nhà xuất bản Mỹ thuật – Âm nhạc, 1971. Includes 'Bài ca năm tấn,' and 'Những cô gái quan họ.'

Discographical References

Anh Ngọc. 'Nỗi lòng.' *Anh Ngọc: Trở về dĩ vãng* [Anh Ngọc: Back to the Past] (CD). Anh Ngọc. *2000*: USA.

Giao Linh. 'Nhẫn cỏ cho em.' *Tiếng hát Giao Linh* (cassette). Băng nhạc Bốn Phương. n.d.: USA.

Hoàng Oanh and Nhật Trường. 'Chuyện tình Lan và Điệp.' *Sóng Nhạc* [Music Waves] (cassette). Sóng Nhạc 5. n.d.: Vietnam.

Hùng Cường and Mai Lệ Huyền. *Kích động nhạc* (cassette). Băng nhạc Bốn Phương. n.d.: USA.

Khánh Ly. *Hát cho quê hương Việt Nam* [Sing For the Homeland Vietnam] (cassette). Băng nhạc Bốn Phương. n.d.: USA. (Includes several of Trịnh Công Sơn's *Ca khúc da vàng*).

Minh Trang. 'Con thuyền không bến' (78 rpm). Polyphon 57.029. *ca. 1950*: Vietnam.

Music of Vietnam (CD). Caprice Records CAP 21406. *1991*: UK.

Musics of Vietnam (4 cassette set). World Music Enterprises. Tape 6. n.d.: USA.

Mỹ Linh. 'Thì thầm mùa xuân.' *Mỹ Linh* (CD). Trung tâm Băng nhạc Trẻ. *1997*: Vietnam.

'My Native Land Quảng Bình' [Quảng Bình quê ta ơi]. *Vietnam Will Win: Liberation Songs of the Vietnamese People Recorded in Vietnam* (LP). Paredon P1009. *1971*: USA.

Nguyễn Cường: Tuổi thơ Hà Nội [Nguyen Cuong: A Hanoi Youth] (cassette). Nhà xuất bản Âm nhạc, Dihavina. n.d.: USA.

Pham Duy. *Music of Viet Nam* (LP). Folkways Records FE 4352. *1965*: USA.

Phương Dung. 'Những đồi hoa sim.' *Phương Dung* (cassette). Sóng Nhạc 6. n.d.: Vietnam.

Quốc Hương. 'Tình ca,' 'Trường Sơn đông, Trường Sơn tây.' *Giọng ca Quốc Hương* [Voice of Quoc Huong] (cassette). Nhà xuất bản Âm nhạc, Dihavina. n.d. [ca. 1995]: Vietnam.

Thái Thanh. 'Giấc mơ hồi hương,' *Những bài ca giã từ* [Songs of Farewell] (cassette). Tú Quỳnh 10. n.d.: Vietnam.

Thanh Thúy. '24 giờ phép.' *Những bản tình ca buồn* [Sad Songs] (cassette). Thanh Thúy 7. n.d.: Vietnam.

Thanh Tuyền. 'Kiếp nghèo.' *Tiếng hát Thanh Tuyền* [Voice of Thanh Tuyen]. Băng nhạc Bốn Phương. n.d.: USA.

Thu Phương. 'Dòng sông lơ đãng.' *Nghệ thuật* [The Arts] (CD). Kim Lợi Productions. *1998*: USA.

Thúy Hà and Duy Tân. 'Việt Nam quê hương tôi.' *Việt Nam quê hương tôi* [Vietnam My Native Country] (33 rpm). Dihavina CKS-0004. n.d.: Vietnam.

Trung Đức. 'Em đi Chùa Hương.' *Em đi Chùa Hương* [I'm Going to the Perfume Pagoda] (cassette). Hoa Phượng Đỏ. *1990*: Vietnam.

Trung Đức. 'Sao em nỡ vội lấy chồng.' *Trần Tiến Thái Bảo nhạc tuyển* [Tran Tien and Thai Bao Music Selections] (cassette). Hoguom Audio HG 104. n.d.: Vietnam.

Út Trà Ôn. 'Dạ cổ hoài lang.' *Traditional Songs of Vietnam 2* (CD). Viet Nam Musicology Institute. n.d.: Vietnam.

Văn Lý. 'Giọt mưa thu' (78 rpm). Oria 506. *1949*: France.

Filmography

Mưa bụi 2 [Rain Dust 2], dir. Trần Cảnh Đôn. 1994. USA. 120 mins. Variety. Original music by Vinh Sử, Hoài Nam, Giao Tiên, Minh Tâm.

Internet Audio

Radio the Voice of Vietnam.
http://www.vovnews.com.vn/index.htm [viewed May 1, 2004].

Trang Âm nhạc [Music Page].
http://www.vov.org.vn/amthanh1/tiengviet/Amnhac/amnhac.htm [viewed May 1, 2004].

Bích Liên. 'Bài ca năm tấn.' *Trang B* [Page B].
http://www.vovnews.com.vn/amthanh1/tiengviet/Amnhac/nhungbaicakhongquen/trangb.htm

Cẩm Vân. 'Bài ca không quên.' *Trang B* [Page B].
http://www.vovnews.com.vn/amthanh1/tiengviet/Amnhac/nhungbaicakhongquen/trangb.htm

Cao Minh. 'Tình đất đỏ miền đông.' *Trang T* [Page T]. http://www.vovnews.com.vn/amthanh1/tiengviet/Amnhac/nhungbaicakhongquen/trangt.htm

Dàn hợp xướng Đài Tiếng Nói Việt Nam và Đội Sơn Ca [Chorus and Ensemble of the Radio Voice of Vietnam and the Son Ca Group]. 'Như có Bác trong ngày đại thắng.' *Trang N* [Page N]. http://

www.vovnews.com.vn/amthanh1/tiengviet/
Amnhac/nhungbaicakhongquen/trangn.htm

Đăng Dương, Trọng Tấn, and Việt Hoàn. 'Đường
chúng ta đi.' *Trang D* [Page D].
http://www.vovnews.com.vn/amthanh1/tiengviet/
Amnhac/nhungbaicakhongquen/trangd.htm

Đăng Dương, Trọng Tấn, and Việt Hoàn. 'Việt
Nam quê hương tôi.' *Trang V* [Page V]. http://
www.vovnews.com.vn/amthanh1/tiengviet/
Amnhac/nhungbaicakhongquen/trangv.htm

Đoàn Nghệ thuật Quân khu 2. [Artistic Unit of the
2nd Military Zone]. *Trang H* [Page H]. http://
www.vovnews.com.vn/amthanh1/tiengviet/
Amnhac/nhungbaicakhongquen/trangh.htm

Hồng Liên. 'Những cô gái quan họ' *Trang N* [Page
N]. http://www.vovnews.com.vn/amthanh1/
tiengviet/Amnhac/nhungbaicakhongquen/
trangn.htm

Hợp xướng Đài Tiếng Nói Việt Nam [Chorus of
the Radio Voice of Vietnam]. 'Diệt phát xít' and
'Tiến quân ca' (Quốc ca Việt Nam). *Tư Liệu Lịch
Sử* [Historical Documents].
'http://www.vovnews.com.vn/amthanh1/
tiengviet/tulieulichsu/tulieulichsu.htm [viewed
May 1, 2004].

Ngọc Lan. 'Mùa xuân trên Thành Phố Hồ Chí
Minh.' *Trang M* [Page M].
http://www.vovnews.com.vn/amthanh1/tiengviet/
Amnhac/nhungbaicakhongquen/trangm.htm

Quang Lý. 'Em ơi Hà Nội phố.' Trang E [Page E].
http://www.vovnews.com.vn/amthanh1/tiengviet/
Amnhac/cakhuctrutinh/trange.htm

Vietnamese Music/Âm nhạc Việt Nam. [Vietnam
News Network]. http://www.vnn.vn/vnn3.music
[viewed May 1, 2004].

JASON GIBBS

CITIES

Ha Nôi

Population: 2,841,7000 (2001)

Ha Nôi, capital of the Socialist Republic of Vietnam, is located in the heart of the Red River Valley in the north of the country. Historically the nation's administrative and educational center, Ha Nôi was under French colonial rule from the late nineteenth century until 1954. Until the early twentieth century, traditional songs and music theater were the most popular forms of entertainment. The first musicians conversant in Western popular music during the colonial era provided entertainment at hotels, restaurants and dance halls. By the 1940s, a substantial number of musicians were performing and publishing their own songs.

In December 1946 the city emptied when it became an open battleground for an eight-year war of resistance by the communist Việt Minh against the French. As non-combatants or opponents to the resistance returned to the city in the late 1940s, they helped to create a vital musical scene of cafés, dance halls and radio bands. At the same time, Ha Nôi remained a powerful symbol for the resistance fighters. Songs like 'Người Hà Nội' (People of Ha Nôi, 1947) by Nguyễn Đình Thi, and 'Tiến về Hà Nội' (Advancing back to Ha Nôi, 1949) by Văn Cao expressed a longed for victorious return to the capital.

After 1954 Vietnam was partitioned and Ha Nôi became the capital of North Vietnam. The new communist government nationalized all cultural activity, causing many musicians to migrate to the south. Ha Nôi became the center for radio, recording and music publishing for North Vietnam. After 1975 Ha Nôi remained the capital of unified Vietnam. In the late 1980s a move toward economic renovation loosened the government control of music. While its importance as a musical and media market is second to Hô Chi Minh City, Ha Nôi continues to be an source of creative talent for the Vietnamese musical market.

Bibliography

1984. *Hà Nội tập bài hát* [Ha Nôi: A Collection of Songs]. Ha Nôi: Sở Văn hóa và Thông tin Hà Nội.

Discographical References

Mai Khanh. 'Người Hà Nội. *Giọng ca Mai Khanh nghệ sĩ ưu tú* [The Voice of Mai Khanh Eminent Artist]. Nhà xuất bản Âm nhạc, Dihavina. *1994*: Vietnam.
Quang Lý. 'Tiến về Hà Nội.' *Ca khúc Văn Cao* [Songs of Văn Cao]. Nhà xuất bản Âm nhạc, Dihavina. *ca. 1990*:. Vietnam.

JASON GIBBS

Hô Chi Minh

Population: 5,378,100 (2001)

Hô Chi Minh, Vietnam's largest city, was known as Saigon prior to 1975. It is located on the Saigon River, a tributary of the Dong Nai River. Founded in the late eighteenth century, it has been Vietnam's main port and commercial center since the time of French colonial rule. During the colonial era it was the administrative capital of Cochin China.

At the beginning of the twentieth century theatrical genres like *hát bội* and later *cải lương* were the dominant forms of musical entertainment. French popular music and musical theater also became popular among the Vietnamese upper classes. Dance and hotel orchestras made up of French, Philippine and Vietnamese musicians performed in the city center and in the Chinese district, Chợ Lớn. French-operated Radio Saigon broadcast *cải lương* both in live performance and on 78 rpm records, and by the 1940s, broadcast Vietnamese popular songs as well.

During World War II, all of French Indochina came under Japanese control. On Japan's surrender in August 1945, the people of Saigon participated in an uprising in hope of averting a French return, singing martial patriotic songs. As the French regained control, the resistance movement was driven to the countryside and Saigon resumed its role as a French administrative and commercial center.

The partition of Vietnam in 1954 brought an influx of musicians and composers from the North. The US military spending that boosted the economy helped develop a vibrant music industry with several music publishers like An Phú, Diên Hồng, Minh Phát, Tinh Hoa Miền Nam (Southern Quintessence), and record companies such as Việt Nam, Continental and Sóng Nhạc (Music Waves). Saigon boasted a number of *phòng trà* (tea rooms), hotel orchestras and live bands that performed on radio stations such as Đài Phát Thanh Sài Gòn (Saigon Radio), Đài Phát Thanh Quân Đội (Armed Forces Radio) and, later, on Vietnam Television (Đài Truyền Hình Việt Nam). It became known as a lively, fun-loving, if not decadent city. The southern government tried to curb this at various times by banning dances like the twist, or shutting down dance clubs and tea rooms. *Cải lương* remained popular, in part owing to the assimilation of influences from foreign motion pictures and music. Saigon's music displayed an eclectism ranging from love songs often using Latin rhythms, to propaganda and protest songs. Many rock groups were formed, both to entertain the lucrative GI market and for the enjoyment of college-aged Vietnamese.

Upon their victory in 1975, the northern regime viewed the culture of the South with horror, and systematically destroyed recordings and sheet music. Songwriters found their works banned and singers had to change their repertoires entirely. Many joined the masses of Vietnamese who left their country by boat. Despite government suppression, music from before 1975 remained very popular.

As Saigon, the city remained a powerful symbol for overseas songwriters. Renamed Hô Chi Minh in 1976, it became a hopeful symbol of a unified Vietnam. The late 1980s brought relaxation of the proscription of pre-1975 music, with tea rooms and karaoke establishments spreading through the city. By the early 1990s Hô Chi Minh reassumed its role as a thriving music and media center with recording and video companies like Bến Thành, Kim Lợi Studio, Phuong Nam, and Saigon Audio that produce music for the domestic and overseas market.

Bibliography

Phạm Duy. 1991. *Hồi ký: Thời phân chia quốc công* [Memoirs: Times of a Divided Nation]. Midway City, CA: Pham Duy Cuong Productions.

Trường Kỳ. 2002. *Một thời nhạc trẻ: Bút ký* [A Time of Youth Music: Sketches]. Montréal, Canada: Trường Kỳ.

Vương Hồng Sển. 1968. *Hồi ký 50 năm mê hát* [50 Years of Passion for the Theater]. Saigon: Cơ sở Xuất bản Phạm Quang Khai.

Xuân Hồng, ed. 1997. *Hồi ức 50 năm âm nhạc cách mạng miền Nam* [Recollections of 50 Years of Southern Revolutionary Music]. Hô Chi Minh: Nhà xuất bản Văn nghệ TP. Hồ Chí Minh: Hội Âm Nhạc TP. Hồ Chí Minh.

JASON GIBBS

DIASPORA

Vietnam Diaspora
Population: ca. 2,000,000 (2000)

From the early twentieth century, Vietnamese were living overseas as colonial subjects throughout the Francophile world. The earliest Vietnamese in France were students, factory workers, and spouses or mixed-race children of French nationals; a number had French citizenship. Most emigrants assimilated French culture and were receptive to popular song, ballroom dancing and film. After World War II, overseas Vietnamese began to play a role in their native country's political and cultural life. During the early 1950s, the radio program *Việt Kiều Ba-Lê* (Overseas Vietnamese in Paris) originated in France and was broadcast in Saigon (now Hô Chi Minh). Furthermore, some Vietnamese living in France, like the musicologist Trần Văn Khê (using the stage name Hải Minh), recorded songs for the Oria label that were sold in their homeland. During the period of conflict between North and South Vietnam (1954–75), overseas Vietnamese in France continued their musical activities but on a smaller scale. More notably, several musical troupes from both sides toured France to perform for the overseas community.

The defeat of the South in 1975 set off a mass exodus in three waves. The first was the airlifted evacuation of April 1975 to the United States. The second wave, lasting from 1976 through the mid-1980s, was of those who escaped by boat or across the border. These refugees spent substantial time in camps in Southeast Asia and Hong Kong. The final wave was of those who left through official sponsorship. As a result there are significant Vietnamese populations in the United States, France, Canada and Australia, and smaller communities in many other nations. Vietnamese from the communist North also studied and lived in the former Soviet Union and Warsaw Pact nations and some have settled there.

The first songs written in North America, such as 'Sài Gòn ơi! Vĩnh biệt' ('Oh Saigon! Goodbye Forever,' 1975) by Nam Lộc, reflected a yearning for the homeland. The first overseas Vietnamese recording produced in the United States was a cassette released in 1976 by the singer Thanh Thúy. Soon several companies emerged that produced and distributed Vietnamese music to Vietnamese businesses in the United States and across the world. The overseas Vietnamese recording industry came to be concentrated in Orange County, California, in an enclave popularly known as 'Little Saigon.' Many of the most popular Vietnamese recordings produced in the United States featured singers and songs from before 1975, now with an electronic music accompaniment. Much of the music of Saigon had already been concerned with separation and nostalgia, reflecting the waves of refugees first moving from North Vietnam to the South, and then from rural Vietnam to the cities.

One of the most successful entertainments created overseas was a video series entitled 'Paris by Night.' First produced in 1985 these videos were modeled after the *Đại nhạc hội* (Grand Music Festivals) popular in South Vietnam before 1975. These variety shows were cast in the style of an opulent Las Vegas-style stage show and featured the greatest stars and entertainers of pre-1975 Saigon as well as new entertainers who started their careers overseas. The success of this series (by 2004 they were up their 72nd release) was due to its ability to distribute professional entertainment to Vietnamese now scattered across the globe. These videos, despite being banned, have remained popular in Vietnam.

Though there are occasional performances of *cải lương* and other traditional music overseas, the music created and performed has tended to be more strongly influenced by international pop music currents. One of the more successful overseas songwriters is Đức Huy who played in Saigon rock bands before migrating to the United States in 1975. His songs, in a light rock idiom, like 'Người tình trăm năm' (Lover of a Hundred Years, 1989) and 'Trái tim ngục tù' (Imprisoned Heart, 1992), are popular both overseas and in Vietnam. Other popular composers living in the United States include Trịnh Nam Sơn, Vũ Tuấn Đức and Jimmi J.C. Nguyễn.

Another genre, the *Hưng ca* (arising songs) are songs that have opposed the communist government in Vietnam. These songs have been performed on anti-communist radio programs in diasporic communities or at demonstrations demanding human rights for Vietnam. Dance music has also enjoyed wide popularity, often in the form of extended multilingual medleys of Vietnamese and Western songs in a single tempo. Both non-native Vietnamese as well as some who were born in the country have become recording stars. The overseas music scene has also been sustained by a number of performers who defected or migrated from Vietnam.

The overseas community long had a technological edge over Vietnam, producing the first Vietnamese language videotapes, karaoke recordings and compact discs. They also became conversant in Internet technologies ahead of artists residing in Vietnam, producing many Web sites devoted to the performing arts and that sell recordings and videos online. Since 1996, a number of overseas performers have returned to perform in Vietnam, causing the anti-communist diasporic community to denounce and boycott them. At the same time popular singers from Vietnam have been performing overseas, although only recently in the United States, where, since they are mistakenly thought to be emissaries of the Vietnamese government, they have sparked demonstrations. Up until the mid-1990s songs and singers in Vietnam held little appeal for overseas Vietnamese audiences. However, since the late 1990s, the quality of recordings made in Vietnam has improved greatly and produced singers and songs following contemporary musical styles and using up-to-date lyrics that appeal to the overseas community, particularly to younger audiences.

Bibliography

Arnett, Elsa C. 2001. 'Heartbreak Shares the Stage with Vietnam's Elvis in Exile.' San Jose *Mercury News* (18 March): 1, 5.

Blackburn, Philip. 2000. 'Vietnam.' *World Music: The Rough Guide*, Vol. 2, ed. Simon Broughton and Mark Ellingham. London: Rough Guides, 262–69.

Đức Hà. 2001. 'Họ đã đến, đã hát, được tán thường và bị chống đối' [They Came, Sang, Were Appreciated and Were Opposed]. *Việt Mercury* (9 March): 1, 45.

Kicon Viet Space: Music.
http://vietspace.kicon.com/vietspace/music

Lull, James, and Wallis, Roger. 1992. 'The Beat of West Vietnam.' *Popular Music and Communication.* 2nd ed. Newbury Park, CA: Sage, 207–236.

Nguyễn Long. 1994. *Ký ức của một người Việt 1934–1994* [Memoirs of a Vietnamese 1934–1994]. Westminster, CA: Nguyễn Long.

Marosi, Richard. 2000. 'Vietnam's Music Invasion.' *Los Angeles Times* (8 August): A1, A5.

Nguyên Sa. 1993. *Nghệ sĩ Việt Nam ở hải ngoại* [Vietnamese Performing Artists Living Overseas]. Irvine, CA: Đời.

Nguyễn Thuyết Phong. 1989. *Thế giới âm thanh Việt Nam: 12 nhạc luận về những vấn đề hôm nay* [The World of Vietnamese Music: 12 Music Essays About Problems of Today]. San Jose, CA: Nhà xuất bản Hoa Cau.

Reyes, Adelaide. 1999. *Songs of the Caged, Songs of the Free: Music and the Vietnamese Refugee Experience.* Philadelphia: Temple University Press.

Rutledge, Paul James. 1992. *The Vietnamese Experience in America.* Bloomington, IN: University of Indiana Press.

Trần Quang Hải. n.d. 'Khái quát về 22 năm tân nhạc Việt Nam hải ngoại (1975–1997)' [A Summary of 22 Years of Overseas Vietnamese Music]. In *Trường Kỳ*, n.d.: 287–99.

Trần Văn Khê. 2001. *Hồi ký Trần Văn Khê, tập 2* [The Memoirs of Tran Van Khe, Vol. 2]. n.p: Nhà xuất bản Trẻ.

Trường Kỳ. 1995. *Tuyển tập Nghệ sĩ, tập 1* [A Selection of Performing Artists, Vol. 1]. Montréal, Canada: Trường Kỳ.

Trường Kỳ. n.d. *Tuyển tập Nghệ sĩ, tập 3* [A Selection of Performing Artists, Vol. 3]. Montréal, Canada: Trường Kỳ.

Wong, Deborah. 1994. '"I Want the Microphone": Mass Mediation and Agency in Asian American Popular Music.' *Drama Review* 38/3 (Fall): 152–67.

Song Books

Đức Huy. 1992. *Người tình trăm năm* [Hundred Year Lover]. n.p.: Nhạc mới.

Nguyễn Hữu Nghĩa. 1985. *Chiến ca [Battle Songs].* Toronto, Canada: Viet Publication.

1987. *Hưng ca Việt Nam: tuyển tập thơ nhạc đấu tranh* [Vietnamese Arising Songs: A Selection of Music and Poetry of Struggle]. Springfield, VA: Phong trào Hưng ca Việt Nam.

Trịnh Nam Sơn. 1995. *Những sáng tác mới trong thập niên 90* [New Works From the 90s]. Fremont, CA: Asian Top Music Productions.

Discographical References

Đức Huy and Thảo My. 'Trái tim ngục tù.' *Vầng trăng năm xưa* [The Moon's Glow in Years Past] (cassette). Nhạc mới Productions 16. *1992*: USA.

Đức Huy. *Người tình trăm năm.* Nhạc Mới Productions 1. *1989*: USA.

Hải Minh. 'Lửa rừng đêm' [Fires in the Night Forest] (78 rpm). Oria. n.d.: France.

Hoàng Lan. 'Nhớ người xa vắng' [Missing Someone Far Away] (78 rpm). Oria. n.d.: France.

Khánh Hà, Tuấn Ngọc, Anh Tú and Lưu Bích. *Tình khúc Vũ Tuấn Đức* [Love Songs of Vu Tuan Duc] (CD). Khánh Hà Productions 30. *1995*: USA.

Jimmii J.C. Nguyễn. *Người con gái/The Girl* (CD). Jimmii Music Entertainment CD2003. *1994*: USA.

Liên khúc cha cha cha bolero. Mimosa Productions 66. *1995*: USA.

Technowave Remix. Asia Entertainment. *1998*: USA.

Thanh Thúy. 'Vĩnh biệt Sài Gòn.' *Vĩnh biệt Saigon: Tiếng hát Thanh Thúy.* Thanh Thúy 1. n.d.: USA.

Trịnh Nam Sơn. *Trịnh Nam Sơn và những sáng tác mới* [Trinh Nam Son and his New Works] (CD). O.S.A. Productions CD-VS-003. *1992*: USA.

Văn Lý. 'Giọt mưa thu' [Autumn Rain Drops] (78 rpm). Oria 506. *1949*: France.

Visual Recording

Paris by Night, vol. 2. 1985. USA. 65 mins. Music by Nguyễn Văn Đông, Song Ngọc, Phạm Thế Mỹ, Vũ Đức Nghiêm, Trường Sa, Lam Phương, Vân Tùng, Thông Đạt, Khánh Băng, Trịnh Lâm Ngân and Lê Dinh.

JASON GIBBS

Part II
Oceania

6. Australia

Australia

Population: 19,731,984 (2003)

With a population widely reported in the media as having reached 20 million in late 2003, Australia covers 2,966,195 sq miles (7,682,300 sq km) on the southwestern rim of the Pacific Ocean, and has a complex indigenous culture of great antiquity. The taxonomy that identifies popular music dates from the first permanent European settlement at Sydney Cove on 26 January 1788. Australia was founded as a penal colony, and its cultural history is traversed by tensions arising from origins in which British class divisions were schematically institutionalized. The colony's great distance from its origins, the vast internal distances over unfamiliarly harsh terrain and climate, and the infamous doctrine of *Terra Nullius*, which declared the continent to be uninhabited at the time of European invasion, all produced a particular tautness in the relationship between high and demotic cultures.

The cultural custodians viewed with suspicion unregulated popular recreations, considering them likely to promote criminality or savagery. There was also a tendency to construct national mythologies in terms of a struggle against a harsh and uncultivated landscape. The colonial administration thus centralized Eurocentric artistic culture as a marker of civilization, an attitude intensified among the genteel middle classes emerging from the mid-nineteenth century anxious to distance themselves from convict roots.

Early coastal settlements became the major cities, with expansion inland and along coastal strips. Wool and cattle industries were established early, but gold strikes in the 1850s generated enormous wealth and stimulated a wave of immigration that diversified what had been basically a white monoculture. Notwithstanding twentieth-century industrialization, masculinist frontier mythology inscribed in 'the bush' and 'the outback' has continued to retain great mythopoeic power. One of the popular rural and, more recently, urban heroes of this mythology is 'the battler,' the ordinary (usually male) individual stoically confronting adversity.

Since the beginning of permanent European settlement, Australia evolved separate administrative territories; currently these are Australian Capital Territory (ACT), New South Wales (NSW), Northern Territory (NT), South Australia (SA), Queensland (Qld), Tasmania (Tas), Victoria (Vic) and Western Australia (WA). Each has a capital city and its own parliamentary government. Distinctions and rivalries between these regions, and especially between the cities of Melbourne and Sydney, have influenced every sociocultural and economic level, including the establishment and location of a new city, Canberra (ACT), as the center of national government following the federation of states and territories into the Commonwealth of Australia in 1901.

Australia's official language remains English and, at the end of the twentieth century, its formal head of state was still the British monarch, though from the colonial period on there have been republican aspirations. In addition to the nationalism accompanying Australia's involvement in World War I, a turning away from imperial roots accompanied increasing US influence, particularly operating through twentieth-century mass mediations. Film and sound recordings constituted a major conduit to US-accented modernity, fortified by the US presence in Australia during World War II. In the postwar period, immigration programs further diversified Australian culture, particularly the abandonment in 1966 of the 1901 'White Australia' immigration policy. Since the late 1980s, that diversity has increasingly embraced the indigenous people, who had not even enjoyed political enfranchisement until the 1960s. The pressures of cultural diversity and other manifestations of globalism increased strikingly as the new millennium approached. The resonance of this was amplified by the 100th anniversary of federation in 2001.

1788 to the 1890s: From White Invasion to Federation

In addition to instruments brought by civilians, the First Fleet, by which the first permanent European settlers traveled to Sydney Cove, carried military musicians and, on 7 February 1788, the Royal Marines played drums and fifes for their first official ceremony in Sydney Cove. The first settlers, numbering just over one thousand, brought with them eighteenth-century Anglo-Irish traditions that ranged from art and religious music to popular dance, folk music and everyday musical practices. The first theater, convict-built, opened in 1796 and presented ballad-opera. Early nineteenth-century theaters performed material ranging through opera, pantomime, ballads and comic songs, all under the scrutiny of an administration anxious to regulate the recreations of the lower orders. In addition to the earliest folk dances, quadrilles and couple dances arrived in the early nineteenth century.

Oral/aural dissemination was supplemented by imported sheet music, handwritten scores and song lyrics published in newspapers; local music publishers were established by mid-century. While there are records of orally disseminated convict ballads, surviving local composition dates from the early nineteenth century, in the work of regimental and civilian musicians. Their work included essays in opera, ballad-opera, chamber and dance music, and marches. In addition, new lyrics to traditional melodies invoked remembered homelands and colonial life.

Gold discoveries of the 1850s radically changed the colony's economy and demography. Immigration diversified and increased, with the population trebling during the decade. Gold-fields money attracted international entertainers and musicians, increasing the range and quality of public music

performances from music hall to art music and early vaudeville. This development also led to a rapid expansion of entrepreneurial activity, as in agencies and performance circuits, the most influential of which was the J.C. Williamson organization.

Prosperity flowed to major centers, consolidating a genteel middle-class culture fortified by free settlers and free-born Australians, who found the pleasures of music enhanced by its function as a class marker along ethnic, racial and economic lines. The European parlor repertoire, overlapping both art and popular music traditions, and augmented by Australian composers like Hamilton Hill, played an increasing role in domestic life. As girls were more likely to have received music tuition, the growth of parlor music-making foregrounded the significance to Australian music of women, who were also increasingly prominent in public performance. In 1888, an eminent visiting French musician and music administrator estimated that 700,000 pianos had been imported into Australia since European settlement a century earlier, a figure described by a twentieth-century historian as 'remarkable even by prevailing European standards' (Covell 1967, 19–20). While this figure was an unconfirmed estimate, in the next year alone the number of pianos imported was 5,170, and there were 'at least ten local manufacturers' (Whiteoak and Scott-Maxwell 2003, 516), suggesting the instrument's importance in proclaiming civilization and gentility in a remote outpost of empire. It also produced an increase in demand for sheet music and music education that enlarged the music retailing and publishing industry. The sol-fa singing instruction method was also important in the approved music-making of the lower orders.

By the end of the nineteenth century, the dominance of British traditions in popular music was under challenge. In performance, US-modeled minstrelsy and vaudeville were achieving ascendancy over English music hall, but more far-reaching was the arrival of sound recordings, first demonstrated in Australia in 1878. They were little more than a passing novelty until the 1890s, when local entrepreneurs, the McMahon brothers, promoted cylinder recordings. They also installed five Edison Kinetoscopes in Sydney, the first moving pictures seen in Australia.

1890s to 1950s: From Recordings to Rock

The developments introduced by sound recording were accelerated by the microphone, which improved recording standards, made possible radio and sound cinematography, and transformed live performance during the 1930s. Internationally decisive, these technologies had an especially important impact on Australia because of the country's distance from seminal centers of modern popular music.

Sound recordings initiated the displacement of the piano as the center of domestic music-making, although player pianos remained a significant form of home entertainment, at least until improvements in recording and playback equipment were made. The gradual replacement of the piano by the gramophone was also seen as threatening the nineteenth-century artistic values that it embodied. From the 1890s, this destabilization was associated with depression in rural areas and failing gold fields, and the growth of urban manufacturing and bureaucratization. One reaction was a nostalgic and xenophobic nationalism fortified by federation in 1901, but at other levels there was a turning toward New World modernity. Both tendencies found expression in popular music. On the one hand a renewal of romanticized rural and colonial narratives and ballad forms would help to feed later country and folk music movements. On the other hand beckoned the United States, whence flowed the most influential developments in the new century: African-American jazz-based popular music.

World War I (1914–18) catalyzed both reactions. Australia's military contribution fueled a nationalism that flowed into popular music in the form of patriotic songs. But the war also awakened an emancipative spirit that embraced social and technological modernity. Sound recordings provided a musical conduit for such developments. Cylinder recordings, made and marketed in Australia from the 1890s, were gradually overtaken by discs, imported in growing numbers from the United States following the war, then supplemented, beginning in the mid-1920s, by the first local manufacturers established in Sydney and Melbourne. *Music Trader* estimated that there were 1 million gramophones in Australia by 1925. While catalogs covered a range of musics, the dissemination of aural/performance-based popular forms was particularly favored by a medium that could provide mass exposure with minimal class, gender and educational constraints. Contemporary advertising emphasized the connection between the phonograph and US jazz, examples of which were available in increasing numbers from 1920.

Radio officially arrived in 1923, providing a further alternative to the piano as a source of domestic music experience and, with its niche programming, accentuating the division between art and popular music. It also provided new employment opportunities for local popular musicians, particularly with the establishment of commercial stations, which began forming their own dance orchestras, expanding a new category of 'studio musicians.' These orchestras were frequently associated with the large dance halls that burgeoned in all major centers beginning in the teens of the century. Along with cabaret/restaurant venues that evolved into the later nightclub scene, the dance halls became major public dance venues, accommodating thousands. The size of these halls reflected Australia's increasing urban density, and provided a new focal point for the conceptualization of 'the masses,' contributing to several significant changes in popular music, which again reflected US influences. Larger halls necessitated bigger orchestras, with a concomitant need for vocal amplification. By 1934, microphones had become standard accessories, opening the way for the dominant vocal styles of twentieth-century mass-mediated popular music.

Even before sound cinematography, film also influenced popular music. Australia developed a robust early film industry; by 1919 cinema attendance in Australia had outstripped church attendance, and in 1928 it exceeded 110 million. The musical accompaniment to this new recreation represented a local mediation that drew heavily on popular music approaches, and in particular provided a workshop for improvisational and collagist modes. Silent films also addressed the competing claims of tradition and modernity, constructing rural mythologies as well as disseminating modern life-style models in which popular music and jazz were central. Both converged in movies dealing with problems faced by the 'modern woman' choosing between traditional roles and the possibilities embodied in the flapper. As women constituted 70 percent of Australian cinema audiences, and the majority of silent film pianists were also women, a gendered link was developed between film, popular music and emancipated modernity.

This link was consolidated by the ambiguous impact of sound cinematography. Initially, as an alternative recreation, the 'talkies' diminished music performance opportunities and gradually displaced cinema musicians. The simultaneous onset of the Great Depression also produced a conservative reaction against the good-time irresponsibility of jazz, leading to a resurgence of earlier popular music forms, including nostalgic bush ballads and parlor songs. There was also a brief reinvigoration of the brass band movement, though it too was damaged by the economics of the Depression, and subsequently fell into steady decline.

At the same time, the 'talkies' reinforced cinema as a channel of contemporary US influences, especially when the diminishing rigors of the Depression encouraged a renewal of interest in African-American–based popular music in the form of swing. This was accentuated by the simultaneous rise of US cinema to market dominance through control of distribution networks, fundamentally weakening the Australian industry. This further Americanized popular music, flooding Australia with the latest styles, dances and repertoire. Furthermore, a hitherto exotic accent and enunciation were now increasingly assimilated to popular song, with consequences that included the elimination of vocally constructed class distinctions projected through, for example, music hall and parlor song. The influence of the microphone on vocal styles also increased, as local singers attempted to reproduce in live performance venues the sounds heard on screen.

The opening of Sydney's Trocadero ballroom in 1936 consolidated swing as the new sound in popular music. The outbreak of World War II in 1939 again revived imperial nostalgia, which flowed into popular music, but the entry of the United States into the war, with some 1 million of its service personnel passing through Australia, accelerated the Americanization of mainstream popular music. This was generally dispersed through the middle-of-the-road (MOR) popular styles of the postwar decade. However, in terms of the values expressed and the lyrical/musical forms, this music reflected a 'back-to-normal' conservatism, which thrived on the economic boom and the Cold War climate and which produced such fashions as square dancing.

Against this there flowed musical countercultures with more overt US influences. The jazz movement bifurcated in the postwar period into modern and traditional schools. The most influential of these was traditional, in which Graeme Bell figured prominently. He was influential in the establishment in 1946 of the Australian Jazz Convention, the world's first and now longest-running annual jazz festival, and in the development of the 'Australian style,' regarded as the most distinctive contribution made to the jazz tradition outside the United States. Through European touring Bell also projected this style internationally, inspiring emulators, transforming the English popular music scene and virtually founding the durable and politically resonant jazz movement in Czechoslovakia. No other form of Australian music has exercised such a strong influence internationally.

In the postwar decade the jazz concert movement, based in local municipal halls, provided a forum as well as performance protocols for the next major development in popular music – rock 'n' roll. While African-American sources dominated developments, other significant strands of mass-mediated popular music had emerged through the 1920s, all serviced by the cultural and technological shifts described above. Hawaiian music maintained a presence well into the postwar era, but perhaps the most robust and durable was country music. New Zealand-born Tex Morton was an important pioneer who made his first recordings in 1936. With radio, recordings became the most important vehicle for the dissemination of the music beyond its rural centers. Urban demand was increased by postwar movement from the country to the booming urban centers, and later exponents like Smoky Dawson and Slim Dusty became nationally and internationally known. US films also played a decisive role in constructing a US-accented version of country music through the genre of the western.

Increasingly technologized music mediation steadily eroded a range of traditional popular music practices. Brass bands, parlor singing, vaudeville and burlesque all lost purchase, and music publishing was marginalized. By the 1950s long-playing recordings, cheaper reel-to-reel tape recorders and television had altered the domestic recreational environment, while the transistor radio facilitated the dissemination of popular music beyond those confines. These were central to radical transformations, in conjunction with demographic and economic factors. From 1941 to 1945 the birthrate had increased at an unprecedented rate; by the late 1950s, the resulting large adolescent population, in a climate of high employment, possessed an unprecedented level of disposable income. These conditions manifested themselves musically in the emergence of rock 'n' roll.

1950s to 2004: From Rock to a Hard Place

Prior to the mid-1950s Australia's rather ad hoc exposure to the United States had produced an

Australian popular music that was in US terms erratic, highly syncretic and, for all that, distinctive. Increasingly coordinated US international cultural marketing strategies altered the relationship between Australian and US popular music. This was particularly evident when the film *The Blackboard Jungle* opened in 1955, converging with a virgin teenage market as yet unclaimed by local commercial interests. The playing of Bill Haley's 'Rock Around the Clock' over the credits signaled the channeling of this market energy into rock 'n' roll.

Although early performers like Johnny O'Keefe and Col Joye broadly took their cue from US models, there was a high level of original composition in the recorded repertoire, initially dominated by the Festival label. Following initial resistance, Australians also found that the stage performance of these local musicians was often more effective than that of visiting US performers, partly because live performance, as opposed to recordings and film, had been basic to their apprenticeships. There were other local inflections that were inevitable prior to the importation of rock's ready-made musical and life-style appurtenances. In many respects the youthful musicians and followers showed a strong 'do-it-yourself' impulse, setting up their own fan clubs, taking recording initiatives, organizing dances and improvising instruments, public-address equipment and uniforms. 'Surf rock' of the early 1960s was rooted in Sydney's surf club culture, and showed little musical debt to apparent US models like the Beach Boys.

Early forums for the music included the town hall concerts in which rock gradually displaced jazz, a shift duplicated in the Sydney Stadium concerts presenting US performers, promoted by innovative US-born entrepreneur Lee Gordon. Rock was thus focused on a live scene with a circuit initially centered on Sydney. The audience was largely working class, a section of the youth market with a disposable income, as opposed to the middle-class youth, who were increasingly extending their education in the expanding university system and who displayed a disdain for the rawness and class connotations of rock.

This disdain was initially shared by the mainstream media; apart from Melbourne broadcaster Stan Rolfe, radio largely ignored rock until its commercial possibilities were grasped. Through the late 1950s there was a gradual takeover by an 'industry' made up of music mediators and mediations. Fan clubs were absorbed into music magazine subsidiaries of the print media; radio developed

new rock formats. Television presented a distinctive case study of this phase of recuperation, because the date of its arrival in Australia (1956) roughly coincided with the advent of rock. It thus took some time to define its position as a mediator of music and society, producing two competing models in the ABC's *Six O'Clock Rock* (which commenced February 1959) and *Bandstand* (November 1958). The sleeker and more domesticated production style of the latter, and a musical content that was closer to MOR, found broader favor, and the show's durability (it ended in 1972) is a metaphor for the sanitization that patterns the earliest phase of the music.

The Beatles' Australian tour in 1964 represented the consolidation of a pop industry that was now upwardly mobile, percolating through the middle classes and robbing other forms (notably jazz) of their market. Maintained by immigration, Australia's British connections provided a congenial environment for the new sound, eclipsing earlier US-modeled rockers with a new generation, in which the Easybeats, the Seekers and the Bee Gees were prominent. This phase changed from the late 1960s into an exploratory psychedelia that broadened the mainstream of popular music. Jazz-rock, folk-rock, country rock and ventures into Eastern and art musics paved the way for an omnivorous syncretism that, with the increasing promiscuity of mass mediations, drew virtually all genres into the category of popular music, one culmination of which would become world music.

The consolidation of a local popular press and of recording and media industries, even though they were still US- and UK-derived, provided a foundation for the emergence of an Australian pop identity, which has proceeded through several distinct stages. In the early 1970s, alternative approaches allied with youth politics became institutionalized. The Vietnam War, racism and urban development provided issues, and pop festivals (in Ourimbah, NSW and Sunbury, Victoria) provided forums for the movement. University circuits and the pub-rock scene flourished as a result of more liberal licensing laws, enabling the development of grass-roots regionalism and youth pop networks. Industry developments also contributed to this movement. The dominance of the major record companies, which with the exception of Festival were foreign owned, was challenged by the emergence of a more significant independent pop sector, the most successful manifestation of which was the Mushroom label (established in

1972). Community FM radio, which arrived in 1974, exposed niche markets, encouraged local recording and promoted alternative formats that had been largely ignored by commercial radio. This included other noncommercial musics, notably jazz, which also benefited from related infrastructural initiatives during this period. In Sydney, the first of many tertiary conservatory-based jazz studies programs was proposed by Don Burrows, who had virtually become the public face of mainstream/progressive jazz in the postwar period, and who later served as the program's director. In 1983, the government-funded Jazz Co-ordination Association of New South Wales was inaugurated, later duplicated in other states and as a national body, with transforming effects on work and touring opportunities and on the public consciousness. This initiative was associated with the establishment of festivals and the Australian Jazz Archives, housed in the National Film and Sound Archive.

In the pop/rock sector, the Australian Broadcasting Commission (later, Corporation) (ABC) established a youth radio station, 2JJJ (later, Triplejay, with national transmission), and a pop television program, *Countdown*, which provided national prime-time coverage, benefiting from the advent of color transmission shortly afterward. The success of bands like Skyhooks and Sherbert, and, later, Jimmy Barnes with Cold Chisel, and singer John Farnham, reflected the power of these convergences. While Sydney and Melbourne remained the major centers, regional activity has also been strengthened, with increasingly coordinated entrepreneurial and infrastructural support, as in Ausmusic, founded in 1989 initially with private sponsorship and government funding to promote the development of every aspect of Australian contemporary music. 2JJJ (Triplejay) has also played a crucial role in establishing national networks – for example, in the discovery through its traveling talent show of the group Killing Heidi in Violet Town in rural Victoria in 1997. The band has achieved international success, and was a multiple winner at the 2000 Australian Record Industry Association (ARIA) awards. The technologically facilitated continuing proliferation of independent labels since the 1980s – labels such as Au-go-go, Volition, Missing Link and Shock – has also coincided with the infiltration of alternative groups into the mainstream charts.

The emergence of local punk/new wave, notably through such bands as Radio Birdman, the Saints and the Birthday Party, although echoing UK and US developments, assumed a distinctive political coloration. The effects also registered beyond Australia: AC/DC, INXS, Nick Cave, the Little River Band, Men At Work, Crowded House, Renée Geyer, Kylie Minogue and, most recently, Natalie Imbruglia exemplify unprecedented international recognition in a range of sub-categories cutting across hard rock, punk, metal, MOR and gothic. At the same time, Australian popular music has been enriched by arrivals from elsewhere, particularly New Zealand, including jazz musicians such as Julian Lee and Judy Bailey, and rock-based groups like Dragon and Split Enz.

Over the last decade of the twentieth century, in a development that calls for closer examination, Australian groups led the phenomenon known as the 'tribute band,' which re-creates the look as well as the sound of earlier groups. The Australian groups included the Beatnix (the Beatles), Head Injuries and Oils Ain't Oils (both Midnight Oil), ABCD (AC/DC), the White and the Zep Boys (both Led Zeppelin), and Bjorn Again (ABBA), the last-named of whom found a place among the 10 highest-paid entertainers in Australia, and who achieved international success.

Although pop has been the dominant form, the expansion of performance and media infrastructures has also allowed other popular musics to thrive in local conditions. Jazz, folk and country have evolved local syncretions that have increasingly overlapped with the world music phenomenon. All popular forms have enjoyed the benefits of developments in sound technology that have produced cheaper, more diverse and more accessible means of music production. These technologies have also been disseminated in a proliferating range of sites. Generally, the term 'popular music' evokes what might be called 'stand-alone' musical experiences, ranging from recordings to attendance at special-purpose live music venues. It is important to remember, however, that most music is experienced in conjunction with other leisure or vocational activities. Apart from homes and workplaces, these sites include leisure spaces such as sporting events, public dining and drinking venues, shopping malls, telephone 'on hold,' and travel by car, aircraft and on foot. Much of the music performed in religious contexts is arguably 'popular,' and indeed the Christian rock group Newsboys was financially even more successful than the high-profile tribute band Bjorn Again. Film has also become one of the most significant and profitable vehicles for various forms of popular music. The dominance of what may be termed 'pop' in the popular music imaginary is not confined to Australia, but for historical reasons it has a particular intensity that is arguably an echo of the earliest colonial period when, as noted above, demotic leisure was largely that of a criminal class.

Conclusion

In spite of the increasing pervasiveness of music, the end of the twentieth century saw a number of changes in legislative and economic environments that were not likely to encourage a regional popular music. The crucial pub scene declined with the advent of random breath testing, entertainment license requirements, central business district development and, particularly in some centers, the displacement of bands by poker machines. The abandonment of local quota broadcasting stipulations in 1992 and the subsequent introduction of 'parallel importing' of CD recordings weakened the leverage of local acts in the industry. Protests by musicians against such developments were conspicuous in the 1998 general election.

The 1995 Contemporary Music Summit called by industry and government disclosed a nervousness in the face of new formations and dynamics that indicated alternative linkages between local subcultures and global markets. The tension between grass-roots and multinational control is the most important dynamic in contemporary popular music in Australia, affecting the means of (re)production and creative consumption. While this is an international phenomenon, two major shifts in its configuration have had particular importance for Australia.

Out of an Australian population of 19.4 million in 2001, 4,105,444 (21.9 percent) were born overseas, and 410,003 identified themselves as 'indigenous,' compared with 352,970 in the 1996 census. In 20 percent of households English was not the only language spoken, if at all (a rise of 2.9 percent since 1991), and well over 100 religious denominational affiliations were recorded. In 2002, it was recorded that over 200 languages were spoken in Australian households, of which 48 were indigenous. 'Multiculturalism' provides a hospitable environment for so-called 'world music,' and there is growing interest in Australia's ethnic and indigenous music, embracing cognate social, political and environmental issues exemplified in the work of Midnight Oil and indigenous and mixed-race groups like Yothu Yindi. Each of these bands exemplifies a further stage in the emergence of what is perceived as a distinctively Australian popular music, sustained not simply by lyrics that address local issues such as indigenous land rights, but also through syncretisms involving musical instruments. Most Aboriginal popular music is stylistically eclectic and strongly influenced by Western popular forms, as in the pioneering country-gospel work from the mid-1950s of the recently resurgent Jimmy Little. But it is the use of the didjeridu and, to a lesser degree, clapsticks that has become a universal marker of 'Australian-ness' in popular music. Indeed, notwithstanding the cultural problematics of its incorporation into mainstream popular music, the didjeridu is probably the most recognizable contribution made by Australia to the international genre known as 'world music.' While the generally masculinist conservatism of mainstream Australian popular music is inscribed in the category 'heritage rock,' the emergence of increasing numbers of women instrumentalists in post-1970s indie/new wave is another reminder of the importance of local, grassroots, independent scenes and technologies in the renewal of the music.

Over the same period, the various techno-based forms, including dance and hip-hop, have radically reconfigured the dynamics of popular music. Performance practices reconceptualize the musician, the audience, the venue and the dancer. The formal properties of contemporary dance music also displace traditional concepts of musical foreground as articulated in such models as melody/backing, words/music and soloist/band. In dance music, one consequence of this change is a dissipation of the traditional channels of meaning and affect for localized ideologies, encouraging an apparently placeless style, though much the same may be said for recent developments in the old radio/television 'talent quest' format, such as *Australian Idol* (2003). Another such development – in which bands are created – is represented through miniseries such as *Popstars*, a program that takes the audience through the musicians' audition process. At the same time, non-geographical social formations, in particular the gay and lesbian communities, may define themselves through the dance party scene. There are also claims made for dance culture that its carnivalesque 'reclamation' of spaces constitutes a form of local activism. At the same time, since the 1980s and particularly through the 1990s, hip-hop has become a significant vehicle for the creation and articulation of local identities within Australia, particularly though not solely by teen male 'crews' who feel marginalized ethnically, geographically and socioeconomically. Aspects of this profile were exemplified in the aggressively suburban ethos of Def Wish Cast in the early 1990s. The fact that much of this is 'indie' to the point of being produced in the home or, literally, as 'garage music' is a reminder of the increasing democratization of the means of production and distribution of techno-based styles. Nonetheless, taken together, dance and hip-hop suggest that the way in which recent developments in popular music production and consumption might mediate localized ideologies remains unpredictable. The extraordinary flourishing of tribute bands in Australia, the sales figures for covers in the local industry, and the enormous success of the nationally touring annual rock/pop show Big Day Out, which features what are regarded as imported and local alternative acts, are counterbalances to a simplistic conception of such binaries as 'alternative/mainstream' and 'authentic/commercial' in Australian pop at this stage in the development of mass mediations. Similarly, the aggressive action by the majors against the unauthorized traffic in on-line music files underlines the ethical, aesthetic and economic ambiguities of music 'glocalization.' Particularly in relation to the synchronous rise of 'world' musics, with their putative focus on local specificity, this marks a particularly sensitive moment in the negotiations between local and global, especially for a country as culturally diverse as Australia. At the very least, it signals the need for more ethnographically oriented studies, taking greater account of the local functions and uses of music.

Bibliography
The following either have been of particular value in the preparation of the foregoing or they take up subjects mentioned in some detail. A longer bibliography can be found in John Shepherd et al., eds., *Popular Music Studies: A Select International Bibliography* (London and Washington: Mansell, 1997); see 'Australia (Settler),' 319–21 and 'Indigenous Australian,' 322–24. A link to an even more extensive and continually updated bibliography of Australian popular music can be accessed at http://www.arts.unsw.edu.au/english/staffprofiles/brucej.htm

Australian Bureau of Statistics (ABS). *Year Book Australia*. Canberra: Australian Bureau of Statistics No. 80, Cat. No. ABS 1301.0. A number of these annual publications were consulted. For 2001 figures, the source was the ABS Web site (http://www.abs.gov.au/ausstats/abs@nsf/cat/).
Australian Record Industry Association. http://www.aria.com.au/

Baker, Glenn A. 1982. *The Beatles Down Under: The 1964 Australia and New Zealand Tour*. Glebe, NSW: Wild & Woolley.
Baker, Glenn A., ed. 1987. *Australian Made: Gonna Have A Good Time Tonight*. Sydney: Fontana Collins.
Bambrick, Nikki, and Miller, Jeremy. 1994. 'Exotic Hula – "Hawaiian" Dance Entertainment in Post-War Australia.' *Perfect Beat: The Pacific Journal of Research into Contemporary Music and Popular Culture* 2(1): 68–87.
Bebbington, Warren, ed. 1997. *The Oxford Companion to Australian Music*. Melbourne: Oxford University Press.
Beilby, Peter, and Roberts, Michael, eds. 1981. *Australian Music Directory*. North Melbourne: Australian Music Directory Pty Ltd.
Bell, Graeme. 1988. *Graeme Bell, Australian Jazzman: His Autobiography*. Frenchs Forest, NSW: Child & Associates.
Bisset, Andrew. 1987. *Black Roots White Flowers: A History of Jazz in Australia*. Rev. ed. Sydney: ABC Enterprises.
Blunt, Bob. 2001. *Blunt: A Biased History of Australian Rock*. Northcote, Victoria: Prowling Tiger Press.
Breen, Marcus, ed. 1987. *Missing in Action: Australian Popular Music in Perspective*. Kensington, Victoria: Verbal Graphics.
Breen, Marcus, ed. 1994. *Australia/New Zealand Issue. Popular Music* 13(3).
Breen, Marcus. 1999. *Rock Dogs: Politics and the Australian Music Industry*. Annandale, NSW: Pluto Press.
Brisbane, Katharine, ed. 1991. *Entertaining Australia: An Illustrated History*. Sydney: Currency Press.
Brokenmouth, Robert. 1996. *Nick Cave: The Birthday Party and Other Epic Adventures*. London: Omnibus.
Bryden-Brown, John. 1982. *J O'K: The Official Johnny O'Keefe Story*. Sydney: Doubleday.
Byrell, John. 1995. *Bandstand and All That*. Kenthurst, NSW: Kangaroo Press.
Bythell, D. 1991. 'The Brass Band in Australia: The Transplantation of British Popular Culture, 1850–1950.' In *Bands: The Brass Band Movement in the 19th and 20th Centuries*, ed. Trevor Herbert. Milton Keynes: Open University Press, 146–64.
Clare, John (aka Gail Brennan). 1995. *Bodgie, Dada and the Cult of Cool*. Sydney: University of New South Wales Press.
Cockington, James. 2001. *Long Way to the Top: Stories of Australian Rock & Roll*. Sydney: ABC Books.

Coupe, Stuart, and Baker, Glenn A. ca. 1983. *The New Rock 'n' Roll: The A-Z of Rock in the '80s.* London: Omnibus Press.

Covell, Roger. 1967. *Australia's Music: Themes for a New Society.* Melbourne: Sun Books.

Cox, Peter. 2001. *Spinning Around: The Festival Records Story.* Sydney: Powerhouse Publishing.

Cox, Peter, and Douglas, Louise. 1994. *Teen Riots to Generation X: The Australian Rock Audience.* Haymarket, NSW: Powerhouse Publishing.

Coyle, Jackey, and Coyle, Rebecca. 1995. 'Aloha Australia – Hawaiian Music in Australia (1920–1955).' *Perfect Beat: The Pacific Journal of Research into Contemporary Music and Popular Culture* 2(2): 31–63.

Coyle, Rebecca, ed. 1997. *Screen Scores: Studies in Contemporary Australian Film Music.* Sydney: AFTRS.

Cunningham, Stuart, and Turner, Graeme, eds. 1997. *The Media in Australia.* 2nd ed. St Leonards, NSW: Allen & Unwin.

Dawson, Herbert Henry. 1985. *Smoky Dawson: A Life.* North Sydney: George Allen & Unwin.

Department for Communications and the Arts. 1995. *Contemporary Music Summit, 27th April 1995: A Report to the Minister for Communications and the Arts.* Canberra: ACT.

Doyle, Peter. 1999. 'Flying Saucer Rock and Roll: The Australian Press Confronts Early Rock and Roll.' *Perfect Beat: The Pacific Journal of Research into Contemporary Music and Popular Culture* 4(3): 24–47.

Dreyfus, Kay. 1999. *Sweethearts of Rhythm: The Story of Australia's All-Girl Bands and Orchestras to the End of the Second World War.* Sydney: Currency.

Dunbar-Hall, Peter. 1995. *Discography of Aboriginal and Torres Strait Islander Performers.* Sydney: Australian Music Center.

Dusty, Slim, and McKean, Joy. 1996. *Slim Dusty: Another Day, Another Town.* Sydney: Pan Macmillan Australia.

Eliezer, Christie. 1976. *Sherbert On Tour.* Melbourne: Dabble Productions.

Evans, Mark. 1998. '"Quality" Criticism: Music Reviewing in Australian Rock Magazines.' *Perfect Beat: The Pacific Journal of Research into Contemporary Music and Popular Culture* 3(4): 38–50.

Forbes, Clark. 1989. *Whispering Jack: The John Farnham Story.* New South Wales: Hutchinson.

Ford, Joan. 1995. *Meet Me at the Trocadero.* Cowra, NSW: Joan Ford.

Garde, Murray. 1998. 'From a Distance: Aboriginal Music in the Maningrida Community and on Their Internet Site.' *Perfect Beat: The Pacific Journal of Research into Contemporary Music and Popular Culture* 4(1): 4–18.

Gibb, Barry, Gibb, Robin, and Gibb, Maurice, with Leaf, David. 1979. *Bee Gees: The Authorized Biography.* New York: Delta Books.

Gorham, Rachael, and Nakache, Arielle. 1993. 'Star Moves: Choreography, Choreographers and Australian Music Video.' *Perfect Beat: The Journal of Research into Contemporary Music and Popular Culture* 1(3): 23–37.

Guldberg, H.H. 1987. *The Australian Music Industry: An Economic Evaluation.* Sydney: Australia Council.

Harley, Ross. 1995. 'Acts of Volition: Volition Records, Independent Marketing and the Promotion of Australian Techno-Pop.' *Perfect Beat: The Pacific Journal of Research into Contemporary Music and Popular Culture* 2(3): 21–48.

Hayton, Jon, and Isackson, Leon. 1990. *Behind the Rock: The Diary of a Rock Band 1956–66.* Milsons Point, NSW: Time-Life Books.

Hayward, Philip, ed. 1992. *From Pop to Punk to Postmodernism: Popular Music and Australian Culture from the 1960s to the 1990s.* St Leonards, NSW: Allen & Unwin.

Hayward, Philip. 1993. 'Safe, Exotic and Somewhere Else: Yothu Yindi, "Treaty" and the Mediation of Aboriginality.' *Perfect Beat: The Journal of Research into Contemporary Music and Popular Culture* 1(2): 33–42.

Hayward, Philip, ed. 1998. *Sound Alliances: Indigenous Peoples, Cultural Politics and Popular Music in the Pacific.* London and New York: Cassell.

Hayward, Philip. 2001. *Tide Lines: Music, Tourism and Cultural Transition in the Whitsunday Islands [and Adjacent Coast].* Lismore, NSW: The Music Archive for the Pacific Press.

Hayward, Philip, et al., eds. 1991–. *Perfect Beat: The Pacific Journal of Research into Contemporary Music and Popular Culture.* For its first three issues the journal's title was *Perfect Beat: The Journal of Research into Contemporary Music and Popular Culture.* This is the major scholarly journal on Australian popular music. A number of its relevant articles, listed under separate city location entries for Australia, are also collected in Hayward (1998).

Homan, Shane. 2002. 'Access All Eras: Careers, Creativity and the Australian Tribute Band.' *Perfect Beat: The Pacific Journal of Research into Contemporary Music and Popular Culture* 5(4): 45–59.

Hutchison, Tracee. 1992. *Your Name's on the Door: 10 Years of Australian Music*. Sydney: ABC Enterprises.

Inglis, Ken. 1983. *This Is the ABC: The Australian Broadcasting Commission 1932–1983*. Melbourne: Melbourne University Press.

Jarosiewicz, Diane. 1992. 'Music Power: Kylie, Bowie and *The Delinquents*.' *Perfect Beat: The Journal of Research into Contemporary Music and Popular Culture* 1(1): 17–24.

Jenkins, Jeff. 1994. *Ego Is Not a Dirty Word: The Skyhooks Story*. Fitzroy, Victoria: Kelly and Withers.

Johnson, Bruce. 1987. *The Oxford Companion to Australian Jazz*. Melbourne: Oxford University Press.

Johnson, Bruce. 1995. 'Australian Jazz in Europe: A Case Study in Musical Displacement.' *Perfect Beat: The Pacific Journal of Research into Contemporary Music and Popular Culture* 2(3): 49–64.

Johnson, Bruce. 2000. *The Inaudible Music: Jazz, Gender and Australian Modernity*. Sydney: Currency Press.

Johnson, Bruce. 2003. 'Naturalizing the Exotic: The Australian Jazz Convention.' In *Jazz Planet*, ed. E. Taylor Atkins. Jackson, MS: University Press of Mississippi, 151–68.

Johnson, Vivien. 1990. *Radio Birdman*. Melbourne: Sheldon Booth.

Laird, Ross. 1997. *A Discography of Popular Music Recorded in Australia or by Australians Overseas, 1924–1950*. 5th (rev.) ed. Canberra: Discographic Researchers.

Latta, David. 1991. *Australian Country Music*. Sydney: Random House.

Luckman, Susan. 2001. 'What Are They Raving On About?: Temporary Autonomous Zones and "Reclaim the Streets."' *Perfect Beat: The Pacific Journal of Research into Contemporary Music and Popular Culture* 5(2): 49–68.

Magowen, Fiona. 1994. '"The Land Is Our Marr (Essence), It Stays Forever": The Yothu Yindi Relationship in Australian Aboriginal Traditional and Popular Musics.' In *Ethnicity, Identity and Music: The Musical Construction of Place*, ed. Martin Stokes. Oxford: Berg, 135–56.

Maxwell, Ian. 2003. *Phat Beats, Dope Rhymes: Hip Hop Down Under Comin' Upper*. Middletown, CT: Wesleyan University Press.

McFarlane, Ian. 1999. *The Encyclopedia of Australian Rock and Pop*. St Leonards, NSW: Allen & Unwin.

McGrath, Noel. 1978. *Australian Encyclopedia of Rock*. Collingwood, Victoria: Outback Press.

McGrath, Noel. 1979. *Australian Encyclopaedia of Rock 1978–79 Yearbook*. Collingwood, Victoria: Outback Press.

Milsom, W., and Thomas, H. 1986. *Pay to Play: The Australian Rock Music Industry*. Ringwood, Victoria: Penguin.

Mitchell, Tony. 1994. 'World Music and the Popular Music Industry: An Australian View.' *Ethnomusicology* 37(3): 309–38.

Mitchell, Tony. 1996. 'Real Wild Child: Australian Popular Music and National Identity.' In *Popular Music and Local Identity: Rock, Pop and Rap in Europe and Oceania*. Leicester: University of Leicester Press, 173–214.

Morrow, Guy. 2002. 'Calling Australia Home: The "Arrivals" Segment of the Opening Ceremony of the Sydney 2000 Olympic Games.' *Perfect Beat: The Pacific Journal of Research into Contemporary Music and Popular Culture* 6(1): 68–79.

Murphie, Andrew. 1996. 'Sound at the End of the World as We Know It: Nick Cave, Wim Wenders' Wings of Desire and a Deleuze-Guattarian Ecology of Popular Music.' *Perfect Beat: The Pacific Journal of Research into Contemporary Music and Popular Culture* 2(4): 18–42.

Myers, Eric, ed. 1994 (updated in 1998). *Australian Jazz Directory*. Sydney: Jazz Co-ordination Association of New South Wales.

National Film and Sound Archive. 1998. *The First Wave: Australian Rock & Pop Recordings, 1955–1963: A Complete Discography, Including Listings of Newsreel and Television Footage, Documentation and Other Archival Materials Held by the National Film and Sound Archive*. Canberra: National Film and Sound Archive. http://www.aa.gov.au/nfsa/nfsa.htm

Neuenfeldt, Karl. 1993. 'Yothu Yindi and *Ganma*: The Cultural Transposition of the Aboriginal Agenda Through Metaphor and Music.' *Journal of Australian Studies* 38: 1–11.

Nicol, Lisa. 1993. 'Culture, Custom and Collaboration: The Production of Yothu Yindi's "Treaty" Videos.' *Perfect Beat: The Journal of Research into Contemporary Music and Popular Culture* 1(2): 23–32.

Nicholson, Dennis Way. 1997. *Australian Soundtrack Recordings 1927–1996: A Discography of Soundtracks and Associated Recordings Relating to Australian Film and Television Productions*. The Rocks, NSW: Australian Music Centre.

Powerhouse Museum et al. 1997. *Real Wild Child!: Australian Rock Music 1950s–90s*. CD-ROM. Australia: Produced by Powerhouse Museum, ABC/

Triple J, Pacific Advanced Media and Mushroom Pictures.

Prices Surveillance Authority. 1990. *Inquiry into the Prices of Sound Recordings*. Canberra: Australian Government Publishing Service.

Rawlins, Adrian. 1986. *Festivals in Australia: An Intimate History*. Spring Hill: D.T.E. Publishers.

Rickwood, Julie. 1998. 'Embodied Acapella: The Experience of Singing a Displaced Eclectic Repertoire.' *Perfect Beat: The Pacific Journal of Research into Contemporary Music and Popular Culture* 3(4): 68–84.

Rogers, Bob, and O'Brien, Denis. 1975. *Rock 'n' Roll Australia: The Australian Pop Scene 1954–1964*. Stanmore, NSW: Cassell Australia.

Ryan, Robin. 1999. 'Gumleaf Playing Competitions: Aboriginal and Non-Aboriginal Performance Styles and Socio-Cultural Contexts.' *Perfect Beat: The Pacific Journal of Research into Contemporary Music and Popular Culture* 4(3): 66–85.

Scott-Maxwell, Aline. 1997. 'Oriental Exoticism in 1920s Australian Popular Music.' *Perfect Beat: The Pacific Journal of Research into Contemporary Music and Popular Culture* 3(3): 28–57.

Scott-Maxwell, Aline. 2002. 'Negotiating Difference: Peter Ciani's Italian-Australian Journey.' *Perfect Beat: The Pacific Journal of Research into Contemporary Music and Popular Culture* 6(1): 33–48.

Sly, Leslie. 1993. *The Power and the Passion: A Guide to the Australian Music Industry*. North Sydney: Warner Chappell Music.

Smith, Graeme. 1992. 'The Country Voice.' *Arena Magazine* 1: 38–40.

Smith, Graeme. 1994. 'Australian Country Music and the Hillbilly Yodel.' *Popular Music* 13(3): 297–311.

Smith, Graeme. 2001. 'Celtic Australia: Bush Bands, Irish Music and the Nation.' *Perfect Beat: The Pacific Journal of Research into Contemporary Music and Popular Culture* 5(2): 3–18.

Smith, Jazzer, ed. 1984. *The Book of Australian Country Music*. Gordon, NSW: Berghouse Floyd Tuckey Publishing Group.

Spencer, Chris. 1990. *Australian Rock Discography: A Discography of Vinyl Product Released by Australian Artists 1960–1989*. Rev. 2nd ed. Golden Square, Victoria: Moonlight Publishing.

Spencer, Chris. 1995. *An Australian Rock Discography 1990–1994*. Golden Square, Victoria: Moonlight Publishing.

Spencer, Chris. 1996. *An Australian Rock Discography 1956–1969*. Golden Square, Victoria: Moonlight Publishing.

Spencer, Chris. 1997. *An Australian Rock Discography 1980–1984*. Golden Square, Victoria: Moonlight Publishing.

Spencer, Chris, and Nowara, Zbig. 1996. *Who's Who of Australian Rock*. 4th ed. Knoxfield, Victoria: Five Mile Press.

Spencer, Chris, with McHenry, Paul, and Nowara, Zbig. 1997. *An Australian Rock Discography 1995*. Golden Square, Victoria: Moonlight Publishing.

St John, Graham. 2001. 'The Battle of the Bands: ConFest Musics and the Politics of Authenticity.' *Perfect Beat: The Pacific Journal of Research into Contemporary Music and Popular Culture* 5(2): 69–90.

St Leon, Mark. 1983. *Spangles and Sawdust: The Circus in Australia*. Melbourne: Greenhouse Publications.

Stone, Sasha. 1990. *Kylie Minogue: The Superstar Next Door*. London: Omnibus.

Stubington, Jill, and Dunbar-Hall, Peter. 1994. 'Yothu Yindi's "Treaty": *Ganma* in Music.' *Popular Music* 13(3): 243–59.

Sturma, Michael. 1991. *Australian Rock 'n' Roll: The First Wave*. Kenthurst, NSW: Kangaroo Press.

Sutcliffe, Mike. 1989. *Australian Record and Music Review*. Sydney.

Turner, Graeme. 1993. 'Who Killed the Radio Star: The Death of Teen Radio in Australia.' In *Rock and Popular Music: Politics, Policies, Institutions*, ed. Tony Bennett et al. London and New York: Routledge, 142–55.

Van Straten, Frank. 2003. *Tivoli*. South Melbourne: Thomas C. Lothian Pty Ltd.

Walker, Clinton. 1982. *Inner City Sound*. Glebe, NSW: Wild & Woolley.

Walker, Clinton. 1984. *The Next Thing: Contemporary Australian Rock*. Kenthurst, Victoria: Kangaroo Press.

Walker, Clinton. 1994. *Highway to Hell: The Life & Times of AC/DC Legend Bon Scott*. Chippendale, NSW: Sun Books, Pan Macmillan.

Walker, Clinton. 1996. *Stranded: The Secret History of Australian Independent Music 1977–1991*. Sydney: Pan Macmillan Australia.

Walker, Clinton. 2000. *Buried Country: The Story of Aboriginal Country Music*. Annandale, NSW: Pluto Press.

Waterhouse, Richard. 1990. *From Minstrel Show to Vaudeville: The Australian Popular Stage 1788–1914*. Kensington, NSW: University of New South Wales Press.

Watson, Eric. 1982. *Eric Watson's Country Music in Australia*. Sydney: Angus & Robertson. (First published Kensington, NSW: Rodeo Publications, 1975.)

Watson, Eric. 1983. *Eric Watson's Country Music in Australia*, Vol. 2. Sydney: Angus & Robertson.

Watterson, Ray. 1988. 'The Role of Commercial Radio in the Development of Australian Rock Music.' In *Rock Music: Politics and Policy*, ed. Tony Bennett. Griffith, Queensland: Institute for Cultural Policy Studies, Division of Humanities, Griffith University, 7–12.

Webb, H. 1987. 'The Reggae-Folk Protest: Australian Pop Music and Ideology.' *Australian Journal of Cultural Studies* (Special Edition): 69–76.

Whiteoak, John. 1993. 'From Jim Crow to Jazz: Imitation African-American Improvisatory Practices in Pre-Jazz Australia.' *Perfect Beat: The Journal of Research into Contemporary Music and Popular Culture* 1(3): 50–74.

Whiteoak, John. 1999. *Playing Ad Lib*. Sydney: Currency Press.

Whiteoak, John, and Scott-Maxwell, Aline, eds. 2003. *Currency Companion to Music and Dance in Australia*. Sydney: Currency Press.

Williams, Mike. 1981. *The Australian Jazz Explosion*. Australia: Angus & Robertson.

Wilmoth, Peter. 1993. *Glad All Over: The Countdown Years 1974–1987*. Ringwood, Victoria: McPhee Gribble.

Yunupingu, Mandawuy. 1994. 'Yothu Yindi – Finding Balance.' In *Voices from the Land – 1993 Boyer Lectures*. Sydney: ABC Books, 1–11.

Zion, Lawrence. 1987. 'The Impact of the Beatles on Pop Music in Australia: 1963–66.' *Popular Music* 6(3): 291–311.

Zion, Lawrence. 1988. 'The Sound of "Australian" Music.' In *Constructing a Culture: A People's History of Australia Since 1788*, ed. Verity Burgmann and Jenny Lee. Fitzroy, Victoria: McPhee Gribble/Penguin, 209–22.

Zion, Lawrence. 1989. 'Disposable Icons: Pop Music in Australia, 1955–63.' *Popular Music* 8(2): 165–75.

Discographical Reference

Haley, Bill, and His Comets. '(We're Gonna) Rock Around the Clock.' Decca 29124. 1955: USA.

Discography

AC/DC. *Back in Black*. Albert/EMI 477089-2. *1980*: Australia.

Bell, Graeme. *Czechoslovak Journey*. Supraphon 0 15 1455. *1973*: Czechoslovakia.

Bell, Graeme. *The EMI Australian Recordings*. Axis CDAX 701583. *1990*: Australia.

Birthday Party, The. *The Bad Seed*. 4AD BAD. *1983*: Germany.

Blunt/Who Cares Wins: A Biased History of Australian Rock. Issued with Blunt (2001); see Bibliography.

Burrows, Don. *Don Burrows: The First Fifty Years* (5 CDs). ABC Music/PolyGram 514 296-2, 297-2, 298-2, 299-2, 300-2. *1993*: Australia.

Bush Traditions. Larrikin Records 007. *1976*: Australia.

Cave, Nick, and the Bad Seeds. *From Her To Eternity*. Mute STUMM 17. *1984*: Germany.

Cold Chisel. *Circus Animals*. WEA 600113. *1982*: Australia.

Dawson, Smoky. *I'm A Happy-Go-Lucky Cowboy*. Kingfisher KF-AUS 16. *1991*: Australia.

Def Wish Cast. *Knights of the Underground Table*. Random Records. *1993*: Australia.

Dusty, Slim. *Country Classics: Slim Dusty* (3 CDs). Reader's Digest 300701300. *1996*: Australia.

Farnham, John. *Whispering Jack*. BMG SFCD 0149. *1986*: Australia.

From the Bush. M 314. *1989*: Australia.

History of Jazz in Australia 1925–1989 (2 CDs). National Film and Sound Archive/Soundabout Australia AH 05 2005. *1996*: Australia.

Imbruglia, Natalie. *Left of the Middle*. RCA 67634. *1998*: UK.

INXS. *Kick*. WEA 255080-1. *1987*: Australia.

Joye, Col. *Very Best 22 Golden Hits* (5 LPs). *1980*: Australia.

Killing Heidi. *Reflector*. Wah Wah/Roadshow. *2000*: Australia.

Little, Jimmy. *An Evening with Jimmy Little*. Festival L45825-6. *1978*: Australia.

Little, Jimmy. *Messenger*. Festival D32064. *1999*: Australia.

Little River Band, The. *Diamantina Cocktail*. EMI EMC 2575. *1977*: Australia.

Men At Work. *Business As Usual*. CBS SBP 237700. *1981*: Australia.

Midnight Oil. *Diesel and Dust*. CBS 460005. *1986*: Australia.

Minogue, Kylie. *Kylie*. Mushroom TVL 93277. *1988*: Australia.

No Worries (2 LPs). Hot Worriedone. *1984*: Australia.

O'Keefe, Johnny. *20th Anniversary Album* (2 CDs). Festival L 45137-8. *1972*: Australia.

Pacific Circle Music: Sydney Australia 1998. Pacific Circle Music PMC98 1 (Major Label Artists), PMC98 2 (Independents). *1998*: Australia. For information on these samples, see the Pacific Circle Music Convention Web site (http://www.pcmc.com.au).

Radio Birdman. *Radios Appear*. Trafalgar TRL 1001. *1977*: Australia.

Real Australian Blues (3 CDs). Studio 52 52CD-018RAB1, 52CD-032RAB2, 52CD-172RAB3. *1991, 1993, 1997*: Australia.

Rockin' 'Neath the Southern Cross 1958–64. Time-Life Music RRC-E31. *1990*: Australia.

Saints, The. *The Monkey Puzzle*. Festival 19353. *1981*: Australia.

Seekers, The. *The Silver Jubilee Album*. EMI 781408-2. *1999*: UK.

The Great Bands. Soundabout Australia AHS 04-2CDS. *1996*: Australia.

The Troc. MBS Jazz 8 Linehan Series. *1991*: Australia.

While My Guitar Gently Kills My Mother. Studio 52 52CD-031/MN. *1991*: Australia.

Yothu Yindi. *Tribal Voice*. Mushroom D30602. *1991*: Australia.

Since 1991, Studio 52 has produced the Nu-Music sample series, presenting as yet unsigned Australian bands, beginning with 52CD-007NU#1 and so far running to Series 15, 52CD-169#13. For further information, e-mail *kool@co31.aone.net.au* or visit the Web site (http://www.koolskools.com.au).

Filmography

The Blackboard Jungle, dir. Richard Brooks. 1955. USA. 101 mins. Urban Drama. Original music by Charles Wolcott.

BRUCE JOHNSON

Australia: Indigenous Popular Music

Population: Aborigine: 314,120 (2001); Torres Strait Islander: 26,240 (2001); both Aborigine and Torres Strait Islander: 17,630 (2001)

Geographical, Sociocultural, Political and Economic Factors

Australia is an island continent located in southwestern Oceania to the southeast of Asia. It has a range of climates (desert, temperate and tropical), but large areas regularly experience drought conditions. The landmass is very ancient and the soils are of low fertility. The population of almost 20 million (Australian Bureau of Statistics 2001) resides primarily in the major capital cities (Sydney, Melbourne, Brisbane, Perth, Adelaide), all of which are located near the coast. Socioculturally, linguistically and musically, Australia has been shaped primarily by the British (and Irish) colonization/invasion, which began in 1788. More recently, the United States has been the predominant influence, especially in politics, the media and popular culture. In addition, Australia has had one of the largest, most diverse and most successful immigration programs in the post-World War II era.

Politically, Australia is a liberal-democratic nation-state with a Westminster system of representative government. It is also a Western, capitalist, developed nation-state in terms of cultural networks, monetary policies and military alliances. Economically, it has a good transportation and business infrastructure. It is a large exporter of minerals, grains and animal products, and an importer of many manufactured and cultural goods. Tourism has been a major source of revenue in recent years, and the continent's unique flora, fauna and natural wonders, as well as its cultures, are vigorously marketed overseas. These geographical, sociocultural, political and economic factors have had a profound impact on the music cultures of Australia, especially those of indigenous Australians.

Demographics, the Colonial Experience and Current Politics

Indigenous peoples in Australia make up approximately 2 percent of the population (2001) and are comprised of several distinct groups. They differ substantially as to cultures, languages and music, reflecting their Australnesian and Melanesian heritages. However, as indigenous peoples, they share broadly similar experiences of colonization/invasion. These experiences varied and occurred in different parts of Australia but included, until quite recently, extensive and repressive governmental control. Aborigines were subjected to genocide, wholesale dispossession of lands, and forced missionization and assimilation (Kidd 1997; Reynolds 1987). Torres Strait Islanders were generally able to remain on their ancestral lands but were compelled to work in maritime industries and were not permitted to leave the islands until after World War II (Beckett 1987; Sharp 1993). Aborigines and Torres Strait Islanders live throughout urban and regional Australia, with Aborigines having sizable communities in some rural areas and Torres Strait Islanders having sizable communities on both the islands of the Torres Strait and the mainland.

It is important to note the resurgence of overt race-based hatred in Australia in the mid-1990s because it significantly affects indigenous peoples and their artistic expressions such as popular music. There was a brief period in the 1980s and early 1990s when cultural and social diversity was recognized and even celebrated (at least at an official level). However, since the election of a conservative coalition government under John Howard in the mid-1990s, mainstream Australia has returned to its deep-seated xenophobic and discriminatory tendencies toward internal and external 'Others,' especially indigenous peoples, Middle-Eastern refugees and Asian immigrants. Indigenous popular music is not just about politics; however, politics has been, and continues to be, a determining factor in how indigenous Australians are positioned within the broader society and how artistic expressions are produced, performed and consumed.

The most commercially and critically successful indigenous song to date, 'Treaty,' recorded by the band Yothu Yindi, deals directly with the politics of indigenous/non-indigenous relationships. Indigenous popular music in Australia may be a 'micro-music' (Slobin 1992) in terms of the international entertainment industry, but nationally it deals frequently with key extramusical macro issues such as land rights, social justice and cultural maintenance. Although themes such as love, personal relationships and everyday life are not absent altogether, songs (and albums) are commonly used to convey overtly or covertly political messages, often about the fundamental connection between indigenous peoples and the land (Dunbar-Hall 1997; Gibson and Dunbar-Hall 2000). This focus is succinctly summarized on the cover of a recording featuring many of the major indigenous artists: *Our Home, Our Land . . . Something to Sing About* (1995).

Indigenous Musical Practices

Many indigenous Australians practice aspects of both traditional and modern music. In some areas, such as the Northern Territory, Queensland, and Western and South Australia, traditional Aboriginal music (and dance) has continued to be an integral part of sociocultural, political and religious life. It is used in public and private ceremonies, which may be of a secular or sacred nature. It is primarily a vocal art form (centered on songs) rather than an instrumental one. Verses commonly use a small number of words with multiple meanings, and the songs connect the singer and the community with the past and the present (Ellis 1979). Percussion (idiophones such as clapsticks, rasps and seed rattles) and the didjeridu (an aerophone, with sound produced through air vibration) also provide accompaniment to both song and dance. These primarily add rhythm, rather than overshadowing the vocal melody and the words; there are no truly melodic instruments (Wild 1988). In Torres Strait

Islander communities in the Torres Strait region and on the Australian mainland, traditional music featuring singing, percussion (drums, rolled mats and clapsticks), instruments (pan pipes and notched flutes) and dance has always been a significant part of social life. It provides musical accompaniment to many aspects of everyday life (Lui and York 2003). The more recent music that has evolved also features strong religious influences, in particular singing styles and hymns introduced by European and Pacific Islander Christian missionaries (Lawrence 1998), along with instruments such as the guitar and the ukulele. For many diasporic Islanders living on the mainland, the performance of traditional music (and dance) is an important part of public and private expressions of identity, and is augmented by a full range of contemporary popular music styles (Neuenfeldt and Lawe-Davies 2004).

In areas where traditional Torres Strait Islander and Aboriginal music was destroyed or decimated, dynamic music cultures have evolved, incorporating elements of traditional indigenous music and performance and those of the modern Western world. It is inaccurate and overly simplistic, however, to dichotomize traditional versus modern forms of indigenous musical artistic expression as if somehow they are discrete entities or antithetical. Because indigenous cultures are vibrant and not static, in practice and praxis traditional and modern forms may overlap or be appropriate in different contexts. Aspects of the above-mentioned elements are still often present, and it can be difficult to separate traditional from modern forms because there are forms in between. There are also often complementary processes of change in continuity and continuity in change at work simultaneously. This is occurring not just in music; it also occurred, during the latter part of the twentieth century, in the overall renaissance of indigenous artistic expression (art, dance, film, theater) and the increased national political activism and international marketing of indigenousness.

Modern Indigenous Popular Music

Two caveats should be kept in mind with regard to modern indigenous popular music. First, Torres Strait Islander and Aboriginal traditional music is also 'popular' to those who create, use and enjoy it. Second, the syncretic music created and practiced by many indigenous (and collaborative non-indigenous) Australians combines or draws on elements from numerous musical and cultural sources.

The popular music that is associated with indigenous Australians encompasses a range of contemporary music genres (for example, rock, reggae, country, pop, rap). It transposes those influences idiosyncratically as to the particulars of performance style and musical and poetic texts (Breen 1989). Defining indigenous popular music is problematic because many indigenous Australians participate in the global cultural economy of popular music and the universal pop aesthetic in the same way as other Australians. As well, the functions and uses of popular music always reflect both individual and group-based talents and preferences. Consequently, rather than attempting a specific definition, it is more useful to acknowledge the eclecticism of indigenous popular music and how it socially, culturally and politically serves different strategies and objectives. There are Torres Strait Islander and Aboriginal solo artists, bands, songwriters, composers, educational institutions and media organizations that have been influential in developing an Australian popular music genre identifiable as indigenous, and it is important to chronicle their noteworthy contributions.

Prior to the emergence of a more widely disseminated and critically recognized genre of indigenous popular music in the late 1980s, there were active indigenous performers entertaining mainly for local and regional audiences (Walker 2000). Country and rock were favorite styles, and performers such as Candy Williams, Essie Coffey, Herb Laughton, Aurial Andrew, Johnny Nicol, Bobby McLeod, Dougie Young, Vic Sims, Isaac Yamma, and Gus, Harry and Wilga Williams were popular. A small number of Aboriginal artists, such as Howard Blair, Lionel Rose and Jimmy Little, were singing, writing and performing nationally, although their indigenousness was not necessarily always emphasized. World War II had also provided opportunities for some performers. The Pitt Family Singers (Heather, Sophie, Dulcie and Walter) from Cairns began performing at military shows and on local radio and eventually entertained at high-profile venues such as the Tivoli Theatre in Sydney. As a soloist, Dulcie Pitt – using the stage name Georgia Lee – performed overseas, as did her niece Wilma Reading.

One notable but no longer popular form of Aboriginal popular music was the solo and ensemble gumleaf music that flourished in some areas (Ryan and Patten 1998). In the Torres Strait in the 1950s, songwriters such as Sonny Kaddy, George Passi, Solkos Tabo and Weser Whaleboat pioneered the *Kole Kabem Wed* style ('song for European dances'), which differed from the 1920s innovations found in the *Segur Kaba Wed* style ('play song and dance'). More 'modern style' songwriters and performers such as Jaffa Ah Mat, the Mills Sisters (Cessa, Ina and Rita) and George Mye documented life in the Torres Strait, including work in the maritime industries (Neuenfeldt 2002a). Songwriting and singing (and dancing) continued as a feature of individual and group competition and pride (Mabo 1984).

There are several well-known contemporary solo artists writing compelling songs documenting the individual and group experiences of indigenous Australians. Most also perform or record with small ensembles. Christine Anu, Getano Bann, Kev Carmody, Kerrianne Cox, Henry (Seaman) Dan, Joey Geia, Ruby Hunter, Bob Randall, Archie Roach, Bart Willoughby and Frank Yamma have been at the vanguard of contemporary singer-songwriters. Songs such as 'Black Deaths in Custody' (Carmody), 'Took the Children Away' (Roach), 'Brown Skin Baby' (Randall) and 'We Have Survived' (Willoughby) have become unofficial indigenous anthems. Other performers, such as Maroochy Barambah, Richard Frankland, Toni Janke and Leah Purcell, also present insightful and varied perspectives on contemporary indigenous life. Similarly, country-oriented artists such as Troy Cassiar-Daley, Roger Knox, Warren Williams and Isaac Yamma maintain high standards of musicianship and songwriting. Didjeriduists Mark Atkins, Alan Dargin, Ashley Dargin, Matthew Doyle, David Hudson, Adrian Ross, Richard Walley and the late David Blannasi have been some of the solo artists performing, composing and teaching both nationally and internationally with Australia's most unique musical instrument (Neuenfeldt 1997).

There are numerous rock-oriented bands that have produced high-quality recordings, songs and albums addressing vital issues in their home state, territory or local community. Amunda (Northern Territory), Blackfire (Victoria), Blekbala Mujik (Northern Territory), Coloured Stone (South Australia), Letterstick Band (north-central Arnhem Land), Nerkep (New South Wales), NoktUrNL (Central Australia), Pad Boys (Queensland), Rygela Band (Tasmania) and Scrap Metal (Western Australia), as well as the most internationally successful band, Yothu Yindi (northeast Arnhem Land), all combine indigenous and Western forms in their musical and poetic texts. In the areas of theater, film and dance, Jimmy Chi, David Milroy and

David Page produce songs, soundtracks and compositions, respectively, that garner national and international acclaim. All across Australia there are Torres Strait Islander and Aboriginal music and dance troupes performing in schools (Neuenfeldt 1998a; Kartomi 1988; Neuenfeldt and Costigan 2002), and for the mass tourism and convention industries. In addition, there are regular indigenous festivals such as Survival Day (Sydney, New South Wales) and Stompen Ground (Broome, Western Australia). For school-age children there are Croc Festivals (predominantly, but not solely, indigenous festivals presented in remote tropical areas of Australia) at various locations in Queensland and the Northern Territory. There is also an extensive indigenous program at the largest folk festival in the Southern Hemisphere, the Woodford Folk Festival (Queensland) (Neuenfeldt 2002b), as well as similar programs at numerous local and regional festivals. They provide regular opportunities for artists to access large audiences.

Yothu Yindi (the name is a kinship term meaning 'mother/child' in the Yolngu language of northeast Arnhem Land) has been the most successful 'indigenous' band to date. Its performances and recordings combine strong and dynamic cultural traditions with high tech and elaborate dancing and stage lighting. The band is also highly politicized in the sense that the main thrust of many of its songs is indigenous relationships to land and livelihood. This arises from a long connection between the clans, moieties and families of the indigenous band members and land rights issues. Interestingly, Yothu Yindi – as the quintessential 'indigenous' band – has always had non-indigenous members and management, in effect implementing its espoused 'both ways' and *ganma* ethos (Neuenfeldt 1993). It is also important to note that there are other influential bands that are collaborations between indigenous and non-indigenous musicians. Examples include Lewis and Young (featuring didjeriduist Tommy Lewis and woodwind player Chris Young); Tiddas (featuring vocalists Lou Bennett, Amy Saunders and Sally Dastey); and the Warumpi Band (featuring singer/didjeriduist George Rurrambu and guitarist/songwriter Neil Murray). Similarly, both indigenous and non-indigenous popular music with indigenous themes is being used in primary, secondary and tertiary school systems (Neuenfeldt 1998b).

Finally, educational institutions and media organizations such as the Centre for Aboriginal Studies in Music (CASM) at the University of Adelaide, the Aboriginal and Islander College of Music in Perth and the Central Australian Aboriginal Media Association (CAAMA) in Alice Springs have been crucial in recruiting, training and encouraging indigenous musicians. They provide positive, professionalized environments where the opportunities for and challenges of achieving change in continuity and continuity in change are being addressed by the makers of modern indigenous popular music.

Conclusion

Indigenous popular music in Australia is an important form of artistic expression that often addresses extramusical issues such as land rights, social justice and cultural maintenance, which, in turn, affect musical issues such as appropriation, collaboration and syncretism. Although Torres Strait Islanders and Aborigines constitute a small percentage of the population, they and their cultures (including their popular music) are pivotal to how Australia presents itself to the world and how non-indigenous Australia perceives itself. Overall, the way indigenous Australians engage with popular music is similar to how many other minority indigenous peoples worldwide both adopt and adapt musical and extramusical elements from the societies and cultures that dominate them (Neuenfeldt 1991). In Australia, what results is distinctly indigenous, even when Western forms, aesthetics and conventions of presentation are used to varying degrees.

By way of conclusion, in the specific context of Aboriginal popular music, Yothu Yindi's Mandawuy Yunupingu (1996) believes that, 'In a general sense ... [it] gives a preliminary aspect of Aboriginal knowledge, Aboriginal culture, [and that of] indigenous Australia, as far as non-Aboriginal Australia is concerned.' He also believes that 'it's going to be even bigger because there is a tendency in Aboriginal communities right now where cultural centers [which include popular music] are being considered the roots level for the next form of education. That form of education will allow Aboriginal people in their own community to sustain their livelihood, sustain their lifestyle, and relate to what is the big picture.' Indigenous popular music celebrates the survival (and, in some cases, revival) of Aboriginal and Torres Strait Islander cultures while at the same time reminding the rest of Australia that there are things, such as popular music, that are shared and can act as bridges rather than barriers to communication.

Bibliography

Australian Bureau of Statistics (ABS). 2001. *Census*. Canberra: Australian Government Printing Service.

Beckett, Jeremy. 1987. *Torres Strait Islanders: Custom and Colonialism*. Cambridge: Cambridge University Press.

Breen, Marcus, ed. 1989. *Our Place, Our Music*. Canberra: Australian Institute of Aboriginal Studies.

Dunbar-Hall, Peter. 1997. 'Music and Meaning in Aboriginal Rock Albums.' *Australian Aboriginal Studies* 1: 38–47.

Ellis, Catherine. 1979. 'Functions and Features of Central and South Australian Aboriginal Music.' In *Australian Aboriginal Music*, ed. Jennifer Isaacs. Sydney: Aboriginal Artists Agency, 23–26.

Gibson, Chris, and Dunbar-Hall, Peter. 2000. 'Nitmiluk: Place and Empowerment in Australian Aboriginal Popular Music.' *Ethnomusicology* 44(1): 39–64.

Kartomi, Margaret. 1988. 'Forty Thousand Years: Koori Music and Australian Music Education.' *Music in Australian Education* 1: 11–28.

Kidd, Rosalind. 1997. *The Way We Civilise: Aboriginal Affairs – The Untold Story*. St Lucia: University of Queensland Press.

Lawrence, Helen Reeves. 1998. '"Bethlehem" in Torres Strait: Music, Dance and Christianity in Erub (Darnley Island).' *Australian Aboriginal Studies* 2: 51–63.

Lui, Lizzie, and York, Frank. 2003. 'Torres Strait Islander Traditions.' In *Currency* Companion to Music and Dance in Australia, ed. John Whiteoak and Aline Scott-Maxwell. Sydney: Currency Press, 662–65.

Mabo, Eddie Koiki. 1984. 'Music of the Torres Strait.' *Black Voice* (James Cook University of North Queensland) 1(1): 33–36.

Magowen, Fiona. 1994. '"The Land Is Our Marr (Essence), It Stays Forever": The Yothu Yindi Relationship in Australian Aboriginal Traditional and Popular Musics.' In *Ethnicity, Identity and Music: The Musical Construction of Place*, ed. Martin Stokes. Oxford: Berg, 135–56.

Neuenfeldt, Karl. 1991. 'To Sing a Song of Otherness: Anthros, Ethno-pop and the Mediation of "Public Problems."' *Canadian Ethnic Studies* 23(3): 92–118.

Neuenfeldt, Karl. 1993. 'Yothu Yindi and *Ganma*: The Cultural Transposition of the Aboriginal Agenda Through Metaphor and Music.' *Journal of Australian Studies* 38: 1–11.

Neuenfeldt, Karl, ed. 1997. *The Didjeridu: From Arnhem Land to Internet*. Sydney: John Libbey/Perfect Beat Publications.

Neuenfeldt, Karl. 1998a. 'Performance, Politics and Pedagogy: Australian Aboriginal Didjeriduists as Culture Workers and Border Crossers.' *Journal of Intercultural Studies* 19(1): 5–20.

Neuenfeldt, Karl. 1998b. 'Sounding Silences: The Inclusion of Indigenous Popular Music in Australian Curricula.' *Discourse: Studies in the Cultural Politics of Education* 19(2): 201–18.

Neuenfeldt, Karl. 2002a. 'Examples of Torres Strait Songs of Longing and Belonging.' *Journal of Australian Studies* 75: 111–16.

Neuenfeldt, Karl. 2002b. 'From Silence to Celebration: Indigenous Australian Performers at the Woodford Folk Festival.' *World of Music* 43(2-3): 63–89.

Neuenfeldt, Karl, and Costigan, Lyn. 2002. 'Torres Strait Islander Music and Dance in Informal and Formal Educational Contexts in Australia.' *Research Studies in Music Education* 19: 46–55.

Neuenfeldt, Karl, and Lawe-Davies, Chris. 2004. 'Mainland Torres Strait Islanders and the "Magical Islands" of the Torres Strait: The Music of Gaetano Bann and Ricardo Idagi as Metaphor and Remembering.' In *Island Musics*, ed. Kevin Dawes. London: Berg, 137–51.

Reynolds, Henry. 1987. *Frontier: Aborigines, Settlers, and Land*. Sydney: Allen and Unwin.

Ryan, Robin, and Patten, Herbert. 1998. 'Gumleaves.' In *The Garland Encyclopedia of World Music. Vol. 9: Australia and the Pacific Islands*, ed. Adrienne L. Kaeppler and J.W. Love. New York and London: Garland Publishing, 134–35.

Sharp, Nonie. 1993. *Stars of Tagai: The Torres Strait Islanders*. Canberra: Aboriginal Studies Press.

Slobin, Mark. 1992. 'Micromusics of the West: A Comparative Approach.' *Ethnomusicology* 36(1): 1–87.

Walker, Clinton. 2000. *Buried Country: The Story of Aboriginal Country Music*. Annandale, NSW: Pluto Press.

Wild, Steven. 1988. 'Aboriginal Music and Dance.' In *The Australian People: An Encyclopedia of the Nation, Its People and Their Origins*, ed. James Jupp. Sydney: Angus and Robertson, 74–181.

Yunupingu, Mandawuy. 1996. Interview with author, 3 April.

Discographical References

Carmody, Kev. 'Black Deaths in Custody.' *Pillars of Society*. Larrikin Records. *1990*: Australia.

No Fixed Address. 'We Have Survived.' *Building Bridges*. ABC Records 846 715-2. *1990*: Australia.

Our Home, Our Land ... Something to Sing About. Mushroom CAAMA 253. *1995*: Australia.

Randall, Bob. 'Brown Skin Baby.' CAAMA FES015. *2000*: Australia.

Roach, Archie. 'Took the Children Away.' *Charcoal Lane*. Aurora/Mushroom D30386. *1990*: Australia.

Yothu Yindi. 'Treaty (Filthy Lucre Remix).' Razor Records C14987. *1991*: Australia.

Discography

Anu, Christine. *Stylin' Up*. White MUSH32059. *1995*: Australia.

Chi, Jimmy. *Bran Nue Dae*. BND Records 002. *1993*: Australia.

Dan, Henry (Seaman). *Follow the Sun*. Hot Records 1075. *1999*: Australia/UK.

Dan, Henry (Seaman). *Perfect Pearl*. Hot Records 1094. *2004*: Australia/UK.

Dan, Henry (Seaman). *Steady Steady*. Hot Records 1079. *2001*: Australia/UK.

Singing Up the Country: Traditional and Contemporary Songs from the Kimberleys, Western Australia. JCK 92CS1. *1992*: Australia.

Tiddas. *Sing About Life*. PolyGram CD 5183482. *1993*: Australia.

Williams, Warren. *Country Friends and Me*. CAAMA CDM309. *1998*: Australia.

Yamma, Frank. *Solid Eagle*. CAAMA M302. *1997*: Australia.

Yothu Yindi. *Tribal Voice*. Mushroom D30602. *1991*: Australia.

KARL NEUENFELDT

CITIES

Adelaide

Population: 1,107,986 (2001)

Adelaide is sited beside the River Torrens on Gulf Saint Vincent, and its origins as a free settlement with early Protestant Anglo-Saxon and German stock remain visible. Subsequent diversified immigration included those of Italian and Greek descent. Its population constitutes around 70 percent of the state of South Australia, of which Adelaide is the capital. It is serviced by highway and railway systems, international and domestic air terminals, and port facilities. Its agricultural economy shifted to industry in the postwar period, with tourism and service industries becoming increasingly important. The city has three universities.

The Teutonic strand woven through Adelaide's history made early and durable musical impact, including the establishment of German music groups such as the Adelaider Liedertafel in 1849. While British patriotism during World War I led to a break in such traditions, they have been subsequently rejuvenated, as in the boisterously demotic annual Adelaide Schützenfest, which includes music and dance and which was revived with great success in the 1960s.

Adelaide has supplied a disproportionate number of Australia's popular musicians. In some genres, particularly jazz, this was largely attributable to the Adelaide College of Music, established by John Ellerton Becker in 1932. During the first wave of rock during the 1950s, the Penny Rockets were central to the local scene. In the same decade, assisted immigration from the United Kingdom led to the establishment of a satellite city, Elizabeth, 16 miles (26 km) to the northeast of Adelaide. The Beatles-led 'British invasion' found Adelaide a rich incubation site, with many young immigrants personally familiar with the musical background. Adelaide thus played a leading role in the next phase of Australia's popular music, with bands like the Twilights, the Master's Apprentices, the Zoot and the Angels gaining national prominence in the 1970s. A local industry was established away from the eastern seaboard, nurturing bands that achieved national and international success, including Cold Chisel and the group Redgum, which anticipated social-issue and indie pop. In 1977, the local group Red Rufus relocated to Melbourne and, under the new name X-Ray-Z, became a leading new wave band. In the same year, the band Young Modern was formed in Adelaide, moving to Melbourne in 1978 where its founder, John Dowler, formed the influential country rock group the Zimmermen. Adelaide also nurtured the early career of folk/pop performer Doug Ashdown, who enjoyed a period of international success, and of Dave Graney, later of the Moodists in Melbourne, who toured with Nick Cave and who, while working with the Coral Snakes, was named Best Australian Male Artist of 1996 by the peak industry body, the Australian Record Industry Association (ARIA). Bands that have chosen to remain in Adelaide have consolidated a strong local following but at the expense of a national reputation, as in the case of the durable Screaming Believers (1981–91), although the Superjesus, founded in 1994, became one of the country's most successful indie groups. The Centre for Aboriginal Studies in Music, which evolved in Adelaide in the early 1970s, has decisively fostered indigenous popular music, a notable early example being the band No Fixed Address.

World music has been particularly evident since the establishment in 1992 of the Womadelaide Festival in partnership with Peter Gabriel's WOMAD (World of Music, Arts and Dance) organization. The very substantial local content draws on a national pool of acts made available by the high level of Australia's cultural diversity, including indigenous music, and participation in Womadelaide can often lead to international success through the WOMAD network. The festival's agenda was underlined in its 2004 presentation, which was conducted in partnership with Amnesty International. While this festival has raised the national profile of world music, the city has evolved 'scenes' in all late twentieth-century popular music genres, with impetus from the annual Music Business Adelaide event, inaugurated in 1997, and devoted to the promotion of all forms of contemporary music.

Bibliography

Bebbington, Warren, ed. 1997. *The Oxford Companion to Australian Music*. Melbourne: Oxford University Press.

Breen, Marcus, ed. 1989. *Our Place, Our Music*. Canberra: Aboriginal Studies Press.

Breen, Marcus. 1992. 'Desert Dreams, Media, and Interventions in Reality: Australian Aboriginal Music.' In *Rockin' the Boat: Mass Music and Mass Movements*, ed. Reebee Garofalo. Boston, MA: South End Press, 149–70.

Castles, John. 1992. '*Tjungaringanyi*: Aboriginal Rock.' In *From Pop to Punk to Postmodernism: Popular Music and Australian Culture from the 1960s to the 1990s*, ed. Philip Hayward. North Sydney: Allen & Unwin, 25–39.

Clunies-Ross, Bruce. 1979. 'An Australian Sound: Jazz in Melbourne and Adelaide 1941–51.' In *Australian Popular Culture*, ed. P. Spearitt and D. Walker. Sydney: Allen & Unwin, 62–79.

Day, David, and Parker, Tim. 1987. *S.A. Great: It's Our Music, 1956–1986*. Adelaide: Wakefield Press.

Ellis, Catherine. 1985. *Aboriginal Music: Education for Living – Cross-Cultural Experience from South Australia*. Brisbane: University of Queensland Press.

Hutchison, Tracee. 1992. *Your Name's on the Door: 10 Years of Australian Music*. Sydney: ABC Enterprises.

Johnson, Bruce. 1987. *The Oxford Companion to Australian Jazz*. Melbourne: Oxford University Press.

Kelton, Tim. 1986. *Underground in the City of Churches*. Adelaide: WAV Press.

McCredie, Andrew D., ed. 1988. *From Colonel Light into the Footlights: The Performing Arts in South Australia from 1836 to the Present*. Norwood, South Australia: Pagel.

McFarlane, Ian. 1999. *The Encyclopedia of Australian Rock and Pop*. St Leonards, NSW: Allen & Unwin.

Spencer, Chris. 1996. *Adelaide Bands*. 5 vols. Victoria: Moonlight Publishing.

Van Straten, Frank. 2003. *Tivoli*. South Melbourne: Thomas C. Lothian Pty Ltd.

Walker, Clinton. 1996. *Stranded: The Secret History of Australian Independent Music 1977–1991*. Sydney: Pan Macmillan Australia.

Whiteoak, John, and Scott-Maxwell, Aline, eds. 2003. *Currency Companion to Music and Dance in Australia*. Sydney: Currency Press.

Zion, Lawrence. 1987. 'The Impact of the Beatles on Pop Music in Australia: 1963–66.' *Popular Music* 6(3): 291–311.

Discography

Angels, The. *Face to Face*. Albert Productions APLP 031. *1978*: Australia.

Ashdown, Doug. *Leave Love Enough Alone*. Billingsgate L35294. *1974*: Australia.

Cold Chisel. *Cold Chisel*. Atlantic 600038. *1978*: Australia.

Dowler, John. *Low Society*. In-Law MOTHER001. *1995*: Australia.

Graney, Dave, with the Coral Snakes. *You Wanna Be There But You Don't Wanna Travel*. Id 522381-2. *1994*: Australia.

Master's Apprentices, The. *Short Cuts*. Columbia SCXO 7983. *1970*: UK.

No Fixed Address. *Wrong Side of the Road*. EMI/Black Records YPRX-1905. *1981*: Australia.

Redgum. *If You Don't Fight You Lose*. Larrikin LRF 037. *1978*: Australia.

Screaming Believers. *Communist Mutants from Space*. Greasy Pop. *1985*: Australia.

Twilights, The. *The Twilights*. Columbia 330SX 7779. *1966*: Australia.

X-Ray-Z. *X-Ray-Z*. Polyester. *1988*: Australia.

Zoot, The. *Just Zoot*. EMI/Columbia. *1970*: Australia.

BRUCE JOHNSON

Alice Springs

Population (Local Government Area): 27,520 (2001)

Alice Springs is situated on the Todd River in the Northern Territory, 926 miles (1,490 km) by road south of Darwin. Surveyed in 1888 as Stuart, in

1933 it took its present name from the nearby springs discovered during construction of the Overland Telegraph in 1871. A railhead for cattle stations, which were established from 1870, Alice Springs has also become a distribution point for mining, natural gas and oil deposits. During World War II, its centrality made it an important military base, and in 1967 a joint US-Australian facility was established at nearby Pine Gap. Alice Springs is serviced by air, road and rail. The town's proximity to major scenic attractions, including Uluru, and its increasing accessibility have made tourism its major industry since the 1980s. Its multi-campus tertiary college services central Australia.

The substantial indigenous presence is strongly represented in culture and tourism. The town's position makes it literally central to a vast rural musical touring and production network, in which country, folk, indigenous and rock hybridities are prominent. The nearby Hermannsburg Aboriginal mission station produced a Lutheran-oriented choir, which was founded in 1877. This choir provided a grounding for many later popular music performers from the 1950s, particularly as its repertoire was secularized somewhat during the 1960s. Alumnus Gus Williams, who with Herb Laughton inaugurated Aboriginal country music shows, established the first Northern Territory Aboriginal Country Music Festival in 1978. His son, Warren Williams, has achieved wide acclaim since his first solo album, *Western Wind*, in 1996.

Alice Springs is home to the Country Music Association and to veteran singer Ted Egan, and is also the site of the Central Australian Aboriginal Media Association (CAAMA). Founded in 1980, the association includes television and radio studios, with a broadcasting servicing area covering one-third of the continent. In conjunction with these and the local tourist industry, the CAAMA record label Imparja has been decisive in developing the reputations of indigenous popular musicians, including the Warumpi Band and non–locally based groups like Coloured Stone, originally from South Australia. The importance of family traditions in indigenous music was exemplified in the case of early CAAMA broadcaster/performer Isaac Yamma (aka Yama), who worked with the Pitjantjatjara Country Band. His son Frank later emerged as a significant performer, particularly through his 1999 award-winning CD *Playing with Fire*. His work, along with the CAAMA catalog, reflects the wide-ranging hybridity of contemporary Australian indigenous popular music.

Bibliography

Bebbington, Warren, ed. 1997. *The Oxford Companion to Australian Music*. Melbourne: Oxford University Press.

Breen, Marcus, ed. 1989. *Our Place, Our Music*. Canberra: Aboriginal Studies Press.

Breen, Marcus. 1992. 'Desert Dreams, Media, and Interventions in Reality: Australian Aboriginal Music.' In *Rockin' the Boat: Mass Music and Mass Movements*, ed. Reebee Garofalo. Boston, MA: South End Press, 149–70.

CAAMA. 1989. *The CAAMA Group*. Alice Springs: The CAAMA Group of Companies.

Castles, John. 1992. '*Tjungaringanyi*: Aboriginal Rock.' In *From Pop to Punk to Postmodernism: Popular Music and Australian Culture from the 1960s to the 1990s*, ed. Philip Hayward. North Sydney: Allen & Unwin, 25–39.

Kelly, Aidan. 1995. *Floods, Sweat and Beers: Rockin' Around the Northern Territory*. Victoria: Moonlight Publishing.

McFarlane, Ian. 1999. *The Encyclopedia of Australian Rock and Pop*. St Leonards, NSW: Allen & Unwin.

Michaels, Eric. 1986. *Aboriginal Invention of Television in Central Australia 1982–1986*. Canberra: Aboriginal Studies Press.

Mitchell, Tony. 1992. 'World Music, Indigenous Music and Music Television in Australia.' *Perfect Beat: The Journal of Research into Contemporary Music and Popular Culture* 1(1): 1–16.

Neuenfeldt, Karl. 1997. 'The Didjeridu in the Desert: The Social Relations of an Ethnographic Object Entangled in Culture and Commerce.' In *The Didjeridu: From Arnhem Land to Internet*, ed. Karl Neuenfeldt. Sydney: John Libbey/Perfect Beat Publications, 107–22.

Walker, Clinton. 2000. *Buried Country: The Story of Aboriginal Country Music*. Annandale, NSW: Pluto Press.

Whiteoak, John, and Scott-Maxwell, Aline, eds. 2003. *Currency Companion to Music and Dance in Australia*. Sydney: Currency Press.

Discographical References

Williams, Warren. *Western Wind*. CAAMA. *1996*: Australia.

Yamma, Frank. *Playing with Fire*. CAAMA. *1999*: Australia.

Discography

Coloured Stone. *Human Love*. RCA SPCD 1208. *1986*: Australia.

Egan, Ted. *Faces of Australia* (5 albums). EMI TCT ELP 1001-1005. *1989*: Australia.

From the Bush. M 314. *1989*: Australia.

Sundowner Campfire Concert: Aboriginal Songs Recorded in Palm Valley – Central Australia; with Aborigines of the Hermannsburg Mission. EMI Custom Service PR 3471. *ca. 1970*: Australia.

Warumpi Band, The. *Warumpi Band Go Bush.* CAAMA. *1983*: Australia.

Yamma, Isaac. *Isaac Yamma and the Pitjantjatjara Country Band, Number 1.* CAAMA cassette. *1983*: Australia.

BRUCE JOHNSON

Brisbane
Population: 1,650,422 (2001)

Originally a penal camp at the mouth of the Brisbane River, with open settlement from 1842, Brisbane became the capital of the new colony of Queensland in 1859, and from 1867 gold strikes gave impetus to infrastructural development. Queensland is Australia's least urbanized state, relying heavily on primary production and a postwar mining boom, with subsequent state-encouraged manufacturing and tourism. The baby boom accelerated growth, but with relatively little immigration during the national postwar intake. Notwithstanding a large, primarily Anglophone, increase since the mid-1970s, Brisbane has the lowest proportion of foreign-born inhabitants among mainland capitals. The city has three publicly funded universities. It is served by railway and highway networks, port facilities, and international and domestic air terminals.

During World War II, Brisbane served as general headquarters for both the Australian army and General MacArthur's US forces, becoming largely a garrison city. Apart from boosting recreational and service sectors, the US presence accentuated the general Americanization of popular youth music that was proceeding nationally. The postwar effects, however, included strong reaction in some quarters, reflecting a conservatism that continued to respond abrasively to cultural innovation, notably in the case of punk/new wave popular music. This coincided with extremely repressive state governments during the 1970s and 1980s, which clashed with politicized urban youth. One effect was the development of a strong oppositional music scene incorporating early punk and new wave. With a dearth of media and venue exposure for alternative groups, this increased the pull to the south and led, in some cases, as with the earlier Bee Gees, to international recognition – as, for example, for the

Saints (1974) and the Go-Betweens (1977). Members of both bands, such as Ed Kuepper and Lindy Morrison, respectively, have remained influential in the Sydney indie scene. Other significant Brisbane expatriates include Tex Perkins (the Cruel Sea, the Beasts of Bourbon), and Peter Wells, whose prolific and diverse career in Sydney included membership in one of the archetypal pub-rock groups, Rose Tattoo.

Brisbane was also a 'way station' for performers from regional Queensland. Fur (1993) and Gaslight Radio (1995) were both from the Gold Coast. One of Townsville's only punk groups in the 1980s, the Madmen, relocated to Brisbane where, as Screamfeeder from 1991, they gained success in the burgeoning alternative scene that also saw the emergence into national mainstream success of such bands as Custard (1990 – originally Custard Gun), Powderfinger (1990), Regurgitator (1993) and Savage Garden (1994). Among the most successful performers to emerge from regional Queensland at the turn of the millennium has been Cairns-born dancer/singer/composer Christine Anu, of Torres Strait Islander background, who was named Best Female Artist of 1996 by the Australian Record Industry Association (ARIA). Apart from a change in the political culture, other developments in the 1990s, such as the foundation of independent community radio station 4ZZZ, have enabled local groups to gain greater exposure. The setting up of the brispop.com Web site by the band Lancaster in 2000 has also provided an international forum for emerging young bands like Flat World Folded, Wipsnade Zoo and Intercooler.

Bibliography
Bebbington, Warren, ed. 1997. *The Oxford Companion to Australian Music.* Melbourne: Oxford University Press.

Gibb, Barry, Gibb, Robin, and Gibb, Maurice, with Leaf, David. 1979. *Bee Gees: The Authorized Biography.* New York: Delta Books.

Hutchison, Tracee. 1992. *Your Name's on the Door: 10 Years of Australian Music.* Sydney: ABC Enterprises.

Johnson, Bruce. 1987. *The Oxford Companion to Australian Jazz.* Melbourne: Oxford University Press.

Nichols, David. 1997. *The Go-Betweens.* St Leonards, NSW: Allen & Unwin.

Van Straten, Frank. 2003. *Tivoli.* South Melbourne: Thomas C. Lothian Pty Ltd.

Walker, Clinton. 1996. *Stranded: The Secret History of*

Australian Independent Music 1977–1991. Sydney: Pan Macmillan Australia.

Discography
Anu, Christine. *Stylin' Up*. White MUSH32059. *1995*: Australia.

Bee Gees, The. *Spicks and Specks*. Spin EX 1474. *1966*: Australia.

Custard. *Weisenheimer*. Ra 2068300007. *1995*: Australia.

Fur. *The Betty Shakes*. Fellaheen/Shock. *1997*: Australia.

Go-Betweens, The. *Beggar's Banquet*. BBL 2002 CD. *1996*: UK.

Go-Betweens, The. *Lee Remick*. Able AB 001. *1978*: Australia.

Go-Betweens, The. *The Go-Betweens*. Silk 002, 004, 005, 006, 007. *1996*: Australia.

Lancaster. *Self Titled Debut*. 103 Records. *2004*: Australia.

Powderfinger. *Transfusion*. Polydor 859727-2. *1993*: Australia.

Regurgitator. *Tu-Plang*. Warner. *1996*: Australia.

Saints, The. *I'm Stranded*. Fatal MA 7158. *1976*: Australia.

Savage Garden. *Savage Garden*. Roadshow/Warner. *1997*: Australia.

Screamfeeder. *Burn Out Your Name*. Survival SUR532CD. *1993*: Australia.

BRUCE JOHNSON

Broome
Population (Local Government Area): 13,196 (2001)

Broome, on Roebuck Bay in Western Australia, is Australia's major northwest port. Early pastoral ventures from 1865 were defeated by the region's climate and isolation – it is 1,390 miles (2,237 km) by road from the nearest state capital, Perth. Settlers turned to pearling, which became a major industry. Although beef processing and offshore gas and oil drilling have risen to economic significance and the pearling fleet is much contracted, there is still significant pearl-farming activity. Officially established in 1883, Broome suffered Japanese air attack in 1942. It is served by domestic airlines, road and rail, and its port facilities were enhanced with the construction of a deep-water jetty to compensate for tide falls of up to 36 ft (11 m).

Popular music hybridity was an inevitable product of the extraordinary diversity of the influences of mission education and the pearling community made up of British and a wide cross section of Asian and Pacific peoples. Since the late 1970s, these hybridities have benefited from a national consciousness of multiculturalism and indigenous popular music, especially as institutionalized at Adelaide's Centre for Aboriginal Music Studies, attended by a number of Broome musicians. With Alice Springs and Darwin, Broome is part of a sprawling indigenous popular music network that has benefited from recently developed infrastructural and technical support, including recording facilities and the Broome Music Aboriginal Corporation. The latter collaborated with the Australian Broadcasting Corporation (ABC) to establish the annual Stompen Ground Festival in 1992. Prominent musicians and bands that have their bases in Broome include Jimmy Chi, his reggae-influenced band Kuckles, and Scrap Metal. Both bands participated in Chi's first musical, *Bran Nue Dae*, which, since its debut in 1991, has brought him national recognition. Along with his later *Corrugation Road*, it addresses the dilemmas of cultural hybridity, incorporating a wide range of musical styles and languages and with an admixture of humor that represents a deconstructive variation on the solemnity with which such issues are usually handled. The musical director for *Bran Nue Dae*, Steven Pigram, is one of six brothers, three of whom were in Scrap Metal, who have been central to contemporary music in Broome for two decades. In 1996 they joined forces, with Paul Mamid, to form the country/rock band the Pigram Brothers. The Kimberley region, to which Broome is central, has also produced what has been described as a local guitar sound in country music (Walker 2000, 271–79), the most conspicuous exponent of which is Kevin Gunn.

Bibliography
Breen, Marcus, ed. 1989. *Our Place, Our Music*. Canberra: Aboriginal Studies Press.

Breen, Marcus. 1992. 'Desert Dreams, Media, and Interventions in Reality: Australian Aboriginal Music.' In *Rockin' the Boat: Mass Music and Mass Movements*, ed. Reebee Garofalo. Boston, MA: South End Press, 149–70.

Castles, John. 1992. '*Tjungaringanyi*: Aboriginal Rock.' In *From Pop to Punk to Postmodernism: Popular Music and Australian Culture from the 1960s to the 1990s*, ed. Philip Hayward. North Sydney: Allen & Unwin, 25–39.

Davies, Chris Lawe. 1993a. 'Aboriginal Rock Music: Place and Space.' In *Rock and Popular Music: Politics, Policies, Institutions*, ed. Tony Bennett et al. London and New York: Routledge, 249–65.

Davies, Chris Lawe. 1993b. 'Black Rock and Broome: Musical and Cultural Specificities.' *Perfect Beat: The Journal of Research into Contemporary Music and Popular Culture* 1(2): 48–59.

Granich, M. 1990. 'Aboriginal Music, Broome Style: Towards a Bran Nue Dae.' *Artlink* 10(1/2): 58–59.

Kelly, Aidan. 1995. *Floods, Sweat and Beers: Rockin' Around the Northern Territory*. Victoria: Moonlight Publishing.

Walker, Clinton. 2000. *Buried Country: The Story of Aboriginal Country Music*. Annandale, NSW: Pluto Press.

Discography

Chi, Jimmy. *Bran Nue Dae*. BND Records 002. *1993*: Australia.

Gunn, Kevin. *Travellin' Man*. Matilda. *1980*: Australia.

Scrap Metal. *Scrap Metal*. ABC Records 846519-1/2. *1990*: Australia.

BRUCE JOHNSON

Darwin

Population: 106,842 (2001)

The capital of the Northern Territory, established (1869) as Palmerston on Beagle Gulf, was renamed Darwin in 1911. Australia's northernmost city, its proximity to Asia gave it a strategic importance that was increased by the Overland Telegraph (1872) linking the south with the submarine cable to Europe. During World War II, Darwin was devastated by 64 Japanese air raids. In a tropical zone, it has frequently been destroyed by cyclones, most recently in 1974. Rebuilding changed a pioneer town into a small, modern, high-rise city, with one university. It has port and airport facilities, but the only road link with the south is the Stuart Highway. In 2003, a long-awaited rail link with the south was completed. Following a 1950s minerals-based boom, most employment is in the public sector, defense industries and tourism. The population is one of Australia's most cosmopolitan, with around 60 ethnic groups: indigenous and long-established Chinese, Greek and Italian communities and, increasingly, Southeast Asians.

Long peripheral to mainstream Australian popular music, Darwin's country, indigenous, ethnic and rock hybridities have recently benefited from a climate of multiculturalism, which in particular reflects the strong Pacific Islander and Asian presence. Darwin's position also enables it to make important links with musicians from Papua New Guinea.

While indigenous music has come to greatest prominence with the rise of world music, in 'Brown Skin Baby' (from the early 1960s) Darwin-based Aboriginal singer/composer Bob Randall wrote one of the first, most famous songs against the assimilationist policies. This theme was taken up again in such songs as Archie Roach's 'Took the Children Away' almost 20 years later. More recently, the Darwin Aboriginal Rock Festival has featured a range of indigenous musicians, including Apaak Jupurrula (Peter Miller), chair of the Top End Aboriginal Musicians Association and leader of the band Blekbala Mujik. With Alice Springs (Northern Territory) and Broome (Western Australia), Darwin is pivotal to an indigenous popular music network spread over an immense, sparsely populated area. It is the city closest to Arnhem Land, the base of such bands as Yothu Yindi, which in 1990 gave its name to a Foundation to help preserve the Yolngu culture. Although Yothu Yindi remains Darwin's best-known musical export, the rock group the Poor (founded as the Poor Boys in 1988) relocated to Sydney in 1991 and gained international recognition, touring the US west coast with the Angels and signing with Epic Records.

Bibliography

Bebbington, Warren, ed. 1997. *The Oxford Companion to Australian Music*. Melbourne: Oxford University Press.

Breen, Marcus, ed. 1989. *Our Place, Our Music*. Canberra: Aboriginal Studies Press.

Breen, Marcus. 1992. 'Desert Dreams, Media, and Interventions in Reality: Australian Aboriginal Music.' In *Rockin' the Boat: Mass Music and Mass Movements*, ed. Reebee Garofalo. Boston, MA: South End Press, 149–70.

Castles, John. 1992. '*Tjungaringanyi*: Aboriginal Rock.' In *From Pop to Punk to Postmodernism: Popular Music and Australian Culture from the 1960s to the 1990s*, ed. Philip Hayward. North Sydney: Allen & Unwin, 25–39.

Dunbar-Hall, Peter. 1997. 'Site as Song – Song as Site: Constructions of Meaning in an Aboriginal Rock Song.' *Perfect Beat: The Pacific Journal of Research into Contemporary Music and Popular Culture* 3(3): 58–76.

Hayward, Philip. 1993. 'Safe, Exotic and Somewhere Else: Yothu Yindi, "Treaty" and the Mediation of Aboriginality.' *Perfect Beat: The Journal of Research into Contemporary Music and Popular Culture* 1(2): 33–42.

Kelly, Aidan. 1995. *Floods, Sweat and Beers: Rockin'*

Around the Northern Territory. Victoria: Moonlight Publishing.

Magowen, Fiona. 1994. '"The Land Is Our Marr (Essence), It Stays Forever": The Yothu Yindi Relationship in Australian Aboriginal Traditional and Popular Musics.' In *Ethnicity, Identity and Music: The Musical Construction of Place*, ed. Martin Stokes. Oxford: Berg, 135–56.

McFarlane, Ian. 1999. *The Encyclopedia of Australian Rock and Pop*. St Leonards, NSW: Allen & Unwin.

Mitchell, Tony. 1992. 'World Music, Indigenous Music and Music Television in Australia.' *Perfect Beat: The Journal of Research into Contemporary Music and Popular Culture* 1(1): 1–16.

Neuenfeldt, Karl. 1993. 'Yothu Yindi and *Ganma*: The Cultural Transposition of the Aboriginal Agenda Through Metaphor and Music.' *Journal of Australian Studies* 38: 1–11.

Neuenfeldt, Karl, ed. 1997. *The Didjeridu: From Arnhem Land to Internet*. Sydney: John Libbey/ Perfect Beat Publications.

Nicol, Lisa. 1993. 'Culture, Custom and Collaboration: The Production of Yothu Yindi's "Treaty" Videos.' *Perfect Beat: The Journal of Research into Contemporary Music and Popular Culture* 1(2): 23–32.

Stubington, Jill, and Dunbar-Hall, Peter. 1994. 'Yothu Yindi's "Treaty": *Ganma* in Music.' *Popular Music* 13(3): 243–59.

Walker, Clinton. 2000. *Buried Country: The Story of Aboriginal Country Music*. Annandale, NSW: Pluto Press.

Whiteoak, John, and Scott-Maxwell, Aline, eds. 2003. *Currency Companion to Music and Dance in Australia*. Sydney: Currency Press.

Discographical References

Randall, Bob. 'Brown Skin Baby.' CAAMA FES015. *2000*: Australia.

Roach, Archie. 'Took the Children Away.' *Charcoal Lane*. Aurora/Mushroom D30386. *1990*: Australia.

Discography

Blekbala Mujik. *Come-n-Dance*. CAAMA 226. *1993*: Australia.

Poor, The. *Who Cares?*. Sony/Columbia 57552. *1994*: USA.

Randall, Bob. *Ballads by Bob Randall*. CAAMA cassette. *1983*: Australia.

Yothu Yindi. *Tribal Voice*. Mushroom D30602. *1991*: Australia.

BRUCE JOHNSON with KARL NEUENFELDT

Hobart

Population: 197,282 (2001)

Hobart is at the mouth of the Derwent River, on the south coast of Australia's largest offshore island, the state of Tasmania (formerly Van Diemen's Land), south of Melbourne. Established as a penal colony in 1804, it is Australia's southernmost capital, with a mild climate. It prospered through shipbuilding and whaling, challenging colonial Sydney as a cultural and commercial center, though as development closer to the mainland proceeded, its growth slowed. Hydroelectric development stimulated secondary industry, but population growth was slower than in any other capital, and there was little immigration, but steady emigration to the mainland. The state is served by highways, freight railway, and ferry and air services to the mainland. It has one university. Heavily reliant on tourism and service industries, the island benefited from the establishment of Australia's first legal casino, Wrest Point (1973), which increased work for popular musicians.

Hobart's insularity and small population relative to the state have discouraged a wide range of musics, a self-perpetuating cycle as alternative-minded pop musicians move to the mainland. International developments arrived late and were further narrowed by the constraints of few musicians accommodating small markets: early rock was sustained by dance and jazz musicians. Radio, television and recordings have thus had particular importance. Jazz musicians Tom Pickering and Ian Pearce, who began their careers in the 1930s, were durable linchpins, contributing significantly to the Australian jazz style. The strong folk movement is reinforced by the Folk Federation of Tasmania, and by special-interest organizations such as the Irish Association of Tasmania and the Tascal Scottish Dance Group. There has been broadening non-Anglophone activity – shading into world music – with bands like Balkanology and the Chilean group Arauco Libre, which has been active since 1987. A well-established focus for such activity is the Cygnet Folk Festival, held south of Hobart in the Huon Valley.

Although not all from Hobart, other Tasmanian musicians who have exerted a strong influence include blues/rock performer Phil Manning (who worked with the seminal band Chain in Melbourne), and bassist Tim Partridge. Among Tasmanian bands to achieve a national reputation after relocating to Melbourne are the Fish John West

Reject, originally founded in 1985, and the Odolites, who relocated a year after their formation in 1984. Wild Pumpkins at Midnight (1984) went to Europe via Melbourne, where they established a strong cult following and, more recently, Monique Brumby has also attracted international recognition. In 2001, the independent organization Tasmusic was established as the peak body for the state's contemporary music industry.

Bibliography

Bebbington, Warren, ed. 1997. *The Oxford Companion to Australian Music*. Melbourne: Oxford University Press.

Johnson, Bruce. 1987. *The Oxford Companion to Australian Jazz*. Melbourne: Oxford University Press.

Madden, Dudley. 1986. *A History of Hobart's Brass Bands and Most Impressive Musicians*. Devonport: C.L. Richmond & Sons.

McFarlane, Ian. 1999. *The Encyclopedia of Australian Rock and Pop*. St Leonards, NSW: Allen & Unwin.

Spencer, Chris. 1993. *Rockin' with the Devil in Tasmania*. Golden Square, Victoria: Moonlight Press.

Whiteoak, John, and Scott-Maxwell, Aline, eds. 2003. *Currency Companion to Music and Dance in Australia*. Sydney: Currency Press.

Discography

Brumby, Monique. *Thylacine*. Sony 4871962. *1997*: Australia.

Chain. *History of Chain*. Mushroom D 45531/2/. *1991*: Australia.

Fish John West Reject, The. *Fin*. Shock Records 0009. *1991*: Australia.

Manning, Phil. *Can't Stop*. Tamborine TM103CD. *1992*: Australia.

Odolites, The. *Face Down in the Violets*. Rampant. *1988*: Australia.

Pearce, Ian. *Tasmanian Jazz Composers*, Vol. 3. Little Arthur LACD 03. *1994*: Australia.

Pearce-Pickering Ragtime Five, The. *Jazzmania*. Swaggie S 1272. *1970*: Australia.

Tasmanian Jazz Composers, Vol. 1. Little Arthur LACD 01. *1992*: Australia.

Tasmanian Jazz Composers, Vol. 2. Little Arthur LACD 02. *1993*: Australia.

Wild Pumpkins at Midnight. *Low-Fi Lucy's Mobile Temple*. Way Over There Records WOT013. *1995*: Australia.

BRUCE JOHNSON with PHIL GRINHAM

Melbourne

Population: 3,471,625 (2001)

Astride the River Yarra on Port Phillip Bay, in a mild to cool latitude, Melbourne evolved from settlement by pastoralists from Tasmania and Sydney, becoming a municipality in 1842. Mid-century gold strikes inland made it, as the capital of Victoria, Australia's largest city and, as its financial center, one of the world's wealthiest and most technologically sophisticated. Although Melbourne was the temporary Commonwealth capital from Federation (1901) until Canberra assumed the role in 1927, it lost ground to Sydney's growth from the turn of the century. Immigration has made a major contribution to its population, in which Greek and Italian have been the most significant non-Anglophone components. The city is serviced by road, rail and port facilities, and by domestic and international air terminals. It has the main campuses of five universities. With fossil-fuel supplies from nearby La Trobe Valley, and oil and gas from Bass Strait, Melbourne is central to Victoria's industry, which includes heavy engineering, petrochemicals, automobiles and agricultural machinery, clothing and electrical goods.

Melbourne and Sydney vie as Australia's major centers. With musicians frequently commuting between them, together they have defined the main contours of the country's popular music history. Culturally, Melbourne has been more Anglocentric and, at historical moments when that bias has weakened, a stronger parochial component has become palpable than is apparent in Sydney's US orientations. In terms of twentieth-century popular music, one manifestation of this is the general recognition that the Australian jazz style evolved out of activity centered on the coterie led by brothers Graeme and Roger Bell and by Ade Monsbourgh in Melbourne. The focus of the traditional jazz movement has broadly remained in Melbourne, and has done so to a distinctive degree compared to Sydney. This is partly due to a higher degree of eclecticism that bridges the old traditional/modern divide. This eclecticism is in turn partly due to the open-minded approach of Brian Brown, a major figure in more progressive styles since the 1950s. Brown also served as the founding director of the Victorian College of the Arts jazz studies program, which he established in 1980. Contemporary to avant-garde styles have also been served by such organizations as the Melbourne Jazz Cooperative, which was established in 1983.

It is arguable that Melbourne also produced a rock/pop approach that can be distinguished from Sydney's, although the increasing homogenizing effect of post-1950s mass mediations has muted the distinctions. The multinational major recording companies have their Australian bases in Sydney, so that local grass-roots activity has a different kind of presence in Melbourne, operating through its own vigorous independent pop press, performance circuit and recording activity, in which Mushroom enterprises have been of particular importance. With Sydney, Melbourne made a decisive contribution to the Australian pop identity that is held to have developed from the 1970s. The television show *Countdown* emanated from Melbourne, which is more central than Sydney to the southeastern network that embraces Adelaide, Canberra and Hobart, and is closer to Perth. Formed by the durable and ubiquitous Ross Wilson, the Melbourne band Daddy Cool achieved breakthrough national and US success throughout 1970–72, and the unprecedented sales of the Skyhooks' 1974 album *Living in the Seventies* are regarded as signaling the confirmation of a competitive Australian pop identity. In different ways this identity would also manifest itself in the work of musician/composer Paul Kelly, who emerged on the Melbourne scene during the 1970s before moving to Sydney in the 1980s. Among his many other projects, he became involved in the career of Aboriginal singer-songwriter Archie Roach, who wrote the classic 'stolen child' song 'Took the Children Away.' Kelly assisted in the production of Roach's Aboriginal social issues album *Charcoal Lane* (Best Indigenous Album, Australian Record Industry Association, 1990). Kelly has also collaborated with Queensland-born Kev Carmody on other musical projects related to similar indigenous issues.

Another important Melbourne band was Jo Jo Zep and the Falcons (formed in 1975), which brought to national recognition Joe Camilleri. Camilleri had worked with the Adderley Smith Blues Band (formed in 1964), and he went on to form the blues/zydeco–influenced Black Sorrows (1984). In the 1970s, other Melbourne bands, including AC/DC (formed in 1973) and the Little River Band (formed in 1975), continued to be prominent in the Australian surge. In 1983, David Bridie and John Phillips formed the successful and durable group not drowning, waving, which became a major focal point in the local development of world music. Melbourne's inner suburban pub circuit and café culture also nurtured a new-wave scene that attracted groups from other capitals where alternativity was less viable, particularly Adelaide and Perth. Pioneer Melbourne groups, including the Boys Next Door (formed in 1975) – later the Birthday Party – with Nick Cave, Cave's later group the Bad Seeds, and Whirlywirld, which pioneered extended use of synthesizers in a punk context in 1978, also laid the foundations of post-punk developments in the 1990s.

To a great extent these developments have been dominated by grunge/thrash–influenced styles, the most successful example of which has been provided by the band Spiderbait, made up of musicians from Finley on the Victoria/New South Wales border, but formed in Melbourne in 1990. Spiderbait's recording debut was on Au-go-go, which also released recordings by alternative groups like the Meanies and the Guttersnipes. Au-go-go is one of the many new indie labels that have helped to sustain a generically eclectic scene so diverse that a brief review becomes little more than a sample listing. Pop-rock groups like Snout and the Dirty Three (both formed in 1992), vocalist Rebecca Barnard (Rebecca's Empire, formed in 1994), and the sometimes disorientingly eclectic Paradise Motel (1995) established strong followings, as did Abremalin (1993) and iNsuRge (1994) in different metal subgenres. Groups like Bodyjar (1994) and the Powdermonkeys (1991) represented the punk ethos that had been reinforced during the 1980s by Vicious Circle (1983) and Depression (1982). While the dance party scene has suffered from negative media coverage relating to drug-taking, particularly in connection with the Victoria Dock dance party in 2000, it remains well established, and Melbourne's DJ Dexta came second in 1999 and 2000 at the World DJ Championships. Through the 1990s a hip-hop scene also developed, particularly as an aggressively western suburbs phenomenon. The local femrock movement was given powerful impetus through the Rock'n'Roll High School, established in 1990 by girls' high-school teacher Stephanie Bourke. It has generated an impressive number of successful 'grot grrrl' groups, including Leviathan, Sourpuss and Midget Stooges. Aside from indie and alternative scenes, the middle-of-the-road (MOR) genres have high-visibility representation in the work of such performers as singer/composer Tina Arena, who has enjoyed international success through recordings.

Bibliography

Bebbington, Warren, ed. 1997. *The Oxford Compa-*

nion to Australian Music. Melbourne: Oxford University Press.

Bendrups, Dan. 2001. 'Melbourne's Latin American Music Scene.' Perfect Beat: The Pacific Journal of Research into Contemporary Music and Popular Culture 5(2): 19–29.

Brokenmouth, Robert. 1996. Nick Cave: The Birthday Party and Other Epic Adventures. London: Omnibus.

Clunies-Ross, Bruce. 1979. 'An Australian Sound: Jazz in Melbourne and Adelaide 1941–51.' In Australian Popular Culture, ed. P. Spearitt and D. Walker. Sydney: Allen & Unwin, 62–79.

Finnriorden, Michael. 1995. An Historical Anthology About Punk, Gothic, Industrial and Dark Wave Music in Melbourne 1978–Present. Melbourne: Moonlight Publishing.

Hutchison, Tracee. 1992. Your Name's on the Door: 10 Years of Australian Music. Sydney: ABC Enterprises.

Jenkins, Jeff. 1994. Ego Is Not a Dirty Word: The Skyhooks Story. Fitzroy, Victoria: Kelly and Withers.

Johnson, Bruce. 1987. The Oxford Companion to Australian Jazz. Melbourne: Oxford University Press.

Johnson, Bruce. 2000. The Inaudible Music: Jazz, Gender and Australian Modernity. Sydney: Currency Press.

Johnson, Bruce. 2003. 'Naturalizing the Exotic: The Australian Jazz Convention.' In Jazz Planet, ed. E. Taylor Atkins. Jackson, MS: University Press of Mississippi, 151–68.

Mathieson, Craig. 1996. Hi Fi Days – The Future of Australian Rock: Silverchair, Spiderbait, You Am I. St Leonards, NSW: Allen & Unwin.

Maxwell, Ian. 2003. Phat Beats, Dope Rhymes: Hip Hop Down Under Comin' Upper. Middletown, CT: Wesleyan University Press.

McFarlane, Ian. 1999. The Encyclopedia of Australian Rock and Pop. St Leonards, NSW: Allen & Unwin.

Murphie, Andrew. 1996. 'Sound at the End of the World as We Know It: Nick Cave, Wim Wenders' Wings of Desire and a Deleuze-Guattarian Ecology of Popular Music.' Perfect Beat: The Pacific Journal of Research into Contemporary Music and Popular Culture 2(4): 18–42.

Riley, Vikki. 1992. 'Death Rockers of the World Unite! Melbourne 1978–80 – Punk Rock or No Punk Rock?' In From Pop to Punk to Postmodernism: Popular Music and Australian Culture from the 1960s to the 1990s, ed. Philip Hayward. North Sydney: Allen & Unwin, 113–26.

Ryan, Robin. 1994. 'Tracing the Urban Songlines – Contemporary Koori Music in Melbourne.' Perfect Beat: The Pacific Journal of Research into Contemporary Music and Popular Culture 2(1): 20–37.

Van Straten, Frank. 2003. Tivoli. South Melbourne: Thomas C. Lothian Pty Ltd.

Walker, Clinton. 1996. Stranded: The Secret History of Australian Independent Music 1977–1991. Sydney: Pan Macmillan Australia.

Whiteoak, John, and Scott-Maxwell, Aline, eds. 2003. Currency Companion to Music and Dance in Australia. Sydney: Currency Press.

Wilmoth, Peter. 1993. Glad All Over: The Countdown Years 1974–1987. Ringwood, Victoria: McPhee Gribble.

Discographical References

Roach, Archie. Charcoal Lane. Aurora/Mushroom D30386. 1990: Australia.

Roach, Archie. 'Took the Children Away.' Charcoal Lane. Aurora/Mushroom D30386. 1990: Australia.

Skyhooks, The. Living in the Seventies. Mushroom K5628. 1974: Australia.

Discography

AC/DC. Highway to Hell. Albert/EMI 477088-2. 1979: Australia.

Arena, Tina. In Deep. Sony SME 4933349. 1997: USA.

Bell, Graeme. The EMI Australian Recordings. Axis CDAX 701583. 1990: Australia.

Birthday Party, The. Prayers on Fire. Missing Link LINK 14. 1981: Australia.

Black Sorrows. Lucky Charm. Sony 4773372. 1994: USA.

Boys Next Door, The. Boots Are Made for Walking. Suicide 103140. 1978: Australia.

Brown, Brian. Carlton Streets. 44 records 6357 700, 9288 001. 1974: Australia.

Carmody, Kev. Eulogy for a Black Person. Festival D30692. 1991: Australia.

Cave, Nick, and the Bad Seeds. From Her To Eternity. Mute STUMM 17. 1984: Germany.

Daddy Cool. Daddy Who? Daddy Cool. Sparmac SPL 001. 1971: Australia.

Jazz Notes: Fourth Australian Jazz Convention. Linehan Series/NFSA CD/NFSA/TA003. 1998: Australia.

Kelly, Paul. Live, May 1992. Mushroom D16061. 1992: Australia.

Little River Band, The. Curiosity Killed the Cat. EMI 10900. 1975: Australia.

Melbourne in the 1920s (5 CDs). Chris Long Antiquarian CL101, CL102, CL104, CL105, CL106. 2000: Australia.

not drowning, waving. *Tabaran.* Warner Reprise 903172999-2. *1991*: USA.

Spiderbait. *The Unfinished Spanish Galleon of Finley Lake.* Polydor 5291552. *1995*: Australia.

Vicious Circle. *Reactivate.* Def DEF0018. *1995*: Australia.

Whirlywirld. *Window to the World.* Missing Link MLS 3. *1979*: Australia.

BRUCE JOHNSON

Newcastle

Population: 563,586 (2001)

Australia's sixth-largest city, Newcastle is located 93 miles (150 km) north of Sydney, on the eastern seaboard of Australia at the mouth of the Hunter River on the north coast of New South Wales. Discovered in 1797 as the second European settlement in Australia, it prospered first as a penal colony before establishing itself as Australia's heavy industry center through its shipping and export of coal and steel.

The city benefited from close contact with leading Sydney jazz musicians between the 1940s and the 1960s, with a small commercial circuit – led by the Steel City Jazz Club – offering exposure to significant performers such as Frank Coughlan, Bob Gibson, Bob Henderson and Frank Marcy. The traditional Maryville Jazz Band in the 1970s provided a nucleus of activity into the mid-1980s (Johnson 1987). Newcastle University's Conservatorium (established in 1952) has provided a context for local performers and composers that incorporates drama studies and a rich theater tradition. Drawing upon rock, pop and cabaret traditions, the Castanet Club, formed from 1980s university students, spawned a group of characters and comedic personnel that has continued to enjoy national media exposure. Newcastle has a strong working-class tradition of music festival activity, encompassing eisteddfods, colliery bands and the Workers' Cultural Action Committees of the 1960s, 1970s and 1980s. The city hosts the annual This Is Not Art festival, which includes the Sound Summit, an event that enjoys national standing.

'The Newcastle Song,' written and performed by Bob Hudson, charted nationally at number one in March 1975 as a satire of local masculine weekend rituals. The Star Hotel riot of 19 September 1979 – a battle between drinkers and police over the closure of a favored live music pub, resulting in dozens of arrests – was documented in song ('The Star Hotel') by Cold Chisel's Don Walker. With 14 police

injured, 31 people arrested and two police vehicles overturned, the event has entered Oz Rock folklore (Homan 2003). The city's music pubs epitomize Oz Rock mythologies, hosting hard rock bands of powerful sonic attack underpinned by virtuosity in the best 'guitar hero' traditions, playing to hard-drinking and hard-to-please working-class audiences (Homan 2003). This is exemplified in the brief national success of the bands Rabbit, DV8, Heroes and the 'new wave' Pel Mel in the 1970s and 1980s, and of the Screaming Jets and the Porkers in the 1990s. Combining grunge with the local heavy rock tradition of bands such as AC/DC, Silverchair stands as the city's single global success. Silverchair's albums – *Frogstomp, Freak Show, Neon Ballroom* and *Diaroma* – have sold more than 6 million copies worldwide.

The ongoing decline in heavy industry and related trade career paths for local youth has led the city council to begin long-term projects designed to position Newcastle as a 'post-industrial' city, with music-making leading cultural and tourism industry strategies integral to both city reinvestment and reimaging (Stevenson 1998). The rich divide between 'smokestack economy' life styles and artistic escape through music is captured in the Australian films *Blackrock* (1997) and *Bootmen* (2000).

Bibliography

Homan, Shane. 2003. *The Mayor's a Square: Live Music and Law and Order in Sydney.* Newtown: Local Consumption Publications.

Hunter Valley Research Foundation (HVRF). 2003. *Newcastle and the Hunter Region.* Newcastle: HVRF.

Johnson, Bruce. 1987. 'Newcastle.' In Bruce Johnson, *The Oxford Companion to Australian Jazz.* Melbourne: Oxford University Press, 219–21.

Mathieson, Craig. 1996. *Hi Fi Days: The Future of Australian Rock.* St Leonards, NSW: Allen & Unwin.

Newcastle Trades Hall Council. 1984. *Working Class, Working Culture: The Workers' Cultural Action Committee of Newcastle.* North Sydney: NSW Community Arts Board.

Octapod. 2001. *This Is Not Art 2001.* http://www.octapod.org.au

Spencer, Chris. 1994. *Rockin' and Shakin' in Rock City: A Documentation of Some Rock and Pop Bands Which Had Their Origins in Newcastle, NSW.* Golden Square, Victoria: Moonlight Publishing.

Stevenson, Deborah. 1998. *Agendas in Place: Urban and Cultural Planning for Cities and Regions.* Rockhampton: Central Queensland University.

Discographical References

Cold Chisel. 'The Star Hotel.' *Swingshift*. WEA Records MX 197924. *1980*: Australia.

Hudson, Bob. 'The Newcastle Song.' *The Newcastle Song*. M7 Records MS-087. *1975*: Australia.

Silverchair. *Diaroma*. Murmur/Sony ELEVENCD8. *2002*: Australia.

Silverchair. *Freak Show*. Murmur/Sony MATTCD043. *1997*: Australia.

Silverchair. *Frogstomp*. Murmur/Sony MATTCD009. *1995*: Australia.

Silverchair. *Neon Ballroom*. Murmur/Sony MATTCD084. *1999*: Australia.

Discography

Pel Mel. *Out of Reason*. GAP LP 2001. *1982*: Australia.

Screaming Jets, The. *Better*. RooArt/Phonogram 878814-7. *1991*: Australia.

Filmography

Blackrock, dir. Steven Vidler. 1997. Australia. 100 mins. Drama. Original music by Steven Kilbey.

Bootmen, dir. Dein Perry. 2000. Australia/USA. 92 mins. Musical Drama. Original music by Cezary Skubiszewski.

SHANE HOMAN

Perth

Population: 1,393,002 (2001)

The capital of Australia's largest state, Western Australia, Perth lies on the estuaries of the Swan and Canning rivers. Founded in 1829 by free settlement, much of the city's early infrastructure was the work of imported convict labor. Development was accelerated by inland gold strikes in the 1890s and, later, by mineral and gas deposits. Population growth has resulted mainly from immigration (including internal), particularly from the United Kingdom. The city has four universities. Its economy is based on services, trading and administration, with an industrial sector well below that of major eastern capitals. On the southwest of the continent, 1,305 miles (2,100 km) across arid terrain from the nearest capital (Adelaide), Perth is one of the world's most isolated major cities. Only shipping, with telegraphy from 1877, linked Perth to the rest of the country until the opening of the Transcontinental Railway in 1917; the establishment of highway and air services followed.

Perth's isolation meant that it relied largely on its own resources to maintain performance traditions, and these have been dependent on media technology for access to external models. The state's small population (10 percent of the country's population) and its vast size are obstacles to touring circuits, although ex-Sydney musicians Rick and Thel Carey established a valuable country music touring circuit in the late 1960s. Generally, however, there has been a steady drift of career musicians, ranging from jazz and swing players (Keith Hounslow, Bob Gibson) to 1950s middle-of-the-road musicians (Rolf Harris). The 1978 Leederville Punk Festival signaled a new wave, in which seminal forces were Perth's first punk group, the Cheap Nasties (formed in 1976), which included Roddy Radalj, James Baker and its founder Kim Salmon, and the Victims (formed in 1977), which included Dave Faulkner. With the dissolution of the Cheap Nasties in 1977, Radalj and Baker went on to Manikins, while Salmon joined the Invaders, which became the Scientists (formed in 1978). The Scientists split up in 1981, to be re-formed in Sydney; they then went on to prominence on the Melbourne circuit by 1983, before relocating to the United Kingdom where they achieved considerable success before disbanding in 1987. Salmon later formed the Surrealists in 1988, and also worked with Sydney-based Beasts of Bourbon. In the meantime, Faulkner ultimately moved to Sydney, where he founded the immensely successful Hoodoo Gurus, which included Baker and Radalj. This lineage is an instructive case study in the way in which the popular music community transcends distance and geography and, in the case of Perth, is also a reminder of the fact that the east has remained the magnet. Perth groups gaining recognition from eastern and even international bases include the Dugites (formed in 1978), the Eurogliders (1980) and the Triffids (1978). A performer gaining similar recognition is English-born Dave Hole, one of Australia's preeminent blues guitarists.

The lure of the east means that the local pop/rock scene is largely sustained by young musicians. In the 1980s and 1990s, they sustained a wide generic range, embracing new wave (the Helicopters, formed in 1980), metal-influenced groups (Black Alice, 1982; Allegiance, 1990; and iNFeCTeD, 1992) and various pop/rock forms (the Stems, 1984; the Kryptonics, 1985; Martha's Vineyard, 1986; V Capri, 1984; Ammonia, 1993; the Goth-based Effigy, 1993; and Jebediah, which debuted in 1997).

Bibliography

Bebbington, Warren, ed. 1997. *The Oxford Compa-*

nion to Australian Music. Melbourne: Oxford University Press.

Hutchison, Tracee. 1992. *Your Name's on the Door: 10 Years of Australian Music*. Sydney: ABC Enterprises.

Johnson, Bruce. 1987. *The Oxford Companion to Australian Jazz*. Melbourne: Oxford University Press.

Kornwiebel, A.H. 1973. *Apollo and the Pioneers: The Story of the First Hundred Years of Music in Western Australia*. Perth: Music Council of Western Australia.

McFarlane, Ian. 1999. *The Encyclopedia of Australian Rock and Pop*. St Leonards, NSW: Allen & Unwin.

Van Straten, Frank. 2003. *Tivoli*. South Melbourne: Thomas C. Lothian Pty Ltd.

Walker, Clinton. 1996. *Stranded: The Secret History of Australian Independent Music 1977–1991*. Sydney: Pan Macmillan Australia.

Whiteoak, John, and Scott-Maxwell, Aline, eds. 2003. *Currency Companion to Music and Dance in Australia*. Sydney: Currency Press.

Discography

Allegiance. *Destitution*. Id ID00172. *1994*: Australia.

Ammonia. *Mint 400*. Murmur MATTCD 023. *1995*: Australia.

Black Alice. *Trilogy Albums: Life on Earth*. Bonsai Records. *1985*: Australia.

Dugites, The. *Cut the Talking*. Mercury 814691-1. *1984*: Australia.

Eurogliders, The. *This Island*. CBS SBP 237 994. *1984*: Australia.

Gibson, Bob. *Bob Gibson at the Surreyville*. Columbia 330S-7569. *1957*: Australia.

Harris, Rolf. *Tie Me Kangaroo Down Sport*. Columbia 45-DO-4131. *1960*: Australia.

Helicopters, The. *The Helicopters*. Warped/Tempo. *1982*: Australia.

Hole, Dave. *Steel on Steel*. Festival D 31383. *1995*: Australia.

Hoodoo Gurus, The. *Stoneage Romeos*. Big Time BT 7018. *1984*: Australia.

Hounslow, Keith. *Keith Hounslow's Jazzmakers: At Last*. Emanem 3605. *1988*: Australia.

Kryptonics, The. *Tonka Stuff*. Zero Hour ZERO801. *1991*: Australia.

Manikins. *Manikins*. CBS. *1988*: Australia.

Martha's Vineyard. *More of the Same/Suntanned Faces*. RooART 872960. *1990*: Australia.

Scientists, The. *Absolute Greatest Hits*. Polydor 849882-1. *1991*: Australia.

Triffids, The. *Australian Melodrama*. White D 31182. *1994*: Australia.

V Capri. *In My World*. Mushroom/Festival. *1986*: Australia.

Victims, The. *All Loud on the Western Front*. Timberyard. *1989*: Australia.

BRUCE JOHNSON

Sydney

Population: 4,128,272 (2001)

Sydney is the oldest and largest city in Australia. Situated on Port Jackson and with a temperate climate, it is a water-oriented city, recreationally, visually and infrastructurally. Established in 1788 as a penal colony with just over a thousand administrators, marines and convicts, its initially slow growth was accelerated by hinterland agriculture, but secondary industry was slow to develop until protective policies were introduced with Federation (1901). Two world wars stimulated industrialization, making Sydney the country's main base for manufacturing and financial interests and, likewise, for Australia's communications and media activity, including satellite, coaxial and optical fiber links; it also became the headquarters for major print, television and film enterprises. It is serviced by road, rail and shipping, and by Australia's busiest domestic and international airport. The harbor bridge (1932) and tunnel (1992) have linked the central business district with the northern suburbs, but motor traffic is placing environmental and logistical strains on a relatively unplanned metropolis. Particularly in conjunction with preparations for the 2000 Olympic Games, massive infrastructural development has continued since the late 1990s. Sydney's population is highly cosmopolitan: in 2001, 31 percent of its inhabitants were foreign-born, and English was the sole language spoken in only 67 percent of households, with the most common foreign languages being Chinese (5 percent), Arabic, including Lebanese (4 percent) and Greek (2 percent). The metropolitan area has five universities.

Sydney, with Melbourne, has largely defined the national profile of Australian popular music, generally with a more pervasive US orientation than its southern rival. A major port for US shipping, Sydney also hosted US service personnel through World War II and the Vietnam War. It thus led the way in twentieth-century US-influenced developments through the jazz, swing and rock eras. Sydney dominated record production from the mid-1920s, and it has been the Australian base for US and multinational majors, so that their increased investment in local acts from the 1970s tended to encourage the 'house style.' Sydney jazz was more directly responsive to US developments, as in the work of Frank Coughlan in the 1930s, and with a more sustained postwar modern movement. Its later rock/pop phase is regarded as manifesting a distinctive emphasis on the aggressiveness of US hard rock and its derivatives. The city's size, its port (frequently hosting foreign naval units), and its diverse and generally liberal recreational life styles have also provided a higher level and greater range of performance opportunities, particularly through alcohol-related recreational spaces. The licensing of non-proprietary clubs (that is, in particular sporting and service clubs) for poker machines in 1956 introduced revenue that often subsidized bands. Similarly, the extension of hotel (pub) hours from 6:00 p.m. to 10:00 p.m. in 1955 was the first move toward even later closing times. These later closing times saw the onset of the pub band era, providing increasing performance opportunities for the full range of popular musics, including durable and still active blues and jazz groups like Foreday Riders (formed in 1966) and Eclipse Alley Five (formed in 1969), respectively. While traditional jazz has been in decline since the mid-1980s, the Sydney Improvised Music Association, which was established in 1984, has helped to sustain the 'contemporary' jazz movement, in which veterans John Pochée (Ten Part Invention) and Bernie McGann have been significant forces. More recently, the members of the ambient/jazz group the Necks have broken out of the prevailing contemporary jazz aesthetic, receiving acclaim in the English press as one of the most significant of all contemporary bands.

The earliest wave of rock in Sydney focused on suburban halls and surf clubs, as in the distinctively Australian 'surf' sound represented in the work of Little Pattie. The new pub band venue engendered the pub-rock tradition that nurtured most of Sydney's rock/pop musicians from the 1970s to the mid-1990s. In addition to internationally profiled bands like Midnight Oil (formed in 1976) and Cold Chisel (formed in 1973), those with a more localized reputation included Rose Tattoo (1976), Mental As Anything (1976), the Sunnyboys (1980), Flaming Hands (1980), the Hoodoo Gurus (1981), the strongly punk-influenced Celibate Rifles (1979), Lime Spiders (1981) and the Hard-Ons (1982). Later representatives of the tradition included Box the Jesuit (1986), You Am I (1989) and

the Whitlams (1993), and hard grunge acts like the Screaming Jets (1989) and Noise Addict (1993). Sydney's distinctive recreational culture has thus produced many of the acts that have gained unprecedented international recognition for Australian pop, from the Easybeats in the 1960s to INXS in the 1990s. Sherbert, formed in 1969, did much to establish national touring circuits and media coverage for Australian acts and, with Melbourne's Skyhooks, was a groundbreaker in the development of the late-1970s Australian scene.

Sydney's inner-city pub scene, pop press and independent recording activity also fostered a new-wave/punk movement. The aggressive Radio Birdman was an influential pioneer, and the punk/jazz hybrid Laughing Clowns, formed by Brisbane's ex-Saints Ed Kuepper in 1979, achieved international recognition. The ethos defined through these pioneers was developed through the 1980s and 1990s by such bands as Massappeal (formed in 1985) and Frenzal Rhom (1992), and 'grot grrrl' group Nitocris (1992).

A number of factors have led to the decline of the pub music scene. These include closer policing of public consumption of alcohol, the displacement of music in small pubs by gaming machines following the recent liberalization of gaming legislation, noise problems in increasingly gentrified inner-city precincts, and also changes in the technology of music recreation. This process has been accompanied by the rise of other musical forms, most notably the techno-based genres of dance and hip-hop. As early as 1979, Severed Heads was pioneering techno-dance, and it was followed by Boxcar (originally from Brisbane) and Single Gun Theory, both formed in 1986. In the 1990s, the Lab (1991) and Itch-E & Scratch-E (1992) were prominent, aided by the independent Volition label. Def FX (1990) united techno with a range of other influences. The scene suffered in terms of public perception with the closure of the Phoenician Club in 1995 after a drug-related fatality, but the genre has remained tenacious, particularly in relation to the gay and lesbian Mardi Gras community. Hip-hop has also decentered the popular music scene, not simply in terms of performance venues and protocols but geographically, being dispersed throughout the suburbs (particularly in the west and southwest), where crews such as Westside Posse/Sound Unlimited, Def Wish Cast and 046 present unashamedly suburban narratives.

As with all state capitals, Sydney has attracted popular musicians in all genres from other regions.

The majority of jazz musicians listed as Sydney-based in *The Oxford Companion to Australian Jazz* (Johnson 1987) are from elsewhere. It seems likely that the same is true of rock/pop-derived musicians. From Canberra came the early punk groups Tactics (formed in 1977) and Falling Joys (1985). Grunge group Tumbleweed (1990) came from near Wollongong in the south, Grinspoon (1994) came from Lismore to the north, and one of the most successful recent arrivals, Silverchair (1994), is from Newcastle. Likewise, many seminal individuals such as Tex Perkins, who formed the Dum Dums (1982) in Brisbane, came from elsewhere. The Dum Dums broke up in Sydney in 1983, but Perkins stayed on to become an eclectically ubiquitous presence, notably fronting the Cruel Sea and the Beasts of Bourbon. He exemplifies a Sydney profile that through its history has included more non-locally born musicians than any other major center.

Bibliography

Bebbington, Warren, ed. 1997. *The Oxford Companion to Australian Music*. Melbourne: Oxford University Press.

Fitzgerald, Jon. 2002. 'Another Front: The Impact of British Pop Within New South Wales (Australia) 1963–1966.' *Perfect Beat: The Pacific Journal of Research into Contemporary Music and Popular Culture* 6(1): 49–67.

Ford, Joan. 1995. *Meet Me at the Trocadero*. Cowra, NSW: Joan Ford.

Gibb, Alex, and Loader, Meagan. 1997. 'Displaced Acappella: The Bulgarian Choral Tradition and Sydney's Martenitsa Choir.' *Perfect Beat: The Pacific Journal of Research into Contemporary Music and Popular Culture* 3(2): 1–14.

Harley, Ross. 1995. 'Acts of Volition: Volition Records, Independent Marketing and the Promotion of Australian Techno-Pop.' *Perfect Beat: The Pacific Journal of Research into Contemporary Music and Popular Culture* 2(3): 21–48.

Homan, Shane. 1998. 'After the Law: Sydney's Phoenician Club, the New South Wales Premier and the Death of Anna Wood.' *Perfect Beat: The Pacific Journal of Research into Contemporary Music and Popular Culture* 4(1): 56–83.

Homan, Shane. 2003. *The Mayor's a Square: Live Music and Law and Order in Sydney*. Newtown, NSW: Local Consumption Publications.

Hutchison, Tracee. 1992. *Your Name's on the Door: 10 Years of Australian Music*. Sydney: ABC Enterprises.

Johnson, Bruce. 1987. *The Oxford Companion to Australian Jazz*. Melbourne: Oxford University Press.

Johnson, Bruce. 2000. *The Inaudible Music: Jazz, Gender and Australian Modernity*. Sydney: Currency Press.

Johnson, Bruce. 2004. 'An Interview with Patricia Thompson (Little Pattie).' *Popular Music and Society* 27(1): 55–78.

Johnson, Bruce, and Homan, Shane. 2003. *Vanishing Acts: An Inquiry into the State of Live Popular Music Opportunities in New South Wales*. Sydney: The Australia Council and NSW Ministry for the Arts. http://www.ozco.gov.au; http://www.arts.nsw.gov.au

Johnson, Vivien. 1990. *Radio Birdman*. Melbourne: Sheldon Booth.

Mathieson, Craig. 1996. *Hi Fi Days – The Future of Australian Rock: Silverchair, Spiderbait, You Am I*. St Leonards, NSW: Allen & Unwin.

Maxwell, Ian. 1997. 'Goa Trance Fred Cole and Michael Hannan on the Flow: Dancefloor Grooves, Rapping "Freestyle" and "the Real Thing."' *Perfect Beat: The Pacific Journal of Research into Contemporary Music and Popular Culture* 3(3): 15–27.

Maxwell, Ian. 2003. *Phat Beats, Dope Rhymes: Hip Hop Down Under Comin' Upper*. Middletown, CT: Wesleyan University Press.

Maxwell, Ian, and Bambrick, Nikki. 1994. 'Discourses of Culture and Nationalism in Contemporary Sydney Hip Hop.' *Perfect Beat: The Pacific Journal of Research into Contemporary Music and Popular Culture* 2(1): 1–19.

McFarlane, Ian. 1999. *The Encyclopedia of Australian Rock and Pop*. St Leonards, NSW: Allen & Unwin.

Van Straten, Frank. 2003. *Tivoli*. South Melbourne: Thomas C. Lothian Pty Ltd.

Walker, Clinton. 1996. *Stranded: The Secret History of Australian Independent Music 1977–1991*. Sydney: Pan Macmillan Australia.

Whiteoak, John, and Scott-Maxwell, Aline, eds. 2003. *Currency Companion to Music and Dance in Australia*. Sydney: Currency Press.

Discography

Beasts of Bourbon, The. *The Low Road*. Red REDCD26; Polydor 511725. *1991*: Australia.

Cold Chisel. *Chisel*. East West 903175021. *1991*: Australia.

Coughlan, Frank. *King of the Trocadero*. Larrikin LRH 428. *1996*: Australia.

Cruel Sea, The. *The Honeymoon Is Over*. Red Eye REDCD 35. *1993*: Australia.

Def Wish Cast. *Knights of the Underground Table.* Random Records. *1993*: Australia.

Easybeats, The. *She's So Fine.* Parlophone A8157. *1965*: Australia.

Hoodoo Gurus, The. *Crank.* Limburger 7432113496 23/94. *1994*: Australia.

INXS. *Shabooh Shoobah.* WEA 600133. *1982*: Australia.

Laughing Clowns. *Mr. Uddich-Schmuddich Goes to Town.* Prince Melon PM 5000. *1981*: Australia.

Little Pattie. *20 Stompie Wompie Hits.* EMI EMY 504. *1980*: Australia. Reissue: Little Pattie. *20 Stompie Wompie Hits.* EMI CD 7243 5 22386 2 0. *2000*: Australia.

Mental As Anything. *Chemical Travel.* Regular/Festival D 31094. *1993*: Australia.

Midnight Oil. *Diesel and Dust.* CBS 460005. *1986*: Australia.

Necks, The. *Sex.* Spiral Scratch 0002. *1989*: Australia.

Nitocris. *Screaming Dolorous.* Phantom PHMCD 42. *1994*: Australia.

Radio Birdman. *New Race.* Trafalgar TRS 11. *1977*: Australia.

Rose Tattoo. *Nice Boys Don't Play Rock 'n' Roll.* Sony 465469. *1993*: Australia.

Severed Heads. *Gigapus.* Volition VOLT. *1994*: Australia.

Sherbert. *Howzat.* Sherbert L35905. *1976*: Australia.

Sound Unlimited. *A Postcard from the Edge of the Underside.* Columbia. *1992*: Australia.

Sydney 1926: The First Discs (2 CDs). Chris Long Antiquarian CL107 and CL108. *2002*: Australia.

Ten Part Invention. *Tall Stories.* Rufus RF006. *1994*: Australia.

Whitlams, The. *Introducing ... The Whitlams.* Phantom PHMCD 27. *1993*: Australia.

You Am I. *Sound As Ever.* Ra 4509939582. *1993*: Australia.

BRUCE JOHNSON

Tamworth
Population: 42,510 (2001)

The city of Tamworth is located on the Peel River in the New England region of New South Wales, 281 miles (453 km) by road northwest of Sydney. It began as a station for the Australian Agricultural Company, with which it remained formally linked until 1985. A village was established by 1839, and Tamworth was gazetted as a town in 1850. Local gold strikes brought benefits to the region and Tamworth was a coach station in the 1860s. Its growth was constrained by large pastoral interests, although when leases expired in 1890 small farms proliferated. In 1888 it became the first Southern Hemisphere town operating its own electric streetlighting. On a plateau with a mild climate, Tamworth serves the medical, educational, administrative and commercial needs of a primary producing region with allied processing (dairy, flour mills, abattoirs) and light industries. It has road, rail and air links to Sydney and to Brisbane, although the rail link to the latter is not direct.

Tamworth is the 'Country Music Capital of Australia.' Local performances and broadcasts on Radio 2TM led to the inauguration of the annual Tamworth Country Music Jamboree (later, 'Festival') in 1966, now the largest music festival in Australia. In conjunction with the festival, since 1973 the Australasian Country Music Awards have been presented on Australia Day, 26 January. Apart from broadcasting, the city fostered independent specialist country record labels Hadley, Opal and Selection, the monthly newspaper *Capital Country* (1978) and a country music museum. In 1992, Tamworth became the headquarters of the Country Music Association of Australia, which set up the Australian College of Country Music in 1997.

The predominant country style in Tamworth looks back to the tradition evolved by pioneers like Tex Morton and Buddy Williams, through Slim Dusty and June Holm, with relatively little space for the 'new country' that emerged in association with the radicalized folk movement of the 1960s. Significant figures at the festival have included John Williamson, the extraordinary yodeler Mary Schneider, and particularly Lee Kernaghan, whose father Ray was also a significant figure in the movement. Aboriginal performers have had a presence, including Jimmy Little and local veteran Roger Knox, whose band Euraba includes his son Buddy. Recently emerging Aboriginal stars include Troy Cassar-Daley and Emma Lee Donovan. With the festival attracting up to 50,000 people – more than the city's normal population – Tamworth exemplifies the potential of music in cultural tourism.

Bibliography

Allan, Monika. 1988. *The Tamworth Country Music Festival.* Sydney: Horowitz Grahame.

Bebbington, Warren, ed. 1997. *The Oxford Companion to Australian Music.* Melbourne: Oxford University Press.

Capital News Country Music. http://www.capitalnews.com.au/custom.asp?page_id=5&y=2002&m=2

Forrest, Bill. 2000. *Saturday Night: A History of Dance Bands in Country New South Wales*. Tamworth, NSW: W.J. Bill Forrest.

Latta, David. 1991. *Australian Country Music*. Sydney: Random House.

McFarlane, Ian. 1999. *The Encyclopedia of Australian Rock and Pop*. St Leonards, NSW: Allen & Unwin.

Smith, Graeme. 1994. 'Australian Country Music and the Hillbilly Yodel.' *Popular Music* 13(3): 297–311.

Smith, Jazzer, ed. 1984. *The Book of Australian Country Music*. Gordon, NSW: Berghouse Floyd Tuckey Publishing Group.

Walker, Clinton. 2000. *Buried Country: The Story of Aboriginal Country Music*. Annandale, NSW: Pluto Press.

Watson, Eric. 1982. *Eric Watson's Country Music in Australia*. Sydney: Angus & Robertson. (First published Kensington, NSW: Rodeo Publications, 1975.)

Watson, Eric. 1983. *Eric Watson's Country Music in Australia*, Vol. 2. Sydney: Angus & Robertson.

Watson, Eric. 1987. 'Country Music: The Voice of Rural Australia.' In *Missing in Action: Australian Popular Music in Perspective*, ed. Marcus Breen. Kensington, Victoria: Verbal Graphics, 48–77.

Whiteoak, John, and Scott-Maxwell, Aline, eds. 2003. *Currency Companion to Music and Dance in Australia*. Sydney: Currency Press.

Discography

Cassar-Daley, Troy. *A Long Way Home*. EMI/Essence CD 5399092. *2002*: Australia.

Country Music in Australia 1936–1959. EMI 814090-2. *1993*: Australia.

Kernaghan, Lee. *Three Chain Road*. EMI 4797672. *1993*: Australia.

Knox, Roger. *The Gospel Album*. Enrec ENC 020. *1986*: Australia.

Schneider, Mary. *Yodelling the Classics*. Crossover Music CD 3 6660 2. *2000*: Australia.

Williamson, John. *Australia Calling – All the Best*. EMI 8301732. *1992*: Australia.

Winners 7, Featuring All the Finalists from the 1999 Toyota Country Music Awards. EMI CD 7243 4 99304 2 1. *1999*: Australia.

http://www.countrymusic.asn.au/winners7.html

BRUCE JOHNSON

7. Aotearoa/New Zealand

Aotearoa/New Zealand: Maori and Pacific Islander Music

Population: Maori: 383,277 (2003); Pacific Islander: 150,150 (2003)

From Hawaiian Combos to Acid Rock

The native inhabitants of Aotearoa ('the land of the long white cloud'), the Maori, who arrived in canoes in the tenth century, constituted approximately one in seven of the population of Aotearoa/New Zealand in the 2001 census. Nine-tenths of the Maori population live on the North Island, and one in four speak *te reo Maori* (the Maori language). Since the 1980s, the Maori, supported by various government initiatives in education, arts funding and broadcasting, have taken increasing steps to revive their cultural, linguistic and social traditions. The establishment of 24 *iwi* (tribal) radio stations around the country since 1990 has provided an important outlet for Maori-language broadcasting and music. In addition, the *Iwi Hit Disc*, a CD compilation of new tracks distributed to all radio stations by the government-funded NZ On Air (Tirangi Te Motu) since July 1998, has provided a boost to media airplay of Maori music. Nonetheless, Polynesians, who include Maori and a growing number of Pacific Islander immigrants, continue to be in the lowest income group in New Zealand, and some of the music they produce deals strongly with social and political concerns, cultural sovereignty and a sense of dispossession. One in 16 of the total population of New Zealand is of Pacific Islander descent; about one-half of these are Samoan, one-quarter Cook Island Maori, one-fifth Tongan, and approximately 20,000 are from the Niuean islands, 7,000 from Fiji, 6,000 from Tokelau and 2,000 from Tuvalu.

Many Maori popular groups and performers have syncretized aspects of traditional Maori *waiata* (song) and pre-European musical instruments with imported African-American and other musical forms throughout the history of Maori popular music. Pacific Islander musicians have produced similar hybrid musical forms, such as 'Samoan soul.'

Since Victorian times Maori concert parties, featuring the polyphonic harmonies of traditional songs and dances of Maori folklore like the *poi* dance, the *haka* (war dance) and the *karanga* (call to ancestors), have been performed in various colonial contexts, often touring outside New Zealand or performing for tourists from abroad. The most notable such performance was at the Christchurch Exhibition of 1907–1908 (McLean 1996, 316). The first popular song to be recorded and pressed in New Zealand (in 1949), however, was the strongly Hawaiian-influenced love song 'Blue Smoke,' sung by 19-year-old Pixie Williams and the Ruru Karaitiana Quartet and later recorded by Dean Martin (Eggleton 2003, 11), which preserved few traces of traditional Maori elements. This Hawaiian influence continued into the 1950s, and was prominent in 'Haka Boogie,' a 1955 composition by Lee Westbrook sung by Morgan Clarke with Benny's Five, which signaled a hybridization of traditional Maori *waiata* and popular dance music, as did Rim D. Paul's 'Poi Poi Twist' in 1962. In the 1950s, Maori show bands, such as the Maori Hi Five (which ended up in Las Vegas in the 1960s as a lounge act), Prince Tui Teka and the Maori Troubadours, and the Volcanics, began performing largely Anglo-American and Italian-American repertoires on cabaret circuits, sharing the indigenous popular music scene with Hawaiian-styled combos and US-influenced country and western singers (Eggleton 2003, 12).

In 1955, a Maori country music artist, Johnny Cooper, known as 'the Maori Cowboy,' was prevailed upon to record a cover version of Bill Haley's 'Rock Around the Clock' in an unsuccessful attempt to launch an indigenous rock 'n' roll scene. In his encyclopedic study of New Zealand popular music from 1955 to 1988, John Dix (1988, 331) has claimed that Cooper's recording was probably the first rock 'n' roll recording made outside the United States. Cooper also made a significant contribution to the local rock 'n' roll scene with his own composition, 'Pie Cart Rock and Roll,' celebrating 'pea pie and pud' and an antipodean institution, the pie cart. He later tutored the pakeha (literally 'non-Maori,' mostly referring to white British settlers) singer Johnny Devlin, who became a rock 'n' roll legend in Australia and New Zealand in the late 1950s.

In the 1960s, three Maori recording artists achieved local prominence: Sir Howard Morrison and his famous quartet; comedian Billy T. James; and ballad-singer John Rowles, who had two hits in the British charts. In the 1970s, the pyrotechnical blues and acid rock of black US guitarists Jimi Hendrix and Carlos Santana were an important influence on Maori guitarists like Billy Tekahika (aka Billy TK), who combined Hendrix-like inflections with blues and aspects of *waiata* and Polynesian guitar rhythms in the band Human Instinct and the all-Maori Powerhouse. They also had an influence on Maori groups Butler, Golden Harvest and Taste of Bounty. Guitarist Tama (Tama Renata), who later provided the powerful theme song for the 1994 Maori film *Once Were Warriors*, combined Hendrix-like lead guitar with reggae, soul, blues and funk rhythms.

Polynesian Soul, Funk and Reggae

The 1980s saw the emergence of soul music as a dominant Maori form. In Auckland the soul scene was spearheaded by 'fonk' group Ardijah, which later relocated to Sydney. But the most distinctive figure in Maori popular music of the 1980s was Dalvanius Prime, who died in 2002. Prime produced 'E Ipo' for the popular ballad-singer Prince Tui Teka, a song that won two New Zealand Record Industry Awards in 1982. This was followed by 'Poi E,' written and produced by Dalvanius on his Maui label and performed by the Patea Maori Club, which reached number one in the New Zealand charts in 1983. 'Poi E' combined traditional Maori

vocal chants, *poi* dancing and Polynesian drumming with funk and break dancing, and was even named Single of the Week by Britain's *New Musical Express*. It eventually won the 1988 New Zealand Recording Industry's Best Polynesian Record award, five years after it was first released.

As in Australia, Bob Marley's performances in New Zealand in 1979 had a strong influence on local indigenous and Pacific Islander musicians, who adopted reggae music and Rastafarian philosophy, with their own adaptations. Aotearoa and Dread Beat and Blood (later Dread Beat, which was associated with another Maori reggae group, Sticks and Shanty) were both formed in 1985. They combined mellifluous Maori and Pacific vocal harmonies with Jamaican rhythms. These groups also used reggae rhythms to express the Maori militancy in their lyrics, and Aotearoa's 1985 single 'Maranga Ake Ai' (Wake Up People) was a plea to young Maori to become politically aware and 'take up the cause.' The Rastafarian collective Twelve Tribes of Israel explored the more religious side of reggae, combining Rastafarian rhetoric with Maori and Pacific Islander elements on their 1990 album *Shine On*, written and produced by Jamaican-born Hensley Dyer. This album featured a song entitled 'The Land of the Long White Cloud,' characterizing Maori and Pacific Islanders as children of Jah.

The most prominent and longest-surviving Polynesian reggae group, Herbs, was formed in 1980 and continued to perform in various mixed Maori and Pacific Islander formations until 1998. The group's 1986 collaboration with Dave Dobbyn, 'A Slice of Heaven,' became the theme song of the New Zealand Tourist Board. Herbs' first single, 'French Letter,' which portrayed the French as 'unwelcome guests making nuclear tests' in the Pacific, went to number 11 in the national charts in 1982, and enjoyed a revival during the anti-nuclear protests against French tests in the Pacific in 1995. Herbs has been described by Duncan Campbell (1993, 51) as 'epitomizing the common purpose of Maori and Islander at a time when the youth of the two communities were more intent on gang warfare,' and its 1981 debut EP, *What's Be Happen?*, as setting 'a standard for Pacific reggae which has arguably never been surpassed.' Herbs' soft brand of politically oriented Polynesian reggae, which includes the occasional song in Maori, became highly successful throughout the Pacific Island region. The twin bothers Ruia and Ranea, a notable Maori reggae duo, followed their 2000 album *Whare Maori* (Maori House) with two albums of songs by Bob

Marley translated into *te reo Maori*, the first of which won a New Zealand Music Award in 2002. Dub has also flourished among Polynesian musicians in New Zealand. Six albums of roots-oriented Pacific inflections by Christchurch-based Salmonella Dub – fronted by Tiki Taane, also known as MC Rizzla – have gained the group a wide following in Australasia and elsewhere. The Wellington-based Trinity Roots has combined jazz, dub and roots reggae to express 'spiritual roots and a sense of *tangata whenua* (the people of the land)' (Eggleton 2003, 187). Katchafire, an eight-piece mixed-race reggae band based in Waikato in the North Island, had an award-winning hit single 'Giddyup' in 2002, and the band's Bob Marley-styled songs have had high-rotation airplay on the popular Mai FM radio network, which specializes in Polynesian and African-American music.

Besides the internationally successful Maori opera singer Kiri Te Kanawa, there have been a number of successful Maori and Pacific Islander women singers of popular music. Soul singer Margaret Urlich's first album *Safety in Numbers* sold nearly a quarter of a million copies in Australia in 1989, and she settled there soon afterward. Her music, like that of other Maori and Pacific Islander women singers in the 1990s (such as Moana Maniapoto-Jackson and her group the Moahunters, Annie Crummer and Emma Paki), has often tended to incorporate the influences of black US dance music and R&B. The disco-soul singer Ngaire (Ngaire Fuata), who is from Ratuma near Fiji, made some impact on the local dance scene with her eponymous album in 1991. It featured a disco cover version of Lulu's 1960s hit 'To Sir with Love,' going to number one in the local charts. Maree Sheehan combines soul, funk and rap with Maori percussive instruments like the *poi* and sticks, and she has stressed the importance of using aspects of *waiata* in her music in order to make it distinctively local. The dominance of black US influences over aspects of *Maoritanga* (Maori culture) in the music of a number of Maori female singers has brought criticism of cultural imperialism from Mahinarangi Tocker, a respected but commercially unrecognized half-Jewish, half-Maori folk singer–songwriter who is a veteran of the New Zealand music industry. But the musical paths taken by a number of young Maori and Pacific Islander women are dictated more by musical preferences and the need for a marketable image in the industry than by indigenous ideological choices. Their use of black US idioms is also a response to a global musical culture of sounds

and images that relates to a shared black aesthetic, against which local notions of 'brownness' can be defined.

Soul singer Sulata, from the Tokelau islands, released a notable album, *Kia Koe*, in 1996, before joining Te Vaka (the Canoe), a 10-piece world music group founded by her uncle. Te Vaka performs a syncretic mixture of traditional Pacific Islander music (featuring log drums), soul and funk, and even incorporates a didjeridu. The most successful female singer-songwriter in New Zealand is half-Maori, half-Chinese Bic Runga, daughter of a former Maori show-band pianist. Her 1997 debut album, *Drive*, which she also produced, sold more than 90,000 copies, the highest-selling album ever in New Zealand by a local artist, and she won a number of awards at the 2003 Tui New Zealand Music Awards for her second album, *Beautiful Collision*. Her sister, Boh Runga, fronts the post-grunge band Stellar*, whose 1999 album *Mix* sold 80,000 copies. In 2000, the female Maori duo Wai 100% released a highly distinctive eponymous album of Maori *waiata* combined with the percussive sounds of *poi*, *piu piu* (flax skirts), body slaps, birds' wings and other sounds. Nineteen-year-old half-Maori, half-pakeha singer Anika Moa's album *Thinking Room* went double platinum in 2001, and she won the 2002 songwriter of the year award for her single 'Youthful.'

Maori and Pacific Islander Hip-Hop

African-American influences are even stronger in Maori and Pacific Islander manifestations of hip-hop. According to Tania Kopytko (1986, 21–22), break dancing first arrived in New Zealand in 1983 via Western Samoa, and by 1994 local break-dance teams, consisting mostly of young Maori and Pacific Islanders, were appearing on local television programs, with Television New Zealand even sponsoring a national break-dance competition. Kopytko claims that break dancing provided Maori youth with a substitute for their own culture, which was largely inaccessible to them. Kerry Buchanan (1993, 27) has argued that hip-hop's associations with African-American culture quickly became an important reference point and example for musical expressions of a local Maori and Pacific Islander vernacular culture, with which it shared strong roots in church and gospel singing. Rap music and hip-hop culture also became an inevitable medium for musical expressions of Maori militancy. The Upper Hutt Posse's Public Enemy–influenced hardcore rap first drew attention in both New Zealand

and Australia in the late 1980s. Upper Hutt Posse released the first hip-hop record in New Zealand in 1988, the 12" (30 cm) single 'E Tu' (Stand Proud), which combined Nation of Islam–influenced rhetoric with an explicitly Maori frame of reference. This track opened the 1998 compilation *Aotearoa Hip Hop, Vol. 1*, which celebrated 10 years of rap music in New Zealand and featured most of the prominent Maori and Polynesian rappers and posses up to that point: Raumoko, 3 the Hard Way, Teremoana Rapley, Sisters Underground, OMC, Dam Native, Ermehn, Urban Disturbance, DLT and Che Fu, Losttribe, Dei Hamo and King Kapisi, whose effort to take 'Samoan hip hop worldwide' has been relatively successful in both Australia and New Zealand. Che Fu, who is of mixed Maori and Niuean descent, and is the son of Tigi Ness of 1970s reggae band I Unity, is a particularly important figure. He featured in the successful soul-funk group Supergroove before emerging as a solo artist and releasing an album with former Upper Hutt Posse member DLT. Eggleton (2003) describes Che Fu's 1998 debut solo album *2b Spacific* as establishing him 'as one of the foremost talents in New Zealand rock music, someone capable of crafting gorgeous soul grooves. Che Fu – who has been described as having the best voice in New Zealand pop history – artfully blends American rhythm and blues and Jamaican reggae with the home-grown rhythms of Polynesian gospel and urban rap' (182). In 1998 a Maori rap-R&B group, Iwi (Tribe), consisting of five vocalists and 12 musicians, released an eponymous album that was the first hip-hop album in Aotearoa/New Zealand to be almost entirely in *te reo Maori*. Apart from a few passages in English, the Maori lyrics to the album are printed on the CD sleeve without any translation. Formed in 1995 at a *hui* (meeting) in a *marae* (community center), Iwi was founded to express the predominant concerns of Maori people in the twenty-first century, based on four key principles: the Maori language, the Maori people, the *marae* and self-government.

However, it is Upper Hutt Posse's uncompromising *kia kaha* (be strong) style of hip-hop that has remained the most distinctive blend of traditional aspects of Maori musical culture, local urban realities, political diatribe and African-American rap music in New Zealand. The group's leader, Te Kupu (D Word), released a solo album, *Ko Te Matakahi Kupu* (The Word That Penetrates), in both *te reo Maori* and English versions in 2000. He also released two exclusively Maori-language albums with Upper Hutt Posse, *Ma Te Wa* (2000) and the

Tui Music Award-winning *Te Reo Maori Remixes* (2002), which consisted of Maori-language versions of the group's previous single releases. Since 2000, a second generation of Maori and Pacific Islander hip-hop artists has emerged, encouraged by the commercial success of Che Fu and DLT (whose single 'Chains' was the first hip-hop release to reach number one in the local charts in 1996), by Pauly Fuemana's 1997 international hit with OMC, 'How Bizarre,' and by the establishment of the annual Aotearoa Hip Hop Summit in 2000. The most successful of these second-generation hip-hop artists, the mixed Maori and Pacific Islander group Nesian Mystik, mentored by Che Fu, released a chart-topping, triple platinum album *Polyunsaturated* in 2002. This group was closely followed by Christchurch-born Samoan rapper Scribe, whose 2003 debut album *The Crusader* and singles 'Not Many' and 'Stand Up,' the latter an anthem to New Zealand hip-hop, reached number one in the local charts. Unfortunately, Scribe appears to have adopted a US accent, verbal idioms and 'gangsta' hip-hop values and attitudes that tend to obscure expressions of local identity and ethnicity. A number of other Polynesian rappers have done the same, particularly those in the South Auckland Dawn Raid collective (named after a police raid on Polynesian immigrant 'overstayers'), such as Mareko, the Deceptikonz, K.A.O.S. and 4 Corners. A notable exception is Ill Semantics, a hip-hop trio that includes the Maori woman rapper Nemesis, whose intelligent soul, R&B and rap debut album *Theory of Meaning* was an important release in 2002. Pacific Islander hip-hop group 3 the Hard Way, whose pop-rap single 'Hip Hop Holiday' (a hip-hop transposition of 10CC's 'Dreadlock Holiday') topped the local charts in 1994 for several weeks and went gold, reaching number 12 on the Australian Top 20, had a surprising comeback in 2003 with two singles and an album of much more R&B-inflected material. Scribe's cousin Ladisix, initially part of the all-female Christchurch-based Pacific Islander rap group Sheelaroc, is one of the few current prominent women MCs ('mic chanters' or 'mike controllers'), performing with her group Verse Two and as a solo artist.

The bestselling soundtrack of Lee Tamahori's highly successful 1994 film *Once Were Warriors* provided a showcase for a wide range of Maori popular music. The Maori musician Hirini Melbourne, who died in 2003, specialized in reconstructing and playing traditional Maori musical instruments from bone, wood, stone, shells and even flax snails, and was the film's musical consultant. Melbourne's Maori songs have been sung by children in schools throughout New Zealand, and his demonstrations and recordings with Richard Nunns of the more than 70 traditional Maori musical instruments (of 34 different kinds that Nunns has collected) have made him the most distinctive indigenous musician in the country. The results of Melbourne's and Nunns' restoration of *nga taonga puoro* (traditional musical instruments) have also surfaced in recordings by popular Maori musicians like Moana and the Moahunters – their 1994 album *Tahi* (One) opens with Melbourne's composition 'Tihore Mai' (Split Apart) – and Hinewehi Mohi (who sings with the group Oceania), Maree Sheehan and Emma Paki, who are all featured on the *Once Were Warriors* soundtrack, along with Herbs, Tama Renata, Upper Hutt Posse, reggae group Southside of Bombay and others. The music for *Once Were Warriors* was recorded for posterity by Tangata Records, an important label established in the early 1990s to promote indigenous recording artists. Other labels, such as Deepgrooves, Southside, Tai E, Urban Pacifika Records, Dawn Raid and Maori Music.Com, have also specialized in music by Maori and Pacific Islander artists.

Proud, an 'Urban-Pacific Streetsoul Compilation' of South Auckland Pacific Islander rap, reggae, soul, a cappella, swing beat and traditional musicians, topped the New Zealand compilation charts for three weeks in 1994, and was re-released due to popular demand in 2001. The recording was the result of a community project in the predominantly Polynesian South Auckland suburb of Otara which involved Samoan, Tongan, Niuean, Fijian and Cook Islander as well as Maori musicians in a 25-date nationwide tour. Produced by Alan Jansson, the album included Sisters Underground, the Semi MCs, DJ Payback, the Pacifican Descendants and the ironically named Otara Millionaires Club (OMC), fronted by Pauly Fuemana. Pauly's brother Phil, a prominent performer and producer in his own right, established Urban Pacifika Records in 1996 to showcase the 'New Urban Polynesian' sound of Pacific Islander groups and performers. The label released the compilation *Gifted & Maori Vol. One* in 2003. But although there is a rich variety of musical idioms and styles in Maori and Polynesian popular music in Aotearoa, and Polynesian hip-hop has enjoyed commercial success, much of this music has remained a relatively marginal phenomenon in commercial, media and industrial

terms due to its limited accessibility within Aotearoa/New Zealand and its near-inaccessibility abroad. Outside Aotearoa, a country still marked by its geographical isolation in the global economy of popular music, the international attention paid to independent label Flying Nun and the pakeha noise-oriented bands and musicians of the 'deep south' of New Zealand in the 1980s and early 1990s has yet to be extended to its rich range of Maori and Polynesian groups and performers.

Bibliography

Buchanan, Kerry. 1989. 'The Upper Hutt Posse: Music with a Message.' *Music in New Zealand* (Summer): 34–35.

Buchanan, Kerry. 1993. 'Ain't Nothing But a G Thing.' *Midwest* 3: 25–27.

Campbell, Duncan. 1993. '"Jah Life" and "Dread Beat."' *Planet* 10 (Autumn): 51.

Dart, William. 1994. 'Te Ku Te Whe: Rediscovering a Tradition.' *Music in New Zealand* 24 (Autumn): 25–27.

Derby, Mark, and Wilson, Helen. 1995. 'Pacific Islander Radio and Music in Auckland.' *Perfect Beat: The Pacific Journal of Research into Contemporary Music and Popular Culture* 2(2): 83–91.

Dix, John. 1988. *Stranded in Paradise: New Zealand Rock'n'roll, 1955–1988*. Wellington: Paradise Publications.

Duff, Alan. 1990. *Once Were Warriors*. Auckland: Tandem Press.

Eggleton, David. 2003. *Ready to Fly: The Story of New Zealand Rock Music*. Nelson: Craig Potton.

Frizzell, Otis. 1994. 'Hip Hop Hype.' *Pavement* 8 (December): 44–50.

Ihaka, Jodi. 1993. 'Why the Kids Wanna Be Black.' *Mana* (August/September): 12–15.

Kopytko, Tania. 1986. 'Breakdance as an Identity Marker in New Zealand.' *Yearbook for Traditional Music* 18: 21–28.

Lealand, Geoff. 1988. *A Foreign Egg in Our Nest?: American Popular Culture in New Zealand*. Wellington: Victoria University Press.

McLean, Mervyn. 1996. *Maori Music*. Auckland: Auckland University Press.

Mitcalfe, Barry. 1974. *The Singing Word: Maori Poetry*. Wellington: Victoria University Press.

Mitchell, Tony. 1994. 'He Waiata Na Aotearoa: Maori & Polynesian Music in New Zealand.' In *North Meets South: Popular Music in Aotearoa/New Zealand*, ed. Philip Hayward, Tony Mitchell and Roy Shuker. Sydney: Perfect Beat Publications, 53–72.

Mitchell, Tony. 1995. 'New Urban Polynesians: *Once Were Warriors*, the *Proud* Project and the South Auckland Music Scene.' *Perfect Beat: The Pacific Journal of Research into Contemporary Music and Popular Culture* 2(3): 1–20.

Mitchell, Tony. 1996. 'The Sounds of Nowhere?: Bicultural Music in Aotearoa/New Zealand.' In Tony Mitchell, *Popular Music and Local Identity: Rock, Pop and Rap in Europe and Oceania*. Leicester: Leicester University Press, 215–62.

Mitchell, Tony. 2001. 'Kia Kaha! (Be Strong!): Maori and Pacific Islander Hip-Hop in Aotearoa-New Zealand.' In *Global Noise: Rap and Hip-Hop Outside the USA*, ed. Tony Mitchell. Middletown, CT: Wesleyan University Press, 280–305.

Reece, Doug. 1997. 'Huh!/Mercury's OMC Finding Fans at Top 40.' *Billboard* 109(27) (3 July): 1, 36.

Reid, Graham. 1992a. 'New Zealand Awards Display Diversity.' *Billboard* 104(1) (25 April): 36.

Reid, Graham. 1992b. 'New Zealand's Maori Music a Genre Melange.' *Billboard* 104(22) (30 May): 1, 34.

Reid, Graham. 1993. 'Kiwi Scene Makes Strong '93 Showing.' *Billboard* 105(30) (24 July): 19, 93.

Reid, Graham. 1994. 'Tour Teaches Pride.' *NZ Herald* (25 March).

Reid, Graham. 1996. 'Polygram's OMC Unearths Polynesia.' *Billboard* 108(27) (6 July): 1, 16.

Russell, John. 1997a. 'Review of Losttribe, "Summer in the Winter."' *Rip It Up* 241 (September): 33.

Russell, John. 1997b. 'Rhymes and Real Grooves: Dam Native.' *Rip It Up* 240 (August): 18.

Russell, John. 1998. 'As Easy as 1, 2 . . . Moana and the Moahunters.' *Rip It Up* 247 (March): 22.

Vui-Talitu, Sara. 1996. ' "AEIOU" – Music Video and Polynesian Communication.' *Perfect Beat: The Pacific Journal of Research into Contemporary Music and Popular Culture* 2(4): 78–88.

Walker, Clinton. 1995. 'Pacific Pride.' *Rolling Stone* (Australian Edition) 510 (June): 28.

Zemke-White, Kirsten. 2001. 'Rap Music and Pacific Identity in Aotearoa: Popular Music and the Politics of Opposition.' In *Tangata o te Moana Nui: The Evolving Identities of Pacific Peoples in Aotearoa/New Zealand*, ed. Cluny Macpherson, Paul Spoonley and Melani Anae. Palmerston North: Dunmore Press, 228–42.

Zepke, S. 1993. 'Dean Hapeta: The Medium Is the Message.' *Music in New Zealand* 23 (Summer): 2–4.

Discographical References

Aotearoa. 'Maranga Ake Ai.' *Tihei Mauriora*. Jayrem JAY-318. *1985*: New Zealand.

Aotearoa Hip Hop, Vol. 1. BMG 74321599162. *1998*: New Zealand.

Che Fu. *2b Spacific*. BMG CD 74321 629924. *1998*: New Zealand.

Clarke, Morgan, with Benny's Five. 'Haka Boogie.' *Rock and Roll from New Zealand, Vol. 7–8*. Collector/White Label 7756. 1955; *2003*: New Zealand.

Cooper, Johnny. 'Pie Cart Rock and Roll.' *Pie Cart Rock'N'Roll: New Zealand Rock'N'Roll 1957–1962*. Zerox Records/Festival Mushroom CD DZER-OX02. *2003*: New Zealand.

DLT. 'Chains.' *The True School*. BMG 74321 393512. *1996*: New Zealand.

Fuemana, Pauly, with OMC. 'How Bizarre.' *How Bizarre*. Mercury 533435. *1997*: USA.

Gifted & Maori Vol. One. Urban Pacifika UPMG 2002. *2003*: New Zealand.

Haley, Bill, and His Comets. '(We're Gonna) Rock Around the Clock.' Decca 29124. 1955: USA.

Herbs. 'French Letter.' *Listen: The Very Best of*. Warner Music NZ CD 0927419502. *2002*: New Zealand.

Herbs. *What's Be Happen?* (EP). Warrior Records/WEAZ 20012. *1981*: New Zealand.

Herbs, with Dobbyn, Dave. 'A Slice of Heaven.' *Listen: The Very Best Of*. Warner Music NZ CD 0927419502. *2002*: New Zealand.

Ill Semantics. *Theory of Meaning*. Dawn Raid Entertainment/Universal DRECD004. *2002*: New Zealand.

Iwi. *Iwi*. Tangata Records/BMG CD TANGD541. *1998*: New Zealand.

Katchafire. 'Giddyup.' Mai Music/Shock Records KCDSP 01. *2002*: New Zealand.

Lulu. 'To Sir with Love.' Epic 10187. *1967*: UK.

Moa, Anika. 'Youthful.' *Thinking Room*. Atlantic 83530. *2001*: USA.

Moana and the Moahunters. *Tahi*. Festival/Southside Records CDD30787. *1994*: New Zealand.

Nesian Mystik. *Polyunsaturated*. Bounce/Universal 99292. *2002*: New Zealand.

Ngaire. 'To Sir with Love.' *Ngaire*. Festival/Southside Records C 30582. *1991*: New Zealand.

Once Were Warriors (Original soundtrack). BMG/Tangata Records CD74321253034. *1994*: New Zealand.

Patea Maori Club, The. 'Poi E.' *Poi E*. Maui Records/WEA CD0630170282. *1996*: New Zealand.

Paul, Rim D. 'Poi Poi Twist.' *Rock and Roll from New Zealand, Vol. 7–8*. Collector/White Label 7756. 1962; *2003*: New Zealand.

Prince Tui Teka. 'E Ipo.' RCA. *1981*: New Zealand.

Proud, An Urban-Pacific Streetsoul Compilation. Volition/Second Nature CD77. *1994*: Australia.

Ruia and Ranea. *Waiata of Bob Marley*. Maori Music.Com CDMMDC100. *2001*: New Zealand.

Ruia and Ranea. *Waiata of Bob Marley Vol. 2*. Maori Music.Com CDMMDC110. *2002*: New Zealand.

Ruia and Ranea. *Whare Maori*. Jayrem/Tangata Records TANGD546. *2000*: New Zealand.

Runga, Bic. *Beautiful Collision*. Columbia CD 5084032000. *2002*: New Zealand.

Runga, Bic. *Drive*. Columbia 488580.2. *1997*: New Zealand.

Scribe. 'Not Many.' *The Crusader*. Dirty Records/Festival Mushroom CD DRT005/337432. *2003*: New Zealand.

Scribe. 'Stand Up.' *The Crusader*. Dirty Records/Festival Mushroom CD DRT005/337432. *2003*: New Zealand.

Stellar*. *Mix*. Epic CD494884.2. *1999*: New Zealand.

Sulata. *Kia Koe*. Deepgrooves/Festival DG026. *1996*: New Zealand.

Te Kupu. *Ko Te Matakahi Kupu*. Kia Kaha/Universal 98342 (Maori version); 98402 (English version). *2000*: New Zealand.

10CC. 'Dreadlock Holiday.' Mercury 6008 035. *1978*: UK.

3 the Hard Way. 'Hip Hop Holiday.' *Old Skool Prankstas*. Deepgrooves/Festival D39915 DG 037. *1994*: New Zealand.

Twelve Tribes of Israel Band (featuring Hensley Dyer). *Shine On*. Twelve Tribes of Israel TTI CAS 1. *1990*: New Zealand.

Upper Hutt Posse. 'E Tu.' Jayrem Records JAY 143. *1988*: New Zealand.

Upper Hutt Posse. *Ma Te Wa*. Kia Kaha/Universal 98842. *2000*: New Zealand.

Upper Hutt Posse. *Te Reo Maori Remixes*. Kia Kaha 0239079. *2002*: New Zealand.

Urlich, Margaret. *Safety in Numbers*. CBS 465652 4. *1989*: Australia.

Wai 100%. *Wai 100%*. Jayrem CDJAY 361. *2000*: New Zealand.

Williams, Pixie, and the Ruru Karaitiana Quartet. 'Blue Smoke.' *Nature's Best: New Zealand's Top 30 Songs of All Time*. Sony Music 5054952000. 1949; *2002*: New Zealand.

Discography

Apanui, Ngahiwi. *Te Hono Ki Te Kainga*. Jayrem JAY-333. *1989*: New Zealand.

Ardijah. *Take a Chance*. WEA CD2556832. *1987*: New Zealand.

Crummer, Annie. *Seventh Wave*. East/West CD0630159462. *1996*: New Zealand.

Dam Native. *Kaupapa Driven Rhymes Uplifted*. BMG/Tangata Records CD0528. *1995*: New Zealand.

Deceptikonz, The. *Elimination*. Dawn Raid Entertainment/Universal CD 99122. *2002*: New Zealand.

DLT. *Altruism*. BMG CD74321806642. *2000*: New Zealand.

Dread Beat and Blood. *No More War*. Jayrem TC-JAY-141. *1987*: New Zealand.

Early Rock & Roll from New Zealand – Vols. 5 and 6. Collector Records CLCD7755/A/B. *2003*: New Zealand.

Ermehn. *Samoans: Part 2*. Deepgrooves/Festival CD DG050 D31811. *1988*: New Zealand.

Fuemana. *New Urban Polynesian*. Deepgrooves CD. *1994*: New Zealand.

Human Instinct. *Stoned Guitar*. Ascension Records ANCD 003. *2001*: Australia.

Katchafire. *Revival*. Mai Music/Shock KCDSP3. *2003*: New Zealand.

King Kapisi. *Savage Thoughts*. Festival Mushroom D32110. *2000*: New Zealand.

Losttribe. *Summer in the Winter*. Urban Pacifika Records/BMG CD74321426144. *1997*: New Zealand.

Mareko. *White Sunday*. Dawn Raid Entertainment/Universal CD 99662. *2003*: New Zealand.

Melbourne, Hirini, and Nunns, Richard. *Te Ku Te Whe*. Rattle Records. *1994*: New Zealand.

Melbourne, Hirini, and Nunns, Richard, with Yates-Smith, Aroha. *Te Hekenga-a-rangi*. Rattle Records RAT DV010. *2003*: New Zealand.

Moana. *Toru*. Tangata Records TANG548. *2003*: New Zealand.

Moana and the Moahunters. *Rua*. BMG/Tangata Records CDD532. *1998*: New Zealand.

Oceania. *Oceania*. Point Music/Universal CD536 775-2. *1999*: New Zealand.

OMC. *How Bizarre*. huh! CD6. *1996*: New Zealand.

Paki, Emma. *Oxygen of Love*. Virgin Records CD4713182. *1996*: New Zealand.

Salmonella Dub. *One Drop East*. Virgin CD 7243 5 92475 0 2. *2003*: Australia.

Sheehan, Maree. *Drawn in Deep*. Arista/Roadshow Music CD 17522-2. *1995*: New Zealand.

Tama (Tama Renata). *Workshop*. Jayrem/Te Aroha Records TCTA 1001. *1989*: New Zealand.

Te Rangatahi: When the Haka Became Boogie's Greatest Bits. BMG/Tangata Records TANG 50A. *1992*: New Zealand.

Te Vaka. *Original Contemporary Pacific Music*. ARC Music Productions EUCD 1401. *1997*: UK.

275

Trinity Roots. *True*. Trinity Roots TR.02. *2002*: New Zealand.

Twelve Tribes of Israel Band NZ. *Showcase Album*. Twelve Tribes of Israel TTI CA 003. *1991*: New Zealand.

Upper Hutt Posse. *Against the Flow*. Southside/Festival L30177. *1989*: New Zealand.

Upper Hutt Posse. *Movement in Demand*. BMG/Tangata Records CD519. *1995*: New Zealand.

Urban Disturbance. *37 a-ttitude*. Festival/Deep-grooves CD DG031. *1994*: New Zealand.

Filmography

Once Were Warriors, dir. Lee Tamahori. 1994. New Zealand. 99 mins. Marriage Drama. Original music by Murray Grindlay, Murray Mcnabb.

TONY MITCHELL

Aotearoa/New Zealand: Pakeha (European)

Population: 3,951,307 (2003)

New Zealand, or Aotearoa (the frequently used Maori name), is a South Pacific country, physically roughly the size of the United Kingdom. It consists of two large islands, along with a number of closely situated smaller islands. The country became a British colony in 1840, and is now a self-governing member of the British Commonwealth.

New Zealand's population of nearly 4 million is predominantly of British origin, with the indigenous Maori and more recent Polynesian island migrants making up approximately 15 percent of the population. The majority of the main urban centers are located on the coast, greater Auckland being the dominant city; indeed, some 75 percent of the population are in the North Island, and a northward drift continues. The country remains heavily dependent on a vulnerable export-oriented agricultural economy.

In 2000–2003, the local economy was buoyant, with low interest rates, low unemployment, rising immigration, and rapidly rising house prices and valuations. By 2004, growth had slowed, with interest rates beginning to rise, the dollar weakening against overseas currencies and a dip evident in the housing market. Despite the threat of recession and the increasing polarization of incomes, living standards are on a par with those in the United Kingdom and the United States.

The Music

The indigenous inhabitants of New Zealand, the Maori, enjoyed a rich musical culture, employing a variety of traditional instruments. The Maori flute-like *koauau* accompanied *waiata* – chants of lament, war, hunting and tattooing – while the Maori also had numerous songs of everyday life: love songs, lullabies, and *poi* and stick games. Some of these songs and instruments have survived, at times being incorporated into new forms. The contribution of several early Maori songwriters was considerable. Tuini Ngawai wrote about 180 songs, mostly for *marae* occasions, and her 'Arohaina Mai' (1939) became the official hymn of the Maori Battalion. Maewa Kaihau is best known for the much-covered 'Haera Ra (Farewell) Waltz Song,' setting new lyrics to 'Po Atarau,' from the Ratana church hymnbook. British singer Gracie Fields recorded it, as 'Now Is the Hour,' after her 1947 tour of New Zealand, and the song became a smash hit internationally. The wistful 'Blue Smoke' (1949), sung by Pixie Williams and the Ruru Karaitiana Quartet, eventually sold 50,000 copies; a TaNew Zealanda-label 78, it has been described as the first record wholly produced in New Zealand.

While Maori has become an officially recognized and supported New Zealand language, songs sung in it rarely receive radio airplay or achieve chart success. (A notable exception was the traditional song 'Poi E,' performed by the Patea Maori Club on the Maui label, which topped local charts in 1984.)

While the Maori language remains marginalized, more evident is the strong historical presence of Maori and Polynesian performers on the local music scene. Prominent examples include: Johnny Cooper, known as 'the Maori Cowboy,' and Maori show bands in the 1950s; the Howard Morrison Quartet in the 1960s; John Rowles in the 1970s; Herbs, and Dalvanius Prime in the 1980s; and Moana and the Moahunters, Ngaire, DLT and Che Fu, and King Kapisi in the 1990s. In 2004, the local version of the television show *Pop Icons* was dominated by young Maori/Polynesian performers. These performers were interweaving elements of soul, funk, rap, reggae and mainstream pop/rock with elements of traditional Maori music.

The first European settlers brought their music with them: the folk songs of early Victorian England, ballads and operatic arias. Choral and instrumental societies were soon formed. Colonial balls and tours by visiting opera companies were an important part of nineteenth-century musical life in the colony. Subsequently, other musical traditions and influences filtered through the country's ports. Hawaiian and country music were prominent during the 1930s Depression period, with country-oriented singers playing ukuleles and steel guitars.

Tex Morton ('the Singing Cowboy') enjoyed a lengthy career, taking in Australia and North America as well as New Zealand. His first recordings, in 1932, were possibly the first country records to be made outside the United States. After his local success, Morton moved to Australia, a career path that has been followed by many subsequent New Zealand performers. The Tumbleweeds' 'Maple on the Hill' (1949) sold more than 80,000 copies and became a New Zealand hillbilly classic. Early record companies (such as Viking or Zodiac) were run from suburban garages by enthusiasts working in the evenings, after their day jobs, with fairly basic equipment. Musical instruments and recording technology were frequently homemade modifications of what was available overseas.

In the 1950s, the arrival of rock 'n' roll created the first truly national local star: Johnny Devlin. *The Lever Hit Parade* (1954–) and subsequent radio chart shows helped popularize rock 'n' roll. The establishment of television in the 1960s, with popular music shows *C'Mon, Let's Go!* and *Happen Inn*, consolidated the careers of a variety of performers: the British beat-influenced music of Ray Columbus and the Invaders and Larry's Rebels; the R&B of the La De Das; the smooth chart pop of Dinah Lee, Shane, the Chicks and the Avengers; and the progressive rock of the Hi-Revving Tongues and Human Instinct (see Flint 1994).

Leading performers through the 1970s and 1980s included the following: singer-songwriters Shona Laing, Jenny Morris and Sharon O'Neill; smooth, 'big-voice' male vocalists John Rowles, Jon Stevens and Mark Williams; rock bands DD Smash (and a solo Dave Dobbyn), the Mockers, Mi-Sex, Dragon and Hello Sailor; pop-oriented bands such as Peking Man and the Exponents; the alternative Flying Nun bands – the Chills, JPS Experience and Headless Chickens; bands mixing Polynesian rhythms and instrumentation with Western styles such as rap and reggae – Herbs, Ardijah, and Moana and the Moahunters; and country singers and country rockers John Hanlon, Maria Dallas, Patsy Rigger and the Warratahs. Many of these went on to be based in Australia, and some enjoyed international success – most notably Split Enz and John Rowles. Some have continued to perform successfully.

The 1990s saw the increasing prominence of Polynesian/Maori performers, particularly in Auckland (OMC, Supergroove, Annie Crummer). Critical and chart success has also been attained by the Mutton Birds, Shihad, Strawpeople, Bic Runga (the biggest-selling local solo artist), Head Like a Hole,

Headless Chickens, Jan Hellriegel and Ngaire. The most internationally successful performers during the 1990s were Crowded House (and later Tim Finn as solo performer), the Mutton Birds, Shihad and OMC, whose single 'How Bizarre' was an international chart topper in 1996.

During 2003, chart success was enjoyed by Auckland hip-hop group Nesian Mystick (number four on the Top 50 album list) and Raglan reggae group Katchafire (number 23). Local rapper Scribe's double A-side 'Stand Up'/'Not Many' spent a record 10 weeks at number one on the singles charts, while his debut album enjoyed major sales. Other leading local performers in 2003–2004 were Auckland nu-metallers Blindspot; Auckland pop rockers Elemenop; Christchurch dance dub collective Salmonella Dub; ex-Wellington rockers Pacifier (formerly Shihad); and singer-songwriter Bic Runga, whose album *Beautiful Collision* was the biggest-selling album in New Zealand in 2003.

Several New Zealand musicians made an international impact during 2002–2003. Teen soprano Hayley Westenra's album *Pure* debuted at number eight on the British pop charts and at number one on the classical charts. By the end of 2003 it had sold 700,000 copies, making it the biggest-selling classical debut album to date (Houlihan 2004). Overseas success was also enjoyed by Kiwi garage rockers the Datsuns and the D4 (especially in the United Kingdom), and drum 'n' bass group Concord Dawn.

The strength of the local scene was also evident in the success of a series of compilation releases from Sony, *Nature's Best*, based on a poll of the all-time best New Zealand recordings. A stronger sense of local musical history was also fueled by a major television series, *Give It A Whirl*, screened during 2003 and accompanied by a double CD 'soundtrack.' Adding to this sense of a vibrant musical scene were two books celebrating local music-making: a highly readable general history by David Eggleton (2003), and Matthew Bannister's more personal account of his 1980s Flying Nun band Sneaky Feelings (1999).

The Music Industry

New Zealand's consumption of recorded music is extremely small, although significant in per capita terms. In 2002, the retail value of the New Zealand music market (all music formats combined) was NZ$192.1 million, with the share of New Zealand artists at an estimated 9 percent (http://www.rianz.org.nz).

The local scene remains insufficient to support more than a handful of full-time professional performers. At the end of the twentieth century, there was still only limited radio and television exposure for local artists, and initiatives to support the industry remained few. Radio New Zealand's musically conservative monopoly was broken by pirate station Radio Hauraki in the late 1960s, and by the mid-1990s over 180 radio stations were continuously on air. Most are privately owned, and represent a proliferation of popular music–oriented radio formats, dominated by Classic Rock and Contemporary Hit Radio. There is also a small group of student radio stations. The proportion of New Zealand music played on radio remained small through the 1990s, varying between approximately 5 percent on some commercial stations and 15–20 percent on student radio, and considerable support existed for a local content quota. Several MTV-style channels operated between 1994 and 1998, but all subsequently folded.

The situation improved quite dramatically in 2002–2003, with the introduction of a virtually compulsory radio airplay code (while not mandatory, the new targets were 'strongly encouraged,' with the threat of non-license renewal). This was reinforced by NZ On Air's increased use of 'song pluggers,' and the formation in 2001 of a New Zealand Music Industry Commission, charged simply with 'growing the industry.'

New Zealand has a small but robust music press, led by the influential monthlies *Rip It Up* and *Real Groove*.

Reflecting the character of these developments, there is an emphasis on a do-it-yourself ethic throughout the infrastructure of the New Zealand music industry.

There are a number of established New Zealand independent labels, along with local branches of the majors that dominate the global music industry. The multinational record companies have continued to supply approximately 90 percent of the domestic market, and most leading local artists record for them (for example, Neil Finn – EMI; Bic Runga – Sony Music). The operation of the majors in New Zealand has been controversial, with some commentators seeing them as exploitative of the local music scene, only picking up and promoting those artists who have international sales potential. Others see the relationship between the majors and the independents as symbiotic.

Independent labels in New Zealand have a long history. Of the now-defunct indie labels, the most significant was Propeller Records, which enjoyed short-lived success in the 1980s with Blam Blam Blam and the Screaming Meemees. Flying Nun is New Zealand's best-known and most successful label. Founded in 1981 to create an outlet for South Island bands, Flying Nun became associated with the 'Dunedin sound.' The Chills developed into Flying Nun's most popular act, the label's first band to tour overseas and the first to sign to an overseas label, their *Kaleidoscope World* album selling 20,000 copies in the United Kingdom.

In the late 1980s, Flying Nun expanded its operations, as popular bands like Straitjacket Fits, the Bats and Headless Chickens had ambitions, partially realized, of reaching both the local and the international markets. A manufacturing and distribution deal was struck with Australia's Mushroom Records in 1990, and similar arrangements were subsequently made to reach the North American market. The Clean, the Chills, JPS Experience, Straitjacket Fits and the Verlaines appeared on US labels, following considerable exposure on US college radio stations. Pagan Records, begun in 1985, initially had Shona Laing, who followed local success with a formidable career overseas, eventually moving to Atlantic (and on to Sony). Pagan's artists have included Paul Ubana Jones, the Warratahs (and Barry Saunders) and Greg Johnson, and the label has a distribution deal with Virgin Records. Other prominent contemporary independent labels are LOOP, Kog Transmission, Mai Music, Wildside, Birthday Records, huh!, Tangata, Urban Pasifika, Rattle Records and Antenna Records (an offshoot of Pagan). The independent labels have recently formed an association to better promote their interests and existence: Independent Music NZ.

The music industry has traditionally handed out awards for artistic significance and sales success; these historically have included the Loxene Gold Disc Awards, the Rheineck Rock Awards and the Just Juice Awards. The Smokefree Rock Quest is a well-established annual competition for high-school bands. These usually offer some assistance to record on a more professional basis, while winning them is also obviously important in terms of status and audience recognition. There are annual New Zealand music awards for recording and records, songwriting and music videos. Most tertiary institutions have music departments, and music is part of the compulsory school curriculum.

There is some significant government support for popular music, especially from NZ On Air, which originally received a proportion of the broadcasting fee legally required of all television owners. When this ended in 2001, NZ On Air received equivalent direct government funding. It has initiated a number of schemes, beginning in 1991 with a subsidy for local music videos. This contributed to a snowball effect, whereby television playlisting led to record sales, which put the records on radio playlists, in turn making the videoclips more popular with the television shows, leading to more sales and higher chart listings. NZ On Air has also funded radio shows featuring local music; a 'Radio Hits Production Scheme' whereby 'significant' commercial airplay is rewarded with partial reimbursement of costs; and a *Kiwi Hit Disc*, a CD compilation of new tracks, supplied free to all radio stations five times a year. The success of the latter encouraged the development of similar compilations complementing the mainstream orientation of the *Kiwi Hit Disc*, and aimed at niche radio audiences: the *Iwi Hit Disc* (Maori radio) and the *Indie Hit Disc*. During 2002–2003, NZ On Air increasingly began using 'song pluggers' to promote its releases to radio playlist programmers.

Boosted by the emergence of several high-profile local acts, and some performers' international success, the NZ On Air schemes contributed to a marked increase in the proportion of New Zealand artists gaining local airplay (some 14 percent across all radio formats during 2003).

Creative New Zealand also subsidizes local recordings. These schemes are run in consultation with radio and recording interests.

New Zealand supports the Berne Convention, the major international agreement on copyright, while locally copyright is regulated under the *Copyright Act* of 1962. Several agencies administer the application of copyright. The most important are AMCOS (the Australasian Mechanical Copyright Owners Society), which represents virtually all music publishers in Australia and New Zealand and, by way of reciprocal arrangements, the vast majority of the world's composers, writers and music publishers; and APRA (the Australasian Performing Right Association).

Conclusion

The bulk of New Zealand popular music is imitative of overseas styles, although frequently inflecting these with local references and the distinctive 'Kiwi' accent. The most innovative and distinctive music has been produced within the alternative, 'lo-fi' tradition, and by artists blending Polynesian/Maori forms with the various African-American musics, especially rap and reggae.

Bibliography

Australasian Performing Right Association (APRA). http://www.apra.com.au

Bannister, Matthew. 1999. *Positively George Street*. Wellington: Reed Books.

Bourke, Chris. 1997. *Crowded House: Something So Strong*. Sydney: Macmillan.

Chunn, Mike, and Chunn, Jeremy. 1995. *The Mechanics of Popular Music: A New Zealand Perspective*. Wellington: GP Publications.

Davey, Tim, and Puschman, Horst. 1995. *Kiwi Rock: A Reference Book*. Dunedin: Kiwi Rock Publications.

Dix, John. 1988. *Stranded in Paradise: New Zealand Rock'n'roll, 1955–1988*. Wellington: Paradise Publications.

Eggleton, David. 2003. *Ready to Fly: The Story of New Zealand Rock Music*. Nelson: Craig Potton.

Flint, Michael. 1994. 'What the Air Was Like Up There – Overseas Music and Local Reception in the 1960s.' In *North Meets South: Popular Music in Aotearoa/New Zealand*, ed. Philip Hayward, Tony Mitchell and Roy Shuker. Sydney: Perfect Beat Publications, 1–15.

Hayward, Philip, Mitchell, Tony, and Shuker, Roy, eds. 1994. *North Meets South: Popular Music in Aotearoa/New Zealand*. Sydney: Perfect Beat Publications.

Houlihan, Mike. 2004. 'Vintage Year for Kiwi Artists.' *Dominion Post* (1 January): A12.

Independent Music NZ. http://www.indies.co.nz

Lealand, Geoff. 1988. *A Foreign Egg in Our Nest?: American Popular Culture in New Zealand*. Wellington: Victoria University Press.

Mansfield, John. 1991. *The Oxford History of New Zealand Music*. Oxford: Oxford University Press.

Mitchell, Tony. 1995. 'New Urban Polynesians: *Once Were Warriors*, the *Proud* Project and the South Auckland Music Scene.' *Perfect Beat: The Pacific Journal of Research into Contemporary Music and Popular Culture* 2(3): 1–20.

Mitchell, Tony. 1996. 'The Sounds of Nowhere?: Bicultural Music in Aotearoa/New Zealand.' In Tony Mitchell, *Popular Music and Local Identity: Rock, Pop and Rap in Europe and Oceania*. Leicester: Leicester University Press, 215–62.

New Zealand Music Industry Commission. http://www.nzmusic.org.nz

New Zealand Official Yearbook 1998. 1998. Wellington: Statistics New Zealand/GP Publications.

Pickering, Michael, and Shuker, Roy. 1994. 'Struggling to Make Ourselves Heard: Music, Radio and the Quota Debate.' In *North Meets South: Popular Music in Aotearoa/New Zealand*, ed. Philip Hayward, Tony Mitchell and Roy Shuker. Sydney: Perfect Beat Publications, 73–97.

Recording Industry Association of New Zealand. http://www.rianz.org.nz

Scapolo, Dean. 1997. *New Zealand Music Charts 1966 to 1996 Singles.* Wellington: JPL Books.

Shuker, Roy, and Pickering, Michael. 1994. 'Kiwi Rock: Popular Music and Cultural Identity in New Zealand.' *Popular Music* 13(3): 261–78.

Spittle, Gordon. 1997. *Counting the Beat: A History of New Zealand Song.* Wellington: GP Publications.

Staff, Bryan, and Ashley, Sheran. 2002. *For the Record: A History of the Recording Industry in New Zealand.* Auckland: David Bateman.

Thomas, Ben. 2003. 'So You Wanna Be a Rock'n'Roll Star?' *Listener* (29 March): 58–59.

Discographical References

Chills, The. *Kaleidoscope World.* Creation 008. *1986*: UK.

Fields, Gracie. 'Now Is the Hour.' London 110. 1947: UK.

Give It A Whirl: The Soundtrack from the Major Television Series. Universal Music New Zealand 99632/REV504. *2003*: New Zealand.

'Haera Ra (Farewell).' *Oceania.* PolyGram 536775. *2000*: New Zealand.

Nature's Best: New Zealand's Top 30 Songs of All Time. Sony Music 5054952000. *2002*: New Zealand.

Nature's Best, Vol. 2. Sony 5088102000. *2002*: New Zealand.

OMC. 'How Bizarre.' Polydor 5776202. *1996*: UK.

Patea Maori Club, The. 'Poi E.' *Poi E.* Maui Records/WEA CD0630170282. *1996*: New Zealand.

Runga, Bic. *Beautiful Collision.* Columbia CD 5084032000. *2002*: New Zealand.

Scribe. 'Not Many.' *The Crusader.* Dirty Records 337432. *2003*: New Zealand.

Scribe. 'Stand Up.' *The Crusader.* Dirty Records 337432. *2003*: New Zealand.

Tumbleweeds, The. 'Maple on the Hill.' *The Golden Years of the Tumbleweeds, 1949–1989.* Viking VPS 490 CD. 1949; *1990*: New Zealand.

Westenra, Hayley. *Pure.* Decca 473300. *2003*: USA.

Williams, Pixie, and the Ruru Karaitiana Quartet. 'Blue Smoke.' *Nature's Best: New Zealand's Top 30 Songs of All Time.* Sony Music 5054952000. 1949; *2002*: New Zealand.

Discography

Ardijah. *Take a Chance.* WEA CD2556832. *1987*: New Zealand.

A Trip To The Moon. *Jazz Hop.* Antenna/Pagan 8572792. *1997*: New Zealand.

Chills, The. *Soft Bomb.* Slash/Liberation 26787. *1992*: USA.

Crowded House. *Woodface.* Capitol C2-93559. *1991*: USA.

Finn, Neil. *Try Whistling This.* Sony/Work 69372. *1998*: USA.

Garageland. *Last Exit to Garageland.* Foodchain 70001. *1997*: New Zealand.

Headless Chickens. *Donde Esta La Pollo.* Flying Nun 011113. *1992*: New Zealand.

Herbs. *Listen: The Very Best of.* Warner Music NZ CD 0927419502. *2002*: New Zealand.

How Was the Air Up There?. EMI 5332812. *2001*: New Zealand.

Johnson, Greg. *Vine Street Stories.* Pagan 4713122. *1995*: New Zealand.

Jones, Paul Ubana. *Uniquely Ubana: The Best of Paul Ubana Jones.* Pagan 5418382. *2002*: New Zealand.

La De Das, The. *Rock 'n' Roll Decade 1964–74.* EMI 50819. *1981*: Australia.

Morris, Jenny. *The Story So Far: The Best of Jenny Morris.* East/West 450991118. *1993*: New Zealand.

Mutton Birds, The. *The Mutton Birds.* Bag Records 4353002. *1992*: New Zealand.

Once Were Warriors (Original soundtrack). BMG/Tangata Records CD74321253034. *1994*: New Zealand.

Paki, Emma. *Oxygen of Love.* Virgin Records CD4713182. *1996*: New Zealand.

Poynton, Dan. *You Hit Him He Cry Out.* Rattle Records RAT D006. *1997*: New Zealand.

Runga, Bic. *Drive.* Columbia 488580.2. *1997*: New Zealand.

Shihad. *Killjoy.* Wildside Records D31340. *1995*: New Zealand.

Upper Hutt Posse. 'E Tu.' Jayrem Records JAY 143. *1988*: New Zealand.

Warratahs, The. *The Collection.* Pagan PACD 1148. *1992*: New Zealand.

Wild Things: Wild Kiwi Garage 1966–1969. Flying Nun FNMC 190 C30620 (audiocassette). *1991*: New Zealand.

Visual Recording

'Long Way to the Top: Stories of Australia and New Zealand Rock'n'Roll.' 2001. ABC (Australian Broadcasting Corporation) video/DVD series.

ROY SHUKER

CITIES

Auckland

Population: 1,074,510 (2001)

Auckland, New Zealand's largest metropolitan center, is situated in the northern part of the country. During the nineteenth century, its economy and port were closely linked to the colony's primary industries (especially agriculture and forestry). Later, although these remained important, Auckland increasingly became the country's dominant manufacturing center, as well as a focus for finance, transport and administrative services. Rapid population growth (in 1936 Auckland accounted for 14 percent of New Zealand's population; by 2001 this figure had reached 29 percent) has made Auckland the dominant New Zealand metropolis.

As a major seaport, Auckland was open to the importation of a myriad of musical influences. Blues, jazz, rock 'n' roll, pop, rock, reggae and rap have historically all been absorbed, and at times reworked in more local idioms. Since the 1950s, thanks to significant immigration of Pacific Islanders and rural Maori, Auckland has emerged as a major Polynesian/Maori center, epitomized by the annual Otara and Pasifika festivals, both with strong musical programs. As the dominant urban center in New Zealand since the turn of the century, Auckland has always attracted musicians from elsewhere in the country, as well as nurturing its own talent.

During the 1950s, jazz performers, big bands and Maori show bands dominated the popular music scene in Auckland. Influenced by the success of the Shadows, instrumental performers then came to the fore, most notably the Keil Isles (1957–67) and guitarist Peter Posa. Auckland increasingly attracted emergent artists from elsewhere in New Zealand, including Johnny Devlin, New Zealand's first local rock 'n' roll star (from Wanganui) and Ray Columbus and the Invaders (from Christchurch). At the same time, considerable local talent emerged, especially during the 1960s, often emulating the styles and covering the releases of various leading British bands (including the Beatles, the Rolling Stones, the Searchers and the Who, all of which toured New Zealand). The La De Das, Larry's Rebels, the Pleasers, Mr. Lee Grant (New Zealand's 'Mr. Mod') and Dinah Lee all had considerable chart success, before trying their luck in Australia. This pattern of Auckland attracting talented national artists, only to have them then relocate overseas,

has continued. Examples include Split Enz and Dragon (1980s).

In recent years, Auckland has become the location for the bulk of the country's popular music activity. The majority of the local and international record labels have their head offices there. Sony New Zealand is the most active major. Leading 'independent' labels include Kog Transmissions, whose electronica has had some success internationally, Arch Hill Recordings, Pagan and Wildside. Local music magazines *Real Groove* and *Rip It Up* are based in Auckland.

There is a strong local club scene, and established venues include the Powerstation, Auckland Town Hall, Western Springs Stadium and the North Shore Events Centre. Prominent festivals include the annual Big Day Out show, involving international and local acts, and Sweetwaters.

The city has a number of major recording studios – Revolver, York Street, Mandrill and Stebbing – and the local offices of the Australasian Performing Right Association (APRA) and the Australasian Mechanical Copyright Owners Society (AMCOS) are located there. Auckland has some 20 radio stations, and it is the main center for New Zealand television production.

Reflecting the strength of the local scene, many of the leading New Zealand musicians are based in Auckland. Much of their output is successfully imitative of major Western pop and rock forms, albeit with local lyrical references (for example, Bic Runga, Dave Dobbyn). Some performers emphasize the intermixing of standard pop and rock forms with Polynesian and Maori musical elements, along with rap and reggae (for instance, 3 the Hardway, Ardijah, Supergroove and OMC).

Bibliography

Mitchell, Tony. 1995. 'New Urban Polynesians: *Once Were Warriors*, the *Proud* Project and the South Auckland Music Scene.' *Perfect Beat: The Pacific Journal of Research into Contemporary Music and Popular Culture* 2(3): 1–20.

Watkins, Roger. 1995. *Hostage to the Beat: The Auckland Scene, 1955–1970*. Auckland: Tandem Press.

Discography

Feelers, The. *Supersystem*. Warner 3984274442. *1998*: New Zealand.

How Was the Air Up There?. EMI 5332812. *2001*: New Zealand.

Katchafire. *Revival*. Mai Music KCDLP001. *2003*: New Zealand.

OMC. *How Bizarre*. PolyGram NZ 533435-2 (huh! 6). *1996*: New Zealand.

Pagan in a Pagan Land. Pagan Records Pal 1036. *1988*: New Zealand.

Salmonella Dub. *Outside the Dubplates*. Virgin Records 07243-5-84631 25. *2002*: New Zealand.

ROY SHUKER

Christchurch
Population: 334,000 (2001)

Situated on the east coast of the South Island, Christchurch is New Zealand's third-largest metropolitan center. The city was one of the original 'Wakefield Company planned settlements' of the 1850s, with most of the early settlers coming from England. As a consequence, Christchurch has well-established traditions of cathedral/church music, brass bands (in 1880 New Zealand's first national brass band contest was held in Christchurch) and folk music. Like other major local centers, the city was on the itinerary of the touring opera companies during the nineteenth century, and in 1906 the country's first professional orchestra was formed for an International Exhibition held in Christchurch. While these musical traditions have been maintained into the twenty-first century, at times the city has suffered from the more rapid growth in New Zealand's North Island – for example, appearing less frequently on the touring schedules of major international performers.

In the 1960s, several leading pop groups originated in Christchurch, most notably Ray Columbus and the Invaders, and Max Merrit and the Meteors. Both drew on British rock 'n' roll for much of their inspiration, along with black US soul, the latter influence stemming from the large number of US Air Force personnel stationed at the Antarctic Operation Deep Freeze base in Christchurch. Establishing what was to be an ongoing trend, however, both groups soon moved to Auckland, and then on to commercial success in Australia.

Christchurch continued to produce nationally prominent pop and rock bands into the 1980s, including Pop Mechanix (founded in 1978 as Bon Marche), the Newz and the Narcs. Most commercially successful were the Dance Exponents, originally from nearby Timaru, with charismatic singer Jordan Luck. Later simply 'the Exponents,' the band enjoyed a long run of chart hits into the 1990s.

Christchurch also supported significant low-key, alternative and experimental scenes, at times constrained by a lack of venues. In the late 1970s, the city became a punk stronghold, initially centered around the Club Da Roux and the Gladstone, with performers such as Bill Direen and the Builders. While associated more with Dunedin, the Flying Nun label was started in Christchurch in 1981, and it soon signed the Gordons, the Playthings and the Newtones, all leading local bands.

The contemporary popular music scene has maintained a marked do-it-yourself emphasis. Local recording companies and labels include Aire Records and Onset Offset (Storm Records); recording studios include Nightshade, Tandem and Sonic Boom. These cater mainly to 'lo-fi' alternative performers, such as Salmonella Dub. More commercial mainstream bands are Zed, and the Feelers, considered New Zealand's answer to 'Britpop.' Following the now well-trodden path, however, they signed with Warners and moved to Auckland in 1997.

Bibliography
Dix, John. 1988. *Stranded in Paradise: New Zealand Rock'n'roll, 1955–1988*. Wellington: Paradise Publications.

Eggleton, David. 2003. *Ready to Fly: The Story of New Zealand Rock Music*. Nelson: Craig Potton.

Mitchell, Tony. 1997. 'Flat City Sounds: A Cartography of the Christchurch Music Scene.' *Popular Music & Society* 21(3) (Fall): 83–106.

Discography
Accident. Failsafe Records SAFE 002. *1982*: New Zealand.

Exponents, The. *Something Beginning with C*. PolyGram 512 210-4. *1992*: New Zealand.

Feelers, The. *Supersystem*. Warner 3984274442. *1998*: New Zealand.

How Was the Air Up There?. EMI 5332812. *2001*: New Zealand.

Pop Mechanix. *Cowboys and Engines*. XFS XS 007. *1982*: USA.

ROY SHUKER

Dunedin
Population: 112,000 (2001)

Situated in the South Island, Dunedin was settled by Europeans in the 1840s – mainly Scottish immigrants, who brought with them the music and instruments of their homeland. Pipe bands, Scottish country dancing and country music have remained features of the region.

While it enjoyed a brief period of national dominance in the mid-nineteenth century due to the Otago gold rushes, Dunedin gradually became more of a regional center for the lower South Island. Its seaport and rural hinterland cemented the city's folk and country music associations. The Tumbleweeds are the most prominent example of this. Formed in Otago in 1949, they were inspired by North America's Carter Family and the *Grand Ole Opry*. Signed to local label TANZA in 1949, they enjoyed a succession of hits through the 1950s, with their 'Maple on the Hill' still the country's bestselling country and western recording (with some 80,000 copies sold).

Dunedin's relative geographical isolation from the rest of New Zealand has produced musical traditions heavily centered on a frequently non-commercial, do-it-yourself ethic. Dunedin was home to an arguably distinctive alternative music sound that developed during the 1980s, associated primarily with the independent label Flying Nun, founded by Roger Shepherd in 1981. Leading bands included the Chills, the Verlaines, the Clean, Sneaky Feelings, the Enemy and Toy Love, the latter two fronted by the anarchic and gifted Chris Knox.

The 'Dunedin sound' was generated through a cultural geography of living on the margin, producing a 'mythology of a group of musicians working in cold isolation, playing music purely for the pleasure of it' (McLeay 1994). As with similar local sounds, there has been debate over its constituent elements, distinctiveness and coherence. Guitar-based pop melodies are featured, along with an initial tendency toward low-tech production values, and a shared aesthetic of the primary importance of the song and the 'roughness' of the music.

For many, especially overseas followers of alternative music, Dunedin and Flying Nun became a metonym for New Zealand music as a whole, although the Flying Nun label embraced a range of performers and styles (see Mitchell 1996). Flying Nun rarely achieved local commercial success, but built up a considerable reputation in the international indie/alternative scene. In the 1990s, Flying Nun relocated to Auckland, and then to London.

Dunedin popular music has remained dominated by the do-it-yourself, 'lo-fi' approach to performing and recording, exemplified in the work of Chris Knox, Peter Jefferies, and the experimental and avant-garde output of the Xpressway label. More recent performers working in this tradition are HDU (techno-inflected experimental rock) and Cloudboy (formerly Mink; electronic rock fusion).

Bands with more commercial ambitions tend to relocate to Auckland. These have included new wave groups the Knobz, the Netherworld Dancing Toys with their infectious 'whiteboy' soul sound ('For Today' [1985] remains one of the bestselling local singles) and King Loser.

Currently, local labels include Yellow Eye Music and Infinite Regress Music.

Bibliography

Bannister, Matthew. 1999. *Positively George Street*. Wellington: Reed Books.

Dix, John. 1988. *Stranded in Paradise: New Zealand Rock'n'roll, 1955–1988*. Wellington: Paradise Publications.

Eggleton, David. 2003. *Ready to Fly: The Story of New Zealand Rock Music*. Nelson: Craig Potton.

McLeay, Colin. 1994. 'The "Dunedin Sound": New Zealand Rock and Cultural Geography.' *Perfect Beat: The Pacific Journal of Research into Contemporary Music and Popular Culture* 2(1): 38–50.

Mitchell, Tony. 1996. 'The Sounds of Nowhere?: Bicultural Music in Aotearoa/New Zealand.' In Tony Mitchell, *Popular Music and Local Identity: Rock, Pop and Rap in Europe and Oceania*. Leicester: Leicester University Press, 215–63.

Discographical References

Netherworld Dancing Toys, The. 'For Today.' *Nature's Best, Vol. 2*. Sony 5088102000. *2002*: New Zealand.

Tumbleweeds, The. 'Maple on the Hill.' *The Golden Years of the Tumbleweeds, 1949–1989*. Viking VPS 490 CD. 1949; *1990*: New Zealand.

Discography

Chills, The. *Submarine Bells*. Flying Nun FN 30340. *1990*: New Zealand.

Clean, The. *Compilation*. Flying Nun FN 30294. *1988*: New Zealand.

Getting Older, 1981–1991: The Flying Nun Retrospective Compilation. Flying Nun FN L30636. *1991*: New Zealand.

Jefferies, Peter. *Electricity*. AJAX 039. *1994*: USA.

Xpressway Pile-Up. Xpressway X/WAYS 5. *1998*: New Zealand.

ROY SHUKER

Wellington

Population: 339,000 (2001)

Wellington is the capital city of New Zealand, having been the official home of Parliament since 1865. The city is situated at the southern end of the North Island, on Cook Strait, around one of the world's greatest natural harbors.

Because of Wellington's position as a major port, its music scene has traditionally been subject to a mix of imported influences, resulting in the development of local jazz, blues and folk performers and venues, in addition to those of rock and pop.

Music was a major part of entertainment in the young colony in the late nineteenth century, with touring operas and musicians of all styles regularly performing. During the 1920s and 1930s, Wellington became the center of government broadcasting activities, a tradition that continued until the 1990s when a significant proportion of national television and radio management and activities shifted to Auckland, following their commercial counterparts.

In 1948, HMV set up its headquarters in Wellington, and the company became the dominant presence on the New Zealand recording and distribution scene though the 1950s. In 1949, the country's first 78 pressing plant was established in Wellington.

In the late 1950s and through the 1960s, Wellington developed a strong club scene, with a number of nationally prominent pop and rock performers. A significant reason for the strength of live music was the pubs (hotel bars), then closing at 6:00 p.m., with clubs and coffee bars consequently becoming the focus of evening entertainment. In mid-1966, there were seven youth clubs distributed across the central city and into the suburbs, 'all of them providing one or two bands at each session as well as guest artists'; 10 weekly public dances; 20 'nite' spots; and some 80 coffee bars, 'many of them featuring folk singers, groups or juke-boxes' (Watkins 1989, 87). Furthermore, Wellington musicians had access to what was then New Zealand's best recording facilities (at HMV), and were also well placed for appearances on the Wellington-produced national television chart pop shows, *Let's Go!* and *C'Mon.*

Performers in the 1960s were mainly influenced by British beat and pop (the Avengers, the Fourmyula), R&B (Bari and the Breakaways) and progressive rock (Mammal). Setting a national trend, however, many of these performers relocated to Auckland for greater national exposure, before venturing overseas, usually to Australia. Much of their material was covers of British and US releases. For example, Bari and the Breakaways' *The Two Albums*, a CD reissue of the band's 1965 and 1966 LPs, includes their largely faithful versions of songs by Chuck Berry, John Lee Hooker, the early Rolling Stones and so on, along with a sprinkling of largely weaker original material. At times, however, original compositions shone through. The Fourmyula were among the most prolific and talented composers of that era, with a string of self-penned local Top 10 singles. In 2000, in a comprehensive poll, their song 'Nature' (1969), written by keyboardist Wayne Mason, was voted New Zealand's best-ever song.

While national broadcaster Radio New Zealand has remained based in Wellington, the operations of national television providers (the state-owned enterprises Television One and Two) have increasingly shifted to the more populous north of the country. Wellington currently has six commercial radio stations.

In the 1990s, the Wellington popular music scene was dominated by heavy metal and 'alternative' rock performers, such as Shihad (now Pacifier), Head Like a Hole and Emulsifier. Rap has also had a strong presence – for example, Upper Hutt Posse. Most recently, although various styles of 'alternative' music have remained evident, electronica has been more prominent.

The city is also a bastion of classical and jazz music. It is the home of the National Symphony Orchestra, a prestigious annual International Arts Festival, and a major jazz school. Several performers (such as pianist Dan Poynton) are seeking to blur the boundaries between classical and jazz music and more 'popular' music styles, with some commercial and critical success.

Local record labels historically included Blue Smoke (with artists such as Johnny Cooper and Chloe) and Jayrem Records (Charlotte Yates, Six Volts, Otis Mace, and the Brainchilds). Currently, leading local labels are Capital Recordings (electronica) and LOOP Records (featuring 'urban New Zealand music,' with major acts being Trinity Roots, and the Black Seeds). Recording studios include Stooges and Vision.

Major local venues are the Queen's Wharf Events Centre, the new Michael Fowler Centre and the Wellington Town Hall. The Wellington Stadium, designed as the capital's major sporting venue, has also been used for larger-scale 'rock' concerts (for example, David Bowie in 2004), but it has proved a controversial venue because of seating and sound issues. Major clubs that regularly feature live music include Bodega's, Indigo and Happy's.

Bibliography

Watkins, Roger. 1989. *When Rock Got Rolling*. Wellington: Hazard Press.

Discographical References

Bari and the Breakaways. *The Two Albums.* Jayrem Records Legenz Series D30874. *1992*: New Zealand.

Fourmyula, The. 'Nature.' *Nature's Best: New Zealand's Top 30 Songs of All Time.* Sony Music 5054952000. 1969; *2002*: New Zealand.

Discography

How Was the Air Up There?. EMI 5332812. *2001*: New Zealand.

LOOP 13. LOOP Select Edition CD.08. *2000/2001*: New Zealand.

Poynton, Dan. *You Hit Him He Cry Out.* Rattle Records RAT D006. *1997*: New Zealand.

Shihad. *Killjoy.* Wildside Records D31340. *1995*: New Zealand.

ROY SHUKER

8. Pacific Islands

Hawai'i (Hawaii)

Population: 1,200,000 (2000)

Located at a latitude of between 19 and 22 degrees north, Hawai'i consists physically of an archipelago of high volcanic islands and coral atolls spanning some 200 miles (322 km). The islands were first settled by Polynesian seafarers from the Marquesas and Society Islands, beginning circa A.D. 400. Long-distance seafaring ceased circa A.D. 1500, after which the inhabitants were isolated until the arrival of European voyagers in 1778. Dramatic social transformations effected throughout the nineteenth century included the rise of capitalism, importation of laborers from Asia (especially China, Japan and the Philippines) and Portugal to work on sugar plantations, and the overthrow of the independent Hawaiian monarchy by North American businessmen in 1893, culminating in annexation to the United States in 1898 and statehood in 1959. Residents populate seven of the eight volcanic islands southernmost in the archipelago; a US naval installation is located on northernmost Midway Island.

In contemporary Hawai'i, popular culture consists of three coexisting and overlapping threads: native Hawaiian traditions, a 'local' culture that mixes the islands' multicultural and multiracial traditions freely in celebratory – yet politically exclusionary – ways, and mainstream North American popular culture. Musicians move fluidly among multiple idioms, despite the music industry's focus on Hawaiian music.

'Hawaiian music' is an umbrella term that embraces multiple genres of repertoire and performance styles. Hawaiian performance traditions held

to be directly continuous from indigenous practices are considered 'ancient,' and contrast with Westernized traditions considered 'modern.' While modern Hawaiian music traditions constitute the core of Hawai'i's popular music industry, ancient performance traditions experienced a vigorous revitalization in a cultural renaissance that began in the 1970s.

Modern Hawaiian music includes genres that fuse indigenous Hawaiian poetic, vocal and instrumental performance practices with melody and harmonization acquired via Christian hymnody, called *hīmeni*. Hymnody, musical rudiments and notational literacy were introduced by North American Calvinist missionaries in the 1820s. The various verse-chorus forms of *hīmeni* served as models for notationally literate Hawaiian songwriters who had begun composing secular songs, called *mele Hawai'i*, by the 1860s. The fusion of Hawaiian vocal and movement styles with Western musical elements resulted in the Westernized genre of strophic song called *hula ku'i* by the 1870s.

By the early 1900s, Hawaiian songwriters had begun writing songs about Hawai'i or Hawaiian culture with English lyrics, creating the category of *hapa haole* song. Together, *hula ku'i* and *hapa haole* song types were mainstays in tourist entertainment throughout the twentieth century, and their performance styles and instrumentation are representative of 'Hawaiian music' as it has become known outside Hawai'i. *Hapa haole* songs caught the attention of commercial songwriters in New York's Tin Pan Alley in the years just prior to 1920 and throughout the following decade; the outpouring of Hawaiian-themed songs, exploiting exoticist fantasizing and gross stereotyping, solidified the use of the 32-bar 'popular song form' (AABA) that was continued by songwriters in Hawai'i.

Modern Hawaiian music genres are accompanied by introduced instruments. The guitar, brought to the islands in the early nineteenth century by Mexican cowboys, initially provided strummed rhythmic accompaniment. The invention of the technique of melodic picking, in which the player holds an acoustic guitar horizontally across the lap and uses a metallic object to stop the strings, is attributed to schoolboy Joseph Kekuku in 1885. In the 1930s, physical alterations, including electric amplification and the addition of sustaining pedals, yielded the 'steel guitar.' In the 1950s, a rural-based acoustic guitar tradition known as kī hōʻalu, or slack-key guitar, became widely popular through the recordings of guitarist Gabby Pahinui. Using a variety of tunings ('slackening'), a guitarist picks a melody line on the higher-pitched strings while simultaneously picking an accompaniment pattern on the lower-pitched strings.

Since World War II, the core instrumental ensemble for modern Hawaiian music has consisted of guitar, ʻukulele and string bass, augmented by piano and steel guitar. The basic four-string ʻukulele was crafted in the islands in the early 1880s by immigrant Portuguese instrument makers, who used the braginha as a model. Performers mix instruments, accompaniment styles and repertoire freely. Early twentieth-century photographs depict ensembles that included flute and violin. Swing bands during the 1930s and 1940s were associated with band leaders such as Johnny Noble, Dick McIntire, Lani McIntire and Harry Owens.

In the performance practice of hula kuʻi songs, singing in the falsetto register is highly valued, combined with liberal use of articulatory techniques that descend from ancient chant styles. Women as well as men sing in the higher falsetto register. Generally, falsetto singers exploit the timbral differences between the registers, and emphasize crossings between chest and falsetto registers, usually using a yodel-like technique. Among prominent male falsetto singers are Tony Conjugacion, George Kainapau, Bill Lincoln and Clyde Sproat; among women are Amy Hanaialiʻi, Genoa Keawe, Karen Keawehawaiʻi and Lena Machado. Choral harmonization, heard in recordings in the 1920s by groups such as the Kalama's Quartet, has been continued into the twenty-first century by groups such as Hoʻokena, the Makaha Sons and Na Leo.

Since the late 1960s, Hawaiʻi songwriters and

performers have used popular song to comment on issues and struggles common to Hawaiʻi's multi-ethnic population, particularly the socioeconomic displacement of long-time residents by waves of foreign investment. Musicians turned to reggae (often dubbed 'Jawaiian' over musicians' objections) in the 1980s and hip-hop in the 1990s. Experiments by hula masters such as Frank Hewett, Tony Conjugacion and Mark Hoʻomalu to set Hawaiian-language texts to electronica settings are assertions of cultural self-determination by native Hawaiians. The contemporary movement for federal recognition and sovereignty for indigenous native Hawaiians gained momentum after the 1993 centennial observance of the overthrow of the independent monarchy by US businessmen and subsequent annexation to the United States in 1898. Native Hawaiian performers such as Sudden Rush and Big Island Conspiracy draw on rap and hip-hop to deliver their messages of native Hawaiian political discontent. Two CDs, *Hawaiian Nation: A Call for Sovereignty* and *Aloha March 2000: Beyond the Apology*, are devoted entirely to protest songs popular at rallies and other pro-sovereignty events.

Commercial dissemination of modern Hawaiian music began in the nineteenth century. Markets included the continental United States as well as Hawaiʻi, owing to multiple national and even international fads. Its popularity stems from multiple sources, including the rise of tourism in the late 1800s, the presence of touring Hawaiian performers at events such as the 1893 Columbian Exposition in Chicago and the 1915 Panama-Pacific Exposition in San Francisco, and the establishment of Hawaiian entertainment venues such as the Hawaiian Room in New York's Lexington Hotel and the South Seas Restaurant in Hollywood.

Sheet music publication of secular *mele Hawaiʻi* songs began in 1869; over 200 songbooks have been published since then. National companies have maintained a presence in commercial recording, starting with Victor in 1905. Other national companies involved in recording Hawaiian music include Columbia, Brunswick, Decca and Capitol. Hawaiʻi-based recording companies began with Hawaiian Transcription Productions in 1936; major labels since then include 49th State, Bell, Hula, Lehua, Liko, Mountain Apple, Poki and Waikiki. Local companies cater more to local consumers, especially hula dance studios with their clientele of instructors and students. Two labels, Cord and Harlequin, have extensive offerings of remastered recordings. Dancing Cat specializes in slack-key guitar recordings. A proliferation of independent labels since the 1970s accounts for the vibrant production and marketing of popular music by Hawai'i-based performers, and the frequent issue of compilations bearing titles such as *Island Love Shack* (Neos Productions, three volumes since 2001), *Hawaiian Style* (Neos Productions, three volumes since 2001) and *Still Pounding* (Poi Pounder Records, two volumes since 2001).

Bibliography

Akindes, Fay Yokomizu. 2001. 'Sudden Rush: *Na Mele Paleoleo* (Hawaiian Rap) as Liberatory Discourse.' *Discourse* 23(1): 82–98.

A Short History of Hawaiian Slack Key Guitar (Kī hōʻalu). n.d. Santa Cruz, CA: Dancing Cat Records. http://www.dancingcat.com/dancingcat/BlueBook.pdf

Beloff, Jim. 1997. *The Ukulele: A Visual History.* San Francisco: Miller Freeman.

Buck, Elizabeth. 1984–85. 'The Hawaii Music Industry.' *Social Process in Hawaii* 31: 137–53.

Buck, Elizabeth. 1993. *Paradise Remade: The Politics of Culture and History in Hawai'i.* Philadelphia: Temple University Press.

Kanahele, George S., ed. 1979. *Hawaiian Music and Musicians: An Illustrated History.* Honolulu: University Press of Hawaii.

Lewis, George. 1992. 'Don' Go Down Waikiki: Social Protest and Popular Music in Hawaii.' In *Rockin' the Boat: Mass Music and Mass Movements*, ed. Reebee Garofalo. Boston, MA: South End Press, 171–82.

Ruymar, Lorene. 1996. *The Hawaiian Steel Guitar.* Anaheim Hills, CA: Centerstream.

Stillman, Amy Kuʻuleialoha. 1987. 'Published Hawaiian Songbooks.' *Notes* 44(2): 221–39.

Stillman, Amy Kuʻuleialoha. 1996. 'Beyond Bibliography: Interpreting Hawaiian-Language Protestant Hymn Imprints.' *Ethnomusicology* 40(3): 469–88.

Stillman, Amy Kuʻuleialoha. 1998. 'Hula Hits, Local Music, and Local Charts: Some Dynamics of Popular Hawaiian Musics.' In *Sound Alliances: Indigenous Peoples, Cultural Politics and Popular Music in the Pacific*, ed. Philip Hayward. London: Cassell, 89–103.

Tatar, Elizabeth. 1987. *Strains of Change: The Impact of Tourism on Hawaiian Music.* Honolulu: Bishop Museum Press.

Weintraub, Andrew. 1998. 'Jawaiian and Local Cultural Identity in Hawai'i.' In *Sound Alliances: Indigenous Peoples, Cultural Politics and Popular Music in the Pacific*, ed. Philip Hayward. London: Cassell, 78–88

Discographical References

Aloha March 2000: Beyond the Apology. Koi Koi KK2002. *2000*: Hawai'i.

Hawaiian Nation: A Call for Sovereignty. Mamo MRCD-3. *1990*: Hawai'i.

Hawaiian Style. Nā Leo Pilimehana 10052. *2001*: Hawai'i. Reissue: *Hawaiian Style*. Neos Productions 52. *2003*: Hawai'i.

Hawaiian Style, Vol. 2. Neos Productions 63. *2003*: Hawai'i.

Hawaiian Style, Vol. 3. Neos Productions 73. *2003*: Hawai'i.

Island Love Shack, Vol. 1. Neos Productions 31054. *2001*: Hawai'i.

Island Love Shack, Vol. 2. Neos Productions 61. *2003*: Hawai'i.

Island Love Shack, Vol. 3. Neos Productions 70. *2003*: Hawai'i.

Still Pounding. Poi Pounder 7005. *2001*: Hawai'i.

Still Pounding, Vol. 2. Poi Pounder PRCD 7012. *2003*: Hawai'i.

Discography

Big Island Conspiracy. *Reflective But Unrepentent.* Deep Ka'a Ka'a Records DKCD 1999. *1999*: Hawai'i.

Conjugacion, Tony. *TC2000.* Mountain Apple MACD 2051. *2000*: Hawai'i.

Conjugacion, Tony. *The Collection.* Aloha Records ARCD 003. *1994*: Hawai'i.

de Mello, Jack. *Music of Hawai'i.* Mountain Apple MACD 2044. *1999*: Hawai'i.

Hanaiali'i, Amy. *Hawaiian Tradition.* Mountain Apple MACD 2040. *1997*: Hawai'i.

Hawaiian Slack Key Guitar Masters. Dancing Cat 08022-38032-22. *1995*: USA.

Hawaiian Slack Key Guitar Masters Collection, Volume 2. Dancing Cat 08022-38046-2. *1999*: USA.

Hewett, Frank Kawaikapuokalani, and Paraz, Freddy Boy. *Native Grooves.* Pa'ani PR10008. *1998*: Hawai'i.

History of Hawaiian Steel Guitar. Cord International HOCD34000. *1999*: USA.

Ho'okena. *Ho'okena 5.* Ho'omau HICD-1005. *1999*: Hawai'i.

Ho'omalu, Mark Kealii. *Call It What You Like ....* MKH MKHD 0003. *2003*: n.p.

Keawe, Genoa. *Hana Hou! Volume 1.* Hula CDHS-586. *1990*: Hawai'i.

Legends of Falsetto. Cord International HOCD 35000. *2000*: USA.

Legends of Ukulele. Rhino R2 75278. *1998*: USA.

Made in Hawai'i: The Hawaiian Steel Guitar. Sma'Kine SKCD-1210. *1996*: Hawai'i.

Makaha Sons, The. *Kuikawa*. Poki SPCD 9059. *1996*: Hawai'i.

Na Kumu Hula: Songs from the Source, Volume 1. State Council on Hawaiian Heritage SCHH-CD-7001. *1997*: Hawai'i.

Na Kumu Hula: Songs from the Source, Volume 2. State Council on Hawaiian Heritage SCHH-CD-7101. *1999*: Hawai'i.

Nā Leo. *Anthology I, 1984–1996*. Mountain Apple 3002. *1996*: Hawai'i.

Sproat, Clyde Halema'uma'u. *Clyde Halema'uma'u Sproat Sings Songs and Stories of Hawai'i*. Pololu PPCD195-1. *1996*: Hawai'i.

Sudden Rush. *Ku'e!!*. Way Out West WOWCD 9702. *1997*: Hawai'i.

The History of Slack Key Guitar. Vintage Hawaiian Treasures Vol. 7. Cord International HOCD24000. *1995*: USA.

Tickling the Strings 1929–1952. Harlequin HQ CD 28. *1993*: UK.

AMY KU'ULEIALOHA STILLMAN

Melanesia

Population: New Caledonia: 210,798 (2003); Papua New Guinea: 5,295,816 (2003); Solomon Islands: 509,190 (2003); Vanuatu: 199,414 (2003)

Composed of the Pacific Ocean's 'black islands,' Melanesia is one of the three large groups of islands that together form Oceania. Located in the southwestern Pacific, north of Australia and west of Polynesia, the region includes the island states of Papua New Guinea, the Solomon Islands, Vanuatu (formerly the New Hebrides), New Caledonia and, culturally, Indonesian West Papua and the eastern region of Fiji. Approximately one thousand distinct languages are spoken in Melanesia, and the region is culturally diverse.

The development of a range of popular music styles in Melanesia was encouraged by conditions of intense social, cultural and political change during the colonial era (beginning in the early nineteenth century and continuing in some island nations into the 1990s) and the Pacific War period (1942–45). By the end of the nineteenth century, Protestant missionaries of various denominations had introduced and established gospel hymnody in many of these islands, which provided the preconditions necessary for the development of a popular musicality (including familiarity with diatonicism and simple triadic harmony, as well as group choral singing).

Prior to the Pacific War, new musical ideas – predominantly guitar- and ukulele-based music styles of Hawai'i, Tahiti and Samoa – were introduced or transmitted by way of: (a) instruments (ukulele, guitar and, to a lesser extent, banjo, mandolin and violin, as well as accordion and harmonica) played by ships' Polynesian and Melanesian crewmen; (b) phonograph records (played or sold by ships' captains and crew, missionaries, plantation labor recruiters and Chinese traders); and (c) live performances (for studies of colonial performance culture in an island's urban center, see Webb 1997, 2000). New Melanesian repertoires included islander interpretations of waltzes, fox trots, barn dances, two-steps and schottisches (see, for example, Low 1962, 81), as well as Polynesian guitar songs.

For more than three years from 1942, Melanesian islands were bombarded with the new sounds of (especially) US musics that were popular at the time – jive and swing, and popular songs of various styles (including Tin Pan Alley, show tunes, 'folk' and 'hillbilly'). Armed forces radio, phonograph records and movies, as well as live entertainment shows and numerous informal impromptu performances (Pate 1986; Priday 1944, 51; Webb 1995), ensured musical saturation. New musical styles began to appear. Troops from a Fijian battalion stationed on Bougainville Island, for example, combined swing and hymnic elements in the song 'Bu Bu' ('Drinking Coconut').

The war period is notable for the performance exchanges between islanders and Allied troops (each group was moved by the music of the other (Webb 1995, 231–79)) (see Lindstrom and White 1990). Such exchanges had the effect among Melanesians of sustaining a postwar mood of optimism and confidence, and of assisting villagers to envision and create a new postwar order. This optimism was expressed in the lyrics and sound patterns of energetic new syncretic forms, which attempted to incorporate the power of whites by appropriating and recombining various features of their popular musical styles.

By the late 1950s – and, in some cases, earlier (see Mytinger 1942, 269) – guitar- and ukulele-based sub-styles of a Polynesian prototypical string band ensemble and sound proliferated across Melanesia. 'String band' came to refer to a particular set of musical features: acoustic instrumentation, including ukulele, guitars, single-string bass, miscellaneous percussion, and blended (usually male) voices singing in triadic harmony; performance contexts (such as nonspecific social gatherings); and instrumentation and stylistic elements. Extant recordings from this period (such as those made in the field by anthropologists M. Young in Vanuatu and M. Groves in Papua New Guinea) indicate a familiarity with the films of the Hollywood singing cowboys and the records of Hank Williams, Elvis Presley and, later, Johnny Cash and Jim Reeves. A range of nonstandard guitar tunings was developed, the names of which share an affinity with Hawaiian slack-key guitar or kī hō'alu, and its Tahitian and Samoan derivative styles (Crowdy 2000; Webb 1998).

A postwar choral movement flourished in some coastal towns and was linked with loyalty to Empire (see Webb 1995, 280–338). Choirs began to expand their repertoires to include a range of Western secular and popular music. In Rabaul in northeastern New Britain, German priest Fr Josef Reischel was a significant musical mentor to numerous choirs and conductors – notably, Resin ToLop of Vunairoto, active into the 1990s – between the late 1940s and the early 1960s. Stopping in Rabaul while on a world tour in 1957, Baroness Von Trapp praised the local choral movement (Webb 1995, 311). Women conductors enjoyed recognition during this time, Lila IaMatalau and Regina IaTade being prominent among them. Choralism played a vital role in honing the ensemble skills and choral harmonizing central to the Melanesian string band sound.

The string band era, a richly creative period that saw the development of innumerable variant substyles, reached its peak and then began to lose momentum by the 1980s (see Webb 1993). The names of many of the most innovative musicians have never been widely known (Rabaul's John Wowono and Stenly ToKulupa, or the Duke of York Islands' Jack Tonga, for example), because string band performance was a local and musically communal movement. Some of Melanesia's earliest popular musicians emerged from the string band movement, while others established themselves independently. In the 1970s, New Caledonia string band Bethela developed a distinctive, complexly textured sub-style and produced many bestselling cassettes. Bethela's lead singer, Lexis, became a solo recording artist and was popular well into the 1990s. Fijian singer Sakiusa Bulicokocoko, who recorded a studio album in Australia in the early 1970s and had a Pacific-wide following, came from

Fiji's guitar-based Bulicoko Band. Fred Maedola in the Solomon Islands (who recorded for New Zealand's Viking Records), popular in the late 1960s and 1970s, modeled himself on Australia's Slim Dusty while incorporating style elements of rock 'n' roll into his acoustic guitar playing. Maedola's counterpart in Papua New Guinea was the Rabaul-based musical raconteur Blasius ToUna.

Born of Yugoslav immigrants, New Zealand guitarist Peter Posa toured Fiji (where he was made an honorary chief), New Caledonia (where he was known as 'King Peter') and Vanuatu in 1963–64. With albums titled Peter Posa in Fiji and Peter Posa in Nouméa, Posa, who 'recorded prolifically and across all genres, from traditional Pacific music through country, Irish folk and into pop'n'roll' (Reid 2004), inspired a generation of Melanesian guitarists, who heard his music through radio request programs.

Melanesia's first 'rock' bands were formed in the mid-1960s in urban centers, including Nouméa and Port Moresby, by so-called mixed race and Chinese musicians and, occasionally, expatriate Australian musicians who could afford the necessary instruments and equipment. One example of expatriate Australian musicians in Papua New Guinea was Johnny Dee Why and the Splinters, Dee Why being an Anglicized pun on the pidgin word for wood. The repertoires of these bands included surf-style rock instrumentals such as those by Peter Posa, the Ventures and the Shadows, as well as other international pop hits. The imitative nature of these bands is captured in their regional-style label, kopikat. Mixed-race popular musician Paul Cheong was acclaimed as a live performer in Rabaul in the late 1950s and 1960s for his ability to imitate various popular music balladeers, including Johnny Ray, Slim Whitman, Harry Belafonte and Tom Jones (Webb 2000). Hotel bands such as Jack Cheung's (later named) Clockwork Orange, and Gwadu, both from Hanuabada near Port Moresby, did stints as resident bands in hotels in several major Melanesian ports from the 1970s, and epitomize the spirit of musical eclecticism of the period.

The establishment of Melanesia's recording industry coincided with the availability of cassette technology in the mid-1970s, and for the first five years it produced tapes mainly of local string bands that either traveled to regional radio station studios or were recorded on mobile equipment in villages. Commercial studios had sprung up in larger urban centers by the end of the 1970s (see Niles 1984), with several, including Papua New Guinea's

Pacific Gold and Chin H. Meen studios, expanding their distribution network regionally by the 1990s.

The West Papuan band the Black Brothers was politically and musically influential across Melanesia for more than a decade from 1979, residing and performing or recording variously in Papua New Guinea, Vanuatu, the Netherlands and Australia. Through their recordings and live performances, the Black Brothers had a musically unifying influence, singing in several different Melanesian pidgins. In the 1980s, they founded the label Vanuwespa (combining the names Vanuatu and West Papua), which contributed to the establishment of the genericized Melanesian reggae sound that has become fundamental to Melanesian popular musicianship at the beginning of the twenty-first century.

Mangrove Studio in New Caledonia was the first Melanesian label to produce compact discs on a larger scale, its initiative riding on (from the late 1980s) the style coalescence and popularity of a new indigenous fusion known as *kaneka* (see Lecren 1998). Reggae-like features are significant in *kaneka* (for aesthetic and political reasons), as in many other forms of Melanesian popular music since the late 1980s. New Caledonian reggae band Flamengo recorded its 1996 album *Legalize Us* (a pun on a Peter Tosh album title and a statement about *kanak* political status) in Paris where the band now resides. Mangrove Studio has continued to record and promote the reggae-influenced music of bands such as Huarere and Naio from Vanuatu, and Apprentice from the Solomon Islands.

Melanesia has not been isolated from the world music vogue, with George Telek of the Rabaul area receiving critical recognition for a 1997 self-titled solo album produced in Australia by David Bridie. In 1999, Telek traveled to the United Kingdom to record a second world music album, *Serious Tam*, this time for Peter Gabriel's Real World label. Other Melanesian world music projects include ethnomusicologist Steven Feld's soundscapes *Voices of the Rainforest* (recorded in the Bosavi area of Papua New Guinea), *Melanesian Choirs – The Blessed Islands: Chants from the Thin Red Line* (a spinoff from the 1998 movie), and the forthcoming collaboration between US world music guitarist Bob Brozman and string band musicians from Papua New Guinea (http://www.pr.mq.edu.au/researcher/showitem.asp?ItemID=331).

World music opportunism is evident in such recordings as Belgian group Deep Forest's 1992 hit 'Sweet Lullaby,' which sampled without license a Solomon Islands traditional song (see Feld 1996), Anthony Copping's 1997 pan-Melanesian pastiche

Siva Pacifica, and its projected follow-up, *Siva Pacifica: Last Voices from Heaven* (National Geographic Channel 2003). Occasional exoticist imaginings and curiosities have also appeared, such as the synth-pop soundscape *Papua New Guinea* by Future Sound of London (2001).

Other recent Western interaction with Melanesian musicians resulting in various kinds of popular music products includes albums by O-shen, an Anglo-American raised in Papua New Guinea who blends Jawaiian sounds with Melanesian pidgin rap, and the Australian musical activists Justin Tonti-Filippini, Fred Smith and David Bridie. Tonti-Filippini released a recording of inspirational music from the years of political upheaval in Bougainville, *Bougainville Voices* (2000). Smith's *Bagarap Empires* (2002) was the result of time spent as a peace monitor in the late 1990s in Bougainville and the Solomon Islands; while in Bougainville, he 'worked with local musicians to release 20,000 copies of an album of Peace Songs in Melanesian Pidgin' (http://www.fredsmith.com.au/pages/mainpage.html). David Bridie produced the compilation *West Papua: Sound of the Morning Star* (2003), which features pieces by electronica, remix and soundscape artists based around recordings of West Papuan traditional songs, village ambiance, news reports and interviews. Bridie is possibly the only Western musician in whose music one can hear, after more than 15 years of sustained collaborative work with Papua New Guinea musicians, reciprocal influences. Examples of these influences can be found in Bridie's 'The Kilana Stringband Song' on My Friend the Chocolate Cake's *Curious* (2002) and his award-winning feature film soundtrack *In a Savage Land*, which incorporates ambient sounds recorded in various Melanesian locations, including the Trobriand Islands.

Bibliography

Crowdy, Denis. 2000. *Guitar Style, Open Tunings and String Band Music in Papua New Guinea*. Unpublished M.A. thesis, University of New England, Armidale.

Feld, Steven. 1996. 'pygmy POP: A Genealogy of Schizophonic Mimesis.' *Yearbook for Traditional Music* 28: 1–35.

Fred Smith. 2004. http://www.fredsmith.com.au/pages/mainpage.html

Lecren, Hervé. 1998. 'Kaneka: Political Music of Kanaky.' In *The Garland Encyclopedia of World Music. Vol. 9: Australia and the Pacific Islands*, ed. Adrienne L. Kaeppler and J.W. Love. New York and London: Garland Publishing, 213–14.

Lindstrom, Lamont, and White, Geoffrey M. 1990. *Island Encounters: Black and White Memories of the Pacific War*. Washington, DC: Smithsonian Institution Press.

Low, Lema. 1962. *A Family in Fiji*. Sydney: Pacific Publications.

'Macquarie's Globetrotting Guitarist Touches Down in PNG.' n.d. *The Macquarie Researcher*. http://www.pr.mq.edu.au/researcher/showitem.asp?ItemID=331

Mytinger, Caroline. 1942. *Headhunting in the Solomon Islands Around the Coral Sea*. New York: The Macmillan Company.

National Geographic Channel. 2003. *National Geographic Channel Celebrates the Siva Pacifica: Last Voices from Heaven*. http://www.nationalgeographic.com.au/front/news/more.asp?id=24_01_03

Niles, Don, comp. 1984. *Commercial Recordings of Papua New Guinea Music, 1949-1983*. Boroko: Institute of Papua New Guinea Studies.

Pate, Michael. 1986. *An Entertaining War*. Sydney: Dreamweaver Books.

Priday, H.E. Lewis. 1944. *Cannibal Island: The Turbulent Story of New Caledonia's Cannibal Coasts*. Wellington, NZ: Reed.

Reid, Graham. 2004. *Peter Posa: My Pick*. http://www.nzherald.co.nz/entertainment/entertainmentstorydisplay.cfm?storyID=3543707&thesection=entertainment&thesubsection=music&thesecondsubsection=reviews

Webb, Michael. 1993. *Lokal Musik: Lingua Franca Song and Identity in Papua New Guinea*. Boroko: Cultural Studies Division, National Research Institute.

Webb, Michael. 1995. *'Pipal bilong music tru'/'A Truly Musical People': Musical Culture, Colonialism, and Identity in Northeastern New Britain, Papua New Guinea, After 1875*. Unpublished Ph.D. thesis, Wesleyan University.

Webb, Michael. 1997. 'A Long Way from Tipperary: Performance Culture in Early Colonial Rabaul, New Guinea, and the Genesis of a Melanesian Popular Music Scene.' *Perfect Beat: The Pacific Journal of Research into Contemporary Music and Popular Culture* 3(2): 32–59.

Webb, Michael. 1998. 'Guitars in the New Guinea Islands.' In *The Garland Encyclopedia of World Music. Vol. 9: Australia and the Pacific Islands*, ed. Adrienne L. Kaeppler and J.W. Love. New York and London: Garland Publishing, 387–88.

Webb, Michael. 2000. 'Rabaul's "Johnny Ray": Early Popular Music in the New Guinea Islands.' In *Papers from Ivilikou: Papua New Guinea Music Conference and Festival (1997)*, ed. Don Niles and Denis Crowdy. Boroko: Institute of Papua New Guinea Studies and University of Papua New Guinea, 20–30.

Discographical References

'Bu Bu' ('Drinking Coconut'). *'Isa Lei': Traditional Music of Fiji* (vinyl LP). Columbia 330SX 7604. n.d.: New Zealand.

Copping, Anthony. *Siva Pacifica*. Virgin 7243 8 44575 2 5. *1997*: Australia.

Deep Forest. 'Sweet Lullaby.' *Deep Forest*. Sony 57840. *1992*: USA.

Feld, Steven. *Voices of the Rainforest*. Rykodisc RCD 10173. *1991*: USA.

Flamengo. *Legalize Us*. Mangrove MGVCD 620. *1996*: New Caledonia.

Future Sound of London. *Papua New Guinea*. Jumpin' & Pumpin' CD TOT52. *2001*: UK.

In a Savage Land. EMI B00003ZKYA. *1999*: Australia.

Melanesian Choirs – The Blessed Islands: Chants from the Thin Red Line. RCA 63470. *1999*: USA.

My Friend the Chocolate Cake. 'The Kilana Stringband Song.' *Curious*. EMI 7243 5401 6622. *2002*: Australia.

Posa, Peter. *Peter Posa in Fiji*. Viking VE 240. *1967*: New Zealand.

Posa, Peter. *Peter Posa in Nouméa*. Viking VE 241. n.d.: New Zealand.

Smith, Fred. *Bagarap Empires*. Self-issued. *2002*: Australia.

Telek, George. *Serious Tam*. Real World 49543. *2000*: UK.

Telek, George. *Telek*. Origin OR 030. *1997*: Australia.

Tonti-Filippini, Justin. *Bougainville Voices*. Ecosonics. *2000*: Australia.

West Papua: Sound of the Morning Star. EMI 7243 5818 5522. *2003*: Australia.

Discography

Lexis and Bethela. *Best of Lexis and Bethela*. Mangrove MGVCD 350. *1994*: New Caledonia.

O-shen. *Iron Youth*. Cinnamon Red CRR0019. *2000*: New Caledonia.

Posa, Peter. *The Best of Peter Posa*. BMG New Zealand 74321508642. *1998*: New Zealand.

Filmography

In a Savage Land, dir. Bill Bennett. 1999. Australia. 116 mins. Drama. Original music by David Bridie.

The Thin Red Line, dir. Terrence Malick. 1998. USA. 180 mins. War Drama. Original music by Hans Zimmer.

MICHAEL WEBB

Micronesia

Population: 433,000 (2004)

Micronesia is situated in the North Pacific between Hawaii and the Philippines and is made up of three major chains of islands: the Marianas in the north, the Marshall Islands in the east and the Caroline Islands, stretching east to west, in the south. The Gilbert Islands form the western part of Kiribati, which also takes in part of Polynesia; Nauru is situated south of the Marshalls; and Wake Island lies to the north. While the total area of the region is greater than that of the United States, the total landmass of the approximately 2,100 islands is only 1,094 sq miles (2,800 sq km). While most of the main islands (Guam and the northern Marianas, Yap, Palau, Chuuk, Pohnpei, Kosrae and Majuro) are linked by air travel, most of the Outer Islands and atolls can be reached only by sea.

Politically the region is divided into six distinct countries: the Commonwealth of the Northern Marianas; the Republic of Belau; the Federated States of Micronesia; the Republic of the Marshall Islands; Kiribati; and Nauru. Wake Island remains under the control of the United States, and Guam is an Unincorporated Territory of the United States of America.

The biggest center for popular music is Guam. With strong North American and Hispanic influences, it has developed a unique blend of traditional Chamorro and contemporary North American music. The popular music scene is strong, with 10 radio stations, six of which play rock, easy listening and jazz. Rock concerts are held occasionally at the University of Guam. Local bands perform at the many hotels on the island, and karaoke is popular. The university has a music department with a jazz band. Guam boasts two 'megaplex' cinemas, and movie theme scores are becoming more accessible and popular among young people and students. Four music stores sell acoustic and electric guitars and related accessories, sheet music, and a wide range of the latest rock and pop CDs from the United States. Cable television offers MTV; Planet Hollywood, the Hard Rock Café and TGI Fridays all opened in the mid- to late 1990s, offering a total music and dining experience.

The distances between the islands of Micronesia, and the diversity of the cultures and languages, have produced a wide range of distinct musical styles throughout the region. Now linked by a common second language (English), currency (US dollars) and regular airline flights, the main islands of Micronesia have access to a steady diet of popular music imported from the United States. Blues, country, Top 40 pop hits, reggae and hip-hop are the main styles favored by the Islanders, and local radio stations cater to the musical needs of each major island center.

Although much of the popular music listened to hails from the United States, successive influences by missionaries, whalers, copra traders, and Spanish, German and Japanese administrations have led to the creation of popular music styles that are unique to the region. The nineteenth century saw the introduction of three- and four-part harmony to several of the islands, plus guitars, ukuleles, mandolins, harmonicas and accordions. Tin cans were, and in some areas have continued to be, used as percussion instruments. Contemporary instrumentation includes electric guitars, keyboards and synthesizers.

A number of surveys conducted since the beginning of the twentieth century have documented several of the more locally specific popular music styles of the region. While many of these styles are now rarely performed, *teempraa utaa* (songs in mixed languages) have continued to be performed on Yap. Iwakichi Muranushi, a Japanese anthropologist, first recorded examples of *teempraa* in 1936. *Teempraa utaa* combine Yapese and Japanese lyrics with a Japanese melody. More contemporary versions use North American melodies. Muranushi recorded another style, *derebuchsul* (a youth's song), on Palau during the same expedition. Like *teempraa*, it displayed evidence of Japanese musical influence.

Since the 1950s, local performers have been making their mark both on the local music scene and among expatriates abroad, particularly on Guam. With the enormous increase in tourism, many hotels and clubs offer a range of musical styles from jazz to Polynesian. Much of the music produced on Guam has an international flavor. For the rest of Micronesia, however, the music tends to be more locally specific, depending on language and particular social and cultural influences.

From the 1960s on, commercial recordings of local artists on Guam and Saipan have been produced and released for sale. Many Palauan artists record in the Philippines, meeting the demand for recordings by local artists on Palau. But there are no facilities for musicians in the less-developed centers. Radio stations may record and broadcast local artists, but these recordings are not available commercially. This has been the case on Yap for a number of years, with radio station WSZA occasionally selling tape recordings of local artists on request. Cassette players are widely available, and many local artists record themselves on audiocassette and simply dub copies for family and friends. It is difficult to name particular bands and artists, as their fame tends to be restricted to the centers in which they live and work. This restriction is due mostly to the absence of a local commercial recording industry. Such an absence isolates local artists from the wider community. Also, language barriers mean that the most widely spoken language is English, a second language to most residents of all centers except Guam. In addition, most bands tend not to remain together for long. They disappear as suddenly as they appeared, as their members' circumstances change or the members move off-island to seek employment.

Live performances are associated with entertainment in the hotels and nightclubs in the major centers such as Guam, or else with festivals or special celebrations. Guam has two major festivals, Guam Discovery Day in March and Liberation Day on 21 July. In addition, there are 29 fiestas each year. Yap celebrates Yap Day on 1 March with a cultural festival. The Belau Arts Festival is held on 9 July in Palau, and there are arts festivals on Saipan in May and in Majuro in August.

Bibliography

Hannan, Michael. 1996. 'Music Archive for the Pacific.' *Perfect Beat: The Pacific Journal of Research into Contemporary Music and Popular Culture* 2(4): vii–ix.

Malm, William P. 1977. *Music Cultures of the Pacific, the Near East and Asia.* 2nd ed. Englewood Cliffs, NJ: Prentice-Hall.

Marshall, Deirdre. 1992. 'Transculturation in Yapese Music.' *Context* 3 (Winter): 31–33.

Marshall-Dean, Deirdre. 1996. 'Cross-Cultural Connections: An Overview of Musical Exchange on the Yap Islands of Micronesia.' *Perfect Beat: The Pacific Journal of Research into Contemporary Music and Popular Culture* 2(4): 89–97.

Marshall-Dean, Deirdre. 1998. 'Yap.' In *The Garland Encyclopedia of World Music. Vol. 9: Australia and the Pacific Islands,* ed. Adrienne L. Kaeppler and J.W. Love. New York and London: Garland Publishing, 729–33.

Puryear, Mark. 1998. 'Popular Music: Micronesia.' In *The Garland Encyclopedia of World Music. Vol. 9: Australia and the Pacific Islands,* ed. Adrienne L. Kaeppler and J.W. Love. New York and London: Garland Publishing, 158–61.

Discography

Call of the Morning Bird: Chants and Songs of Palau, Yap and Ponape Collected by Iwakichi Muranushi, 1936 (ed. Elizabeth Tatar). Bernice Pauahi Bishop Museum. *1985*: Hawaii.

Spirit of Micronesia. Saydisc Records 414. *1995*: UK.

DEIRDRE MARSHALL

Polynesia

Population: American Samoa: 70,260 (2003); Cook Islands: 21,008 (2003); Fiji: 868,531 (2003); French Polynesia: 262,125 (2003); Niue: 2,145 (2002); Pitcairn Island: 47 (2003); Samoa: 178,173 (2003); Tokelau: 1,418 (2003); Tonga: 108,141 (2003); Tuvalu: 11,305 (2003); Wallis and Futuna Islands: 15,734

The term 'Polynesia' refers to a large number of islands and island groups in the Pacific Ocean. The area forms a triangle, with Hawai'i (Hawaii) at its northern apex, Rapa Nui (Easter Island) at its southeast and Aotearoa (New Zealand) at its southwest. The two main geocultural regions of the area are East and West Polynesia, but a third region comprises the 'outlier' islands, which have a Polynesian population, but are located to the west of the triangle.

The ancestors of Polynesian peoples started migrating from Southeast Asia about 50,000 years ago, but Polynesia itself has been populated for only about 3,500 years (New Zealand Maori arriving in their homeland as recently as 1,000 years ago). Despite vast ocean distances between these scattered island groups, the Polynesian area displays a strong degree of cultural homogeneity, perhaps due to its late settlement. Polynesian economies are traditionally based on subsistence fishing and farming, and social organization is based on rank determined by blood and marriage relationships, with political power residing with chiefs at the apex of the sociopolitical system. In many parts of modern Polynesia, the village is still the main operational unit, despite the presence of some medium-size cities in the region.

The term 'Polynesian music' includes several distinct musical streams or categories. So-called 'ancient' or 'traditional' styles are often chant-based genres which have survived (or have been revived) from pre-European contact times; such music may have evolved over time and include some modern aspects. Contact with European cultures, from explorers in the 1700s to missionary activities of the 1800s, and more recently cassettes, radio airplay and live concert tours of US rock in the 1950s and reggae in the 1980s, has had a formative influence on the development of several other regional music styles in Polynesia. These include various types of Christian music, as well as modern 'popular' forms used primarily in secular entertainment contexts. Both Christian and secular forms are syncretic, combining indigenous and imported musical traits.

Modern popular music in Polynesia can be loosely divided into two main coexisting streams or traditions – acoustic 'string band' music and electric pop. String bands were popular in several areas of Polynesia by the late 1800s. This older-style popular music is acoustic – homophonic songs sung by vocal groups, and accompanied by strummed guitars and ukuleles. Voices usually sing in three- or four-part closely spaced harmony, and male falsetto is a common practice. Acoustic string band songs are traditionally sung by all-male groups in some areas (for example, Fiji and Tonga). This is mainly because men rather than women participate in the extended informal beer- or kava-drinking sessions with which such singing is associated. Such group singing is a shared community experience, designed to engender group solidarity as well as while away the evening leisure hours. The standard Western acoustic guitar and the ukulele are the main instruments; they usually provide chordal strumming, sometimes highly syncopated, as in Cook Island and Tahitian string bands. Some Polynesian guitars and ukuleles have distinctive tunings, developed over the years to best suit particular styles of playing. In most acoustic bands, the guitar(s) and ukuleles strum chords, but in some areas (such as Samoa) the acoustic guitars may adopt the divided lead, rhythm and bass functions of electric bands or Western pop groups. Other stringed instruments can also be found in some traditions – for example, the banjo (penisio), which is very popular in Tonga, and the one-string bass (called selo in Tonga and Samoa). String bands may also include one or more percussion instruments, such as an indigenous log drum, the tini (tin can) or even an upturned bucket.

The second stream of popular music in Polynesia is defined initially by its electric dimension. These more modern styles of Polynesian 'electric' pop feature the use of electric instruments, modern upbeat rhythms and a wider range of harmonies than older string band songs. Instruments commonly employed include electric/bass guitars, amplified ukulele, keyboards, saxophone, and drumkit or drum machine. Most songs are set in the

standard 'verse-chorus' form of Western pop songs, and include instrumental introductions and breaks. Modulation as a contrastive device, sometimes to link songs in medleys, is also practiced. The songs may be used to accompany modern, Western-style dancing, but people also sometimes use steps and movements of traditional dance in such contexts. Some songs are common to both acoustic and electric groups, but the latter tend to play more covers of Western pop songs – electric pop in Polynesia includes adaptations of all the major Western rock varieties, including rock 'n' roll, heavy rock, funk and disco. Reggae, in particular, has had a big impact on the Pacific musical scene. Electric bands may include recent 'originals' in their repertoire, and some bands also include experimental or 'fusion' pieces, setting musical elements from pre-European contact styles in a modern musical context.

Live performances of popular music in Polynesia are associated with a variety of contexts and venues, including private parties in houses or outdoors (often in conjunction with informal drinking sessions), and more formal contexts such as festivals, competitions, and cultural celebrations connected with special events such as national days. Hotels, bars, clubs and tourist resorts also feature Polynesian bands as nightly entertainment.

Local radio stations often provide a major service in broadcasting local as well as imported popular music throughout the region. Locally produced cassettes still form the primary basis for commercial dissemination of popular music in Polynesia, although CDs are becoming more common in the region. Several Polynesian countries may have local recording studios producing cassettes or CDs (these studios often being located in major towns, such as Papeete in Tahiti [French Polynesia]), but the music industry is on the whole small-scale. In some cases, more substantial recording studio production of Polynesian popular music occurs outside Polynesia in new homelands such as Auckland, New Zealand, which feature large immigrant populations of Polynesian peoples. Videos of performances are sometimes an important means of disseminating popular music from 'back home' to these new homelands, and may be used by some groups and musicians for extending or updating their repertoire.

Each tradition of popular music in Polynesia has its own individual identity, established initially by linguistic aspects, as the standard local language is the favored option in most cases. Some songs are in

English or French, or are macaronic, combining English/French and indigenous words/verses. A distinctive local identity may also be conferred by musical features; these include a preference for certain instruments, rhythms or harmonies, as well as aspects that have persisted from indigenous music traditions. In the Cook Islands, for example, older chant and secular song styles (*pe'e* and *ute*) also surface in some popular song contexts.

Popular music traditions in Polynesia do share many common features. Common themes for song texts are love, beauty of nature/homeland and bereavement. In many parts of Polynesia, tune appropriation is common. Imported Western tunes may be fitted with local words. For other songs, both text and tune are composed, but are influenced by Western or Caribbean music. 'Authorship' is a flexible and sometimes disputed concept. Many older-style string band songs have no known or remembered composer. In some cases, the appellation 'composer' may apply to the text (not to the borrowed tune). Some songs of recent origin do have a known composer of both words and melody. Melodies of Polynesian popular songs tend to set texts syllabically, and musical phrasing is often text-determined, possibly a reflection of indigenous approaches to music-making.

Melodies often exhibit evidence of a Western triadic structure. Melodic form is predominantly strophic, with or without a distinct musical refrain. Songs may be in slow or fast tempo, and are commonly in 4/4 time. Instruments often employ only the three basic chords of Western diatonic harmony – tonic, subdominant and dominant, with occasional secondary dominants or a minor chord. Tonic and dominant sevenths, and tonic with added sixth are also common. Keys are most often major. The tonic chord may have an added sixth (basic ukulele tuning) as a distinctive harmonic feature of several Polynesian styles. Some aspects of Polynesian popular songs are not derived from standard Western practice – these include asymmetrical and extended harmonic phrases, in some cases related to the text-determined melodies.

Bibliography

Christensen, Dieter, and Kaeppler, Adrienne L. 1974. 'Oceania, Arts of (Music and Dance).' In *The New Encyclopaedia Britannica*, Vol. 13. 15th ed. Chicago: Encyclopaedia Britannica, 456–61.

Goldsworthy, David. 1997. 'Music, Dance and Piety in the Cook Islands.' *Esplanade: The Arts Magazine* (March/April): 58–59.

Goldsworthy, David. 1998a. 'Fijian Music.' In *The Garland Encyclopedia of World Music. Vol. 9: Australia and the Pacific Islands*, ed. Adrienne L. Kaeppler and J.W. Love. New York and London: Garland Publishing, 774–76.

Goldsworthy, David. 1998b. 'Popular Music: Fiji.' In *The Garland Encyclopedia of World Music. Vol. 9: Australia and the Pacific Islands*, ed. Adrienne L. Kaeppler and J.W. Love. New York and London: Garland Publishing, 161–62.

Hannan, Michael. 1996. 'Music Archive for the Pacific.' *Perfect Beat: The Pacific Journal of Research into Contemporary Music and Popular Culture* 2(4): vii–ix.

Linkels, Ad. 1995. *Fa'a-Samoa. The Samoan Way ... Between Conch Shell and Disco*. Tilburg, The Netherlands: Mundo Étnico Foundation.

Linkels, Ad. 1998. *Sounds of Change in Tonga: Dance, Music and Cultural Dynamics in a Polynesian Kingdom*. Tilburg, The Netherlands: Mundo Étnico Foundation.

McLean, Mervyn. 1999. *Weavers of Song: Polynesian Music and Dance*. Auckland: Auckland University Press.

DAVID GOLDSWORTHY

Index

Page numbers in bold indicate major headwords

Index

Index

Index